Beginning JSP 2.0

Ben Galbraith
Peter den Haan
Lance Lavandowska
Sathya Narayana Panduranga
Krishnaraj Perrumal
Erick Sgarbi

Wrox Press Ltd. ®

Beginning JSP 2.0

First printed March 2003

Published by Wrox Press Ltd,
Arden House, 1102 Warwick Road, Acocks Green,
Birmingham, B27 6BH, UK.
Printed in the USA
ISBN 1-86100-831-7

Trademark Acknowledgments

Wrox has endeavored to adhere to trademark conventions for all companies and products mentioned in this book, such as the appropriate use of capitalization. Wrox cannot however guarantee the accuracy of this information.

Credits

Authors
Ben Galbraith
Peter den Haan
Lance Lavandowska
Sathya Panduranga
Krishnaraj Perrumal
Erick Sgarbi

Additional Material
Vikram Goyal
Peter Den Haan

Project Manager
Nicola Phillips

Managing Editor
Laurent Lafon

Commisioning Editor
Paul Jeffcoat

Technical Editors
Emma Costelloe
Richard Deeson
Robert Shaw

Indexers
Martin Brooks
John Collin
Andrew Criddle

Technical Reviewers
Kashif Anwar
Ersin Eser
Greg Feirer
Vikram Goyal
Margarita Isayeva
Andrew Jones
Sachin Surinder Khann
Brad Maiani
Kirk Montgomery
Steve Parker
Phil Powers de George
David Schultz
John Timney
David Whitney

Production Coordinator
Neil Lote

Production Assistant
Paul Grove

Cover Design
Natalie O'Donnell

Series Editor
John Collin

Proof Readers
Dev Lunsford
Chris Smith

About the Authors

Ben Galbraith

At the tender age of six, Ben Galbraith wrote his first computer program. He continued writing code for fun and profit throughout his youth, starting his career in IT when twelve years old. By the time he was seventeen, Ben led a development team for Acer America Corporation. His responsibilities included developing and maintaining nearly a dozen various enterprise systems with international deployments and hundreds of users.

When the Web craze hit in '95, Ben dove in, using Perl and vi to build countless web applications throughout the end of the last century. Mr. Galbraith was introduced to server-side Java in '99, and has since become something of a Java enthusiast. He has written dozens of Java/J2EE applications for numerous clients and actively tinkers on several open source projects. He has also co-authored a gaggle of books on various Java and XML-related topics.

Ben currently resides in Provo, Utah with his wife and daughter.

Peter den Haan

Peter den Haan is a senior systems engineer at Objectivity Ltd, a UK-based systems integration company. He started out programming at 13 on a Radio Shack TRS-80 model I with 16KB of memory, but has progressed since to become J2EE systems architect and lead developer for Internet and intranet projects for customers ranging from the UK Football Association Premier League to Shell Finance.

Peter has previously written the security and cryptography chapters for Wrox Press's *Beginning Java Networking.* He is a Sun Certified Java 2 developer, a JavaRanch bartender, self-confessed geek, holds a doctorate in theoretical physics, and plays bass in the local worship band. You can reach him at bjsp@peterdenhaan.info.

I would like to thank the Lord and my wife Inger for their support – I wouldn't be able to do without either of you.

Lance Lavandowska

Lance Lavandowska has been working with JavaServer Pages since 1998. He has contributed to several Apache Jakarta projects, the Castor project, and the Roller weblogger project. Lance has also served as a technical reviewer on several JSP books and was a co-author on *Professional JSP Site Design* from Wrox.

As usual, I'd like to thank my family for supporting me while working on this book. I'd also like to thank the fine people at Wrox for the opportunity to work with them again; may they not regret it. You can visit me, and check out my blog, at http://www.brainpolis.com/roller/page/lance.

Sathya Narayana Panduranga

Sathya is a Software Design Engineer living in the Software Capital of India, Bangalore. He has expertise in Microsoft and Java technologies and has worked in the domains of Internet, telecom, and convergence. His favorite areas of interest are distributed and component-based application architectures, and object oriented analysis and design. Contributing to a range of technical articles and books is a hobby that gives him the immense satisfaction of sharing his knowledge. He can be contacted at sathyanp@hotmail.com.

I would like to thank my loving wife Ramya, whose patience and cooperation made it possible for me to contribute to this book.

Krishnaraj Perrumal

Krishnaraj Perrumal is founder and director of Adarsh Softech, at Salem. He has successfully developed and managed a number of software projects and e-projects, and his programming experience spans the past 15 years. He regularly gives presentations on Java technology, XML, information systems security, and audit.

He is a Sun Certified Java Programmer, a Certified Novell Netware Engineer, and also a Certified Information Systems Auditor. Currently he spends most of his time providing consultancy and solutions for computer security, in addition to web development. He loves to spend all his free time with children, but being tech savvy, Information Technology constitutes both his profession and his hobby. You can contact Krishnaraj at adasoft@sancharnet.in.

I dedicate my contribution to my mother who recently passed away. I'm indebted to the Wrox team for this opportunity and for making my work presentable. I'm grateful to Girija, Adarsh, dad, and my sisters' (Suja and Gaye) families for their support.

Erick Sgarbi

Erick Sgarbi has several years' experience in software development and as a consultant in e-commerce. He holds MCAD, JCP, and MCSD certifications and after all these years working in the field, he will shortly be returning to academia to complete a Bachelor degree in Information Systems. During his career, he has worked for many companies, developing applications in Java, C#, VB.NET, J#, Visual C++, and Visual Basic, among others. Currently, Erick's focus is on the bridge between .NET and Java Technologies, in particular the development of applications for Mobile and Smart devices in distributed environments.

I would like to thank the whole Wrox Press team, especially Richard Deeson, Paul Jeffcoat, Emma Batch, and Nicola Phillips for their great work and patience with this book :-)

Gratitude also to all the other authors, who have worked so hard and given great input on each others' work.

I also wish to thank the Australian Catholic University and the Australian Computer Society (ACS) for their excellent efforts in passing knowledge and networking Australian IT professionals.

Lastly, I want to thank mum & dad, Tia Ottilia & Seu Altair, Chris & Ale and Pat for their continuous support.

Table of Contents

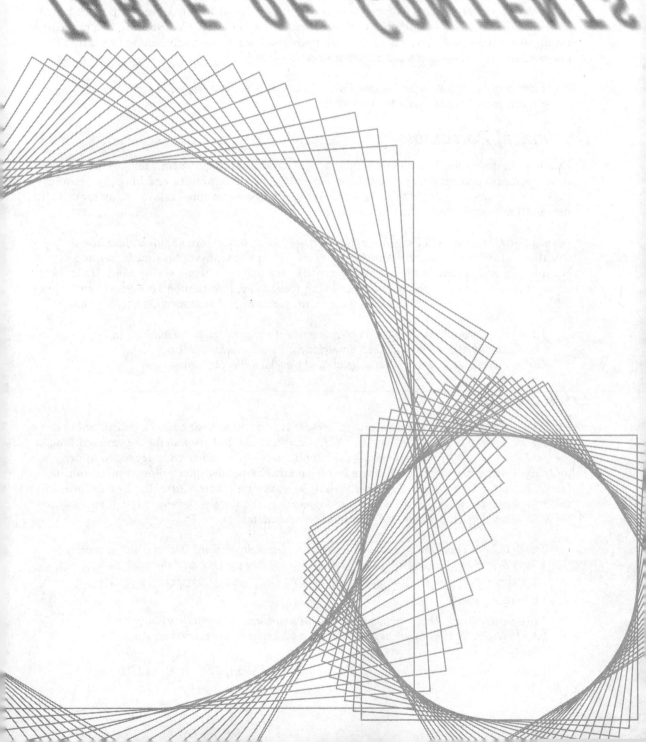

Table of Contents

Chapter 3: Working with Data   67

Chapter 4: Reusing Code   99

Table of Contents

Table of Contents

Chapter 16: A Struts Web Application — 659

Table of Contents

INTRODUCTION

Introduction

Over the course of its short life, the Internet, or more specifically, the World Wide Web, has metamorphosed from a drab collection of publicly visible documents into a virtual Aladdin's cave of interactive content. There's an array of sites where anyone with the right equipment to go online can get hold of almost everything that crosses their mind; from consumer goods to information on virtually any topic.

Despite this apparent transformation, the nature of the sites themselves is still fundamentally the same: pages are laid out using the language of HTML which has changed little since the early days, and this is no coincidence. The standardized nature of HTML enables the greatest number of people to access the Web, so how is it that browsing today is such a richer experience? The key is **server-side programming**. Rather than simply dishing out static pre-written HTML pages to browsers, the servers that power modern web sites assemble pages on the fly. These **dynamic pages** can respond to changing conditions, to present the latest information, or to display information according to the user's preferences or job role.

Web sites made up of dynamic pages are called web applications, reflecting their programmatic nature. There are many technologies that can be used on the server to support web applications, and the most popular leverage existing programming languages into the web sphere. The Java language is one of the most widely used languages in the world today, and in spite of the recent shakedown of the computing industry, skilled Java developers still command salaries that could inspire envy in the Pope.

JavaServer Pages, or **JSP** for short, is a server-side technology that takes the Java language, with its inherent simplicity and elegance, and uses it to create highly interactive and flexible web applications. In today's unsure economic climate, having the Java language behind it makes JSP particularly compelling for business: Java is an open language, essentially meaning it doesn't require expensive licenses and thus JSP solutions can be highly cost-effective.

The founding premise of JSP is that HTML can be used to create the basic structure of a web page, and Java code can be mixed in with it to provide the dynamic components of the page that modern web users expect. If you have an understanding of the concepts of HTML and web pages, JSP provides an unbeatable way to learn about creating creative and interactive content as well as to get to grips with the popular language of Java. This book will be your guide as you step into this exciting, but sometimes frustrating, world. We'll teach you:

❑ How to get JSP web applications up and running.

❑ Java, from the elementary principles through to more advanced techniques.

❑ How to put Java to use to build interactive and dynamic web sites.

As you progress through the book, your knowledge and confidence of JSP and Java will be steadily built up, with the help of plenty of step-by-step working examples, until by the end, you're ready to apply these techniques in the professional arena.

Who is this Book For?

As one of Wrox Press's *Beginning* series, this book will show you everything you need to know, from scratch. All we assume is a basic understanding of web pages written in HTML.

We don't assume any programming experience, and teach you all you need to know about Java as well as JSP, from the essential syntax and rules, to where to download the required software for free. However, this book will also suit you if you have a little programming experience in a language other than Java, or would like to turn your hand towards web programming.

What's Covered in this Book?

In the early chapters, this book runs through the process of creating and deploying some simple JSP applications, and looks into the fundamentals of the Java language. We go on to build on this start by introducing new techniques, and gradually increasing the complexity and sophistication of the code the example applications demonstrate.

The book's chapters can be summarized as follows:

In **Chapter 1**, *A First JSP*, we lay the foundation for the rest of the book by walking through the process of installing the software that JavaServer Pages and Java require. We then test that everything's working by creating our very first working JSP page. The chapter also contains some background discussion on the origins of today's Web, explaining a little of the various technologies you may encounter in your work.

Chapter 2, *How It Works*, builds on the lessons from Chapter 1 to show how HTML and JSP code can work together to create dynamic web pages. We look at some key HTML elements that are particularly useful in this context, and look at some special JSP tags, called the **JSP Standard Tag Library**, or **JSTL**.

Chapter 3, *Working with Data*, looks at a crucial aspect of almost all interactive web sites: the storage and retrieval of data. Web sites can either entertain or educate, or if you're lucky they do both. In either case it takes relevant and up-to-date content. Often, such content is stored in databases, and incorporating such dynamic information into web pages is the subject of this chapter. We look at how the popular and powerful (and free) MySQL tool can be used to store data in combination with JSP.

Chapter 4, *Reusing Code*, takes a look at how web sites are designed and built in the real world of business. The efficiency of this process is often what sets professional development teams apart from the amateurs, and an essential technique to aid efficiency is that of code reuse. This chapter examines why it is so important, and introduces a technique that facilitates it in the world of JSP applications – the **JavaBean**.

Chapter 5, *Decisions, Decisions*, takes an in-depth look at an essential technique for any dynamic page: conditional logic. We look at the constructs that we have available, and how and when our web applications should use each.

In order to develop anything other than the most simplistic web sites, you'll need a solid grasp of the concepts of **OOP (Object Oriented Programming)**. **Chapter 6**, *More on Objects*, examines and reveals all that you need to know, from constructors and casting, to interfaces and inheritance.

Chapter 7, *Utility Classes and the Expression Language*, examines the most useful of the J2SE class library that comes with the Java language. These classes perform a variety of common tasks, such as dealing with **collections**, and dates and times. We finish off by looking at how the Expression Language (or EL) simplifies using these utility classes from our web pages.

Chapter 8, *When It All Goes Wrong*, deals with that essential part of any professional quality application: handling errors. It's an unfortunate but inescapable fact that things don't always go according to plan, and so Java provides a mechanism for handling and recovering from such mishaps: the system of **exceptions**. We look at these here, as well as providing some useful techniques when tracking down errors (bugs) in our code.

When creating JSP pages, we don't have to place our code in the page itself. We've already seen one way to encapsulate code elsewhere, when we looked at JavaBeans in Chapter 4 (and elsewhere). In **Chapter 9**, *Writing Tag Libraries*, we examine the other main technique: creating our own **custom tags**, which we can then use in our pages just as if they were standard JSP tags.

Chapter 10, *Behind the Scenes*, takes a useful and interesting journey into what goes on in order to make our pages work. It looks at the key concept of the **servlet**, and the part that it has to play. We also have a first look at the concepts of authentication and state.

Chapter 11, *Keeping Track of Users*, comes back to the **session** and **application** objects introduced in the previous chapter. We investigate how they, in conjunction with **cookies**, let our applications deal intelligently with users by tracking who's using our site, and what they are currently doing.

Chapter 12, *Securing Web Applications*, examines the all-important issue of web site **security**. We look at how to secure our applications using Tomcat, and how to require various levels of authentication when users try to access particular resources. We finish with a step-by-step example of how to create our own custom security tags.

In **Chapter 13**, *JDBC and Advanced Queries*, we revisit the topic of Chapter 4 to add some more technical details to your data access knowledge, such as **connection pooling**, executing **SQL commands** through JDBC (Java Database Connectivity), and **transactions**, illustrated by worked examples as usual.

XML is an increasingly popular format for sharing information over the Web, and in **Chapter 14**, *JSP and XML*, we look at the principles of the XML standard, and run a few JSP samples that manipulate XML using freely available tag libraries.

Chapter 15, *Structuring Applications with Struts*, takes a detailed tour of the JSP application framework known as **Struts**. This framework is widely used in the industry, and it supplies a structure that we can apply to our web applications. This structure takes care of a lot of the groundwork required by professional-level applications, and can handle aspects such as internationalization and security.

We've come a long way since the start of the book, and **Chapter 16**, *A Struts Web Application*, rounds things off with a case study, based on Struts as many real-world JSP applications are. We walk through this complex database-powered application, providing an invaluable overview of how the components of a working application fit together in practice.

At the end of the book, four **appendices** cover a range of useful reference material on the syntax of JSP and its implicit objects, the details of the various configuration files you'll encounter during the course of the book, and sources of useful information that will continue to be useful throughout your web development career.

What You Need to Use this Book

The first thing you'll need to use this book is a computer that supports the Java programming language. This includes computers that run Microsoft Windows (including Windows 95, 98, Me, NT, 2000, and XP) or Linux.

All the software we'll use is open source, so it is available free of charge over the Internet. Consequently, an Internet connection is pretty much essential in order to get hold of this software.

As we need further software components during the course of the book, we'll indicate clearly where to download them from and the installation procedure to follow.

Conventions

We've used a number of different styles of text and layout in this book to differentiate between different kinds of information. Here are examples of the styles used and an explanation of what they mean.

Code has several fonts. If we're talking about code in the text, we use a non-proportional font like this: `for...next`. If it's a block of code that can be typed as a program and run, then it will also appear within a gray box:

```
public java.util.List getDependants()
{
  return _jspx_dependants;
}
```

Sometimes we'll see code in a mixture of styles, like this:

```
import javax.servlet.http.*;

public class SessionTracker2 extends HttpServlet
{
  public void doGet(HttpServletRequest req, HttpServletResponse res)
```

When this happens, the code with a white background is code we are already familiar with; the line highlighted in gray is a new addition to the code since we last looked at it.

Advice, hints, and background information come in this type of font.

> **Important pieces of information are placed inside boxes like this.**

Bullets appear indented, with each new bullet marked as follows:

❑ **Important Words** are in a bold type font.

❑ Words that appear on the screen, or in menus like File or Window, are in a similar font to the one you would see on a Windows desktop.

❑ Keys that you press on the keyboard, such as *Ctrl* and *Enter*, are in italics.

Customer Support

We always value hearing from our readers, and we want to know what you think about this book: what you liked, what you didn't like, and what you think we can do better next time. You can send us your comments, either by returning the reply card in the back of the book, or by e-mail to feedback@wrox.com. Please be sure to mention the book title in your message.

How to Download Sample Code for this Book

Visit the Wrox site at http://www.wrox.com/, and locate the title through our Find a Book facility. Open the book's detail page and click the Download Code link. Alternatively, click the DOWNLOAD CODE link at the top of the Wrox homepage, and select the book in the text box there.

Before you download the code for this book, you may register your book by providing your name and current e-mail address. This is a purely optional step which allows us to contact you should issues with the code download arise, or should the code download package be updated at a later date. Be assured that Wrox will never pass any details supplied during registration to any third party. Full details are contained in our Privacy Policy, linked to from the download page.

Download files are archived in a zipped format, and need to be extracted with a decompression program such as WinZip or PKUnzip. The code is typically arranged with a suitable folder structure, so ensure your decompression software is set to use folder names before extracting the files.

Errata

We've made every effort to make sure that there are no errors in the text or in the code. However, no one is perfect and mistakes do occur. If you find an error in one of our books, such as a spelling mistake or a faulty piece of code, we would be very grateful to hear about it. By sending in errata, you may save another reader hours of frustration, and of course, you will be helping us provide even higher quality information. Simply e-mail the information to support@wrox.com, where your information will be checked and posted on the errata page for the title, or used in subsequent editions of the book.

To view errata on the web site, go to http://www.wrox.com/, and locate the title through the Find a Book search box. Clicking the View errata link that appears below the cover graphic on the book's detail page brings up a list of all errata for that book reported to date.

E-mail Support

If you wish to directly query a problem in the book with an expert who knows the book in detail then e-mail support@wrox.com, with the title of the book and the last four numbers of the ISBN in the subject field of the e-mail. A typical e-mail should include the following things:

- ❏ The **title of the book, last four digits of the ISBN**, and **page number** of the problem in the Subject field.

- ❏ Your **name, contact information**, and the **problem** in the body of the message.

We **won't** send you junk mail. We need the details to save your time and ours. When you send an e-mail message, it will go through the following chain of support:

- ❏ Customer Support – Your message is delivered to our customer support staff, who are the first people to read it. They have files on most frequently asked questions and will answer anything general about the book or the web site immediately.

❑ Editorial – Deeper queries are forwarded to the technical editor responsible for that book. They have experience with the programming language or particular product, and are able to answer detailed technical questions on the subject.

❑ The Authors – Finally, in the unlikely event that the editor cannot answer your problem, he or she will forward the request to the author. We do try to protect the author from any distractions to their writing; however, we are quite happy to forward specific requests to them. All Wrox authors help with the support on their books. They will e-mail the customer and the editor with their response, and again all readers should benefit.

The Wrox Support process can only offer support to issues that are directly pertinent to the content of our published title. Support for questions that fall outside the scope of normal book support is provided via the community lists of our http://p2p.wrox.com/ forum.

p2p.wrox.com

For author and peer discussion join the P2P mailing lists. Our unique system provides **programmer to programmer**™ contact on mailing lists, forums, and newsgroups, all in addition to our one-to-one e-mail support system. If you post a query to P2P, you can be confident that it is being examined by the many Wrox authors and other industry experts who are present on our mailing lists. At p2p.wrox.com you will find a number of different lists that can help you, not only while you read this book, but also as you move on and develop your own applications.

To subscribe to a mailing list just follow these steps:

1. Go to http://p2p.wrox.com/

2. Choose the appropriate category from the left menu bar

3. Click on the mailing list you wish to join

4. Follow the instructions to subscribe and fill in your e-mail address and password

5. Reply to the confirmation e-mail you receive

6. Use the subscription manager to join more lists and set your e-mail preferences

Why This System Offers the Best Support

You can choose to join the mailing lists or you can receive them as a weekly digest. If you don't have the time, or facilities, to receive the mailing list, then you can search our online archives. Junk and spam mails are deleted, and your own e-mail address is protected by the unique Lyris system. Queries about joining or leaving lists, and any other general queries about lists, should be sent to listsupport@p2p.wrox.com.

CHAPTER 1

A First JSP

Welcome! In recent years, Java has risen to become one of the dominant development platforms for the Web, and knowledge of Java and often JSP is required for a wide variety of situations throughout the industry. You probably already knew that, and that's why you're reading this book right now.

In this book, we set out to make it easy for anyone of only modest computing skills to learn enough about Java and JSP to create web applications using the very latest technologies in this arena, such as JSP 2.0 and Tomcat 5.0 (you'll learn what these are in just a few paragraphs).

The goal of this first chapter is to install all the tools on your machine that you'll need to develop JSP web applications. We'll walk through the process of writing a simple web application as well, and discuss some fundamental principles of the Web itself, looking at the role that Java and related technologies have to play.

Subsequent chapters of this book will gradually ramp up your knowledge of JSP and Java as it pertains to JSP applications. By the end of the book, you will be confident enough to start writing your own JSP web applications.

Installing the Software

Fortunately, all the software that we'll use throughout this book is available without charge. In this chapter, we'll install the essentials for creating Java web applications, namely:

❑ **Java 2 Standard Edition Software Development Kit (J2SE SDK)**. There are three different versions of Java that software developers use: Java 2 Micro Edition (J2ME), Java 2 Standard Edition (J2SE), and Java 2 Enterprise Edition (J2EE). J2ME is used for developing applications for small devices such as phones or PDAs. It is a stripped down version that is highly optimized for these devices' limited capabilities. J2SE is the standard version of Java for developing everything else, from games to business applications. J2EE is built on top of J2SE, adding a plethora of features geared towards applications for very large businesses (so-called "enterprises"). All the extras included with J2EE can be downloaded separately and used with J2SE.

❑ **Apache Jakarta Tomcat**. Tomcat is what's known as a **servlet container**. In the Java world, a servlet container is responsible for receiving web requests and passing them to Java web applications. We discuss servlet containers and Tomcat in greater detail later in this chapter.

We will provide instructions for installing these applications on Windows 2000/XP and Red Hat Linux. If you're using a different version of Windows or a different distribution of Linux, and you can't figure out what's going on from the instructions given, don't panic; both of these applications come with their own installation instructions. In a pinch, you can simply refer to them.

Downloading Java Standard Edition

Sun Microsystems, the creator and maintainer of Java, make it available for download from their web site. At the time of writing, the latest version is 1.4.1, which can be found at the following URL:

http://java.sun.com/j2se/1.4.1/download.html

This URL takes you to a page offering the various flavors available depending on the platform you use. There is also the choice between the JRE and the SDK. The JRE (Java Runtime Environment) is for folks who wish to run Java applications but aren't developing Java software, so you'll want the SDK (Software Development Kit). If you're using Windows, download the one labeled:

Windows (all languages, including English)

If you're on Linux, download this one:

Linux RPM in self-extracting file

> **Be sure to download the J2SE SDK, not the JRE.**

Because web sites are subject to change, and books sadly are unchanged after they've been printed, these links may no longer work. In that event, the general directions are to visit http://java.sun.com and download the latest version of Java for your operating system that you can find. Sun does a pretty good job of providing help and instructions to get you this far.

Installing Java on Windows

The file you've downloaded is a self-extracting EXE file, so double-click it once it's downloaded. You then need to enter the name of the folder where Java is to be installed. Choose something like `C:\java\jdk1.4`, but if you install to somewhere else be sure to note down the location for future use. Now finish off the installation, leaving any options at their default values.

Installing Java on Red Hat Linux

The RPM (Red Hat Package Manager) file you downloaded is wrapped in a self-extracting binary format that you'll need to execute before you can install. Open a shell prompt to the location you've downloaded Java, and type the following:

```
chmod a+x j2sdk-1_4_1_01-linux-i586-rpm.bin
./j2sdk-1_4_1_01-linux-i586-rpm.bin
```

You will then be presented with a long license. Read it carefully and copiously (wink), and then agree to it, at which point an RPM file will be extracted into the same directory. Before you can install it, you must become the `root` user by typing the following:

```
su
```

Once you've entered the `root` password at the prompt, you can then install Java by typing:

```
rpm -U j2sdk-1_4_1_01-linux-i586-rpm
```

Of course, if you've downloaded a different version of Java, you'll need to use that filename in place of the one shown here.

The RPM will install Java to the following path: `/usr/java/j2sdk1.4.1_01`.

Downloading Tomcat

This book has been written for the latest incarnation of the Apache Foundation's Tomcat web server, version 5.0. However, Tomcat 5.0 was not quite ready for release at the time of writing, so we can't provide an absolutely definitive URL for downloading it. A good place to start is at the following URL:

> http://jakarta.apache.org/site/binindex.html

That link should pull up a page with (among other things) assorted links under the headings of **Release Builds**, **Milestone Builds**, and **Nightly Builds**. Look for anything starting with **Tomcat 5** in the **Release Builds** section and click it. In the event that there is no release build of Tomcat 5, download the latest Tomcat 5 release under the **Milestone Builds** heading, or try the following URL:

http://jakarta.apache.org/builds/jakarta-tomcat/release/v5.0.0-alpha/

The Tomcat 5 link takes you to a screen that begins with a file listing. Click on the folder marked bin, and from the list of files that then appear, Windows users should select the latest version of Tomcat 5 that ends with .exe, and Linux users should download the latest version ending with .tar.gz.

> Do not download any files that have **LE** in the filename, as this indicates the "Light Edition" of Tomcat. Although the Light Edition avoids downloading duplicate copies of libraries that are now included in the 1.4 version of J2SE, it also excludes two libraries, JavaMail and the Java Activation Framework, that we will be using later in this book.

If you can't find any links to download Tomcat 5, that probably means that Tomcat 5 hasn't yet been officially released. In this case, navigate to the following location, and click the link that starts v5.x.x to get hold of a pre-release version:

http://jakarta.apache.org/builds/jakarta-tomcat/release/

Installing Tomcat on Windows

Just as with Java, all you need to do to install Tomcat is double-click on the file you've downloaded. You'll need to select a directory for the installation, such as C:\java\tomcat50. As with Java, you'll need to remember this location for later use. Do not click on the checkbox labeled **NT Service** should you see it. This option means that Windows will start Tomcat automatically every time the system boots up, and stop it when Windows is shut down. This is really only useful when web applications are finished, rather than when applications are being created, as in this book.

Installing Tomcat on Linux

To install Tomcat, you'll need to create a suitable directory with the mkdir command, and extract Tomcat into that directory with the following command (assuming you are in the same directory where you downloaded Tomcat):

```
tar -xzf jakarta-tomcat-5.0.tar.gz -C /usr/local/java/tomcat50
```

Of course, change the names of the file and directory as appropriate.

Configuring Your Environment

The final step of the installation is to set some **environment variables** which applications can use to find components required for proper operation. Tomcat needs us to set two environment variables, and we'll also modify the PATH variable so that the Java and Tomcat files are accessible from any other folder.

Windows 2000 / XP

1. Open the System item in Control Panel, and select the Advanced tab.

2. Click the Environment Variables button to open the Environment Variables dialog. You should see a window like this one:

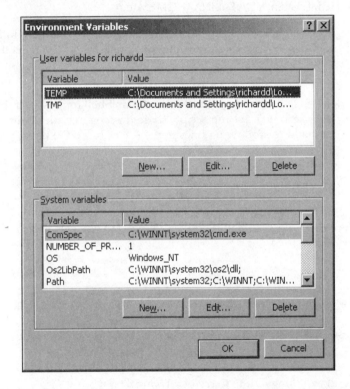

3. Click the New button in the lower System Variables section. When the New System Variable dialog appears, enter a name of JAVA_HOME, and enter the full path to your JDK (such as C:\java\jdk1.4) for the value.

4. Repeat steps 3 and 4 to create another variable called CATALINA_HOME, the value of which specifies the location of your Tomcat installation (such as C:\java\tomcat50).

5. Create one last variable by following the same process. Call it **CLASSPATH**, and give it a value of %CATALINA_HOME%\common\lib\servlet.jar;.

   *If you already have an environment variable called **CLASSPATH**, place the above at the end of the existing value, with a semi-colon (;) at the end of the old value and before the value given above.*

6. Locate the variable named **Path** in the System variables list, and double-click it or click the **Edit** button to bring up the Edit System Variable dialog.

   Chances are, a few different paths are already given for this variable, each path separated by a semi-colon. Select the value box and press the *End* key on your keyboard. Type in the following, including the semicolon at the beginning:

   ;%JAVA_HOME%\bin;%CATALINA_HOME%\bin

7. Once you're done, click on **OK** to close the **Edit System Variable** window, and **OK** a couple more times to close the Environment Variables and Systems dialogs.

Red Hat Linux

Red Hat Linux's default shell is the popular Bourne Again Shell (or **bash**). If this is your shell, you'll need to edit your account's startup script. To do this, log in under your own account (usually *not* root) and add the following lines to the ~/.bashrc file using your editor of choice:

```
export JAVA_HOME=/usr/java/j2sdk1.4.1_01
export CATALINA_HOME=/usr/local/java/Jakarta-tomcat-5.0
export PATH=${PATH}:${JAVA_HOME}/bin:${CATALINA_HOME}/bin
```

If by chance you're using the TC Shell (**tcsh**), you'll need to edit ~/.tcshrc by adding the following lines:

```
setenv JAVA_HOME /usr/java/j2sdk1.4.1_01
setenv CATALINA_HOME /usr/local/java/Jakarta-tomcat-5.0
setenv PATH ${PATH}:${JAVA_HOME}/bin:${CATALINA_HOME}/bin
```

Again, if you've chosen different directories for the above, change them as necessary, and if you're not sure which shell you're using, type **echo $SHELL** to find out.

We're all done with installing – time to try out Tomcat!

Try It Out   Testing Tomcat

1. On Windows, the installer created a group in your start menu, probably called Apache Tomcat 5.0. To run Tomcat, select the **Start Tomcat** item in this menu. Alternately, if you prefer the Windows command line, you can execute the following command:

> **%CATALINA_HOME%\bin\startup**

However, as we've added `%CATALINA_HOME%\bin` to the path, you can just type `startup` and it'll work.

On Linux, you can start Tomcat by executing the following script:

`/usr/local/java/tomcat50/startup.sh`

As we've added Tomcat to the `PATH` variable, you can simply type `startup.sh`.

2. Once Tomcat is up and running, open your favorite web browser and navigate to http://localhost:8080/. You should see a page something like the following:

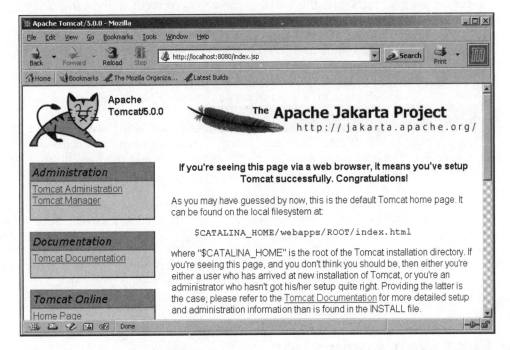

3. Scroll down to the Examples box on the left hand side, click the JSP Examples link, and try out a couple of the sample programs to verify that everything is working properly. If you can't get the examples to work, double check that you have correctly followed the above instructions.

4. At some point, you'll want to shut Tomcat down. On Windows, you can do this by clicking the Stop Tomcat item in the Start menu. The command line version of this is `%CATALINA_HOME%\bin\shutdown`, or just `shutdown`. Normally, you should avoid simply closing the Tomcat window, as that may result in loss of data.

On Linux, execute the script `shutdown.sh`.

When Things Go Wrong

If Tomcat did not start up like it was supposed to, try the following suggestions to figure out where things went wrong.

1. On Windows, open a command prompt (look for the Command Prompt in the Start menu, or type cmd or command in the Run option given on the Start menu). Type the command cd %CATALINA_HOME%. On Linux, type cd $CATALINA_HOME, also without the quotes. Verify that you are now in the directory where you installed Tomcat. If not, repeat the step for creating that environment variable in the *Configuring Your Environment* section above.

2. Repeat the same process using %JAVA_HOME% or $JAVA_HOME. If you're not in the correct location, make sure this variable was set up correctly in the *Configuring Your Environment* section.

3. From the Windows command line, type java and press *Enter*. If you see a message starting with something like 'java' is not recognized as..., try typing %JAVA_HOME%\bin\java and pressing *Enter*. If that still produces the same error message, it indicates that Java was not properly installed for some reason.

    Verify that you properly followed the instructions for installing Java, and check the java.sun.com web site for help. If the first command failed but the second one succeeded, repeat the section for setting the PATH variable in the *Configuring Your Environment* section.

    The same applies to Linux users, but you'll need to use $JAVA_HOME in place of %JAVA_HOME% in the above instructions. Also note that Windows uses a back-slash (\) for its paths, whereas Linux uses a forward-slash (/).

4. If you've made it this far, check and see if Tomcat was properly installed at the path you selected. If not, reinstall it, referring to the jakarta.apache.org/tomcat web site for any special guidance.

Our First Web Application

Okay, we've got Java, we've got Tomcat: now we're ready to write a little web application. This example will be our first look at **JavaServer Pages (JSP)** technology, which mixes Java code with standard HTML, and what could be better for our first application than a version of the timeless "Hello World" program? Far be it from us to break from long-standing tradition. To add a dynamic touch, we'll make it perform some hard-core number crunching too.

Try It Out	A Simple Web Application

1. We'll start by creating a new web application called `helloJSP`. To do this, use Windows Explorer to create a new folder with that name in the `webapps` subdirectory off the Tomcat installation folder. This will create the directory structure shown below:

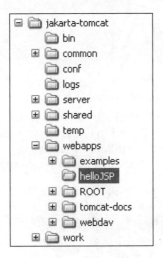

2. Inside this folder, we need to create another folder. We won't actually *use* it in this chapter, but it must be present for Tomcat to recognize our web application.

Inside the `helloJSP` folder you just created, create a folder called `WEB-INF`. As we'll see in later chapters, this folder is the location for essential files for the web application.

We can now place all sorts of resources in our `helloJSP` web application folder that form part of the web application itself. This might include HTML files and JSP pages, which can be placed directly inside the `helloJSP` folder, and we could view them by navigating in your web browser to a URL such as http://localhost:8080/helloJSP/filename.html.

3. We are going to create a JSP page, which can include Java code that is run *by the web server* (in other words, by Tomcat) to alter what is sent to the browser. It's important to be clear that the code is running on the server – although as you run examples in this book, you'll probably have the browser running on the same machine as the web server, that's not the case for applications that have been deployed.

Create a new text file in your `helloJSP` folder, and call it `index.jsp`. When writing code files, be they JSP or Java, you'll need to use a text editor such as Notepad rather than a word processor like Microsoft Word as the latter will insert special formatting characters that will render our code useless.

4. Open the new `index.jsp` file, and add the following code:

```html
<html>
  <head>
    <title>My First JSP</title>
  </head>
  <body>
    Hello, world!
    <p/>
    2 + 2 is ${2 + 2} and 4 * 4 is ${4 * 4}
  </body>
</html>
```

Save the file, and we're done.

5. Now, let's see how our JSP page appears in a web browser. Start Tomcat (if it's still running from earlier, you'll need to shut it down and restart it so it will recognize our new `helloJSP` web application) and then navigate to http://localhost:8080/helloJSP/index.jsp in your browser.

You should see a screen that looks something like this:

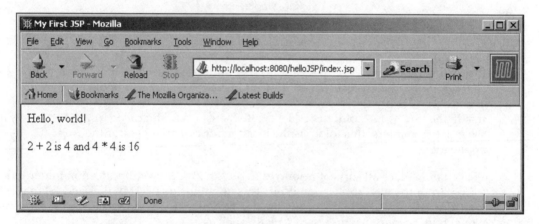

Congratulations! You've created your first JSP, and you're on the way to a larger world of Java fun. If all this still seems a bit hazy at the moment, don't worry, as things will become clearer as you progress through the book.

If it didn't work for you, make sure that Tomcat is running, and that you have capitalized the URL just as the `index.jsp` file and `helloJSP` folder are capitalized on disk.

How It Works

If you've done any work with HTML, the JSP we wrote should have looked very familiar to you. In fact, the only JSP-centric code we wrote was this line:

```
2 + 2 is ${2 + 2} and 4 * 4 is ${4 * 4}
```

JSP uses the special notation, `${ ... }`, to distinguish itself from normal HTML. The servlet container (that is, Tomcat) will then attempt to evaluate the expression within those tags.

In this case, we've created code that completes two simple mathematical expressions: 2 + 2 and 4 * 4. Of course, you will soon learn how to do much more than simple math.

While we're here, select **View | Source** in your browser to see exactly what HTML the browser received. Notice that it's entirely HTML – the JSP code elements have been replaced with the result of the contained expressions – the Java code was run *on the server* and never made it as far as the browser:

```
<html>
    <head>
        <title>My First JSP</title>
    </head>
    <body>
        Hello, world!
        <p/>
        2 + 2 is 4 and 4 * 4 is 16
    </body>
</html>
```

The URL we used to request the page, http://localhost:8080/helloJSP/index.jsp, comprises five distinct parts:

- ❑ http – This indicates that our request and response are carried over the Hypertext Transfer Protocol, HTTP, which is the standard mode of communication between browsers and servers on the World Wide Web.

- ❑ localhost – This is the name of the web server. localhost is a reserved name to indicate the local machine, that is, the machine the browser is running on. Normally, a web browser will access a server somewhere else in the world, in which case this part would be substituted with the domain where you are making the application available, such as www.myJSP.com. During development and testing however, pages are often accessed from a browser running on the same machine as the web server, in which case the localhost shortcut can be used.

  Technically, localhost is an **alias** for the IP address 127.0.0.1, sometimes called the **loopback address**, and which indicates the local machine.

19

❑ 8080 – This is the port number that the web server is listening on. A computer can have various server programs each waiting for clients (such as web browsers) to connect to them. To avoid clashing, each server program must have a unique port number. Normally web servers use port 80, so Tomcat uses port 8080 by default in order to coexist with any other web server that may be running on the same machine.

❑ helloJSP – This is the name of the web application we created, and tells Tomcat which subfolder of `webapps` contains the resources for this application.

❑ index.jsp – This is the name of the actual document we requested. The `.jsp` extension tells Tomcat to treat the file as a JSP file, and execute any Java code it contains. Files that have the `.html` extension are left untouched and sent directly to the browser.

We can also create subfolders off our `helloJSP` folder to hold other web resources, such as images. Such subfolders do not become web applications in their own right though – only folders directly within Tomcat's `webapps` folder are web applications.

Brief History of Java and the Web

For the curious, the following sections present a summarized history of the Web and the role that Java plays in it. Feel free to skip to the next chapter if you'd rather just get straight down to business.

The Web

Back in the sixties, as computers began their prolific distribution across the nation, the United States military constructed a computer network called ARPANET, which was designed to link key computers across the nation. The network was based on a peer-to-peer model, that is, instead of a single machine acting as the server, all computers on the network passed messages along. The idea was that this made the network resistant to disruption caused by a nuclear attack on the United States knocking out key computers.

Fortunately, this resistance to nuclear attack was never tested, but the network's well-designed and robust architecture ensured its survival. As well as the military, the academic community was connected to it, and soon the network became primarily used for scientific research and collaboration. It was renamed the **Internet** because it linked up many local area and wide area networks.

The early days of the Internet were not for the layman. Few people outside of the scientific disciplines were even aware that it even existed, and fewer still had access to it. Ease of use was not a priority, and the first generation of Internet users used command-line utilities such as Telnet, FTP, and Gopher to get anything useful done.

The seeds of a more user-friendly Internet, and hence one that was open for more widespread use, were sown in 1989 when Tim Berners-Lee, a computer scientist working for the European Organization for Nuclear Research (CERN), came up with the concept of the **World Wide Web**. Berners-Lee envisaged an interactive **hypertext** system on top of the existing Internet to facilitate communication amongst the world community of physicists. Hypertext refers to any system where certain words function as links to other documents or sections of a document – Macintosh users might remember the classic HyperCard, which was the first hypertext application used by many.

The Web began to gain momentum, and by 1993 comprised around 50 web servers. At this time an event occurred that would light the fuse of the Internet skyrocket: the National Center for Supercomputing Applications (NCSA) at the University of Illinois released the first version of the Mosaic web browser for Unix, PC, and Macintosh systems. Prior to Mosaic, the only fully featured browser available was on the NeXT platform.

With the Mosaic foundation in place, 1994 saw the emergence of the Web into popular culture, and members of the general public began to explore the Internet for themselves. In the same year, a small Silicon Valley company, that would eventually become Netscape, was founded by some of the same folks who had created Mosaic. The so-called "New Economy" consisting of e-land grabs and irrationally over-valued companies was just around the corner. And the rest is, well, history.

For more information on the history of the Internet, see *http://www.isoc.org/internet/history/.*
For more information on the history of the Web, see *http://www.w3.org/History.html*

How The Web Works

There can be confusion as to what exactly the Internet is and how it's different from the Web. The Internet is the physical computer network that links computers around the world. The Web on the other hand is a **service** that sits on the foundation of the Internet. The Web allows computers to communicate with each other. The Web is one of many different services that utilize the Internet; others include e-mail, streaming video, and multiplayer games.

As a service, the Web defines how two parties, a **web client** (generally a web browser) and a **web server**, use the Internet to communicate. When you visit a web site, a relationship is created between your browser and the web site server. In this relationship, the browser and server communicate through the exchange of messages. First, your browser sends a message to the web server requesting the particular web page that you have asked for, and the web server responds with an appropriate message containing the HTML for the page if it is available. For each additional page that is viewed, the web browser sends additional requests to the web server, which likewise responds with the appropriate messages.

This type of relationship is called a **request-response model**. The client, in this case the web browser, requests a specific resource (for instance, a web page) and the server then responds with the requested resource, if it's available. The requests and responses travel over the Web using the **Hyper Text Transfer Protocol** (**HTTP**). Just as a diplomatic protocol dictates how two governmental parties should conduct discussions, HTTP defines what messages should be exchanged when two computers communicate remotely. The request the client sends to the server is the HTTP **request**, and the response sent by the server back to the client is the HTTP **response**.

The Responsive Web

The web today doesn't consist solely of static pages that return an identical document to every user, and many pages contain content that is generated independently for each viewer. While static files still have their place, the most useful and appealing pages are dynamically created in response to the users' preferences.

The **Common Gateway Interface** (**CGI**) provided the original mechanism by which web users could actually execute programs on web servers, not just request HTML pages. Under the CGI model:

1. The web browser sends a request just as it would for an HTML page.

2. The web server recognizes that the requested resource corresponds to an external program.

3. The web server executes the external program, passing it the HTTP request that it received from the browser.

4. The external program does its work, and sends its results to the server.

5. The web server passes the program's output back to the browser as an HTTP response.

CGI was enormously popular in the early days of the Web as a means of generating web pages on the fly. Almost every programming language imaginable has been used to implement some kind of CGI-based solution, but Perl is perhaps the most popular language for CGI development.

However, as the Web grew in popularity and the traffic demands placed on web sites increased, CGI wasn't efficient enough to keep up. This is because, with CGI, each time a request is received the web server must start running a new copy of the external program.

If only a handful of users request a CGI program simultaneously, this doesn't present too much of a problem, but it's a different story if hundreds or thousands of users request the resource at the same time. Each copy of the program requires its own share of CPU time and memory, and the server's resources are rapidly used up. The situation is even bleaker when CGI programs are written in interpreted languages such as Perl which result in the launch of large run-time interpreters with each request.

Alternatives to CGI

Over the years, many alternative solutions to CGI have surfaced. The more successful of these all provide an environment that exists *inside* an existing web server, or even functions as a web server on its own.

Many such CGI replacements have been built on top of the popular open-source **Apache web server** (http://www.apache.org/). This is because of Apache's popular modular API, which allows developers to extend Apache's functionality with persistent programs. The modules are loaded in memory when Apache starts up, and Apache passes the appropriate HTTP requests to these in-memory modules and passes the HTTP responses back out to the browser. This means that the cost of loading an interpreter into memory is removed, and scripts can begin executing faster.

While few developers actually create modules themselves (because they are relatively difficult to develop), many third-party modules exist that provide a basis for developers to create applications that are much more efficient than normal CGI. A few examples:

❑ **mod_perl** – Maintains the Perl interpreter in memory, thus freeing Perl scripts from the overhead of loading a new copy of the Perl interpreter for each request. This module is very popular.

❑ **mod_php4** – Speeds up code in the popular PHP language in the same way that mod_perl speeds up Perl.

❑ **mod_fastcgi** – Similar to plain vanilla CGI, but enables programs to stay resident in memory rather than terminate when each request is completed.

While the Apache name originally referred only to the Apache web server, a legion of open-source programs have been developed under the auspices of the Apache Project, including the Tomcat server which we're using in this book.

One CGI replacement technology you may well have already heard of is Microsoft's **Active Server Pages**, or **ASP**. Initially, Microsoft attempted to create an interface to their IIS web server, called **ISAPI** for **Internet Server Application Programming Interface**. This didn't spawn the large following that Apache's equivalent API did, but it is nevertheless a high-performance API that many businesses use, including eBay. However, because of its complexity, ISAPI is rarely suited to the beginning developer. Microsoft's IIS web server itself, however, is widely used, largely because it comes free with many versions of Windows. Incidentally, IIS can be configured to work with Tomcat.

Microsoft followed up ISAPI with its ASP technology, which lets us embed programming code, typically VBScript, into standard HTML pages. This model has proved extremely successful, and acted as the catalyst driving the development of Java web technology, which we will discuss shortly.

Java and the Web

At last we come to Java. Java was initially released in the mid-1990's as a way to liven up dull, static web pages. It was platform-independent (the same Java code can run on computers running a variety of different operating systems, rather than being tied to just one) and allowed developers to have their programs executed right in the web browser. Many an industry sage prognosticated that these Java **applets** (applet being a "mini-application" that executes within another application – the browser) would catch on, making the Web more exciting and interactive, and changing the way we bought computers, reducing all the various operating systems into mere platforms for web browsers.

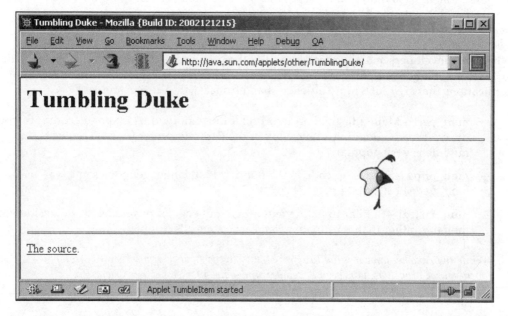

One of many applets available at http://java.sun.com/applets/. If you enter the URL shown in the screenshot above, don't forget to capitalize it as it appears.

However, Java applets never really caught on to the degree such people predicted, and other technologies such as Macromedia Flash became more popular ways of creating interactive web sites. However, Java isn't just good for applets: it can also be used for creating standalone platform independent applications. While these too could threaten the monopolies of entrenched incompatible operating systems, Java applications haven't really caught on yet either. This is probably because Java's support for creating GUI (Graphical User Interface) applications – applications with windows, icons, buttons, and so on – has until very recently been quite poor and quite slow. This situation is changing, and in fact today's versions of Java do enable developers to create cutting-edge GUI applications.

But like a prizefighter that won't stay down, those innovative Java architects kept on fighting, releasing Java **servlets** into the arena. Servlets (a "mini-server") are another alternative technology to CGI. Servlets are not stand-alone applications, and must be loaded into memory by a **servlet container**. The servlet container then functions as a web server, receiving HTTP requests from web browsers and passing them to servlets which generate the response, typically an HTML document. Alternatively, the servlet container can integrate with an existing web server – for example, a popular Apache module integrates Apache with the Tomcat servlet container.

The simplicity of the Java programming language, its platform independent nature, Sun's open-source and community-driven attitude towards Java, and the elegance of the servlet model itself have all made servlets an immensely popular solution for providing dynamic web content.

JavaServer Pages (JSP)

To make creating dynamic web content even easier, Sun introduced **JavaServer Pages** (**JSP**). While writing servlets can require pretty extensive knowledge of Java, a Java newbie can learn some pretty neat tricks in JSP in a snap. JSP represents a viable and attractive alternative to Microsoft's ASP.

> *JSP technology is actually built on top of servlets. As we'll see later in the book, the two technologies actually work well together, and it is common to use both in the same web application.*

More On Servlet Containers

As mentioned earlier, JavaServer Pages and servlets require a special kind of server to operate: a servlet container. Tomcat, which we installed earlier, is known as a reference implementation of a JSP servlet container, but this is not to say that it is not worthy of use in production systems. Indeed, many commercial installations do use Tomcat, but there are many other servlet containers available. These include Caucho Resin (http://www.caucho.com), which is very popular, and somewhat faster than Tomcat, but is a commerical product that must be purchased. Jetty (http://jetty.mortbay.org) is perhaps the most popular open source competitor, and there are many alternatives.

The Java Community

In fact, the multiplicity of servlet containers is another example of the biggest strength of the Java family of technology: choice. All the Java technologies are controlled by a community of developers and corporations who together form the **Java Community Process** (**JCP**). The JCP system enables anyone to contribute to the future of Java by participating on expert committees that shape new features of the language, or simply by issuing feedback to Java's architects.

Through the JCP and the documents it publishes into the public domain, anybody can develop Java extensions and features as defined by the JCP. The JCP's main purpose is to prevent the Java language degenerating into a chaos of incompatible, duplicated, and redundant functionality by setting standards. However, because of the freedom to create Java technology based on these standards, Java developers have a great deal of choice of development tools offered by a variety of competing vendors.

This philosophy is often referred to as "agree on standards, compete on implementation". It is in direct contradiction to Microsoft's philosophy embodied in such technologies as its .NET platform. Microsoft controls the standards used in .NET, and creates most of the development tools associated with .NET. Considering the benefits and pitfalls of each model – Java's community driven approach versus Microsoft's benevolent dictatorship approach – is a complex and often emotionally charged issue that will be left out of this book.

Web Applications

To create a web application of any significant utility, a developer usually creates many different JSP pages and/or servlets. Additionally, the developer may have a number of images and HTML pages they wish to associate with the JSP pages and servlets, and there may be code libraries and other files that form part of the same application.

Keeping track of all of these files can be a bit difficult, and configuring a servlet container to know where to find them all can seem quite a nightmare. Hang on – actually, it's really rather easy. It turns out that Java defines a standard directory layout for web applications. Furthermore, Java defines a standard configuration file for web applications that tells servlet containers how the web application works.

By following this standard layout, Java developers don't have to worry about how to configure different servlet containers; it all happens automatically. We will discuss this standard directory layout in greater detail in the next chapter.

Application Servers

Servlet containers are only part of the Java story. Since the development of servlet and JSP technology, many additional Java technologies have been created that ease the development of large and complex business applications, either for use on the Internet or private intranets. Examples of these technologies include Enterprise JavaBeans, which aims to make it easier for developers to distribute sophisticated Java objects onto many different servers (as opposed to having all of the code for an application on one server), and the Java Connector Architecture, which helps developers include older, pre-Java applications and data sources in their applications. These advanced technologies geared towards large businesses compose the J2EE standard, which we briefly mentioned at the start of this chapter.

A servlet container alone is not sufficient to power J2EE applications. Instead, an **application server** is required. This supports all of the J2EE technologies, is usually much more feature rich than a servlet container like Tomcat, and often includes features that enable it to service many more users than a typical servlet container. However, because JavaServer Pages and servlets compose a key part of the J2EE platform, application servers also must support the same features that a servlet container does – and often, an application server simply integrates with one of the existing servlet containers.

While application servers can set you back tens of thousands of dollars, some free application servers are available, such as jBoss (www.jboss.org).

JavaScript

In closing, let's talk about JavaScript. JavaScript is a technology that enables web pages to have some programmatic functionality *in the browser*. While Java applets are isolated applications that are simply displayed on a web page, JavaScript works with and can manipulate the HTML page in which it is embedded.

Some folks, after coding some JavaScript code here and there, are under the impression that they know Java and have programmed in Java, but this isn't really true. JavaScript is **not** Java; it's an entirely distinct programming language that was developed about the same time that Java was released.

Originally called LiveScript, the name was changed by Netscape to JavaScript because it employed a syntax similar to Java's, and because those behind it wanted to capitalize on the exposure and popularity of the Java language. However, Microsoft introduced its own scripting language, JScript, and after a while a neutral standard was developed, with the decidedly less appealing name of **ECMAScript**. Today, JavaScript and JScript are based on this open standard (also called ECMA-262), but Netscape and Microsoft persist in using their proprietary names for their implementations.

To better understand the distinction between JavaScript and JavaServer Pages, it may help you to remember that **JavaScript code is generally executed by the web client (browser)** after the web server sends the browser the HTTP response, while **JavaServer Pages are executed by the web server** before the web server sends the HTTP response. In fact, the JSP is what creates the HTTP response. Thus, JavaScript is said to be a "client-side" technology and it is code that can be viewed (and copied) by web users, while JavaServer Pages are a "server-side" technology where the code is not visible to web users as it is processed by the web server before it reaches the client.

Summary

In this chapter, we've tried to get you up and running as a budding web developer. We've:

❑ installed the basic tools we need to create Java web applications

❑ created our first simple web application

❑ examined the history of the web, the difference between static and dynamic web content, and approaches to creating dynamic content, and the difference between client-side programming (such as JavaScript) and server-side programming (like JSPs or servlets)

In subsequent chapters, we'll build on this foundation to create increasingly complex and useful web applications, and we'll also be taught more details about the workings of the Java language.

CHAPTER 2

How It Works

In Chapter 1, we downloaded and set up the tools necessary to develop JSP applications. We also covered some background information that will help put that development into context. In this chapter, we'll carry on consolidating the foundation that you'll build upon as you establish your JSP career.

We'll start out with a quick rundown of HTML, looking at what makes up a simple HTML page. Once the HTML refresher is out of the way, we'll introduce JSP's major features in order to get a feel for what's possible with JSP.

We'll conclude the chapter by demonstrating several key features of JSP through two examples.

A Brief Summary of HTML

JavaServer Pages consist of normal HTML with additional JSP-specific code. For readers with HTML experience, this means that writing JSPs will be a piece of cake – you simply add a few JSP elements to your existing HTML pages where you want JSP to create dynamic features and you're good to go.

However, if you've never written HTML before, or are quite rusty, don't panic. In this section, we'll provide a brief introduction of HTML. You won't be an HTML expert after this crash course, but you will learn enough to lay a solid foundation upon which we can build with JSP.

Tags

HyperText Markup Language (HTML) consists of two basic elements: tags and text. To understand the relationship between the tags and the text, let's take a look at a snippet of HTML:

```
<h1>Header</h1>
Normal text.
```

This HTML would be displayed by a web browser in a format similar to the following:

Header

Normal text.

The <h1> tag, short for "Header 1", instructs web browsers to display the text within it as a large header. The </h1> tag, which compliments the <h1> tag, marks the end of text that should be formatted as a header.

We can extract a few key points from this example:

❑ HTML tags are enclosed in angle brackets, < and >. Examples of HTML tags are <h1>, <body>, <table>.

❑ HTML tags have two types:

❑ Tags that contain text, such as <h1>text</h1> and text. Such tags should always have a matching beginning and ending tag.

❑ 'Standalone' tags that do not contain text, such as <p /> and <br />. Such tags should always end with " />". Although the final /> was not a requirement of versions prior to XHTML, it has been changed in order to comply with the rules of XML, and it also makes it clear if a tag is a container tag or not. While today's browsers support both formats, you are strongly encouraged to use />, where it is compatible.

❑ The primary purpose of tags is to modify the appearance and behavior of text. There are, however, some other uses, as we will see later in this chapter.

Important Principles

There are ninety different HTML tags. However, an HTML page should contain at least two tags: <html> and <body>. The following example therefore represents the smallest possible HTML page:

```
<html>
  <body>
  </body>
</html>
```

Generally speaking, all of the content of the HTML page that is displayed by the web browser should be nested in the <body> tag.

Attributes

Most HTML tags can have various **attributes** set to alter their behavior or appearance in some way. Such attributes appear after the tag name, within the opening tag itself. For instance, the HTML `<table>` tag, which is used to organize output in the form of rows and columns, has the attribute `border` which can be set as follows:

```
<table border="1">
```

In this case, we've assigned `border` a value of 1, which indicates the size of the border to draw around the table and its cells.

Note that all values given to attributes should be enclosed in quotes (either single or double quotes, but they must match and be consistent throughout the page). Previous versions of HTML didn't require the quotes, and you may encounter code that doesn't use them, but in general that style should be avoided.

In this book, we will introduce those attributes that are useful for our examples and case studies. The complete list of HTML tags (elements) and their attributes can be obtained at the following URLs:

http://www.w3.org/TR/REC-html40/index/elements.html
http://www.w3.org/TR/REC-html40/index/attributes.html

Formatting HTML Output

One of the key concepts of HTML is that any sequence of whitespace is rendered on the browser screen as a single space. In other words, any line breaks or groups of more than one space character will appear on screen as a single space. For example, the following three different HTML pages would all be displayed in the same way:

```
<html>
  <body>
    Hello
    World!
  </body>
</html>
```

```
<html><body>Hello        World!</body></html>
```

```
<html><body>Hello World!</body></html>
```

A browser would display all of these pages as:

Hello World!

To display text on two or more different lines, we use the `<br />` tag to instruct the browser to insert a line break. The following code:

```
<html><body>Hello<br />World!</body></html>
```

would therefore be displayed as:

> Hello
> World!

Paragraphs

The `<p />` tag is used to separate two paragraphs of text. It is similar to the `<br />` tag, with two important differences. First, the `<p />` inserts space in between two paragraphs, whereas the `<br />` tag simply breaks the line. Second, the `<p />` can also be used as a container tag (that is, `<p></p>`).

The following HTML:

```
<html><body>Hello<p />World!</body></html>
```

would be displayed as:

> Hello
>
> World!

Using Tables

A great many HTML pages place text into tables, as a simple yet robust means of formatting data. HTML tables are defined by the `<table>` tag, which contains a `<tr>` tag for each row in the table, and a `<td>` tag for each cell in a row. Thus, the following code:

```
<html>
  <body>
    <table border="1">
      <tr>
        <td>
          Hello
        </td>
        <td>
          World!
        </td>
      </tr>
      <tr>
        <td>
          This is
        </td>
        <td>
```

```
        a table!
      </td>
    </tr>
  </table>
  </body>
</html>
```

would appear in a browser as the following:

Hello	World!
This is	a table!

A Little Style

So far we've talked about inserting line breaks and creating tables, but we haven't addressed how to change other details about the appearance of your HTML, such as font size or color. The style of HTML text is controlled by a special attribute that belongs to almost every tag: the `style` attribute. Some examples of the `style` attribute are shown below:

```
<html>
  <body>
    <p style="color: red">
      This text will be in red!
    </p>
    <p style="color: blue; font-size: 20pt">
      This big text will be in blue!
    </p>
  </body>
</html>
```

The preceding example if rendered would be appear in a browser as follows:

This text will be in red!

This big text will be in blue!

Note that we used the <p> tag as a container in order to apply its style to the text inside. Let's take a closer look at one of the style attributes we added to the <p> tags:

```
style="color: blue; font-size: 20pt"
```

The value of the style attribute, the `"color: blue; font-size: 20pt"` bit, controls how the contents of the container tag are displayed using the style language called **Cascading Style Sheets** (**CSS**). CSS is a way of defining rules which modify how HTML tags are rendered. A CSS rule takes the form of:

```
css_attribute: css_value
```

Multiple CSS attributes can be assigned to a tag's style attribute by joining them together with a semicolon, as shown in the example above. Here are some examples of valid CSS attributes:

Attribute Name	Example(s)	Description

color	`color: blue`
	
	`color: white`
	
	`color: #FFFFFF`
	
	Possible values for `color` include: `aqua`, `black`, `blue`, `fuchsia`, `gray`, `green`, `lime`, `maroon`, `navy`, `olive`, `purple`, `red`, `silver`, `teal`, `white`, and `yellow`
		Controls the font color. Either a name of a color may be provided (some 16 colors are supported by name), or an RGB value in hexadecimal format. The hexadecimal (hex) format starts with a #, and then is composed of three groups of two characters. Each character can be 0-9 or A-F. Using the letter characters lets each character represent 16 values instead of just 10. For example, A represents 11, B is 12, and so on to F, which is 16. The first two characters determine the value for red, the second two for green, and the third two for blue. Thus, the hex color for pure red is #FF0000, for blue is #0000FF, and white is #FFFFFF.

background -color	`background-color: black`	Determines the background color of a region. As for the `color` attribute, this may either be a name or a value.

font-size	`font-size: 12pt`
	
	`font-size: 12px`
	
	`font-size: smaller`
		Controls the size of the font. The values can be given in either the pt (font point size) or px (exact height in pixels) format. Relative font sizes are also possible with the words larger and smaller.

font -family	`font-family: Arial`
	
	`font-family: Tahoma, sans-serif`
		Sets the font to be used.

That's enough CSS to get us started, but there's a lot more that CSS enables us to do, and if you're interested, look at http://www.w3.org/TR/REC-CSS2/.

Creating Style Classes

If you want to apply the same style to multiple parts of your HTML document, it would be rather tedious to repeat it all over the place, as in the following HTML fragment:

```
<p style="font-size: 20pt; color: blue; font-family: sans-serif">
   Paragraph 1 Text.
</p>
<p style="font-size: 20pt; color: blue; font-family: sans-serif">
   Paragraph 2 Text.
</p>
<p style="font-size: 20pt; color: blue; font-family: sans-serif">
   Paragraph 3 Text.
</p>
```

CSS enables us to create classes that consist of a set of style rules, defined in a <style> tag within the HTML <head> section. We can then associate these styles to HTML tags by setting the class attribute as shown in the following example:

```
<html>
  <head>
    <style type="text/css">
      .bigblue {
        font-size: 20pt;
        font-family: sans-serif;
        color: blue;
      }
    </style>
  </head>
  <body>
    <p class="bigblue">
       Paragraph 1 Text.
    </p>
    <p class="bigblue">
       Paragraph 2 Text.
    </p>
    <p class="bigblue">
       Paragraph 3 Text.
    </p>
  </body>
</html>
```

The <head> tag, which precedes the HTML <body>, is a special area of an HTML document called the HTML head section. It contains tags which describe the HTML document (so-called meta information) or provide other information required for the document, such as the CSS class definitions in the above example.

Try It Out   **Creating a Simple HTML page**

1. First, we need to set up folders in Tomcat's webapps directory to create a new JSP application for this example, call it PhoneBook, and create a folder inside it called WEB-INF. Inside that, create two further folders, one called classes, and the other called lib.

    As you may remember from the first chapter, these folders must exist for Tomcat to recognize our files as a new web application.

2. Save the following code as phoneNumbers.html in the PhoneBook folder:

```html
<html>
  <head>
    <style type="text/css">
      BODY {
        font-family: sans-serif;
        font-size: 10pt;
        background-color: gray;
        color: white;
      }
      TABLE {
        border: 1px solid black;
        font-family: sans-serif;
        font-size: 10pt;
      }
      .row1 {
        background-color: gray;
        color: black;
      }
      .row2 {
        background-color: silver;
        color: black;
      }

    </style>
  </head>
  <body>
    These are some of my friends.
    <p />
    <table>
      <tr>
        <th>
          Name
        </th>
        <th>
          Phone
        </th>
      </tr>
      <tr class="row1">
```

```
         <td>
           Amy
         </td>
         <td>
           415-555-1212
         </td>
       </tr>
       <tr class="row2">
         <td>
           Geoff
         </td>
         <td>
           415-555-1213
         </td>
       </tr>
     </table>
   </body>
 </html>
```

3. Start Tomcat and view the file by navigating to the following URL in your browser:

http://localhost:8080/PhoneBook/phoneNumbers.html

If you've entered everything correctly, you should see a page similar to this:

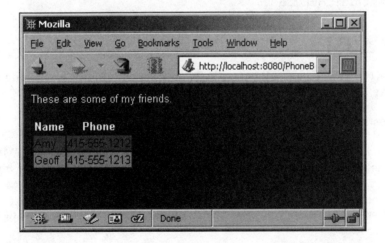

This HTML file is a good example of the tags introduced earlier in this section. We added a few new twists to the CSS in the `<style>` tag, such as the ability to redefine a tag's default style (the BODY and TABLE style names) and the `border` attribute.

It is important that you save the HTML file with a name that ends in .html or .htm, as we have done, so that the web server (in this case, Tomcat) knows that the file contains HTML markup.

HTML Summary

Well, this is a JSP book, not an HTML book, so we're going to wrap up our brief introduction to HTML. This section has provided all you need to know to create working JSP pages, and you'll build on this foundation and broaden your understanding of HTML as time goes on.

By studying the subsequent examples and case study, you'll learn more about what you can do with HTML. If you are interested in learning more about HTML and CSS, we recommend the following resources:

Getting started with HTML by Dave Raggett
http://www.w3.org/MarkUp/Guide/

The Official HTML 4.01 Specification
http://www.w3.org/TR/html401/

The Offical CSS Specification
http://www.w3.org/TR/REC-CSS1

The Official CSS-2 Specification (adds more features to CSS)
http://www.w3.org/TR/REC-CSS2/

Creating a JSP

We can make our HTML page a JSP page by simply using the .jsp extension in place of .html (or .htm). We can then open it by visiting the following URL:

http://localhost:8080/begjsp-ch02/phoneNumbers.jsp

We'll see that as a JSP page, it doesn't appear any different to the original HTML page. The only difference might be a small delay in delivery from Tomcat, as the web server must now check the page for JSP code before sending it off to our browser.

Code in JSP pages can take one of five major types which we'll look at in the next section.

JSP Code Types

With JSP, as with many other programming tools, there's more than one way to skin a cat. In all, there are five main ways that we can incorporate dynamic functionality into a JSP page. Each has its own advantages and disadvantages. Don't worry if the different types seem confusing right now; the distinctions between them will become clearer as we put them to use throughout this book.

Expression Language

JSP has a special syntax for incorporating the results of simple expressions into a page. This syntax is the **Expression Language** (**EL** for short), and it uses the following syntax:

```
${EL_expression}
```

Be aware that unlike other ways of adding dynamic content to JSP pages, EL does not use standard Java, but a syntax all its own, although there is considerable overlap between the two.

The following EL fragment displays the user-agent value given in the header part of the HTTP request that was sent by the browser when asking for the page:

```
${header["user-agent"]}
```

The user-agent value in the HTTP header specifies the type of browser that is making the request for the page. For example, Mozilla 5.0 running on Windows XP Professional would display:

Mozilla/5.0 (Windows; U; Windows NT 5.1; en-US; rv:1.2) Gecko/20021126

We'll look at the Expression Language in more detail in Chapter 7.

Scriptlets

Scriptlets allow Java code to be embedded directly into JSP pages by placing it within <% and %> delimiters. For illustration, we'll create a simple page containing a scriptlet that displays either **Good Morning** or **Good Afternoon** according to the time of day. Insert the following code in a file called goodAfternoon.jsp in the existing begjsp-ch02 folder:

```jsp
<%@ page import="java.util.Calendar"%>
<html>
  <body>
    Good
    <%
      Calendar calendar = Calendar.getInstance();
      if (calendar.get(Calendar.AM_PM) == Calendar.AM) {
        out.print("Morning");
      } else {
        out.print("Afternoon");
      }
    %>
  </body>
</html>
```

When executed in the afternoon, this JSP will generate the following output:

```
<html>
  <body>
    Good
    Afternoon
  </body>
</html>
```

While scriptlets are certainly powerful, their use is generally discouraged in professional Java development circles for two main reasons:

❑ Scriptlets result in JSP pages that are almost always horribly structured and difficult to maintain.

❑ Effective use of scriptlets requires an understanding of the Java programming language. Since the people who actually design pages are often not the people who add the code, a JSP littered with scriptlets would be very difficult for a page designer to reformat.

This dim view of scriptlets is universally accepted, and JSP even allows scriptlet support to be disabled entirely. Throughout this book, we will follow good design practice and refrain from their use.

Expressions

A JSP expression is similar to a scriptlet, except that instead of containing arbitrary amounts of Java code, it returns the result of a single Java expression. The syntax is also similar, except that the opening delimiter finishes with an equals sign. The following simple expression is equivalent to the EL example we saw above:

```
<%= request.getHeader("user-agent") %>
```

When placed in a JSP page, the above line would display code similar to the following:

Mozilla/5.0 (Windows; U; Windows NT 5.1; en-US; rv:1.2) Gecko/20021126

(This is if the computer was running Mozilla 5.0 on Windows XP Professional.)

Expressions are primarily used to display values that are either automatically provided by your servlet container or to display already existing values that have been created by other means in your web application or JSP page. Contrast this with scriptlets, which are primarily used to create new values through the use of custom Java code.

Expressions, like scriptlets, should be avoided in favor of the JSP Expression Language.

JSP Tags

As you know, HTML consists of dozens of tags that page authors can use, to which JSP adds about a dozen new ones of its own. These special JSP tags (also called **standard actions**) are processed by the servlet container before the page is sent to the browser. Consider the following example:

```
<html>
  <body>
    This is a JSP.<br />
    <jsp:include page="anotherPage.jsp" />
  </body>
</html>
```

Here, `<jsp:include>` is a JSP tag which tells the servlet container to insert the page indicated by the `page` attribute, which here is `anotherPage.jsp`. The page sent to the browser will then contain the contents of `anotherPage.jsp` in place of the `<jsp:include>` tag, as well as the content of the containing JSP page. There's a little more to it than this, as we'll see when we come back to such issues in Chapter 4.

JSP tags are very powerful ways of accomplishing a wide range of tasks, and as we proceed through the book, we'll come up against more of these tags as and when they are needed.

Custom Tags

JSP lets page authors define their own custom tags. These tags resemble regular JSP tags in appearance and in how they are used, but the developer defines their specific function.

Custom tags are a neat way of extending the standard functionality available through JSP, and they also provide an excellent means for sharing code with others. There are dozens of custom tag libraries floating around the Internet that you can download and use in your applications.

We'll discuss custom tags in detail in Chapter 4.

Java Standard Tag Library (JSTL)

In addition to the regular JSP tags, the Java community has created a standard library of custom tags to be used in JSP pages. This collection is called, appropriately enough, the **JSP Standard Tag Library**, or **JSTL**. While the JSTL isn't an official part of the JSP feature set, you'll find that it is an almost indispensable tool.

We will make use of the JSTL extensively throughout this book, and we'll have a first go at using it a little later in the chapter.

Viewing Request Headers

Now let's look at a couple of examples that put these JSP techniques into action. Our first example will use the JSTL to display the information contained in the HTTP header section. As we've already mentioned, a browser sends an HTTP Request to the server when the user wishes to view a page held on that server. The HTTP Request details which page the user wishes to see, and the server sends the browser a HTTP Response that contains the requested page.

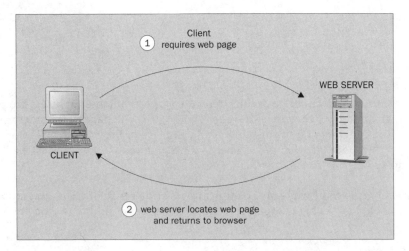

HTTP Requests contain certain details about the browser in an intial section called the **HTTP header**, and it is these details that our first sample JSP will display. First, though, we need to download and install the JSTL.

Downloading the JSTL

You can download the JSTL from the Apache Software Foundation, the same place we obtained Tomcat. Navigate to the following URL:

http://jakarta.apache.org/builds/jakarta-taglibs/releases/standard/

Download the latest version you see (click the Last modified link at the top of the listing twice to order the files in descending order of date). At the time of writing, the latest version was 1.0.2. Windows users should download the file ending .zip, while Linux users should download the file ending in .tar.gz.

Installing the JSTL on Windows

The JSTL is distributed as a ZIP file, as this format allows multiple files to be included in a single, compressed package. You'll need to extract the files from the ZIP archive for use. Windows XP has built-in support for ZIP files, and just double-clicking on it will open it as if it were a folder in its own right. Other versions of Windows require a separate program to extract ZIPs, such as WinZip, which is available over the Internet as shareware (http://www.winzip.com/).

Extract the files to somewhere appropriate. `C:\java` would be a good choice. When you extract the files (or copy if using Windows XP), a directory is created called `jakarta-taglibs` that contains the JSTL files in various subfolders.

Installing the JSTL on Red Hat Linux

Once you've downloaded the JSTL, you must decompress it into a directory of your choice, say `/usr/local/java/`. The appropriate command is:

```
tar -xzf jakarta-taglibs-standard-1.0.2.tar.gz -C /usr/local/java
```

Try It Out   **Viewing Request Headers**

1. Set up a new Tomcat web application by creating a directory called `RequestHeaders` under `webapps`. As before, create a folder called `WEB-INF` within it, and two folders called `classes` and `lib` inside that.

2. To use the JSTL, we need to copy the JSTL files into our web application's `lib` subdirectory. The files we need to copy are those within the `lib` folder off the `standard-1.0.2` directory within `jakarta-taglibs`. (If you have a version of JSTL other than 1.0.2, the path will vary accordingly).

3. Now create a file called `request.jsp`, which starts with the line:

```
<%@ taglib uri="http://java.sun.com/jstl/core_rt" prefix="c" %>
```

This is a **taglib directive**, and it tells Tomcat that tags that start with the letters given in the `prefix` attribute belong to the tag library specified by the `uri` attribute. We'll see this in action in a minute, when we use some JSTL tags.

4. The next few lines of our JSP are simple HTML tags to start a table:

```
<html>
  <body>
    You sent the following request headers:
    <p />
    <table border="1">
      <tr>
        <th>
          Header
        </th>
        <th>
          Value
        </th>
      </tr>
```

5. This table will format the different request headers for display, and we do this by looping through every header, inserting its name (`entry.key`) and value (`entry.value`) into a row of the table:

```
<c:forEach var="entry" items="${header}">
  <tr>
    <td>
      ${entry.key}
    </td>
    <td>
      ${entry.value}
    </td>
  </tr>
</c:forEach>
```

6. We perform the loop through the use of the `<c:forEach>` custom tag. Note the prefix `c:` indicating that this tag belongs to the JTSL library.

7. Finally, our JSP ends by closing the HTML tags and should be saved to the `RequestHeaders` folder:

```
    </table>
  </body>
</html>
```

8. Now restart Tomcat, open up your web browser, and navigate to http://localhost:8080/ RequestHeaders/request.jsp. You should see a screen similar to the following:

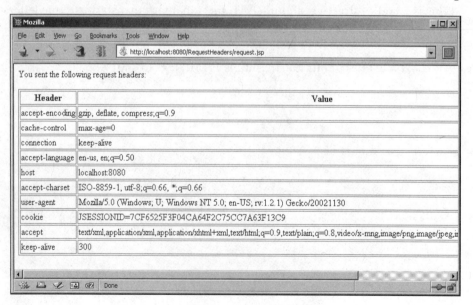

We've created a table that lists the name and value of each request header that your browser sent to Tomcat (of course, your system may have different values to those shown). Most of these headers aren't values that you're likely to be interested in as a developer, as they are more for the server's benefit. For example, the connection header's value is Keep-Alive, which tells the server that the browser wants to keep the connection open, because subsequent requests are likely.

One header that is often used by JSP developers, as seen in earlier examples, is the user-agent header that specifies the type of web browser in use. This enables a web application to change its behavior according to the capabilities of the browser, or to keep statistics about which browsers users have.

How It Works

Let's start with another look at the taglib directive:

```
<%@ taglib uri="http://java.sun.com/jstl/core_rt" prefix="c" %>
```

The uri attribute (uniform resource indicator) provides a unique name for the tag library. Note although this takes the form of a regular URL you might type into a browser, it does not necessarily correspond to a valid web location, and it only needs to be a unique name to identify tags that belong to a particular library. Tomcat can then find the required tag library, not by visiting the URI, but by searching all the files in the lib subdirectory of the current web application for a tag library that matches this URI, which in this case will be the JSTL.

The prefix attribute sets what custom tags from this library are to start with, to distinguish them from other tags in the page. Here, the prefix is c, as seen on the JSTL <forEach> tag. This tag is what's known as an **iterator** tag. It iterates – or steps through – each item in a **collection**, applying the code inside the tag to each item. A collection can be any group of data items stored together in a single place.

The <forEach> tag has attributes called items and var, which specify which collection to iterate through and a name for the item currently selected by the loop respectively. In our example, we've used EL in the items attribute to make the loop cycle through the collection of request headers. We've set the var attribute so that we can access each header in turn by the identifier entry.

Items in the HTTP headers are stored as key-value pairs, where the key is a name that can be used to retrieve a particular value. In our case, we can access the key name using ${entry.value} and the value using ${entry.key}.

Thus, our <forEach> tag iterates through each header, and prints out its name and value inside a table. Note that the <forEach> tag, as a custom tag dealt with by JSP, is not received by the browser. Instead, it is replaced by the result of its operation, which is a bunch of <tr> tags containing the header names and values, as you can see by viewing the source for our JSP in your browser.

There you have it – using EL and the JSTL in tandem lets us create JSP pages that are quite a bit more complicated (and useful) than our first example back in Chapter 1.

HTML Forms

Our next example is interactive, and captures data from an HTML form. This is the usual way of getting information from the client for use by a server-based web application. The information that the user provides may be textual (for instance the user's name), or it may be a selection from a number of options in dropdown lists, radio buttons, and so on. Once complete, the user clicks a button to submit the data to the server.

HTML provides a number of different controls for requesting information from the user in a form. We will meet these shortly; first let's look at the basic building block of any HTML form – the `<form>` element itself.

The `<form>` Element

Forms on HTML pages are defined with the `<form>` tag, but note that the `<form>` element doesn't directly produce any visual effects in the browser. We need to place controls within the `<form>` element to provide information for the user and the means for them to input any information we require.

The `<form>` tag's attributes let us specify certain configurations for the form, and we'll look more closely at these attributes over the following pages.

The action Attribute

The `action` attribute specifies what is to happen when the user has completed the form and submitted it. We can specify a server-side resource – for example, a JSP – that processes the form data submitted by the user. This server-side resource may then produce an HTML page that is sent back to the client.

We indicate such resources using a URL, as shown below:

```
<form action="http://myServer.com/process.jsp">
```

On form submission (for example, when the user clicks on a Submit button), the page will jump to the stated URL. For example, this could be the URL http://myServer.com/process.jsp.

Note that URLs can also be supplied as a *relative* path based on the location of the page that contains the form:

```
<form action="process.jsp"></form>
```

In this case, `process.jsp` needs to be in the same folder as the page containing the form. For instance, if the current page were at http://myServer.com/input.jsp, the request would be sent to http://myServer.com/process.jsp.

Finally, if a form has no `action` attribute, the page that contains the form is reloaded when submitted, but we can have it take a different course of action than when it was first loaded.

The name Attribute

When we pass data from the form, we can use the name specified in the form's `name` attribute to identify which form or form control the data belongs. This is necessary as there may be more than one form on the page. We will use this attribute in examples to come.

The method Attribute

As well as a choice of where to send the form data, we also have a choice of how to send it, which we specify using the `method` attribute. Two commonly used methods for sending the data are:

- ❑ GET (the default)
- ❑ POST

When a form is submitted, the browser collates the data entered or selected by the user into name-value pairs, where the name corresponds to the `name` attribute of the control, and the value denotes the value chosen. **The way the browser sends this information to the server differs according to the method used.**

The GET method of transferring data appends data as a list of name-value pairs after the URL of the page that we are sending the form to. The list is separated from the URL itself by the ? character, and any subsequent pairs begin with an ampersand (&), as in this example:

```
process.jsp?userName=John+Doe&tummy=large&head=square
```

Data appended to a URL like this is said to form a **query string**. The target page will then be able to get hold of these values by using the associated name.

As you may be thinking, placing name-value pairs in the URL is a rather public way of passing information. The POST method provides an alternative that sends name-value hidden away inside the body of the HTTP request.

The main drawback of POST is that if the user bookmarks the page, the name-value pairs won't be stored in the bookmark, potentially causing problems. Also, be aware that although POST is more secure than GET, POST data is not encrypted, and it would not be very difficult for someone to get hold of the data if they really wanted to.

The target Attribute

We noted earlier that the server-side resource identified in the action attribute might produce an HTML page when the form is submitted. The target attribute may be used to identify a frame or window within the browser to which the resulting HTML page should be sent, if it is different from the frame or window containing the form. This attribute may take one of the following values:

- ❑ _blank – the resulting HTML page is sent to a new window.

- ❑ _parent – the resulting HTML is sent to the parent of the current frame.

- ❑ _self – the resulting HTML page overwrites the current page. This is the default value used when one is not specified.

- ❑ _top – the resulting HTML page will occupy the entire browser window, ignoring all the nested framesets.

Now that we know how to create a form, let's find out how to fill it with elements.

Using HTML Elements

HTML form controls are used for rendering the textboxes, dropdown lists, and checkboxes that forms use to get data from the user. The following HTML elements may be used:

- ❑ <input> – renders controls such as textboxes, radio buttons, and checkboxes

- ❑ <select> – renders multi-select listboxes and dropdown listboxes

- ❑ <textarea> – renders multi-line edit controls

Let's review each of these elements in turn.

The <input> Element

The HTML <input> element creates textboxes, radio buttons, or checkboxes, depending on the value of the type attribute. There are other attributes that set other properties, and we'll look at the most common of these in this section.

The type Attribute

This is perhaps the most important attribute, as it defines the type of control we want, according to the values given in the following table:

Attribute Value	Description
text	Renders a textbox. This is the default if the attribute is not specified.
password	Renders password controls. These are the same as textboxes, but input is represented on-screen by an asterisk character.
hidden	Defines hidden controls, for storing information on the page that is not to be displayed on-screen. These values typically store values used by the server across multiple requests.
checkbox	Renders checkboxes.
radio	Renders radio buttons.
reset	Renders a button control that resets the form controls to their original default values.
submit	Renders the button control that submits the form.
image	Uses an image for the button instead of the default look.
button	Renders a button control that may be linked to client-side script.
file	Renders a file control that allows the user to browse to and select files from their local file system to be uploaded to the server.

Here's an example that creates a textbox:

```
<input type="text">
```

The name Attribute

After we have chosen the type of control we need, we must give it a name if the data the control contains is to be passed to the server on form submission. We do this using the name attribute:

```
<input type="text" name="address">
```

The code above would create a textbox called address. Therefore, when we submit the form to the server, the information in this textbox can be obtained by using the name address.

The maxlength Attribute

The maxlength attribute may only be used if the type attribute is either text or password, and specifies the maximum number of characters that may be entered into the control. For instance, we could impose a limit of 30 characters on the textbox we created earlier like so:

```
<input type="text" name="address" maxlength="30">
```

The size Attribute

This attribute can also be used if the type attribute is either text or password. It sets the control's visible width in characters (note that maxlength doesn't change the actual width of a textbox, just the number of characters that will be accepted). So, we could define a width for the address textbox like this:

```
<input type="text" name="address" maxlength="30" size="30">
```

These attributes are enough for us to create a simple HTML form, so let's do so now. We'll come back to look at other attributes of the <input> element afterwards.

Try It Out   **Adding Textboxes to an HTML Form**

1. In this example and the next, we'll build up a form that could be used to order a pizza over the Internet. Create a folder called Pizza in webapps, and one called WEB-INF inside it, and finally, create the classes and lib folders within this folder.

2. Create a file called pizza.html in the Pizza folder. It starts off with the usual HTML for beginning a page:

```
<html>
  <head>
    <title>Take The Pizza</title>
    <style type="text/css">
      H1 {
        font-size: 12pt;
        font-weight: bold;
      }
    </style>
  </head>
  <body>
```

Notice that we defining a default style here for HTML <h1> elements.

3. Now we have to add the HTML form that will get the information from the user. We'll set the form to submit its data to a page called process.jsp using HTTP POST:

```
<form action="process.jsp" method="post">
```

4. Once we've got the explanatory text in the form out of the way, we'll set up a table that contains a couple of textboxes for the user's name and address by adding the following code:

```
Welcome to Take the Pizza Online! We're eager to take your order
for pizza via our new web form!
<p />
Please fill out the fields below and click on "Place Order" when
you're done!
<p />
<h1>Your Information:</h1>
<table>
  <tr>
    <td>
      Name:
    </td>
    <td>
      <input type="text" name="name" size="30">
    </td>
  </tr>
  <tr>
    <td>
      Address:
    </td>
    <td>
      <input type="text" name="address" size="70">
    </td>
  </tr>
```

5. Now we just have to close all our HTML elements by adding the following code and then saving the page:

```
      </table>
    </form>
  </body>
</html>
```

6. Restart Tomcat and navigate to localhost:8080/Pizza/pizza.html. You should see something similar to the following:

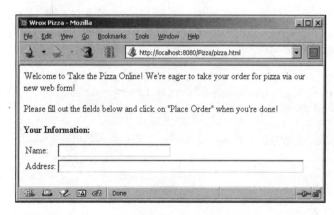

How It Works

As it stands, our page doesn't actually do much. OK, the textboxes are there for our hungry user to enter their name and address but there's no **Place Order** button yet. There's not even a way for our corpulent friend to let us know what type of pizza they're after.

You can see though that creating textboxes on a form is far from rocket science. We simply have to place <input> elements at appropriate places, specifying a type attribute of text and a suitable value for the name attribute.

Note that because our first page didn't require any special JSP features, we simply used a normal HTML page. This is good practice, as HTML pages have less overhead than a JSP; the server does less to serve an HTML page to the user than with a JSP page. However, our pizza order page is still under construction; after all, we haven't given our client a choice of pizzas or even provided a submit button so that we can send the form data! Before we fix that, let's first discuss some more of the attributes of <input>.

The checked Attribute

This attribute may be used on the <input> element if the type attribute is either radio or checkbox. If the attribute is present, the radio button or the checkbox is checked by default. For example:

```
<input type="radio" name="someValue" checked="true" />
```

This code would create a radio button called someValue that is checked by default.

The value Attribute

The behavior of the value attribute depends on what the type attribute is set to. Button controls display the contents of this attribute on the button. In other words, a button defined by the HTML below:

```
<input type="button" name="bob" value="Press Me!" />
```

will appear in the browser like this:

Press Me!

Along the same lines, here's an example of creating a submit button called dataSubmit with **Submit Form** as the button text:

```
<input name="dataSubmit" type="submit" value="Submit Form" />
```

For text and password controls, the `value` attribute supplies the default value to use for the control, as in this example:

```
<input type="text" name="marge" value="Pigsy" />
```

This creates a textbox called `marge` that contains the string Pigsy by default, like so:

Pigsy

Finally, for selectable controls like radio buttons and checkboxes, this attribute defines the value that is sent as part of the name-value pair for the option represented by that particular radio button or checkbox.

Note that more than one control in a form might share the same value for the `name` attribute when we have a group of controls that we intend using together. For example, we might have a group of radio buttons for selecting one of a set of choices. Each choice would be represented by its own <input> element, but all the elements would have a `name` attribute with the same value:

```
<input type="radio" name="delivery" value="express" />
<input type="radio" name="delivery" value="surface" />
<input type="radio" name="delivery" value="pigeon" />
```

This would create three radio buttons, where only one may be selected at one time. If the first radio button is selected when the form is submitted, a name-value pair of `delivery=express` would be sent to the server. If the second radio button is selected, the name-value pair `delivery=surface` would be sent instead, and similarly for the third button.

For other controls, which are grouped by sharing a `name` attribute, users may select any combination of them. In such scenarios, the key-value pairs sent to the server can contain duplicate values for the key. For instance:

```
<input type="checkbox" name="limbs" value="arms">
<input type="checkbox" name="limbs" value="legs">
```

Both these checkboxes could be checked at once, and if that is the case when the form is submitted, the name-value pairs `limbs=arms` and `limbs=legs` would both be sent back to the server.

Now let's incorporate some of these extras into the page we started earlier. We'll start with a pair of radio buttons that let the user specify whether they want the pizza delivered or whether they intend to drop in and pick it up themselves.

1. Open the `pizza.html` file, and add the following highlighted code, immediately after the `<table>` element we've already got:

```
      ...
      </tr>
    </table>
    <p />
    <h1>Order Type:</h1>
    <table>
      <tr>
        <td>
          <input type="radio" name="purchaseType" value="Home Delivery">
        </td>
        <td>
          Home Delivery
        </td>
      </tr>
      <tr>
        <td>
          <input type="radio" name="purchaseType" value="Take Away">
        </td>
        <td>
          Take Away
        </td>
      </tr>
    </table>
  </form>
 </body>
</html>
```

2. Next we'll add another table, this time creating a set of checkboxes for the user to choose the toppings they want. Place these lines after the table from Step 1:

```
      </tr>
    </table>
    <p />
    <h1>Please Select Any Additional Toppings:</h1>
    <table>
      <tr>
        <td>
          <input type="checkbox" name="peppers" value="Yes">
        </td>
        <td>
          Peppers
        </td>
      </tr>
      <tr>
        <td>
```

```
            <input type="checkbox" name="sweetcorn" value="Yes">
          </td>
          <td>
            Sweetcorn
          </td>
        </tr>
        <tr>
          <td>
            <input type="checkbox" name="mouse" value="Yes">
          </td>
          <td>
            Mouse Innards
          </td>
        </tr>
      </table>
    </form>
  </body>
</html>
```

3. The last thing we'll add at this stage is a submit button that submits the form data containing the order to the process.jsp page:

```
        </tr>
      </table>
      <p />
      <input type="submit" value="Place Order">
    </form>
  </body>
</html>
```

4. Save the file, and navigate to http://localhost:8080/Pizza/pizza.html. You'll see something similar to this:

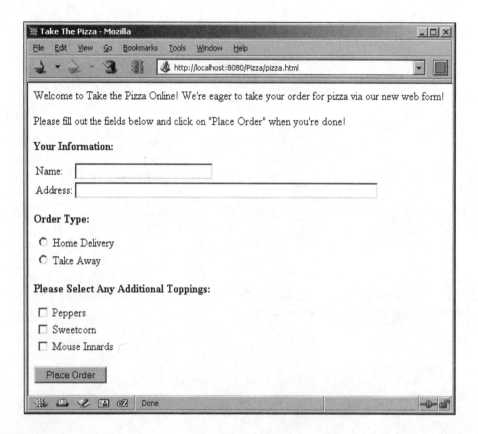

How It Works

When we added the two radio buttons, we gave both the name purchaseType to ensure that only one of the two may be selected at any one time. The value to use for each radio button is given with the value attribute:

```
<input type="radio" name="purchaseType" value="Home Delivery">
<input type="radio" name="purchaseType" value="Take Away">
```

A description for each option is provided as straight text in the next cell on the row.

Next we present three checkboxes that offer a (rather limited) selection of toppings. Remember that the value attribute for a checkbox indicates the value that will be sent if that checkbox is checked:

```
<input type="checkbox" name="peppers" value="Yes">
<input type="checkbox" name="sweetcorn" value="Yes">
<input type="checkbox" name="mouse" value="Yes">
```

So we now have a form that the user can use to provide a range of information. We also have a submit button, but why should clicking it result in an error message?

The reason is that the page attempts to send the form data to process.jsp, which doesn't exist yet. We'll come to writing that page towards the end of the chapter, once we've got our HTML form finished.

The <select> Element

The <select> element provides the means for rendering dropdown lists and multi-select listboxes within HTML forms. One such control is represented by a single <select> element, which contains an HTML <option> element for each item in the list as shown:

```
<select>
  <option>Item 1</option>
  <option>Item 2</option>
  ...
  <option>Item N</option>
</select>
```

We configure details of the control's appearance and behavior by setting attributes on the <select> and <option> elements.

Let's review some of these attributes, starting with attributes for the <select> element.

The name Attribute

As usual, the name attribute for a <select> element specifies the name in the name-value pair that is sent back to the server when the form is submitted.

The size Attribute

If the value of the size attribute is 1, the control is rendered as a dropdown listbox; if it is greater than 1, the control is rendered as a listbox, and the value of the attribute indicates the number of items that are visible in the list at once. The default value is 1.

The multiple Attribute

If the multiple attribute is present, the control will allow multiple items in the listbox to be selected together. If a form is submitted with multiple items selected, all the selected values are sent as name-value pairs using the name defined for the <select> element.

Next, there are two attributes for the <option> element that are particularly useful, value and selected:

The value Attribute

If no value attribute is present, the data that appears between the start and end <option> tags is passed as the value when an option is selected. For instance:

```
<select name="caller">
  <option>Dobber</option>
  <option>Yasser</option>
  <option>Mio Mio</option>
</select>
```

If the user now selects the third option from this list, and submits the form, the name-value pair `caller=Mio+Mio` would be sent.

In many cases, this wouldn't be suitable, and the `value` attribute lets us provide the value that we'd rather use.

So we could change the above example to return the caller's phone number rather than their name:

```
<select name="caller">
  <option value="212 421 5532">Dobber</option>
  <option value="212 336 7205">Yasser</option>
  <option value="431 771 8027">Mio Mio</option>
</select>
```

If we selected the last option this time, we would now get `caller=431+771+8027`.

The selected Attribute

If this attribute is set to `true` for an `<option>` element, the contents of this `<option>` are displayed in the control by default.

We'll now apply this knowledge to incorporate a listbox into our pizza application.

Try It Out   **Adding Listboxes to HTML Forms**

1. We'll add a listbox that gives the customer three sizes of pizza to choose from. As before, we'll place the control in an HTML table. Add this highlighted code to the end of `pizza.html`:

```
    ...
      <td>
        Mouse Innards
      </td>
    </tr>
  </table>
<p />
<h1>Pizza Size:</h1>
<table>
  <tr>
    <td>
```

```
        Size:
      </td>
      <td>
        <select name="size">
          <option>Small</option>
          <option selected="true">Medium</option>
          <option>Large</option>
        </select>
      </td>
    </tr>
  </table>
  <p />
  <input type="submit" value="Place Order">
  </form>
  </body>
</html>
```

2. Save the file, and navigate to http://localhost:8080/Pizza/pizza.html in your browser. You will see something similar to the following:

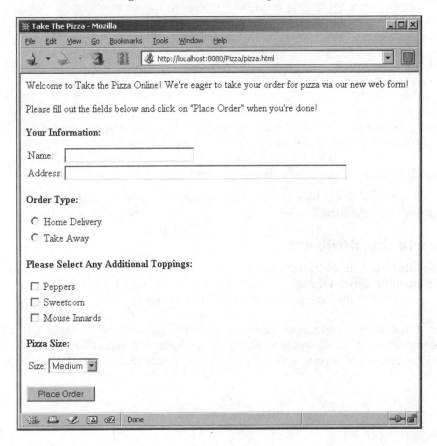

We added a `<select>` element called `size` to create a listbox. It contains three `<option>` elements, one for each available size: small, medium, and large. The second of these, medium, is the option that is selected by default when the page loads:

```
<select name="size">
  <option>Small</option>
  <option selected="true">Medium</option>
  <option>Large</option>
</select>
```

We're nearly finished with our pizza order page now. We have just one minor modification left to make.

The `<textarea>` Element

The `<textarea>` element is used in an HTML form to render multi-line textboxes. All the text appearing between the start and end tags are displayed in the control:

```
<textarea>
line of text
another line of text
</textarea>
```

Note that unlike normal HTML, the `<textarea>` will preserve spaces and carriage returns. Let's have a look at the attributes of the `<textarea>` element.

The name Attribute

As with the other controls, the `name` attribute sets the name in the name-value pair that is sent to the server when the form is submitted.

The rows and cols Attributes

The `rows` attribute defines the number of rows of characters displayed in the control. Similarly, the `cols` attribute defines the width of the control in characters. The default value of these attributes varies with the browser and the operating system.

Let's now finish off our pizza example by incorporating a multi-line textbox. Our pizza order page looks pretty cool at the moment, but there is one improvement we could make. Since an address is composed of several lines of text, the Address textbox would be better as a multi-line textbox.

Adding Multi-line Textboxes to HTML Forms

1. Open up `pizza.html`, and replace the line:

```
<input type="text" name="address" size="70">
```

with this one:

```
<textarea rows="4" cols="40" name="address"></textarea>
```

2. Now save the file and reload it in your browser once again. You'll see that the original one-line text field has now been replaced with a multi-line textbox:

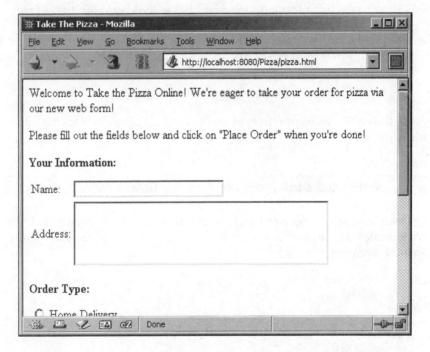

Creating multi-line textboxes in HTML isn't hard. Here, our `<textarea>` element specifies a textbox of size 4 rows by 40 columns. As an empty element, the textbox will appear without any text when the page first loads.

Request Processing

So far, our examples have shown how HTML forms and form elements may be used for rendering different input controls in the user's browser for collecting information. Now we'll look at the other half of the picture: what happens when a user submits their form. The data on the form is sent back to the server, which must read and interpret this data by some means. In our case of course, we're using JSP to process this information.

Using the param Collection

In a previous example, we saw that the Expression Language has access to the `header` collection, which contains information about a particular HTTP request. The `param` collection is similar, except that it contains data sent to the server from HTML forms, and so in this case, it gives us a way to access the information the user has entered into our pizza form.

Using the `param` collection is quite simple, as long as we know the names of the name-value pairs. The EL code below would obtain the value corresponding to the name `delivery`:

```
${param.delivery}
```

Let's now use the `param` collection to read and display all of the values that our pizza HTML form sends to the server.

Try It Out   Retrieving Data From the Request Object

1. The form on our `pizza.html` page sends its data to a JSP page called `process.jsp`. We'll create this file now, in our `Pizza` directory. It starts out with standard HTML opening elements:

```html
<html>
  <head>
    <title>Take The Pizza</title>
    <style type="text/css">
      H1 {
          font-size: 12pt;
          font-weight: bold;
      }
    </style>
  </head>
  <body>
    <h1>Order Confirmation</h1>
    <p />
    Please review this data to ensure that it is correct.
    <p />
```

2. We'll simply display the information that has come from the pizza form in an HTML table:

```html
<table border="1">
  <tr>
    <td>Name:</td>
    <td>${param.name}</td>
  </tr>
  <tr>
    <td>Address:</td>
    <td>${param.address}</td>
  </tr>
  <tr>
    <td>Order Type:</td>
    <td>${param.purchaseType}</td>
  </tr>
  <tr>
    <td>Peppers:</td>
    <td>${param.peppers}</td>
  </tr>
  <tr>
    <td>Sweetcorn:</td>
    <td>${param.sweetcorn}</td>
  </tr>
  <tr>
    <td>Mouse Innards:</td>
    <td>${param.mouse}</td>
  </tr>
  <tr>
    <td>Size:</td>
    <td>${param.size}</td>
  </tr>
</table>
</body>
</html>
```

3. Now open `pizza.html` in your browser. Fill in your order, and click **Place Order** to submit the information to `process.jsp`. This page should then appear, displaying a summary of your order details, like so:

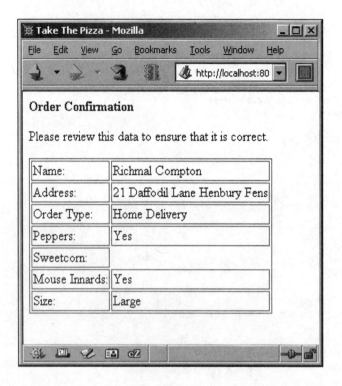

This page shows how simple it is to get information from another web page, thanks to the `param` collection.

Summary

It's time to take a step back and review what we've covered in this chapter. First, let's go over the major points of our HTML review:

❑ HTML consists of tags and text. Tags take the form `<tagname>`. They are either container tags of the type `<tag></tag>` or stand-alone tags of the type `<tag />`.

❑ HTML tags typically modify how text appears on screen.

❑ HTML tags may have attributes that affect their behavior and appearance.

❑ The `class` and `style` attributes may be used to further control the behavior of tags and the appearance of text.

Now let's sum up the key points related to JavaServer Pages:

❑   JSP page are very similar to HTML pages but end in `.jsp`. JSP pages have access to a wealth of features not available to 'vanilla' HTML pages.

❑   JavaServer Pages use the following to achieve these extra features:

   ❑   Scriptlets, which consist of embedded Java code in the JSP. Scriptlets are viewed as poor programming practice and are generally avoided.

   ❑   Expressions, which display data and values in the JSP.

   ❑   Expression Language Expressions are a fast and efficient way to display data in a JSP.

   ❑   JSP tags, which are somewhat like normal HTML tags but produce JSP-specific functionality.

We also learned about the JSP Standard Tag Library (JSTL), which are a set of custom tags that grant us a wealth of functionality. Finally, we wrapped up the chapter with a look at using the `param` collection for extracting data from HTML forms.

CHAPTER 3

Working with Data

Data can be stored in several ways, including XML files, plain text files, relational databases, object databases, spreadsheets or in memory. This chapter will introduce you to relational databases, how to request data from them using their "native" language, and how this knowledge can be used in JSPs.

In this chapter you will learn:

- ❑ About relational databases
- ❑ About concepts associated with databases, such as normalization
- ❑ How to install MySQL
- ❑ The basics of Structured Query Language (SQL)
- ❑ How to use a JSP page to connect to a database and display information
- ❑ How to use a JSP to add information to a database

Let's start by establishing what databases are, and why we would want to use them.

Introducing Databases

Chapter 2 introduced some mechanisms for handling user input. For this input to be useful, it must be stored somewhere, so it can be retrieved later. While it would be certainly possible to store the information as plain text files, it would quickly become inadequate if your information became increasingly complex. Structured information, such as that found in an on-line shopping site or on a message-board, usually necessitates the use of a database.

> A database is a collection of data organized such that its contents can be easily accessed and manipulated.

To understand this definition better, consider an example of an unsorted pile of papers. How do you find a particular page within the pile? You would probably start from the top of the pile and work your way down until you got to the page you want. This could be a time-consuming process if the pile was large and your page was near the bottom. This unorganized environment is analogous to data that is stored in a normal "flat" file on a computer, where data is held in no particular order and has to be searched from beginning to end (known as **sequential access**) to locate information relevant to a particular task.

Now, consider a library or bookshop. When you need a particular book, you might have to search through a card catalog. This is an example of a (non-electronic) database. It is a well-organized system in which data is stored in specific locations, and because of its structure and organization, any data can be retrieved quickly and easily. This also allows both direct and random access to the information.

A software program for creating and modifying databases is called a **Database Management System (DBMS)**. The DBMS removes the complexities of storing the database information in specific locations, within the particular files, directories and disk volumes used by the server. The server keeps track of where the data is stored, so as a database user you don't have to worry about it.

Using Tables

One of the most common ways to organize data is by arranging it into **tables**. For instance, referring back to our bookshop analogy, we could make a table of books. Each book's data (author(s), title, price, and so on) would fill a **row** (or **record**) of the table. Since we would want to use the table to compare data from different books, we would arrange the data we wish to compare (the price, say) into a **column** (or **field**). Assuming our wise bookshop owner stocks Wrox books, a portion of the Book table might look something like this:

Title	Author(s)	Price
Beginning JSP Web Development	John Timney, Ben Galbraith, Casey Kochmer, Jayson Falkner, Meeraj Kunnumpurath, Romin Irani, Perrumal Krishnaraj, Sathya Narayana Panduranga	$39.99
Professional JSP Site Design	Kevin Duffey, Richard Huss, Vikram Goyal, Ted Husted, Meeraj Kunnumpurath, Lance Lavandowska, Sathya Narayana Panduranga, Krishnaraj Perrumal, Joe Walnes	$59.99
Profession JSP, 2nd Edition	Sing Li, Grant Palmer, John Timney, Steve Wilkinson, Dan Malks, Sameer Tyagi, Geert Damme, Rod Johnson, Larry Kim, Ben Galbraith, Bob Sullivan, Mark Nelson, Casey Kochmer, Jayson Falkner, Geoff Taylor, Robert Burdick, Simon Brown, Thor Kristmundsson	$59.99

As you can see, the table groups the data about each individual book into a separate row, and data about each **attribute** of a book into separate column.

Now, if we were to construct a database to contain this data, we would do exactly the same thing – organize the data into a table. In fact, a database will probably contain more than one table, each holding data about a different **entity** – books, computers, movies, or whatever. These things are all different so you wouldn't want them all jumbled together in one place.

> An entity is a "thing" that a database holds information on. Usually, each entity you identify will have a table of its own in the database.

Of course, the fact that we create tables to hold information about a particular entity implies that the records within the table share common attributes – in other words, the records within a table are related. After all, it makes no sense to store unrelated information, like mixing up the information related to your movie collection with the information about the books in your bookstore. While they all have titles, books have authors, movies have running time, and computers have processor speeds.

Relational Databases

Let's go back to our `Book` table. While it is perfectly logical to store related data about books in a table, this table is not as efficient at storing this data as it may first appear.

Look at the way we are storing the information about our authors. You'll see that a couple of authors are listed for more than one book. If we wanted to look for books co-authored by a certain individual, we would need to look through the author list for each book. Not only that, but by repeating this information in each book entry, we are introducing the possibility of typographical errors. For instance, if an author of an existing book releases a new book, there's a chance that whoever enters the new book's details into the database may misspell the author's name, and the new book would not come up if someone searched for all books by that author.

If on the other hand, we were to have a separate list of authors, we could link each book to authors in that list. This would eliminate the possibility of misspellings (well, outside the first time the name is entered), and we could more easily look for a particular author's books as they will be explicitly linked to that author. A system that links data across more than one entity (table) is referred to as a **Relational Database Management System (RDBMS)**.

Relationships Between Data

This second problem arises due to the nature of the relationships between attributes *within* the table. We have no problem storing data within a table when all of the attributes map **one-to-one** (1:1) or **one-to-many** (1:M). In a one-to-one relationship, each column involved in the relationship contains unique values. Say for instance, a business has a separate table holding e-mail addresses for its customers. There would then be a one-to-one relationship between the customers table and the e-mail table (assuming that each customer can have only one e-mail address on file). You should note that one-to-one relationships are pretty rare.

On the other hand, we already have several one-to-many relationships in our table. An example is between title and price; a book can only have one price in the store, but we can have more than one book selling at the same price. We don't have a problem organizing 1:M relationships within a table, although we can encounter the data repetition problem discussed earlier.

The big problem comes when we encounter **many-to-many** (M:M) relationships. Such a relationship exists in our data between titles and authors, where a book can have more than one author, and an author may have written more than one book. Organizing many-to-many relationships in a table is a difficult task, as we have seen, and one that reduces our ability to modify the table later.

The Relational Model

One common way to solve the problems discussed above is to break up any tables with M:M relationships into smaller ones that together hold the same data. This multi-table approach is called the **relational model**, because there are relationships between the data in different tables. Obviously, we need a way to preserve these relationships even though the data is now in separate tables. To do this, we share one attribute per table with another table; these attributes that are shared between tables are called **keys**.

For instance, we might choose to place information about authors in one table, and data about Books in another, and link the two tables using the author name attribute as a key. In this case, if we looked up information on a particular book title in the `Book` table, and then wanted to find out about the authors of that book, we would note the names of the book authors and scan down the `Authors` table until we found the correct records. Note that in this case, the author name column of the Author table would have to contain unique values; otherwise we would get confused when we try to track down the record for a particular author. A key column like this, that is only allowed to contain unique values, is called a **primary key**. The corresponding author name column in the `Book` table is called a **foreign key**, because it refers to values from a key column in another table.

Title	Price	Author_ID
Beginning JSP Web Development	$39.99	1
Professional JSP Site Design	$59.99	2
Profession JSP, 2nd Edition	$59.99	3

Author_ID	Author(s)
1	John Timney, Ben Galbraith, Casey Kochmer, Jayson Falkner, Meeraj Kunnumpurath, Romin Irani, Perrumal Krishnaraj, Sathya Narayana Panduranga
2	Kevin Duffey, Richard Huss, Vikram Goyal, Ted Husted, Meeraj Kunnumpurath, Lance Lavandowska, Sathya Narayana Panduranga, Krishnaraj Perrumal, Joe Walnes
3	Sing Li, Grant Palmer, John Timney, Steve Wilkinson, Dan Malks, Sameer Tyagi, Geert Damme, Rod Johnson, Larry Kim, Ben Galbraith, Bob Sullivan, Mark Nelson, Casey Kochmer, Jayson Falkner, Geoff Taylor, Robert Burdick, Simon Brown, Thor Kristmundsson

> **A primary key is a column in a table that has a unique value for each row, and can thus be used to identify any one row unambiguously. A foreign key is a column in a table that itself refers to a primary key in another table. Foreign key values are not necessarily unique – that is, several rows can refer to the same row in the related table.**

But how do we decide what attributes to use as keys? We need to follow a process that enables us to optimize our database table split. Luckily, this process exists, and is called **normalization**.

Normalization

The process towards database normalization progresses through a series of steps, typically known as **normal forms**, a concept introduced in the 1970s by a fellow called E. F. Codd.

Normalizing a database aims to:

❑ Arrange data into logical groupings such that each group describes a small part of the whole

❑ Minimize the amount of duplicate data stored in a database

❑ Organize the data in such a way that, when you modify it, you make changes in only one place

❑ Build a database in which you can access and manipulate the data quickly and efficiently without compromising the integrity of the data in storage

> **Normalization minimizes redundancy in data by dividing a database into two or more tables and defining relationships between them. This allows for changes, additions, and deletions to fields to be made in just one table but to be reflected in the others via the relationships defined.**

There are three sets of rules that are listed below for database normalization. If the first set of rules as presented below is observed, the database is said to be in **first normal form**. Likewise, if all three sets of rules are observed, the database is considered to be in **third normal form**.

The rules that you should follow for converting the database to its first normal form are:

❑ Eliminate repeating groups in individual tables

❑ Create a separate table for each set of related data

❑ Identify each set of related data with a primary key

Book_ID	Title	Price
1	Beginning JSP Web Development	$39.99
2	Professional JSP Site Design	$59.99
3	Profession JSP, 2nd Edition	$59.99

Author_ID	Author(s)
1	John Timney, Ben Galbraith, Casey Kochmer, Jayson Falkner, Meeraj Kunnumpurath, Romin Irani, Perrumal Krishnaraj, Sathya Narayana Panduranga
2	Kevin Duffey, Richard Huss, Vikram Goyal, Ted Husted, Meeraj Kunnumpurath, Lance Lavandowska, Sathya Narayana Panduranga, Krishnaraj Perrumal, Joe Walnes
3	Sing Li, Grant Palmer, John Timney, Steve Wilkinson, Dan Malks, Sameer Tyagi, Geert Damme, Rod Johnson, Larry Kim, Ben Galbraith, Bob Sullivan, Mark Nelson, Casey Kochmer, Jayson Falkner, Geoff Taylor, Robert Burdick, Simon Brown, Thor Kristmundsson

The rules to convert the database to its **second normal form** are (the database should already be in its first normal form):

❑ Create separate tables for sets of values that apply to multiple records

❑ Relate these tables with a foreign key

Book_ID	Title
1	Beginning JSP Web Development
2	Professional JSP Site Design
3	Profession JSP, 2nd Edition

Price_ID	Price
1	$39.99
2	$59.99

Author_ID	Author(s)
1	John Timney, Ben Galbraith, Casey Kochmer, Jayson Falkner, Meeraj Kunnumpurath, Romin Irani, Perrumal Krishnaraj, Sathya Narayana Panduranga
2	Kevin Duffey, Richard Huss, Vikram Goyal, Ted Husted, Meeraj Kunnumpurath, Lance Lavandowska, Sathya Narayana Panduranga, Krishnaraj Perrumal, Joe Walnes
3	Sing Li, Grant Palmer, John Timney, Steve Wilkinson, Dan Malks, Sameer Tyagi, Geert Damme, Rod Johnson, Larry Kim, Ben Galbraith, Bob Sullivan, Mark Nelson, Casey Kochmer, Jayson Falkner, Geoff Taylor, Robert Burdick, Simon Brown, Thor Kristmundsson

Continuing on the quest for complete normalization of the database, the next step in the process would be to satisfy the rule of the third normal form:

❑ Eliminate transitive dependencies (where a non-key attribute is dependent on another non-key attribute). For example, say we have a `Contacts` table with names and addresses, and the `Author` table links to it using the name field. This would be a problem if the name in the `Contacts` table or `Author` table were changed, as we'd break the link between the tables. A row's primary key should never be altered, thus it is not transitive.

Adhering to the third normal form, while theoretically desirable, is not always practical. For instance, if you wanted to create a database of friends' addresses, you would need to eliminate all possible inter-field dependencies, creating separate tables for cities, ZIP codes, and so on. In theory, full normalization is worth pursuing. However, many small tables may degrade performance or exceed open file and memory capacities. It may be more feasible to apply third normal form only to data that changes frequently. If some dependent fields remain, design your application to require the user to verify all related fields when any one is changed.

Although normalization forms can go up to the fifth form, third normal form is considered the highest level necessary for most applications. As with many formal rules and specifications, real world scenarios do not always allow for perfect compliance. If you decide to violate one of the first three rules of normalization, make sure that your application anticipates any problems that could occur, such as redundant data and inconsistent dependencies. As an example, we won't be splitting out our price information as demonstrated above. Creating a new table to hold one column of data creates more work (linking the tables) and complexity than we would save by not repeating pricing information in each book row.

Given the guidance from the normalization process, let's now split our Books table into the most efficient set of relational tables. Before, we mentioned that we could split the table into Book and Author tables, but this still presents us with inefficiencies:

❑   Although this is not the case at the moment, as we add new books to the table, we might encounter different authors with the same name, and different books with the same title – so it would not be wise to use either of these columns as primary keys.

❑   Each title in the Book table can still have many authors, which makes it difficult to match entries in the author name column of the Book table with corresponding entries in the author name column in the Author table.

However, we can solve these problems. To get around the first problem, we create another table to hold authors. This Author table will contain an author name column, and another column that contains a unique ID for that author. This author ID column can then be used as the primary key for this table. Since author ID values rather than author names will be used by other tables, we are then free to modify an author's name without having to modify every record that belongs to this author.

Solving the last problem, of multi-author entries, takes a bit more effort. One way to address it would be to create the concept of an "author contribution". We'll have a third table, the Contribution table, which simply consists of the author's ID, the ID of the book associated with that author, and a contribution ID (the primary key for this table).

Here's the structure of our database model now:

Table	Column	Key
Book	ID	Primary Key
	Title	Not a key field
	Price	Not a key field
Author	ID	Primary Key
	Author_Name	Not a key field
Contribution	ID	Primary Key
	Title_ID	Foreign Key
	Author_ID	Foreign Key

We are now almost ready to implement this database structure (or **schema**) on our machines. However, there is one last aspect of relational databases we must consider: referential integrity.

Referential Integrity

Let's consider what happens when you start manipulating the records in our tables. You can edit the book information at will without any ill effects, but what would happen if you needed to delete a title? The entries in the `Contribution` table will be left linking to a non-existent book. Clearly you can't have a contribution detail without the associated book title being present. So you must have a means in place to enforce a corresponding book title for each contribution. This is the basis of enforcing **referential integrity**. There are two ways that you can enforce the validity of the data in this situation. One is by cascading deletions through the related tables; the other is by preventing deletions when related records exist.

> **Referential integrity prevents inconsistent data from being created in the database by ensuring that any data shared between tables remains consistent. To put it another way, it ensures that the soundness of the relationships remains intact.**

Database applications have several choices available for enforcing referential integrity, but if possible, you should let the database engine do its job and handle this for you. Database engines allow you to use declarative referential integrity. You specify a relationship between tables at design time, indicating if updates and deletes will cascade through related tables. If cascading updates are enabled, changes to the primary key in a table are propagated through related tables. If cascading deletes are enabled, deletions from a table are propagated through related tables.

Before you go ahead and enable cascading deletes on all your relationships, keep in mind that this can be a dangerous practice. If you define a relationship between the Author table and the Title table with cascading deletes enabled, and then delete a record from Author, you will delete all Title table records that come under this category. Be cautious, or you may accidentally lose important data.

Introducing SQL

In a moment, we are going to install a **Relational Database Management System (RDBMS)** so that we can create and manipulate databases. First, however, let's introduce you to the language we use to communicate with relational databases: **Structured Query Language**, or **SQL** for short. A **query** is simply a statement that we send to an RDBMS in order to retrieve and manipulate data.

There are actually three languages within SQL itself:

❑ **Data Definition Language (DDL)** – used to create databases and tables

❑ **Data Maintenance Language (DML)** – used to add, remove, and change data in tables

❑ **Data Query Language (DQL)** – used to retrieve data from tables

As we will see later, SQL resembles a human language, and reads almost like a form of broken English (SQL originates from the Structured English Query Language of the 70s, and although the 'English' has now been dropped from the acronym, SQL is still widely pronounced 'SEQUEL'). SQL itself is platform independent, although each relational database management system usually has a few quirks in its SQL implementation. There are many different RDBMSs available, with different capabilities, from simple systems with limited features, to sophisticated databases capable of handling large numbers of concurrent users and offering advanced features such as distributed transactional support and powerful search algorithms. However, almost all use SQL as the data access language. Some common RDBMSs are:

❑ Oracle

❑ Sybase

❑ Informix

❑ Microsoft SQL Server

❑ Microsoft Access (through the so-called Jet engine)

❑ MySQL

In addition to being easy to use and having great performance and reliability, the last RDBMS on that list, MySQL, has another feature that makes it popular: free availability under the terms of the GNU Public License (GPL). It's a feature that appeals to us too, and so we'll use it throughout this book. For more information about the GPL, or the GNU Project, visit http://www.gnu.org.

Installing MySQL

Go to http://www.mysql.com/downloads/index.html and download the latest zipped binary version, which should be version 3.23.38 or higher. The current version at the time of writing is 3.23.54a, with version 4.0 under development.

Here's how to install MySQL on Windows 2000 or XP (or even Windows NT 4):

1. Download MySQL.

2. Unzip it in some empty directory and run the `setup.exe` program. By default, MySQL will be installed in `C:\mysql`.

    To start MySQL as a service (meaning MySQL will run when your machine starts up), you will need to open a command console and move to the `mysql\bin` folder, where the MySQL programs are kept. Now type:

    > mysqld-nt --install

    This will install MySQL as a service. Running MySQL as a service means that each time you restart your computer MySQL will be started automatically.

To install MySQL on Windows 98, you will need to follow the same instructions as above, but you should note that MySQL can only be installed as a service on Windows NT/2000/XP.

Troubleshooting

Here are some useful starting points that should help if you encounter problems during installation:

❑   Check the `C:\mysql\mysql.err` file for helpful information.

❑   Move to the `C:\mysql\bin` folder and start up MySQL manually with the following command:

    > mysqld --standalone

    This may display some useful information on screen that could help solve your problem.

❑   Start `mysqld` with the `--standalone` and `--debug` options. this tells `mysqld` to write a log file in `C:\mysqld.trace` that should indicate why `mysqld` won't start.

You can use the information you gather with these techniques to perform searches on Google.com (one of the best way's to find solutions in my experience), or to ask intelligent questions on a MySQL mailing list (information on the mailing lists can be found at http://www.mysql.org/documentation/lists.html).

You can test whether MySQL is working by executing the `mysqlshow` command from MySQL's `bin` folder, which lists the databases available. If installation went correctly, you should see the following two default MySQL databases:

```
+-----------+
| Databases |
+-----------+
| mysql     |
| test      |
+-----------+
```

Using MySQL

Now that we have MySQL installed, let's have a little play with its command line tool, `mysql`, located in the `C:\MySQL\bin\` folder. Open a command prompt window, change to the appropriate directory, and type `mysql`. The MySQL prompt should then appear:

mysql>

Note that when MySQL is installed on Windows, all local users have full privileges to all databases by default. Although you can skip it for the purposes of the samples in this book, production scenarios require MySQL to be more secure, and you should set an individual password for all MySQL users, and remove the default record in the `mysql.user` table that has `Host='localhost'` and `User=''`, using the following command:

mysql> USE mysql
mysql> DELETE FROM user WHERE Host='localhost' AND User='';
mysql> QUIT

The first command tells SQL to use the `mysql` database, and the second removes the appropriate record from the `user` table of that database (don't forget the final semicolon!). Lastly we exit the `mysql` tool using the `QUIT` command (alternatively, we can use `EXIT` if we wish).

Note that SQL commands, such as DELETE, WHERE, and QUIT, are not case-sensitive, although, according to convention, we'll capitalize them in this book. Do be aware though that the names of SQL tables and columns, as well as values themselves, are case-sensitive, and must use the casing applied at definition.

Now, you should also add a password for the **root user**. The root user, also called the **admin user**, has full privileges to the database, and so anyone logged into MySQL as root has the power to change the database in any way they please (or to make costly mistakes). To change the password, make sure that you are in the C:\MySQL\bin\ folder, and use another command line tool, mysqladmin:

> **mysqladmin reload**
> **mysqladmin -u root password your_password**

where your_password is the password you wish to use. Make sure you type this correctly, as you won't be asked to confirm it. Once the password is set, you then shut down the mysql server with the following command:

> **mysqladmin --user=root --password=your_password shutdown**

Now that you can get the MySQL server up and running securely, you can experiment with some basic database administration issues. For more help getting up to speed with MySQL, check out Wrox Press's *Beginning Databases with MySQL*, ISBN 1-86100-692-6.

Accessing the MySQL Server Remotely

To connect to the server, you'll usually need to provide your MySQL username when you invoke mysql and, most likely, a password (don't worry about creating a new user account yet – we'll come back to that in a little while). If the server runs on a machine other than the one where you log in, you'll also need to specify a hostname:

> **mysql -h hostname -u username -p**

When you hit *Enter*, you'll be prompted for the password for that user:

Enter password:

When you have entered it, you should see some introductory information followed by the **mysql>** prompt – this prompt indicates that you are connected to the MySQL server. After you have connected successfully, you can disconnect at any time by typing QUIT at the prompt or by pressing *Control-D*:

mysql> QUIT
Bye

Issuing SQL Commands

Run the following simple command that requests the current date from the server:

    mysql> SELECT CURRENT_DATE;

Note the semicolon that ends the SQL statement. It should produce output something like the following:

```
+--------------+
| CURRENT_DATE |
+--------------+
| 2002-11-21   |
+--------------+
1 row in set (0.07 sec)
```

This query illustrates several points about the `mysql` tool:

❑ A command normally consists of a SQL statement followed by a semicolon, although there are cases where the semicolon is not needed. `QUIT`, mentioned earlier, is one of them.

❑ When you issue a command, it is sent to the server for execution. Any results are displayed in the form of a grid. The first row typically shows the names of the columns, and below appear results from the query.

❑ `mysql` shows how many rows were returned and how long the query took to execute, as a rough idea of server performance.

We have just entered is a single-line command consisting of a single SQL statement, but more complex commands can comprise multiple statements. All the statements can either be added on a single line one after the other, or they can be entered on multiple lines by simply pressing *Enter* before the final semicolon is typed. `mysql` indicates what is expected next by changing the prompt to one of the following:

Prompt	Meaning
mysql>	Ready for new command.
->	Waiting for next line of multiple-line command.
'>	Waiting for next line, collecting a string that begins with a single quote.
">	Waiting for next line, collecting a string that begins with a double quote.

SQL Data Types

When we create a database table in our database, we must define the data type for each column, along with the lengths of any strings where appropriate. The data types that MySQL supports for columns may be grouped into three categories:

- ❑ Numeric
- ❑ Date and Time
- ❑ String

Numeric Data Types

Data Types	Desciption	Range/Format
INT	Normal-sized integer	(-2^{31} to 2^{31}-1), or (0 to 2^{32} -1) if UNSIGNED
TINYINT	Very small integer	(-2^{7} to 2^{7}-1), or (0 to 2^{8} -1) if UNSIGNED
SMALLINT	Small integer	(-2^{15} to 2^{15}-1), or (0 to 2^{8} -1) if UNSIGNED
MEDIUMINT	Medium-sized integer	(-2^{23} to 2^{23}-1), or (0 to 2^{24} -1) if UNSIGNED
BIGINT	Large integer	(-2^{63} to 2^{63}-1), or (0 to 2^{64} -1) if UNSIGNED
FLOAT	Single-precision floating-point number	Minimum non-zero $\pm1.176\times10^{-38}$; maximum non-zero $\pm3.403\times10^{+38}$
DOUBLE/REAL	Double-precision floating-point number	Minimum non-zero $\pm2.225\times10^{-308}$; maximum non-zero $\pm1.798\times10^{+308}$
DECIMAL	Float stored as string	Maximum range as DOUBLE

Note that INT is an alias for INTEGER, and both can be used interchangeably.

Data/Time Data Types

Data Types	Desciption	Range/Format
DATE	A date	YYYY-MM-DD format. Range 1000-01-01 to 9999-12-31
DATETIME	A date and time	YYYY-MM-DD hh:mm:ss format. Range 1000-01-01 00:00:00 to 9999-12-31 23:59:59
TIMESTAMP	A timestamp	YYYYMMDDhhmmss format. Range 19700101000000 to sometime in 2037

Data Types	Desciption	Range/Format
TIME	A time	hh:mm:ss format. Range -838:59:59 to 838:59:59
YEAR	A year	YYYY format. Range 1900 to 2155

Character Data Types

Data Types	Desciption	Range/Format
CHAR	Fixed-length string	0-255 characters
VARCHAR	Variable-length string	0-255 characters
BLOB	Binary Large OBject	Binary data 0-65535 bytes long
TINYBLOB	Small BLOB value	Binary data 0-255 bytes long
MEDIUMBLOB	Medium-sized BLOB	Binary data 0-16777215 bytes long
LONGBLOB	Large BLOB value	Binary data 0-4294967295 bytes long
TEXT	Normal-sized text field	0-65535 bytes
TINYTEXT	Small text field	0-255 bytes
MEDIUMTEXT	Medium-sized text	0-16777215 bytes
LONGTEXT	Large text field	0-4294967295 bytes
ENUM	Enumeration	Column values are assigned one value from a set list
SET	Set value(s)	Column values are assigned zero or more values from a set list

As the table above shows, MySQL offers two ways of storing strings, CHAR and VARCHAR. The difference between them is that CHAR is **fixed-width**, while VARCHAR is **variable-width**. Suppose we had two columns set to a size of 20 characters, name1 and name2, of type CHAR and VARCHAR respectively. If we entered the name "Bob" into both of them and then retrieved the values, name2 would return exactly "Bob" – those three letters and nothing more. name1, however, would return this string followed by 17 spaces: "Bob   ". So what are TEXT fields, you may ask? Suffice to say that they behave like VARCHARs, except that they are specified in bytes instead of characters, and have certain limitations when it comes to querying data.

SQL Modifiers

Certain modifiers can be applied to a column to further define its properties, a few of which are specific to MySQL. The most common are:

Modifier	Description
AUTO_INCREMENT	Allows a numeric column to be automatically updated when records are added. Useful for creating a unique identification number for each row.
DEFAULT *value*	Specifies the default value for a column.
NULL	Specifies that a column may contain undefined, or NULL, values.
NOT NULL	Requires that the column must contain a non-NULL value.
PRIMARY KEY	Makes the column the primary key. It must also have a NOT NULL modifier.

Our next task is to use this information to create a MySQL database and tables. Let's first familiarize ourselves with the necessary SQL statements.

Creating Databases and Tables with SQL

Let's start with an example of creating a SQL database. The database that we create, publish, will be used throughout the remainder of the book, so make sure you set it up as described here.

Try It Out   **Creating a Sample Database**

1. The CREATE DATABASE statement creates an entirely new empty database. You must be the administrative user (the root user) for MySQL to be able to use this statement. Open the mysql prompt, and run the command below to create our sample database, which is called publish:

    mysql> CREATE DATABASE publish;

2. To check that we created the database successfully, list all of the databases in MySQL with the following command:

    mysql> SHOW DATABASES;

You should see the following output:

```
+----------+
| Database |
+----------+
| mysql    |
| publish  |
| test     |
+----------+
3 rows in set (0.00 sec)
```

3. While we're here, we can remove a database using the DROP DATABASE command:

mysql> DROP DATABASE publish;

Feel free to try this, but if you do, make sure to recreate the publish database by running the CREATE DATABASE command again.

4. Since it isn't good practice to use your root account for general database access, so let's create a new user named publish for use with our examples:

mysql>   grant all privileges
mysql>   on publish.*
mysql>   to publish@localhost
mysql>   identified by 'wrox';

5. Now we have a database, but it contains no tables as yet. Before we can add them, we have to tell mysql to work with our database with the USE command:

mysql> USE publish;

The Database changed message will tell us that our change was successful.

6. Now we use the CREATE TABLE statement to define the structure for new tables in the database. This statement consists of the name of the new table followed by the list of each column in the new table. The list provides the name of the column followed by its data type, then any modifiers (as described earlier). The definition for each column is separated from the next by a comma, and the whole list is enclosed in parentheses.

Now go ahead and use this syntax to create the book table like so:

mysql> CREATE TABLE book (

The first column we want is an ID field, which will be used as the primary key for the table, so must be unique (and not null). This is an ideal candidate for the AUTO_INCREMENT modifier:

-> id INTEGER NOT NULL AUTO_INCREMENT PRIMARY KEY,

Now we want a few strings, for the title, author, and editor details. Only the title is required, so we use the NOT NULL modifier:

-> title VARCHAR(255) NOT NULL,
-> authors VARCHAR(255),
-> editor VARCHAR(255),

Lastly add some other fields that we'll need later in this book:

-> chapters TEXT,
-> page_count INTEGER,
-> status CHAR(1) NOT NULL);

If you're wondering where the price field is, don't worry, as we'll come to that in a moment.

7. We can use the SHOW TABLES command to check that our book table is in our database:

mysql> SHOW TABLES;

You should see something like this:

```
+-------------------+
| Tables_in_publish |
+-------------------+
| book              |
+-------------------+
1 row in set (0.00 sec)
```

Altering Tables

As we develop new applications, a fairly common requirement we encounter is the need to modify a table that has already been created by us – or by some other developer before us. We do so using the ALTER TABLE statement, which lets us add, change, rename, or remove columns from an existing table.

Try It Out   **Changing the Structure of an Existing Table**

1. First we will add our Price field to the table, using the ADD command, and specifying the properties of the field:

mysql> ALTER TABLE book ADD (price INTEGER);

So here we've added a field called Price that contains integer values.

2. Why would we represent price as an integer, when a decimal would seem much more logical? Well, it was a deliberate mistake, so remove this field using the DROP command:

mysql> ALTER TABLE book DROP price;

3. Now add the field again, but this time as a decimal field, with maximum of five characters, two of which are after the decimal point:

mysql> ALTER TABLE book ADD (prize DECIMAL(5,2));

4. Whoops, we've done it again: another boo-boo. This time, the data type of the field is correct (a decimal field) but the name of the field is wrong. We'll modify the field using the CHANGE command, rather than deleting it and creating a new one:

mysql> ALTER TABLE book CHANGE prize price DECIMAL(5,2);

At last, our field is just how we want it. Note that we had to specify all of the properties of the new field when we used the CHANGE command, even though we just wanted to change the field name.

5. There are a couple of other SQL commands used with ALTER TABLE that are worth being aware of. The first is the ALTER command for changing field definitions. For instance, if we wanted to set the status field to a default value of 'P', we could use:

mysql> ALTER TABLE book ALTER status SET DEFAULT 'P';

6. The other command is MODIFY, which can change the entire definition of a particular field. Let's say, to be awkward, we wanted to change the Price field back into an integer field. Then we could use:

mysql> ALTER TABLE book MODIFY Price INTEGER;

If you try this last command, change the field back to a decimal after, as we'll need it to be that type when we start inserting data.

Manipulating the Database

We now have our database set up, but it's not a whole lot of use without any data, so let's move on to see how to add some records.

Inserting Data into Tables

Now that we have created the table we need to add the data about our books to it. To do this, we need to use the INSERT INTO...VALUES command.

This command inserts the column values given in parentheses after VALUES into the table named after INTO. Let's see it in action on our sample database.

Try It Out   Inserting Data

1. For example, to insert data for a book entitled *Lord of the Things*, we would enter the following:

**mysql> INSERT INTO book (title, price) VALUES
    -> ('Lord of the Things', 9.99);**

Note that we specify the fields (or columns) that are to be populated by this command after the table name, and then list the values for these fields in the same order. All fields and values are separated by commas, and strings are delimited by single or double quotes.

2. To check that the data has been placed in our table correctly, run the following command:

mysql> SELECT id, title, price, status FROM book;

This should display something similar to this:

```
+----+--------------------+-------+--------+
| id | title              | price | status |
+----+--------------------+-------+--------+
|  1 | Lord of the Things |  9.99 |   P    |
+----+--------------------+-------+--------+
```

Notice that as an auto-increment field, the `id` column has automatically been set to 1 for this first record. Also, the `status` column has the value 'P' as this is the default we set earlier.

3. Now let's add details for another couple of books. We can insert more than one record at a time by giving more than one set of values, each separated by commas. Run the following SQL command:

**mysql> INSERT INTO book (title, price) VALUES
    -> ('Mr Bunny\'s Guide to ActiveX', 14.99),
    -> ('Parachuting for You and Your Kangaroo', 19.99);**

Notice that the first of these two books demonstrates a title string that contains a single quote character. We can't use a quote character as is, because MySQL would assume that we were finishing the string at that point, and return an error when it came to the rest of our string.

To get round this, we have to use **escape characters**, where we precede the quote with a \ backslash character to make \ '. Awkward readers might be wondering what we'd do if our book title contained the sequence \ ' – we'd then need to use the \ \ escape character for the backslash, followed by the one for the single quote, to make \ \ \ ' altogether. Alternatively, we could simply change our string to use double-quotes at either end, because as long as the type of quotes (single or double) surrounding the string is different to those inside it, there won't be any confusion.

4. Check that all three books have been added as expected by running the same SELECT statement we used in Step 2. Note how the id field is incremented for each new record.

Querying the Database

As we were inserting data into our database, we checked that new records had been correctly using the SQL SELECT statement to query the database. Let's have a closer look at the command we ran:

mysql> SELECT id, title, price, status FROM book;

Running this command produces output something like this:

```
+----+---------------------------------------------+-------+--------+
| id | title                                       | price | status |
+----+---------------------------------------------+-------+--------+
|  1 | Lord of the Things                          |  9.99 |   P    |
|  1 | Mr Bunny's Guide to ActiveX                 | 14.99 |   P    |
|  1 | Parachuting for You and Your Kangaroo       | 19.99 |   P    |
+----+---------------------------------------------+-------+--------+
3 rows in set (0.04 sec)
```

The command asks for the columns called id, title, price, and status for all rows in the book table. The general form for a SELECT statement that retrieves all of the rows in the table is:

> SELECT Column1Name, ... , ColumnXName FROM TableName;

There is also a special form that returns *all* columns from a table, without our having to type the name for every column:

> SELECT * FROM TableName;

If you run this, you'll see that other columns for which we didn't specify a value are set to NULL.

As a rule, you should avoid using **SELECT * FROM** except for testing or debugging purposes, unless you really do need every single column from the table. Performance will be enhanced if you only request those fields that you actually intend to use. Additionally, **SELECT *** offers no control over the order of the returned fields, as they are returned in the order in which they were declared in the **CREATE TABLE** statement.

When retrieving data with a SELECT query, we can order the returned rows by adding an ORDER BY clause to the command. The ORDER BY statement is followed by the column that we wish to sort on, and finally we specify whether to order highest to lowest – a descending sort as indicated by DESC – or lowest to highest – an ascending sort, indicated by ASC. ASC is the default sort, so it is assumed if neither DESC nor ASC is specified. For instance, the command below displays books in order of price, highest price first:

```
mysql> SELECT price, title FROM book
    -> ORDER BY price DESC;
```

We'll see something like this:

```
+--------+-------------------------------------------+
| price  | title                                     |
+--------+-------------------------------------------+
|   9.99 | Lord of the Things                        |
|  14.99 | Mr Bunny's Guide to ActiveX               |
|  19.99 | Parachuting for You and Your Kangaroo      |
+--------+-------------------------------------------+
```

You'll see that the column order has changed because of how we've ordered the column names in the SELECT statement.

Modifying Data

We've already seen how to modify the structure of existing tables, so now let's look at how to modify the data that our tables contain, using the UPDATE...SET command. When using this syntax, we simply specify the table where we wish to change column values after the UPDATE statement, and specify which column or columns are to be affected after the SET statement.

Hence, we could change the status column for all books to 'O' using this command:

```
mysql> UPDATE book SET status = 'O';
```

You should see a confirmation that all 3 rows in the table were affected by the command, and you can verify that by executing the SELECT statement we used earlier.

> Likewise you could use an **UPDATE** to modify the `title`, or any other fields. Note that it is not a good idea to modify the `id` field once it has been set. Changing a primary key field could impact other parts of your system which rely on the `id` keeping the same value, such as maintaining referential integrity.

The WHERE Clause

While the UPDATE command we've just seen is a quick way to change all values for a given column or set of columns in a table, we generally only wish to change certain specific rows. To specify criteria that rows must match for a command to be applied, we append a WHERE clause.

For instance, the command below would change the price of the book with an ID of 1 to $8.99:

mysql> UPDATE book SET price = 8.99 WHERE id = 1;

Run it now and see. Can you guess what SQL command we should use to retrieve the information shown below for just that book?

```
+----+-------------------------------------------------+-------+
| id | title                                           | price |
+----+-------------------------------------------------+-------+
|  1 | Lord of the Things                              |  8.99 |
+----+-------------------------------------------------+-------+
```

We simply use the same WHERE clause on a SELECT statement:

mysql> SELECT id, title, price FROM book WHERE id = 1;

Deleting Data

To delete a given row or set of rows, we use the DELETE FROM. . .WHERE command. For instance, we can delete the book called *Mr Bunny's Guide to ActiveX* with this command:

mysql> DELETE FROM book
-> WHERE title = "Mr Bunny's Guide to ActiveX";

Now execute a SELECT command to retrieve all books from the table, and you'll see that the record for that book no longer appears:

```
+----+-------------------------------------------------+-------+
| id | title                                           | price |
+----+-------------------------------------------------+-------+
|  1 | Lord of the Things                              |  8.99 |
|  1 | Parachuting for You and Your Kangaroo           | 19.99 |
+----+-------------------------------------------------+-------+
```

Do be careful when using DELETE as once a row is removed, it is lost forever. Hence be particularly wary when specifying a non-unique column in the WHERE clause, such as we have here. In our small database, we know that only a single row will be deleted, but in a real-world database, we can easily end up accidentally deleting a whole bunch of records if we use a badly thought-out WHERE clause. We can reduce the chances of this happening by specifying a WHERE clause on a uniquely valued field (such as a primary key).

We've now covered enough of the basics of the SQL syntax to move on to see how we can use it to access databases in a JSP page.

Displaying Data Using the JSTL SQL Tags

In Chapter 2 you were introduced to the JavaServer Pages Standard Tag Library. The JSTL is divided into four functional groupings, one of which is the SQL tag library for querying a database, and performing inserts and updates. In the following sections, we'll apply what we've learned about SQL to a simple JSP page that displays the information in the book table.

Try It Out   Querying Data with the JSTL

1. Create a new web application folder called DataAccess inside Tomcat's webapps folder. Create a folder inside it with the name WEB-INF.

2. Next we need to give our web application access to the JSTL by copying the JSTL lib folder into WEB-INF just as we did in the previous chapter. Be sure to copy the entire lib folder, not just its contents.

3. We also need to make the MySQL **Java DataBase Connectivity (JDBC)** classes available as well. These can be found at http://www.mysql.com/downloads/api-jdbc-stable.html. Once downloaded, unzip the file and copy mysql-connector-java-2.0.14-bin.jar into your webapp's WEB-INF/lib directory (the filename may be slightly different if a newer version has been released).

4. Create the following JSP page in the DataAccess folder as bookDB.jsp:

```
<%@ taglib prefix="c" uri="http://java.sun.com/jstl/core_rt" %>
<%@ taglib prefix="sql" uri="http://java.sun.com/jstl/sql_rt" %>

<sql:setDataSource var="datasource"
            driver="com.mysql.jdbc.Driver"
            url="jdbc:mysql://localhost/publish"
            user="publish" password="wrox" />

<sql:query var="books" dataSource="${datasource}">
  SELECT id, title, price FROM book
</sql:query>
```

```
<html>
  <head>
    <title>A First JSP Database</title>
  </head>
  <body>
    <table border="1">
      <tr>
        <td>id</td><td>title</td><td>price</td>
      </tr>
<c:forEach items="${books.rows}" var="row">
      <tr>
        <td><c:out value="${row.id}" /></td>
        <td><c:out value="${row.title}" /></td>
        <td><c:out value="${row.price}" /></td>
      </tr>
</c:forEach>
    </table>
  </body>
</html>
```

5. Start up Tomcat and navigate to `localhost\DataAccess\bookDB.jsp`:

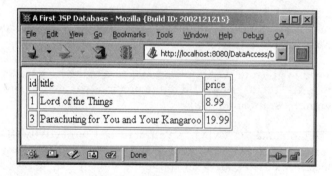

How It Works

First we declared the `core` and `sql` libraries so that they will be available to us in the page. This should look familiar from the examples in the Chapter 2.

Before we can issue a query, we'll need to make a connection to the database using `<sql:setDataSource />`. We declare the JDBC `driver` we are using, the `url` where the database is located, and our `username` and `password` combination. The JDBC driver and URL will be the same no matter where in your Java applications you use them (well, the URL could be different if your application isn't running on the same machine as the database). And of course you will need to use a username and password that has read and write permissions (if your application won't do any inserts or updates, you should configure a user without these permissions and use this new user for your application).

The resulting JDBC Data Source is assigned to the variable var, which we've named datasource (aptly enough). In JDBC, all queries (including inserts and updates) are performed against a Data Source. There are several ways to obtain a Data Source for use, and some others will be seen later in this book.

A familiar SQL query appears in the body of the <sql:query /> tag. Since all queries must be performed against a data source, we assign the dataSource and declare that the resulting data be held by a variable var, named books. Unlike the examples using the mysql command-line tool, we are responsible for handling the display of the data ourselves.

> JDBC queries return a resultset, a mechanism for holding each row of data returned by the query. If you are unfamiliar with the concept of looping (or iteration), consider it like flipping through a notepad where each page of the notepad represents a row from the database. Each page (or row) contains one set of data for that entry: in our example the "page" contains an ID, title, price, and the other fields that we're currently ignoring.

Now that we have loaded our books data, we can display the data using the JSTL core tags. The JSTL provides <c:forEach /> tag for looping over data, which requires two arguments: the set of data to loop over and the variable which will hold each row of data, represented as items and var respectively (to be strictly accurate, these two arguments are not required but are one possible set of options). We will cover looping with the JSTL in more detail in Chapter 5, for now just rest assured that it is used to present each row of data. Once each row is assigned to variable row, the fields of data can be accessed directly by column name as you see in the <c:out /> tags.

Hold on to your hats, because next we look at using JSTL tags to insert information into our database.

Manipulating Data With JSTL SQL Tags

In order to create or edit data we are going to make use of another JSTL tag. As you saw above, data is edited using an UPDATE query. Developers have a strange passion for granting objects the most obvious of names (well, good developers do), so the JSTL tag we will be using is the <sql:update> tag. That said, perhaps you're expecting to see an <sql:insert> and <sql:delete> tag, but they don't exist – <sql:update> is used for all three operations. Let's have an example:

```
<sql:update>INSERT INTO book (title, price) VALUES (?, ?)
  <sql:param value="${param.title}" />
  <sql:param value="${param.price}" />
</sql:update>
```

If you've used SQL and JDBC in the past the INSERT statement will look familiar. If not, you may be wondering about the question marks in the query above. The <sql:update /> tag acts like a prepared statement, into which the <sql:param /> tags insert their values in order of appearance. Look again and you will see param.title and param.price specified in the same order as in the insert SQL. You will learn more about Prepared Statements later, in Chapter 13.

The use of ${param.title} above should be familiar to you from the previous chapter, as the Expression Language syntax for getting the value for the new title from the request, which is then inserted into the stored procedure (and thence into the database).

Try It Out   Inserting Data with the JSTL

1. You learned about HTML form handling in the previous chapter, so let's create a form that will allow users to insert new books into our database.

Create the following JSP page as bookDB2.jsp:

```
<%@ taglib prefix="c" uri="http://java.sun.com/jstl/core_rt" %>
<%@ taglib prefix="sql" uri="http://java.sun.com/jstl/sql_rt" %>

<sql:setDataSource var="datasource"
    driver="com.mysql.jdbc.Driver"
    url="jdbc:mysql://localhost/publish"
    user="publish" password="wrox" />

<c:if test="${param.title != null}">
    <sql:update dataSource="${datasource}">
      INSERT INTO book (title, price) VALUES(?, ?)
        <sql:param value="${param.title}" />
        <sql:param value="${param.price}" />
    </sql:update>
</c:if>

<sql:query var="books" dataSource="${datasource}">
  SELECT id, title, price FROM book
</sql:query>
<html>
  <head>
      <title>A First JSP Database</title
  </head>
  <body>
    <form method="post">
      <table border="1">
        <tr>
        <td>id</td><td>title</td><td>price</td>
        </tr>
<c:forEach var="row" items="${books.rows}">
        <tr>
          <td><c:out value="${row.id}" /></td>
```

```
        <td><c:out value="${row.title}" /></td>
        <td><c:out value="${row.price}" /></td>
      </tr>
</c:forEach>
      <tr>
        <td> </td>
        <td><input type="text" name="title" size="30" /></td>
        <td><input type="text" name="price" size="5" /></td>
      </tr>
      <tr>
        <td colspan="3" align="center">
        <input type="submit" value="Save New Book" />
        </td>
      </tr>
    </table>
  </form>
  </body>
</html>
```

2. Navigate to `localhost\DataAccess\bookDB2.jsp`. It looks pretty similar to how it did before, except the last row in the table now lets us add new book details:

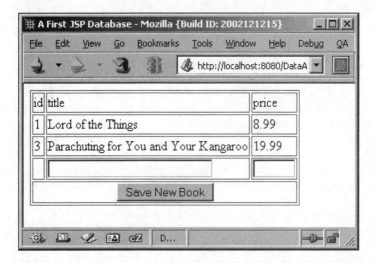

3. Enter a title and price (including the decimal point), and click **Save New Book**. Notice that we don't have to explicitly set the ID of the new book, as that field is set to `AUTO_INCREMENT`, and so MySQL assigns the "next available" number as the value of the new row's id column.

4. Even though we've already deleted the row that had an ID of 2, the database does not take the deleted record's ID as available. MySQL has kept track of the last value it assigned as a book's ID and considers the next available number to be 4:

95

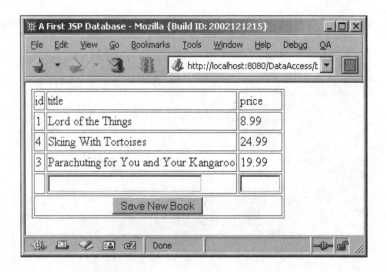

How It Works

The `taglib` declaration should be familiar by now, and we saw the `<sql:setDataSource>` tag in our first example. We repeat that code here.

The `<c:if>` tag lets us apply the standard conditional logic: "if the test is true, then perform the following actions", and it's covered in detail in Chapter 5. We use it here to prevent the page from trying to INSERT a new record when someone is just viewing (that is, the `submit` button hasn't been clicked). This prevents the page causing an error by attempting to insert "blank" entries into the `book` table, since both of these fields are declared NOT NULL (meaning **some** value has to be entered).

Inside the `<c:if>` tag, we have the same INSERT code shown earlier. This checks the request, and if a title has been submitted it creates an INSERT query to be executed.

Next we reload the books for display. Since this happens after the INSERT query, our new book should show up in the list.

Now add the HTML form tags (again, see Chapter 2) which allow the user to enter a title and price, and you've got the means by which to enter your new books.

Now you have the core of a library management system. You can view the books in your "library", and add more as you please. All without a bit of Java code! The power of the JSTL should be readily apparent, and you've had but a taste. Thirsting for more?

Summary

We've covered a lot of information in this chapter – firstly we examined the fundamental concepts of relational databases, and then we installed and configured our own personal RDBMS – MySQL – and used it to create a books database. This demonstrated the basics of SQL queries, including how to add, remove, and read information from a database. Finally, we took a peek at how the JSTL provides a means to put that database to use in a JSP page.

Why Not Try?

At this point you may be ready to try something a bit more complicated. Here are a few challenges to test what you've learned so far:

❑ How should our last example be changed so that it can be used to delete a book?

HINT: You'll need to add a mechanism for selecting which book to delete, and use a DELETE query.

❑ How could that example be revised to allow users to update a book's title or price?

HINT: You'll need to add a mechanism for selecting which book to edit, and rewrite the SQL query as an update.

❑ Change the example to give each of the books an arbitrary value for status, and show the status field on the HTML form, colored according to its value.

HINT: you'll need to UPDATE each of your books with a status value. Then use the <tr> tag's color attribute to color each row dependent on each book's status value. You can make up your own status values and colors, or color "P" and "O" as "green" and "white", respectively.

❑ There's one large potential problem with the last example we looked at in this chapter – can you spot what it is?

The problem is that there is no guarantee that a user will submit appropriate data. For instance, an error would occur if the user typed a title in the price field (since price must be a number). Before we can resolve this issue however, we need to study conditional logic and the JSTL in more depth, so we'll come back to this question in Chapter 5.

CHAPTER 4

Reusing Code

In professional environments, a formal process typically guides the development of applications. There are in fact dozens – probably hundreds – of different processes that can be followed, and indeed the topic of managing software development is so rich and complex that we won't even attempt to cover it in this chapter or book.

Most of these design processes, however, share the following overall flow, or as it is sometimes called the development life cycle:

- ❑ First, you gather all the **requirements** of the software – that is, what it should do.
- ❑ Next, you **design** how the software will fulfill those requirements.
- ❑ Armed with a design, you **develop** the application according to the design – the actual programming.
- ❑ Once the software is created, it is **tested** and debugged.
- ❑ The product is then released, or **deployed**.
- ❑ It then enters the **maintenance** phase during which new bugs are fixed as they are discovered, and features are added or changed as the users' requirements change.

Of these phases, which do you suppose is the most time consuming and therefore most costly? You might be surprised to discover that it is in fact the **maintenance** phase – businesses spend far more maintaining software once it has been deployed than they do actually developing it in the first place.

The lesson here applies to even the smallest of software projects: develop your applications with an emphasis on making future maintenance as easy as possible, because chances are that this is where you'll be spending the majority of your time.

One of the best ways to ease the maintenance burden of any application is to design to **maximize reuse** of code. Therefore, this chapter will show how to reuse JSP code and thus make applications easier to maintain.

As we discuss code reuse, we will also talk about how to integrate standard Java code into JSP pages. This topic, covered in the last half of this chapter, is in fact very important, as it enables us to create web pages that have the power and extensive features of one of the most popular programming language on the planet.

And so, off we go!

Code Reuse

Reusing code *sounds* like a great idea; after all, reusing homework got me through most of school, but that's an entirely different yarn. We've said that designing for reuse makes an application easier to maintain, so let's now examine why this is.

Imagine our web site contains several JSP pages that each has a certain element in common, such as the following HTML table of shipping charges:

```
<table border="1">
    <tr>
        <td colspan="2">
            Shipping Rates
        </td>
    </tr>
    <tr>
        <td>
            Small
        </td>
        <td>
            $5.75
        </td>
    </tr>
    <tr>
        <td>
            Large
        </td>
        <td>
            $10.25
        </td>
    </tr>
</table>
```

For the benefit of those who don't speak HTML natively, here's what the table actually looks like:

Shipping Rates	
Small	$5.75
Large	$10.25

Now let's say that, one day, we need to change this information, say to add a new shipping category for medium items. If each of the many pages in our web site contains its own copy of the code, we'd have to go through and change each one in turn, which is tedious at best. And what if we make a mistake on one of the pages, or miss one altogether? Ugh.

It would be so much better if we could simply create this code once, and somehow instruct all our pages to insert this single file, we'd be able to change it once and all our pages would then show the new version straight away. This gives a taste of how code reuse can make applications easier to maintain.

Planning for Reuse

Code reuse makes maintenance easier, but does it let us create applications faster? This might *seem* to be the case, but in reality, the answer is more complex. Maximizing code reusability takes planning, and sometimes the extra planning effort, and building the reusable component itself, can take more time than just copying and pasting the same code over and over again.

Reusing code is primarily a mechanism for easing maintenance, and not necessarily a mechanism for accelerating development. Sometimes people get confused on this point, and sidestep the reusability issue because they think addressing it in their situation would require unnecessary time and effort. While it often does take longer to design for reuse, it's generally more than worth it in the long run. Poorly designed code not only requires more work to maintain, but it may make improvements too costly, forcing users to put up with unsatisfactory applications, or to simply drop applications that you've poured a lot of sweat into.

> **So planning for reuse can be time consuming, but it is worth it. It requires sitting down and considering what an application needs to accomplish, what different JSP pages will be required, and always looking for opportunities to reuse the same chunk of code. There are numerous professional methodologies for doing this, but common sense isn't a bad way to start.**

We should also mention, however, that once you've designed code for reuse on a few projects, you may indeed start to experience dramatic accelerations in new application development as you are able to reuse code from previous projects.

Inevitably, however, while developing an application we discover new reuse opportunities we hadn't spotted during the design stage. Often it is worth adjusting the design to cater for such opportunities – a process known as **refactoring**. There are many tools in the marketplace to make refactoring easier by automating certain aspects of changing the code. Most of these tools aren't geared towards JSP in particular, but many are designed with Java in mind.

The Web Catalog Application

Just as "a picture is worth a thousand words", a good code example is worth pages of well-worded explanations. So let's see a small example application that does *not* reuse code as well as it could, and then as we introduce ways to reuse code, we'll modify the application appropriately.

Try It Out   A Badly Written JSP Application

1. Our example application will be a web catalog comprising two JSP pages powered by the MySQL database program introduced in Chapter 3. The first thing we need to do is create a suitable database. Open `mysql`, and run the following command:

```
mysql> CREATE DATABASE catalog;
mysql> USE catalog;
mysql> CREATE TABLE products (
    -> id INTEGER NOT NULL AUTO_INCREMENT PRIMARY KEY,
    -> name VARCHAR(15),
    -> description VARCHAR(50),
    -> price DECIMAL(7,2));
```

2. We'll create a user for this database called `catalogDBA`:

```
mysql> GRANT ALL PRIVILEGES ON catalog.*
    -> TO catalogDBA@localhost
    -> IDENTIFIED BY 'wrox';
```

3. Now we need to populate the database with some data. Run the following commands at the `mysql>` prompt:

```
mysql> INSERT INTO products (name, description, price)
    -> VALUES ("Widget A", "A nice entry level widget", 5000),
    -> ("Widget B", "An even better widget", 5625),
    -> ("Widget C", "This widget is the coolest, you need it", 6403),
    -> ("Widget D", "Customers of means will appreciate this widget",
    -> 7500),
    -> ("Widget E", "This widget will bring you friends and popularity",
    -> 8950),
    -> ("Widget F", "We distilled happiness & made it into this widget",
    -> 15023),
    -> ("Widget G", "The widget to make you happier than a March Hare",
    -> 35075),
    -> ("Widget H", "Exclusivity has a price, and it's $750", 75000);
```

4. Now we need a location for our sample application, so create a new folder in Tomcat's webapps directory called GoodDesign. Inside it, create another folder called WEB-INF, and copy the JSTL lib folder inside that. Finally, copy the JAR file for MySQL JDBC support into the lib directory as we did in the previous chapter, and we're good to go.

First page – page1.jsp

1. Create a file called page1.jsp in the GoodDesign folder. This page will list the less expensive items available from our catalog database. It starts with taglib directives for the JSTL core, SQL, and formatting tags:

```
<%@ taglib uri="http://java.sun.com/jstl/core_rt" prefix="c" %>
<%@ taglib uri="http://java.sun.com/jstl/sql_rt" prefix="sql" %>
<%@ taglib uri="http://java.sun.com/jstl/fmt_rt" prefix="fmt" %>
```

2. First, we have some setup details to get out of the way, starting with an HTML <style> tag:

```
<html>
    <head>
        <title>WROX Catalog</title>
        <style type="text/css">
            BODY {
                font: 10pt sans-serif;
            }
            DIV.header {
                background: gray;
                color: white;
                padding: 5px 5px 5px 10px;
                font: bold 16pt sans-serif;
            }
            TABLE {
                border-collapse: collapse;
            }
            TH {
                background: black;
                color: white;
                margin: 1px;
            }
            TD {
                border: 1px solid silver;
            }
            .price {
                text-align: center;
            }
        </style>
    </head>
    <body>
```

```
<div class="header">
    WROX Catalog
</div>
<p/>
Welcome to the WROX Catalog.
<p/>
We have inexpensive items, shown below, and
<a href="page2.jsp">expensive items</a>.
<p/>
```

3. Now we set up the connection details for our database in a JSTL SQL
   <setDataSource> element. We also create a query that will grab all items below $100:

```
<sql:setDataSource url="jdbc:mysql://localhost/catalog"
                   driver="com.mysql.jdbc.Driver"
                   user="catalogDBA" password="wrox"/>

<sql:query var="catalog">
    SELECT * FROM products
    WHERE price < 10000
    ORDER BY price
</sql:query>
```

4. We use an HTML table to display the information pulled from the database:

```
<table width="100%">
    <tr>
        <th>
            Item
        </th>
        <th>
            Description
        </th>
        <th>
            Price
        </th>
    </tr>
```

5. Now that's the table heading set up, so we move onto the content. We'll create a new
   row in the table for each row in the results returned from our query using a JSTL
   <forEach> element:

```
<c:forEach varStatus="status" var="row"
           items="${catalog.rows}">
    <tr>
        <td>
            ${row.name}
```

```
                </td>
                <td>
                    ${row.description}
                </td>
                <td class="price">
                    <fmt:formatNumber value="${row.price / 100}"
                                      type="currency"/>
                </td>
            </tr>
        </c:forEach>
```

6. Close our HTML tags, and the first page is done:

```
        </table>
    </body>
</html>
```

Second page - page2.jsp

1. Our application has a second page that lists items aimed at those customers with less sense than money. Again, we start with some taglib directives, and an HTML <style> element:

```
<%@ taglib uri="http://java.sun.com/jstl/core_rt" prefix="c" %>
<%@ taglib uri="http://java.sun.com/jstl/sql_rt" prefix="sql" %>
<%@ taglib uri="http://java.sun.com/jstl/fmt_rt" prefix="fmt" %>
<html>
    <head>
        <title>WROX Catalog</title>
        <style type="text/css">
            BODY {
                font: 10pt sans-serif;
            }
            DIV.header {
                background: gray;
                color: white;
                padding: 5px 5px 5px 10px;
                font: bold 16pt sans-serif;
            }
            TABLE {
                border-collapse: collapse;
            }
            TH {
                background: black;
                color: white;
                margin: 1px;
            }
            TD {
                border: 1px solid silver;
            }
```

```
            .price {
                text-align: center;
            }
        </style>
</head>
<body>
    <div class="header">
        WROX Catalog
    </div>
    <p/>
Welcome to the WROX Catalog.
    <p/>
We have expensive items, shown below, and
<a href="page1.jsp">inexpensive items</a>.
    <p/>
```

2. The connection details are the same, but our query is slightly different:

```
<sql:setDataSource url="jdbc:mysql://localhost/catalog"
                   driver="com.mysql.jdbc.Driver"
                   user="catalogDBA" password="wrox"/>

<sql:query var="catalog">
    SELECT * FROM products
    WHERE price >= 10000
    ORDER BY price
</sql:query>
```

3. Our query results are formatted as a table just as before:

```
<table width="100%">
    <tr>
        <th>
            Item
        </th>
        <th>
            Description
        </th>
        <th>
            Price
        </th>
    </tr>
    <c:forEach varStatus="status" var="row"
            items="${catalog.rows}">
        <tr>
            <td>
                ${row.name}
            </td>
            <td>
                ${row.description}
```

```
                </td>
                <td class="price">
                    <fmt:formatNumber value="${row.price / 100}"
                                      type="currency"/>
                </td>
            </tr>
        </c:forEach>
    </table>
  </body>
</html>
```

4. Navigate to localhost:8080/GoodDesign/page1.jsp in your browser:

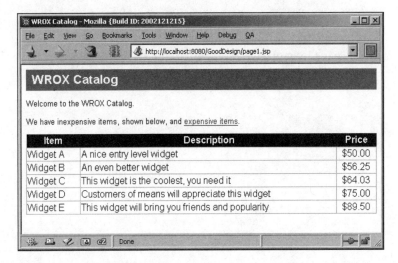

5. Click the **expensive items** link to see the second page:

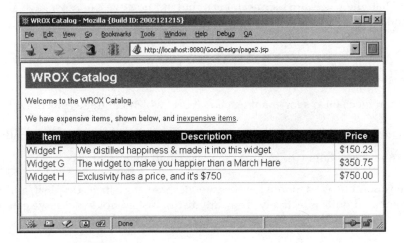

How It Works

As you have probably noticed, the two pages are nearly identical. If you have a closer look at the code, you'll see that there are in fact only two places where it is different. Firstly, the descriptions at the top of each page:

page1.jsp

```
          We have inexpensive items, shown below, and
          <a href="page2.jsp">expensive items</a>.
```

page2.jsp

```
          We have expensive items, shown below, and
          <a href="page1.jsp">inexpensive items</a>.
```

The second difference is the query we run against the database:

page1.jsp

```
          <sql:query var="catalog">
              SELECT * FROM catalog
              WHERE price < 10000
              ORDER BY price
          </sql:query>
```

page2.jsp

```
          <sql:query var="catalog">
              SELECT * FROM catalog
              WHERE price >= 10000
              ORDER BY price
          </sql:query>
```

Other than that, the pages are identical. Let's find out how we can repackage all this duplicated material and make our pages more elegant and reusable at a stroke.

Mechanisms for Reuse

JSP has several mechanisms for enabling code reuse, which fall under one of two basic categories:

- ❑ **Includes** – enable the contents of one file or JSP to be inserted into another JSP
- ❑ **Custom tags** – allow developers to create their own JSP tags

There is considerable overlap in what the two mechanisms can accomplish, and the two can often be combined quite effectively. They are distinguished not by *what* we can do with them, but rather, *how* we can do it.

Includes

As stated earlier, "includes" are all about taking data from one file and inserting them in another. There two types of includes are:

- ❏ **translation-time** includes
- ❏ **request-time** includes

The difference between these two is best understood by reviewing how JSP works. Recall that any JSP tags are translated into HTML when web browsers request a JSP page. Thus, the following JSP code:

```
My name is ${name}
```

would be **translated** by swapping the JSP Expression Language for some appropriate HTML, which depending on the value of name, might be something like this:

```
My name is Steve "Dancing Monkey Boy" Ballmer
```

when the page is **requested** by the browser. These two incarnations of a JSP page are the key to the difference between the two types of includes. Translation-time includes will include the content of an external resource, such as another JSP or an HTML file, *before* the JSP is translated into a servlet. Request-time includes will include the content of another JSP or HTML file *after* the JSP is translated into a servlet.

We look at servlets and the process of compiling JSP pages into them in Chapter 10. Until then, you just need to know that translation-time includes are appropriate when the page we are including needs access to all the JSP variables and data in the page that is including it. The source code of the included JSP page combines with the source code of the including JSP page, and the two become one big page that is then translated into a servlet together.

When the included JSP *doesn't* need access to internal data of the including JSP, a request-time include will do just fine.

This doesn't tell the whole story, however. There is another compelling feature of request-time includes: they let us pass settings (called **parameters**) to the included JSP page. This makes it easier to reuse included JSPs, as we can tailor them to the page that is including them.

The Include Directive

We'll now look at how these include thingies work. The first include we will look at is the **include directive**. An include directive is a translation-time include, and it looks like this:

```
<%@ include file="filename.jsp" %>
```

In this case, the file `filename.jsp` located in the same directory as the JSP will be included. You can specify any file path you want, relative to the path of the JSP.

The Include Action

The second include we will consider is the **include action**. This include is a request-time include. It has this form:

```
<jsp:include page="filename.jsp" />
```

We can pass parameters to JSP pages included with an include action in the following way:

```
<jsp:include page="filename.jsp">
    <jsp:param name="someName" value="someValue">
</jsp:include>
```

To access the parameter, the included JSP would use the following syntax:

```
The value for "someName" that you gave me is ${param.someName}.
```

The word someName should of course be replaced with your parameter name. You can use both the include directive and the include action anywhere you want to in a JSP page.

Try It Out   Creating a Header and Footer

1. Now, we'll apply this technique to our sample application and reduce some of that duplicated code. Create a new directory in the GoodDesign folder for our new files, and call it Include.

2. The code that creates the top of each page is completely identical, so we'll move it into a new file called header.jspf. Create this file in the Include directory, and enter the following code in it:

```
<html>
    <head>
        <title>WROX Catalog</title>
        <style type="text/css">
            BODY {
                font: 10pt sans-serif;
            }
            DIV.header {
                background: gray;
                color: white;
                padding: 5px 5px 5px 10px;
                font: bold 16pt sans-serif;
            }
```

```
        TABLE {
            border-collapse: collapse;
        }
        TH {
            background: black;
            color: white;
            margin: 1px;
        }
        TD {
            border: 1px solid silver;
        }
        .price {
            text-align: center;
        }
    </style>
</head>
<body>
    <div class="header">
        WROX Catalog
    </div>
    <p/>
    Welcome to the WROX Catalog.
    <p/>
```

3. The very bottom of each page is also identical. Create a file called `footer.jspf` containing the following code in the `Include` folder:

```
    <hr/>
    &copy; Copyright 2003 Wrox Widgets Ltd
  </body>
</html>
```

*We use the `.jspf` extension rather than `.jsp` because these files are not complete JSP files in themselves – they are **JSP fragments**. JSP fragments are intended to be used only within other JSP pages. There's nothing stopping our using the `.jsp` extension, but `.jspf` makes their intended use clear.*

4. To use these fragments in our catalog application, we simply need to replace the code they contain with an appropriate include directive. Make a copy of `page1.jsp` with the name `page1include.jsp`, and change it as highlighted:

```
<%@ taglib uri="http://java.sun.com/jstl/core_rt" prefix="c" %>
<%@ taglib uri="http://java.sun.com/jstl/sql_rt" prefix="sql" %>
<%@ taglib uri="http://java.sun.com/jstl/fmt_rt" prefix="fmt" %>
<%@ include file="/Include/header.jspf" %>
        We have inexpensive items, shown below, and
        <a href="page2include.jsp">expensive items</a>.
        <p/>
```

```
<sql:setDataSource   url="jdbc:mysql://localhost/catalog"
                     driver="com.mysql.jdbc.Driver"
                         user="catalog" password="wrox"/>

<sql:query var="catalog">
    SELECT * FROM catalog
    WHERE price < 10000
    ORDER BY price
</sql:query>

<table width="100%">
    .
    .
    .
</table>
<%@ include file="/Include/footer.jspf" %>
```

5. Similarly, make a copy of page2.jsp called page2include.jsp, and change it as
    shown below:

```
<%@ taglib uri="http://java.sun.com/jstl/core_rt" prefix="c" %>
<%@ taglib uri="http://java.sun.com/jstl/sql_rt" prefix="sql" %>
<%@ taglib uri="http://java.sun.com/jstl/fmt_rt" prefix="fmt" %>
<%@ include file="/Include/header.jspf" %>
    We have expensive items, shown below, and
    <a href="page1include.jsp">inexpensive items</a>.
    <p/>
    <sql:setDataSource   url="jdbc:mysql://localhost/catalog"
        driver="org.gjt.mm.mysql.Driver"
         user="catalogDBA" password="wrox"/>

    <sql:query var="catalog">
        SELECT * FROM products
        WHERE price >= 10000
        ORDER BY price
    </sql:query>

    <table width="100%">
        .
        .
        .
    </table>
<%@ include file="/Include/footer.jspf" %>
```

6. If you now open the new pages in a browser, you'll see that the headers appear just as
    they did originally and that the footers now also appear:

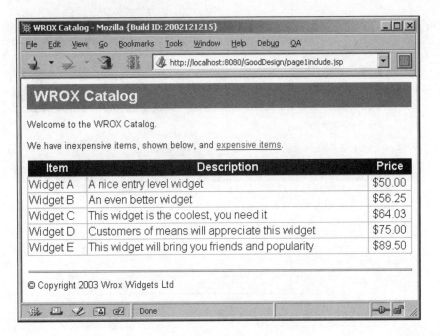

7. We're already starting to reduce the needlessly repeated code, and make our code more maintainable. As a demonstration of the advantages this offers, let's pretend the powers that be have decided to revamp our site's appearance. Open `header.jspf`, and change the highlighted lines as shown:

```
<html>
    <head>
        <title>WROX Catalog</title>
        <style type="text/css">
            BODY {
                font: 10pt sans-serif;
            }
            DIV.header {
                background: blue;
                color: yellow;
                padding: 5px 5px 5px 10px;
                font: bold 16pt sans-serif;
            }
            TABLE {
                .
                .
                .
```

8. As they are in the header, these changes will be immediately reflected on all pages that include that header, as you'll see if you open them now:

113

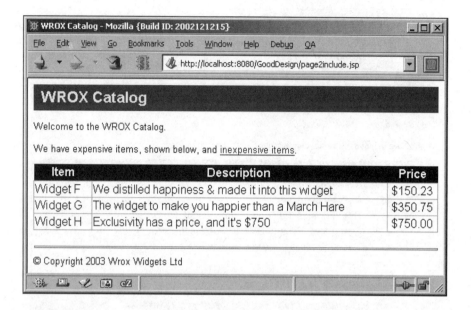

How It Works

We extracted the static HTML that creates the top part of pages on our site and placed it in the file `header.jspf`. There was nothing stopping us including the `taglib` directives in the header, but this isn't generally good practice as not all pages that have the header would require all the libraries, and some might require other libraries, so we're best to leave them on the pages where they are used.

It's always a good idea to place related files of a web application in suitably named directories, as it makes them much easier for others to make sense of. Thus, we placed our header and footer in a new directory called `Include`.

Try It Out   An External Stylesheet

1. Our `<style>` element in our header file defines the CSS styles that are apply to the web page. Rather than mix these style definitions in with our JSP, we can move them into a separate file, allowing styles to be readily shared with other applications.

To do this, create a new folder called `Styles` in the `GoodDesign` folder, and create a text file there called `style.css`. Place all the CSS rules in it like so:

```
BODY {
    font: 10pt sans-serif;
}
```

```
DIV.header {
    background: gray;
    color: white;
    padding: 5px 5px 5px 10px;
    font: bold 16pt sans-serif;
}
TABLE {
    border-collapse: collapse;
}
TH {
    background: black;
    color: white;
    margin: 1px;
}
TD {
    border: 1px solid silver;
}
.price {
    text-align: center;
}
```

2. Now we can replace this information in `header.jspf` with a `<link>` element for the stylesheet:

```
<html>
    <head>
        <title>WROX Catalog</title>
        <link rel="stylesheet" href="Style/style.css"
              type="text/css">
    </head>
    <body>
        <div class="header">
            WROX Catalog
        </div>
        <p/>
        Welcome to the WROX Catalog.
        <p/>
```

3. Open both pages in your browser, and you'll see the separate stylesheet produces the same display as previously. If we make any changes to the stylesheet, or link our header to an entirely different one, our pages will reflect the changes immediately.

Custom Tags

Underneath the banner of "custom tags", we in fact find three distinct species:

❑ **Classic tag handlers** – the original JSP custom tag mechanism, and rather complex to create. Generally, we wouldn't create our own custom tags of this type, although we may use them often enough. The JSTL is an example of classic tag handlers.

❑ **Simple tag handlers** – allow JSP developers who know Java to do some pretty complex things and package them up so they can be used just as a regular JSP tag. Don't let the title fool you – if you don't know how to program in Java, simple tag handlers are not simple at all. However, the original JSP custom tag mechanism, introduced many years ago, does indeed make these look very easy to create, hence the name.

❑ **Tag files** – these are JSP files with certain features that allow them to be included in another JSP through a tag interface. Think of them as a sort of bridge between includes and custom tags.

In this chapter, we're just going to look at tag files. We'll come back to simple and classic tag handlers later, in Chapter 9.

Tag Files

Tag files are the simplest way to create custom JSP tags. They require no knowledge of Java programming, and they resemble the include action (a request-time include) in terms of functionality.

Perhaps the best way to explain how to use a tag file is to show it in action. Returning to our example application, there is one chunk of code that is begging for reuse: the catalog table itself. It is an ideal candidate for implementation as a tag file.

Try It Out   **Creating a Custom Tag**

1. Create a directory for our tag files named `tags` off `WEB-INF` folder for the `GoodDesign` application. Tag files don't have to be placed in this folder, but it can be easier, as we find out in Chapter 9.

2. Inside the tags folder, create a file called `catalogTable.tag` with the following content:

```
<%@ taglib uri="http://java.sun.com/jstl/fmt_rt" prefix="fmt" %>
<%@ taglib uri="http://java.sun.com/jstl/core_rt" prefix="c" %>
<%@ taglib uri="http://java.sun.com/jstl/sql_rt" prefix="sql" %>
<sql:setDataSource  url="jdbc:mysql://localhost/catalog"
                driver="com.mysql.jdbc.Driver"
                  user="catalogDBA" password="wrox"/>
```

```
<sql:query var="catalog">
    <jsp:doBody/>
</sql:query>

<table width="100%">
    <tr>
        <th>
            Item
        </th>
        <th>
            Description
        </th>
        <th>
            Price
        </th>
    </tr>
    <c:forEach varStatus="status" var="row"
            items="${catalog.rows}">
        <tr>
            <td>
                ${row.name}
            </td>
            <td>
                ${row.description}
            </td>
            <td class="price">
                <fmt:formatNumber value="${row.price / 100}"
                                  type="currency"/>
            </td>
        </tr>
    </c:forEach>
</table>
```

This file contains the code that should be executed whenever we use our custom tag. You'll notice that it is pretty much the same code that already creates the table in both pages.

3. Now we need to use our new tag in our application's JSP pages. Make a copy of `page1include.jsp` called `page1tag.jsp`, and do the same for the second page.

4. As all the functionality is now housed in the `catalogTag` tag we've just created, we can remove all three existing `taglib` directives. However, we need a new one for our own tag:

```
<%@ taglib tagdir="/WEB-INF/tags" prefix="tags" %>
<%@ include file="/Include/header.jspf" %>
    .
    .
    .
```

117

Notice that our tag file's `taglib` directive is different from the other three. This difference is down to the fact that the first three are classic tags and ours is a simple tag. We will explain this in greater detail in Chapter 9, which covers custom tags.

5. Now we can use our tag in place of the SQL tags and table that create our catalog. Change `page1tag.jsp` as shown below:

    .
    .
    .

```
    We have inexpensive items, shown below, and
    <a href="page2tag.jsp">expensive items</a>.
    <p/>
    <tags:catalogTable>
        SELECT * FROM products
        WHERE price < 10000
        ORDER BY price
    </tags:catalogTable>
<%@ include file="/Include/footer.jspf" %>
```

6. `page2tag.jsp` is changed similarly:

    .
    .
    .

```
    We have expensive items, shown below, and
    <a href="page1tag.jsp">inexpensive items</a>.
    <p/>
    <tags:catalogTable>
        SELECT * FROM products
        WHERE price >= 10000
        ORDER BY price
    </tags:catalogTable>
<%@ include file="/Include/footer.jspf" %>
```

7. Open the new pages in your browser, and you'll see the output is just the same as it was previously.

How It Works

Look at how much smaller these files are! We've taken two highly inefficient files (in terms of reuse) and made them much more efficient and maintainable.

Let's have a closer look at our tag file. It starts off with the familiar tag library directives because our tag uses the JSTL. Secondly, where we previously had SQL statements, we now have a single JSP tag:

```
<jsp:doBody/>
```

This tag will be replaced by whatever appears between the start and end tags of our custom tag when used on a JSP page. Thus, when we use it on our first JSP page like so:

```
<tags:catalogTable>
    SELECT * FROM products
    WHERE price < 10000
    ORDER BY price
</tags:catalogTable>
```

the `<jsp:doBody>` tag will be replaced with the given SQL query.

Beyond JSP

We've spent the first part of this chapter learning how to reuse code using nothing but JSP features. As you've seen, there's some powerful stuff that can be done. But sooner or later, you'll need to tap into a far larger and more flexible resource of features: the Java language itself.

One of the easiest ways to use Java in JSP is through **JavaBeans** in conjunction with the JSP mechanisms that we've already seen. JavaBeans are reusable objects created with the Java programming language. However, as you may well have never programmed in Java before, the next part of this chapter concentrates on teaching the basic principles, and then we'll move on to use JavaBeans in JSP.

What are Java Objects?

Java is an **object oriented programming** (OOP) language. That means that coding is all about creating objects that can be used over and over again, in either their original form, or in new forms created by extending those original forms.

Objects in the programming sense of the word might seem awkward and unnatural at first, but once you get to grips with the concept, they are actually a very logical way to think about problems and organize code.

An object in OOP represents some particular "thing", just as it does when we use the word in language. For instance a *Newspaper* is an object. It has certain properties that make it distinct from any other object – a *Tree*, a *Car*, or whatever.

Java defines an object's distinctive properties in what is known as a **class**. A class constitutes a template or a mould that we can then use to create objects of that class: this is known as **instantiating** the class. Each object of a particular class is said to be an **instance** of that class.

A class specifies the variables that are needed to hold necessary information about any instance of that class, and it also specifies code that we can use to manipulate and retrieve that information in the form of **methods**. The information is stored in variables called **attributes**. When we create an object belonging to a certain class, the Java compiler needs to see the definition of the attributes and methods. To make this possible, we have to define each class in its own file with the .java extension, and a filename that exactly matches the class name. Don't forget that class and file names are case sensitive in Java, so a class called Bodkin would have to be defined in a file called Bodkin.java if it is to be publicly accessible.

When we call a method to access the attributes of an object, we can pass extra information that may be relevant to that method by enclosing it in parentheses after the method name. Such items of information are called **arguments** or **parameters**. Methods sometimes compute a useful value, and this can be passed back to the code that calls the method (the method is said to **return** a value). Actually, we have already encountered and used methods in Chapter 3 when we invoked methods on the request object.

One of the great advantages of object orientation is that we can build new class templates on top of existing ones. This is known as **inheritance**. For example, we could make a new class of objects, *Sunday Newspaper*, that "inherits" all of the attributes and methods of *Newspaper* objects but adds new ones of its own too. We say that the *Sunday Newspaper* class is a **subclass** of *Newspaper*, while *Newspaper* is the **superclass** of *Sunday Newspaper*. We will discuss inheritance in greater detail in Chapter 6.

Classes let us separate functionality and associated data into methods and attributes. Classes provide "black box" functionality that we can use without needing any knowledge of how they work. Class **inheritance** enables our code to be more reusable, as we'll see in Chapter 6.

Introducing JavaBeans

JavaBeans are Java objects that expose data through what are called **properties**. For instance, we might have a bean that models a bank account, and such a bean might have account number and balance properties.

Formally, a JavaBean is really nothing more than a Java class that maintains some data (the properties) and follows certain coding conventions. These conventions provide a mechanism for **automated support** – that is, the JSP engine, for example Tomcat, can inspect the bean and discover what properties it has. This mechanism is called **introspection**.

Properties

Each item of information that a bean exposes is called a **property**. For an example of public properties we need look no further than HTML.

```
<p style="font-family: sans-serif; color: blue">
    Did you like that "blue" song that was popular a while back?
</p>
```

In HTML with reference to the <p> tag for example, `style` is an example of a property that can be set against the standard HTML <p> tag. You may already be very familiar with this type of property.

Like HTML properties, properties in JavaBeans provide a simple approach to being able to pass information to set or retrieve a value to use in your JSP code.

The properties of a JavaBean are publicly exposed using getter and setter methods. These methods follow simple naming conventions, easiest understood by example. If we have a property called `style` the getter and setter methods would be called `getStyle()` and `setStyle()`. The method names are simply the capitalized name of the property preceded by either `get` or `set`. This capitalization is required.

To build a JavaBean of our own all we have to do is to write a Java class, and obey these rules.

Building a JavaBean

So what does a JavaBean look like? Let's define a JavaBean class called `CarBean` that we could use as a component in a car sales web site. It will be a component that would model a car and will have one property – the make of the car.

```java
public class CarBean
{
   private String make = "Ford";

   public CarBean() {}

   public String getMake()
   {
     return make;
   }

   public void setMake(String make)
   {
     this.make = make;
   }
}
```

There are several things of note here. The first line is where we define the name of the class:

```
public class CarBean
```

Don't worry about the `public` keyword; we'll explain this later. The definition of the contents of the class goes inside the braces following the class name. First up, we define a `String` property called `make`, and set its value to "Ford":

```
private String make = "Ford";
```

Again, ignore the `private` keyword for the time being.

Next we see the definition of a special method called the **constructor**:

```
public CarBean() {}
```

A constructor is a special method called when an instance of a new bean is requested, and always has the same name as the class. You should note that this constructor is empty (there is nothing between the braces) but this is often not the case: we can set properties at instantiation time between these braces.

Moving through the code we can see this property has "getter" and "setter" methods.

```
public String getMake()
{
   return make;
}
```

The `getMake()` method returns the value of `make`. It does not get passed any arguments. The `setMake()` method is however passed an `String` argument also called `make`, which is used to set the `make` property to the same value as the argument:

```
public void setMake(String make)
{
   this.make = make;
}
```

The `void` keyword indicates that this method returns no value. `this` is a way of referring to the current `CarBean` object, so `this.make` is simply the `make` property of the current object.

Variable Scope

In the last section, we ignored the presence of two Java keywords associated with the attributes and methods within the class:

❑   `public`

❑   `private`

These keywords refer to the **scope** of an attribute, variable, or method. The scope defines the parts of the code in which the variable or method is recognized, and so we can use them. The scope of a variable or method depends upon where it is **declared** (defined).

Variables that are defined within a method have **local** scope. This means that they can only be used within the confines of the method in which they were declared. However, variables declared as attributes within the class can be used anywhere within the class definition.

But what about when we come to use an object of this class? Which variables declared within the class can we use? The answer to this is that it depends. We cannot directly access variables (with local scope) declared within class methods. If an attribute is declared as being `public`, we can access the attribute from outside the class. However, if an attribute is declared as being `private`, we can only use it within the class.

The same is true for the scope of methods in the class. If the method is declared as being `public` it can be called from outside the class; if it is `private`, it cannot.

You should note that the all our attributes have been made `private`, while all of the getter/setter methods are `public`. There is a good reason for this: it forces us to use these methods to access and modify attribute values. This is much safer than allowing direct access to attributes. For example, using the setter method forces us to provide a value for the attribute that is of the correct data type, otherwise the resetting of the value won't work. In other words, we can make sure that any user who wants to access the data in the bean does so without modifying the data in unpredictable ways.

We now understand the code required for a JavaBean, but there is another step to take before it can be used – compilation.

Class Files and Compilation

Before a JavaBean, or any class, can be used in an application it must be **compiled**. The process of compilation is converting **source code** into **byte code**. It is this byte code that the **Java Virtual Machine (JVM)** that runs Java programs can understand and execute.

Classes are compiled using the **javac** compiler that comes as part of the Java SDK you installed in Chapter 1. We will see exactly how this is done in the example to follow.

However, if we want to use a compiled JavaBean in a JSP web application, the JSP engine, for example Tomcat, also needs to know where to look for it.

You saw in Chapter 1 that web applications are stored under the `%CATALINA_HOME%/webapps` directory. If you had a web application called "cars" you would create a directory `cars` in `%CATALINA_HOME%/webapps`.

By default Tomcat (and any other servlet container) checks for classes in the `/WEB-INF/classes` directory under the web application directory, and any subdirectories of this. So, for our "cars" web application Tomcat would look for JavaBeans in directory `%CATALINA_HOME%/webapps/cars/WEB-INF/classes` and all directories below this. While it is possible to store your JavaBeans elsewhere, in this chapter we will store our JavaBeans in this default location.

Using a JavaBean

We have now defined a JavaBean, and we know that we need to compile it and put in a directory where Tomcat can see it. But that's now the whole story. How do we use it in a JSP page?

Remember how we insisted that the getter and setter methods followed a strict naming convention? In the previous example the need for this convention wasn't clear. Next, we will introduce **bean tags**, which will allow us to remove the need for scriptlets to call bean methods from the JSP.

JSP provides an approach to utilizing JavaBeans that is based on the concept of tags. These tags are really no more complicated than the standard HTML tags; they have a name and they take attributes.

Tags are designed to make the page developer's job easier as they allow the designer to use JavaBeans without knowing any Java. There are three tags provided by the specification to support the use of JavaBeans in your JSP pages:

- `<jsp:useBean>`
- `<jsp:setProperty>`
- `<jsp:getProperty>`.

In this section we will tell you about each of these tags and how to use them when working with your JavaBeans.

The <jsp:useBean> Tag

The `<jsp:useBean>` tag locates and instantiates a JavaBean. For example:

```
<jsp:useBean id="myCar" class="com.wrox.cars.CarBean" />
```

Here, an object of class `com.wrox.cars.CarBean` will be located and created if an instance doesn't already exist. We can refer to this bean later in the page, using the value set for the `id` attribute (`myCar`).

Note that for the `<jsp:useBean>` tag we have two ways of closing the tag. We can use the short notation of `/>` shown above to close the tag. Or, if you wish to populate values at instantiation rather than after instantiation you can use the full `</jsp:useBean>` end tag instead:

```
<jsp:useBean id="myCar" class="com.wrox.cars.CarBean" ></jsp:useBean>
```

The <jsp:setProperty> Tag

The `<jsp:setProperty>` element sets the value of a property of a bean using the setter method.

If we have instantiated a JavaBean with an `id` of `myCar`, as we did in the previous section, we can use the following tag to set the value of a property of the bean.

```
<jsp:setProperty name="myCar" property="make" value="Ferrari" />
```

Here we are setting the property `make` to the value `Ferrari`. This is where the usefulness of the method naming conventions becomes apparent. This tag takes the bean instance with an `id` of `myCar` and calls the `setMake()` method on it. It passes `Ferrari` to the method as the argument.

The <jsp:getProperty> Tag

The `<jsp:getProperty>` element gets a property value using the getter method and returns the property value to the calling JSP page.

As with the `<jsp:setProperty>` tag, you must create or locate a bean with `<jsp:useBean>` before you can use `<jsp:getProperty>`. Here's an example of using the tag:

```
<jsp:getProperty name="myCar" property="car" />
```

We get the value of the property `car` from the bean instance `myCar`.

> Remember to specify the `<jsp:useBean>` tag before using either the `<jsp:setProperty>` or the `<jsp:getProperty>` tags, otherwise your JSP page will throw a compile error.

Now we will create the `CarBean` class we described in the previous section and use it in a JSP page with the bean tags we just reviewed.

Try It Out   Using a JavaBean in JSP

1. First, create a folder called `Reuse` for our new application in Tomcat's `webapps` directory. Create a `WEB-INF` subfolder as usual, and a folder called `classes` inside it.

Inside here, create another folder called `com`, one called `wrox` inside that, and finally, one called `cars` inside the new `wrox` folder. Don't worry about the directory structure at this point – we'll explain it in a moment.

2. Create a new file in the `cars` directory called `CarBean.java`, and insert the following code:

```java
package com.wrox.cars;

import java.io.Serializable;

public class CarBean implements Serializable
{
  private String make = "Ford";

  public CarBean() {}

  public String getMake()
  {
    return make;
  }

  public void setMake(String make)
  {
    this.make = make;
  }
}
```

3. Now create a JSP page in the `Reuse` folder called `carPage.jsp` to demonstrate our bean:

```html
<html>
    <head>
        <title>Using a JavaBean</title>
    </head>
    <body>

    <h2>Using a JavaBean</h2>

    <jsp:useBean id="myCar" class="com.wrox.cars.CarBean" />

    I have a <jsp:getProperty name="myCar" property="make" /> <br />

    <jsp:setProperty name="myCar" property="make" value="Ferrari" />
```

```
    Now I have a <jsp:getProperty name="myCar" property="make" />

    </body>
</html>
```

4. We first need to compile `CarBean.java`. From a command prompt, change to the `classes` directory in the `Reuse` application's `WEB-INF` folder, and enter the following command:

> **> javac com/wrox/cars/CarBean.java**

If you get any errors go over the code and make sure you entered it exactly as it is written. When compilation is complete you will have a file called `CarBean.class` in the directory.

5. Now start up Tomcat, and open http://localhost:8080/Reuse/carPage.jsp in your browser. You should see something like this:

How It Works

Let's walk through our code and explain it. The first line in our JavaBean class is:

```
package com.wrox.cars;
```

What is this? Java classes are stored in collections called **packages**. These packages provide an easy way to organize related classes. The names of packages follow a very simple structure. You have already come across packages in Chapter 1 when you used the `Date` class. The `Date` class is stored in the `java.util` package.

The name of the package has a direct relation to the directory in which the class is stored under the `classes` folder. For example, since the `Date` class is in the package `java.util`, it would need to be stored under a `/classes/java/util` directory structure. Similarly our `CarBean` class is stored under the `classes/com/wrox/cars` directory within our `webapps` directory.

Next we have to import a class to use with our class:

```
import java.io.Serializable;
```

This tells the compiler that we want to use the `Serializable` class which is in the `java.io` package. Now we declare our class:

```
public class CarBean implements Serializable
```

You don't need to worry too much about what `implements Serializable` means. It simply allows the class and its data to be saved to disk and reloaded again by Java programs that use the JavaBean.

We've seen and explained the rest of the class, so we don't need to go through it again. Now let's take a look at the JSP code in `carPage.jsp`.

We start off with some simple HTML, defining the title of the page and displaying a heading of **Using a JavaBean**:

```
<html>
  <head>
    <title>Using a JavaBean</title>
  </head>
  <body>

    <h2>Using a JavaBean</h2>
```

Next we issue a `<jsp:useBean>` request to the tag handler which in turn instantiates the JavaBean:

```
<jsp:useBean id="myCar" class="com.wrox.cars.CarBean" />
```

The `<jsp:useBean>` tag provides an `id` for this instance called `myCar`. The `id` can be used to identify the JavaBean in the page. Because each bean instance is given an `id` you could instantiate many JavaBeans of the same type if you wanted to, all with different `id` attributes.

The `<jsp:useBean>` tag also identifies a class that is the location of the compiled code for the JavaBean.

Next we use the `<jsp:getProperty>` and `<jsp:setProperty>` tags to retrieve the initial value of the `make` property for this instance, and display it, then reset this property to "Ferrari".

```
I have a <jsp:getProperty name="myCar" property="make" /> <br />

<jsp:setProperty name="myCar" property="make" value="Ferrari" />
```

We finish by displaying this new property value:

```
Now I have a <jsp:getProperty name="myCar" property="make" />
```

A Closer Look at JavaBean Methods

Although we have only used getter and setter methods in our bean so far, you should realize that we don't have to have just methods that get and set properties. Methods in our bean could contain any kind of functionality. For example, we might include a method that establishes a database connection, and this method is called from another method in the bean. However, the important thing to remember is that unless you include getter and setter methods, you will not be able to retrieve or set values in the bean using tags.

Another important point that may not be clear to you at the moment is that the properties we get do not have to be bean attributes. Although the bean we created earlier uses accessor methods to retrieve and set attribute values, we can return the value of any variable from a get accessor using a tag, not just object attributes.

For example, say we wanted to calculate the cost of a car after sales tax. We could add two new attributes to our class, which represent the cost before tax (cost) and the tax rate (taxRate):

```
private double cost = 10000.00;
private double taxRate = 17.5;
```

We can also easily add a method that calculates the sales tax:

```
public double getPrice()
{
  double price = (cost + (cost * (taxRate/100)));
  return price;
}
```

Now note that this method follows the standard conventions for a getter method; it returns a value but takes no argument, and it follows the standard naming convention. However, as you'll notice, there is no underlying price attribute for in our class. It turns out that we don't necessarily need an underlying attribute – we can generate the attribute on the fly as we've done here. Note that we don't need a setter for the price property. This is because this property is generated from other properties, and cannot itself be set to any particular value. If we did allow someone to pass us a new value of price via a hypothetical setPrice(double price) method, we would have no way of determining the cost and taxRate variables from it.

Since the name of the getter method implies that the value returned by the method corresponds to a property called `price`, we can retrieve this value from a bean instance using a `<jsp:getProperty>` tag:

```
<jsp:getProperty name="myCar" property="price" />
```

Here the bean instance ID is `myCar`. Let's now create a new version of our `CarBean` bean that includes the ability to get the price of the car.

Try It Out   Bean Methods

1. Make the highlighted changes to `CarBean.java`:

```
package com.wrox.cars;
import java.io.Serializable;

public class CarBean implements Serializable
{
  private String make = "Ford";
  private double cost = 10000.00;
  private double taxRate = 17.5;

  public CarBean() {}

  public String getMake()
  {
    return make;
  }

  public void setMake(String make)
  {
    this.make = make;
  }

  public double getPrice()
  {
    double price = (cost + (cost * (taxRate/100)));
    return price;
  }
}
```

2. Open a command prompt, change to the `classes` directory, and run the following command to recompile the JavaBean:

> javac com/wrox/cars/CarBean.java

3. Now create a new JSP page, `carPage2.jsp`, in the `Reuse` folder, and enter the following code in it:

```html
<html>
    <head>
        <title>Using a JavaBean</title>
    </head>
    <body>

    <h2>Using a JavaBean</h2>

    <jsp:useBean id="myCar" class="com.wrox.cars.CarBean" />

    I have a <jsp:getProperty name="myCar" property="make" /> <br />

    My car costs $<jsp:getProperty name="myCar" property="price" />

    </body>
</html>
```

4. Restart Tomcat and open http://localhost:8080/Reuse/carPage2.jsp in your browser. You should see something like this:

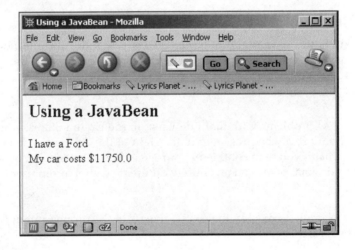

How It Works

Let's skip to the new bits we've added. Two new attributes, `cost` and `taxRate`, hold the pre-tax cost of the car and the sales tax rate:

```java
private double cost = 10000.00;
private double taxRate = 17.5;
```

Then we have our method for getting the taxed price of the car:

```
public double getPrice()
{
    double price = (cost + (cost * (taxRate/100)));
    return price;
}
```

Now let's see how we use the `getPrice()` method in the JSP. As usual we use the `<jsp:useBean>` tag to create a bean instance, which is given an ID of `myCar`:

```
<jsp:useBean id="myCar" class="com.wrox.cars.CarBean" />
```

Then we retrieve the `make` of the car as in our previous example:

```
I have a <jsp:getProperty name="myCar" property="make" /> <br />
```

Finally we retrieve the post-tax cost of the car, represented by the property `price`, and display it on the webpage:

```
My car costs $<jsp:getProperty name="myCar" property="price" />
```

A Problem Of Currency

So, are we done with this example? Not quite. Take a look at the output of our JSP once again. Do you notice something that doesn't look quite right? Look at the last line:

```
My car costs $11750.0
```

There are quite a few problems with that line. First, in the United States, where this example is run, two digits should really be presented to the right of the decimal, instead of the one zero shown here. But what if you're in continental Europe or Latin America? You might very well use a comma for your decimal point and an entirely different symbol to represent the appropriate currency instead.

Let's change our example to display the cost of the car in the proper amount, no matter where you happen to be located.

Try It Out   Formatting Currency

1. The only file we'll need to change for our example is `carPage2.jsp`. Modify it as highlighted below:

```
<%@ taglib uri="http://java.sun.com/jstl/fmt_rt" prefix="fmt" %>
<html>
```

```
<head>
    <title>Using a JavaBean</title>
</head>
<body>

<h2>Using a JavaBean</h2>

<jsp:useBean id="myCar" class="com.wrox.cars.CarBean" />

I have a <jsp:getProperty name="myCar" property="make" /> <br />

My car costs <fmt:formatNumber value="${myCar.price}"
                                type="currency" />

</body>
</html>
```

2. Navigate to http://localhost:8080/Reuse/carPage2.jsp in your browser once again. You should now see a properly formatted currency value customized for your part of the world:

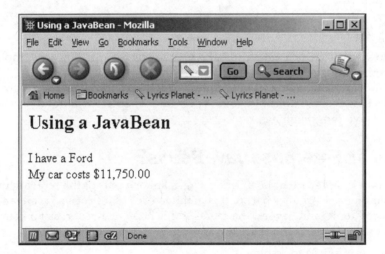

How It Works

We could have placed logic in CarBean's getPrice() method to format our price the way we want it, and indeed, this would have worked fine. However, the JSTL comes with a series of tags designed to format currency, as we've seen earlier in this chapter. We decided to leverage these tags in our JSP instead of making the change in our JavaBean.

However, we can't use the JSTL tag in conjunction with the `<jsp:getProperty>` tag that we used to have because JSP cannot use other JSP tags as tag attributes – only text or EL expressions. But not to worry! The `<jsp:useBean>` tag makes JavaBeans available for use with the `<jsp:getProperty>` and `<jsp:setProperty>` tags, as you already know, but it also makes the JavaBean available for use with the JSP Expression Language (EL).

So, to solve our problem, we simply replaced the original line:

```
My car costs $<jsp:getProperty name="myCar" property="price" />
```

with a new line that uses the JSTL and EL in place of the `<jsp:getProperty>` tag:

```
My car costs <fmt:formatNumber value="${myCar.price}"
                               type="currency" />
```

And so we see that you can use either the `<jsp:getProperty>` and `<jsp:setProperty>` tags to access your JavaBeans, or the EL. Which you choose is entirely up to you, and it is simply a matter of preference. However, to access a JavaBean within tag attributes, you need to use the EL.

More with JavaBeans

You now know how to fuse together JSP and Java to create quite powerful applications. We will build on this knowledge as we continue through the book. In Chapters 5 and 6, we'll teach you more about the Java language, and in Chapter 7, we'll be finding out more about Java's existing code libraries that you can utilize in your code. Other chapters will build on your budding knowledge of Java programming.

JavaBeans or Enterprise JavaBeans?

We explained in Chapter 1 that Java Server Pages are one part of the J2EE architecture, namely the "presentation tier". Another part of this architecture is **Enterprise JavaBeans** (**EJBs**). EJBs are an advanced topic, and beyond the scope of this book. However, as you create bigger and better JSP web applications you will inevitably come across the term.

Our intention here is to warn you not to confuse the JavaBeans we have learnt about in this chapter with Enterprise JavaBeans. Although they share a similar name they have very different capabilities, design, and uses.

JavaBeans are designed to be general-purpose components that can be used in a variety of different applications, from very simple to very complex.

EJBs, on the other hand, are components designed intended for use in complex business applications. They support features commonly used in these types of programs, such as: automatically saving and retrieving information to a database, performing many tasks in a single transaction that can be safely aborted if parts of the transaction fail, or communicating either other Java components across a network, and so on. While you could accomplish any one of these EJB features with normal JavaBeans, EJBs make using these complex features easier.

However, EJBs are considerably more complicated to understand, use, and maintain than JavaBeans, and frankly, we'll have our hands full discussing JSP technology in this book, so we won't discuss EJBs at all within this text.

Summary

We introduced this chapter by discussing the virtues of code reuse. To summarize our earlier discussion: code reuse makes it easier to maintain your applications after they are developed. Ease of maintenance is important, because in the business world, more effort is spent maintaining software than developing it.

After establishing the importance of code reuse, we showed you two mechanisms for reusing code:

- ❑   Includes
- ❑   Custom tags

We showed how an example program was transformed by using these mechanisms.

Finally, we wrapped up the chapter by introducing you to object oriented programming. We covered the basics of using object methods, and showed you how to compile a class, and where to store it in a web application.

We then looked at a specific type of Java class, a JavaBean. You saw how to use these beans to organize your code. You also learnt how to use bean tags to instantiate a bean, and to set and retrieve data values from the beans. We noted how the simplicity of these tags can make your JSP code easier to understand and maintain.

In Chapter 5, we are going to look at Java control statements, which allow us to make decisions within our code and then change the flow of execution through our code. You will see that using control statements wisely can allow us to reuse even more of our code. We will also introduce the idea of an array, as a way to collect together groups of variables. We will see how this can make our code simpler too.

CHAPTER 5

Decisions, Decisions

Only the most simplistic JSP page can get away without needing to perform one of a selection of actions according to some condition or other. These conditions are used to control the flow that your code follows as it executes, and they do so through **control statements**. Such statements evaluate an expression to determine the condition, and direct the flow of execution accordingly.

So the kinds of program flow control we will meet in this chapter are:

❑   Conditional statements – evaluating a condition in the program and executing code depending on whether the condition evaluates to "true" or "false"

❑   Iterative statements – repeating (*looping* through) sections of code

❑   Branching statements – transferring execution of the program to a particular section of the code

We will discuss the syntax Java provides for all of these in this chapter, and also look at the flow control constructs of the JSTL. We'll also look at how Java lets us store and manipulate groups of variables of the same type using **arrays**. In short, we will be covering:

❑   How to compare values

❑   How to easily incorporate logic in your code

❑   The if, if...else, and switch statements

❑   The while, do...while and for loops

❑   The break, continue, and return statements

❑   How to use arrays, and when

In each case we'll present the standard Java techniques, followed by a JSTL example if appropriate.

Comparing Data Values

The data values being compared are known as **operands** and these operands can be variables, constants or expressions. The basic syntax for comparing two data values is shown below:

```
operand1  relational_operator  operand2
```

where `relational_operator` is one of those shown in the following table. The table also shows the JSTL equivalents. In a JSTL tag, you are free to use either form of operator.

Operator	JSTL	Operator Name	Explanation
<	lt	Less Than	Evaluates to `true` if operand1 is less than operand2, otherwise `false`.
<=	le	Less Than Or Equal To	Evaluates to `true` if operand1 is less than, or equal to, operand2, otherwise `false`
>	gt	Greater Than	Evaluates to `true` if operand1 is greater than operand2, otherwise `false`.
>=	ge	Greater Than Or Equal To	Evaluates to `true` if operand1 is greater than, or equal to, operand2, otherwise `false`.
==	eq	Equal To	Evaluates to `true` if operand1 is equal to operand2, otherwise `false`
!=	ne	Not Equal To	Evaluates to `true` if operand1 is not equal to operand2, otherwise `false`.

Logical Operators

These relation operators form the basis of all logical tests, and they can be combined into more complex tests using the logical operators listed below to construct more complex expressions that consist of two or more conditions. Remember that operands can be values, variables, or expressions.

Operator	Syntax	Explanation
||	*operand1* || *operand2*	This is the logical OR operator, which returns `true` if operand1 *or* operand2 is `true`. It only returns `false` if both the operands are `false`. It evaluates operand2 only if operand1 is `false`.

Operator	Syntax	Explanation
&&	*operand1* && *operand2*	This is the logical AND operator, which returns `true` if operand1 *and* operand2 are `true`. In other words, if any of the operands are `false`, it returns `false`. Note that operand2 is evaluated only if operand1 is `true`.
!	!*operand1*	Returns `true` if operand1 is `false`. Else if operand1 is `true`, it returns `false`.

As an illustration, say an online store offers free shipping to customers who purchase four or more items of total value above $100. If we have a couple of variables that indicate number of items bought and total cost, called `itemcount` and `totalcost` respectively, then the following expression will determine whether or not shipping is free:

```
itemcount >= 4 && totalcost >= 100
```

If we're going to be using this expression regularly, we can store the result in a boolean variable, say `freeShipping`:

```
freeShipping = (itemcount >= 4 && totalcost >= 100);
```

So for instance, if a customer buys six items and pays $130, then `freeShipping` will be `true`. Now say the store changes its policy so that customers need to meet only one of the criteria (4 items or more, or $100 or more spent) to qualify for free shipping. We could implement this by simply changing the logical operator in the expression:

```
freeShipping = ((itemcount >= 10) || (totalcost >= 100));
```

Let's have a look at another example, which demonstrates the use of the compliment operator, !, applied to an integer, n:

```
!(n >= 0)
```

In this case, when n is negative, the part of the expression within parenthesis results in `false`. The ! operator takes the complement of that to give the result of the expression as a whole; in other words, `true` when n is negative. Conversely, if n is zero or greater, then the part in brackets will be `true`, and so the whole expression will evaluate to `false`. This expression is in effect just a more convoluted way of writing:

```
n < 0
```

Making Decisions

What we've learned thus far – how to compare values and how to use Boolean logic to create more complex expressions (or "decisions") – are the basic tools for controlling the flow of a program. There are many situations where such expressions are useful, and you'll find very few programming problems that do not require them at one point or another.

Most often, such expressions are combined with **control statements**, which are statements that control the flow of program execution. There are three basic kinds of control statement:

1. **Conditional statements** – here the statement is evaluated, and the code block executed depends upon the value returned by the statement

2. **Iterative statements** – the same block of code is executed again and again ("iterated")

3. **Branching statements** – the statement moves execution to a particular point within the code

In this section, we'll examine each of these in turn.

Introducing Conditional Statements

While writing programs we continually come across situations where we need to evaluate a condition and proceed according to the result. Java has two main types of conditional statement:

❑   if statement (and its variations)

❑   switch statement

The main difference between the two is that an if statement requires an expression that results in either true or false, while switch allows one of many blocks of code to be executed, depending on the outcome of the expression.

The if Statement

Let's start with an example of an if statement:

```
if ( itemQuantity > 0 )
{
  System.out.println("The Quantity is greater than 0");
  System.out.println("No. of items : " + itemQuantity);
}
```

In English, what this basically means is "if the value of itemQuantity is greater than zero, then display:

The Quantity is greater than 0

No. of items :

followed by the value of itemQuantity."

Note that this if statement follows the general form of if statements:

```
if (expression)
{
    Statement Block
}
```

You may recognize the correspondence with the JSTL <if> tag that we've already used in earlier chapters' examples:

```
<c:if test="expression">
    Statement Block
</c:if>
```

The expression is evaluated first, and if it evaluates to true, the statement block (which consists of one or more Java statements) is executed. In a JSP page the statement block could consist of other tags (HTML or JSP tags) or even plain text.

Be aware that here we show the syntax using a statement block, as denoted by enclosing curly braces. Java does not require that statement blocks be used, and if only a single line is to be executed if the expression evaluates to true, the braces can be omitted, as shown below:

```
if (itemQuantity > 0)
    System.out.println("The Quantity is greater than 0");
```

This applies to all other Java constructs as well as if, with the exception of do...while loops. Note that this doesn't apply to JSTL. JSTL's <if> tag, for instance, always requires a closing tag:

```
<c:if test="expression">Statement Block</c:if>
```

This requirement is the same as numerous HTML tags, which also require a closing tag, such as the table (<table></table>), heading (<h1></h1>), and font (<font></font>) tags. While most web browsers are lenient about this rule, JSP tags are not: you must supply the closing tag.

The if...else Statement

The if statement is often found used in conjunction with else, which allows us to specify code that should be executed when the expression doesn't evaluate to true like so:

```
if (expression)
{
   Statement Block 1
}
else
{
   Statement Block 2
}
```

As before, the expression is evaluated first, and if it results in `true`, then statement block 1 is executed. If the expression is not true, then statement block 2 is executed instead.

Here's an example of the `if...else` statement that evaluates whether we have four or more items to ship. If this is the case, the customer incurs no shipping costs. If we have less than four items, the shipping cost is found by multiplying the number of items to ship by the cost of shipping an item:

```
if (itemQuantity >= 4)
{
   shippingCost = 0.0;
}
else
{
   shippingCost = basicShippingCost * itemQuantity;
}
```

So for orders of four or more items, the `shippingCost` variable will be set to zero. For fewer items than that, the cost will depend on the value of `basicShippingCost` and the total number of items ordered.

The if...else if Statement

Many situations are little more involved, and we don't simply want to execute one of two options depending on whether a single condition is true or not. For instance, our online store might offer several levels of discount to customers, depending on how much they spend. There might be no discount for purchases below $100, but between $100 and $500 the customer gets 10% off, while above $500 they get 15% off.

We can quite easily code such behavior in Java by simply placing further `if` statements for each `else` keyword, as shown below:

```
if (expression1)
{
   Statement Block 1
}
else if (expression2)
{
```

```
Statement Block 2
}
.
.
More else if Blocks !
.
.
```

Here, the only statement block that will be evaluated will be the first one where the associated expression evaluates to `true` (and all previous expressions have come up as `false`).

Consider the code snippet shown below. Here we test the value of the integer variable n against several possible values. Firstly, we check if it is less than zero (negative), then if it is equal to zero, and lastly if it is greater than zero (positive):

```
int n = 10;

if (n < 0 )
{
   System.out.println("n is negative");
}
else if (n == 0)
{
   System.out.println("n is zero");
}
else if (n > 0)
{
   System.out.println("n is positive");
}
```

Since n is set to 10 at the start of the code snippet, the output will be n is positive. This is a simple example, but it illustrates the flow of execution well enough for our purposes.

Variable Scope in Statement Blocks

Before we move any further, it's time to throw in a cautionary note about variable scope and statement blocks. A statement block is a number of statements grouped together by being enclosed within two curly braces, {}. Look at the following code snippet:

```
int myVar1 = 100;
System.out.println(myVar1);

if (myVar1 > 0)
{
   int myVar2 = myVar1 * 2;

   System.out.println(myVar1);
   System.out.println(myVar2);
}
System.out.println(myVar2);
```

In this code, we create two integer variables called `myVar1` and `myVar2`, set them to 100 and 200 respectively, and attempt to print them out twice. Therefore we might expect the execution of this code to result in:

```
100
100
200
200
```

Actually, attempting to print `myVar2` for the second time, once we're outside the statement block following the `if` statement, will result in a compiler error. This is because `myVar2` is declared *inside* the `if` statement block, so its scope is **local** to that block. Outside of the block, the variable doesn't actually exist, and so an error is thrown. For this code to compile and run, we'd need to move the declaration of `myVar2` outside of the `if` block, or alternatively remove the last `System.out` line.

You should note, however, that variables declared *outside* of the statement block may be used within the statement block as well, and we are able to access `myVar1` inside and outside of the `if` block.

Let's now put into practice what we have learned about conditional statements. Due to the way tag libraries work and variable scope, we can't simply add a tag after a JSTL `<if>` to provide `else` functionality, and we have to turn to a different construct: the JSTL `<choose>...<when>` form.

Try It Out   The JSTL choose...when Construct

1. We're going to create a simple shopping cart where users enter the number of items they wish to buy, and then submit their order. First off, create a new folder under `webapps` to hold the pages we will create in this chapter. Call the new directory `Decisions`. Create a folder called `WEB-INF` within it, and then copy the JSTL `lib` folder inside that.

2. Then create a file called `whenexample.html` in your new directory. This file starts out with the standard HTML opening tags:

```html
<html>

  <head>
    <title>Chapter 5 Examples</title>
  </head>

  <body>
```

3. Now we start an HTML form. This is a neat way of getting data from users. When the user presses the submit button (which we come to in a minute), all the data entered on the form can be sent off to a server for processing, or sent to another page where it can affect the content of that page. We're taking the latter of these two options, and as the action attribute indicates, the second page is called whenexamplehandler.jsp:

```
<form method="POST" action="whenexamplehandler.jsp">
```

4. The form itself will be laid out as an HTML table with three columns:

```
<table border="0" cellpadding="0" cellspacing="0" width="439">
  <tr>
    <td width="157"><b>Shopping Cart</b></td>
    <td width="128"></td>
    <td width="148"></td>
  </tr>
  <tr>
    <td width="157" bgcolor="#C0C0C0">
      <font color="#FFFFFF">Product</font>
    </td>
    <td width="128" bgcolor="#C0C0C0">
      <font color="#FFFFFF">ListPrice</font>
    </td>
    <td width="148" bgcolor="#C0C0C0">
      <font color="#FFFFFF">Quantity</font>
    </td>
  </tr>
```

5. Each row of the table represents a single item available for purchase:

```
<tr>
  <td width="157">Beginning JSP</td>
  <td width="128">$49.99</td>
```

6. The last column is a textbox where users can enter the quantity they wish to order:

```
<td width="148">
  <input type="text" name="quantity" size="4" />
</td>
</tr>
```

7. Then we close the table, and set up the submit button for when the user has entered all necessary details. This button uses the POST method to pass the form values to the destination given by the <form>'s action attribute:

```
</table>
<p>
```

```
            <input type="submit" value="Place Order" name="PlaceOrderBtn"/>
        </p>
```

8. Now we close the other HTML tags, and we're done with the HTML file:

```
    </form>

  </body>
</html>
```

9. When the user submits the form, the form data entered – which here is just that in the `quantity` field – is submitted to the `whenexamplehandler.jsp` page. Create a file with this name now, again in the `Decisions` folder. This is quite a short file, and I'll explain it in detail in the *How It Works* section. Here it is in full:

```
<%@ taglib prefix="c" uri="http://java.sun.com/jstl/core_rt" %>
<%@ page info="If Example JSP"%>
<html>

  <head>
    <title>Conditional Statements</title>
  </head>

  <body>
    <b>WHEN Statement Example ( Response ) <br /></b>
    <br />

    <c:choose>
      <c:when test="${param.quantity > 0}" >
        Thank you for your order!!
      </c:when>
      <c:otherwise>
        Sorry, please enter a positive quantity
      </c:otherwise>
    </c:choose>
  </body>
</html>
```

10. Now start up Tomcat, and browse to the following URL in your browser:

http://localhost:8080/Decisions/whenexample.jsp

Enter a positive number in the Quantity field as shown:

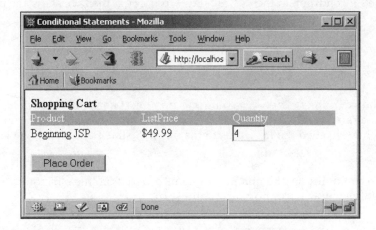

Click **Place Order** and you should see the following output:

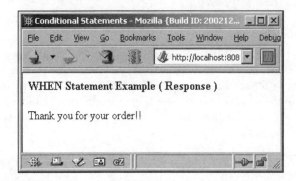

11. Click your browser's **Back** button, and try it again, but this time enter zero in the quantity box and click **Place Order**. You should see the message asking you to supply a positive quantity.

How It Works

We've already examined the HTML code quite closely, so let's now concentrate on the second file, `whenexamplehandler.jsp`. This file checks whether `quantity` is greater than zero using EL inside a JSTL `<when>` tag:

```
<c:when test="${param.quantity > 0}">
```

If this is `true`, what appears before the closing `<when>` tag will be used for the final page, which here is simply the message **Thank-you for your order!!**. As you see, the `<c:when ></c:when>` tags act like the `if { }` block in normal Java code.

If however the EL condition in the `<when>` tag is not `true`, then we show the message **Sorry, please enter a positive quantity**:

```
<c:otherwise>
  Sorry, please enter a positive quantity
</c:otherwise>
```

In this case, the `<c:otherwise></c:otherwise>` tags behave like a Java `else` block. Be warned that the relationship between `if...else` and `<c:if>...<c:otherwise>` is not perfect. Some have likened the JSTL tags to the `switch` statement, which we will cover in a little bit.

Notice that we could display the quantity of items ordered on this page quite easily, by inserting the following EL in `whenexamplehandler.jsp`:

```
<c:when test="${param.quantity > 0}" >
  Thank you for your order of ${param.quantity} items!!
</c:when>
```

A Note About Input Validation

The final question in the Try It Out section at the end of Chapter 3 touched on the problem of ensuring our users submit meaningful data. In this example for instance there's nothing to stop a user entering letters or other non-numeric characters in the **Quantity** box. The JSTL will attempt to convert the parameter value to an appropriate type (an integer in this case), but often conversion simply isn't possible, resulting in a screenful of user-scaring error messages, as you can see if you try it yourself:

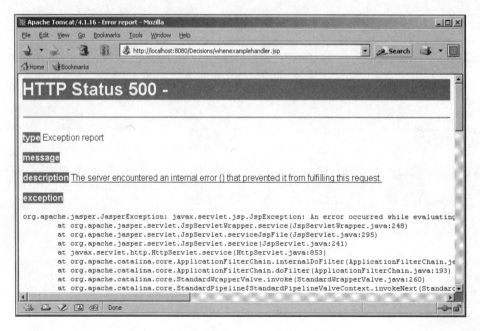

It is very important to prevent such unprofessional outcomes in your programs, and you do it by the process of input validation. Validation involves anticipating places where inappropriate input is possible, and handling such eventualities by checking the submitted input, and displaying a warning of your own if the input is not of the correct type. This could involve adding code to the page to perform this task, or you could pass the responsibility off to another component. In Chapter 15, we'll introduce Struts, a framework that, among many other things, makes the validation of user input fairly simple.

We can use an `if` statement to gain some simple protection. The final example in Chapter 3 checked that the `title` was not `null`, but not the `price`. And it didn't check to see that the `price` was not a negative number. As a partial solution, the conditional logic could be changed to:

```
<c:if test="${(param.title != null) && (param.price > 0)}" >
```

Unfortunately, it's still possible that an error could occur should `price` not be a number. The handling of errors (known as **exceptions** in Java) that may occur is an important consideration for any programmer, and we'll cover this topic in detail in Chapter 8.

Nested if Statements

We can model this "choice within a choice" in Java by embedding an `if` statement or an `if...else` statement inside another `if` or `if...else` statement. This is known as the **nesting** of `if` statements, and is shown in a general way below. The nested statements are highlighted:

```
if (expression1)
{
  if (expression2)
  {
    Statement Block 1
  }
}
else
{
  if (expression3)
  {
    Statement Block 2
  }
  else
  {
    Statement Block 3
  }
}
```

This ability to nest statements should not be entirely unexpected. Since a statement block is simply one or more lines of Java code, there is no reason why an `if` statement block should not contain further `if` and `if...else` statements.

Let's see a code snippet to illustrate our point. We'll return to our earlier shipping cost scenario. Here, our customer is only allowed free shipping if more than 4 items are purchased. If he spends more than $100 on his 5 or more items then the customer gets 5% discount as well. However, if over $2000 is spent on the 5 or more items, the customer gets a free television:

```
if ( itemQuantity > 4 )
{
  System.out.println("Free Shipping for You!!");
  if (itemCost > 100)
  {
    System.out.println("5% Discount for You!!");
    if (itemCost > 2000)
    {
      System.out.println("Free Television for You!!");
    }
  }
}
```

Notice that we have more than one level of nesting here: we can have as many levels as we need, and the same construct can be created with JSTL <choose> tags:

```
<c:choose>
  <c:when test="${itemQuantity > 4}" >
    <c:choose>
      <c:when test="${itemCost > 2000}">
        You've earned a free television, plus a 5% discount and
        free shipping.
      </c:when>
      <c:when test="${itemCost > 100}">
        5% discount on your purchase, in addition to no shipping
        charge.
      </c:when>
      <c:otherwise>
        We will ship your order free of charge.
      </c:otherwise>
    </c:choose>
  </c:when>
</c:choose>
```

The Conditional Operator

Java provides a very concise way of writing conditional logic with the ?: operator. As this operator takes three operands, it is known as the **ternary operator**. Most operators take two operands, and are thus known as binary operators, and there are a few unary operators also that take just one operand, such as the complement operator.

operand1 ? operand2 : operand3

operand1 is evaluated, and if it works out to true, then operand2 is returned, otherwise operand3 is returned. Look at the following line:

```
boolean freeShipping = (itemCost > 100) ? true : false;
```

In the above example, `freeShipping` will be set to `true` if `itemCost` is above 100, otherwise it will be set to `false`.

Take a look at another example:

```
int x = 20;
int y = (x > 50)? x + 10 : x - 15;
```

Here the integer variable x is initialized to 20. Since `(x > 50)` evaluates to `false`, the variable y is assigned the value of the third operand, which has the value `x - 15` (which in turn evaluates to 5). While there is no JSTL equivalent for the `?:` operator, it can be useful in Java code elsewhere.

The switch Statement

We have already seen that there is a way to deal with a selection of options using `if...else if` statements. However this method can be somewhat untidy. A cleaner alternative is to use the `switch` statement, the basic syntax of which is shown below:

```
switch (expression)
{
  case <expressionValue 1>
    StatementBlock1;
    break;
  case <expressionValue 2> :
    StatementBlock2;
    break;
  default :
    DefaultStatementBlock;
    break;
}
```

The first thing to note is that there is a single expression to evaluate, which follows the initial `switch` keyword. The `switch` keyword is then followed by a sequence of `case` statements, each of which has an associated **expression value**. At the end of the list of case statements, the `default` keyword may appear.

What happens when a `switch` statement is encountered is this:

1. The expression is evaluated, and the result is compared to each `case` statement's expression value in turn.

2. When a `case` statement is found where the expression value matches the result of the expression, the statements belonging to that `case` are executed.

3. If no matching `case` statement is found, the statements given for the `default` case are executed.

There are a couple of important things to note about the `switch` block:

❑ The expression must return a value of type `byte`, `char`, `short` or `int`.

❑ If a `break` statement is not placed at the end of a particular `case` statement's code block, all the code for all subsequent `case` statements will be executed too. The `break` statement exits the `switch` construct, and execution continues from the following statement.

This is required because expression values cannot contain logical operators, and this behavior allows one block of code to match several case statements. However, it is a pitfall that can often trap the unwary programmer.

> If you do not include the **break** statement, program flow will fall through to the remaining case options, and execute all statement blocks until **break** is encountered or the **switch** statement ends.

The JSTL contains no parallel, though a similar effect can be created using `choose...when` as we'll see in the next Try It Out. The example below shows a `switch` statement that displays a list of options according to the value of the `bookChosen` variable:

```
switch (bookChosen)
{
  case 1 :
    System.out.println("Beginning JSP");
    System.out.println("Price : $39.99, September 2001");
    break;
  case 2 :
    System.out.println("Professional JSP 2.0");
    System.out.println("Price : $59.99, April 2003");
    break;
  default :
    System.out.println("No Book Chosen");
    break;
}
```

In the above code snippet, if `bookChosen` is 1, the output produced would be:

```
Beginning JSP
Price : $39.99, September 2001
```

If however `bookChosen` were 5, it wouldn't match any case expression values, and so the `default` code would be executed, displaying the message No Book Chosen.

There is no direct equivalent to the switch statement in JSTL, but we can achieve a similar effect using the <choose> tag. In the next example, we'll present a dropdown list that lets the user select a particular book and see details on that book by clicking a button. We'll use a JSTL <choose> tag to select the details for the chosen book.

Try It Out   The choose...when...when Construct

1. First we'll create an HTML file to build the initial form displayed to the user. This file will be called whenexample2.html, and should be placed in your Decisions folder. It starts out identically to our previous HTML file:

```html
<html>
  <head>
    <title>Conditional Statements</title>
  </head>
  <body>
```

2. As before, we create an HTML form, containing a table, that will post its data to a JSP:

```html
<form method="POST" action="whenexamplehandler2.jsp">
  <table border="0" cellpadding="0" cellspacing="0" width="100%">
    <tr>
      <td><b>View Book Details</b></td>
      <td></td>
      <td></td>
    </tr>
    <tr>
      <td colspan="3">
```

3. This time, we create a dropdown list, with the following HTML:

```html
<select size="1" name="book">
  <option selected value="1">Beginning JSP</option>
  <option value="2">Professional JSP 2.0</option>
  <option value="3">Beginning Java</option>
</select>
```

4. We need a submit button again, this time labeled Get Details:

```html
<input type="submit" value="Get Details"
       name="GetDetailsBtn" />
      </td>
    </tr>
  </table>
</form>
  </body>
</html>
```

5. When the user clicks the **Get Details** button, they will be passed to the
`whenexamplehandler2.jsp` file. This is fairly short, and appears below in its entirety:

```
<%@ taglib prefix="c" uri="http://java.sun.com/jstl/core" %>
<html>
  <head>
    <title>Decisions Examples</title>
  </head>
  <body>
    <b>Book Details Page</b><br /><br />
    <c:choose>
      <c:when test="${param.book eq 1}" >
          Beginning JSP<br />
          Price : $39.99, September 2001<br />
      </c:when>
      <c:when test="${param.book eq 2}" >
          Professional JSP 2.0<br />
          Price : $59.99, April 2003<br />
      </c:when>
       <c:when test="${param.book eq 3}" >
          Beginning Java<br />
          Price : $49.99, July 2000<br />
      </c:when>
    </c:choose>
  </body>
</html>
```

6. Now browse to **localhost:8080/Decisions/whenexample2.jsp** in your browser. Select a
book from the dropdown list:

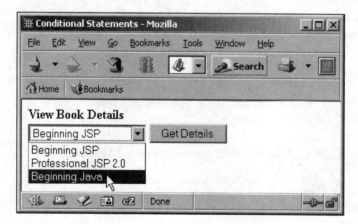

7. If you choose **Beginning Java** and click **Get Details**, you will see the following information:

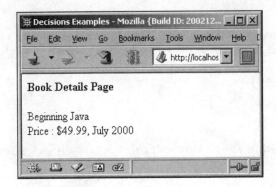

How It Works

The book selected in the initial HTML page is stored in a form field called (unsurprisingly) book, and we use it in the test attribute of JSTL <when> tags in our JSP page:

```
<c:when test="${param.book eq 2}" >
    Professional JSP 2.0<br />
    Price : $59.99, April 2003<br />
</c:when>
```

Notice the JSTL relational operator eq which has the same function as the equals sign. Also note the similarity between the <c:when> tag and the case statement in Java's switch construct.

Loops and Iteration

There are many programming situations where we need to execute the same logic repeatedly. While we could simply write out the code several times in sequence, this is clearly not a great idea. Firstly there's a much greater chance that we'll make an error in one of the duplicated blocks, and that error would consequently be harder to track down as there'd be no clear indication of which duplicated block contained the error. Secondly, in many cases, we rarely know in advance how many times we need to repeat the same steps. Consequently, just about every programming language ever has constructs that allow a single block of code to be repeated a given number of times.

Executing the same block of code over and over is known as **iteration**, or **looping**. Java has three types of iterative logic, each represented by one of the following statements:

❑ while statements

❑ do...while statements

❑ for statements

We will have a look at each of these in this section.

The while Loop

In many situations, we want to repeat a block of code for as long as a given expression remains true, and in such cases, we can use the while loop. Its syntax is pretty simple:

```
while (expression)
{
    Statement Block
}
```

For example, the following while loop will print out the digits 1 through 5:

```
int count = 1;

while (count < 6)
{
    System.out.println(count);
    count = count + 1;
}
```

We have an integer variable, count, which we initialize to 1. The while statement itself says that the statement block should be executed over and over until the value of count reaches 6. Each time we loop through the statement block, the value of count is displayed, and 1 is added to count, so count will be displayed five times before the while expression returns false.

Let's now move on and look at a variation of the while statement, the do...while statement.

The do...while Loop

do...while loops are very similar to while loops, and they repeat a block of code for as long as an expression remains true. The difference is that do...while loops check the value of the expression *after* the code block, and not before as in the plain while loop. This really just means that the code block will always execute at least once (even if the condition is not true when the loop is first encountered).

A pitfall of do...while loops in Java is that a semi-colon is required at the end of the while statement, something that is frequently forgotten.

```
do
{
    Statement Block
} while (expression);
```

Let's now return to our simplistic while loop that counts up to 5. Consider what would happen if we initialize the count variable to 6 instead of 1:

```
int count = 6;
```

```
while (count < 6)
{
  System.out.println(count);
  count = count + 1;
}
```

Since the `while` loop will only iterate while the value of `count` is less than 6, setting the initial value to 6 means that the loop never gets executed.

Now consider what happens if we set up the same counting example using a `do...while` loop:

```
int count = 6;

do
{
  System.out.println(count);
  count = count + 1;
} while (count < 6);
```

In this case, because the expression is not checked until the end of the loop, one iteration is allowed to occur, and we can see the value of `count` displayed:

6

> Use the while loop when you need the condition to be checked before executing the code block, and use **do...while** when the code block should execute at least once.

The for Statement

```
for(initialization; termination; increment)
{
  Statement Block
}
```

The `while` and `do...while` constructs let us create general purpose loops that can be applied to a range of situations. However, in many cases, we want to repeat a block of code a certain number of times, and on each pass through the loop, use the current loop count in some code. Such situations are ideally suited to the `for` loop.

Key to how `for` loops work is a counter variable. This variable can be set to a value on entering the loop, and will be increased or decreased by a certain amount at the end of each execution of the code block forming the body of the loop. There is also a test which determines when enough loops have been performed.

Let's see a simple example of a `for` loop as illustration:

```
for (int num = 1; num <= 5; num++)
{
  System.out.println(num);
}
```

The output of this would be:

```
1
2
3
4
5
```

In this case, the loop uses a counter variable called num, which is declared and initialized to 1 in the first expression in the brackets following the `for` statement. This expression is the **initialization expression**, and it is followed by what is called the **termination expression**. The termination expression gives a condition that must evaluate to true for the code in the loop body to be executed (in this case, the loop will continue for as long as num is less than or equal to five). The last expression of the `for` syntax is the **increment expression**, which is executed every time the end of the loop body is reached (and here, increments num by one).

The `for` statement is very flexible. The increment expression can be any expression that should be executed at the end of each iteration, and need not involve the loop counter at all. The **initialization expression** can set the counter to any value we choose, and we can use any numerical type as well as integers. We can of course use other variables in any of the three `for` expressions.

As you can see, our `for` loop's initialization expression declares and initializes num, but this is not a requirement, and we can just as well use an already existing variable as our counter, and we can even use its existing value by using a 'blank' initialization expression:

```
int num = 1;
for (; num <= 5; num++)
```

JSTL implements for loops using the `<forEach>` tag. Given the concepts of `for` statements that we've just discussed, you should be able to deduce the purpose of most of the attributes shown in the tag below:

```
<%@ taglib prefix="c" uri="http://java.sun.com/jstl/core" %>
<c:forEach begin="3" end="15" step="3" var="index" varStatus="num">

  <c:out value="${index}" />:<c:out value="${num.count}" /><br />

</c:forEach>
```

If you type the above code into a text file and save it as `forexample.jsp` in your `Decisions` directory, it will produce the following output when opened in a browser:

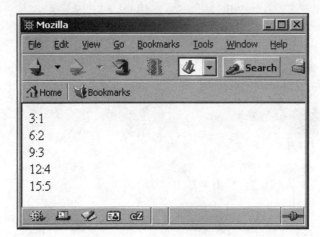

As you can see, this tag in fact requires two variables to function correctly, and we specify which names to give these using the `var` and `varStatus` attributes. `varStatus` specifies the name to use for the loop counter, and `var` is used internally by the JSTL.

This `<forEach>` loop mirrors the Java `for` loop below:

```
for (num = 3; num <= 15; num += 3)
    System.out.println(num);
```

We'll cover other uses of the `<forEach>` tag later in this chapter.

Branching Statements

Statements which direct the flow of execution to a particular point in a program are known as **branching** (or "flow control") statements. We've already seen one of these when we looked at the `switch` construct, where the `break` statement is needed at the end of `case` blocks to exit the switch at that point and continue at the line immediately after the `switch`.

We'll look at this statement in more detail in this section, along with two more:

- ❑ `break`
- ❑ `continue`
- ❑ `return`

Since we've already mentioned the `break` statement, let's start with that.

The break Statement

As well as exiting a `switch` statement, `break` can be used to terminate any enclosing `for`, `do...while`, or `while` loop. Program control continues at the statement immediately following the enclosing loop.

An example of the `break` statement in a `for` loop is shown below (this is a modification of the example we used to explain the `for` loop):

```
for(int num = 1; num <= 5; num++) {
  System.out.println(num);
  if (num == 3) {
    break;
  }
}
```

In the above code snippet, if the value of the `num` variable is equal to 3, the `break` statement is executed. This will result in the termination of the enclosing `for` statement, so the `for` loop for values of `num` equal to 4 or 5 will not be iterated. The output of the above code snippet will therefore be:

```
1
2
3
```

You should note that a **labeled** `break` statement is also available. This is useful because it means that we can jump to the end of any particular enclosing statement using `break` and a label. To illustrate this, consider what would happen if we nested the `for` statement from the example above inside another `for` statement:

```
OuterLoop:
for(int counter = 1; counter <= 2; counter++) {
  InnerLoop:
  for(int num = 1; num <= 5; num++) {
    System.out.println(num);
    if (num == 3) {
      break OuterLoop;
    }
  }
} // break directs execution flow to this point
```

Note that we have labeled the `for` statements with `OuterLoop` and `InnerLoop` labels respectively, and that we have labeled `break` too:

```
break OuterLoop;
```

Now when program execution reaches this line, it will jump to the end of the outer `for` statement, *not* to the end of the inner `for` statement (as an unlabeled `break` would), because we specifically stated `OuterLoop`. The `break` statement always causes execution to drop to the end of the enclosing code block.

Note that this use of `break` is generally considered poor programming, and better encapsulation should be employed in its place (here for instance, we could put the `InnerLoop` in a separate method and replace the `break` statement with a `return`). However, sometimes it is valid to "break the rules", and so you should be aware of this possible usage.

We will see that other types of statement can be labeled in a similar way.

The continue Statement

Inside a `for`, `do...while`, or `while` loop, the `continue` statement will skip to the next iteration of the loop. `continue` can be used with a label to skip the current iteration of the loop that is referred to by that label.

An example of the `continue` statement is shown below:

```
for(int num = 1; num <= 5; num++) {
   if (num == 3)
      continue;

   System.out.println(num);
}
```

when num is 3, the expression in the `if` statement, num `==` 3, evaluates to `true`, and the `continue` statement is called. This terminates the current iteration of the `for` loop at that point, and the incremental expression will be called. Therefore this `for` statement will not show the number 3:

```
1
2
4
5
```

The return Statement

The `return` statement is used within a method, and it returns control back to the code that called the method. That is, on reaching a return statement, the method ends, and the calling code continues from where it left off. If the method should return a value, then the `return` statement **must** include a variable of the required data type. We will see many examples of this in later chapters.

Introducing Arrays

We have now discussed all of the important control statements and it's time to move on to discuss how variables of the same data type can be grouped together into arrays. We'll also see how combining control statements with arrays can make our code simpler and easier to manage.

So what exactly is an array? Well, imagine that our program needed a thousand `String` variables, each one storing a different value as shown below:

```
String name1 = "Richmal";
String name2 = "Tobian";
String name3 = "Rozzle";
.
.
.
String name1000 = "Joey";
```

Remembering and managing them all would be troublesome to say the least! Also, there would more than likely be many situations where we need to perform the same action on every variable. Even something as simple as printing out a list of all the names would require us to type the same code for each `String`:

```
myPrintMethod(name1);
myPrintMethod(name2);
myPrintMethod(name3);
.
.
.
myPrintMethod(name1000);
```

To address such situations, we have the concept of the array variable, which allows many instances of a single data type to be grouped together and greatly simplifies using groups of variables as we will see.

Arrays can contain groups of any of the basic primitive data types, such as `int`, `String`, `char`, and `float`, and they can also handle other data types such as user-defined objects. We can even have arrays of arrays (of arrays...)! Note, however, that we cannot have an array of mixed data types – every element of an array must be of the same type.

Array Elements and Index Values

Each variable in an array is known as an **element**. In order to be able to reference a particular element within the array, we use its **index**, which indicates the element's offset from the start of the array. The fact that array indices start at zero is a source of many programming errors, and you always need to remember that the first element has an index of zero (not one), the second has an index of one, the fifteenth has an index of 14, and so on.

Creating Arrays

There are three steps when creating an array:

1. Declare

2. Define

3. Initialize

The third step isn't always required, but the other two are necessary for an array to be usable.

Declaring an Array

We declare an array by specifying the type of array elements followed by a pair of empty square brackets, and finally the name of the array, like so:

```
int[] numbers;
```

The above line declares an array of integers called `numbers`. However, the square brackets can be placed after the array name, as in this example which declares an array of strings called names:

```
String names[];
```

Defining an Array

Before we can use an array we have declared, we need to **define** it by stating its size – the number of elements that it will contain. This step is necessary so that the correct amount of memory can be allocated for it. We use the `new` keyword to define an array, like so:

```
numbers = new int[4];
names = new String[1000];
```

Here, we've defined the numbers array as containing four elements, and names as containing one thousand.

On definition, each of the elements in an array is set to the default value for that data type. The default value of any primitive data type (except boolean) in an array is zero, the default value for a boolean is false, and the default value for any `Object` type is `null`.

Initializing and Resetting Array Values

Our final step is to place initial values into our array elements. We can assign values to each of the elements individually, as below:

```
numbers[0] = 39;
names[0] = "Chris";
```

The number between the brackets is the index of the element that we wish to populate.

You should note that we can **reset** the values contained by the elements in an array at any time during the array's lifetime in exactly the same way. So if Chris changed his name to Kurt, we could reset the value of the second element of the `names` array using:

```
names[0] = "Kurt";
```

Creating an Array the Easy Way

There's no need to declare and define arrays in individual steps, and we can perform all of these steps in a single line of code if we wish. For instance, we can create an array of four integers, with values 39, 21, 8, and 93 with this line:

```
int[] numbers = {39, 21, 8, 93};
```

Note that Java uses the number of values provided as initialization to set the size of the array.

Finally, the easiest way to create a new array is to initialize it using an existing array. For instance, now that we have created the `numbers` array, we could use it to initialize a new array, `moreNumbers`:

```
int[] moreNumbers = numbers;
```

In this case, Java creates a new integer array, `moreNumbers`, that has the same number of elements as the `numbers` array, and each element of `moreNumbers` will contain the same value as the corresponding element of `numbers`.

On a JSP page, we could declare an array using this sort of code inside a scriptlet. Generally speaking, however, placing Java code in a JSP page is considered a "breach of contract." This "unwritten contract" states that JSP pages are for HTML and JSP tags, and Java objects are where code belongs. However, JSP actually provides us with arrays whenever data has been submitted to a page, whether using the GET or POST method (review Chapter 2), and the JSTL expression language provides a handy mechanism for getting these arrays as we've already seen:

```
${ paramValues.book_id }
```

This will return a `String` array of the parameters called `book_id` that were submitted to the page. If there were only one `book_id` parameter, it would be a `String` array whose size is one.

Iterating Through Arrays

The `for` loop is very useful when we need to process each element in an array, and is often used in conjunction with the `length` property. This property tells us how many elements the array contains, and therefore can be used in the termination expression:

```
for(int index = 0; index < thisIsAnArray.length; index++)
```

Note that `length` will return the declared size of the array, regardless of how many array elements have been initialized. The `for` loop is particularly suited to arrays because in the loop body, we can use the counter variable to process each element in turn, like so:

```
System.out.println(moreNumbers[index]);
```

This process is often called *iterating through the array*.

In the following example, we'll put our new-found knowledge of arrays and JSTL iteration to use in a JSP page.

Try It Out   Arrays

1. This example consists of a single JSP page that allows us to make changes to the book table we worked with in Chapter 3. The first thing we need to do then is copy the MySQL Connector/j JAR to the `Decisions lib` folder (inside `WEB-INF`).

2. Now we can start writing our JSP page, called `arrayexample.jsp`. We need to include the JSTL and SQL tag libraries:

```
<%@ taglib prefix="c" uri="http://java.sun.com/jstl/core_rt" %>
<%@ taglib prefix="sql" uri="http://java.sun.com/jstl/sql_rt" %>
```

3. Next, we need to provide the connection information for our database:

```
<sql:setDataSource var="datasource"
   driver="com.mysql.jdbc.Driver"
   url="jdbc:mysql://localhost/publish"
   user="publish" password="wrox" />
```

4. The next section of code is used to update our database when changes have been made. Don't worry about why that appears here just now, we'll explain that once the page is done.

```
<c:if test="${!empty param.title}">
  <c:forEach items="${paramValues.title}" varStatus="i">
    <c:if test="${paramValues.price[i.count-1] > 0.0}">
```

```
        <sql:update dataSource="${datasource}">
          UPDATE book
            SET title = ?,
                price = ?
          WHERE id = ?
          <sql:param value="${paramValues.title[i.count-1]}" />
          <sql:param value="${paramValues.price[i.count-1]}" />
          <sql:param value="${paramValues.id[i.count-1]}" />
        </sql:update>
      </c:if>
    </c:forEach>
</c:if>
```

5. Now we run a query on the books table, extracting the id, title and price fields:

```
<sql:query var="books" dataSource="${datasource}">
  SELECT id, title, price FROM book
</sql:query>
```

6. The last thing to create is an HTML form for displaying information from the database:

```
<form method="post">
<table border="1">
  <tr>
  <th>id</td><th>title</td><th>price</td>
  </tr>
```

7. We use another JSTL <forEach> to loop through all books that are to be displayed:

```
<c:forEach var="row" items="${books.rows}">
  <tr>
    <td>
      <input type="hidden" name="id" value="${row.id}" />
      ${row.id}
    </td>
    <td>
      <input type="text" name="title" value="${row.title}" size="30" />
    </td>
    <td>
      <input type="text" name="price" value="${row.price}" size="6" />
    </td>
  </tr>
</c:forEach>
```

8. The last row in this table will contain the form's submit button. As the form doesn't specify an action attribute, this button will post the form information *back to this page itself*:

```
  <tr>
    <td colspan="3" align="center">
    <input type="submit" value="Save Changes" />
    </td>
  </tr>
</table>
</form>
```

9. Open your browser and go to localhost:8080/Decisions/arrayexample.jsp. You should see a page that looks something like this:

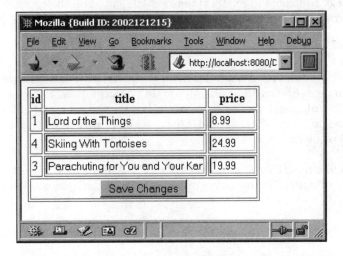

10. Change some values and click on the **Save Changes** button. You should get a response that looks like this (depending on the items you chose):

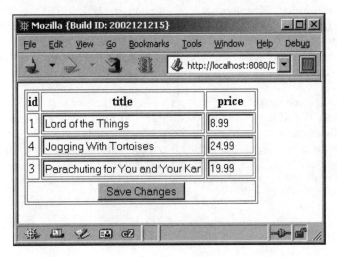

How It Works

In Step 4, we added some code inside the following JSTL `<if>` tag:

```
<c:if test="${!empty param.title}">
```

This tag uses the Expression Language `empty` operator to see if there is a `title` parameter for the page that is neither `null` nor empty. When the page is first accessed from our browser, there won't be any parameters at all, so the `<if>` block is skipped, and we load up the data from our database, and come to the form that will display it on the page. First of all, the form has a hidden form field for the row ID of each book:

```
<input type="hidden" name="id" value="${row.id}" />
```

By storing this as a hidden form field, it will be returned to the server when the user submits the form and thus the server will be able to use it to determine which rows need updating in the database. We could place the ID in a textbox, but then users could edit the value, so we hide it. In this case, we do however want the ID to be visible, so we display it as static text right after the hidden field using EL.

Why do we hide the row ID, you may ask? As you will recall from earlier examples of HTML forms, all values submitted to the server must be contained in one manner of form element or another.

We then create text boxes in the next two rows, one for the price, and one for the title:

```
<input type="text" name="title" value="${row.title}" size="30" />
<input type="text" name="price" value="${row.price}" size="6" />
```

When the form is submitted, it posts back to the page itself. In other words, the page is regenerated, but this time with the data we submitted available as parameters in the `param` array. So, now when we get to the first JSTL `<if>` tag, the `test` attribute, `"${!empty param.title}"`, will evaluate to `true`, and we can use the `<forEach>` tag to iterate over the `String` array returned by `$paramValues.title`.

Remember that when we looked at `<forEach>` earlier, it has `begin` and `end` attributes, and an attribute called `var` that denotes the loop counter. In this case, as the variable given in the `var` attribute holds the current value from the loop, which in this case would be the current `title`, we can't use it as the array index (that must be numerical!). Instead, we take advantage of the fact that the `<forEach>` tag uses its own status mechanism: `varStatus`. But `varStatus` tracks the current iteration starting at one, and as arrays begin their index at zero, we have to do some math:

```
<c:if test="${paramValues.price[i.count-1] > 0.0}">
```

Now we can run through all the parameter values and update the database as necessary using the SQL UPDATE statement. Once the database update is complete, we continue down the page, and extract the updated data from the database and display it in a form just as before.

Multi-Dimensional Arrays

So far, the arrays we've looked at have had a single index value to access elements they contain. They can be visualized as simple lists of data items, where the index specifies the number of the required item in the list. Such arrays are known as **one dimensional**, because just one index can uniquely identify any one particular member.

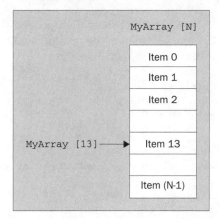

However, arrays can have more than one dimension. For instance, a two dimensional array has two indices. Such arrays can be visualized as a set of pigeon-holes, and in order to locate one specific pigeon-hole, we need to know both how far from the left side it is, and how far down from the top it is:

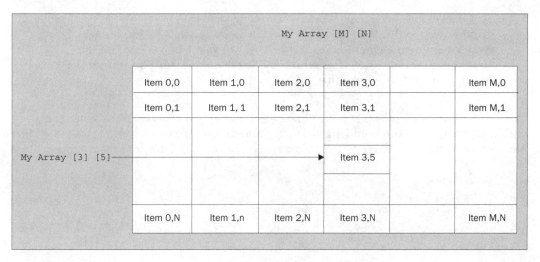

For instance, say we had two houses in our street, and each house had three occupants. We could store the names of the occupants in a two-dimensional `String` array, where the first index would indicate the house in question, and the second one would indicate a particular occupant.

Creating a 2D array is very similar to creating an ordinary 1D array:

```
String[][] houses = {
  { "Joey", "Tommy", "Podlington" },
  { "Pickles", "Scragg", "Floopy" },
};
```

Note that we need two empty brackets after the data type, and that we initialize using a set of values each contained in curly braces. In Java, the general syntax for creating 2D arrays of size *m* x *n* (where *m* and *n* are positive integers) is:

```
DataType[][] array_variable_name = {
  { value1, value2, ..., valuen },
  { value1, value2, ..., valuen },
  .
  .
  .
  { value1, value2, ..., valuen }, // mth array of values
}
```

Referencing elements in a 2D array is equally straightforward. For instance, we could find the name of the second member of the first house using `houses[0][1]` (don't forget that array indices always start at zero!). Also, we can indicate the whole of the first house using `houses[0]`. In other words, if we want to reference all occupants of the *m*th house, we would use `houses[m-1]`, and if we wish to reference the *n*th occupant of the *m*th house, we would use both indices: `houses[m-1][n-1]`.

> **Another way to think of 2D arrays is as an array of arrays – that is, as a 1D array where each element is itself a 1D array. Thus, when we access the array, the first index specifies which 'subarray' to use, and the second index specifies the offset within that subarray.**

One thing to be aware of is that Java allows so-called **jagged arrays**. This is when the arrays within an array are of different length. For instance, if the two houses in our road had different numbers of occupants, we could use an array like the following to store their names:

```
String[][] houses = {
  { "Joey", "Tommy", "Podlington" },
  { "Pickles", "Scragg", "Floopy", "Zuppo" },
};
```

As you can see, the first house has three occupants, while the second has four. In other words, `houses[0].length` will be 3 and `houses[1].length` will be 4.

As with 1D arrays, we don't have to declare, define and initialize an array at the same time. For example, we might not know how many occupants there are in the houses:

```
String[][] houses  = new String[2][];
```

Here, we have told Java that the first dimension of the `newHouses` array will contain two elements which will both be arrays. When you declare a 2D array, we do have to declare at least the first (primary) array dimension. We can then specify the second index before use. Again, we can create jagged arrays in this fashion, as in the following example:

```
String[][] houses = new String[2][];

houses[0] = new String[3];

houses[0][0] = "Joey";
houses[0][1] = "Tommy";
houses[0][2] = "Podlington";

houses[1] = new String[4];

houses[1][0] = "Pickles";
houses[1][1] = "Scragg";
houses[1][2] = "Floopy";
houses[1][3] = "Zuppo";
```

Now, let's finish off the chapter by looking at a common task when working with arrays: sorting.

Sorting Arrays

The standard Java package `java.util` contains a class called `Arrays` that provides a range of methods for array handling. It has methods for searching an array, for comparing arrays, and so on. One method of this class, `Arrays.sort()`, provides a way of sorting the elements of an array. For full details of this class, see the documentation at http://java.sun.com/j2se/1.4.1/docs/api/java/util/Arrays.html.

The `sort()` method sorts an array according to the **natural ordering** of the data type held in the array. Natural ordering is the name given to the default ordering for a particular data type. For example, the natural order for integers is ascending numerical order, and for strings, it is ascending alphabetic order.

For example, if we have an integer array containing five values:

```
int[] sortme = {25, 32, 19, 27, 24};
```

and we printed this array using a loop such as this:

```
for(int i = 0; i < sortme.length; i++)
    System.out.println(ages[i]);
```

then we would expect to see:

```
25
32
19
27
24
```

However, if we first sort the array, and then print it out, like this:

```
Arrays.sort(sortme);
for(int i = 0; i < sortme.length; i++)
    System.out.println(ages[i]);
```

the values would appear lowest first:

```
19
24
25
27
32
```

So what if you need to sort something "unnaturally"? The `java.util` package also contains an interface called `Comparator`. If we implement the `compare` and `equals` methods of this interface, we could use another `Arrays.sort()` method, `Arrays.sort(Object[] array, Comparator c)`, to order elements according to a different pattern. Implementing comparators is beyond the scope of this book, but if you wish to find out more, *Beginning Java 2* (Wrox Press, ISBN 1-86100-569-5) makes a good place to start.

Summary

This chapter has covered the basics of specifying decisions in our code, and how these decisions can be used to affect program flow using control statements. There are three key types of control statements:

❑ **Conditional Statements** (`if`, `if...else`, and `switch`) – execution of a block of code is controlled by the result of evaluating an expression.

❑ **Iterative Statements** (`for`, `while`, `do...while`) – repeat the same code block a certain number of times.

❑ **Branching Statements** (break, continue, return) – used to exit a loop, or the current loop iteration, or a method respectively.

We also covered arrays, which are groups of the same data type. They simplify the maintenance and processing of large numbers of variables. The for loop (or <forEach> tag in a JSP page) is a great tool for processing all the elements of an array in sequence. We looked at two-dimensional arrays and jagged arrays, which are invaluable in many situations. We closed by looking at the sort method of the java.util package.

The main reason for using arrays and control statements is that they make our code simpler, easier to maintain, and more reusable. In the next chapter we are going to introduce tag libraries, which can simplify JSP scripts still further.

Why Not Try?

❑ Extend the first example (whenexample.jsp) to add a set of conditional statements that grant a 10% discount for the first 14 days of each month, and an additional 5% if the number of items ordered is greater than 3. Grant a 25% total discount if the total items is greater than 10, regardless of the day of the month.

For this example, just add a field for the user to enter the current day of the month, so you can read it as $param.dayOfMonth. Of course, a real system would get this information from the server, but we need not worry about that here.

❑ Change the second example (whenexamplehandler2.jsp) so that it displays each book name up to and including the one selected. Put another way, if the user selects book 2, print the information for book 1 and book 2.

❑ Use the JSTL <forEach> and <when> tags on a JSP page to count from one to one hundred by ones, printing every third number (3, 6, 9, ...). Now rewrite it again so that it counts by threes. Use the var and varStatus attributes to verify your output.

❑ Create an array of first names in "random" order. Use any one of the looping techniques to print out the names. Then use Arrays.sort() to order the names alphabetically, and print them again.

CHAPTER 6

More on Objects

We introduced object orientation in Chapter 4, where we learned how to create our own classes and use them as JavaBeans in JSP.

This chapter expands on the theme of code reuse, following the sequence below:

- ❑ A review of objects
- ❑ A closer look at methods and constructors
- ❑ How to create classes based on existing classes
- ❑ How to create a general design for a set of classes
- ❑ A look at an essential feature for the creation of extensible programs – that of **inheritance**
- ❑ A discussion of type conversion, or **casting**
- ❑ How to define and implement classes and interfaces, a closely related concept
- ❑ A look at static members

Let's begin by quickly reviewing what we learned about objects in Chapter 4.

A Quick Review of Objects

In programming, an object can be anything – literally. This is because objects are nothing more than computer representations of real-world things. Objects have characteristics and behaviors that the programmer can define – they are software constructs that encapsulate data and the means to use or modify that data into a single entity. Fully object oriented programs are made up of a set of cooperating objects, which exchange messages to achieve a common objective.

A Real World Analogy

To get a better example of what objects actually are, let's have a look at a simple example. The code below defines a very simple class called `Book`:

```
package booklibrary;

public class Book implements Serializable
{

  private String title;

  Book() {}

  public String getTitle()
  {
    return this.title;
  }

  public void setTitle(String newTitle)
  {
    this.title = newTitle;
  }

}
```

From this code, we see that the `Book` class:

❑ has a member variable called `title` that has `private` access. `private` access means that `title` can only be accessed directly from within the class.

❑ has a special method called a **constructor** that has the same name as the class itself. If a class has a constructor, Java calls it when an object is created to perform any necessary initialization. We will come back to the issue of constructors in the next section.

❑ has two methods, `getTitle()` and `setTitle()`, that have `public` access. `public` access means that they can be accessed by any code where an object of the class is used. The two methods, `getTitle()` and `setTitle()`, are known respectively as the getter and setter methods, or **get and set accessors**. They follow the JavaBean coding conventions, which mean that the class may be used as a JavaBean and may be accessed using the bean tags within a JSP page.

If it should be treated as a bean, the class should implement the `java.io.Serializable` interface. This means that instances of the class can be stored outside of system RAM, such as in a file. A feature of the servlet container, known as **session persistence**, only works if beans implement `Serializable`.

We will be using this `Book` class, and variations of it, throughout the chapter, so let's create and test it.

A Simple Class

1. First we need a web application to host our code. Create a folder called `Objects` within Tomcat's `webapps` folder, and create a subfolder in it called `WEB-INF`, and another one within that called `classes`.

2. As the Java code for classes used by our web application will be placed in a package called `booklibrary`, they must be placed in a subfolder of `classes` called `booklibrary`. Create that directory, and create a file there called `Book.java`, and enter the code for the `Book` class that we've already seen:

```java
package booklibrary;

public class Book
{

  private String title;

  public String getTitle()
  {
    return title;
  }

  public void setTitle(String newTitle)
  {
    this.title = newTitle;
  }

}
```

3. Now we need to compile our java class. From a command prompt, change to the `classes` directory and run the following command:

   > javac booklibrary\Book.java

   This will create a file called `Book.class` in that directory.

4. Next, we'll write a JSP page that uses this class. Create a file called `bookPage.jsp` in the `Objects` directory, open it, and enter the following code:

```html
<html>
  <head>
    <title>A Simple Class</title>
  </head>

  <body>
    <jsp:useBean id="myBook" class="booklibrary.Book" />
```

```
      <jsp:setProperty name="myBook"
                       property="title"
                       value="Beginning JSP 2.0" />
    Book Title: <jsp:getProperty name="myBook" property="title" />
  </body>
</html>
```

5. Let's check it out! Start up Tomcat, and open localhost:8080/Objects/bookPage.jsp in your browser. You should see something like:

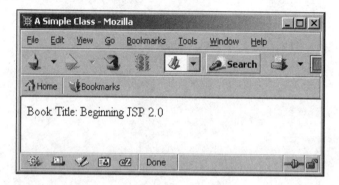

There isn't anything in this example that we've not already seen Chapter 4. The Book class we have created is a simple JavaBean with a single attribute, `title`. Note the accessor methods that were introduced in Chapter 4, and allow us to use the class as a JavaBean and access the `title` property using the bean tags.

A Closer Look at Objects

In order to understand object oriented programming (OOP), you need to understand the following three very important concepts:

❑ Encapsulation

❑ Inheritance

❑ Polymorphism

The idea of encapsulation is that, ideally, objects do not require knowledge of their inner workings in order to be useable. In other words, we expose our objects through a set of `public` methods which are all that an application needs to know about. As long as the arguments, names and return values of the methods stay the same, we can entirely rewrite the code that implements a given method, and any applications that use those objects will still work.

178

As we progress through this chapter, these terms, and other key concepts of OOP, will be explained in more depth, and you'll soon get a feel for what the terminology represents. We'll start off with a look at method overloading, and constructors.

Method Overloading

A method's signature includes its name and the list of parameters it requires. Java allows us to create two or more methods with the same name and return type, but with different argument lists. This is **method overloading**, and it allows our classes to expose different methods that perform closely related functionality in a natural and intuitive way. Java uses the number and type of arguments to choose which method definition to execute.

Note that differences in argument names are not significant, and also that although an overloaded method may have a different return type, that alone is not sufficient to distinguish an overloaded method, and it must also have a different parameter list.

For instance, we may decide to create an `Author` class to complement our `Book` class:

```
package booklibrary;

public class Author
{

  private String lastName;
  private String firstName;
  private String otherNames;

  public void setName(String firstName,
                      String lastName,
                      String otherNames)
  {
    this.lastName = lastName;
    this.firstName = firstName;
    this.otherNames = otherNames;
  }

  public String getName()
  {
    return firstName + " " + otherNames + " " + lastName;
  }

}
```

This class has `private` attributes that store the names of an author, a `public` method to set these, and another `public` method to retrieve the name as a single string.

If an author did not have any middle names, we could use our set accessor like this:

```
Author myAuthor = new Author();
myAuthor.setName("Shakespeare", "William", "");
```

However, a preferable way might be to overload the set accessor in the author class, so that we can just miss out the `otherNames` parameter, like so:

```
public void setName (String firstName, String lastName)
{
   this.lastName = lastName;
   this.firstName = firstName;
   this.otherNames = "";
}
```

In fact, this isn't the only way to implement this overloaded method. It is generally preferable to simply call the other form of the `setName()` method:

```
public void setName (String lastName, String firstName)
{
   this.setName (lastName, firstName, "");
}
```

This is better because, should we at some later date change how we store names (perhaps we want to update a database when the name is changed), we would only have to alter the first `setName()` method, and all the overloaded forms would then use the new technique automatically.

Method overloading provides a convenient way for us to interact with our objects. Instead of creating methods with names like `setFullName()` or `setShortName()`, we can create a single, logical method name and keep the interaction simple.

Method overloading is especially useful when used with constructors, because it allows us to code several constructors (the name is predetermined by the name of the class), each taking a different set of parameters for initializing the object.

Constructors

A constructor is a special method that is employed when an object of the class is created (instantiated), and it specifies any special actions that need to be performed when an object is created. A constructor is just like any other method of a class, except that it always has the same name as the class itself, and there is no return type. Here is the simplest constructor we could have:

```
public Author()
{
}
```

This simple constructor doesn't do anything beyond what is normally performed for the creation of an object. In fact, the Java compiler adds a constructor of this form by default to all classes where it is not already included.

We might wish to provide a constructor which allows us to set the name of an author when we create an `Author` object, and it might look like this:

```
public Author(String firstName, String lastName, String otherNames)
{
  this.firstName = firstName;
  this.lastName = lastName;
  this.otherNames = otherNames;
}
```

Or, we may provide a constructor which sets some default values when names aren't provided:

```
public Author()
{
  this.firstName = "Anne";
  this.lastName = "Orther";
  this.otherNames = "";
}
```

Thanks to method overloading, we can define both of these (and more), and we could then instantiate the `Author` class in two different ways:

```
Author author1 = new Author();
Author author2 = new Author("Douglas", "Adams", "");
```

Let's extend our `Book` class to take advantage of multiple constructors to set the title of a book at instantiation.

Try It Out   Method Overloading and Constructors

1. Open `Book.java`, and add a new constructor as highlighted:

```
package booklibrary;

public class Book
{

  private String title;

  public String getTitle()
  {
    return title;
  }
```

```
  public void setTitle(String newTitle)
  {
    this.title = newTitle;
  }

  public Book(String title)
  {
    this.title = title;
  }

}
```

2. Recompile the Book class using the same command line as before:

> **javac booklibrary\Book.java**

3. Now copy bookPage.jsp and rename it bookPage2.jsp. Replace the content of the
<body> element with the following:

```
<html>
  <head>
    <title>A Simple Class</title>
  </head>

  <body>
    <%
      booklibrary.Book myBook =
                    new booklibrary.Book("Beginning JSP 2.0");
    %>
    Book Title:
    <%= myBook.getTitle() %>
  </body>
</html>
```

4. Restart Tomcat and open **bookPage2.jsp** in your browser. You should see the same
page as that produced by the first example:

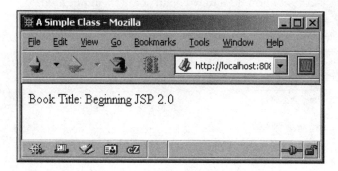

Although scriptlets are generally frowned upon, they are useful in certain situations. Most web applications produce different output based on runtime conditions, such as the state of a bean, and scripting elements can be used to control which parts of the JSP page are sent to the browser depending on the conditions. However, it is preferable to wrap up any such code in a custom tag rather than placing it directly in the JSP page. We look at custom tags in detail in Chapter 9.

In this example, we cannot use the Book class as a JavaBean because JavaBeans may only use the empty constructor, so instead we must resort to scriptlets to create and use our Book object. We can then use our Book constructor to provide the book title on creation.

We then use a standard scriptlet expression to return the title, to verify that our constructor has indeed worked as planned:

```
<%= myBook.getTitle() %>
```

Inheritance

The classes that we've looked at here have been rather simple to say the least. In the real world of production software, creating a new class is a long process that can take a lot of time and effort, not only in creating it, but in testing it. So, if a class already exists that is close to what is needed, it may be possible to **extend** that class to produce a new class with the extra functionality required. This will often take far less effort than building a whole new class from the ground up, particularly as the existing class should already have been thoroughly tested.

This is the idea behind **inheritance**, and it also makes code more maintainable, as changes made to an existing class are reflected in any classes that inherit from it. In this section, we'll look at how to extend an existing class to create a new class.

In Java, the existing class is often called the **superclass** and the new class is the **subclass**. The subclass inherits all the members of the superclass, including private and public variables and methods. In use, the new class acts just as any other class, as if it has been written from scratch.

We can illustrate inheritance in our book class, by extending it to create two new classes, one to represent a children's book, and another for technical books. Each type of book has much in common, and we'll keep what is common in the generic Book class. We'll extend that class to add functionality for each of the two book types that is not shared by other. This functionality will be:

❑ For children's books, we need to store the recommended minimum age for the reader.

❑ For the technical book, we need to record a recommended skill level, for example "beginner".

Let's see how this is done in code. We'll start with the ChildrenBook class:

```java
package booklibrary;

public class ChildrenBook extends Book
{

  private int minimumAge;

  public int getMinimumAge()
  {
    return minimumAge;
  }

  public void setMinimumAge(int newAge)
  {
    this.minimumAge = newAge;
  }

}
```

And here's the code for TechnicalBook:

```java
package booklibrary;

public class TechnicalBook extends Book
{

  private String skillLevel;

  public String getSkillLevel()
  {
    return skillLevel;
  }

  public void setSkillLevel(String newLevel)
  {
    this.skillLevel = newLevel;
  }

}
```

Notice the extends keyword that appears in the first line of the class definition which tells the Java compiler that these classes inherit from an existing class called Book. Other than that, the two classes are defined in exactly the same manner as any other class.

There are a couple of pitfalls to be aware of when using inheritance:

❑ When a subclass inherits a superclass, it cannot access any of its private methods or variables; like a parent's bankbook, these are off-limits to children.

❑   Java does not allow a subclass to directly inherit from more than one superclass at once. For instance, say we also had a class called Hardback, we couldn't then inherit from both Hardback *and* Book to create our TechnicalBook class. However, Hardback could inherit from Book, and we could then inherit from Hardback to have that effect.

Constructors are not inherited although the subclass can call public and protected level constructors of a superclass, through use of the super() method. This method invokes the superclass constructor that has a matching signature. We'll come back to investigate the meaning of the protected keyword later in the chapter, in the section headed *Access Modifiers*.

For example, we can create a constructor for our TechnicalBook class that takes the title of the book using super() to call the Book constructor as follows:

```
public TechnicalBook(String title)
{
   super(title);
}
```

Let's see how inheritance works in practice.

Try It Out   Inheriting from Book

1. First create a file called ChildrenBook.java in the same folder as Book.java. Enter the following code:

```
package booklibrary;

public class ChildrenBook extends Book
{

   private int minimumAge;

   public int getMinimumAge()
   {
      return this.minimumAge;
   }

   public void setMinimumAge(int a)
   {
      this.minimumAge = a;
   }

   public ChildrenBook(String title)
   {
      super(title);
   }
}
```

2. Then create the second class in another file, called `TechnicalBook.java`:

```java
package booklibrary;

public class TechnicalBook extends Book
{

   private String skillLevel;

   public String getSkillLevel()
   {
     return this.skillLevel;
   }

   public void setSkillLevel(String s)
   {
     this.skillLevel = s;
   }

   public TechnicalBook(String title)
   {
     super(title);
   }

}
```

3. Open a command prompt and change to the `classes` directory. Run the following commands to compile our two new classes:

> **javac booklibrary\TechnicalBook.java**
> **javac booklibrary\ChildrenBook.java**

4. Now we need a JSP page to demonstrate these derived classes. Enter the code below in a file called `bookPage3.jsp` in the `Objects` directory:

```jsp
<%@ page import="booklibrary.*" %>

<html>
  <head>
    <title>Inheritance</title>
  </head>

  <body>
    <%
      TechnicalBook techBook = new TechnicalBook("Car Mechanics");
      ChildrenBook childBook = new ChildrenBook("The Three Bears");
    %>

    Technical Book Title: <%= techBook.getTitle() %>
    <br />
```

```
      Childrens Book Title: <%= childBook.getTitle() %>

  </body>
</html>
```

5. Now we're all set, so restart Tomcat, and point your browser at
localhost:8080/Objects/bookPage3.jsp. You should see something like this:

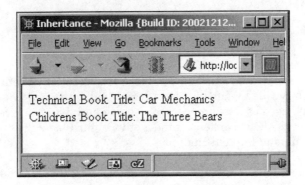

How It Works

Both the `ChildrenBook` and `TechnicalBook` classes inherit from our `Book` class using the
`extends` keyword, and they both also have a constructor, which calls the corresponding
constructor in the superclass using the `super()` method.

As before, our JSP page uses scriptlets to create instances of both `ChildrenBook` and
`TechnicalBook` using the constructor that takes the title of the book as its only argument:

```
<%
   TechnicalBook techBook = new TechnicalBook("Car Mechanics");
   ChildrenBook childBook = new ChildrenBook("The Three Bears");
%>
```

The titles of the book are then retrieved using the `getTitle()` method that `ChildrenBook`
and `TechnicalBook` inherit from `Book`:

```
Technical Book Title: <%= techBook.getTitle() %>
<br />
Childrens Book Title: <%= childBook.getTitle() %>
```

So now you should have a good idea of how to create and use classes that inherit from another
class. You may be surprised to discover that you have already been doing this every time you
created a class – all classes can trace their lineage through to the `Object` class.

The Object Class

All classes, including the `Book`, `TechnicalBook`, and `ChildrenBook` classes you created earlier, extend the `java.lang.Object` class implicitly through `Book`. In other words, when you create a class like this:

```
public class Book
```

the compiler understands it as:

```
public class Book extends Object
```

Inheriting from the `Object` class means that all our own classes have automatic access to the eleven methods exposed by `Object`. Some of these are potentially useful, such as `equals()`, `finalize()` (which is called when the object is finished with), and `toString()`. Although all these methods can be used as they are, generally we would define our versions of any that might be useful in a class. Our versions of the methods must have the same signature, and are said to **override** the default implementation.

Note that if we create a class that inherits from another class that overrides any of these methods, our class will inherit the overriding method. When that method is then executed, it is the overridden version that determines what happens, not the default. We'll look at overriding in more detail shortly.

The most useful of these, or at least the most commonly used, are `toString()` and `equals()`. These have `public` accessibility.

toString()

The `toString()` method returns a string representation of an object.

The string that the default `toString()` method returns contains the type of the object followed by a `@` character and a number (in hexadecimal). This number is the object's hash code. For instance, if we were to add the following at the end of `bookPage3.jsp`:

```
        .
        .
        .
        Children's Book Title: <%= childBook.getTitle() %>
        <br/>toString() for Children's Book: <%= childBook.toString() %>

    </body>
</html>
```

we'd see the `toString()` value on our page, like so:

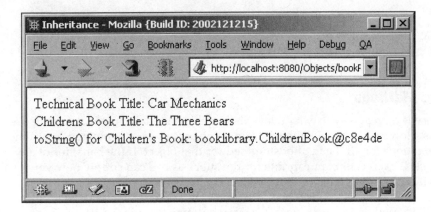

This is rarely useful, and we would usually override it in any classes where we wish to use it.

equals()

Calling the `equals()` method on an object compares the object with the object passed as an argument. If they are the same (not just equal – they must be one and the same object), it returns `true`, otherwise it returns `false`. However, as with `toString()`, classes generally define their own particular ways of determining equality.

This is different to the == operator, as when this operator is used on two object references, it will return `true` only if both references are to the same object. There is a problem with using == with strings, due to the fact that Java saves program memory space by maintaining a pool of unique string objects. In other words, if a program uses the string literal "Yes" in ten different places, only one unique string will actually be created.

Using the comparison operator to compare such strings appears to work, like so:

```
String affirmative = "Yes";
String reply = "Yes";
if (reply == affirmative)    // this condition will evaluate to true
{
```

However the following slight variation causes the creation of separate string objects, and the comparison won't give the result we might be expecting:

```
String affirmative = "Yes";
String reply = new String("Yes");
if (reply == affirmative)    // this condition will evaluate to false
{
```

Thus, when comparing strings, use the `equals()` method (as with object references), and you'll always get the expected behavior:

```
String affirmative = "Yes";
String reply = new String("Yes");
if (reply.equals(affirmative)) // this condition will evaluate to true
{
```

Overriding Methods

Inheritance is a great way to extend an existing object to make its functionality useful in new situations. However, when we inherit from an object, we are not obliged to use the implementations for all the methods defined for that object. If the behavior of any methods of the superclass class is not appropriate for the subclass, we can supply new versions of those methods by **overriding** them in the subclass.

To override a method in a new class, we simply define the method using the same name, argument list, and return type of the original, and provide the new implementation that should apply for our new class. If we don't use the same argument list and return type as the original, we are in fact creating a overloaded version of the method and not an overridden one.

> Note that we can prevent classes that inherit from our classes from overriding any particular method by declaring such methods with the `final` keyword.

To illustrate overriding, we'll override the `toString()` method that the `TechnicalBook` class inherits from `Object`. We will not override it in `ChildrenBook` in order to show the difference.

Try It Out   Overriding the toString() Method

1. Add the following method to `TechnicalBook.java`:

```
package booklibrary;

public class TechnicalBook extends Book
{

  private String skillLevel;

  public String getSkillLevel()
  {
    return skillLevel;
  }

  public void setSkillLevel(String s)
  {
    skillLevel = s;
  }
```

```
   public String toString()
   {
     return getTitle();
   }

   public TechnicalBook(String title)
   {
     super(title);
   }

}
```

2. Now recompile this class from the command prompt as before.

3. Create the following JSP page in the `Objects` directory as `bookPage4.jsp`:

```jsp
<%@ page import="booklibrary.*" %>

<html>
  <head>
    <title>Inheritance</title>
  </head>

  <body>
    <%
      TechnicalBook techBook = new TechnicalBook("Car Mechanics");
      ChildrenBook childBook = new ChildrenBook("The Three Bears");
    %>

    TechnicalBook toString(): <%= techBook.toString() %>
    <br />
    ChildrenBook toString(): <%= childBook.toString() %>

  </body>
</html>
```

4. Start Tomcat and open this page in your browser. You should see something like this:

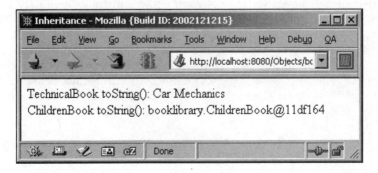

You won't see exactly the same output for the `toString()` method called on the `ChildrenBook` class: the hash value is likely to be different on different systems.

How It Works

By overriding the `toString()` method in the `TechnicalBook` class, this method will now return the book title, which is more meaningful than what we get by default.

We didn't have to do anything special when creating the new `toString()` method; we simply wrote it as we would a normal method. The compiler recognizes that it overrides the inherited method and acts accordingly.

What Can You Override?

When you override a method in a subclass, the signature (method name and parameter list) must be identical to the signature of the method in the superclass. Further restrictions on overriding are the following:

❑ Exceptions thrown – any exceptions declared must be of the same class as those thrown by the superclass, or a subclass of such exceptions.

❑ Return type – the subclass method must have the same return type as the superclass method.

❑ Access modifiers – the overriding method can't be declared with more restrictive access than the superclass method. We look at access modifiers in detail in the next section.

❑ Final methods – methods declared `final` can't be overridden.

❑ Private methods – methods declared `private` can't be overridden simply because they are not visible outside the class. The subclass can declare a method with the same name, but this isn't strictly speaking overriding.

Access Modifiers

Access modifiers are keywords that are used when a class, method, or variable is defined, and indicate where the item in question may be used – they control its **visibility**, or scope. While a class may contain many methods and properties, not all of them will be useful to a consumer of that class and some may even be harmful.

There are four levels of protection that we can apply to restrict access to class members: `public`, `private`, `protected`, and `package`. `package` protection is the default when no modifiers are specified. Methods and properties with `package` protection are only visible to other classes in the same package, but not outside that package.

We've already used the `public` modifier, to allow access from any class, and `private`, to restrict access to the class where the member is defined. The `protected` modifier is sort of a halfway house between `private` and `public`, and it makes a member available to any class within the same package, and also available within any subclass even if outside the current package. `protected` means we can create members that are not visible to users of a class (that is, programmers), but which may be used or overridden by derived classes.

The table below sums up the effects of the access modifiers.

Visibility	`public`	`protected`	`private`	`package`
From the same class	Yes	Yes	Yes	Yes
From any class in the same package	Yes	Yes	No	Yes
From any class outside the package	Yes	No	No	No
From a subclass in the same package	Yes	Yes	No	Yes
From a subclass outside the same package	Yes	Yes	No	No

Abstract Classes

Abstract classes are classes whose sole purpose is to provide necessary information for subclasses. Abstract classes cannot be instantiated directly – they may only be inherited from.

Often, we create a hierarchy of classes that will work together to solve a particular programming problem. Abstract classes can be an essential part of such hierarchies, providing a template that classes that inherit from them can copy, in order to fit in with the overall hierarchy.

Abstract classes can contain anything a normal class can contain. In addition, abstract classes can contain **abstract methods**. These are methods that have signatures (a name, access modifier, parameter list, and return type), but no implementation. Subclasses of the abstract class must then provide the actual implementation, in the same way as they might override non-abstract, or **concrete**, inherited methods.

In our example, now that we have the `ChildrenBook` and `TechnicalBook` subclasses, we don't really need to create instances of `Book` (assuming that our library only contains children's books and technical books). So, we can make our `Book` class abstract by adding the `abstract` keyword:

```
public abstract class Book {
```

And voilà, `Book` can no longer be instantiated. Its subclasses can still be instantiated, which is of course the whole idea. Let's also add an abstract method called `getType()`:

```
package booklibrary;

public abstract class Book
{

  private String title;

  public String getTitle()
  {
    return title;
  }

  public void setTitle(String newTitle)
  {
    this.title = newTitle;
  }

  public abstract String getType();

  public Book(String title)
  {
    this.title = title;
  }

}
```

When you derive a class from an abstract base class, you need to define all the abstract methods in the subclass. If you don't, then the subclass will also be abstract and must be declared as such (with the `abstract` keyword). You will of course be unable to instantiate such a subclass.

Abstract classes and methods provide a mechanism for combining code that is common to multiple objects into a single parent class, even where subclasses must differ in their implementation of other methods. Although we can no longer create an instance of the `Book` class, we can still declare a variable to be of type `Book`. This can very useful, as we shall see in the next section.

Casting Objects

Casting is the process of converting one type to another and is essential for many expressions where multiple types are used together. For example:

```
long longNumber = 0x100000024L;
int littleNumber = 3;
int c = littleNumber + (int)longNumber;
```

Here, a variable of type `long` is cast to a variable of type `int` as it is used in a calculation where the result is assigned to another integer variable (c).

The issue at stake is that of **assignment compatibility** – when assigning a value to a variable, it must be of a compatible type. There is also the risk of **truncation** when casting from a type with a greater range of possible values (such as `long` above) to one with a smaller range (such as `int`). The `long` type holds integers using a total of 64 bits, while `int` uses just 32 bits. Hence, we could try to cast a `long` that is too large to be stored in `int`, in which case the `long` number will be truncated – that is, it will be corrupted and its true value lost.

When we're dealing with objects, or rather references to an object, things are perhaps a little more straightforward than with primitives. The reference to an object of a given class can be assigned to:

❑   Any reference variable of the same type.

❑   Any reference variable for the superclass of the object's class.

❑   Any reference variable for the interface implemented by the object's class.

❑   Any reference variable for an interface implemented by a superclass of the object's class.

Such assignments do not require the use of a cast operator. Also, we can assign a reference to any object to a reference variable of type `Object`, because the `Object` class is a superclass of every other class.

Assignments of references other than those listed above require the use of a cast operator to explicitly change the type of the reference. However, it is not possible to convert the type of a reference in all cases. Generally, a cast can only be performed when both reference types are for classes that belong to the same 'ancestral line' of a class or interface hierarchy.

When we cast a superclass reference to a subclass, we often refer to it as a **downcast**. Casting the other way, from a subclass to a superclass, is automatic, and doesn't require a cast operator. For example, we can assign a `TechnicalBook` object to a `Book` object without an explicit cast, as the `Book` class is the superclass of `TechnicalBook`:

```
TechnicalBook techBook = new TechnicalBook();
Book anyBook = techBook;
```

We can store instances of any subclass in variables of type `Book`:

```
Book anyBook = new TechnicalBook();
anyBook = new ChildrenBook();
```

195

When to Cast Objects

You can cast objects upwards and downwards through a class hierarchy. We've seen how and why you would cast upwards, for example casting a `TechnicalBook` object to a `Book`, so let's now look at when you might cast downwards.

Say we have some `TechnicalBook` and `ChildrenBook` objects held in variables of type `Book`. We would then be unable to call methods specific to the `TechnicalBook` and `ChildrenBook` classes, such as `getMinimumAge()` and `getSkillLevel()`. To call such methods, we would have to cast the `Book` object reference *downwards* to the appropriate subclass:

```
ChildrenBook childBook = (ChildrenBook)bk;
childBook.getMinimumAge();
```

We can avoid using the interim variable `childBook`, and rewrite this in a single line:

```
((ChildrenBook)bk).getMinimumAge();
```

However, you should try to avoid explicitly casting objects like this as it increases the potential for an invalid cast, in which case an error will occur. If you do find that you are explicitly casting objects often, it might be worth thinking about redesigning your classes.

Let's now put some of this theory into practice in an example.

Try It Out — Abstract Methods

1. First of all, make sure you've made the changes to the `Book` class as highlighted in the *Abstract Classes* section.

2. Next, add an implementation for the `getType()` method to the `TechnicalBook` class:

```
package books;

public class TechnicalBook extends Book
{
    .
    .
    .
    public String getType()
    {
      return "TECHNICAL";
    }
    .
    .
    .
}
```

3. Add a similar method to `ChildrenBook`:

```
public String getType() {
  return "CHILDREN";
}
```

4. Now open a command prompt, and navigate to the `classes` folder, and compile all three classes as before. Make sure to compile `Book.java` first.

5. Finally, create a file called `bookPage5.jsp` in the `Objects` folder, and insert the code shown below:

```
<%@ page import="booklibrary.*" %>

<html>
  <head>
    <title>Inheritance</title>
  </head>

  <body>
    <%
      Book techBook = new TechnicalBook("Car Mechanics");
      Book childBook = new ChildrenBook("The Three Bears");
    %>

    TechnicalBook Type: <%= techBook.getType() %>
    <br />
    ChildrenBook Type: <%= childBook.getType() %>

  </body>
</html>
```

6. Start Tomcat and navigate to http://localhost:8080/begjsp-ch06/bookPage5.jsp. You should see something like this:

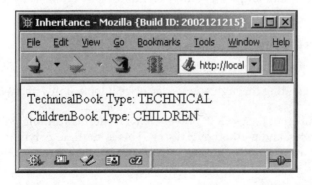

Both the instance of `TechnicalBook` and `ChildrenBook` are stored in a variable of type `Book`:

```
<%
  Book techBook = new TechnicalBook("Car Mechanics");
  Book childBook = new ChildrenBook("The Three Bears");
%>
```

When we call the `getType()` method the output is different for `techBook` and `childBook`:

```
TechnicalBook Type: <%= techBook.getType() %>
<br />
ChildrenBook Type: <%= childBook.getType() %>
```

This shows that even though the objects were stored in a variable of type `Book`, the compiler remembers what the real type of the object is.

Using methods in this way is known as **polymorphism**.

Polymorphism

Polymorphism, from the Greek *poly* meaning many and *morph* meaning shape, refers to the ability of a variable of a certain type to reference other objects of multiple types, and to automatically call methods specific to the type currently referenced.

In other words, we can define a superclass, such as `shape`, and derive several subclasses from it, say `square`, `triangle`, and `circle`. Each derived type can define a method with the same name but a different implementation, such as `area()`. We could then use a single reference variable of type `shape` to refer to any of the derived types, and if we then call the `area()` method, we will get a result appropriate to the subclass currently referenced.

From a practical programming viewpoint, polymorphism manifests itself in three distinct forms in Java:

❑   Method overloading

❑   Method overriding through inheritance

❑   Method overriding through an interface (we'll look at interfaces in the next section)

You will see that much of Java's OOP power stems from this runtime polymorphism using class inheritance, interfaces, and method overriding. This is runtime polymorphism because it is not known until the code is actually running which subclass a superclass reference holds. Runtime polymorphism is also referred to as **late binding**.

Interfaces

All of this talk of abstract classes leads into another mechanism of object oriented programming: **interfaces**. In Java, interfaces are similar to abstract classes but with the following three important differences:

- ❑ An abstract class can define an implementation for some or even all of its methods, but an interface cannot. It is like an abstract class that has *all* its methods declared abstract.

- ❑ A subclass can only descend directly from one superclass, but an object can implement multiple interfaces at once.

- ❑ Members (methods or properties) declared using the `final` keyword may not be overridden.

An interface is essentially a collection of constants and abstract methods. A class that derives from an interface is said to **implement** that interface, and the `implements` keyword replaces `extends`. When a class implements an interface it can be thought of making a contract to implement all the constants and methods defined in the interface and inherited by it. The only way it can avoid having to implement all these, is if it is declared abstract.

Choosing Between Interfaces and Abstract Classes

While there are situations where interfaces are the only way to achieve a certain effect, there are many situations where either an interface or an abstract class would be appropriate.

In general, go for an abstract class when it would be logical to provide some predefined functionality, and subclasses will function as extended versions of the superclass.

Conversely, when it doesn't make any sense to provide any implementation details, or when the subclasses may need to function as radically different objects, you should use an interface.

Static Members

Let's now round up our discussion with a look at **static members**. These members of a class are available across all instances of a class. If a class has a static property, declared with the `static` keyword, every instance of that class will see the same copy of the property. That is, if one instance sets the static property to five say, all other instances would immediately see its value as being five.

Additionally, static members can be used before a class is instantiated and they can be accessed, or invoked, either by using the class name or through an object reference.

In general, static variables should also be declared `final`, as there are very few situations where it would be desirable to allow a static variable to be overridden. (One appropriate use might be to count the number of objects instantiated from a specific class.)

Static methods should generally only be used for actions that have no requirement to remember anything from one invocation to the next. The method should also ideally be **self-contained**, that is all information that it needs to do its job should come either from incoming parameters or from other static properties. A static method only has access to other static members of the class – it cannot use instance variables defined in the class.

Although this book is about JavaServer Pages, standalone Java applications are often useful for testing classes and so we'll now cover the special static method, main().

The main() Method

Every standalone Java application must contain a single method called main() that constitutes the **entry point** for the application – that is, it is the first method called when the application is run.

The main() method must always have the following signature:

```
public static void main(String[] args)
```

It has to be public and static so that it can be called from outside the class without the class having to be instantiated, and it may not return a value, hence it is declared void. It always has an array of String objects as its only parameter. This array contains any arguments passed to the program on the command line.

Try It Out   A Standalone Java Application

1. Open your text editor and enter the following code in a file called BookApp.java:

```
public class BookApp
{

  private String title;

  public String getTitle()
  {
    return title;
  }

  public void setTitle(String newTitle)
  {
    this.title = newTitle;
  }

  public static void main(String[] args)
  {
    BookApp myBook = new BookApp();
    myBook.setTitle("Beginning JSP 2.0");
```

```
        System.out.println(myBook.getTitle());
    }

}
```

2. Compile the class with the following command:

   > javac BookApp.java

3. Now run the Java application with this command:

   > java BookApp

   You should see the following output:

   Beginning JSP 2.0

How It Works

The `BookApp` class contains a static method called `main()`, so we can run it using the java interpreter on the command line.

When we do, the `main()` method creates an instance of the `BookApp` class and sets the title in just the same way that we've already seen in the code run from our JSP pages.

Finally we print out the title of the book using the `println()` method:

```
        System.out.println(myBook.getTitle());
```

Summary

As an object oriented language, Java has many built-in features that encourage and facilitate code reuse. This chapter has introduced the essential principles of OO design to enable you to confidently use classes and objects in your JSP development.

Here is a summary of the key points that you should take away with you:

❏ Access modifiers (`package`, `public`, `protected`, and `private`) control which members of an object are visible and accessible and which are hidden. Hiding an object's members makes future changes to the class's internal behavior possible, as well as simplifying use of those classes.

❏ Constructors can be provided to initialize objects on creation.

❑ Method overloading lets us define multiple methods with the same name and return type, but different parameters.

❑ Inheritance permits us to create hierarchies of classes. A superclass is subclassed by another class that inherits all its functionality and may add some of its own. Subclasses may also override the functionality of methods defined in the superclass. In Java, a class may directly inherit from one superclass only.

❑ An abstract class cannot itself be instantiated, but a subclasses that inherits from it may be, as long as the subclass implements all the abstract methods defined by the abstract class. Abstract classes are mostly useful for housing code that is used by more than one other class but when certain methods must be implemented differently in each subclass.

❑ Interfaces provide no functionality, and simply define methods that an implementing class must provide. A subclass may implement (inherit) multiple interfaces.

❑ Static methods are shared amongst all instances of a class, and can be accessed without instantiating the containing class.

❑ The special static method, `main()`, is used by the Java runtime to determine the entry point for standalone applications.

You can find further coverage of objects in *Beginning Java 2* (ISBN 1-86100-569-5) and *Beginning Java Objects* (ISBN 1-86100-417-6), both by Wrox Press.

Why Not Try?

❑ Create a standalone Java application to illustrate the issues with the comparison operator when used with strings, which we looked at earlier in this chapter.

You may also wish to try casting a `long` to an `int`. See what happens if the `long` variable contains a number outside the range supported by `int` (such as 3 000 000 000).

❑ Derive a new class from `Book` called `Novel`. The new class should have a way of storing the category of novel as a string, such as Horror, Romance, and so on. Create or modify a JSP page to demonstrate the new class.

CHAPTER 7

Utility Classes and the Expression Language

Cast your mind back to Chapter 5, and recall the concept of an array that we introduced and discussed at some length. As you now know, arrays are useful for storing multiple objects into a single object. This aggregation of objects makes tasks simple that would otherwise be rather cumbersome, such as passing multiple objects to another method or performing the same task on multiple objects.

However, there are a couple of areas where arrays fall flat on their face:

❑ Capacity – Arrays are not resizable; once you create an array that can store 10 elements, it can never be changed to hold more or less.

❑ Indexing – The only way to retrieve data from an array is by knowing the position of the element in the array that you want to extract.

Fortunately, we don't have to live with either of these limitations. The Java class library contains numerous **utility classes** which are designed to supplement the capabilities of the core Java language. Among these utility classes is the **collections framework**, which provides solutions to both of these limitations.

There are a few other utility classes, unrelated to arrays or collections, which are quite handy. Since we are already discussing utility classes in this chapter, we will also cover them here. These are the `Date` and `Calendar` classes. Anytime you deal with dates or times, you will want to be aware of these classes and their features.

We will finish the chapter by covering in detail the Expression Language (EL) that we have mentioned so frequently earlier in this book. The EL has special features that make using the collections framework in JavaServer Pages very easy, and so it is quite fitting that we discuss those features, as well as others, in this chapter.

Introducing Collections

A **collection** is simply an object that represents a group of other objects. To allow any collection to be manipulated by a class, regardless of the details of the collection itself, Java also includes a standard architecture for all classes that manipulate collections: this is known as the **collections framework**.

The collections framework provides us with a well-designed collection of interfaces, which classify the different types of collections:

❑   Sets (implemented by the interface `java.util.Set`)

❑   Lists (implemented by the interface `java.util.List`)

❑   Maps (implemented by interface `java.util.Map`)

The framework also provides us with a set of classes that implement the above interfaces, and allow us to manipulate the collections. These are the classes that you will use in your program; however it makes good sense to start with a discussion of the three types of collection.

Sets

A set is probably the simplest collection of all. It is simply a group of objects collected together, without regard to order. In other words, a set consisting of `{object1, object2, object3, object4}` is exactly the same as a set consisting of `{object3, object2, object4, object1}`, and any other variations on this theme. However, since there is no order to the objects, each object added to a set must be unique, or we would not be able to tell between objects inside the set.

You should note that there are variations on the basic set described above; for example, some sets may be ordered.

Lists

The list collection type differs from the set in two important ways. First, unlike the set, the order of the objects is important in a list. The list is therefore what is called an **ordered collection**. Second, while the set cannot contain duplicate objects, in a list the elements do not need to be unique. As a side effect of maintaining the order of objects, we can also select the position at which we add new objects to the list.

Actually, we could say that an **array** is a fixed list, because it has all of the properties described above, except that once we have defined it we cannot add new elements to it, so its size is fixed. Ordinary lists on the other hand are free to expand (and decrease) in size. Like arrays, we can reference a particular object within a list using its index value.

Here's an example of a list of employee names:

Employee Name	Index Value
Ernest	0
John	1
Algernon	2
Ernest	3

Let's say that you wanted to add another employee, Gwendolyn, to this list. If we do not specify an index of where we want to insert a new element, it will be added by default at the end of the list. However, if we specify that we want to add the name Gwendolyn to the second position (index = 1), the list becomes:

Employee Name	Index Value
Ernest	0
Gwendolyn	1
John	2
Algernon	3
Ernest	4

Notice how the index values of all of the names occurring in the list after Gwendolyn have changed. When we used arrays, the value of a particular element did not change unless we manipulated the value of the element directly. With lists, however, adding or removing objects from the list can also affect the values held by other objects. This is a consequence of the ability of lists to fluctuate in size.

Other types of lists include **stacks** and **queues**. Stacks are lists in which new objects are always added or removed from the end of the list (a "last in, first out" mechanism). Queues are "first in, first out" – new objects are added to the end of the list, while objects to be removed from the list are always taken from the start of the list.

Maps

In a map collection, objects are stored in pairs. One of the objects in the pair contains the information we wish to store in the collection, and the other object is a called a **key**. The value of the key uniquely identifies the pair, much as the index of an array element uniquely identifies the element. Unlike an index however, a key does not need to be an integer; it can be any type of object. Obviously, since the key is used to identify an object pair within the map collection, there cannot be duplicate key values in the map.

This means that when we wish to retrieve the information stored in an object pair, we locate the pair by looking up the appropriate key value. This becomes clearer when we use an example. Consider the employee directory shown below:

Employee ID	Employee Name
1001	Ernest
2003	Algernon
3000	John

Every employee has a unique employee ID. It would be most convenient if we could get the employee name if we know the employee ID – in this case we want to use the employee ID as the key. So, if we know the key, we can also retrieve the employee information associated with the object pair.

Collection Classes

In the previous section you were introduced to three collection interfaces:

- ❏ java.util.Set
- ❏ java.util.List
- ❏ java.util.Map

These interfaces define methods that are appropriate for working with each of these types of collections. However, if you recall your lesson on interfaces from the previous chapter, you'll know that you can't actually instantiate (that is, use) an interface. Instead, you must instantiate an object that implements the interface.

Unfortunately, you're going to need to write your own classes that implement these interfaces. It'll be hard, but we know you're up to the challenge. The Java collections framework comes complete with a group of different classes that implement these interfaces. A partial listing of these classes follows:

Interface	Implementation Classes
Set	HashSet, LinkedHashSet, TreeSet
List	ArrayList, LinkedList
Map	HashMap, TreeMap, LinkedHashMap, WeakHashMap

So, with all of these options, which implementation classes are you going to want to use for your application? Ah, the beauty of the collections framework: each of these classes has slightly different features and performance characteristics, but they all conform to their parent interface. Thus, you can pick and choose the implementation you want, but interact with it the same as with any other implementation.

If the above explanation didn't make any sense to you, perhaps the following example will. Let's say we want to make use of a List in a JavaBean we're writing. We can use the List via the following manner:

```
List myList = new ArrayList();
myList.add(someVariable);
```

However, let us further suppose that we don't know how big the List needs to be – it can either contain 5 elements or 5000 elements. Well, it turns out that the ArrayList class isn't very efficient in these situations. While the ArrayList is perfectly capable of expanding its size automatically, it takes time and resources to do so. The other List implementation class, LinkedList, is designed to expand very efficiently – it takes almost no time and few resources to expand. With the collections framework, changing our List from an ArrayList to a LinkedList is as easy as changing one line:

```
List myList = new LinkedList();
```

This is what is meant by the statement that the collections framework lets you swap implementation classes. As long as the class implements the proper interface (Set, List, or Map) you can change a single line of code to use the alternate implementation.

Implementation Classes at a Glance

Now that we've explained why there are multiple implementation classes for each collection interface, let us consider the virtues of each of these implementation classes:

Type	Class	Description
List	ArrayList	Uses an array as its underlying storage. While an array by itself cannot be expanded, when the underlying array becomes full, this class will create a new larger array and copy the old array into the new array. This class is known for being fast at finding items in the list, but slow at expanding its size.
List	LinkedList	A collection of items where each points to the next and previous items in the list. This means that the LinkedList has no penalty for dynamically expanding, but it is slower at finding items.
Map	HashMap	General purpose implementation of Map. Once objects are stored in a HashMap, the order in which they were stored is lost. Performance is very good.
Map	LinkedHashMap	Extends HashMap to preserve the order in which objects are stored in the HashMap. Still performs very well.
Map	WeakHashMap	Modifies the behavior of HashMap such that it automatically removes items from itself that are no longer being used by other components of your application. Performance is only slightly poorer than HashMap.
Map	TreeMap	An alternate Map that sorts its items accordingly to a specific order (you will learn about sorting later in this chapter). Its performance is not as good as that of the HashMap.
Set	HashSet	The basic implementation of Set. The order in which items are added to the Set is not preserved.
Set	LinkedHashSet	Extends HashSet to preserve the order in which items are added.
Set	TreeSet	Like TreeMap, this Set will sort its contents according to specific order. As with TreeMap, TreeSet is outperformed by HashSet.

You may choose the implementation class for the collection you'll be using depending on your application's requirements. In the case where multiple classes will do, you should choose the class that is likely to give you the best performance.

One final comment before we move on. Whenever you use any of the collection classes in your application, you must **import** that class. For example, to use the List interface and the ArrayList implementation class, you must add the following two lines to the top of your source code:

```
import java.util.List;
import java.util.ArrayList;
```

If this strikes you as tedious, you can simply import every class in the collections framework (and quite a few other classes too) with this line:

```
import java.util.*;
```

This latter example is considered stylistically inferior to the former example, as it makes it ambiguous to others which classes you actually use in your code, but you may use it if you wish.

Using a List

We have already discussed the fixed nature of an array – the fact that it cannot fluctuate in length once it has been defined. Often though, we encounter situations where we need more flexibility than this. For example, a shopping cart at an e-commerce site may contain anything from none to dozens of items, and shoppers are welcome to purchase as many of these items as they want. They may then change their minds about their purchases and remove items from their shopping carts. Since the capacity of the collection needed to store the items is unknown and liable to change anyway, we need to be able to dynamically resize the collection as elements are added and removed. This capability is provided in Java by list collections.

Creating a List

Recall that to use a List, we must instantiate one of its implementation classes. Let's use the ArrayList (we could just as easily use the LinkedList). Here's an example:

```
List shoppingCart = new ArrayList();
```

This will create a new List object called shoppingCart. Note that we haven't defined the capacity of this collection. As we have mentioned, an ArrayList grows itself dynamically as you add elements to it. It does this by allocating an initial capacity when you create it. If you continually add elements to the ArrayList, it will fill all the space initially allocated. When this space is filled, the ArrayList, without any intervention on the part of the programmer, increases the capacity by a predetermined increment.

Alternately, you might want to specify the initial capacity of the ArrayList. In this case we can use an alternate constructor, shown below:

```
List shoppingCart = new ArrayList(10);
```

This constructor will create an `ArrayList` with the capacity to hold the (integer) number of objects between the parentheses, which is declared to be 10 here.

Size

Up to this point, we have been using the terms 'capacity' and 'size' interchangeably, to mean the number of objects that a collection can contain. However, this is not strictly true.

When any `List` is first created, it doesn't contain any objects. The technical way of saying this is that the elements of `ArrayList` do not **reference** any objects. The number of object references that `ArrayList` holds is referred to as its **size**; that is, the number of objects that it is currently holding.

The size of a `List` can be retrieved using the `size()` method:

```
int shoppingCart = shoppingCart.size();
```

This method returns an `int` value of the number of objects referenced in `shoppingCart`.

Capacity

Unlike size, **capacity** is a special property that applies only to an `ArrayList`, and not to `List` or `LinkedList`. Recall that the `ArrayList` uses an array to store its objects. This array is just the same as any regular array we might define in Java. This means that it has a fixed size, and so, if we want an `ArrayList` to store more than its array can handle, the `ArrayList` must create a new larger array and copy all of the objects from the old array into the new array. The size of this underlying array is the known as the `ArrayList`'s **capacity**.

Because capacity is a property of `ArrayList`, and not `List`s in general, it cannot be retrieved from a `List` unless the `List` is first cast to an `ArrayList` type, as shown below:

```
List list = new ArrayList();

/* we must first cast the List to an ArrayList */
ArrayList arrayList = (ArrayList) list;
int capacity = arrayList.capacity();

/* or, if we're fancy, we can do it all on one line */
int fancyCapacity = ((ArrayList) list).capacity();
```

Alternately, you could simply opt to work with an `ArrayList` instead of a `List`, as shown below:

```
ArrayList list = new ArrayList();
int capacity = list.capacity();
```

However, this is considered bad style, as your code now requires a specific implementation of a `List`, namely `ArrayList`, rather than being written to support the interface, which is `List`. This means that if at some future point you want to switch to `LinkedList` or `MyCompanysCoolCustomList`, you'll need to change a whole bunch of code.

Adding Objects To a List

To add objects to a `List`, we can use the `add()` method. Let's assume that we want to add instances of a `Product` class (representing products to buy on the e-commerce site). Then we can use the following code to add three more instances of product (`product1`, `product2`, and `product3`) to our `shoppingCart` collection:

```
shoppingCart.add(product1);
shoppingCart.add(product2);
shoppingCart.add(product3);
```

You should note that this method appends an element to the *end* of the list. We can add any Java object to a `List`. The method returns `true` if the collection has changed as a result of the call. We can use an overloaded form of the `add()` method if we want to define the position at which the new object should be added too:

```
shoppingCart.add(2, product4);
```

Here, the first argument (2) is an `int` value that defines the position of the new addition: at index 2 for our example, so `product4` will be the third object in the `shoppingCart` list.

Retrieving Elements From a List

To retrieve an object from a `List`, we first need to know the index of the object that we wish to access. Once we know the index, we can retrieve that object using the `get()` method. By default the `get()` method returns an instance of the `Object` class which is the superclass of all objects. Therefore it is necessary to **cast** this to the correct class type (in other words we change the data type). Let's see an example:

```
Product prod = (Product) shoppingCart.get(2);
```

You can see that we are retrieving the third element (index position 2, remember it is zero based) of `shoppingCart`, which we know corresponds to the `product4` instance from the previous example.

Casting

Lists store all elements as the generic `Object` type. Since we want the `get()` method to return an object of type `Product`, we must change the type from `Object` back to its actual type, `Product`. This is done by **casting** the value using the code `(Product)`. In other words, the standard way to cast any object or variable is to use:

```
(TargetClassName) GivenInstance
```

where `GivenInstance` is the object instance that we want typecast, and `TargetClassName` is the class of object we want it cast to. From the example on the previous page we can see that the object returned after the cast is then placed in the `Product` instance `prod`. Therefore `prod` and `product4` are both references to the same object.

Removing Elements From A List

To remove a particular element from a `List`, we can use the `remove()` method. Again, you will need to specify the index of the element that you want to remove:

```
shoppingCart.remove(2);
```

Here we are completely removing the third object in the `shoppingCart` list (we saw before that this was `product4`). You should note that we can discard all of the objects referenced in a `List`, using the `clear()` method:

```
shoppingCart.clear();
```

Here we are removing every object from `shoppingCart`. Obviously this method should be used with care!

We've covered quite a few methods in this section so far, so now let's try them out by creating a Java console program that uses an `ArrayList` to maintain a list of `User` objects.

Try It Out   **Using an ArrayList**

1. First, we'll create a location for this chapter's example code. In Tomcat's `webapps` folder, create a new directory called `Utility`, containing a `WEB-INF` directory.

Our Java classes will be contained in a package called `com.wrox.utilities`, so we need to create a `classes` directory in `WEB-INF`, and a sub-directory there called `com`, containing yet another with the name `wrox`, and finally a folder in there called `utilities`. It is this 'top-most' folder that will hold all Java code in the `com.wrox.utilities` package.

2. Next create a class called `User` as shown below. The `User` class defines a particular user in an organization. For this simple demonstration, let's assume that a user has only two attributes, a `username` and a `phoneNumber`. Save the following file as `User.java` in the `utilities` folder:

```
package com.wrox.utilities;

public class User
{
    String userName;
    String phoneNumber;
```

```
  public User(String userName, String phoneNumber)
  {
    this.userName = userName;
    this.phoneNumber = phoneNumber;
  }

  public void setUsername(String userName)
  {
    this.userName = userName;
  }

  public String getUsername()
  {
    return userName;
  }

  public void setPhoneNumber(String phoneNumber)
  {
    this.phoneNumber = phoneNumber;
  }

  public String getPhoneNumber()
  {
    return phoneNumber;
  }
}
```

3. Open a command prompt at the `classes` folder and compile this Java file using the following command:

> **javac com\wrox\utilities\User.java**

4. Now, let's take care of the main console program, `ListDemo.java`, that demonstrates the use of a `List`. This class should be created directly in the `classes` directory, and not the `utilities` one as it is not part of that package. However, the first line imports our package allowing us to use the classes it contains:

```
import com.wrox.utilities.*;

import java.util.List;
import java.util.ArrayList;

public class ListDemo
{
  public static void main(String[] args)
  {
    User user1 = new User("H Wyatt", "123-444-4444");
    User user2 = new User("A Brimacombe", "123-555-5555");
    User user3 = new User("K Ibidibbydodah", "123-666-6666");
```

```
    List userList = new ArrayList();
    userList.add(user1);
    userList.add(user2);
    userList.add(user3);

    User user = (User) userList.get(1);
    System.out.print("Second user: ");
    System.out.print(user.getUsername());
    System.out.println(" (" + user.getPhoneNumber() + ")");
    System.out.println("All users:");

    for (int i = 0; i < userList.size(); i++)
    {
      user = (User) userList.get(i);
      System.out.print("  " + user.getUsername());
      System.out.println(" (" + user.getPhoneNumber() + ")");
    }
  }
}
```

5. Now compile this class, again from the `classes` folder, using the following command:

> **javac ListDemo.java**

6. Now run the program using the following command:

> **java ListDemo**

You should see the following output:

```
Second user: A Brimacombe (123-555-5555)
All users:
  H Wyatt (123-444-4444)
  A Brimacombe (123-555-5555)
  K Ibidibbydodah (123-666-6666)
```

How It Works

We'll skim over the `User` class, because it is a simple bean class with two attributes (`username` and `phoneNumber`) and getter/setter accessors for these attributes.

Let's turn our attention to `ListDemo.java`. We first create the `List` and then add the `User` objects to it, as shown below:

```
    List userList = new ArrayList();
    userList.add(user1);
    userList.add(user2);
    userList.add(user3);
```

Then we retrieve the second object from the list, and print out its `User` attributes: `userName` and `phoneNumber`:

```
User user = (User) userList.get(1);
System.out.print("Second user: ");
System.out.print(user.getUsername());
System.out.println(" (" + user.getPhoneNumber() + ")");
```

Finally, we use a `for` loop to iterate through all elements in the list. To be able to set the termination expression, we need to know the number of elements in the list, so we use the `size()` method of the `List` to determine that:

```
for (int i = 0; i < userList.size(); i++)
```

Then, for each index, we use the `get()` method to retrieve the element:

```
user = (User) userList.get(i);
```

Note the correct type casting of the object returned by the `get()` method to `User`. We finish by printing the attribute values for this particular instance:

```
System.out.print("   " + user.getUsername());
System.out.println(" (" + user.getPhoneNumber() + ")");
```

Iterating Through Collections

In Chapter 5, we noted that combining loops with arrays is a useful programming tool. The same is true of using loops with collections, as we demonstrated in the example above. However, there is an easier way than using a `for` loop to iterate through a collection. Any collection object can create another object called an **iterator**, implemented in an interface, `java.util.Iterator`. The `Iterator` object has references to all of the objects in the collection, and provides easy-to-use methods that enable us to walk through the collection selecting objects from it. Let's take a look at how to use them.

If we want to use an iterator, our first step is to make sure we have imported the `java.util.Iterator` class:

```
import java.util.Iterator;
```

To retrieve an iterator, we call the `iterator()` method on the collection class. For instance, referring to the `userList` collection we created in our previous Try It Out:

```
Iterator userIter = userList.iterator();
```

This creates an `Iterator` object called `userIter` that can step through the objects in the `userList` list.

Having created an iterator, we can now use its methods. There are three:

- ❏ `next()`
- ❏ `hasNext()`
- ❏ `remove()`

The `next()` method returns the next object in the list. The first call to `next()` will retrieve the first object, the second call to `next()` the second object, and so on; the iterator keeps track of where we are in the list. The `hasNext()` method peeks forward in the list to see if we have reached the end of it (it returns `false` if we have reached the end of the list, and `true` if not). As you can imagine, these two methods are often found together in code. For example, we could change the `for` loop from our `List` Try It Out to use an `Iterator` like so:

```
        .
        .
        .
      while (userIter.hasNext())
      {
        User user = (User) userIter.next();
        System.out.print("Username: " + usr.getUsername());
        System.out.println(" (" + usr.getPhoneNumber() + ")");
      }
    }
  }
```

For each iteration, we first check if there are any more objects in the list by calling the `hasNext()` method on the iterator. If there are, then the expression evaluates to `true` and we can proceed with retrieving, and printing, the next object. You should take note that we again need to cast the object returned by the `next()` call to the correct type.

We have already seen how we can use the `remove()` method to remove a specific object from a collection, when we discussed `List`. For example:

```
  userIter.remove(2);
```

This will remove the third element from `userlist`. We can also use `remove()` without including an index value as an argument to the method:

```
  userIter.remove();
```

In this case it will remove the last object returned by `next()`, although if the `next()` method has not yet been called, or the `remove()` method has already been called for this object, we will get an error. You should note that not all iterators support this method.

You should also note that there is also a `java.util.ListIterator` interface that extends the `java.util.Iterator` interface, but allows you to traverse a collection of objects forwards or backwards, and to add objects as well as remove them. However, for simplicity's sake, we will stick to using the `Iterator` interface for this chapter.

Sorting a List

Consider the code snippet below that creates a `List` collection `names` and fills it with (unsurprisingly) with names:

```
List names = new ArrayList();
names.add("James");
names.add("Robin");
names.add("Aaron");
```

If we use an iterator now to walk through the collection and print the objects, we find we get the following output:

```
James
Robin
Aaron
```

At some point in the future we might envisage that these names would have to be sorted in alphabetical order:

```
Aaron
James
Robin
```

So, it would be useful if we had a way to sort lists. Fortunately, the collections framework provides a mechanism for sorting. A special class, `java.util.Collections`, contains a static `sort()` method. Static methods, you may recall, are methods which can be utilized without instantiating the class. The `sort` method usually sorts objects in ascending order, alphabetically or numerically. There are, however, exceptions to this rule for some classes, such as for the `Character` class (sorted numerically by Unicode value), and the `Date` class we will be meeting later in the chapter (which is sorted chronologically).

So, in order to sort the `names` list, we would use the following line of code:

```
Collections.sort(names);
```

Now we could use an iterator to print out the alphabetically sorted `names` list. First we create an iterator:

```
nameIter = names.iterator();
```

And then we use the `hasNext()` and `next()` methods of the iterator to cycle through the list. For each iteration, we print out the `String` object representing the name:

```
while (nameIter.hasNext()) {
    String s = (String) nameIter.next();
    System.out.println(s);
}
```

Remember that to do this we would also need to have imported the `java.util.Collections` and `java.util.Iterator` classes at the top of our file.

Now, there is a proviso for using the `Collections.sort()` method in this simple way. This works just fine for pre-defined simple objects that you can fill your collection with, such as `Integers`, `Floats`, and `Strings`. However, if we want to place user-defined objects in a list (like the `User` objects we defined earlier in the chapter), and then sort these, we need a little more work, because we must define how these objects should be sorted.

The Comparable Interface

To allow sorting of your own user-defined classes you will have to implement the `java.lang.Comparable` interface in your classes. The `Comparable` interface has a single method, `compareTo()`, which you will have to *implement* (that is, write) if you want to make your class sortable. This method needs to return a positive value if `object1` should come after the object passed to the method (`object2`), and a negative value if the `object2` should come first. In other words, say we have the following call to the `compareTo()` method:

```
object1.compareTo(object2);
```

If `object1` should come after `object2`, then the call should return a positive value, but if `object2` should come first, then we should get a negative value returned. If they are equal, 0 (zero) should be returned.

It is up to you to decide how to your objects should sort. A common solution is to sort user-defined object instances by the values of one or more of their attributes.

For further analysis, let's consider an example. Suppose we have a simple Java class called `Bovine`:

```
public class Bovine
{
    private String species;
    private int hoofSize;
    private String owner;
    private Boolean bull;

    // accessor methods go here
}
```

For the sake of brevity, we've left out the standard getters and setters. Part of our application involves sorting a `List` of these `Bovine` objects. But, how do you go about sorting cattle? Perhaps they could be sorted by species, hoof size, or ownership; but there's absolutely no way the Java collection's framework will possess any special knowledge to help it sort `Bovine` objects by default.

Fortunately, all we need to do is implement the `compareTo()` interface, and our `Bovine` class can be sorted using the `Collections.sort()` method. Here's how we'd change our `Bovine` class:

```
public class Bovine implements Comparable
{
  .
  .
  .
  public int compareTo(Object o)
  {
    Bovine bovine = (Bovine) o;
    if (getHoofSize() < bovine.getHoofSize())
      return -1;
    else
      if (getHoofSize() > bovine.getHoofSize()) {
        return 1;
      else
        return 0;
  }
}
```

As you can see from this code, we've decided to sort our `Bovine` classes based on the `hoofSize` attribute (alright, alright, so I wouldn't make a good farmer). However, we could have chosen any one of the other attributes, or even a combination of them. Thus, any class can implement its own custom sorting semantics.

The equals() method

While implementing the `Comparable` interface is sufficient for sorting our objects in `List` collections, it is good general practice to provide an implementation for another method: `equals`. We should also mention that you must provide an implementation of `equals` in order for your objects to function with `Set` or `Map` collections.

Recall that every class in Java implicitly inherits the `Object` class. `Object` defines several methods, one of which is `equals`. However, the `equals` method that `Object` defines is not very useful – it only checks if two objects are actually the same object, not if two objects have equivalent contents.

For `equals` to function as it should, we'll need to override it with our own implementation. Overriding a method is quite easy – all we do is create a method with the same name, parameters, and return type as a method we inherit, and our new method will be used instead.

The `equals` method itself is quite simple. It takes one argument, an `Object`, and compares the argument `Object` to itself to see if they are equal. If so, a `boolean` `true` value is returned. Otherwise, `false` is returned.

Let's see this method applied in the our `Bovine` class:

```
public class Bovine implements Comparable
{
   .
   .
   .
   public boolean equals(Object o)
   {
     if (o instanceof Bovine)
     {
       Bovine bovine = (Bovine) o;
       if (getHoofSize() == bovine.getHoofSize()) return true;
     }
     return false;
   }
}
```

We first check to see if the `Object` being passed to the method is of class `Bovine`, using the `instanceof` operator:

```
(o instanceof User)
```

This expression will return `true` if `o` is an instance of the `Bovine` class, and `false` if not. If the expression returns `true`, we then cast `o` to the `Bovine` class. We then compare the values of the `hoofSize` property, which we decided back in our `compareTo` would be our basis for comparing `Bovine` classes:

```
if (getHoofSize() == bovine.getHoofSize())
{
   return true;
}
```

Let's now use what we have learned above to sort a list of names.

Try It Out   Sorting User-Defined Objects

1. In this example, we are going to adapt the `List` Try It Out that we created earlier so that the `User` objects in the `List` can be sorted.

    Save a copy of `User.java` as `User2.java`, and make the changes highlighted below:

```
package com.wrox.utilities;

public class User2 implements Comparable
{
  String userName;
  String phoneNumber;

  public User2(String userName, String phoneNumber)
  {
    userName = userName;
    phoneNumber = phoneNumber;
  }

  public boolean equals(Object o)
  {
    if (o instanceof User2)
    {
      User2 user = (User2) o;
      if (user.getUsername().equals(this.userName)) return true;
    }
    return false;
  }

  public int compareTo(Object o)
  {
    User2 user = (User2) o;
    return (this.getUsername().compareTo(user.getUsername()));
  }

  public void setUsername(String userName)
  {
    userName = userName;
  }

  public String getUsername()
  {
    return userName;
  }

  public void setPhoneNumber(String phoneNumber)
  {
    phoneNumber = phoneNumber;
  }

  public String getPhoneNumber()
  {
    return phoneNumber;
  }
}
```

Now compile the new User2.java class.

2. Next we need to modify the `ListDemo.java` file to sort `User2` objects in the `List`. Make the changes highlighted below, and recompile this class as before.

```
import com.wrox.utilities.*;

import java.util.*;

public class ListDemo {
  public static void main(String[] args) {
    User2 user1 = new User2("H Wyatt", "123-444-4444");
    User2 user2 = new User2("A Brimacombe", "123-555-5555");
    User2 user3 = new User2("K Ibidibbydodah", "123-666-6666");

    List userList = new ArrayList();
    userList.add(user1);
    userList.add(user2);
    userList.add(user3);

    System.out.println("Before sorting:");
    iterateNames(userList);

    System.out.println("After sorting:");
    Collections.sort(userList);
    iterateNames(userList);
  }

  public static void iterateNames(List userList)
  {
    Iterator iterator = userList.iterator();
    while (iterator.hasNext())
    {
      User2 user = (User2) iterator.next();
      System.out.print("  ");
      System.out.println(user.getUsername());
    }
  }
}
```

3. Run the `ListDemo` program using the same command as before. You should see:

```
Before sorting:
  H Wyatt
  A Brimacombe
  K Ibidibbydodah
After sorting:
  A Brimacombe
  H Wyatt
  K Ibidibbydodah
```

We have sorted the names alphabetically (by first initial, mind you, but you get the drift).

How It Works

We have actually already introduced you to most of the new code in this modified version of the List example, so we won't go into it in much depth here.

First of all, we have the bean class User2.java, which now has two new methods:

```
public boolean equals(Object o)
public int compareTo(Object o)
```

We discussed the implementation of these methods in the section before this example, so we won't re-tread old ground here. Note that we also made sure that the User2 class was sortable by implementing the Comparable interface:

```
public class User2 implements Comparable
```

Let's move on to the class that actually performs the sorting, ListDemo. Here we create a List called userList and fill it with names and phone numbers, as in our earlier List example. Now what we want to do is to iterate through all of the names printing them out, sort the names, and then print them out again. Since we want to iterate and print all of the names twice during the program, it makes sense to move this functionality into a method:

```
public static void iterateNames(List userList)
{
  Iterator iterator = userList.iterator();
  while (iterator.hasNext())
  {
    User2 user = (User2) iterator.next();
    System.out.print("  ");
    System.out.println(user.getUsername());
  }
}
```

The method takes a List as argument. The code inside the method should be familiar to you: we create an iterator for the list and then use the hasNext() and next() methods to iterate through the list. We print out each username we find to the console.

In the main() method of the program we make use of this method, by calling it to iterate through the User2 objects and print names before we sort the list:

```
System.out.println("Before sorting:");
iterateNames(userList);
```

Then we sort the `userList` collection:

```
Collections.sort(userList);
```

Finally we print out the sorted list:

```
System.out.println("After sorting:");
iterateNames(userList);
```

Map Collections

At the start of this chapter, we introduced the concept of a map, as a way of storing data values with an associated key. Each key is unique, which enables us to use it to find and retrieve the data we want from the map collection quickly and efficiently. Keys can be any type of Java object. In this section, we are going to look at how to use maps.

Before we get into the methods of the `Map` class, let's throw together a scenario that we can use to demonstrate the use of a `Map` collection. In this scenario, we would like to store company employees' telephone numbers. Therefore, we want to create a key-value map in which the employee's name is the key, and the telephone number is the value we wish to retrieve. Here's a table of employees and their numbers:

Employee Name	Telephone Number
Joey	111-222-3333
Ross	444-555-6666
Chandler	777-888-9999

For our Map implementation class, we'll choose the general purpose `HashMap` class. To create a `Map` with the `HashMap` class, we'll need the following code:

```
Map employeeMap = new HashMap();
```

Here we have named our new `Map` instance `employeeMap`. Now we want to add the names and numbers to this map. To do this we need to use the `put()` method, as demonstrated below:

```
employeeMap.put("Joey", "111-222-3333");
employeeMap.put("Ross", "444-555-6666");
employeeMap.put("Chandler", "777-888-9999");
```

The `put()` method takes two arguments: the first is the object to use as the key (a `String` representing the employee name here); the second is the object which will hold the data we will want to retrieve (telephone numbers stored as `Strings` too).

So once the key-value pairs are in the map, how do we retrieve them? We use the `get()` method:

```
String phoneNum = (String) employeeMap.get("Chandler");
```

The method requires that you know the key associated with the value you wish to retrieve, because this key object must be fed into the method as an argument. Here, the key is `Chandler`. The method returns the value associated with this key, which must be cast back to a `String`.

The table below shows some other useful methods associated with `Map` that we will use in a moment:

Method	Description
`remove()`	Removes the value from the map for the key that you pass the method as argument, and returns the value that has been removed.
`size()`	Returns the number of key-value pairs in the map as an integer.
`putAll()`	Takes a map object as an argument; transfers all key-value pairs from this map object to the current map object.

You should note that we can use iterators with `Map` objects. To do this, we must first create a `Set` object which holds the keys from the key-value pairs, using the `keySet()` method and then obtain an `Iterator` from the `Set`. Let's do this for our `employeeMap` object:

```
Set keys = employeeMap.keySet();
Iterator keyIter = keys.iterator();
```

Some folks reduce this to one step using the following syntax:

```
Iterator keyIter = employeeMap.keySet().iterator();
```

Now that we have the `Iterator`, we can do some iterating using the `hasNext()` and `next()` methods we have already seen. For instance, if we wanted to print out all of the employee names and telephone numbers present in the `employeeMap` map, we could use:

```
while (keyIter.hasNext())
{
  String nextName = (String) keyIter.next();
  String phoneNum = (String) employeeMap.get(nextName);
  System.out.println(nextName + ": " + phoneNum);
}
```

As always, remember to cast objects returned from collection methods. Let's now tie all of the `Map` methods we have skimmed through so far into an example.

Try It Out   Using a Map

1. For this example, we'll create a simple standalone Java application as before, this time using our employee directory scenario to demonstrate the use of the Map class.

Save the Java code below in the classes directory in a file called MapDemo.java. As you can see, the only method this class contains is main():

```java
import java.util.*;

public class MapDemo
{
  public static void main(String[] args)
  {
    Map employeeMap = new HashMap();

    employeeMap.put("Joey", "111-222-3333");
    employeeMap.put("Ross", "444-555-6666");
    employeeMap.put("Chandler", "777-888-9999");

    Iterator keyIter = employeeMap.keySet().iterator();
    while (keyIter.hasNext())
    {
      String nextName = (String) keyIter.next();
      String phoneNum = (String) employeeMap.get(nextName);
      System.out.println(nextName + ": " + phoneNum);
    }

    employeeMap.remove("Chandler");
    System.out.println("Removed Chandler; didn't like him much anyway");

    Map newEmployeeMap = new TreeMap();
    newEmployeeMap.putAll(employeeMap);

    keyIter = newEmployeeMap.keySet().iterator();
    while (keyIter.hasNext())
    {
      String nextName = (String) keyIter.next();
      String phoneNum = (String) newEmployeeMap.get(nextName);
      System.out.println(nextName + ": " + phoneNum);
    }
  }
}
```

2. Compile the example and then run it by entering the following commands from the classes directory:

> **javac MapDemo.java**

> **java MapDemo**

Here's the output you should see:

```
Joey: 111-222-3333
Chandler: 777-888-9999
Ross: 444-555-6666
Removed Chandler; didn't like him much anyway
Joey: 111-222-3333
Ross: 444-555-6666
```

Note that the order of the first three lines will be completely random; the `HashMap` class makes no guarantees as far as the order of items are concerned. The last two lines, however, are stored in a `TreeMap` and are thus guaranteed to be displayed in an order consistent with the behavior of the `compareTo` method on the objects it contains.

How It Works

Let's walk through the class in the example. The first line of note is right at the start:

```
import java.util.*;
```

Because we'll be using a handful of classes, such as `java.util.Map`, `java.util.HashMap`, `java.util.Set` and the `java.util.Iterator` classes, we'll keep things simple and just import all the classes in the `java.util` package.

Moving inside the `MapDemo` class, we encounter a block of code that should be familiar: we create the `employeeMap` collection and then fill it using the `put()` method. We then iterate through the collection, printing out the key-value pairs. Remember that to iterate through the collection we need to make a `Set` of keys, and an iterator for this set:

```
Iterator keyIter = employeeMap.keySet().iterator();
```

After we have printed out the collection, we find out that Bill has actually recently moved to a different company. This means we must remove the corresponding number from the collection:

```
employeeMap.remove("Chandler");
System.out.println("Removed Chandler; didn't like him much anyway");
```

We use the `remove()` method with the key as an argument, to remove the number from `employeeMap`, and then we print out the number we have removed.

We finish off the example by copying all of the data present in `employeeMap` to another `Map`, `newEmployeeMap`. This new `Map` is an instance of a `TreeMap`, which means that all of the entries will be sorted on the basis of their keys. We create the new map, and then we use the `putAll()` method to copy all of the key-value pairs across from `employeeMap` to `newEmployeeMap`:

```
HashMap newEmployeeMap = new TreeMap();
newEmployeeMap.putAll(employeeMap);
```

To demonstrate that our data has been copied, we'll again print out the contents of our `Map` (because we're using a `TreeMap`, the data will automatically be sorted):

```
keyIter = newEmployeeMap.keySet().iterator();
while (keyIter.hasNext())
{
    String nextName = (String) keyIter.next();
    String phoneNum = (String) newEmployeeMap.get(nextName);
    System.out.println(nextName + ": " + phoneNum);
}
```

The hashCode Method

In order for any object to be used as a key in a `Map`, it should provide an implementation of the `hashCode()` method. The `hashCode()` method is used by `Map` to efficiently store and manage its data. Like `equals()`, `hashCode()` is defined by the `Object` class. It returns an `int` value that is used by `Map` to organize its internal data structures.

There are two hard and fast rules for the value that `hashCode` returns:

❑   `hashCode()` must be consistent with `equals()`: it must provide the same `int` result for objects that are equal (as determined by the `equals()` method)

❑   `hashCode()` must be consistent with itself: if an object hasn't changed, it should return the same value every time it is called

While the standard Java objects such as `String` or `Integer` already have an implementation of `hashCode()`, we'll need to write our own implementation for our own classes.
Let's take a look at how we would add a `hashCode()` method to our previous `Bovine` class:

```
public class Bovine implements Comparable {
    private String species;
    private int hoofSize;
    private String owner;
    private Boolean bull;

    .
    .
    .

    public int hashCode()
    {
        int hashCode = 0;
```

```
        hashCode += species.hashCode();
        hashCode += owner.hashCode();
        hashCode += (bull) ? 1 : 0;
        hashCode += hoofSize;

        return hashCode;
    }
}
```

A quick glance at this code will confirm that it meets the two rules we discussed above: two `Bovine` objects that are equal according to `equals` will return the same value from `hashCode`, and `hashCode()` will always return the same value for the same `Bovine` object as long as it hasn't changed.

We should mention that there is an additional guideline for creating a good `hashCode()` method: non-equal objects should return a unique value. This recommendation is not a requirement, but following it results in better performance from your `Map`. However, creating such a `hashCode()` method is a somewhat advanced topic. If the thought tickles your fancy, take a look at Wrox Press's *Beginning Java 2*, ISBN 1-86100-569-5, which covers the topic in some depth.

We now move on to discuss how to incorporate date and time objects into our Java code.

Date and Time Classes

Since dates and times are everyday considerations in our lives, it is inevitable that we will have to deal with them in our programs at some point. In this section, we will learn how to manipulate dates and times in our Java programs. Let's now take a look at the date/time classes which are available in the `java.util` package.

The Date Class

The `java.util.Date` class stores a date and time, with millisecond precision. To create a `Date` object, we need to use the `Date()` constructor. There are two common ways of using this constructor. The first creates a `Date` instance that holds the current date. For example, the following line will result in the creation of a `Date` instance called `currentDate`, which holds the current date:

```
Date currentDate = new Date();
```

You may be interested to know that internally, the `Date` class keeps track of the date by calculating the number of milliseconds that have passed since midnight on January 1, 1970. If we happen to know the number of milliseconds that have passed since that time for any given date, we can use `Date`'s second constructor in this manner:

```
Date myDate = new Date(992710981977);
```

Obviously this is not particularly user-friendly; it was not designed for human use. We'll come back to this issue again in a moment.

Retrieving Dates

Retrieving the date from a `Date` instance is pretty easy. Printing out the date in calendar-style format is a matter of just printing out the instance itself:

```
System.out.println("Current Date: " + currentDate);
```

This line would print:

> Current Date: Sat Jun 16 18:03:01 GMT+01:00 2001

If you can also retrieve the number of milliseconds stored in the instance using the `getTime()`:

```
System.out.println("Current Date (ms): " + currentDate.getTime());
```

Comparing Dates

We will often want to compare two dates to see which one comes first. Since the `java.util.Date` class implements the `Comparable` interface that we covered in the previous section, we can use the `compareTo()` method, as shown below, to do this:

```
myDate.compareTo(currentDate);
```

It compares the value of the invoking instance (`myDate` here) to that of the argument passed (`currentDate`). If the values are equal it returns 0. If the invoking `Date` is later than the argument `Date` passed, then it returns a positive value. If the invoking `Date` is earlier than the argument, then it returns a negative value. So, assuming that the current date is later than the value in `myDate`, this call should return a negative value.

The Calendar Class

The `Date` class really just performs one function: it represents a given moment in time. Often, however, we want to perform rather complex calculations involving dates. Consider some of the date-related problems we may wish to solve:

- ❑ Is January 10, 2030 a Monday?
- ❑ How many working days are between now and December 18, 2004?
- ❑ Which day of the week will Christmas fall on for the next ten years?

In reality, Java makes working with dates pretty simple. The key is the `java.util.Calendar` class, which is an abstract class (that is, you can't use it directly – you must use one of its subclasses) along with its implementation classes. Unlike the collections framework, you don't need to worry about choosing an implementation class. You can create a `Calendar` instance in the following way:

```
Calendar myTime = Calendar.getInstance();
```

The `Calendar.getInstance()` method figures out what part of the world you're in, and creates an appropriate `Calendar` object for you. The `getInstance()` method is static, so you don't need to have an instance of `Calendar` to use it, as shown in the example above.

The `Calendar` class defines a set of constants that make it easy for you to not only format the date stored in the `Calendar` instance, but to also retrieve specific information from the object like the month stored, the year stored, and so on. Here are examples of field constants (although there are many others):

Constant	Example Value
`Calendar.YEAR`	2001
`Calendar.MONTH`	5 (0-11, so 5 is June)
`Calendar.DATE`	16 (1-31)
`Calendar.HOUR`	6 (1-12)
`Calendar.MINUTE`	3 (0-59)
`Calendar.SECOND`	1 (0-59)
`Calendar.AM_PM`	1 (AM is 0, PM is 1)
`Calendar.DAY_OF_WEEK`	7 (1-7, 7 is Saturday)

These constants are all pretty self-explanatory (`DATE` is the day of the month), but do remember that `MONTH` goes from 0 to 11, and not 1 to 12 as you might expect. We can change the values of these constants using `get()` and `set()` methods. For example, if `myTime` is a `Calendar` instance, we can set the day of the month to the 25th like so:

```
myTime.set(Calendar.DATE, 25);
```

You can see that we must specify the field constant and the new constant value as arguments. If we check the value of `Calendar.DATE` now using `get()`:

```
System.out.println("Day of the month: " + myTime.get(Calendar.DATE));
```

We will see the following output:

Day of the month: 25

Note that we need to provide the field constant as an argument to `get()`. If we want, we can retrieve the full date using the `getTime()` method:

```
System.out.println("Date: " + Calendar.getTime());
```

Date: Mon Jun 25 18:03:01 GMT+01:00 2001

The `getTime()` method needs no arguments – notice how the day of the week has been automatically changed to match the rest of the date. The full date returned includes the weekday, the local time zone, and the time down to the second. Now, chances are that you are not going to want to display all of this information to a user, and you will want to be more selective because you have your own standard date format that you want to adhere to. So we'll now look at how Java specifies a date format for objects.

Formatting Dates

You may have noticed that the standard representation for the date and time varies from country to country. For example, the date format for the United States is:

```
MM/dd/yyyy
```

Here, `MM` is a number from 1-12 representing the month, `dd` is the day of the month, and `yyyy` is the year. For June 16th 2001, this would equate to 06/16/2001. The United Kingdom date format reverses the order of the month and day:

```
dd/MM/yyyy
```

There are lots more date/time format variations, and below are some of the most common:

Format Pattern	Examples
dd-MM-yyyy	02-06-2001
dd MMMM yyyy	02 June 2001
EEE, dd MMMM yyyy	Sat, 02 June 2001
HH:mm:ss	06:36:33
hh:mm a	06:37 AM

Notice the use of EEE to represent the weekday, a for AM/PM, and HH, mm, ss to represent hours, minutes and seconds respectively.

Java provides a class, java.text.SimpleDateFormat, that allows us to format Date objects according to user-defined patterns like these. To do this, we must feed a date format to the SimpleDateFormat() constructor, like this:

```
SimpleDateFormat dateFormat = new SimpleDateFormat("EEE, dd MMMM yyyy");
```

In this case we have created a SimpleDateFormat object called dateFormat that will change the format of a Date object to EEE, dd MMMM yyyy. So if we have a Date object called currentDate, we can change it to this new format and print it like so:

```
System.out.println("Date: " + dateFormat.format(currentDate));
```

Notice that we invoked the format() method on the dateFormat object to actually perform the formatting. The Date object we wish to format is fed into this method as an argument, and the formatted date is returned a string.

If we want to format Calendar instances, we must first cast the instance into a Date instance using the getTime() method:

```
String gCalFormatted = dateFormat.format(myTime.getTime());
```

To finish off this section on Date objects, we'll now use them in a quick class. Since we've been concentrating on classes in this chapter far more than JSP pages, let's build a JSP-based example.

Try It Out   Date/Time Classes

1. Remember the millennium counters that displayed the days until New Year's Eve 2000? This example does much the same thing – except that the year 2000 has passed us by, so we have the year 3000 to look forward to instead!

    The example uses a JavaBean defined in the file MillenniumCounter.java. This bean stores the current date and a target date (the new millennium in this case) as attributes, and allows us to get, set, and manipulate these dates.

    Save the following file in the utilities directory (under the classes directory of our Utility web application folder) under the name MillenniumCounter.java:

```
package com.wrox.utilities;

import java.util.*;
import java.text.SimpleDateFormat;
```

```
public class MillenniumCounter
{
  private SimpleDateFormat dateFormat;
  private Calendar targetDate;

  public MillenniumCounter()
  {
    dateFormat = new SimpleDateFormat("EEE, dd MMMM yyyy");

    targetDate = Calendar.getInstance();
    targetDate.set(targetDate.YEAR, 3000);
    targetDate.set(targetDate.MONTH, 0);
    targetDate.set(targetDate.DATE, 1);
    targetDate.set(targetDate.AM_PM, 0);
    targetDate.set(targetDate.HOUR, 0);
    targetDate.set(targetDate.MINUTE, 0);
    targetDate.set(targetDate.SECOND, 0);
  }

  public String getToday()
  {
    return dateFormat.format(new Date());
  }

  public long getDays()
  {
    Calendar now = Calendar.getInstance();
    if (now.after(targetDate))
      return 0;
    else
    {
      long milliseconds = (targetDate.getTimeInMillis()
                            - now.getTimeInMillis());
      long seconds = milliseconds / 1000;
      long minutes = seconds / 60;
      long hours = minutes / 60;
      long days = hours / 24;

      return days;
    }
  }
}
```

2. Compile it from the `classes` directory with this command:

> **> javac com\wrox\Utility\MillenniumCounter.java**

3. Next, we need a JSP page that instantiates the bean and uses it to display how many days there are to go until the new millennium, along with the current date. Save the following file, `MillenniumCounter.jsp`, in the `Utility` folder:

```
<html>
  <head><title>Millennium Counter</title></head>
  <body>

    <jsp:useBean id="counter" scope="page"
                class="com.wrox.utilities.MillenniumCounter"/>

    The current date is ${counter.today}
    <p/>
    Only ${counter.days} days until the new millennium!

  </body>
</html>
```

4. Start Tomcat if it's not already going, and point your browser to the new page at http://localhost:8080/Utility/MillenniumCounter.jsp. You should see something like this (depending on the date of course):

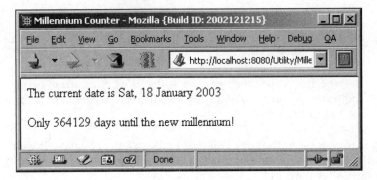

How It Works

Let's start with the bean. We start off by stating the package that the bean is in, and by importing the utility classes that we will need. The class itself has two attributes: a `SimpleDateFormat` object to hold the date format and a `Calendar` object to hold the target date of the new millennium:

```
private SimpleDateFormat dateFormat;
private Calendar targetDate;
```

Next we initialize our attributes in the constructor. First of all we initialize the `SimpleDateFormat` object attribute with the format `"EEE, dd MMMM yyyy"`:

```
dateFormat = new SimpleDateFormat("EEE, dd MMMM yyyy");
```

The next attribute to initialize is the target date. We initialize this to the year 3000 by setting all of the field constants of the `targetDate` instance individually:

```
targetDate = Calendar.getInstance();
targetDate.set(targetDate.YEAR, 3000);
targetDate.set(targetDate.MONTH, 0);
targetDate.set(targetDate.DATE, 1);
targetDate.set(targetDate.AM_PM, 0);
targetDate.set(targetDate.HOUR, 0);
targetDate.set(targetDate.MINUTE, 0);
targetDate.set(targetDate.SECOND, 0);
```

After the constructor we have the `getToday()` method, which retrieves today's date and returns it in the date format we want:

```
public String getToday()
{
  return dateFormat.format(new Date());
}
```

Note that we could have just returned today's date and used the JSTL to format the date, as we have seen done in previous chapters.

The last method, `getDays()`, in the bean class is the most interesting, because it does all the clever stuff. It computes the number of days to go until the target date, and returns this number. Let's see how it does this.

Our first step is to check that the new millennium hasn't already passed us by! We accomplish this by using the `after()` method of the `Calendar` class, which returns true if the passed `Calendar` occurs after the other `Calendar`, as shown:

```
public long getDays()
{
  Calendar now = Calendar.getInstance();
  if (now.after(targetDate))
    return 0;
```

Now, if the present date comes before the year 3000, which is highly likely, we next calculate the number of milliseconds between the present date and the year 3000, as shown:

```
else
{
  long milliseconds = (targetDate.getTimeInMillis()
                       - now.getTimeInMillis());
```

Since humans don't really think in terms of milliseconds, we do some basic math to convert the milliseconds into days:

```
long seconds = milliseconds / 1000;
long minutes = seconds / 60;
long hours = minutes / 60;
long days = hours / 24;
```

Now we just return the value for days and we're done:

```
    return days;
}
```

Well, we've now walked through our bean, so let's check out the JSP page. Ignoring the HTML, we start by instantiating a `MillenniumCounter` called `counter`:

```
<jsp:useBean id="counter" scope="page"
             class="com.wrox.utilities.MillenniumCounter"/>
```

We then use the JSP Expression Language to access the bean methods. First we retrieve and display today's date by accessing the `today` property (via the `getToday()` method):

```
The current date is ${counter.today}
```

Finally we access the `days` property and display the number of days to go until the new millennium:

```
<p/>
Only ${counter.days} days until the new millennium!
```

And that's it!

The Expression Language

Now we come to the Expression Language, which as you should know by now is commonly abbreviated to EL. The EL is a new feature to JSP 2.0; it allows JSP developers to access Java objects via a compact, easy-to-use shorthand style.

Prior to JSP 2.0, to retrieve a value from a Map in a JSP, you would have to use something like the following:

```
<%= ((Map) pageContext.findAttribute("myMap")).get("someKey") %>
```

Not the prettiest code you're likely to see, is it? Let's explain what is going on. The `pageContext` object, which is basically a container for various key JSP functions, has a method `findAttribute()` that searches the four object storage scopes (`page`, `request`, `session`, and `application`) for an object with the passed key. Once we obtain the object we must cast it to its proper type, in this case a `Map`, and then execute the `get` method on the `Map` to obtain our object. Quite a few steps!

If this seems tedious to you, and rather complex, you're not alone. Many of the most experienced Java and JSP developers find this syntax somewhat opaque.

The EL equivalent of the above example is:

```
${myMap.someKey}
```

EL Features

As we learned in Chapter 2, the EL's basic syntax is:

```
${expression}
```

These EL expressions can be used anywhere in a JSP page where HTML or text may appear. They can also be used as attribute values for JSP tags and custom tags if appropriate.

Now that we know where we can use the EL, let's talk about what you can do with it. JSP's Expression Language is actually rather simple. Its key features are:

- Easy syntax for accessing variables
- Special support for collection objects and arrays
- Implicit objects
- Arithmetic

Let's cover each of these in turn.

Easy Syntax for Accessing Variables

When you use JavaBeans with JSP via the `<useBean>` tag, or other mechanisms that introduce variables into your environment, you must have a means of accessing those variables. With the EL, this is trivial. To access any object, just use the following syntax:

```
${object}
```

You learned earlier that JavaBeans and other objects will reside in one of four scopes: `page`, `request`, `session`, or `application`, and this syntax searches all four for any variable of the given name.

However, simply knowing how to reference an object isn't useful in itself, and we generally need to access its properties. The EL makes this easy, too. Recall from Chapter 4 that we can access properties of JavaBeans with the `<getProperty>` tag, like this:

```
<jsp:getProperty name="myBean" property="myProperty"/>
```

The EL equivalent of this tag is the following:

```
${myBean.myProperty}
```

Special Support for Collections

Accessing simple properties, such as a number or a string, is fine and can be easily accomplished via the EL or with a more complex `<getProperty>` tag as you have just seen. But what if the property is a `Map`, `List`, or array? Well, if you're using a `<getProperty>` tag, accessing a property that is a `Map` will display the following:

```
{key1=value1, key3=value3, key2=value2}
```

In other words, it'll display the contents of your `Map`. Probably not something you want displayed. Below is what is displayed when `<getProperty>` is used on an array property:

```
[Ljava.lang.String;@b9b8d0
```

Now that is truly cryptic. In short, while `<getProperty>` and the EL are interchangeable for some properties, the EL enables access to other properties that can't be meaningfully accessed through `<getProperty>`.

EL Map Support

To access the contents of a `Map`, there are two syntactical options:

```
${myMap.myKey}
${myMap["myKey"]}
```

While the first of these two seems the simplest, the second has an advantage: it can be used at run time, while the first cannot. For example, let's say you have a `Map` variable, `myMap`, and another, `myKeyVariable`, which corresponds to a key that you want to access. Let us further suppose that `myKeyVariable` contains the value `aFunKey`. The following syntax would not work:

```
${myMap.myKeyVariable}
```

This doesn't work because the EL searches `myMap` for a key that is literally equal to `myKeyVariable`, which is not what we intend. However, this will do the trick:

```
${myMap[myKeyVariable]}
```

Using `Maps` in JSPs has never been simpler!

List and Array Support

Recall that both `List` objects and arrays can be accessed via an index property. Using these with the EL is quite simple:

```
${anArrayOrList[0]}
```

where 0 is the index of the item you wish to retrieve.

Implicit Objects

Implicit objects are those objects that are always available to JSP developers. The EL gives JSP developers more implicit objects than they've ever had before, making it very convenient to access all sorts of data. Some of these objects are as follows:

Implicit Object	Description
pageScope	A Map of all the objects that have page scope.
requestScope	A Map of all the objects that have request scope.
sessionScope	A Map of all the objects that have session scope.
applicationScope	A Map of all the objects that have application scope.
param	A Map of all the form parameters that were passed to your JSP (for example, the HTML `<input name="myName" type="text">` is passed to your JSP page as a form parameter)
paramValues	HTML allows for multiple values for a single form parameter. This is a Map of all the parameters, just like `param`, but in this object the values are an array containing all of the values for a given parameter in the event that there is more than one.
header	A Map of all the request headers.
headerValues	For the same reasons as `paramValues`, a `headerValues` object is provided.
cookie	A Map of all the cookies passed to your JSP. The value returned is a `Cookie` object. See below for an example of how to interact with this object.

Let's take a look at some examples of how to use these objects:

```
${pageScope.myObject}
${param.firstName}
${paramValues.phoneNumber[0]}
${cookie.someCookie.value}
```

As you can see above, all of these implicit objects follow the simple rules that we've just finished reviewing.

Cookie Class

For your information, we thought we'd tell you a bit about the Cookie class that you'll be dealing with in JSPs. It's a simple, JavaBean-compliant class with the following key properties:

Property	Description
name	The name of the cookie
value	The value of the cookie
domain	The domain name of the cookie; it will only be sent to servers in this domain (for example, www.wrox.com)
maxAge	The length of time in seconds that the cookie will exist; "-1" indicates that the cookie will stick around until the browser quits
path	Restricts the cookie to only be sent to the server when requesting URLs from it that contain this path (for example /companyStore)
secure	true or false indicating whether the cookie will only be sent when connecting via HTTPS (an encrypted form of HTTP)

Arithmetic

The final feature of EL we're going to look at is its ability to evaluate various arithmetic expressions. The following is an example of some of the EL's arithmetic operators at work:

```
${((2 + myVar) * 16) % 5}
```

The EL supports the following arithmetic operators:

Addition	+
Subtraction	-
Multiplication	*
Division	/ or "div"
Remainder (modulo)	% or "mod"

Furthermore, EL supports relational operators to compare two values. These are:

Equals	== or "eq"
Not equals	!= or "ne"
Less than	< or "lt"
Greater than	> or "gt"
Less than or equals	<= or "le"
Greater than or equals	>= or "ge"

Finally, the EL also supports the standard so-called logical operators, which are:

And	&& or "and"
Or	|| or "or"
Not	! or "not"

Summary

Arrays are Java's basic mechanism for storing multiple objects into a single object. However, the size of an array cannot be changed once it is created, and furthermore, arrays don't have a lot of features. Java solves this problem with the **collections framework**. There are three basic types of collections: sets, lists, and maps.

A set is an unordered collection of unique objects. A list is an ordered collection of non-unique objects. A map is a collection of key/value pairs. The keys of a map are a set; that is, all keys are unique. Both the key and value of a map may be of any object type.

There are three interfaces in the collections framework that represent these collection types: Set, List, and Map. There are many classes which implement these interfaces that can be used by developers, such as `HashSet`, `ArrayList`, and `HashMap`.

JSP's Expression Language (EL) makes it easy to access the contents of these collection classes in your JSP pages. Furthermore, the EL provides a "short-cut" syntax for accessing variables in your JSPs, as well as many "implicit objects" that are always available for use. Finally, the EL gives JSP developers to ability to perform basic arithmetic in their pages.

CHAPTER 8

When It All Goes Wrong

Sometimes things go wrong. This is particularly a fact of life in programming, and the first step to reducing errors is simply to get into good programming habits. However, even the best programmer will still encounter bugs and errors that they must deal with. In this chapter, we will learn about Java's error handling mechanism, and how to apply this to JSP.

Java uses the simple but efficient error-handling model of **exception management**. It involves anticipating situations that our code might "take exception to", including external problems such as file system errors, input/output errors and so on. Conditions may arise that our code can't deal with, and we can watch for such 'exceptional events' and catch them by triggering an **exception handler**.

Java offers a set of exception classes that are built just to work with errors, creating an exception-handling framework that allows us to ensure a proper response will be triggered for any given error. We can build on the existing exception classes to create classes tailored for errors specific to our own programs.

This chapter will walk through the process of handling errors in the Java and JSP programming environments. The main focus is on how Java uses exceptions to handle events that need extra care and handling. However, JSP web applications take Java into new areas, which will even be new to many Java programmers. This chapter will examine these areas, and the features that allow JSP to interact with the wider world, by taking an especially close look at handling errors in JSP applications. To this end, we'll give an overview of the types of problems that JSP programmers face and the tools used to make such problems manageable.

As we progress through the chapter, we'll examine the following topics in turn:

- ❏   The different types of error that we can encounter in our applications
- ❏   The details of Java's exception handling mechanism
- ❏   How to apply Java exception management to JSP

❑ How to diagnose and treat HTML and JavaScript-related errors in a JSP page's output

❑ How to make sense of stack trace error messages

❑ Log files, and their place in tracking exceptions over time

❑ Additional resources for solving coding problems

Types of Error

Errors can generally be classified into two types depending on what causes the error:

❑ **System errors**

System errors happen when a program receives an unexpected response from the operating system it is running under. These errors might be due to trying to open a connection to a network that is down, low memory resources, or a bad software driver – such things that, as programmers, we have little control over.

The good news is that these errors tend to be very visible. Handling a system error often means having to update a software driver or another piece of external software outside of your program's control: the bad news is that a programmer doesn't always have control or the authority to update the outside aspects of the system.

❑ **Application errors**

Most errors are caused by a mistake in the application code itself. Generally speaking, these coding errors take one of the following forms:

❑ **Logic errors** – occur when faulty assumptions are made in code. For example, we may use an `if` statement which checks two possible conditions, when really it should check for three. This would mean that the code will work part of the time, but at other times the code contained by the `if` statement won't fire when it should.

❑ **Syntax errors** – These could be caused by simple typing mistakes (typos), or they could be the result of a misunderstanding on our part of how to code a particular technique. A common syntax error in Java is the use of the single = assignment operator within a logical expression, when we really mean to use the comparison operator, ==. While these typos might seem easy to fix, they can be easy to overlook, and hence hard to track down. The compiler catches most of the typos, so they won't make it to your compiled code, but syntax errors, such as the one described above where the assignment operator is confused for the comparison operator, will not.

When faced with an error, determining what type of error is involved can be half the battle. Most programmers develop their own preferred method for tracking down errors. For instance, when an error happens in an application I've written, I'll typically start by verifying the syntax is right, and then switch to reviewing the logic. The point is that different types of error require slightly different approaches to resolve but a common plan can help you in organizing your error handling routine.

Introducing Exceptions

An exception is an event that occurs during the execution of a program that disrupts its normal flow. Many kinds of errors can cause exceptions – ranging from simple programming errors, such as trying to access more elements in an array than it was defined to hold or using an expression that involves division by zero, through to hardware failures, such as a disk crash or network outage.

Regardless of the cause, such errors prevent the code from continuing. The Java approach when such an error is encountered is to **throw an exception**. Note that an exception is something that requires extra attention, and so is not necessarily an error.

The goals of exception handling are:

❑ To separate error handling code from regular code.

❑ To group error types, differentiate errors, and signal an unusual event.

❑ To provide a mechanism that permits the program to recover when something untoward occurs, avoiding a crash.

Java's exception classes make it easy for us to handle exceptions that might occur. While exception handling makes handling application errors easy, it also allows us to do much more than dealing with a fixed number of possible system errors. In fact, the biggest advantage of Java exceptions is that they permit a programmer to create code that can handle both its own errors and any outstanding conditional processing.

Dealing with Exceptions

Now that we have had an introduction to the basic idea of an exception, let's introduce the basic concepts of how Java handles exceptions, and back it up with an example. We'll then move on to explain in more detail what is going on behind the scenes.

Our first step is to look at one basic Java class and four Java keywords:

❑ `Exception` – a Java class that stores information about an "exception" that has occurred during processing of the code.

❑ `throws` – this keyword lets us pass certain exceptions up to the calling code rather than handling the code locally.

❑ `try` – this keyword wraps a block of code where we expect exceptions to occur. A `try` block is used in conjunction with the `catch` keyword to catch and handle exceptions in code.

❑ `catch` – this statement defines a block of code that handles a particular sort of exception. We associate exception handlers with a `try` block by providing one or more `catch` blocks directly after the `try` block where exceptions of that type are likely to occur.

❑   `finally` – this keyword defines code that is *always* executed after a certain `try...catch` block, whether or not the code in that `try` block threw an exception. This provides a place for any code required to tidy up objects used in the `try` block, such as to close files or release other system resources.

Try It Out   The try...catch Construct

1. In this example, we write a really simple JSP that attempts to display the result of dividing a number by zero. This will throw an exception, and is a very common eventuality to code for.

Our first JSP will show what happens if we don't handle this exception, and we'll move on to add suitable exception handling in the form of a `try...catch` block. First we need a web application for our pages, so create folder called `Exceptions` in Tomcat's `webapps` folder, containing another folder called `WEB-INF` as usual.

2. Now create a file in the `Exceptions` folder called `untrappedError.jsp`, and enter the following code:

```
<%@page contentType="text/html"%>
<html>
  <head>
    <title>Looking at Exceptions</title>
  </head>
  <body>
<%
    int i = 10, j = 0;

    i = i / j;

%>

  <p> The value of i is: <%= i%> </p>
  <p> The value of j is: <%= j%> </p>

  </body>
</html>
```

3. Start Tomcat, and open `untrappedError.jsp` in your browser. You'll see the following exception report:

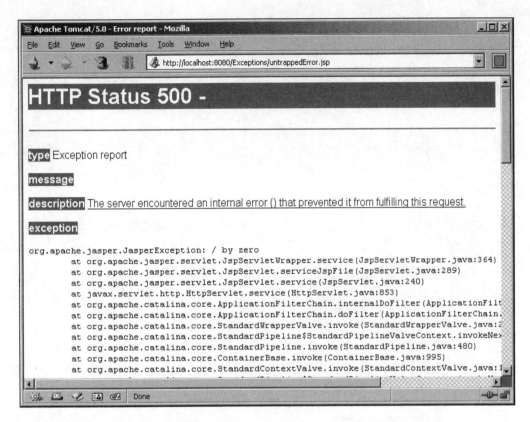

It would be more than a little embarrassing if a visitor to our web site encountered a messy error message such as this. It would quite likely undermine any confidence they may have, and our company could lose business!

4. Fortunately, Java's exception handling makes preventing this quite easy. Make a copy of the page as `trappedError.jsp`, and add the `try...catch` block highlighted below:

```
<%@page contentType="text/html"%>
<html>
  <head>
    <title>Looking at Exceptions</title>
  </head>
  <body>
<%
    int i = 10, j = 0;

    try
    {
      i = i / j;
    }
```

```
      catch (Exception e)
      {
        out.print("An error just occurred with the description:<br>");
        out.print(e.toString());
      }

  %>

  <p> The value of i is: <%= i%> </p>
  <p> The value of j is: <%= j%> </p>

  </body>
</html>
```

5. Open `trappedError.jsp` to see the effect of the new code. The error still occurs, but our page is a lot neater:

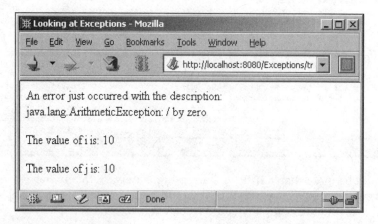

How It Works

When we opened the first page that contained no exception handling, we saw Tomcat's generic error page, which gives a one line description of the exception encountered, followed by a **stack trace** – the long list of apparently impenetrable technicalities. Later in the chapter we'll learn how to decipher the stack trace to see how it can help us locate where in the code this error is being caused.

Note that we have no control over what appears on error pages such as these – it is entirely down to the servlet engine in use. We can, however, tell the servlet engine to use our own error page rather than the default one, as we will do shortly.

We got round the problem by placing the code that we suspect might cause an error (i = i / j;) inside the starting and ending brace ({}) of a `try` block:

```
try
{
  i = i / j;
}
```

When the Java runtime encounters this mathematically insoluble equation, it throws an exception which moves the flow of execution to the `catch` block:

```
catch (Exception e)
```

The code in this simply prints out an error message, which includes the message stored in the `Exception` object (e), got hold of by the `toString()` method:

```
out.print("An error just occurred with the description:<br>");
out.print(e.toString());
}
```

Therefore, the `try...catch` construct allows us to control the behavior in the event of an error, and we can retrieve any specific message from the `Exception` object.

How Exception Handling Works

Let's now dig in a little, and find out how it all works. The previous section introduced the exception handling, and we implemented a simple `try...catch` block.

The exception classes form the first part of the picture, acting as the message carriers for problems that occur within Java code. All exception classes are ultimately derived from the `Throwable` class.

The Throwable Class

Only objects that are instances of `Throwable`, or a subclass of `Throwable`, can be thrown and caught by handler code.

There are two subclasses of `Throwable`: `Exception` and `Error`.

`Error` is designed for non-recoverable internal errors – in other words, error conditions that necessitate program termination. These are conditions internal to the Java Virtual Machine (JVM) and therefore there is little a programmer can do about them. You should neither try to catch these errors nor throw them.

The `Exception` subclass is for conditions that a program can recover from, and continue to execute safely. The `Exception` class is itself subclassed into several other exception classes, which all fall into two broad categories:

❑ **Runtime exceptions** – deriving from the Exception class, the class RuntimeException and its subclasses represent programmatic errors or bugs. These are the exceptions that the JVM will throw at you if your code attempts to do something it shouldn't, such as divide by zero.

❑ **All other exceptions** – sometimes also called **checked exceptions**, these are exception classes that represent conditions that would probably be out of a programmer's hands, and result from a problem with the environment. User mistakes also fall into this category. Of course, a clever programmer would anticipate and code accordingly for these cases. An example of such an exception is ClassNotFoundException.

The Throwable class defines two particularly useful methods that are inherited by all Exception classes:

❑ public String getMessage() – returns a detailed message describing the exception that just occurred.

❑ public String toString() – think of this as a shorter form of the getMessage() method above.

There are dozens of Java exception classes for a wide range of errors. For example, there is a SQLException class which is specifically built to handle SQL database exceptions. This exception object contains extensions for dealing with the ins and outs of SQL errors, such as the getErrorCode() method that returns the database error code. So it's a good idea when working in unfamiliar areas to review what Exception objects might be suitable for your code.

You can, of course, create your own exception classes by deriving them from the Exception class (or one of its subclasses). You may wish to do this if the exception classes provided with Java do not adequately cover the conditions that are faced by your particular application.

If you do create your own exception class, it is usual to have at least two constructors: one standard constructor that takes no arguments, and one which takes a String argument for the error message used to describe the error. This is the error message that would be printed if either the getMessage() or the toString() methods were called.

Throwing and Catching an Exception

Before we create our own custom exceptions, let us look at how to work with Java defined exceptions. Later we will see that working with our own exceptions is no different from working with the built-in ones.

A common situation where exceptions might be expected is when dealing with files. For instance, how can we make our code to handle a file that doesn't contain the expected contents? Such a situation would throw the Java EOFException exception, or a custom exception of our own.

Here's an example:

```
Exception trouble = new Exception("Bad things just happened!");
throw trouble;
```

This could also be written more concisely as:

```
throw new Exception("Bad things just happened!");
```

Once you have created the exception object, you use the throw statement, which passes, or **throws**, it back to the calling method. What the calling method does with the exception is entirely up to it.

Methods that throw particular types of exception advertise that fact using the throws keyword in their signature. This tells any calling method that it needs to catch this exception and deal with it.

Any exception that might be thrown should be handled, unless the method throws the exception up to the calling method. The calling method can then either handle the exception itself, or it can throw it back to the method that called it, and so on.

When passing exceptions from a called method to the calling method like this, we say that exceptions "bubble" up the stack at runtime (the **stack** is the list of methods that have executed to get to the current code position).

For example, imagine a situation where method a() calls method b(), which then calls method c(), and an exception occurs in method c(). Rather than handle the exception itself, method c() throws the exception up to method b().However, method b() can also choose to not to handle the exception and can instead **rethrow** it. This means that an exception occurring in method c() can be passed all the way back to method a() for handling. If no method handles an exception, then the program will be terminated with a default error message, as we saw in the first Try It Out earlier in the chapter.

In practice, the first chance to handle an exception is at the time of the error. If the exception is not handled, it then gets passed back to the method that called the current method. The Java VM steps backwards through the stack, until either it finds code that handles the exception, or the JVM is forced to deal with the error itself. The Java VM's usual method for handling exceptions is to terminate the program with a general exception report in the form of a stack trace. As we've seen, such reports are confusing and unhelpful to users so it is rarely a good idea to leave exceptions for the JVM to handle.

If you try to write code that throws an exception without either catching the error yourself, or declaring that the method can throw the exception, you will get a compiler error like the following:

Exception must be caught, or it must be declared in the throws clause of this method

Note that the above is true only for checked exceptions (exceptions that derive directly from the `Exception` class).

Declaring a method that will throw an exception is a simple matter of using the `throws` keyword in the method declaration. So, for example, we might write:

```
public void validateUser(PageContext page) throws Exception
```

This method can now throw exceptions of type `Exception` back to the previous method in the call stack. Note that methods can throw more than one type of exception, as long as all types appear in the comma-separated list of exception classes after the `throws` keyword:

```
public void validate (PageContext page)
   throws IOException, UserDefinedException
```

Declaring a method in this manner provides the only indication to other programmers that the method might throw an exception that they need to catch.

However, there are two things to note about throwing multiple exceptions:

❑ You don't need to advertise unchecked exceptions (exceptions other than checked, deriving from `RuntimeException`, or the `Error` classes).

❑ All subclasses of an exception class may be thrown from your code as well as the declared superclass exception. So if you advertise that your method throws the `Exception` class for example, your method could actually throw any of its subclasses. You might think that this is a handy mechanism, but by doing this, your method won't tell callers of your methods the types of exceptions that might be thrown.

Try It Out   **Throwing and Catching an Exception**

1. Let's see how this throwing and catching of exceptions works in practice. We'll create a simple HTML form for entering a user name and password which is then posted to a JSP that uses a JavaBean to check whether the supplied values are valid. If not, the bean will throw an exception for the JSP page to handle.

We'll start by creating the form page, which should be placed in our `Exceptions` folder, under the name `loginException.html`. You should be fairly well acquainted with the layout of HTML forms by now – here's how this one should look:

```
<html>
<head><title>Throwing an Exception</title></head>
<body>
<p> This test page shows how to create a basic exception
    within a Javabean and how to use the exception.</p>
```

```
<form action="loginException.jsp" method="post">
  <table>
    <tr>
      <td>User name:</td>
      <td><input name="username" type="text"></td>
    </tr>
    <tr>
      <td>Password:</td>
      <td><input name="password" type="password"></td>
    </tr>
    <tr>
      <td></td>
      <td><input name="submit" value="Log in!" type="submit"></td>
    </tr>
  </table>
</form>
</body>
</html>
```

2. Next, let's create a JavaBean in a file called `User.java`. The file needs to be placed in a folder called `except`, in a folder called `wrox`, itself in a folder called `com` within a `classes` subdirectory of `WEB-INF`:

```
package com.wrox.except;

public class User
{

  private String username;
  private String password;

  public User()
  {
  }

  public void setUsername(String username)
  {
    this.username = username;
  }

  public String getUsername()
  {
    return this.username;
  }

  public void setPassword(String password)
  {
    this.password = password;
  }
```

```
public void validate() throws Exception
{
  if (!(this.username.equals("Dougal")
     && this.password.equals("roundabout")))
  {
    Exception trouble = new Exception("Couldn't validate your"
                                      + " password!");
    throw trouble;
  }
}
}
```

3. Now compile this class by running the following command from the `classes` directory:

> **javac com\wrox\except\User.java**

4. Finally, we create our JSP page where this bean will be used. It needs to be located in the `Exceptions` folder, under the name `loginException.jsp`.

```
<%@ page contentType="text/html"%>
<html>
<head><title>Throwing an Exception</title></head>
<body>
<p> This test page shows how to create a basic exception
    within a Javabean and how to use the exception.</p>

<jsp:useBean id="myUser" class="com.wrox.except.User" scope="page"/>
<jsp:setProperty name="myUser" property="*"/>

<%
   try
   {
     myUser.validate();
     out.print("The user " + myUser.getUsername() + " is registered.");
   }
   catch (Exception e)
   {
     out.print("We encountered a problem: " + e.toString());
   }
%>
</body>
</html>
```

5. Restart Tomcat and direct your browser to `loginException.html`:

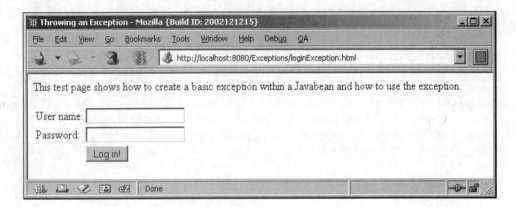

6. Enter a user name of Dougal with the password roundabout, click Log in!, and you should see this screen:

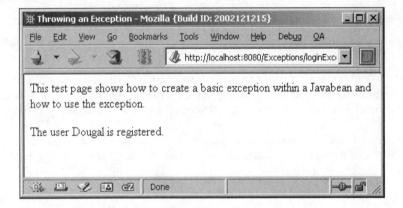

7. Now do it again, but this time, enter an incorrect password. You'll see the following message, indicating that an exception was thrown by our bean:

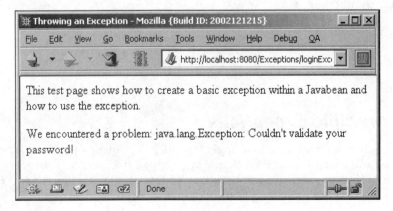

How It Works

The bean is for the most part quite simple: it has accessor methods corresponding to the names of the form fields, and these properties will be filled in by the `<jsp:setProperty>` tag in the JSP.

The action comes in the `validate()` method. If the user name and password aren't recognized then we create an `Exception` object with a suitably descriptive message, and throw it. Since `validate()` declares that it throws `Exception`, we pass the buck to the code that calls the method – in other words, to the JSP page:

```
public void validate() throws Exception
{
   if (!(this.username.equals("Dougal")
      && this.password.equals("roundabout")))
   {
      Exception trouble = new Exception("Couldn't validate your"
                                    + " password!");
      throw trouble;
   }
}
```

The code of the JSP page is relatively simple also. First we create an instance of our `User` object using the `<jsp:useBean>` action, and populate its properties using `<jsp:setProperty>`. We then have to check the user name and password were recognized, by calling `validate()`.

Since calling this method could cause an exception, we place it in a `try...catch` block. If everything is fine we display the name of the validated user, otherwise we report the exception received from the `User` object:

```
<%
   try
   {
     myUser.validate();
     out.print("The user " + myUser.getUsername() + " is registered.");
   }
   catch (Exception e)
   {
     out.print("We encountered a problem: " + e.toString());
   }
%>
```

Catching Multiple Exceptions

So far we've only been interested in a single type of exception at a time; the examples were pretty simple, and a single `catch` block quickly trapped the exception. However, it is possible to catch many different types of exceptions caused by a single `try` block if it is followed by a separate `catch` block for each exception we're interested in.

The order in which the `catch` blocks appear is important, as when an exception is encountered during the processing of the `try` block, the first `catch` block that matches the exception thrown will be invoked. This means that we need to place the more specific types of exceptions before the general types, because otherwise the more general exception would catch the more specific ones too. Consider the following example:

```
try
{
    .
    .
    .
}
catch (FileNotFoundException fne)
{
    // code for file not found error
}
catch (IOException ioex)
{
    // code for IOException
}
```

Here, the `FileNotFoundException` is the more specific exception, as it is a subclass of `IOException`. If the code in the `try` block attempts to use a file that doesn't exist, the `catch` block for `FileNotFoundException` will handle it, which is what we want. Had the order of the catch blocks been reversed and `IOException` were listed before `FileNotFoundException`, `IOException` would catch all `FileNotFoundException` errors (as well as any other I/O exception), and the code inside the `FileNotFoundException` block would never be reached. Fortunately, the Java compiler will alert you of such unreachable code with a compile error.

Try It Out   Catching Multiple Exceptions

1. One problem with our earlier example occurs if we fail to enter any data in the user name or password fields; the relevant JavaBean property value will then be `null`. Let's modify our `User` bean so that it checks for this problem as well.

    Create a copy of `User.java` called `User2.java`, and make the changes highlighted below:

```
package com.wrox.except;

import java.io.IOException;

public class User2
{

    private String username;
    private String password;
```

```
public User2()
{
}

public void setUsername(String username)
{
  this.username = username;
}

public String getUsername()
{
  return this.username;
}

public void setPassword(String password)
{
  this.password = password;
}

public void validate() throws IOException, Exception
{
  if(this.username == null || this.password == null)
  {
    IOException ioex = new IOException("You must supply a username"
                                + " and password!!");
    throw ioex;
  }
  if (!(this.username.equals("Casey")
    && this.password.equals("Kochmer")))
  {
    Exception trouble = new Exception("Couldn't validate your"
                                + " password!");
    throw trouble;
  }
}
}
```

Compile the new class with the following command:

> **javac com\wrox\except\User2.java**

2. Now we just need to change our JSP page to use the new class, and catch the new exception. Make the changes highlighted below to `loginException.jsp`:

```
<%@ page contentType="text/html"%>
<html>
<head><title>Throwing an Exception</title></head>
<body>
<p> This test page shows how to create a basic exception
    within a Javabean and how to use the exception.</p>
```

```
<jsp:useBean id="myUser" class="com.wrox.except.User2" scope="page"/>
<jsp:setProperty name="myUser" property="*"/>

<%
   try
   {
     myUser.validate();
     out.print("The user " + myUser.getUsername() + " is registered.");
   }
   catch (java.io.IOException ioex)
   {
     out.println("We encountered an IOException: " + ioex.toString());
   }
   catch (Exception e)
   {
     out.print("We encountered a problem: " + e.toString());
   }
%>
</body>
</html>
```

3. Restart Tomcat, and open (or refresh) the `loginException.html` page in your browser. This time, leave the text boxes blank, and click **Log in!**. You should see the new error message:

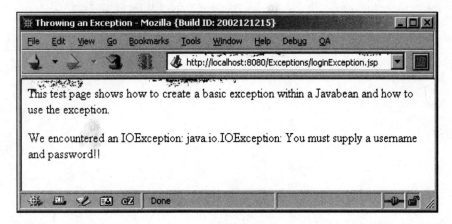

4. If you want, try it again using an incorrect user name or password, and you should see the first error message just as before.

How It Works

This example demonstrates the importance of the order of the `catch` blocks in our code.

If our `try` block throws a `IOException`, the first `catch` block will deal with it, and if it throws an `Exception` or any of its other subclasses, the second `catch` block will handle it.

The finally Clause

The `finally` clause is an important addition to the basic `try...catch` concept. It contains code that will be executed whether or not an exception occurs within the `try` blocks, providing a way for our applications to shut down processes properly. For example, when working with databases, it is a good idea to close connections once they are finished with (because database connections tend to be resource intensive and can be limited due to licensing). Placing the code that closes the database connection within a `finally` block guarantees that the database connection will be closed no matter what.

Try It Out   The finally Clause

1. To understand how the `finally` clause works, let's look at a simple example. Save the code below as finally.jsp, in the `Exceptions` folder:

```
<%@page contentType="text/html"%>
<html>
<head><title>Using the finally Statement</title></head>
<body>
<%
    int i = 10000;
    int j;
    try
    {
        for (j = 5; j > -1  ; j--)
        {
            i = i / j ;
            out.print("Value of i=");
            out.print(i);
            out.print("<br>");
        }
    }
    catch (Exception e)
    {
        out.print("An error just occurred of the following nature:<br>");
        out.print(e.toString());
    }
    finally
    {
```

```
       /* reset i to 10000 */
       i = 10000;
     }
%>

<p> The final value of i is <%= i %> </p>
</body>
</html>
```

2. Now open this page in a web browser. You should see this output:

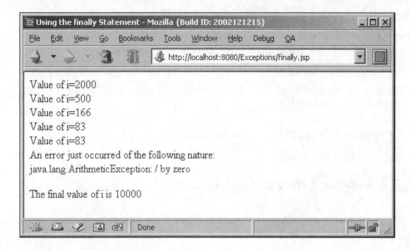

How It Works

This little example shows that the `finally` clause is always executed, even if an exception is thrown.

After the `ArithmeticException` occurs, the processing skips any other code within the `try` block and jumps to the first matching `catch` clause. Once the code in that block has been executed, processing jumps to the `finally` block, and `i` is reset to 10000.

Building New Exceptions

While exceptions are great, they're most useful when exception classes give adequate details about what just happened. Exceptions should always contain a message about the error they represent, but we infer additional information from the actual class of the exception object itself. As an example, when we used the `IOException` class to handle a blank username or password, the exception class didn't give any really useful information about the reason behind the error. If we could code our own exception class, say `NoValuesEnteredException`, it is immediately clear what is the exact nature of the problem.

Creating our own exception objects also makes exception handling more elegant than using a generic `Exception` object, since we have more control over what happens when an exception occurs. For instance, if we wanted to log a message when a certain exception happens, we could do so within the constructors of such exceptions and this way make sure that the event is always logged.

Creating an exception requires us to extend the `Throwable` class, or more normally a subclass of `Throwable` such as `java.lang.Exception`. Our new exception class will:

❑ Define any new properties. While this isn't always required, it can be useful to track additional information within the exception object to give a `catch` block additional information when dealing with our exceptions.

❑ Define the basic constructors – one with no arguments, and one with a `String` argument – and any additional constructors for special initialisation purposes.

❑ Modify methods that were inherited from the base class. For example, the `toString()` function can be enhanced to report on additional properties and other features being tracked by the exception.

All in all it's pretty simple, as the next example will hopefully demonstrate.

Try It Out   Building a New Exception Class

1. We'll create our own exception class for our user object from the previous examples. Enter the code below in a file called `UserException.java` in the `com.wrox.except` folder of our application's `classes` directory:

```
package com.wrox.except;

public class UserException extends Exception
{

  private String userValue = "null";

  public UserException()
  {
  }

  public UserException(String msg)
  {
    super(msg);
  }

  public  String getUserValue()
  {
    return this.userValue;
  }
```

```
   public void setUserValue(String userValue)
   {
     if (userValue == null)
       this.userValue = "null";

     this.userValue = userValue;
   }

   public String toString()
   {
     return (super.toString() + ": The User is " + this.getUserValue());
   }

   public UserException(String msg, String userValue)
   {
     super(msg);
     setUserValue(userValue);
   }
}
```

2. Now we'll upgrade our bean to use this new exception class. Copy `User2.java` as `User3.java`, and change it as highlighted:

```
package com.wrox.except;
```

```
public class User3
{

  private String username;
  private String password;

  public User3()
  {
  }

  public void setUsername(String username)
  {
    this.username = username;
  }

  public String getUsername()
  {
    return this.username;
  }

  public void setPassword(String password)
  {
    this.password = password;
  }
```

```
public void validate() throws UserException, Exception
{
    if(this.username == null)
    {
        throw new UserException("UserName must be supplied !!");
    }
    if(this.password == null)
    {
        throw new UserException("Password must be supplied !!",
                                this.username);
    }
    if (!(this.username.equals("Dougal")
        && this.password.equals("roundabout")))
    {
        Exception trouble = new Exception("Couldn't validate your"
                                    + " password!");
        throw trouble;
    }
  }
}
```

3. As the `User3` class depends on the `UserException` class, the easiest way to compile
    these classes is to compile them all at once like this:

    > javac com\wrox\except*.java

4. We now need to make a couple of changes to `loginException.jsp`:

```
<%@ page contentType="text/html"%>
<html>
<head><title>Throwing an Exception</title></head>
<body>
<p> This test page shows how to create a basic exception
    within a Javabean and how to use the exception.</p>
```

```
<jsp:useBean id="myUser" class="com.wrox.except.User3" scope="page"/>
<jsp:setProperty name="myUser" property="*"/>
```

```
<%
    try
    {
        myUser.validate();
        out.print("The user " + myUser.getUsername() + " is registered.");
    }
    catch (com.wrox.except.UserException usex)
    {
        out.println("We encountered a UserException: " + usex.toString());
    }
    catch (Exception e)
    {
```

```
        out.print("We encountered a problem: " + e.toString());
    }
%>
</body>
</html>
```

5. Restart Tomcat, and open the `loginException.html` page. Leave one of the fields blank, and click the **Log in!** button:

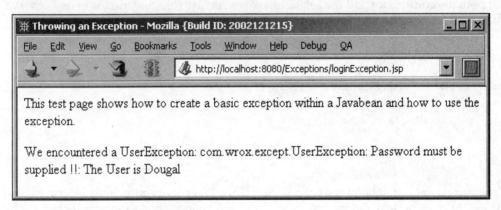

The major new feature in this example is the new exception class. Our `UserException` class extends `Exception` to add a new property called `userValue` and corresponding accessors:

```
private String userValue = "null";

    .
    .
    .

public  String getUserValue()
{
  return this.userValue;
}

public void setUserValue(String userValue)
{
  if (userValue == null)
    this.userValue = "null";

  this.userValue = userValue;
}
```

We also added a new constructor:

```
public UserException(String msg)
{
   super(msg);
}
```

This new constructor calls the parent constructor, passing in the error string. The second step is to set the `userValue` property using the user ID that was passed in. Now, instead of having to call both the constructor and the set accessor, we can use this constructor to do both. We use this constructor in the `User3` class to create a new `UserException` object:

```
throw new UserException("Password must be supplied !!", this.username);
```

`UserException` overrides the `toString()` method:

```
public String toString()
{
   return (super.toString() + ": The User is " + this.getUserValue());
}
```

The `toString()` method of the base `Exception` class only reports basic information about the exception – its class and the message – but our version reports the user ID as well, by calling the superclass's version using `super.toString()` to get the basic error text, and then appending the user ID to the end of that message.

The nice thing is that the new `UserException` class is very easy to use, with almost no modification of the previous code required.

Using Exceptions

Now that we've covered the basics of exceptions, let's examine a number of issues that may not be immediately apparent.

Catching and Identifying Exceptions

As we saw, the `catch` clause specifies what particular subclass of `Exception` it matches, and this is the key. A `catch` block that matches all `Exception` objects makes it hard to tell what type of error we're actually trapping without parsing the error message, which is not very elegant and not very effective for dealing with unknown types of errors. However if our `catch` block matches `EOFFileException`, say, we know immediately that we've tried to read beyond the end of a stream.

Therefore, a more specific class of exception, used in place of the generic `Exception` class, can allow our code to react better when an error occurs. At the same time, it helps to make our code modular, readable, and as a result more maintainable over the long run.

This also means that when creating an exception class you should clearly name it to identify what it is catching, making it easier for use by other programmers.

Checked and Unchecked Exceptions

A **checked** exception is one that the programmer must deal with. In other words, we must either use a `try...catch` block to handle the exception, or declare that our own method can throw that exception. The compiler enforces this rule.

Exceptions based on the `Exception` class, which are the most common, are always checked exceptions, apart from the special subclass of `Exception` called `RuntimeException`. We are not forced to `catch` or `throw` exceptions that are subclasses of `RuntimeException`. Sometimes this type of exception is referred to as an **unchecked** exception.

An example of an unchecked exception is the `ArithmeticException` class, which catches mathematical errors such as division by zero. The possibility of division by zero can be eliminated by always checking that the divisor is not zero, and there would then be no need to catch such exceptions.

This said, exception management is an important tool and short-circuiting it shouldn't be carried out lightly.

Another point is that a method need not declare itself as throwing a `RuntimeException` in order to throw one. This means that the function's users won't necessarily know from the method signature or documentation if that method may throw a `RuntimeException`. The reason is that `RuntimeExceptions` represent errors that can occur anywhere.

> Most exceptions you will build will be checked exceptions derived from the **Exception** class. Classes deriving from **Error** and **RuntimeException** are unchecked exceptions.

Summary of Exceptions

To sum up, here are some key points about Java exceptions:

- ❑ Exception management should be only used for conditions that cannot be easily dealt with at the current level of code you are within. Exceptions should never be used merely to replace simple conditional `if` logic, because throwing an exception requires creation of new objects and additional processing by the JVM. However, a `try...catch` block doesn't itself adversely affect performance unless an exception is actually thrown.

- ❑ A perfect example of when to use an exception is when connecting to outside resources such as databases or networks. At the point of connection, if a driver isn't available to allow you to connect to the resource doesn't exist, the code cannot continue, and it isn't possible for it to try something else. Throwing an exception lets us jump back to the previous logical step to determine how to proceed.

❑   The nice thing about the Java exception model is that it helps to keep code clean.
    Exception management avoids code repetition by allowing a single block of code to
    handle particular problems that occur in a variety of places throughout our code.

❑   Careful thought is required when choosing the Exception subclass to catch
    exceptions. While the Exception class can catch any possible exception, it may be
    preferable to catch more specific exception types in order to apply more intelligent
    handling logic.

❑   The finally block gives us a chance to reset objects and roll data back to an original
    state if something does go wrong – all too often, programmers neglect to reset objects
    after an exception.

Error Handling in JSP

Now that we have a basic understanding of how exceptions and errors are handled in Java, we
can look at how JSP changes the picture. JSP adds the concept of an **error page** that we can set
up to centrally handle errors. There are also some methods to communicate error status to
browsers and other client tools.

JSP Error Pages

A JSP application isn't a single piece of Java code logic, but rather a collection of pages, loosely
connected by URL links. While a Java application runs in a very linear fashion, a JSP
application's life is a chaotic bouncing from one page to the next. To simplify things, JSP lets us
create specialized, centralized error pages to handle errors and exceptions.

Error pages are the same as any other JSP page, with an additional implicit object for tracking
errors. They give JSP a central place for handling problems – instead of handling an exception
within the JSP page where an error occurs, we can jump to a page tailored for handling the type
of error detected. A single project can contain many different error pages for handling different
kinds of errors. There may be an error page just for login errors, while another error page might
be set up to handle general errors that occur within the application itself.

There are two steps when making and using an error page:

❑   Create the error page itself. This is pretty much the same as any other JSP page, except
    that it has a page directive with an isErrorPage attribute set to true.

```
<%@ page isErrorPage="true" %>
```

This tells the JSP container (such as Tomcat) that this is an error page and that it
should create the implicit exception object for it. This exception object refers to
the exception that occurred within the original JSP page and it can be queried for error
information. The error page could simply display a notice saying something went
wrong, or it might provide a complex analysis of the error. In many working JSP web
sites, error pages alert the system administrator by sending a report via e-mail.

❏   Set our JSP pages to use our error page in the event of an error using the `errorPage` attribute on the `page` directive:

```
<%@ page errorPage="error.jsp" %>
```

This tells the page to redirect to `error.jsp` in the event of an exception, although we may name our error pages how we please.

Try It Out   A JSP Error Page

1.   Let's start by creating a JSP page in the `Exceptions` folder that attempts to share 10 apples among zero people. We'll call it `divByZero.jsp`:

```
<%@ page contentType="text/html" errorPage="showError.jsp" %>

<html>
  <head>
    <title>Building a simple error handling page.</title>
  </head>
  <body>

<%
  int apples = 10;
  int people = 0;
  int share = apples / people;
%>

  </body>
</html>
```

2.   Now we'll create the error page specifed in the above JSP page's `errorPage` attribute, `showError.jsp`. It also goes in the `Exceptions` application folder:

```
<%@ page contentType="text/html"%>
<%@ page isErrorPage="true" %>
<html>
  <head>
    <title>Our simple error handling page.</title>
  </head>
  <body>
    <h1>You tried to use an application that has bugs in it!!!</h1>

    Please harass the System Administrator <br>
    Exception: <%= exception.toString() %><br><br>

  </body>
</html>
```

3. Make sure Tomcat is running, and open `divByZero.jsp` in your browser. You should see the following error page:

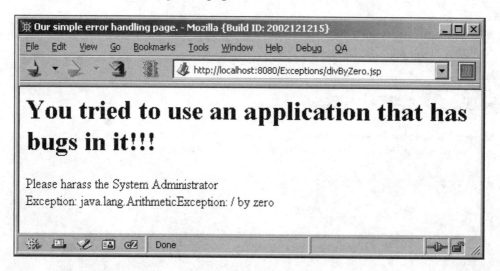

Notice that although this message is produced by our error page, we still see the URL for the JSP that caused the error in the browser's address bar. This is because Tomcat **forwarded** the result to the `showError.jsp` page – we'll see more about forwarding in Chapter 10.

How It Works

`divByZero.jsp` declares its error page in its `page` directive:

```
<%@ page contentType="text/html" errorPage="showError.jsp" %>
```

This tells the JSP container that if anything goes wrong, it should forward the request to the `showError.jsp` page.

Moving on to the error page itself, you should note two things:

❑ The `isErrorPage` attribute on the `page` directive telling the JSP container to build the implicit `exception` object.

❑ We use the JSP `exception` object (note small 'e') to determine what problem occurred:

```
Exception: <%= exception.toString() %><br><br>
```

JSP and Client-Side Errors

Now it's time to take a deeper look into the role that the client has to play in JavaServer Pages. JSP sits between our server-based logic, converting it to HTML and JavaScript, which is in turn interpreted by a remote client (typically a web browser). This twin-faceted nature of JSP can cause problems, particularly for new JSP programmers, as errors can be caused in the client-side code as well as by the server-side code that we've written.

While we can safely leave out the details of client-side coding at this level, this chapter will touch upon some of the more important points. There is a danger that JSP developers focus on the server side of the application to the detriment of the client side. Bad client-side design and programmer sloppiness can combine to create an array of problems. Secondly, because a JSP page can contain a mix of server-side and client-side logic, the client is at risk of receiving somewhat gnarled code that can seriously impact site performance.

Watch the HTML

The first thing to think about to reduce client-side problems is to ensure that our JSP pages generate properly laid-out HTML. That is, it must be syntactically valid and only use tags that are supported by the target browsers. HTML tags should be nested properly, because if they are not, the browser will behave unpredictably, usually resulting in the page not being displayed properly for the user. The types of errors seen due to malformed HTML are varied and strange, and include dropdown boxes not displaying correctly, form elements appearing at the wrong place on-screen, and worse.

For example, here is a snippet of badly formed HTML:

```
<table><form>
<tr><td>WROX</form>
</td></tr>
</table>
```

Note how the start and end `<form>` and `<table>` tags are improperly nested – they overlap each other. Here is the same script laid out correctly:

```
<form>
  <table>
    <tr><td>WROX</td></tr>
  </table>
</form>
```

As you can see, indenting code readably helps track down errors. In addition, specialized tools can help by double-checking the HTML to make sure it is formatted correctly. I recommend the following two products:

❑   **HTML Tidy**, which can be found at http://tidy.sourceforge.net/

❑   The **HTML Validation Service** provided by the W3C organization, at http://validator.w3.org/

One problem with JSP comes from the fact that the client-side code is *dynamically* generated by Java code, making it difficult to check the validity of the HTML that certain JSP code will produce. When checking client-side HTML, a good way around this problem is to use the View | Source option in a browser, and run that HTML through an HTML checker such as HTML Tidy to spot problems.

Finding JavaScript Errors with Mozilla

JavaScript is an important part of almost any HTML-based JSP application. It permits the programmer to perform certain actions client-side rather than making another request to the server (a so-called **server roundtrip**). As well as improving our application's performance by reducing network requests, this also helps by reducing the load each client makes on the server, allowing us to support more simultaneous users.

JavaScript can be used to validate form fields and implement other dynamic interactive features on a page. The price is of course that we then have to ensure our JavaScript code is error-free as well as the JSP, and we should also be aware that not all browsers support JavaScript, or have it enabled.

JavaScript can actually be tougher to debug than Java for many reasons. Firstly, it lacks the true exception handling found in Java proper. It can also be hard to spot bugs in JavaScript as the JavaScript code may only be executed under certain conditions, such as encountering an invalid form field. Another problem arises because, if an error is present in the JavaScript of a page, most of the page may well display just fine, but some features may not work as intended, or perhaps some content doesn't appear as it should. This is because the page's HTML may be intact, but only some of JavaScript has been executed, leaving the page unfinished. Many modern browsers do have a feature to alert the user in the event of JavaScript errors, but by default, these errors are hidden and the browser attempts to provide the best possible page to the user.

Several low-cost methods are available to help locate JavaScript problems. Perhaps the easiest is to use the Mozilla browser (Netscape is based upon the Mozilla browser, and will also work for this), found at http://www.mozilla.org/releases. Mozilla provides a great JavaScript console window that shows a detailed list of all the JavaScript errors that have occurred on a page.

Let's walk through an example to demonstrate this feature.

Try It Out   **Using Mozilla to Track Down JavaScript Errors**

1. Place the code below in a file called `error_javascript.jsp` in the `Exceptions` folder:

```
<%@page contentType="text/html"%>

<html>
  <head><title>JavaScript Error</title></head>
  <body>

    <div id="test">
    </div>

    <script language="JavaScript">

        var l_doc = document.getElementById("test");
        l_doc.innerHTML = "This line should appear on the page<br/>";
        ldoc.innerHTML = l_doc.innerHTML + "As should this one<br/>";
        l_doc.innerHTML = l_doc.innerHTML + "And then this one too";

    </script>

    <p>
      The above JavaScript code, inside the &lt;script> element,
      misspells l_doc as ldoc.
    </p>
    <p>
      Mozilla's JavaScript console makes it possible to find the error
      quickly.
    </p>
  </body>
</html>
```

2. With Tomcat running, open http://localhost:8080/Exceptions/error_javascript.jsp in your browser. You should see this:

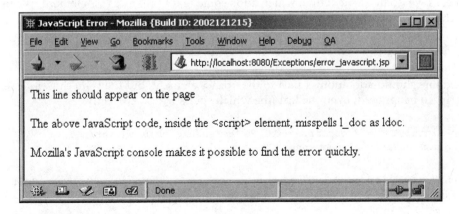

277

Looking at this, it's not immediately clear that an error has even occurred. However, an error has happened, causing two lines not to display.

3. Open the JavaScript console window by choosing **Tools** I **Web Development** I **JavaScript Console** in Mozilla. This window lists all of the JavaScript errors that occurred on this page, like this:

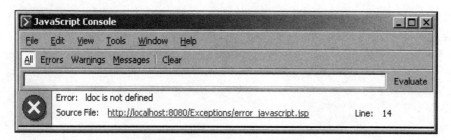

We see a description of the error itself and the line number of the error. In this case we see the code is trying to access a variable that doesn't exist (due to a mistyped variable name).

How It Works

The JavaScript on our JSP page contains a simple typo when the 1_doc variable is used. This one typo isn't enough to stop the page from running, but is enough to prevent two lines from being displayed in the browser.

Note the use of the JavaScript getElementById() method. This returns a reference to the named HTML element on the page:

```
document.getElementById("test");
```

Our JavaScript can then use this reference to modify that HTML element dynamically at runtime, as we do in the next line, which adds some text to that <div> element. We use the innerHTML() property of 1_doc to add the text inside the HTML tag in question:

```
1_doc.innerHTML = "This line should appear on the page<br>";
```

The next line should add another part to the <div> element, but the typo causes *all* remaining JavaScript to be ignored, even the last line which spells 1_doc correctly:

```
1doc.innerHTML = 1_doc.innerHTML + "As should this one<br/>";
1_doc.innerHTML = 1_doc.innerHTML + "And then this one too";
```

Note that both innerHTML() and getElementById() are only supported by newer versions of IE (5.0 and above) and Netscape (6.0 and above) browsers.

You can see that it isn't hard to track down client-side errors with Mozilla. It should be mentioned that this method of tracking down JavaScript bugs does have one serious drawback: applications intended to work only in Internet Explorer may use JavaScript that is not compatible with Mozilla.

Deciphering JSP Errors

When an unhandled JSP error occurs, the message output to the browser can be very confusing, and different JSP containers can handle the display and translation of the error differently. However, in the case of Tomcat, it is possible to walk you through how to translate the error into something more meaningful.

Using the Stack Trace

Earlier in the chapter, when executing the `untrappedError.jsp` page, the JSP container produced a long stack trace as part of the error message. Let's take a closer look at that stack trace, which appears in the lower section of the error message, under the section root cause:

```
java.lang.ArithmeticException: / by zero
  at org.apache.jsp.untrappedError_jsp._jspService(untrappedError_jsp.java:59)
  at org.apache.jasper.runtime.HttpJspBase.service(HttpJspBase.java:136)
  at javax.servlet.http.HttpServlet.service(HttpServlet.java:853)
  at org.apache.jasper.servlet.JspServletWrapper.service(JspServletWrapper.java:315)
  .
  .
  .
```

The first line tells us which exception was thrown, a "division by zero" error in this case.

The remaining lines specify where the error occurred. When you run a JSP page, it is converted into Java code (a servlet, covered in more detail in Chapter 10), and it is when executing this servlet that the error really occurs, rather than the JSP page itself. The servlet (a Java class that provides our page's functionality) is held in the class file called `untrappedError_jsp.java`, and the error occurred in that file at line 59.

This Java file can be found in Tomcat's `work` folder, under a subfolder corresponding to the URL of the page. So, the Java code for this page will be located in a file called `untrappedError_jsp.java` inside the folder `localhost\Exceptions\`, which is found in the `Standalone` subdirectory of the `work` folder (notice how the port number, 8080, is *not* included in the name).

If we open this file and scan down to line 62, we'll see the following line:

```
i = i / j ;
```

So, we have enough information to find the line of code causing the problem, and begin to solve it – it's not normally difficult to match the line in the Java code to the original JSP file.

Using Log Files

Our JSP container keeps a log of any events, activities, or problems that occur when our JSP pages are opened. Often, users can only give a vague description of a problem, or they will not even alert us of problems at all. This makes the log file a very important tool while in pilot and production stages of a project, when users are using the system heavily on a daily basis. Reviewing the log file every once in a while is a good habit to get into. With this in mind, let's now discuss the basics of a log file.

> **Our examples are all based upon Tomcat 5.0. Different JSP containers may maintain their log files in a different directory, and there could be other differences as well.**

In Tomcat's `conf` folder, you'll find a file called `server.xml`. Open it up and browse down to the following section:

```
<!-- Logger shared by all Contexts related to this virtual host.  By
default (when using FileLogger), log files are created in the "logs"
directory relative to $CATALINA_HOME.  If you wish, you can specify
a different directory with the "directory" attribute.  Specify either a
relative (to $CATALINA_HOME) or absolute path to the desired directory.-->
<Logger className="org.apache.catalina.logger.FileLogger"
        directory="logs"  prefix="localhost_log."  suffix=".txt"
        timestamp="true"/>
```

This `<Logger>` element tells us that Tomcat places its web application log files in a directory called `logs`. In addition, the log files will begin with the prefix `localhost_log` and end with the suffix `.txt`. The name will also specify the time the log was made due to the attribute `timestamp="true"`. Have a look in your Tomcat `logs` directory and you will some of the logs that have already been created, and named according to the scheme above.

A quick peek inside a log file reveals entries describing errors such as this:

```
2003-01-09 01:19:51 StandardWrapperValve[jsp]: Servlet.service() for servlet jsp threw
                exception
org.apache.jasper.JasperException: / by zero
  at org.apache.jasper.servlet.JspServletWrapper.service(JspServletWrapper.java:364)
  at org.apache.jasper.servlet.JspServlet.serviceJspFile(JspServlet.java:289)
  at org.apache.jasper.servlet.JspServlet.service(JspServlet.java:240)
  at javax.servlet.http.HttpServlet.service(HttpServlet.java:853)
  .
  .
  .
```

The log file contains the timestamp and stack trace of each error that happened. Note that exceptions handled by code are not listed in the log file: only unhandled exceptions and internal errors make it in. Since we have a stack trace, it is possible to use the techniques discussed in the previous section to find the error within the servlet, and then trace back to the JSP.

Log4j

Log4j is an open source API developed under the Apache Jakarta project, which provides a dedicated logging package. There are many reasons why we might choose to use a separate logging package rather than the logs provided by Tomcat.

Applications need a way to inform developers and administrators about their state, and often the simple log statements provided by Tomcat (or your servlet engine) are not enough. The log entries lack particulars about the state of our application when something does go wrong; that is, there's no information about attributes, the severity of the error, or other contextual information. We could construct our own exception object to output such contextual details, but this would require a fair amount of extra work.

Note that not all entries in a log file need to relate to errors, and might contain other data such as values of certain attributes or variables to give a picture of the state of our application and also to provide a way of gathering statistics, if so desired.

Third party log packages, such as Log4j, generally allow us to control when and where to log and what details to log. In this section, we will look at how to use Log4j to do all these things.

Installing Log4j

Log4j can be downloaded from the Apache web site at http://jakarta.apache.org/log4j by following the download link. The current version is 1.2.7, and you should download either the TAR file or the ZIP depending on whether you're running Linux or Windows. Each download contains full documentation, source code, and examples as well as a JAR file in the `lib` directory that contains the Log4j distributable. This JAR is placed in a web application's `WEB-INF\lib` directory if that application is to use Log4j.

Log4j Concepts

We need to cover a few Log4j concepts before we can move on to some examples. The basic concepts of the Log4j system are **loggers**, **appenders**, and **layouts**.

A logger is a component that is responsible for handling an application's log requests. In technical terms, it is a class supplied by the Log4j API that is used to create log requests. Each class in an application can create a unique logger, use a common logger previously created, or use a root logger. For instance, we could create a logger in the `User` class that we created previously like so:

```
Logger userLogger = Logger.getLogger("com.wrox.Exceptions.User");
```

Loggers are **named entities**, which simply means that each logger is known by a unique name, as passed in to the `getLogger()` method (so the logger above is has the name `com.wrox.Exceptions.User`). If no logger already exists with that name, Log4j will create one which remain available until the application is shut down. New loggers inherit the properties of the default root logger provided by Log4j (unless different properties have been specified in a configuration file).

Once we have a logger, we can use it to write to the log using methods on the logger instance, like so:

```
userLogger.debug("Debug log statement: user is accessing a file");
```

Here we're using a method called `debug()`. There are similar methods for outputting different kinds of messages, including `info()`, `warn()`, `error()`, and `fatal()`.

The appender is special Log4j class that specifies where log statements should be sent. We can choose from a `FileAppender` (for writing to files), a `JDBCAppender` (for writing to a database), a `ConsoleAppender` (for writing to the console), and several others. You can even write your own Appender if necessary.

The style that messages should use when entered into the log is defined by the Layout, so the three conceptual entities of the Log4j system interrelate according to this rule:

> **A logger sends messages to an appender using a given layout.**

An external configuration file details which appenders an application should use and the layout to be applied to log entries. This configuration file is passed to the Log4j `PropertyConfigurator.configure()` method at application startup, and will look something like the following:

```
log4j.rootLogger=debug, root

#
# For this simple example, we are just going to log to the console
#
log4j.appender.root=org.apache.log4j.ConsoleAppender

#
# When logging using the ConsoleAppender, the following value tells how and
# what to log. The SimpleLayout simply logs the level of the message and
# the message itself.
#
log4j.appender.root.layout=org.apache.log4j.SimpleLayout
```

Note the use of the hash character to indicate comments.

Try It Out   Logging With Log4j

1. We'll build on previous examples in this chapter to make them output log statements using Log4j. Start by creating a subfolder off Exceptions called lib. copy log4j-1.2.7.jar from Log4j's dist/lib directory to this new lib folder to make the Log4j classes available to this application. This is all that is required for an application to access and use the Log4j API.

2. Create a file called config.properties in the application's WEB-INF folder, and save the following in it:

```
#
# This defines the logging level for the rootLogger. It is not required
# if you are going to keep the level at debug as the rootLogger by
# default is at the debug level. The value after the comma is the
# appender for the root
#
log4j.rootLogger=debug, root


#
# For this simple example, we are just going to log to the console
#
log4j.appender.root=org.apache.log4j.ConsoleAppender


#
# When logging using the ConsoleAppender, the following value tells how
# and what to log. The SimpleLayout simply logs the level of the
# message and the message itself.
#
log4j.appender.root.layout=org.apache.log4j.SimpleLayout
```

3. Make a copy of User3.java called User4.java, and make the changes highlighted below. Make sure the parameter in the configure() method call matches the location of Tomcat on your system:

```
package com.wrox.except;

import org.apache.log4j.Logger;
import org.apache.log4j.PropertyConfigurator;

public class User4
{

    static Logger logger = Logger.getLogger("com.wrox.except.User");
    private String username;
    private String password;

    static
    {
```

```
              PropertyConfigurator.configure("C:\\java\\tomcat50\\webapps"
                              + "\\Exceptions\\WEB-INF\\config.properties");
      }

      public User4()
      {
      }

      public void setUsername(String username)
      {
        logger.debug("Username set: " + username);
        this.username = username;
      }

      public String getUsername()
      {
        return this.username;
      }

      public void setPassword(String password)
      {
        this.password = password;
      }

      public void validate() throws UserException, Exception
      {
        if(this.username == null)
        {
          throw new UserException("UserName must be supplied !!");
        }
        if(this.password == null)
        {
          logger.error("Password is null for " + username);
          throw new UserException("Password must be supplied !!",
                                  this.username);
        }
        if (!(this.username.equals("Dougal")
          && this.password.equals("roundabout")))
        {
          Exception trouble = new Exception("Couldn't validate your"
                                    + " password!");
          throw trouble;
        }

      logger.info("Validation successful for: " + this.username);
      }
  }
```

4. We now need to compile the User4 class. From the command prompt, navigate to the Exceptions\WEB-INF\classes directory. Before we actually compile, we'll add the Log4j API to the CLASSPATH environment variable with the following command:

> **set CLASSPATH=%CLASSPATH%;..\lib\log4j-1.2.7.jar**

5. Note that this change will be lost when the command prompt window is closed, so you may prefer to change the CLASSPATH using the System properties dialog as described in Chapter 1. We can now compile like so:

> **javac com\wrox\except*.java**

6. Next, change `loginException.jsp` as highlighted:

```
<%@ page contentType="text/html"%>
<%@ page import="org.apache.log4j.Logger" %>
<html>
<head><title>Throwing an Exception</title></head>
<body>
<p> This test page shows how to create a basic exception
    within a Javabean and how to use the exception.</p>

<jsp:useBean id="myUser" class="com.wrox.except.User4" scope="page"/>
<jsp:setProperty name="myUser" property="*"/>

<%
  Logger jspLogger = Logger.getLogger("JSPLogger");

  try
  {
    jspLogger.info("Validating user");
    myUser.validate();
    jspLogger.info("User validated !!");
    out.print("The user " + myUser.getUsername() + " is registered.");
  }
  catch (com.wrox.except.UserException usex)
  {
    out.println("We encountered a UserException: " + usex.toString());
  }
  catch (Exception e)
  {
    out.print("We encountered a problem: " + e.toString());
    jspLogger.fatal("A terrible thing happened !! " + e.toString());
  }
%>
</body>
</html>
```

7. It is now time to see the fruits of our labor. Restart Tomcat. When you start it up again, run the `startup.bat` file in Tomcat's `bin` folder to make the Tomcat console visible – it will whinge about missing `web.xml` files, but just ignore it.

8. When Tomcat's up and running, navigate to the `loginException.html` page. Enter a user name and hit *Enter* without typing anything in the password box. Watch the Tomcat console, and you'll see our Log4j messages appear:

```
Tomcat                                                              _ □ ×
INFO: Processed tld jar  /WEB-INF/lib/xercesImpl.jar 220
16-Jan-2003 15:08:02 org.apache.catalina.startup.ContextConfig tldScan
INFO: Processed tld jar  /WEB-INF/lib/standard.jar 310
16-Jan-2003 15:08:02 org.apache.catalina.startup.ContextConfig tldScan
INFO: Processed tld jar  /WEB-INF/lib/struts.jar 521
16-Jan-2003 15:08:02 org.apache.struts.util.PropertyMessageResources <init>
INFO: Initializing, config='org.apache.struts.util.LocalStrings', returnNull=tru
e
16-Jan-2003 15:08:02 org.apache.struts.util.PropertyMessageResources <init>
INFO: Initializing, config='org.apache.struts.action.ActionResources', returnNul
l=true
16-Jan-2003 15:08:05 org.apache.catalina.startup.ContextConfig applicationConfig

SEVERE: Missing application web.xml, using defaults only StandardEngine[Standalo
ne].StandardHost[localhost].StandardContext[/Utility]
16-Jan-2003 15:08:05 org.apache.coyote.http11.Http11Protocol start
INFO: Starting Coyote HTTP/1.1 on port 8080
16-Jan-2003 15:08:05 org.apache.jk.common.ChannelSocket init
INFO: JK2: ajp13 listening on tcp port 8009
16-Jan-2003 15:08:05 org.apache.jk.server.JkMain start
INFO: Jk running ID=0 time=20/210  config=C:\java\tomcat50\conf\jk2.properties
DEBUG - Username set: Dougal
INFO - Validating user
ERROR - Password is null for Dougal
```

9. Try leaving the user name blank, and see what results you get. Also try using the correct user name and password. You'll see corresponding messages in the Tomcat console:

```
Tomcat                                                              _ □ ×
16-Jan-2003 15:08:02 org.apache.struts.util.PropertyMessageResources <init>
INFO: Initializing, config='org.apache.struts.util.LocalStrings', returnNull=tru
e
16-Jan-2003 15:08:02 org.apache.struts.util.PropertyMessageResources <init>
INFO: Initializing, config='org.apache.struts.action.ActionResources', returnNul
l=true
16-Jan-2003 15:08:05 org.apache.catalina.startup.ContextConfig applicationConfig

SEVERE: Missing application web.xml, using defaults only StandardEngine[Standalo
ne].StandardHost[localhost].StandardContext[/Utility]
16-Jan-2003 15:08:05 org.apache.coyote.http11.Http11Protocol start
INFO: Starting Coyote HTTP/1.1 on port 8080
16-Jan-2003 15:08:05 org.apache.jk.common.ChannelSocket init
INFO: JK2: ajp13 listening on tcp port 8009
16-Jan-2003 15:08:05 org.apache.jk.server.JkMain start
INFO: Jk running ID=0 time=20/210  config=C:\java\tomcat50\conf\jk2.properties
DEBUG - Username set: Dougal
INFO - Validating user
ERROR - Password is null for Dougal
INFO - Validating user
DEBUG - Username set: Dougal
INFO - Validating user
INFO - Validation successful for: Dougal
INFO - User validated !!
```

How It Works

Our configuration file tells Log4j how and where to send log messages. Our file only contains three lines (ignoring comments). The first is this:

```
log4j.rootLogger=debug, root
```

This tells Log4j that the root logger, which we call root and from which the `JSPLogger` and `com.wrox.except.User4` loggers derive, has its logging level set at `debug`. The logging level determines what log statements are actually output from our code. For instance, if we set a level of `info`, then only log messages that use `info` and levels higher than it will be logged. The levels have the following hierarchy:

```
fatal
error
warn
info
debug
```

So using the `debug` level means all log messages will be output. The next line simply tells Log4j that the root appender will output messages to the console, using the built-in `ConsoleAppender`:

```
log4j.appender.root=org.apache.log4j.ConsoleAppender
```

The final line in our configuration file specifies the layout, or the style, in which the `ConsoleAppender` should output log statements. We use `SimpleLayout`, which as we saw in the Tomcat console, outputs the level of the message followed by a hyphen and the actual message.

Having created the configuration file, we need to load it in the `User4.java` class to initialize Log4j:

```
static
{
   PropertyConfigurator.configure("C:\\java\\tomcat50\\webapps"
                    + "\\Exceptions\\WEB-INF\\config.properties");
}
```

The `static` keyword and the `{}` around this code are required here, but don't worry too much about this – it simply means the code will be executed automatically.

Having configured Log4j, we can now use it in any class or JSP page by acquiring access to a Logger object. In our `User4` class itself, we use the following code:

```
static Logger logger = Logger.getLogger("com.wrox.except.User");
```

and within our JSP page, we use:

```
Logger jspLogger = Logger.getLogger("JSPLogger");
```

Notice that we didn't need to configure Log4j in our JSP. This is because, once configured in our User4 class, Log4j is available to any class within the same Java VM (**Virtual Machine** – the environment where Java classes actually run). JSP pages are, after all, Java servlet classes and can therefore access the Log4j details we've set up. Notice also, that the logger has the name JSPLogger when accessed from a JSP page. If we had other JSP pages, which any serious application would, we would use the same call as above and we'd retrieve the same Log4j object.

Finally, having acquired a logger object, we can create log messages at leisure! In the User4 code, we perform some debug, error, and info logging, while in the JSP page, we do info and fatal logging. Prudently placed log messages can be invaluable when attempting to understand what our application is getting up to, which is particularly useful when trying to track down bugs.

Old School Debugging

We'll end the chapter with a quick discussion of a few tried and tested debugging techniques. Exceptions can handle runtime errors within the code, but we almost always encounter bugs that need to be fixed before an application goes into production. Everyone has their own tricks to get to the bottom of such bugs, which might include some of the following:

❑ **Make a logic table**
Many programmers try to keep track of all the possible permutations of what their code will do in their head. However, it can at times be useful to create a logic table, a physical list of all such possibilities. A logic table takes the form of a matrix of required outcomes against the input data that should trigger each outcome. Once the table is created, we can verify each of the outcomes. Sometimes we simply overlook things, and the act of writing it down can help catch such oversights.

❑ **Print the code out**
Printing out code that is causing us problems can give us a fresh perspective, and this is often all it takes to spot an error in the code. When completely stuck this is a great technique, not least because it allows us to take the code somewhere quiet to read through, such as the local café.

❑ **Explain the code to someone else**
We can often acquire a strange blindness to our own errors. Having someone else looking at the code can often be a way to solve a difficult problem. This technique also requires us to explain our the logic out loud, helping us think about what is happening further. Some programmers go as far as to talk to inanimate objects or hapless bystanders (like their mom) when no other people are around, as the simple act of talking through the logic can be a tremendous help in solving problems.

❑ **Use a profiler or debugger**

Code in an application is a static thing, while the application itself is fluid and dynamic. As a result, the logic of the code can be elusive when writing. A debugger lets the programmer examine the state of variables and examine what is going on as the code runs in real time. A profiler is another piece of software that gathers performance statistics on how the code is running, and it can highlight areas that are causing problems. These tools can help us to locate where bad assumptions have been made in the logic. Debuggers are often built into Java **IDEs (Integrated Development Environments)**, while a profiler is usually sold as a separate commercial product.

Be warned that it does take extra time to learn how to use either a debugger or a profiler properly. However, it is worth both the cost and the time for professional programmers to learn how to use these tools, since they can save far more time and effort when solving problems.

❑ **Print statements within the code**

Often a snapshot of what is happening in the code can take us a long way to solving a problem. Debuggers are one way to see inside a running program, or we can add statements to output certain values at key points of our code. While this solution won't offer the robustness of a debugger, and we must take care to remove such statements before our application goes 'live', they can be a quick way to get to the root of things. For example, we could add a line such as this to a JSP page to display the value of a particular variable:

```
<% System.out.println("The value of i is " + i); %>
```

Alternatively of course, we could use the techniques described in the Log4j section to output helpful information.

Resources

In the quest to solve JSP and/or Java problems, half of the battle is knowing where to look. This section provides a list of online resources that may help. The following sites have forums or extensive searchable FAQ lists.

❑ For general questions about Java, try **JavaRanch** (http://www.JavaRanch.com/).

❑ For help on HTML problems, **SiteExperts** (http://www.siteexperts.com/) is a great place to ask questions.

❑ For help tracking down JSP bugs, two sites stand out: **JGuru** (http://www.jGuru.com/), a useful FAQ site for both Java and JSP, and the **Sun** JSP mailing list archive (http://archives.java.sun.com/archives/jsp-interest.html), which is an excellent place to search for answers.

❑ For help on solving JavaScript problems, try **javascript.faqts** (sic), which can be found at http://www.faqts.com/knowledge_base/index.phtml/fid/53/

❑ For general JSP reference materials, **JSPInsider** (http://www.jspinsider.com/) is one of the few JSP sites which concentrates on all aspects of building a JSP application.

❑ For Log4j information and help, head to http://jakarta.apache.org/log4j/docs/documentation.html

❑ Finally, if you need additional information about exceptions, check out **Sun**'s site. Part of the Java Trail has a nice review on exceptions called *Handling Errors with Exceptions*, at http://java.sun.com/docs/books/tutorial/essential/exceptions/.

Summary

There is a surprising amount to learn when dealing with errors in JSP and Java. The biggest problem comes from the sheer range of errors that you will encounter, from system problems to Java coding errors, from typos in Java to typos in HTML and Javascript.

Error handling really requires a new way of thinking. Instead of just allowing errors to happen, Java permits us to be proactive. It requires some time and practice to effectively build exception management into a web-application, but doing so builds a user-friendly and reliable system.

Fortunately, part of JSP's strength is that it is based upon Java. Unlike many of the other server-side web solutions, Java provides JSP with an exception handling system that allows us to easily handle both expected and unexpected problems, so that we can avoid crashed web pages wherever possible. While this means a little additional work during coding, the cost saving of using code that is reliable and able to cope intelligently with errors shouldn't be ignored when building professional sites.

Java's exception management is surprisingly simple, with only five basic keywords: `throw`, `throws`, `try`, `catch`, and `finally`. However, with the addition of the `Throwable` class (and its subclasses) and the ability to add exceptions by creating custom classes, Java's exception management is highly flexible.

We also looked at the challenging environment JSP offers for error handling. With JSP code running on the server, but producing code which will run on a client machine, it presents many areas for things to go wrong. Understanding the nature of JSP is as important for solving problems as using solid exception management based on Java exception management.

We had a good look at how to use Log4j to send log messages that are more flexible than the built-in logging capability of Tomcat and other servlet engines.

Back in Chapter 6, we looked at the concept of JSP **tag libraries**, though we only considered how to make use of pre-existing libraries such as the Jakarta project's request library. We've now learned enough to be able to start writing our very own tag libraries, and that's the subject for the next chapter.

CHAPTER 9

Writing Tag Libraries

As we have seen throughout earlier chapters, the JSTL encapsulates key functionality applicable to many JSP applications. It provides many types of tags, such as iteration tags and tags for accessing databases using SQL. Along with these standard tags, JSP 2.0 technology also provides the facility for creating application-specific custom tags. In other words, we can build and distribute our own tags for use in JSP pages.

Tag libraries simplify JSP coding and make pages easier to maintain. In other words, unlike Java code, JSP tags blend well with the JSP style of coding. Custom tags can be created to send e-mails, manage the flow or logic of an application, access application specific Java beans, and more. There are many tag libraries that are freely available for a variety of such common tasks, and some of these are listed in the *Resources* section at the end of this chapter.

However, not every application's needs are catered for by these third-party libraries, and so at some point you may decide it's appropriate to develop your own new tags. This chapter discusses issues involved in the development of custom tag libraries.

In this chapter you will learn how to:

- ❑ Create and use simple tags
- ❑ Develop different types of classic tags
- ❑ Program with custom tags, including:
  - ❑ Creating cooperating tags
  - ❑ Adding attributes to tags
  - ❑ Creating tags with scripting variables
  - ❑ Accessing variables from JSP using TEI helper classes
  - ❑ Building and packaging tag libraries for distribution/reuse

Custom Tags

> A custom tag is like a JavaBean but with extra functionality such as `request` and `response` objects which contain details about the current HTTP request and response. Also, custom tags remove Java code from a JSP page to allow designers with no Java knowledge to maintain the web site.

JSP 2.0 provides two ways to create custom tags: **simple tags** created with JSP fragments and **classic tags** created with tag handlers.

Simple tags or tag files can be used to develop custom tags that are simple, presentation-oriented, and which can take advantage of existing tag libraries. Simple tags can still be written in Java by tag developers but remain useful for page authors who have no knowledge of Java. A tag file is a source file containing a reusable fragment of JSP code that is translated into a tag handler by the web container. We looked at both these types of tags in Chapter 4.

A tag handler is an object that conforms to the tag interface. You should implement a classic tag when the flexibility and power of the Java programming language is needed to supply the functionality required by the tag. For example, when you want to write a tag for simplifying database access, you would write a classic tag.

Types of Tags

A custom tag can have a rich set of features. It can access all the objects that are normally available to JSP pages, like `request`, `session`, and `application`. It can modify or filter the response generated by the page that contains it. It can be contained or nested within other tags, and it can communicate with other tags.

The following examples aim to introduce you to the different types of tags with the help a fictional `showTime` tag which displays the current time. We will look into the details of creating and using custom tags in later sections.

Simple Tags

Below is the simplest possible tag that doesn't require a body – that is, no code needs be placed within start and end tags. In this example, the tag would be replaced with the current time in the HTML page sent to the client:

```
<time:showTime />  <!-- Displays current time -->
```

Tags With Attributes

Tags can have attributes that customize the tag's output just like HTML elements, in the form `attribute_name="value_name"`. There are three kinds of attributes: **simple**, **fragment**, and **dynamic**.

Simple attributes merely state a value as a string, as in the following tag with a simple attribute named `timezone`, the value of which determines which time zone should be displayed:

```
<time:showTime timeZone="GMT" />
<!-- Displays current time for GMT time zone -->
```

Fragment attributes specify values as portions of JSP code within the `<jsp:attribute>` element as shown below:

```
<time:showTime format="HH:MM:SS:mmm">
  <jsp:attribute name="timeZone">
    GMT
  </jsp:attribute>
</time:showTime>
```

Dynamic attributes allow the tag to specify an unknown number of related attributes as a set that follows the pattern demonstrated by `timeZone` in this example:

```
<time:showTime timeZone1="PST" timeZone2="GMT" timeZone3="EST"/>
```

Tags With a Body

A JSP tag can contain custom tags, core tags, scripting elements, HTML text, or tag-dependent content in the **body** between its start and end tags. In this example, the time zone is passed as body content rather than as an attribute:

```
<time:showTime format="HH:MM:SS">
  GMT
</time:showTime>
```

Cooperating Tags

Tags can cooperate with each other by implicitly sharing objects. In the following example, the `connection` tag creates a named SQL connection object called `con1`, which is then used by the `query` tag:

```
<mySQL:connection id="con1"/>

<mySQL:query id="query1" conn="con1">
  .
  .
  .
</mySQL:query>
```

Building Custom Tags

Now we've seen how custom tags can appear on a JSP page, let's get down to the business of creating custom tags. As mentioned earlier, simple and classic are two kinds of tags. Simple tags can be created from pure JSP code or they can use Java. Classic tags have to be written in Java – they implement interfaces defined by the JSP specification and extend a few of the helper classes provided.

Both types of tags must be declared in a **descriptor file** if they are to be used in a page.

Introducing Tag Library Descriptors

Tag libraries must be described to the JSP container in order for them to be used. This description is placed in an XML configuration file called a **Tag Library Descriptor**, or **TLD**.

Tag libraries may comprise many tags and the TLD file provides details about both the tag library as a whole and each tag it contains. TLD files have the extension `.tld`, and are usually stored in the WEB-INF/tags folder of your web application. Tag files placed in the WEB-INF/tags directory, or a subdirectory, are accessible to JSP pages without the need to explicitly write a Tag Library Descriptor. This makes it easy to create libraries of JSP code by simply creating a new file containing the reusable code in WEB-INF/tags, or a subfolder off it.

TLDs are used by the JSP container to validate the tags and by JSP page development tools to facilitate development. TLDs are a crucial part of JSP tag development and are covered in the *Advanced Simple Tag Programming* section in this chapter. However, if there is no such file provided for a library, the JSP container assumes certain default values.

A TLD must begin with an XML document prolog that specifies the version and the schema (using the `xmlns:xsi` attribute). An XML schema is an XML file that specifies requirements for documents that conform to a particular XML structure. It is then followed by the `<taglib>` element which contains all the details of the library, and specifies the tags it contains within `<tag>` elements:

```
<?xml version="1.0"?>
<taglib xmlns="http://java.sun.com/xml/ns/j2ee"
        xmlns:xsi="http://www.w3.org/2001/XMLSchema-instance"
        version="2.0">
  <tlib-version>1.0</tlib-version>
  <jsp-version>2.0</jsp-version>
  <short-name>time_tag</short-name>
  <uri>http://myserv.com/time_tag</uri>
  <display-name>Time Tag</display-name>
  <description>Time utility library</description>

  <validator>
   <validator-class>
    time.Validator
```

```
      </validator-class>
    </validator>

    <listener>
     <listener-class>
      time.Listener
     </Listener-class>
              </listener>

            <tag>
        <name>showTime</name>
        <tag-class>time.ShowTime</tag-class>
      </tag>
  </taglib>
```

The root element, `<taglib>`, contains a variety of elements, the most important of which are listed below:

Element	Description
`<tlib-version>`	Version of the tag library (above it is 1.0)
`<jsp-version>`	Version of the JSP implementation (above file states 2.0)
`<short-name>`	Short name for the tag library
`<uri>`	URI for referencing this tag library from a JSP page
`<tag-file>`	Descriptor for a simple tag
`<description>`	Descriptive name of the tag library
`<display-name>`	Name that will be displayed by the tag utility tools (if any) for the user
`<validator>` (optional)	Java class which validates or examines the JSP page for conformance to the tag library's requirements
`<listener>` (optional)	Java class which listens for events, such as loading and unloading of the JSP page
`<tag>`	Descriptor for a classic tag

These are **top-level elements** (that is, they must appear as immediate children of the root `<taglib>` element). Also remember that XML is case-sensitive! For more information about JSP and XML, see Chapter 14. The default values for some of these child elements are:

297

❏ `<tlib-version>` – provides a version for the tag library. Defaults to 1.0.

❏ `<short-name>` – derived from the directory name. If the directory is `WEB-INF\tags`, the short name is simply `tags`.

❏ A `<tag-file>` element is considered to exist for each tag file in this directory, with the following sub-elements:

   ❏ `<name>` – the filename of the tag file, without the `.tag` extension.

   ❏ `<path>` – the path of the tag file, relative to the web application root.

Developing Simple Tags

Previously, only developers who were familiar with Java could write custom tag libraries. In JSP 2.0, simple tag handlers allow tags to be developed that do not use any scripting elements in the attribute values or tag body. This makes them accessible to presentation-tier developers who do not know Java.

The body of the JSP fragment must only contain template text and JSP action elements but it cannot contain scriptlets. The recommended file extension for a tag file is `.tag`. The tag may be composed of a master file that can include other files which define complete tags or tag fragments. Let's start writing a simple tag right away.

Try It Out — Writing A Simple Tag

1. Create a new folder called `Libraries` in your `webapps` folder, containing a subfolder called `WEB-INF`. Add a subfolder inside that with the name `tags`.

2. Save the following code in the `tags` folder as `Greetings.tag`:

```
<%--
  - A greeting tag -
--%>

Hello, welcome to the world of Simple tags!
```

3. Next, save the following in the `Libraries` folder as `Greetings.jsp`:

```
<!-- Greetings.jsp -->

<%@ taglib prefix="tags" tagdir="/WEB-INF/tags" %>
<html>
  <head>
    <title>Simple Tag Example</title>
  </head>
  <body>
```

```
         <h1>Greeting Message Using a Tag File</h1>
         <hr>
         <br>
         <b> <tags:Greetings/> </b>
      </body>
   </html>
```

4. Finally, make sure Tomcat is running, open your browser, and navigate to localhost:8080/Libraries/Greetings.jsp:

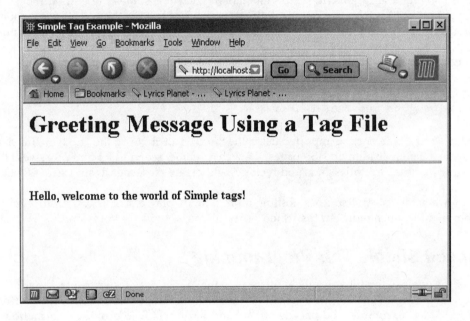

How It Works

The JSP file starts with a `taglib` directive so that it can use our tag from the `WEB-INF\tags` directory with a prefix of `tags`:

```
<%@ taglib prefix="tags" tagdir="/WEB-INF/tags" %>
```

It then uses our `Greetings` tag, which does nothing more than display a simple text message. Note how we've used it in combination with standard HTML markup to embolden the output:

```
<b> <tags:Greetings/> </b>
```

As we've not explicitly created a TLD for our library, Tomcat uses the defaults given at the end of the previous section, equivalent to this file:

299

```
<taglib>
  <tlib-version>1.0</tlib-version>
  <short-name>tags</short-name>
  <tag-file>
    <name>Greetings</name>
    <path>/WEB-INF/tags/Greetings.tag</path>
  </tag-file>
</taglib>
```

As it has no tag descriptions (in <tag> elements), Tomcat assumes the `tags` directory (and any subdirectory off it) is a library of tags defined by the files it finds there. There is no special relationship between subdirectories; they are allowed simply for organizational purposes. For example, a web application with tags held in a subdirectory of `tags` called `time` would contain two tag libraries:

```
\WEB-INF\tags\
\WEB-INF\tags\time\curTime.tag
```

Such tag libraries can only be imported using the `tagdir` attribute on the `taglib` directive. Upon deployment, before loading the JSP pages, the web container searches for and processes all tag files appearing in these directories and subdirectories and makes these tags available to JSP pages.

The tag we have just created does nothing more than display a greeting. Of course, tag libraries can be used for much more sophisticated purposes, as we will see very soon.

Advanced Simple Tag Programming

One of the goals of tag files as a technology is to make it as easy to write a tag handler as it is to write a JSP page. Previously, writing tag handlers was a tedious task, with a lot of effort required to write, compile and package them, and write a TLD to provide information to tools and page authors about them. The packaging of tag files on the other hand is simple and fast, while still providing as much power and flexibility as classic tag handlers.

Packaging Tag Files

Tag extensions written in JSP using tag files can be placed in one of two locations. The first possibility is in the META-INF/tags directory in a JAR file installed in the WEB-INF/lib directory. Tags placed here are typically part of a reusable library of tags that can be easily dropped into any web application. The second possibility is in a subdirectory of web application's WEB-INF folder. Tags placed here are within easy reach and require little packaging.

To be accessible, tag files packed up in a JAR require a TLD, which describes simple tags using <tag-file> elements inside a <taglib> element. The <tag-file> element describes the location of the tag file defining the simple tag, and must contain <name> and <path> child elements to define the tag name and the location of the tag file relative to the TLD respectively.

It is also possible to keep classic tags in the same tag library, although these are described by the <tag> element in the TLD. This means that in most instances the user need not be aware of how a custom tag is implemented.

Tag File Directives

There are many directives that can be used when developing simple tags. These include:

- ❑ taglib – used to make use of another external tag library, just as in a JSP page.

- ❑ include – passes the request to another JSP, similar to in JSP pages.

- ❑ tag – similar to the page directive, but applies to tag files instead of JSP pages. Its most important attributes are:

  - ❑ name : the name of the tag.

  - ❑ display-name : name which will be displayed by the tools.

  - ❑ body-content : provides information on the content of the body of this tag. Can be either empty, tagdependent, or scriptless.

  - ❑ dynamic-attributes : indicates whether this tag supports additional attributes with dynamic names.

  - ❑ description : a description of the tag.

  Here's an example:

```
<%@ tag name="add"
        display-name="Addition"
        body-content="scriptless"
        dynamic-attributes="false"
        description="A Simple tag" %>
```

- ❑ attribute – allows the declaration of custom action attributes. The important attributes are:

  - ❑ name : the name of the attribute.

  - ❑ required : whether this attribute is required (true) or optional (false). Defaults to false if not specified.

  - ❑ type : the runtime type of the attribute's value. Defaults to java.lang.String if not specified.

  - ❑ fragment : indicates if the attribute is a JSP fragment that needs to be evaluated.

  - ❑ rtexprvalue : indicates whether the attribute's value may be dynamically calculated at runtime by a scriptlet expression. Defaults to false.

  - ❑ description : a description of the attribute.

Here's an example:

```
<%@ attribute name="attrib" required="true" fragment="false"
               rtexprvalue="false" type="java.lang.Integer"
               description="Required Attribute" %>
```

❑ `variable` : defines a variable exposed to the calling page by the tag handler. Some important attributes are:

   ❑ `name-given` : defines a scripting variable to be defined in the page invoking this tag.

   ❑ `variable-class` : the name of the class of the variable. The default is `java.lang.String`.

   ❑ `scope` : the scope of the scripting variable defined. Can have values `AT_BEGIN`, `AT_END`, or `NESTED`. Defaults to `NESTED`.

   ❑ `description` : a description of the variable.

   ❑ `declare` : specifies whether the variable is to be declared.

Here's an example:

```
<%@ variable name-given="ADD"
             variable-class="java.lang.Integer"
             scope="NESTED"
             declare="true"
             description="Summation" %>
```

Tag File Standard Elements

The two **standard elements** that create content (which is sent in the response or stored in a scoped attribute for use elsewhere on the containing page) are `<jsp:invoke>` and `<jsp:doBody>`. These elements can only contain whitespace and `<jsp:param>` elements.

The `<jsp:invoke>` standard action takes a fragment name and optional parameter elements, and invokes the fragment, sending the output of the result to a page-scope variable that can be examined and manipulated. This standard action can only be used inside tag files. The following is an example of a fragment invocation with parameters:

```
<jsp:invoke fragment="myfragment">
  <jsp:param name="param1" value="value1"/>
  <jsp:param name="param2" value="${value2}"/>
</jsp:invoke>
```

`<jsp:doBody>` invokes the body of the tag, sending the output of the result to a scoped attribute that can be examined and manipulated. This standard action can only be used inside tag files. `<jsp:doBody>` behaves exactly like `<jsp:invoke>`, except that it operates on the body of the tag instead of on a specific fragment passed as an attribute.

Storing Output

We specify the `var` or `varReader` attributes to send the result of standard tag file elements to a scoped attribute. The result is stored in a scoped attribute with the name specified by `var`. Otherwise, the result is stored in a scoped attribute of type `java.io.Reader` with the name specified by `varReader`. The `Reader` object can be passed to a custom tag for further processing. Only `var` or `varReader` can be specified. A `<scope>` attribute may be included specifying an existing `var` or `varReader` attribute.

Let's now develop a more useful tag. We'll create one that implements a products catalog that stores products with their original and sale prices. It accepts two fragments for customizing the appearance of products on sale and at normal price.

Try It Out   **A Simple Tag with Attributes**

1. Create a text file in our Libraries application's tags folder called `catalog.tag`. The file starts out by defining a couple of attributes for the tag as JSP fragments. Each attribute defines a set of scripting variables that can be accessed in JSP pages using EL, as in `${name}`, `${price}`, and so on:

```
<%@ attribute name="normalPrice" fragment="true" %>
  <%@ variable fragment="normalPrice" name-given="name" %>
  <%@ variable fragment="normalPrice" name-given="price" %>

<%@ attribute name="onSale" fragment="true" %>
  <%@ variable fragment="onSale" name-given="name" %>
  <%@ variable fragment="onSale" name-given="origPrice" %>
  <%@ variable fragment="onSale" name-given="salePrice" %>
```

2. Our tag creates a catalog as an HTML table where each cell contains information about a single item. Each item is either at normal price or on sale. If it is on sale, we invoke the `onSale` fragment and if not we invoke the `normalPrice` fragment. In either case, we set values for attribute variables using the `<jsp:param>` tag:

```
<table border="1">
  <tr>
    <td>
      <jsp:invoke fragment="normalPrice">
        <jsp:param name="name" value="Hand-held Color PDA"/>
        <jsp:param name="price" value="$298.86"/>
      </jsp:invoke>
    </td>
    <td>
      <jsp:invoke fragment="onSale">
        <jsp:param name="name" value="4-Pack 150 Watt Light Bulbs"/>
        <jsp:param name="origPrice" value="$2.98"/>
        <jsp:param name="salePrice" value="$2.32"/>
      </jsp:invoke>
```

```
      </td>
      <td>
        <jsp:invoke fragment="normalPrice">
          <jsp:param name="name" value="Digital Cellular Phone"/>
          <jsp:param name="price" value="$68.74"/>
        </jsp:invoke>
      </td>
      <td>
        <jsp:invoke fragment="normalPrice">
          <jsp:param name="name" value="Baby Grand Piano"/>
          <jsp:param name="price" value="$10,800.00"/>
        </jsp:invoke>
      </td>
      <td>
        <jsp:invoke fragment="onSale">
          <jsp:param name="name" value="Luxury Car w/ Leather Seats"/>
          <jsp:param name="origPrice" value="$23,980.00"/>
          <jsp:param name="salePrice" value="$21,070.00"/>
        </jsp:invoke>
      </td>
    </tr>
</table>
```

Save this file.

3. Now we'll create a JSP page called `shopping.jsp` that uses this catalog tag. We need a `taglib` directive to make our tag library available to the JSP, and then we set up our page with some standard HTML tags:

```
<%@ taglib prefix="tags" tagdir="/WEB-INF/tags" %>
<html>
  <head>
    <title>Shopping: A Simple Tag Example</title>
  </head>
  <body>
    <h1>ABC Store: New Year Sale</h1>
    <hr>
    <h2>$$ Weekend Prices...Hurry$$</h2>
```

4. Now we come to the tag itself. We set it to print the catalog with sale prices in bold and then strikeout the old prices. Normal prices will be displayed in the ordinary font.

```
    <tags:catalog>
      <jsp:attribute name="normalPrice">
        ${name}<br/>
        ${price}
      </jsp:attribute>
      <jsp:attribute name="onSale">
        Item: ${name}<br/>
```

```
        <font color="red"><strike>Was: ${origPrice}</strike></font><br/>
        <b>Now: ${salePrice}</b>
      </jsp:attribute>
    </tags:catalog>
  </body>
</html>
```

5. Ensuring Tomcat is running, navigate to localhost:8080/Libraries/shopping.jsp in your browser and you should see something like the screenshot below:

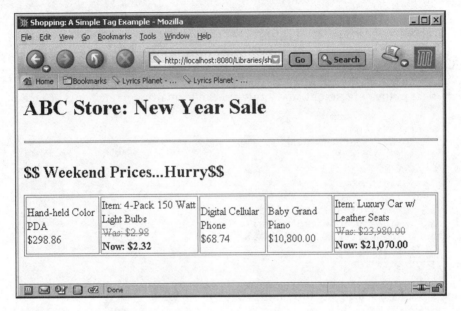

Excellent, we've created a tag that can be placed on a page to create a catalog with very little effort! I'll have a 4-pack of economy light bulbs, and a luxury car, please.

How It Works

In Step 1, we start by creating a JSP fragment `normalPrice` that defines scripting variables name and `price`:

```
<%@ attribute name="normalPrice" fragment="true" %>
  <%@ variable fragment="normalPrice" name-given="name"%>
  <%@ variable fragment="normalPrice" name-given="price"%>
```

Our `catalog` tag displays a set of products in a table with their sale prices. The following code in the tag invokes the `normalPrice` fragment and sets values for the variables name and price using the `<jsp:param>` element:

```
<td>
  <jsp:invoke fragment="normalPrice">
    <jsp:param name="name" value="Hand-held Color PDA"/>
    <jsp:param name="price" value="$298.86"/>
  </jsp:invoke>
</td>
```

As we place the `catalog.tag` tag file in the `tags` folder under `WEB-INF`, it doesn't need a TLD, as the container will generate an implicit TLD for it. We can use the tag in a JSP page that contains the `taglib` directive shown below:

```
<%@ taglib prefix="tags" tagdir="/WEB-INF/tags" %>
```

Our JSP displays prices in the catalog according to the attribute type (`normalPrice` or `onSale`). We accessed the JSP fragment (scripting) variables using EL , allowing us to display regular prices in the default font, and apply special formatting to elements of type `onSale`:

```
<tags:catalog>
  <jsp:attribute name="normalPrice">
      ${name}<br/>
      ${price}
  </jsp:attribute>
  <jsp:attribute name="onSale">
      Item: ${name}<br/>
      <font color="red"><strike>Was: ${origPrice}</strike></font><br/>
      <b>Now: ${salePrice}</b>
  </jsp:attribute>
</tags:catalog>
```

Thus we are able to selectively format the content.

The SimpleTag Interface

Simple tags can also be built by implementing the SimpleTag interface defined in the `javax.servlet.jsp.tagext` package. This interface defines a method called `doTag()` for housing the tag's functionality. Tags created this way do not support scripting variables and they are generally presentation oriented (although simple tags like the one we created in the previous section are in fact compiled into Java objects that implement this interface). `SimpleTagSupport` is an implementation of the `SimpleTag` interface, and it's usually easier to derive our tags from `SimpleTagSupport` rather than implementing our own version of `SimpleTag`.

We could create the `Greetings` tag that we created in the first example by deriving from `SimpleTagSupport` like so:

```
public GreetingsTag extends SimpleTagSupport
{
  public void doTag() throws JspException
```

```
    {
      getJspContext.getOut().write(
                      "Hello, welcome to the world of Simple tags!");
    }
}
```

Describing a Classic Tag with a TLD File

A tag library can contain several tags, in which case each custom tag must have a `<tag>` element in the library's TLD file that links it to a custom tag handler. All `<tag>` elements must contain at least the two sub-elements `<name>` and `<tag-class>`, and no two tags may have the same name. the following snippet shows a TLD that declares two different tags, `Salutation` and `Greetings`:

```xml
<?xml version="1.0" encoding="ISO-8859-1"?>
<taglib xmlns="http://java.sun.com/xml/ns/j2ee"
        xmlns:xsi="http://www.w3.org/2001/XMLSchema-instance"
        version="2.0">
  <tag>
    <name>prayers</name>
    <tag-class>custom.Salutation</tag-class>
    <body-content>empty</body-content>
  </tag>

  <tag>
    <name>greetings</name>
    <tag-class>custom.Greetings</tag-class>
    <body-content>empty</body-content>
  </tag>
</taglib>
```

Some of the most important child elements for the `<tag>` element in a TLD are given in the table below:

Element	Required	Description
`<name>`	Yes	A unique name for the tag. This name corresponds directly to the element name of the custom tag in your JSP.
`<tag-class>`	Yes	The tag handler class that implements the `Tag`, `IterationTag`, or `BodyTag` interface.
`<tei-class>`	No	An optional **Tag Extra Info** class for the tag, which must derive from `TagExtraInfo`. We will discuss the use of these classes later in the chapter.

Table continued on following page

Element	Required	Description
`<display-name>`	Yes	A short name for the tag, intended for display by tools.
`<description>`	No	A short description of the tag.
`<variable>`	No	Creates a scripting variable that can be used by the tag. We will explain the use of scripting variables later in the chapter.
`<attribute>`	No	Information about an attribute used by the tag. We will be covering the use of attributes later in the chapter. If the tag uses more than one attribute, use as many `<attribute>` elements as are needed.

Building Classic Tags

The JSP tag extensions API (Application Program Interface) was designed to execute in any JSP container. It was designed to be simple enough for web designers with limited knowledge of Java to able to use and yet allow Java developers to quickly develop and easily distribute extensions. It was also designed to allow wide range of tags to be built. In this section we will build some custom tags with this API.

To implement a custom tag, a handler class must be created, and then mapped to its corresponding custom tag using a TLD file. For example, if we created a tag called `time` to print the current time, we would have to write a handler class, called something like `TimePrinter`, and then map it to the tag named `time` through the TLD file.

A tag handler must implement one of the following interfaces of the `javax.servlet.jsp.tagext` package:

❑ `Tag` – this interface defines the basic methods needed in tag handlers, which define classic tags. The most important are the `doStartTag()` and `doEndTag()` methods, called when start and end tags are encountered by the container respectively.

❑ `IterationTag` – an extension of the `Tag` interface that provides additional functionality for iterations through a set of data. It defines an additional method called `doAfterBody()`, which is invoked as the container passes through repetitive body evaluations.

❑ `BodyTag` – an extension of `IterationTag` with additional methods for working with the tag's body content. It defines additional methods called `doInitBody()` and `setBodyContent()`.

All tag handlers, except for those which implement the `SimpleTag` interface, must define certain methods, chiefly the `doStartTag()` and `doEndTag()` methods of the `Tag` interface. When the starting tag (such as `<time:curTime>`) is read, the container calls the appropriate tag handler's `doStartTag()` method. When the corresponding closing or end tag (`</time:curTime>`) is read, the container calls the `doEndTag()` method. In general, creating a tag handler is nothing more than writing the code for each of these methods.

The Tag Interface

The `Tag` interface is the base tag handler interface that defines the methods required by all tag handlers. The interface requires six methods to be defined: `doStartTag()`, `doEndTag()`, `getParent()`, `setParent()`, `release()`, and `setPageContext()`. Often though, we only want to implement one or two of these methods in a tag handler class, and we can then derive from the helper class, `TagSupport`. As this class implements all the methods in the `Tag` interface, our tag handler class only needs to define (or specifically, override) the methods we need, such as `doStartTag()` and `doEndTag()`.

When the starting tag is encountered by the JSP container, the `doStartTag()` method is called; the return value of this method determines what is done next. Valid return values include `EVAL_BODY_INCLUDE` or `SKIP_BODY`. If `SKIP_BODY` is returned, the tag's body is not read. It should be used on tags that do not have a body or tags where we don't want the body evaluated. Returning `EVAL_BODY_INCLUDE` will cause the tag body content to be evaluated and available for use in your tag handler. In later sections, we will see other return values of the `doStartTag()` method.

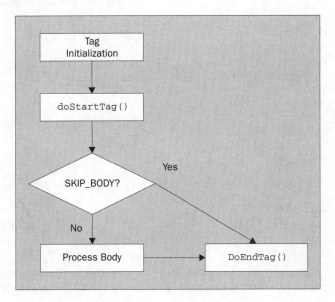

The `doEndTag()` method is called when the end tag is encountered. If it is an empty tag, this method is still called, but straight after `doStartTag()`. Valid return values for this method are `EVAL_PAGE` or `SKIP_PAGE`. If the `doEndTag()` method returns `EVAL_PAGE`, execution of the JSP page continues as normal after the custom tag. However, if `doEndTag()` returns `SKIP_PAGE`, the JSP page will stop after evaluating the custom tag. This means the rest of your JSP will be completely skipped. Be cautious when returning this value, because code appearing after the tag will not be executed.

Now we know the basics, let's create a simple custom tag for ourselves.

Try It Out   Extending TagSupport to Create a Classic Tag

1. We'll create a simple tag that shows the current time in a JSP page. Create a subfolder off `Libraries\WEB-INF\classes` called `custom`, and save the following code there, in a file called `timeTag.java`:

```java
package custom;

import javax.servlet.jsp.tagext.*;
import javax.servlet.jsp.*;
import java.text.SimpleDateFormat;

public class timeTag extends TagSupport
{

  // We need to override only this method for our tag:
  public int doEndTag() throws JspException
  {
    SimpleDateFormat sdf;
    sdf = new SimpleDateFormat("HH:mm:ss");
    String time = sdf.format(new java.util.Date());
    try
    {
      pageContext.getOut().print(time);
    }
    catch (Exception e)
    {
      throw new JspException(e.toString());
    }
    return EVAL_PAGE;
  }
}
```

2. Open a command prompt window, and navigate to the `classes` folder. Run the following command (**all on one line**) to compile the `TimeTag` class:

    > **javac custom\timeTag.java -classpath**

      %CATALINA_HOME%\common\lib\jsp-api.jar

The `-classpath` part of this makes sure that `jsp-api.jar` – the file containing classes such as `TagSupport` – is available for our Java code. If compilation fails, make sure that your `%CATALINA_HOME%` environment variable is set to the location where you installed Tomcat. You can do this from the command line like so:

> **> set CATALINA_HOME=C:\java\tomcat50**

3. Now we must create the Tag Library Descriptor file:

```
<?xml version="1.0" encoding="ISO-8859-1"?>
<taglib xmlns="http://java.sun.com/xml/ns/j2ee"
        xmlns:xsi="http://www.w3.org/2001/XMLSchema-instance"
        version="2.0">
  <tlib-version>1.0</tlib-version>
  <jsp-version>2.0</jsp-version>
  <short-name>ExampleTags</short-name>
  <description>A set of example tag handlers.</description>
  <tag>
    <name>time</name>
    <tag-class>custom.timeTag</tag-class>
  </tag>
</taglib>
```

Save this as `exampleTags.tld` in the `WEB-INF` directory of our `Libraries` application.

4. Now we'll create a JSP page called `currentTime.jsp` to use our new custom tag:

```
<%@ taglib prefix="example" uri="/WEB-INF/exampleTags.tld" %>
<html>
  <head></head>
  <body>
    Welcome to my web page. The current time is <example:time />
  </body>
</html>
```

Save this in the `Libraries` directory as normal.

5. With Tomcat running, navigate to localhost:8080/Libraries/currentTime.jsp. Your browser should display something like this:

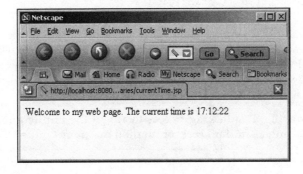

Every time you refresh the page, you should see the time update accordingly.

How It Works

We begin by writing a handler class, `timeTag`, that extends `TagSupport`, which in turn implements the `Tag` interface. To implement your own code you must override the appropriate methods from `TagSupport`.

Recall that `doEndTag()` is called when the JSP container encounters the ending custom tag. For this class, we override the `doEndTag()` method to have our custom code. The other methods will be left as they are. For simple tags, `TagSupport` already does a great job implementing them.

```
public int doEndTag(){
    .
    .
    .
    return EVAL_PAGE;
}
```

The code that outputs the current time is placed within the `doEndTag()` method. To generate the time we create a new instance of the `java.text.SimpleDateFormat` class, specifying a time format of "hours:minutes:seconds".

```
SimpleDateFormat sdf;
sdf = new SimpleDateFormat("HH:mm:ss");
```

The current time is passed to `SimpleDateFormat`'s `format()` method by creating a new instance of the `java.util.Date` class, and we store the formatted date it returns in the string variable `time`:

```
String time = sdf.format(new java.util.Date());
```

Next, we print the current time:

```
pageContext.getOut().print(time);
```

Unlike in a JSP page, the `out` implicit object (used to send output to the client) is not directly available to our tag, so we can't just write `out.print()`. Instead, we use the `pageContext` object, which provides convenient access to implicit JSP objects. We can access the implicit `out` object via the `pageContext` object's `getOut()` method.

> You should note that inside a tag, access to any of the implicit objects is achieved by calling a similar accessor method on **pageContext**.

Now, let's look at the TLD file, which starts with the XML declaration indicating this is an XML document:

```
<?xml version="1.0" encoding="ISO-8859-1"?>
```

The next line opens the `<taglib>` element. This element contains a `version` attribute and XML Schema and namespace definitions that together effectively state that the TLD conforms to the JSP 2.0 specification.

```
<taglib xmlns="http://java.sun.com/xml/ns/j2ee"
        xmlns:xsi="http://www.w3.org/2001/XMLSchema-instance"
        version="2.0">
```

Each TLD must have the `<tlib-version>` and `<jsp-version>` elements. These correspond to the version of your tag library and the JSP version required to implement it:

```
<tlib-version>1.0</tlib-version>
<jsp-version>2.0</jsp-version>
```

The `<short-name>` and `<description>` elements provide a little more information about your tags. These values are arbitrary and provide a unique name for the tag library along with a description of the tag's functionality:

```
<short-name>ExampleTags</short-name>
<description>A set of example tag handlers.</description>
```

The element of the most significance is `<tag>`. Each `<tag>` element appearing inside your TLD links a unique `name` to a tag handler class. The value of the `name` attribute is what we use as the element in JSP pages that use this custom tag. The `<tag-class>` element requires the value of your tag handler class:

```
<tag>
  <name>time</name>
  <tag-class>custom.timeTag</tag-class>
</tag>
</taglib>
```

Now we have a complete TLD for our newly made custom tag. As the chapter progresses, we will add new types of elements to the same TLD and extend the same custom tag library.

```
<%@ taglib prefix="example" uri="/WEB-INF/exampleTags.tld" %>
<html>
  <head></head>
  <body>
    Welcome to my webpage. The current time is <example:time />
  </body>
</html>
```

This being our example set of tags the `example` prefix seemed appropriate. The element name after the colon in our tag must match one of the `<tag>` entries in the TLD.

Real Time/Date Tags

On a side note, this example was inspired by an actual set of commonly used JSP tags. Even though this first example is not the most complex of custom tags, it still simplifies a common task to aid the JSP developer. We will continue to improve on this tag in the next section, but if you are interested in seeing a fully-fledged time/date tag library, the Jakarta `DateTime` Taglib can be found at http://jakarta.apache.org/taglibs/doc/datetime-doc/intro.html.

The IterationTag Interface

The `IterationTag` interface is used when a custom tag needs to repeatedly re-evaluate its body, which can be useful for looping (iterating) through a collection of objects without using a scriptlet. The `IterationTag` accomplishes the looping by extending the `Tag` interface and implementing a new method, `doAfterBody()`. This method is called after the body of a tag is evaluated but only if `EVAL_BODY_INCLUDE` is returned from `doStartTag()`.

The value returned by the `doAfterBody()` method determines if the body should be evaluated again. If `doAfterBody()` returns the value `EVAL_BODY_AGAIN`, then the body should be evaluated again. After evaluation `doAfterBody()` is invoked again, and again, until `SKIP_BODY` or `EVAL_BODY_INCLUDE` is returned.

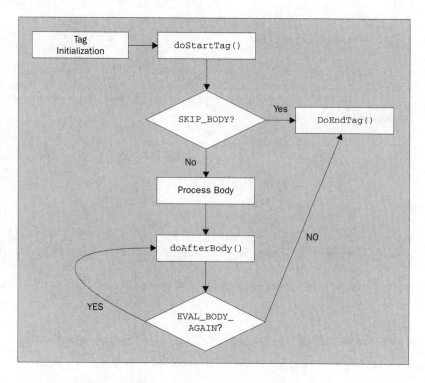

Creating a tag handler that implements `IterationTag` is done by extending `TagSupport` as we did with the `Tag` interface.

The following small example demonstrates the `IterationTag` interface by looping through a collection of objects and displaying some information about each. For simplicity, we will create a static array of strings to loop through, although we'd normally use this in a JSP page to iterate over dynamically generated collections. The procedure however is just the same.

The point to take away from this example is how the basic looping mechanism works with custom tags. Later on in the chapter we will improve the example to implement additional features of custom tags.

Try It Out   **Iterating Over a Collection of Objects Using a Custom Tag**

> **1.** Save the following tag handler code as `iterateTag.java` in the `custom` subdirectory of the `Libraries'` classes folder:

```
package custom;

import javax.servlet.jsp.*;
import javax.servlet.jsp.tagext.*;

public class iterateTag extends TagSupport
{
  private int arrayCount = 0;
  private String[] strings = null;

  public int doStartTag()
  {
    arrayCount = 0;
    strings = (String[]) pageContext.getAttribute("strings");
    return EVAL_BODY_INCLUDE;
  }

  public int doAfterBody() throws JspException
  {
    try
    {
      pageContext.getOut().print(" " + strings[arrayCount] + "<BR>");
    }
    catch(Exception e)
    {
      throw new JspException(e.toString());
    }
    arrayCount++;
    if(arrayCount >= strings.length) return SKIP_BODY;

    return EVAL_BODY_AGAIN;
  }
}
```

2. Open a command prompt, navigate to the `classes` directory, and run the following command, all on one line:

> **> javac custom\iterateTag.java -classpath**
>
> **%CATALINA_HOME%\common\lib\jsp-api.jar**

3. Edit the `exampleTags.tld` file to include the new tag handler:

```xml
<?xml version="1.0" encoding="ISO-8859-1"?>
<taglib xmlns="http://java.sun.com/xml/ns/j2ee"
        xmlns:xsi="http://www.w3.org/2001/XMLSchema-instance"
        version="2.0">
  <tlib-version>1.0</tlib-version>
  <jsp-version>2.0</jsp-version>
  <short-name>ExampleTags</short-name>
  <description>A set of example tag handlers.</description>
  <tag>
    <name>time</name>
    <tag-class>custom.timeTag</tag-class>
  </tag>
  <tag>
    <name>iterate</name>
    <tag-class>custom.iterateTag</tag-class>
  </tag>
</taglib>
```

4. Now we'll create a JSP page that uses the new tag:

Save `iterateTag.jsp` (shown below) in the `Libraries` application folder:

```jsp
<%@ taglib prefix="example" uri="/WEB-INF/exampleTags.tld" %>
<html>
  <head><title>Object oriented programming languages</title></head>
  <body>
    <h1>Object Oriented Programming Languages</h1>
<%
  String[] strings = new String[]{ "Java", "C++", "SmallTalk" };
  pageContext.setAttribute("strings",strings);
%>
 <example:iterate>
   The string is:
 </example:iterate>
  </body>
</html>
```

5. Start Tomcat if necessary, and browse to localhost:8080/Libraries/iterateTag.jsp.

316

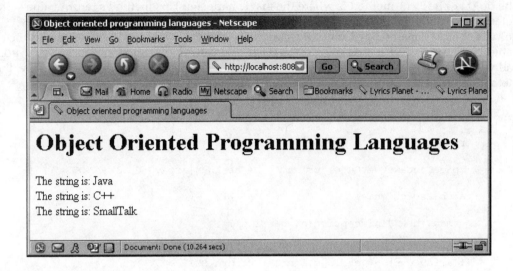

How It Works

The above example takes what we already know about tag handlers and demonstrates the
doAfterBody() method. The tag handler, iterateTag.java, was created in the same
fashion as timeTag.java by extending the TagSupport class:

```
public class iterateTag extends TagSupport
```

In this example, our collection of objects is going to be an array of strings. Some variables are
declared for the array, as well as an integer variable to track our position in the array.

```
private int arrayCount = 0;
private String[] strings = null;
```

The doStartTag() method is overridden to load an array of strings from the current
pageContext object. This tag requires the array to be defined in the pageContext before it
can be used. Notice the return value for the doStartTag() method. The value of
EVAL_BODY_INCLUDE tells the custom tag to evaluate the contents of its body and send the
results to the client. More importantly, the custom tag will then invoke the doAfterBody()
method to see what should be done next.

```
public int doStartTag()
{
    strings = (String[]) pageContext.getAttribute("strings");
    return EVAL_BODY_INCLUDE;
}
```

The `doAfterBody()` method is where the magic happens. This method's return value determines whether the tag should evaluate its body again. In this example, the `doAfterBody()` method prints out the current item in the array and then increments the count value. If the `arrayCount` value is now larger than the array, the method returns `SKIP_BODY` and will not loop again. If the `arrayCount` value is smaller then the length of the array, the method returns `EVAL_BODY_AGAIN` and we'll loop through again:

```
public int doAfterBody() throws JspException
{
  try
  {
    pageContext.getOut().print(" " + strings[arrayCount] + "<BR>");
  }
  catch(Exception e)
  {
    throw new JspException(e.toString());
  }
  arrayCount++;
  if(arrayCount >= strings.length) return SKIP_BODY;

  return EVAL_BODY_AGAIN;
}
```

The logic behind the new tag handler is simple. All we are trying to accomplish here is to use the `doAfterBody()` method to loop through the tag a few times while evaluating the body.

The change in `exampleTags.tld` is nothing more than a new `<tag>` element to describe the new tag handler:

```
<tag>
  <name>iterate</name>
  <tag-class>custom.iterateTag</tag-class>
</tag>
```

Once the tag handler and TLD are done, the tag is ready for use in a JSP page. our example page does two main things. First, an array of strings is created for the custom tag, and then the `strings` property of the `pageContext` object is set to the value of the `strings` array:

```
<%@ taglib prefix="example" uri="/WEB-INF/exampleTags.tld" %>
<html>
  <head></head>
  <body>
<%
  String[] strings = new String[]{ "Java", "C++", "SmallTalk" };
  pageContext.setAttribute("strings", strings);
%>
```

The second part of the JSP page uses the new tag. The tag does not require a body, but we can optionally include some code to be evaluated with each item in the array. For this example we just display a little text before each the array entry:

```
<example:iterate>
  The string is:
</example:iterate>
  </body>
</html>
```

The BodyTag Interface

BodyTag is the largest and most versatile of the three tag interfaces. It extends IterationTag to provide features for manipulating the body content. To fully understand the BodyTag interface, we first need to introduce the javax.servlet.jsp.tagext.BodyContent object.

The BodyContent object holds the results from evaluating the body of our custom tag. BodyContent has methods for clearing its contents, reading its contents, and converting the contents to a String. We can manipulate the BodyContent object each time we loop around and re-evaluate the body of your tag. This continues as long as needed and ends when SKIP_BODY is returned.

With IterationTag, you are restricted in the changes you can make to the content of the body. With BodyTag, there is no such restriction; changes can be stashed in a BodyContent object and used as you wish.

Two new methods are available in the BodyTag interface: doInitBody() and setBodyContent(). If the Tag Library Descriptor file indicates that the action must always have an empty action, by a <body-content> entry of "empty", then the doStartTag() method must return SKIP_BODY. Otherwise, the doStartTag() method may return SKIP_BODY, EVAL_BODY_INCLUDE, or EVAL_BODY_BUFFERED.

If SKIP_BODY is returned the body is not evaluated, and doEndTag() is invoked.

If EVAL_BODY_INCLUDE is returned, setBodyContent() and doInitBody() are not invoked, the body is evaluated and "passed through" to the current out, doAfterBody() is invoked and then, after zero or more iterations, doEndTag() is invoked.

If EVAL_BODY_BUFFERED is returned, setBodyContent() is invoked, doInitBody() is invoked, the body is evaluated, doAfterBody() is invoked, and then, after zero or more iterations, doEndTag() is invoked:

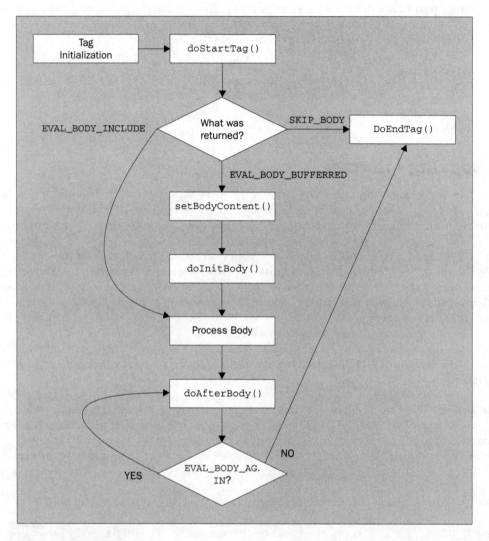

Another pre-built object named BodyTagSupport is used when coding a tag handler that implements the BodyTag interface. In a similar way to how we previously extended the TagSupport object, we can extend the BodyTagSupport object to make a tag handler:

```
public class exampleTag extends BodyTagSupport{
    .
    .
    .
}
```

Using the BodyTag Interface

Accessing the body content can be a very powerful tool for a JSP developer. As an example, let's say we run an online forum, but we've discovered that the built-in profanity filtering isn't quite as puritanical as we'd like. We're naturally disgusted at some of the profanities that now litter our nice gardening site, and so we set off on a mission to code a way around people's (un)natural disgodfulness.

The main tags in this library wrap an entire JSP page and implement the `BodyTag` interface. Accompanying the tags is a list of all the undesired words that we'll filter. The tags work by processing their body once per word on the list. Whenever the current undesired word is encountered, it is replaced by a series of asterisks. After filtering the body content completely, the results are saved and sent back to the client.

The `BodyTag` interface provides a simple solution to our problem. The profanity filter tags can also be reused on any JSP project with content that needs filtering. Manipulating the body of a tag is a powerful and valuable feature of custom tag libraries.

Try It Out   **Iterating Over a Collection of Objects Using a Custom Tag**

1. Our filter searches for all occurrences of the word "Drat" and replaces them with "****". In this example, the text to filter is hard-coded into the JSP page but the principles are the same if we use an external word list dynamically.

Save the following tag handler code as `filterTag.java` in the `custom` subdirectory of the `Libraries classes` folder:

```java
package custom;

import java.util.*;
import javax.servlet.jsp.*;
import javax.servlet.jsp.tagext.*;

public class filterTag extends BodyTagSupport
{
  public int doStartTag()
  {
    return EVAL_BODY_BUFFERED;
  }

  public int doAfterBody() throws JspException
  {
    String cleanString = "";
    BodyContent bc = getBodyContent();

    // Get bc as a string
    String unfiltered = bc.getString();
```

```
  // StringTokenizer splits the string into tokens, using spaces as the
  // delimiters
  StringTokenizer st = new StringTokenizer(unfiltered);

  while (st.hasMoreTokens())
  {
    String temp = st.nextToken();

    // Censor if we find the dreaded word
    if(temp.equalsIgnoreCase("drat"))
      temp = "****";

    // Add a space between each word
    cleanString += " " + temp;
  }
  try
  {
    getPreviousOut().print(cleanString);
  }
  catch(Exception e)
  {
    throw new JspException(e.toString());
  }
  return SKIP_BODY;
  }
}
```

Open a command prompt and navigate to the `classes` directory and run the following command:

> **javac custom\filterTag.java -classpath**

> **%CATALINA_HOME%\common\lib\jsp-api.jar**

2. Edit the `exampleTags.tld` file to include the new tag handler:

```
<?xml version="1.0" encoding="ISO-8859-1"?>
<taglib xmlns="http://java.sun.com/xml/ns/j2ee"
        xmlns:xsi="http://www.w3.org/2001/XMLSchema-instance"
        version="2.0">
  <tlib-version>1.0</tlib-version>
  <jsp-version>2.0</jsp-version>
  <short-name>ExampleTags</short-name>
  <description>A set of example tag handlers.</description>
  <tag>
    <name>time</name>
    <tag-class>custom.timeTag</tag-class>
  </tag>
  <tag>
    <name>iterate</name>
    <tag-class>custom.iterateTag</tag-class>
  </tag>
```

```
    <tag>
      <name>profanityFilter</name>
      <tag-class>custom.filterTag</tag-class>
   </tag>
 </taglib>
```

3. Now we'll create a JSP page that uses the new tag. Save `profanityFilter.jsp` (shown below) in the `Libraries` application folder:

```
<%@ taglib uri="/WEB-INF/exampleTags.tld" prefix="example" %>
<html>
<head>
  <title>Profanity Filter Example</title>
</head>
<body>
  <h1>Gardening Discussion</h1>
  <example:profanityFilter>
    <p>
    Drat ! That cat from next door has ruined my begonias again!
    </p>
    <p>
    Drat drat and double drat that cat!
    </p>
  </example:profanityFilter>
</body>
</html>
```

4. Start Tomcat if necessary, and browse to localhost:8080/Libraries/profanityFilter.jsp:

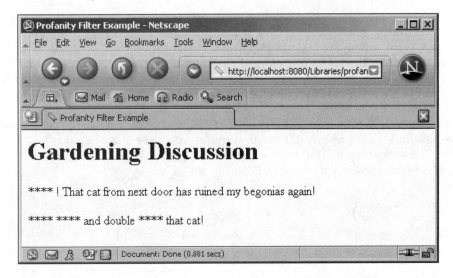

How It Works

Our tag has run through its body content, removing all offensive words. Note that this tag only matches words that end with a space, hence the space before the exclamation mark on the first line. As you'll see if you choose View Source in your browser, the HTML passed to the client looks like this:

```
<head>
  <title>Profanity Filter Example</title>
</head>
<body>
  <h1>Gardening Discussion</h1>
    <p>
    ****! That cat from next door has ruined my begonias again!
    </p>
    <p>
    **** **** and double **** that cat!
    </p>
</body>
</html>
```

Although the BodyTag interface is potentially very powerful, implementing it is a complicated business, beyond the scope of this book. For further information, see *Professional JSP* from Wrox Press, ISBN 1-86100-832-5.

Simple Cooperating Tags

Creating a helper tag can be very beneficial for a JSP developer. Dumping too many features inside one tag is not generally good OOP practice, and it's certainly not a requirement of custom tags. Also, moving scriptlets into custom tags makes them more acceptable, and easier to maintain. We can illustrate these points by placing the script generating the static array for the previous example in a custom tag. Should we later need to use this array on several pages, the custom tag would be readily available.

In general, when two or more tags function together they are referred to as **cooperating tags**. Our next example will illustrate one of the simplest cases where the two tags indirectly work together. The second tag will be the same iteration tag we just made. The first tag will handle the job of creating the array of strings.

Try It Out   Building a Set of Cooperating Tags

1. We'll now create a new tag handler to replace the scriptlet that creates the array in `iterateTag.jsp`.

Save the code below as `createArrayTag.java` in our `Libraries` application's `custom` directory:

```
package custom;

import javax.servlet.jsp.*;
import javax.servlet.jsp.tagext.*;

public class createArrayTag extends TagSupport
{

  public int doStartTag()
  {
    String[] strings = new String[] {"Java", "C++", "SmallTalk"};
    pageContext.setAttribute("strings", strings);

    return SKIP_BODY;
  }
}
```

2. Run the following command from the `classes` directory:

> **javac custom\createArrayTag.java -classpath**

%CATALINA_HOME%\common\lib\jsp-api.jar

3. Now edit `exampleTags.tld` to include the new tag handler information. The tag handler will be called by a custom tag called `<createArray>`:

```
<?xml version="1.0" encoding="ISO-8859-1"?>
<taglib xmlns="http://java.sun.com/xml/ns/j2ee"
        xmlns:xsi="http://www.w3.org/2001/XMLSchema-instance"
        version="2.0">
  <tlib-version>1.0</tlib-version>
  <jsp-version>1.2</jsp-version>
  <short-name>ExampleTags</short-name>
  <description>A set of example tag handlers.</description>
  <tag>
    <name>time</name>
    <tag-class>custom.timeTag</tag-class>
  </tag>
  <tag>
    <name>iterate</name>
    <tag-class>custom.iterateTag</tag-class>
```

```
    </tag>
  <tag>
    <name>createArray</name>
    <tag-class>custom.createArrayTag</tag-class>
  </tag>
</taglib>
```

4. Finally, modify `iterateTag.jsp` to use the new cooperating tags instead of the tag and scriptlet combination:

```
<%@ taglib prefix="example" uri="/WEB-INF/exampleTags.tld" %>
<html>
  <head></head>
  <body>
    <h1>Object Oriented Programming Languages</h1>

    <example:createArray/>
    <example:iterate>
      The string is:
    </example:iterate>
  </body>
</html>
```

5. Browse to `iterateTag.jsp`. You will still get the same results, but using two cooperating tags rather than the scriptlet:

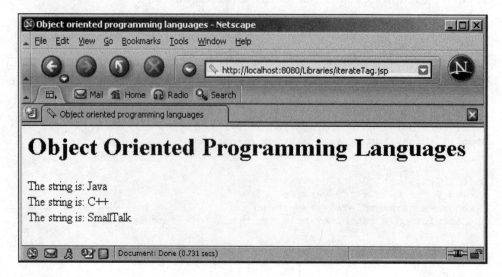

How It Works

No new concepts were needed to make the `<createArray>` tag. Its tag handler code only overrides the `doStartTag()` method to do the same thing that the scriptlet used to. An array is created and stashed inside the current `pageContext` object:

```
public int doStartTag()
{
  String[] strings = new String[]{ "Java", "C++", "SmallTalk" };
  pageContext.setAttribute("strings",strings);

  return SKIP_BODY;
}
}
```

The code for `iterateTag.jsp` does not change much either. Instead of the scriptlet we now use our cooperating tag:

```
<example:createArray/>
<example:iterate>
  The string is:
</example:iterate>
```

The Benefits of Cooperating Tags

At this stage, we should point out some features of our previous example. The first is that two tags can cooperate and share functionality. For this example, we used the two tags indirectly to pass information through the `pageContext` object. For more complex tag libraries, tag handlers also provide a convenient mechanism for nesting and sharing information to the surrounding tags. We will not delve completely into this mechanism because it is not terribly helpful when creating a few simple tags. Some good resources to learn more about this functionality will be listed at the end of the chapter.

Another good point to note is that we now have all of the functionality consolidated inside the custom tags. Should the functionality be needed across many pages the custom tag can be included in each page. A practical example can be related to the `<createArray>` tag. Our `<createArray>` tag loads the array of strings into the `pageContext`. This same array could be reused across many pages and the array used for various tasks. One change to the tag handler's code and all of the implementing pages will be updated. Additionally imagine if the `<createArray>` tag provided some attributes for customizing and performed a more difficult task such as querying a database to generate the array. Then the `<createArray>` tag would become a powerful piece of cooperating logic inside an easy and reusable custom tag.

This example's cooperating tags are simple because the concept is introduced with a contrived static array of strings. In practice, this is rarely the case and the cooperating tags provide a powerful tool for consolidating and reusing complex logic. In general, it is good to examine scriptlets and see if they would better suit a custom tag or work in cooperation with a custom tag. Custom tags work well and provide an easy interface for a JSP developer and those not terribly familiar with Java coding.

Later in this chapter, an additional benefit to custom tag libraries versus scriptlets will also be introduced to help enforce some of the above thoughts. Tag handler code and TLD files may be compressed and packaged in to a single file called a JAR for easy use amongst many JSP projects.

Extending Custom Tag Functionality

In previous sections, we used only a small part of the functionality that custom tag libraries provide. There are three principal ways to extend the functionality of custom tags.

❑   Create Attributes

❑   Create Scripting Variables

❑   Use Tag Extra Info (TEI) classes

In this section we are going to take a close look at each of these. Let's start by discussing tag attributes.

Adding Attributes to Your Tags

The `<time>` custom tag we created earlier works fine but it is not very flexible. What if we wanted to change the formatting of the date displayed? Right now the user is stuck with whatever we coded into the tag. `SimpleDateFormat` has many options for how the formatting looks. We just need a mechanism to customize the output of the tag. We can solve this problem by adding a `format` attribute to the tag and then applying the requested format.

The concept of attributes used with tag handlers may be new to you, but from a coding standpoint, attributes will look very familiar. In Chapter 4, we learned about JavaBeans and accessor methods. The tag handler class implements an attribute using a setter method of the same name in your tag handler's code. These set methods are no different from those seen with a JavaBean.

The <attribute> Element

Attributes for a tag must first be declared in the TLD file. The `<attribute>` element declared in the TLD file is a sub-element of `<tag>`. There must be one `<attribute>` element for every attribute of a custom tag.

```
<tag>
  <attribute>

    .
    .
    .

  </attribute>
</tag>
```

The `<attribute>` element has additional sub-elements that contain more information about the attribute (note that only `name` below is a required attribute):

Element	Description
`<name>`	The name of the attribute.
`<required>`	Specifies if the attribute is required for the tag. You can specify either `true` or `yes` to make the attribute required. The value of `false` or `no` means the attribute is optional. The default value is `false`.
`<rtexprvalue>`	Specifies if the attribute can be created dynamically by a scriptlet at runtime. Values available for this element are `true` or `yes` to allow for a runtime scriptlet value, and `false` or `no` to disallow it.
`<type>`	Optional attribute. Refers to the type of the attribute's value at runtime. If no value is specified, the default, `java.lang.String`, is used.
`<fragment>`	Optional attribute. This attribute can be a fragment to be evaluated by the tag handler (`true`) or a normal attribute to be evaluated by the container prior to being passed to the tag handler. If this attribute is `true`, then the `rtexprvalue` attribute does not need to be specified. The `rtexprvalue` attribute is fixed at `true` by the container. The `type` attribute also does not need to be specified, and is set by the container to `javax.servlet.jsp.tagext.JspFragment`. Defaults to `false`.

Let's now use this knowledge to add an attribute to the `time` tag we created earlier that lets the page designer specify the format the time should be displayed in through an attribute on the `time` tag called `format`.

Try It Out   Adding an Attribute to a Tag Handler

1. First, make the following modifications to the tag handler `timeTag.java`:

```
package custom;

import javax.util.*;
import javax.servlet.jsp.tagext.*;
import javax.servlet.jsp.*;
import java.text.SimpleDateFormat;

public class timeTag extends TagSupport
{
  String format = "HH:mm:ss";

  public void setFormat(String newFormat)
  {
    format = newFormat;
  }
  public int doEndTag() throws JspException
  {
    SimpleDateFormat sdf;
    sdf = new SimpleDateFormat(format);
    String time = sdf.format(new java.util.Date());
    try
    {
      pageContext.getOut().print(time);
    }
    catch (Exception e)
    {
      throw new JspException(e.toString());
    }
    return EVAL_PAGE;
  }
}
```

2. Run the following command from the classes directory:

> **javac custom\timeTag.java -classpath**

   %CATALINA_HOME%\common\lib\jsp-api.jar

3. Now we need to reflect the tag handler class changes in `exampleTags.tld` by adding the following highlighted lines:

```
<?xml version="1.0" encoding="ISO-8859-1"?>
<taglib xmlns="http://java.sun.com/xml/ns/j2ee"
        xmlns:xsi="http://www.w3.org/2001/XMLSchema-instance"
        version="2.0">
```

```
    <tlib-version>1.0</tlib-version>
    <jsp-version>2.0</jsp-version>
    <short-name>ExampleTags</short-name>
    <description>A set of example tag handlers.</description>
    <tag>
      <name>time</name>
      <tag-class>custom.timeTag</tag-class>
      <attribute>
        <name>format</name>
      </attribute>
    </tag>
    <tag>
      <name>iterate</name>
      <tag-class>custom.iterateTag</tag-class>
    </tag>
    <tag>
      <name>createArray</name>
      <tag-class>custom.createArrayTag</tag-class>
    </tag>
</taglib>
```

4. Finally, edit `currentTime.jsp` to use the new attribute:

```
<%@ taglib prefix="example" uri="/WEB-INF/exampleTags.tld" %>
<html>
  <head></head>
  <body>
    Hello, the current date and time is
    <example:time format="dd/MM/yy HH:mm:ss"/>
  </body>
</html>
```

5. Since we have changed the tag handler class, the TLD, and the JSP, we need to make sure the container uses the new version. Restart Tomcat to reload the changes and browse to `currentTime.jsp`. The new message and formatting will appear:

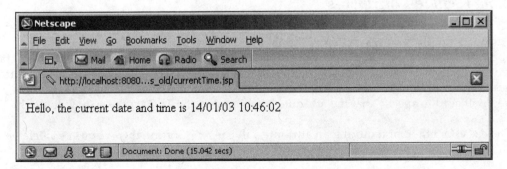

331

How It Works

Adding attributes to tag handlers is not a difficult task. Attributes are represented in a tag handler by a setter method of the same name. Our new attribute is named `format`. To reflect this in our tag handler code, a method is needed, called `setFormat()`. A new variable will also be created in the tag handler called `format`:

```
String format = "HH:mm:ss";

  public void setFormat(String newFormat){
    format = newFormat;
  }
```

The string passed to the `SimpleDateFormat` object is now changed to the value given by the `format` variable. If the user doesn't specify this attribute, the original formatting will apply:

```
sdf = new SimpleDateFormat(format);
```

The possible values for the format attribute are the same as defined in the `SimpleDateFormat` object documentation. In the example we demonstrated this by adding in the date ahead of the current time.

Reflecting the custom tag's new attribute in the TLD is also an easy task. We add a new `<attribute>` element to `exampleTags.tld` inside the `<tag>` element. The `<attribute>` element has a `<name>` child element providing the name of the new attribute. This name also defines the set accessor to call in the custom tag handler:

```
<display-name>time</display-name>
<attribute>
  <name>format</name>
</attribute>
```

Making Required Attributes

There is no restriction on the number of attributes for a custom tag. Adding additional attributes simply requires repeating the above steps for each attribute needed: add the appropriate setter method in your tag handler, and add the attribute to your TLD. By default, any attribute added will *not* be required by the tag. Sometimes it does not matter if an attribute is left optional; however other attributes might be critical to make the tag work. In these cases you will need to specify that the attribute is required in the TLD. Let's see how to do this.

The easiest method of requiring an attribute value is by inserting the `<required>` element as a child of the appropriate attribute element.

```
    <attribute>
      <name>format</name>
      <required>true</required>
    </attribute>
```

Using the `<required>` element like this means that if the user doesn't specify a value for this attribute when using the tag, an exception will be thrown, as shown below:

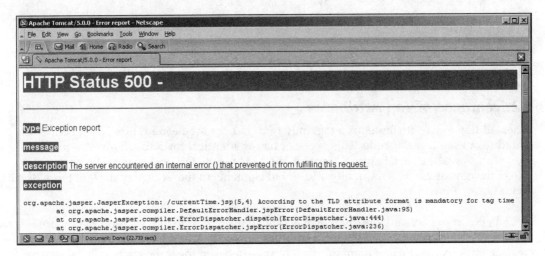

Displaying the error in such a crude manner is not a requirement. The error message does eventually say According to the TLD attribute format is mandatory for tag time, although a custom error page or a `try...catch` statement would pretty up the exception message.

Evaluating Attribute Values at Runtime

The `<rtexprvalue>` element lets us control whether the attribute can accept scriptlet expressions evaluated at request time, or whether they must be static values. For better performance, custom tag attributes default to requiring static values. Additionally, the value of an attribute does not necessarily need to be a string. A more advanced feature of custom tag attributes is to allow any type of object to be passed in to the set accessor. This feature may only be used if the `<rtexprvalue>` element is set to `true`.

For an example, let us pretend `exampleTags.tld` had set the `rtexprvalue` element to `true`:

```
    <attribute>
      <name>format</name>
      <rtexprvalue>true</rtexprvalue>
    </attribute>
```

When using the `time` tag, a scriptlet expression would be perfectly valid for our attribute value. It might look similar to below if the format value had been passed as a parameter in the `request` for the web page:

```
<%@ taglib prefix="example" uri="/WEB-INF/exampleTags.tld" %>
<html>
  <head></head>
  <body>
    Welcome to my webpage. The current time is
    <example:time format="${param.format}"/>
  </body>
</html>
```

This would let the user specify the time format rather than having it statically coded into the JSP.

The Advantages of Tag Attributes

When adding a new attribute for a tag, only two changes are needed. First, a set accessor is added to our tag handler code. This accessor has an identical form to what we've previously seen with a JavaBean in Chapter 4. Second, the TLD for the tag library must be updated to reflect the new attribute. Optionally additional elements in the TLD may declare more details about the attribute.

Overall, it is very easy and worthwhile to add attributes for a custom tag, and in practice it is rare to see a custom tag that does not allow attributes to specify additional information. The method of creating attributes and using them does not change between the three tag handler interfaces.

Scripting Variables

One of the most popular uses for tag libraries is to remove the need for scriptlets in JSP pages, but tag libraries are not limited to this purpose. A tag handler can also create objects and store them in the `pageContext` object for use in JSP code. Such objects created by a tag handler are known as **scripting variables**. In effect, they provide the same functionality as `<jsp:useBean>` action tags, but in a more flexible manner. We are also able to define the scripting variable's scope within the JSP page.

There are two ways that we can retrieve a scripting variable from a JSP page:

❑   Declare the variable in the TLD

❑   Create a helper `TagExtraInfo` class

Let's look at each of these in turn.

Declaring Scripting Variables in the TLD File

If you want to create a variable in your tag handler for access by scriptlet code in your JSP, the simplest way is to declare it is in the TLD file.

Recall from earlier the `<createArray>` tag creates an object and sets it within the pageContext. The `<createArray>` tag was originally designed to cooperate with the `<iterate>` tag, but we can also use `<createArray>` with a scriptlet. So, why do we need to bother declaring a scripting variable in the TLD? After all, we could just retrieve the scripting variable using a scriptlet that calls the `pageContext.getAttribute()` method. To answer this question, let's do exactly that; we'll retrieve a scripting variable using a scriptlet.

This first example may seem like a step backwards from the previous examples. Don't worry. We need to take a quick step back to introduce scripting variables before demonstrating their full potential.

This example removes the code from `iterateTag.java` and places it in a scriptlet.

Try It Out   **Using a Scripting Variable in a JSP Scriptlet**

1. Create a new JSP using the code below and save it as `scriptingVariables.jsp.` in the `Libraries` folder:

```
<%@ taglib prefix="example" uri="/WEB-INF/exampleTags.tld" %>
<html>
  <head></head>
  <body>
    <example:createArray/>
    <%
      String[] strings = (String [])pageContext.getAttribute("strings");
    %>
    There are <%= strings.length %> strings available.<br>
    <%
      for(int i = 0; i<strings.length; i++)
      {
        out.println("The value \"" + strings[i] + "\" is in slot #" + i
                 + " of the array.<br>");
      }
    %>
  </body>
</html>
```

Note the use of the sequence \ " to insert a double-quotes character in the page text.

2. Now browse to http://localhost:8080/Libraries/scriptingVariables.jsp:

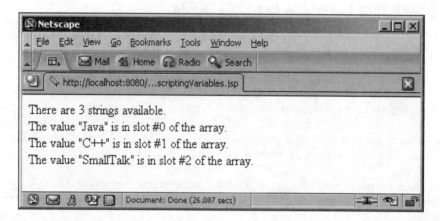

As you can see, the scriptlet can access the array of strings in the same fashion as the custom tag did.

How It Works

The example is quick and to the point. The JSP page looks similar to iterateTag.jsp but instead of using the custom tag, we have placed a few scriptlets on the JSP page. The first scriptlet takes the array stored in the pageContext object by the <createArray> tag and turns it into an array of strings available for the other scripts on the page:

```
<%
   String[] strings = (String [])pageContext.getAttribute("strings");
%>
```

The second section of code uses the new array of strings and shows a little information about them. The looping previously done by the <iterate> tag is now accomplished with a for loop for this single JSP.

```
There are <%= strings.length %> strings available.<br>
<%
   for(int i = 0; i<strings.length; i++) {
     out.println("The value \"" + strings[i] + "\" is in slot #"
                                 + i + " of the array.<BR>");
   }
%>
   </body>
</html>
```

On the plus side, the new JSP shows that a cooperating tag need not always cooperate with other tags. Working with a scriptlet is perfectly valid. However, with the scriptlet there are two points we should look at and improve on. The first is how the scripting variable is introduced to the JSP page. The first scriptlet is not actually needed at all. Consider the `<jsp:useBean>` action, where a scripting variable is directly created in our JSP. Custom tag libraries can also mimic this functionality and directly introduce scripting variables. The easiest method is by declaring the scripting variable in the TLD.

Another justification for eliminating the scriptlet is reusability and maintainability. When using scriptlets we have specific code on each JSP that would need to be modified if we wanted to change something about how it works. If we've got a lot of pages on our site, this can be a very time consuming and error-prone activity. The custom tag puts all of our code in one place making changes much quicker and reliable.

In the previous example, we used a scriptlet in conjunction with a custom tag. This is a double whammy, because if the scriptlet needs changing, we must change it on each implementing JSP, and if the custom tag's logic is changed, it might disrupt the scriptlet's functionality also. We can solve this problem by letting the custom tag be responsible for both setting the variable in the `pageContext` and initializing a new scripting variable.

Adding a scripting variable via the TLD is accomplished by adding a `<variable>` element as a child to the appropriate `<tag>` element.

The `<variable>` Element

The `<variable>` element in the TLD is a sub-element of `<tag>` and declares scripting variables for a particular tag. It contains its own subelements described below:

Element	Description
`<name-given>`	This contains the name of the scripting variable. Note that there is another way for naming a scripting variable, but we don't need to worry about it here – as long as one is used, the TLD is valid.
`<variable-class>`	The value of this element indicates the Java type of the scripting variable.
`<declared>`	The value of this element is `true` (or `yes`) if the scripting variable is new.
`<scope>`	The value for this element defines the scope of the scripting variable. There are three possibilities. If it is `AT_BEGIN`, the scripting variable is in scope after the starting tag. `AT_END` indicates it is in scope after the ending tag, and `NESTED` means the variable is valid between the start and end tags.

In the case of the `<createArray>` tag, we can add the `<variable>` element to remove the need for the first scriptlet in `scriptingVariables.jsp`. Let's see how.

The previous example used a scriptlet dependent on a custom tag. We can solve the problems this creates by letting the custom tag be responsible for both setting the variable in the `pageContext` and initializing a new scripting variable.

Try It Out   Introducing a Scripting Variable into a JSP Page Using the TLD File

1. Add a `<variable>` element for the `<createArray>` tag in `exampleTags.tld`:

```xml
<?xml version="1.0" encoding="ISO-8859-1"?>
<taglib xmlns="http://java.sun.com/xml/ns/j2ee"
        xmlns:xsi="http://www.w3.org/2001/XMLSchema-instance"
        version="2.0">
  <tlib-version>1.0</tlib-version>
  <jsp-version>2.0</jsp-version>
  <short-name>ExampleTags</short-name>
  <description>A set of example tag handlers.</description>
  <tag>
    <name>time</name>
    <tag-class>custom.timeTag</tag-class>
    <attribute>
      <name>format</name>
    </attribute>
  </tag>
  <tag>
    <name>iterate</name>
    <tag-class>custom.iterateTag</tag-class>
  </tag>
  <tag>
    <name>createArray</name>
    <tag-class>custom.createArrayTag</tag-class>
    <variable>
      <name-given>strings</name-given>
      <variable-class>java.lang.String []</variable-class>
      <declare>true</declare>
      <scope>AT_END</scope>
    </variable>
  </tag>
</taglib>
```

2. Now remove the first scriptlet in `scriptingVariables.jsp`:

```jsp
<%@ taglib prefix="example" uri="/WEB-INF/exampleTags.tld" %>
<html>
  <head></head>
  <body>
    <example:createArray/>
```

```
There are <%= strings.length %> strings available.<br>
<%
for(int i = 0; i<strings.length; i++)
{
  out.println ("The value \"" + strings[i] + "\" is in slot #" + i
           + " of the array.<BR>");
}
%>
</body>
</html>
```

3. Restart Tomcat and browse to `scriptingVariables.jsp` to verify it now works without the scriptlet:

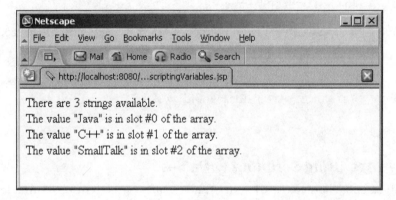

How It Works

Our previous example functions around the new `<variable>` element introduced to the `exampleTags.tld`.

The `<variable>` element is responsible for introducing the new scripting variable. Notice the `<variable>` element is placed inside the `<tag>` element for the `<createArray>` tag. Each of our custom tags may create as many scripting variables as needed. In this case, we only want one and the `<createArray>` tag should create it. Should more variables be needed, we would add additional `<variable>` elements.

The `<variable>` element relies on its four child elements to set up the scripting variable. The first two are fairly straightforward. The `<name-given>` element describes the name to be given to our new scripting variable and also represents the name of the object holding it in `pageContext`. The `<variable-class>` element defines the type of the scripting variable's object. We know the variable stashed in the `pageContext` was an array of type `java.lang.String`.

The `<declare>` child element determines if the scripting variable is a new object, or if it is already available. Give the value `true` is the scripting variable is new for the page, or `false` if the variable has previously been declared for the page.

The `<scope>` element defines when the new scripting variable can be used in the JSP. As we've already discussed, it has three possible values:

Scope	Meaning
AT_BEGIN	Creates the scripting variable at the start tag and keeps it around for the rest of the JSP page.
AT_END	Creates the scripting variable at the end tag and also keeps it around for the rest of the JSP page.
NESTED	The NESTED value will only keep the scripting variable in scope between the start and end tags of the custom tag.

For the `<createArray>` tag, we want to make sure the variable is in scope after the custom tag so either the AT_BEGIN or AT_END values would work:

```
<scope>AT_END</scope>
```

Cooperating Tags Using Scripting Variables

Now we will examine how to use the extra functionality of the scripting variables with a custom tag. The first example of the `<iterate>` tag iterated through an array of strings displaying them in the client browser with some text. In that case, the strings from the array will always appear *after* the text in the body of the tag. The previous example, using scripting variables, gave us the ability to place the array values anywhere we liked inside the results.

We'll now return to the idea of using custom tags to replace scriptlets. The previous two examples required scriptlets to demonstrate the basic functionality of scripting variables. Now we can use this knowledge to improve the `<iterate>` tag and give it much more flexibility.

Try It Out   Improving the Iterate Tag to Work With Scripting Variables

1. First, add the following changes to the `iterateTag.java` tag handler code:

```
package custom;

import javax.servlet.jsp.*;
import javax.servlet.jsp.tagext.*;
```

```
public class iterateTag extends TagSupport
{
  private int arrayCount = 0;
  private String[] strings = null;

  public int doStartTag()
  {
    arrayCount = 0;
    strings = (String[]) pageContext.getAttribute("strings");
    pageContext.setAttribute("currentString", strings[arrayCount]);
    pageContext.setAttribute("arrayCount", new Integer(arrayCount));

    return EVAL_BODY_INCLUDE;
  }

  public int doAfterBody() throws JspException
  {
    arrayCount++;
    if (arrayCount >= strings.length)
      return SKIP_BODY;

    pageContext.setAttribute("currentString", strings[arrayCount]);
    pageContext.setAttribute("arrayCount", new Integer(arrayCount));

    return EVAL_BODY_AGAIN;
  }
}
```

2. Change to the `classes` directory and run this command:

> **> javac custom\iterateTag.java -classpath**

> **%CATALINA_HOME%\common\lib\jsp-api.jar**

3. Now edit `exampleTags.tld` to have the iterate tag create two new scripting variables:

```
<?xml version="1.0" encoding="ISO-8859-1"?>
<taglib xmlns="http://java.sun.com/xml/ns/j2ee"
        xmlns:xsi="http://www.w3.org/2001/XMLSchema-instance"
        version="2.0">
  <tlib-version>1.0</tlib-version>
  <jsp-version>2.0</jsp-version>
  <short-name>ExampleTags</short-name>
  <description>A set of example tag handlers.</description>
  <tag>
    <name>time</name>
    <tag-class>custom.timeTag</tag-class>
    <attribute>
      <name>format</name>
    </attribute>
```

```
    </tag>
    <tag>
      <name>iterate</name>
      <tag-class>custom.iterateTag</tag-class>
      <variable>
        <name-given>currentString</name-given>
        <variable-class>java.lang.String</variable-class>
        <declare>true</declare>
        <scope>NESTED</scope>
      </variable>
      <variable>
        <name-given>arrayCount</name-given>
        <variable-class>java.lang.Integer</variable-class>
        <declare>true</declare>
        <scope>NESTED</scope>
      </variable>
    </tag>
    <tag>
      <name>createArray</name>
      <tag-class>custom.createArrayTag</tag-class>
      <variable>
        <name-given>strings</name-given>
        <variable-class>java.lang.String []</variable-class>
        <declare>true</declare>
        <scope>AT_END</scope>
      </variable>
    </tag>
</taglib>
```

4. Lastly, change `scriptingVariables.jsp` to use the new `<iterate>` tag in place of the remaining scriptlet:

```
<%@ taglib prefix="example" uri="/WEB-INF/exampleTags.tld" %>
<html>
  <head></head>
  <body>
    <example:createArray/>
    There are <%= strings.length %> strings available.<br>
    <example:iterate>
      The value "<%= currentString %>" is in
      slot #<%= arrayCount %> of the array.<BR>
    </example:iterate>
  </body>
</html>
```

5. Restart Tomcat and browse to the modified `scriptingVariables.jsp` page. We should see the same results:

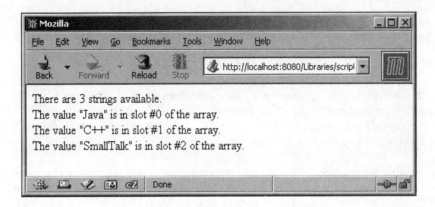

How It Works

The first big change is to the code of the tag handler `iterateTag.java`. Two new values are placed in the `pageContext` to be used later as scripting variables. The tag handler sets the two new values in the `pageContext` at two different times. The first is done during the `doStartTag()` method to initialize the values. Notice when placing our `int` value into the `pageContext` object, we create a new `int` object. This is necessary because `int` is a primitive type but the `setAttribute()` method of `pageContext` requires an object. We are forced to make an `Integer` object from our `int`:

```
public int doStartTag()
{
  arrayCount = 0;
  strings = (String[]) pageContext.getAttribute("strings");
  pageContext.setAttribute("currentString", strings[arrayCount]);
  pageContext.setAttribute("arrayCount", new Integer(arrayCount));
  return EVAL_BODY_INCLUDE;
}
```

The values are set a second time during the `doAfterBody()` method. These methods are called once for each item in the array we iterate through. The set methods are needed to make sure the scripting variable is current for each evaluation of the body. This means that the scripting variable should be assigned the appropriate value at each iteration, since at each iteration the body is evaluated freshly:

```
public int doAfterBody() throws JspException
{
  arrayCount++;
  if(arrayCount >= strings.length)
    return SKIP_BODY;
```

```
        pageContext.setAttribute("currentString", strings[arrayCount]);
        pageContext.setAttribute("arrayCount", new Integer(arrayCount));
        return EVAL_BODY_AGAIN;
    }
```

The next change is to reflect the new scripting variables in the TLD. We added the two new `<variable>` elements under the `<tag>` element for the iterate tag in `exampleTags.tld`. These new elements will create the two scripting variables out of the two objects stashed in the `pageContext` object by the `<iterate>` tag.

The first variable represents the current string from our array of strings. The name used to set the object in `pageContext` was `currentString`. The scripting variable is also named `currentString` for use by the JSP. The type of this object is `java.lang.String`, the scripting variable is newly declared to the JSP, and only stays in scope for the body of the custom tag:

```
        <variable>
          <name-given>currentString</name-given>
          <variable-class>java.lang.String</variable-class>
          <declare>true</declare>
          <scope>NESTED</scope>
        </variable>
```

The second scripting variable is the current index of the array. The variable was stored in the `pageContext` object as `arrayCount` and is initialized as a scripting variable with the same name. The object is of type `java.lang.Integer`. The variable is new and will be in scope only for the body of the custom tag:

```
        <variable>
          <name-given>arrayCount</name-given>
          <variable-class>java.lang.Integer</variable-class>
          <declare>true</declare>
          <scope>NESTED</scope>
        </variable>
```

Advantages of Scripting Variables Within Iterating Tags

With a few scripting variables, our new `<iterate>` tag overcomes some limitations of the previous version. With this example, we are now using the body of the tag to include our scripting variables. The values of these variables change and with each evaluation of the body the correct results are generated. We can take a higher-level view and see the difference directly by comparing the code in `iterateTag.jsp` to the code in `scriptingVariables.jsp`.

Here is the code for `iterateTag.jsp`. It relies on printing out a static message and then appending a string from the array:

```
<%@ taglib prefix="example" uri="/WEB-INF/exampleTags.tld" %>
<html>
  <head></head>
  <body>
    <example:createArray/>
    <example:iterate>
      The string is:
    </example:iterate>
  </body>
</html>
```

Compare it to the code we are now using in `scriptingVariables.jsp`.

```
<%@ taglib prefix="example" uri="/WEB-INF/exampleTags.tld" %>
<html>
  <head></head>
  <body>
    <example:createArray/>
    There are <%= strings.length %> strings available.<br>
    <example:iterate>
      The value "<%= currentString %>" is in
      slot #<%= arrayCount %> of the array.<br>
    </example:iterate>
  </body>
</html>
```

This would not function with the first version of the `<iterate>` tag, but the new `<iterate>` tag can still work using the old syntax. In general, the new tag is a much more practical example of the iteration capability of custom tags. Imagine if the array being iterated through was an array of e-mail messages. The `<iterate>` tag might have a scripting variable for the address, subject, and message of each e-mail that functions in the same way as `currentString` does in this example. The code in the body of the tag would need to be nothing more than the HTML for displaying each message along with the reference to the scripting variables as needed.

Declaring Scripting Variables Using TagExtraInfo Classes

Declaring a scripting variable by way of a TLD is simple and it works, but another method does exist. Each custom tag may have a `TagExtraInfo` (TEI) helper class declared to accompany it. The TEI class can create scripting variables in a similar fashion to the previous section. A bonus with using a TEI class is the ability to dynamically create scripting variables instead of relying on information coded in the TLD. In addition to creating scripting variables, a TEI class can also perform the validation of custom tag attributes at runtime.

Before we go into the details of how to declare a scripting variable using a TEI class, we need to understand two objects:

❑   `TagData` – holds information about tag attributes

❑   `VariableInfo` – describes a new scripting variable

Let's take a closer look at these objects.

The TagData Object

The `TagData` object provides information about a custom tag's attributes at translation time. It is generated automatically by the JSP container based on the corresponding custom tag. From a developer's view, we only use the given `TagData` object to get information about the custom tag the TEI was declared for.

The `TagData` object has a few different methods we can use to get information about the custom tag's attributes. The first is the `getAttributes()` method, that returns an object called an **enumeration** (of class `java.util.Enumeration`). An enumeration object contains a collection of values, not unlike the `Iterator` object that we saw in Chapter 8. The enumeration returned by `getAttributes()` contains all of the attributes in the `TagData` object.

Another useful method is `getAttributeString()`, that takes a `String` representing the name of a particular attribute as an argument, and returns another `String` representing the value of the attribute. The `getAttribute()` method is a variation on this theme, in that it takes a `String` attribute name argument, but returns the attribute value as an `Object`.

The VariableInfo Object

The `VariableInfo` object describes a new scripting variable. To make a `VariableInfo` object, we need the same information used previously when declaring a scripting variable via the TLD. Recall the following snippet from `exampleTags.tld` we have previously used:

```
<variable>
  <name-given>strings</name-given>
  <variable-class>java.lang.String []</variable-class>
  <declare>true</declare>
  <scope>AT_END</scope>
</variable>
```

This snippet is found in the body of the `<tag>` element for the `<createArray>` tag. The snippet creates a new scripting variable of type `java.lang.String` with a name of "strings", and with a scope starting after the end custom tag. When creating a `VariableInfo` object, we use the same information as in the TLD, but as parameters in a constructor instead. For example:

```
VariableInfo vi = new VariableInfo(varName, className, true,
                      VariableInfo.AT_END);
```

The first argument, varName here, represents the name of the new scripting variable as a String. The second, className, is the full class name of the variable's type, represented as a String. The third, true here, is a boolean stating whether the scripting variable is new and so must be declared. The final argument is an integer value representing the required scope of the scripting variable. The available values are shown in the table below:

Field	Description
VariableInfo.AT_BEGIN	The new scripting variable will be in scope after the starting custom tag.
VariableInfo.AT_END	The new scripting variable will be in scope after the ending custom tag.
VariableInfo.NESTED	The scripting variable will only be in scope inside the body of the custom tag.

Creating a Scripting Variable using a TEI Class

New scripting variables are defined via TEI classes by the getVariableInfo() method. This method takes a TagData object as an argument, and returns an array of VariableInfo objects. A scripting variable is created for each VariableInfo object in the returned array. Each VariableInfo object is custom defined by the JSP developer when overriding this method in the TEI class.

Now that we have a general idea of what a TagExtraInfo class does, we can try using one with a custom tag. Luckily, we also already have some tag handlers requiring scripting variables. For this example, we will make the <createArray> tag use a TEI class.

Try It Out   **Using a TEI Class to Declare a Scripting Variable in a JSP page**

1. Modify createArrayTag.java to implement a new attribute called name. This attribute will determine the name of the scripting variable created:

```
package custom;

import javax.servlet.jsp.tagext.*;

public class createArrayTag extends TagSupport
{
  private String name = null;

  public int doStartTag()
  {
    String[] strings = new String[] {"Java", "C++", "SmallTalk"};
    pageContext.setAttribute(name, strings);
```

```
      return SKIP_BODY;
  }
  public void setName(String newName)
  {
    name = newName;
  }
}
```

2. Run the following command from our application's `classes` folder:

> **> javac custom\createArrayTag.java -classpath**
>
>   **%CATALINA_HOME%\common\lib\jsp-api.jar**

3. Next, create a `TagExtraInfo` class to accompany the new tag handler. Extending the `TagExtraInfo` class is the preferred method for creating a TEI class.

Save the following code as `arrayExtraInfo.java` in the `custom` directory:

```
package custom;

import javax.servlet.jsp.tagext.*;

public class arrayExtraInfo extends TagExtraInfo
{

  public VariableInfo[] getVariableInfo(TagData data)
  {

    String variableName = data.getAttributeString("name");

    VariableInfo vi = new VariableInfo(variableName,"String []", true,
                                    VariableInfo.AT_END);
    VariableInfo[] tagVariables = new VariableInfo[1];
    tagVariables[0] = vi;

    return tagVariables;
  }
}
```

6. Compile it with the following command:

> **> javac custom\arrayExtraInfo.java -classpath**
>
>   **%CATALINA_HOME%\common\lib\jsp-api.jar**

7. Now modify `exampleTags.tld` so that we no longer use the `<variable>` element for the `<createArray>` tag. Instead add a new element named `<tei-class>`. The value of this element will be our TEI class name. Also add in the new attribute added to the `<createArray>` tag:

```xml
<?xml version="1.0" encoding="ISO-8859-1"?>
<taglib xmlns="http://java.sun.com/xml/ns/j2ee"
        xmlns:xsi="http://www.w3.org/2001/XMLSchema-instance"
        version="2.0">
  <tlib-version>1.0</tlib-version>
  <jsp-version>2.0</jsp-version>
  <short-name>ExampleTags</short-name>
  <description>A set of example tag handlers.</description>
  <tag>
    <name>time</name>
    <tag-class>custom.timeTag</tag-class>
    <display-name>time</display-name>
    <attribute>
      <name>format</name>
    </attribute>
  </tag>
  <tag>
    <name>iterate</name>
    <tag-class>custom.iterateTag</tag-class>
    <variable>
      <name-given>currentString</name-given>
      <variable-class>java.lang.String</variable-class>
      <declare>true</declare>
      <scope>NESTED</scope>
    </variable>
    <variable>
      <name-given>arrayCount</name-given>
      <variable-class>java.lang.Integer</variable-class>
      <declare>true</declare>
      <scope>NESTED</scope>
    </variable>
  </tag>
  <tag>
    <name>createArray</name>
    <tag-class>custom.createArrayTag</tag-class>
    <tei-class>custom.arrayExtraInfo</tei-class>
    <attribute>
      <name>name</name>
    </attribute>
  </tag>
</taglib>
```

8. Finally, create a JSP page in the `Libraries` directory called `teiExample.jsp`:

```
<%@ taglib prefix="example" uri="/WEB-INF/exampleTags.tld" %>
<html>
  <head></head>
  <body>
  <example:createArray name="strings"/>
  The array has <%= strings.length %> items.
  </body>
</html>
```

9. Now navigate to //localhost:8080/Libraries/teiExample.jsp to see the scripting variable at work with the new `name` attribute:

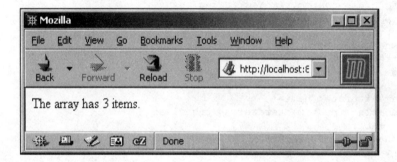

How It Works

This example is focused upon the `name` attribute added to the `<createArray>` tag. The TEI class `arrayExtraInfo` dynamically names the new scripting variable to the value of the `name` attribute. The TEI class knows the value of the attribute because the JSP container passes in a current `TagData` object with that information.

The first change was to the tag handler code in `createArray.java`. We changed the tag handler to have a new attribute of `name`. Adding this attribute requires no new information from this section. It involves adding a set accessor for the `name` variable and a change to the TLD.

We also changed a line to set the `name` variable in to the `pageContext` object. Instead of using a static value of `"strings"`, the `name` variable is now used:

```
pageContext.setAttribute(name, strings);
```

To make the example TEI class, we sub-classed the `TagExtraInfo` class of the Servlet/JSP API. Similar to the `TagSupport` and `BodyTagSupport` objects and tag handlers, the `TagExtraInfo` class is provided for convenience:

```
import javax.servlet.jsp.tagext.*;

public class arrayExtraInfo extends TagExtraInfo
```

We override the methods inside our custom TEI class. The `getVariableInfo()` method determines if any scripting variables should be created. Since one scripting variable is to be created, we must override this method to return an array containing one `VariableInfo` object:

```
public VariableInfo[] getVariableInfo(TagData data)
```

The name of the scripting variable is the same value as the `name` attribute from the custom tag. To get the value of the `name` attribute we call the `getAttributeString()` method from the `TagData` object:

```
String variableName = data.getAttributeString("name");
```

The `VariableInfo` object is created to represent the new scripting variable. the constructor requires a few parameters, including the name of the scripting variable, now held in the `variableName` object, the type of the scripting variable (an array of strings), a boolean indicating that the scripting variable is new to the JSP, and finally an argument to indicate that this variable comes into scope after the ending custom tag:

```
VariableInfo vi = new VariableInfo(variableName, "String []", true,
                                   VariableInfo.AT_END);
```

Finally the `VariableInfo` object is placed in an array to be returned by the method. By returning an array, this method allows us to return as many `VariableInfo` objects as desired:

```
VariableInfo[] tagVariables = new VariableInfo[1];
tagVariables[0] = vi;

return tagVariables;
    }
}
```

Two changes were made to `exampleTags.tld`. The first change was a declaration for the new attribute in the `<createArray>` tag. The second change was replacing the old `<variable>` element with a `<tei-class>` element for the `<createArray>` tag.

```
<tei-class>custom.arrayExtraInfo</tei-class>
```

The `<tei-class>` element functions in the same manner as the `<tag-class>` element but for the `TagExtraInfo` class. Instead of defining the tag handler class the value of this new element defines our custom TEI class. In general if any custom tag is using a TEI class it will implement a `<tei-class>` element in a similar fashion.

The example JSP is nothing more then a simple demonstration of the new functionality the TEI class provides. In the new code we can dynamically name the scripting variable. For the example, we give a value of `"strings"` to the name attribute of the `<createArray>` tag. Later a scripting variable is used of the same name.

```
<example:createArray name="strings"/>
The array has <%= strings.length %> items.<BR>
```

We can now name the new scripting variable anything we like. This little extra bit of flexibility is unavailable when declaring scripting variables with the TLD, and is one of the advantages a TEI class offers over using the TLD when declaring scripting variables. It certainly requires more work, but we can override the `getVariableInfo()` method to achieve much more in practice.

Using TEI Classes For Tag Validation

TEI classes also implement the `isValid()` method, one of the original mechanisms for validating the attributes of a custom tag. This method accepts a `TagData` object as an argument. If the boolean value returned by the method is `true`, the tag will be used, but if it is `false` an error will be thrown.

We won't give a full example of using the `isValid()` method, as this approach to tag validation is rarely used today. The `javax.servlet.jsp.tagext.TagLibraryValidator` class is now the preferred method for validating custom tags, as the error message produced by the `isValid()` method is very crude and not customizable by the JSP developer. Here is a sample that can be added to `arrayExtraInfo.java` to produce this error message:

```
package custom;
import javax.servlet.jsp.tagext.*;

public class arrayExtraInfo extends TagExtraInfo
{

  public VariableInfo[] getVariableInfo(TagData data)
  {
    String variableName = data.getAttributeString("name");

    VariableInfo vi = new VariableInfo(variableName,"String []", true,
                                       VariableInfo.AT_END);
    VariableInfo[] tagVariables = new VariableInfo[1];
    tagVariables[0] = vi;

    return tagVariables;
  }

  public boolean isValid(TagData data)
  {
    return false;
  }
}
```

In general, this is how the `isValid()` may be overridden to verify the tag. However, instead of immediately returning `false`, the `TagData` object would really check to see if tag values met any necessary requirements. As it is, `teiExample.jsp` will now always produce the following error message once this class is recompiled and Tomcat restarted:

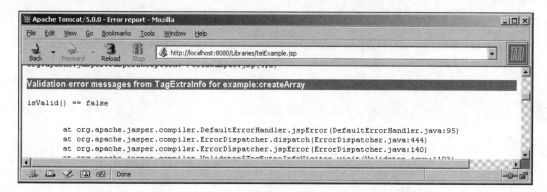

An error page can be used to catch and pretty up this screen, but that is usually not an adequate solution. The error message, **Attributes are invalid according to TagInfo**, doesn't give real detail of what is wrong with the attribute or how to fix the problem. Since there is no convenient method to accomplish this using the `isValid()` method, it is rarely suitable.

The `javax.servlet.jsp.tagext.TagLibraryValidator` class has a similar method to `isValid()` called `validate()`, which returns a string that may describe any problems with the current attributes. The `TagLibraryValidator` class also has access to the entire JSP page instead of just a specific custom tag. these features make `TagLibraryValidator` usually the better solution when validating custom tags. The `TagLibraryValidator` class is covered in *Professional JSP*, Wrox Press, ISBN 1-86100-832-5.

Locating a TLD File

When we use custom tags on a JSP page, the TLD must be referenced so that the JSP container understands what the custom tags look like. Up until now, this chapter has used the real URI to the TLD file in the `taglib` directive:

```
<%@ taglib prefix="example" uri="/WEB-INF/exampleTags.tld" %>
```

The `uri` attribute's value is the actual URI to the TLD, relative to the web-app root. There is nothing wrong with this method, but two other methods also exist, and we'll address them in this section. The first of the other methods creates a fictitious URI and links it to the TLD via a configuration file for the JSP application.

Referencing the TLD via the web.xml Deployment Descriptor

Using web.xml to map a custom tag library is the most commonly used method. While it is slightly less intuitive compared to the method we have been using, it allows for any URI to reference a TLD. When the JSP container sees the URI given in the taglib directive it will try to find the TLD using the URI as a path to the actual file. If this fails, the JSP container will then check web.xml and see if the URI is custom-defined for the web application. If so, the web.xml file will provide the real location of the TLD file. Let's demonstrate this with a small example.

Try It Out   Referencing a TLD Using web.xml

1. The web.xml file is located in the WEB-INF directory of the JSP application. For this chapter, create a file named web.xml in the WEB-INF subdirectory of our Libraries folder. Enter the following code:

```
<?xml version="1.0" encoding="ISO-8859-1"?>
<web-app xmlns="http://java.sun.com/xml/ns/j2ee"
         xmlns:xsi="http://www.w3.org/2001/XMLSchema-instance"
         version="2.4">
  <taglib>
    <taglib-uri>exampleTags</taglib-uri>
    <taglib-location>/WEB-INF/exampleTags.tld</taglib-location>
  </taglib>
</web-app>
```

2. Now take scriptingVariables.jsp and edit the taglib directive to use the new URI:

```
<%@ taglib prefix="example" uri="exampleTags" %>
<html>
  <head></head>
  <body>
    <example:createArray name="strings"/>
    There are <%= strings.length %> strings available.<BR>
    <example:iterate>
      The value "<%= currentString %>" is in
      slot #<%= arrayCount %> of the array.<BR>
    </example:iterate>
  </body>
</html>
```

Notice that we've also included the new name attribute on the createArray tag in line with the changes we made earlier.

3. Be sure to restart Tomcat and then browse to scriptingVariables.jsp:

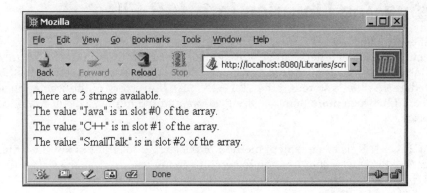

How It Works

This example relies on the `<taglib>` element in the `web.xml` file. `web.xml` is an XML file and always starts with the same basic header and must have a document element of `<web-app>`. We place our `<taglib>` element as a direct child of `<web-app>`:

```
<web-app xmlns="http://java.sun.com/xml/ns/j2ee"
         xmlns:xsi="http://www.w3.org/2001/XMLSchema-instance"
         version="2.4">
  <taglib>
    <taglib-uri>exampleTags</taglib-uri>
    <taglib-location>/WEB-INF/exampleTags.tld</taglib-location>
  </taglib>
</web-app>
```

The elements contained within `<taglib>` are:

❑ `<taglib-uri>`
This element's value is what we will give for the `uri` attribute in a `taglib` directive. Choose something simple and descriptive.

❑ `<taglib-location>`
This element must contain the actual path to the Tag Library Descriptor.

We can now use the new URI in any of our `taglib` directives. This provides a much more robust link to the correct tag library than a relative URI, allowing us to move our JSPs to a subdirectory without breaking the link to the library.

Remember our TLD file has not been changed. Creating a TLD for your tag library and referencing the TLD are distinctly different. These methods are all different ways to reference the same TLD. The final method for referencing a TLD is geared for tag libraries provided in a special package called a JAR.

355

Packaging Tag Libraries into JAR Files

Tag handlers can be made available to a web application in two basic ways. The classes implementing the tag handlers can be stored in an unpacked form in the WEB-INF/classes/ subdirectory of the web application, as we have done so far. Alternatively, if the library is distributed as a JAR, it is stored in the WEB-INF/lib/ directory of the web application. A tag library shared between more than one application is stored in the lib sub-folder of the Java directory.

A Java Archive (JAR) is a convenient method of packaging together many class files in one main file. A JAR file uses compression to combine many resources such as class files and Tag Library Descriptors. In the case of custom tag libraries, a JAR file contains all the tag handler classes and related TLD files.

Packaging a custom tag library in a JAR makes it very portable. Installing a JAR simply requires the JAR file to be placed in the WEB-INF/lib directory of the JSP application and rebooting Tomcat. Compared to copying various files and/or editing the web.xml file, this method is clearly the winner.

The JSP 2.0 specification provides a new method for referencing TLD files in a JAR file. Any number of tag libraries may be packaged in the same JAR as long as all have the appropriate tag handler class files and a TLD in the META-INF directory with the .tld extension. Additionally, each TLD must specify different uri values. There may never be two tag libraries referenced with the same URI regardless of the method used to reference them. This method is demonstrated in the following example.

Try It Out   Packaging a Tag Library With JAR

1. The JDK comes with a tool named jar for creating JAR files. From a command prompt, browse to the %JAVA_HOME%/bin directory and execute this command:

   > jar

2. This provides the following details about how the jar utility may be used:

```
⌐ Command Prompt                                                    _□×
C:\java\jdk1.4\bin>jar
Usage: jar {ctxu}[vfm0Mi] [jar-file] [manifest-file] [-C dir] files ...
Options:
   -c  create new archive
   -t  list table of contents for archive
   -x  extract named (or all) files from archive
   -u  update existing archive
   -v  generate verbose output on standard output
   -f  specify archive file name
   -m  include manifest information from specified manifest file
   -0  store only; use no ZIP compression
   -M  do not create a manifest file for the entries
   -i  generate index information for the specified jar files
   -C  change to the specified directory and include the following file
If any file is a directory then it is processed recursively.
The manifest file name and the archive file name needs to be specified
in the same order the 'm' and 'f' flags are specified.

Example 1: to archive two class files into an archive called classes.jar:
       jar cvf classes.jar Foo.class Bar.class
Example 2: use an existing manifest file 'mymanifest' and archive all the
          files in the foo/ directory into 'classes.jar':
       jar cvfm classes.jar mymanifest -C foo/ .

C:\java\jdk1.4\bin>_
```

3. Before using the `jar` tool, we need to set up our files in a specific hierarchy. First, create a `C:\jarfile\custom` directory and save all of the tag handler class files in there. Next, create a `C:\jarfile\META-INF` directory and copy `exampleTags.tld` into it.

4. Now open up the copy of `exampleTags.tld` and add the following line:

```xml
<?xml version="1.0" encoding="ISO-8859-1"?>
<taglib xmlns="http://java.sun.com/xml/ns/j2ee"
        xmlns:xsi="http://www.w3.org/2001/XMLSchema-instance"
        version="2.0">
  <tlib-version>1.0</tlib-version>
  <jsp-version>2.0</jsp-version>
  <short-name>ExampleTags</short-name>
  <uri>exampleURI</uri>
  <description>A set of example tag handlers.</description>
  <tag>
    .
    .
    .
  </tag>
</taglib>
```

5. Run the `jar` utility from the `C:\jarfile` directory like so:

> **> jar cvf example.jar custom META-INF**

6. We'll then see some output describing the JAR creation:

added manifest
adding: custom/arrayExtraInfo.class(in = 744) (out= 410)(deflated 44%)
adding: custom/createArrayTag.class(in = 694) (out= 442)(deflated 36%)
adding: custom/iterateTag.class(in = 948) (out= 564)(deflated 40%)
adding: custom/timeTag.class(in = 1011) (out= 595)(deflated 41%)
adding: META-INF/exampleTags.tld(in = 1326) (out= 498)(deflated 62%)

7. A new file will be created in the `JAVA_HOME/bin` directory called `example.jar`. This is the JAR file for the custom tag library. Place this file in the `lib` directory in our `Libraries` application's `WEB-INF` folder.

8. To test the new JAR, edit `teiExample.jsp` to use a new URI.

9. Notice this URI is not the real location of our TLD nor is it defined by `web.xml`:

```
<%@ taglib prefix="example" uri="exampleURI" %>
<html>
  <head></head>
  <body>
  <example:createArray name="strings"/>
      We are now using a JAR file!<br>
  The array has <%= strings.length %> items.
  </body>
</html>
```

If you want, you can delete all `*.class` files from the `WEB-INF/classes/custom` directory and also delete the `exampleTags.tld` and `web.xml` files from `WEB-INF`, to make absolutely certain that everything comes from the JAR file.

10. Restart Tomcat to load the new JAR, and browse to `teiExample.jsp`. The example should work as before:

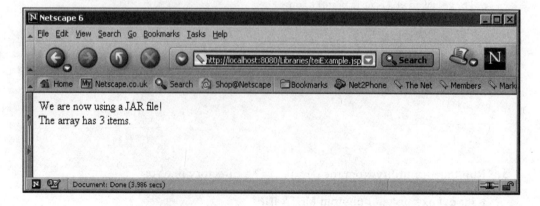

How It Works

Although the example may seem complicated, all we're really doing is making a small addition to exampleTags.tld and placing it inside a JAR.

By default, a JSP 2.0 compliant container will take any file with a .tld extension placed in the META-INF folder of a JAR, and treat it as a TLD. The URI of a TLD read in this manner is defined by the <uri> element of the TLD. One of the steps in this example was to add the following <uri> element to exampleTags.tld:

```
<uri>exampleURI</uri>
```

The value of the <uri> element is exampleURI, but we could use any arbitrary string. In a similar fashion to web.xml in the previous example, the JSP container now uses this information to resolve unknown URIs in a taglib directive. In our case scriptingVariables.jsp uses exampleURI in its taglib directive.

```
<%@ taglib prefix="example" uri="exampleTags.tld" %>
```

If our JAR file included multiple TLD files each must have a unique <uri> element. Tomcat knows that the URI exampleURI is contained in the exampleTags.tld file and links the prefix example to that tag library.

In this section, let's look at an example that illustrates the use of a pre-created custom tag library. We will build an e-mail application around Jakarta's popular Mailer tag libraries, and we'll see how simple it can be to use this tag library.

Try It Out   Using Custom Tag Libraries

The groundwork

1. To use the Jakarta Mailer tag library, install JavaMail 1.2 and the Java Beans Activation Framework. These are available from http://java.sun.com/products/javamail and http://java.sun.com/products/glasgow/jaf.html respectively. Installation instructions are also available at these web pages.

2. Download the Mailer 1.0 tag library from Jakarta.apache.org/taglibs. You will have to download two files, taglibs-mailer.tld and taglibs-mailer.jar.

    The first file is the Tag Library Descriptor. The second is a java archive, which contains Tag Handler classes. We learn about both of these in the next section.

3. Now, copy the Tag Library Descriptor file to the WEB-INF subdirectory of our web application and copy the tag library JAR file to the lib subdirectory of WEB-INF. The TLD file contains the tag library description and the JAR file contains the Java implementation for the library.

4. Add a `<taglib>` element to the web application's web.xml as shown below:

```
.
.
.
<taglib>
  <taglib-uri>http://jakarta.apache.org/taglibs/mailer</taglib-uri>
  <taglib-location>/WEB-INF/mailer.tld</taglib-location>
</taglib>
</web-app>
```

Building the Application

1. Let's create the HTML form which will to submit to the JSP page, which will process the information and send an e-mail. Save this file in Libraries as premailer.html. This form has the typical e-mail fields, **From**, **To**, **CC**, **Subject** and **Message**. Apart from these, it has another field for the mail server name:

```
<!--Premailer.html -->

<html>
  <head>
    <title>mail </title>
  </head>

  <body bgcolor="#FFFFFF">
    <p>Complete the form below to send mail.</p>

    <form method="post" name="interest" action="mailer.jsp">
      <table border="0" width="100" cellspacing="0">
        <tr>
          <td>The name of your mail server if it is other than
            localhost:</td>
        </tr><tr>
          <td><input type="text" name="server" value="localhost"
            size="25"></td>
        </tr><tr>
          <td>From:</td>
        </tr><tr>
          <td><input type="text" name="from" size="25"></td>
        </tr><tr>
          <td>To:</td>
        </tr><tr>
          <td><input type="text" name="to" size="25"></td>
        </tr><tr>
          <td>Cc:</td>
```

```
        </tr><tr>
          <td><input type="text" name="cc" size="25"></td>
        </tr><tr>
          <td>Subject:</td>
        </tr><tr>
          <td><input type="text" name="subject" size="50"></td>
        </tr><tr>
          <td>Message:</td>
        </tr><tr>
          <td>
          <textarea name="message" rows="5" cols="80" wrap></textarea>
          </td>
          <tr>
      </table>
      <p>
        <input type="submit" name="submit" value="submit">
        <input type="reset" name="reset" value="reset">
      </p>
    </form>

  </body>
</html>
```

2. Now let's write the JSP page which sends e-mail using the Jakarta Mailer tag library. Save this JSP in the Libraries folder as Mailer.jsp:

```
<!—Mailer.jsp -->
<%@ taglib uri="http://jakarta.apache.org/taglibs/mailer-1.0" prefix="mt" %>

<html>
<head>
  <title>Example JSP using mailer taglib</title>
</head>
<body bgcolor="#FFFFFF">

<mt:mail server="<%=request.getParameter("server")%>">

  <mt:from>
    <%=request.getParameter("from")%>
  </mt:from>

  <mt:setrecipient type="to">
    <%=request.getParameter("to")%>
  </mt:setrecipient>

  <mt:setrecipient type="cc">
    <%=request.getParameter("cc")%>
  </mt:setrecipient>
```

```
    <mt:subject>
      <%=request.getParameter("subject")%>
    </mt:subject>

    <mt:message>
      <%=request.getParameter("message")%>
    </mt:message>

    <mt:send>
      Errors Occurred. Unable to send message
    </mt:send>
</mt:mail>
<p>The message has been successfully sent.</p>
</body>
</html>
```

3. Navigate to localhost:8080/Libraries/premailer.html in your browser, and fill in some details:

4. Click the Submit button, and you should receive the following message:

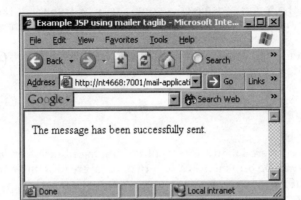

5. To see the result, you can provide your own e-mail in the form. You will need to make sure to provide the right mail server address.

How It Works

Let's start with a look at the `taglib` directive which sets a prefix of `mt` for the mailer tags:

```
<%@ taglib uri="http://jakarta.apache.org/taglibs/mailer" prefix="mt" %>
```

When the container reads a tag prefixed with prefix `mt`, this is mapped to Mailer tag handler. The `<send>` tag sends the message and prints an error if it fails.

More information about the Jakarta Mailer Tag Library can be found by following the links to the Mailer tag at jakarta.apache.org/taglibs.

Resources

As well as the JSTL standard tag library, there are many free custom tag libraries, which support anything from sending e-mail to accessing EJBs. Here are links to some of the larger tag library resources:

- ❑ The **J2EE Tutorial Addendum** at htpp://java.sun.com/j2ee/1.4/docs/tutorial/index.html contains a link to creating custom tags in JSP pages, including detailed information about directives.

- ❑ The **Jakarta Taglibs** project at http://jakarta.apache.org/taglibs/index.html is open-source and designed to be portable between any JSP containers.

❑ **JSPTags.com** at http://www.jsptags.com provides current listings of the most popular tag libraries and a few of its own.

❑ **JSP Insider** at http://www.jspinsider.com is an extensive JSP information site with many tag library resources and includes many articles and tutorials.

Finally, if you are interested in learning more about JAR files, **Sun** provides a free tutorial at http://java.sun.com/docs/books/tutorial/jar/index.html.

Summary

In this chapter, we've covered many aspects of writing tag libraries. In general, the process of writing a tag library can be broken down into two parts: creating tag handlers and linking the tag library with the JSP container.

Tags are either simple or classic tags. Simple tags are easy to develop, and can contain regular JSP code, but classic tags need to be developed in Java.

There are three interfaces to choose from when we create a tag handler: `Tag`, `IterationTag`, and `BodyTag`. Implementing these interfaces can be tedious, especially when only one or two of the methods are of interest. Included in the JSP API are two helper classes, `TagSupport` and `BodyTagSupport`. Extending these helper classes is a quick way to create a tag handler. When you create a tag handler implementing the `Tag` or `IterationTag` interface, you should extend the `TagSupport` object. When creating a tag handler implementing the `BodyTag` interface, extends the `BodyTagSupport` object.

We broke mapping a tag library down into two further main steps: creating a Tag Library Descriptor file (TLD) and linking this TLD with the JSP container.

Linking the TLD with the JSP container can be accomplished using three different methods:

❑ Using the relative URI.

❑ Mapping through `web.xml`, which allows for an arbitrary pseudo-URI.

❑ Finally when packaging your tag library in a JAR, `.tld` files in the `META-INF` directory are mapped automatically.

The last method provides the same functionality as mapping via `web.xml`, but allows the tag library to be easily ported between JSP projects.

Tag libraries are one of the most popular features of JSP and one chapter cannot do justice to the entire specification. We hope though that this chapter has served as a useful starting point.

Why Not Try?

1. Classify JSTL standard tags into the types of tags that we have discussed here.

2. Develop a tag for use in error pages. The tag should get its error information from the `request` object, and could color-code the error depending on its severity.

3. Enhance the Jakarta mailer example to allow the sending of attachments.

CHAPTER 10

Behind the Scenes

When working with JSP, a certain amount of understanding of what goes on behind the scenes helps us to use the technology effectively and can assist the debugging process when things go wrong.

This chapter focuses on the **Java Servlet API** since servlets are the power behind JSP technology. Before any JSP page is run, it is converted into a servlet. The process is as follows:

1. A programmer writes a JSP page and places it in a servlet container.

2. The first time the page is requested, the servlet container converts the JSP into Java source code, creating a servlet that provides the functionality required. The source code is then compiled into a Java class, which the servlet container then loads.

3. Requests from clients are serviced by the servlet, and its responses are returned to the client by the server.

4. If the JSP page is subsequently modified, the server will notice this and recreate the servlet accordingly.

So, servlet technology is an essential part of JSP. This chapter provides an overview of servlets from a programming viewpoint. We'll look at:

❑   The servlet architecture and how servlets work.

❑   What happens behind the scenes when a JSP is converted into a servlet.

❑   More about web applications, the web.xml file that is used to configure them, and advanced configuration options.

❑   Advanced servlet topics: session tracking, the servlet context, and how to forward and include requests.

If what we cover in this chapter whets your appetite for more information about servlets, you may wish to check out the official home of the servlet API at http://java.sun.com/products/servlet/.

Introducing the Java Servlet Technology

A servlet is a Java program that generates dynamic web content. They are written using the **Java Servlet API** and are managed by a **servlet container** such as Tomcat. As we saw in Chapter 1, the HTTP protocol on which the web is built uses a request-response model where the server receives requests from a browser, processes them, and sends an appropriate response back to the browser (or any other web client, such as a search engine indexer). The Java Servlet API enables us to write Java code to process and respond to client requests. For example, a servlet might be responsible for taking data from an HTML order-entry form and using it to update a company's order database.

As we've seen, servlets run inside a Java-enabled server (a **servlet container**) such as Tomcat, as illustrated below:

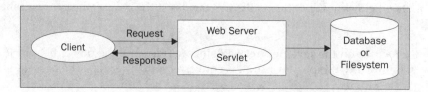

The servlet container does quite a bit of work. It loads the servlets, routes requests to them, and handles their responses, and tries its best to make sure that the servlets can keep up with the number of browsers requesting information from them.

To better understand what happens when a browser sends a request to a servlet, let's have a closer look at the process:

1. The client sends a request to the container.

2. The container determines which servlet (if any) should receive the request.

3. If the servlet isn't already loaded, the container loads it. Once the servlet is loaded, it typically stays in memory until the container shuts down.

4. The container sends the request to the servlet. The servlet container can send multiple requests to the same servlet at the same time, or even load a second copy of a servlet in extreme conditions.

5. The servlet processes the request, builds a response, and passes it to the container.

6. The container sends the response back to the client.

As you can see, the servlet container takes care of the lion's share of this process, relieving us of any requirement to know the complicated details of communicating with web clients over HTTP and TCP/IP.

The Role of Servlets in Web Applications

It is of course fully possible to create complex, exciting web applications using nothing but JavaServer Pages. However, many architects prefer to mix servlets and JSP pages when creating web applications. A common design used in such scenarios works like this: a single servlet acts as a sort of "controller", receiving all requests, performing any necessary tasks, and forwarding the request to a JSP. Manually coded servlets are ideal for the controller component as they can access the Java libraries more easily than a JSP page. They are also much easier to integrate with other, more advanced components, such as Enterprise JavaBeans.

This design is often referred to as the "Model-View-Controller" design pattern, or MVC for short. Let's have a look at an example of MVC architecture:

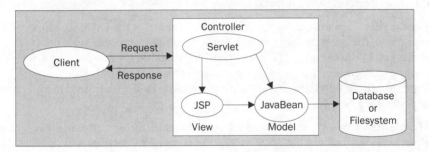

The processing is divided into information (the model) and presentation (the view) components, both orchestrated by the controller. The controller servlet processes requests, and creates components such as JavaBeans for use by the presentation component (that is, JSP). The controller is also responsible for forwarding individual requests to the appropriate JSP page.

The MVC model makes the web application structured and modular – hence easier to develop and extend – by dividing the application into three parts: **model**, **view**, and **controller**.

❑ **Model** – represents the core of the application's functionality – what is often referred to as the **business logic**. This core will be shared between all applications, be they web-based, desktop-based, or whatever. It is quite independent of the view and the controller. JavaBeans can fulfill this function as they can interact with a database or file system in order to maintain the application's data.

❑ **View** – presents the data the model represents to the user. The view can access the model's data, but it should not change the data directly; it must pass requests from the user to change the data. In addition, it knows nothing about the controller. The view will be notified when changes to the model (data) occur. If a view is properly separated from the controller and model, a web interface developer can create the view components without any direct knowledge of what happens in the database or what goes on in the business logic component.

❑ **Controller** – The controller reacts to the user input. It interacts with the model and the view, and coordinates the flow of data from the model to the view.

Generally speaking, the MVC model is the preferred architecture when creating anything but the simplest of applications. There are several reasons for this, some of which include:

❑ **Flexibility** – Because controllers are responsible for determining which JSP pages to display, you can change the order in which JSP pages are displayed, or even which JSP is displayed, without changing links. You could even decide to use something entirely different from JSP at a later data.

❑ **Reusability** – Because the individual components of the MVC application are separated, they can be more easily reused. For example, because the model components don't create HTML output, they can be used with a non-web version of the application. Furthermore, because the view components don't contain any business logic or application data code, they can be more easily changed in order to give the application a new look.

❑ **Maintainability** – It's much easier to make modifications and additions to programs when we know where the code is. If code is spread over a bunch of JSP pages, it's hard to know where to look when changing one particular aspect.

In the early days of servlets, most developers who wanted to use the MVC architecture simply created their own. Nowadays, however, there are many third-party MVC architectures that can be integrated with your applications. One of the most popular is named **Struts**, which we'll be discussing in the last two chapters of the book. There are others, however, such as the official Java MVC framework called JavaServer Faces, to be released soon (http://java.sun.com/j2ee/javaserverfaces).

The Servlet Architecture

In this section, we'll look at how to write a servlet. Servlets are just classes that derive from the abstract class `javax.servlet.http.HttpServlet`. The simplest servlet would be this:

```
import javax.servlet.http.HttpServlet;

public class SimpleServlet extends HttpServlet {}
```

Obviously, this servlet doesn't actually do anything, but it is a legal servlet. Let's now talk about how we can make this servlet *do* something.

Handling Requests

As we have already seen, the servlet container accepts a request from a client (such as a web browser) and forwards it to the servlet, which processes it and sends a response back to the container, which is then forwarded to the client.

The servlet container forwards requests it receives to the servlet by calling the `service()` method on the `HttpServlet` object, passing in two objects: `HttpServletRequest` and `HttpServletResponse`. We can then use the `HttpServletRequest` object to find out details of the request, and various methods on `HttpServletResponse` let us build our response.

The default `service()` method on `HttpServlet` determines the method type of the request, and forwards the `HttpServletRequest` and `HttpServletResponse` objects to the appropriate helper method, which for GET or POST will be either:

❑   `doGet()` for HTTP GET requests

❑   `doPost()` for HTTP POST requests

Thus, instead of overriding the `service()` method, servlet authors can override one of these two methods (or both). These aren't the only two methods, and there are five similar methods that are less commonly used:

❑   `doHead()` handles HTTP HEAD requests. It executes the `doGet()` method, but only returns the headers `doGet()` produces.

❑   `doOptions()` handles HTTP OPTIONS requests. This method determines which HTTP methods are directly supported by the servlet and returns that information to the client.

❑   `doTrace()` handles HTTP TRACE requests. It creates a response containing all the headers sent in the TRACE request.

❑   `doPut()` is called for HTTP PUT requests.

❑   `doDelete()` is called for HTTP DELETE requests.

Because of these additional methods, it's usually a good idea to not to override the `service()` method, and instead to override just those methods for the HTTP methods that we wish to support.

`HttpServlet` has a few extra methods of interest to us:

❑   `init()` and `destroy()`, which allow us to initialize resources in our servlet upon startup and if necessary release resources when the servlet is taken out of service.

❑   `getServletInfo()`, which the servlet uses to provide information about itself.

Try It Out   **An Example Servlet**

1. Let's start with a simple example, creating a servlet class that overrides the
doGet() method to return a simple HTML page to the client when it makes a GET
request. We'll use this example as a reference when explaining the servlet life cycle.

Start by creating a new web application folder called Servlets in Tomcat's webapps
directory. Create a subfolder called WEB-INF, itself containing a directory called
classes. Inside classes, create the folder structure com\wrox\servlets.

2. Create a new file called ExampleServlet.java in the new servlets folder and
save this code in it:

```
package com.wrox.servlets;

import java.io.*;
import javax.servlet.*;
import javax.servlet.http.*;

public class ExampleServlet extends HttpServlet
{

  public void doGet(HttpServletRequest request,
                    HttpServletResponse response)
        throws ServletException, IOException
  {
    response.setContentType("text/html");
    PrintWriter out = response.getWriter();
    out.println("<html><head><title>");
    out.println("Servlet Example");
    out.println("</title></head><body>");
    out.println("<h1>This is an example servlet.</h1>");
    out.println("</body></html>");
    out.close();
  }

  public void doPost(HttpServletRequest request,
                     HttpServletResponse response)
        throws ServletException, IOException
  {
    doGet(request, response);
  }
}
```

3. Now we need to compile our servlet. From the classes directory, enter the following
command, all on one line:

> **javac com/wrox/servlets/ExampleServlet.java
    -classpath %CATALINA_HOME%\common\lib\servlet-api.jar**

4. We've now got a compiled servlet, but we can't use it yet. Before we can access our servlet, we must tell our servlet container (Tomcat in this case) which requests to forward to our servlet by creating a file named `web.xml` in the `WEB-INF` directory. This file should contain the following:

```xml
<?xml version="1.0" encoding="ISO-8859-1"?>
<web-app xmlns="http://java.sun.com/xml/ns/j2ee"
         xmlns:xsi="http://www.w3.org/2001/XMLSchema-instance"
         xsi:schemaLocation="http://java.sun.com/xml/ns/j2ee
                 http://java.sun.com/xml/ns/j2ee/web-app_2_4.xsd" version="2.4">
  <servlet>
    <servlet-name>Example</servlet-name>
    <servlet-class>com.wrox.servlets.ExampleServlet</servlet-class>
  </servlet>
  <servlet-mapping>
    <servlet-name>Example</servlet-name>
    <url-pattern>*.example</url-pattern>
  </servlet-mapping>
</web-app>
```

5. Now start Tomcat and navigate to http://localhost:8080/Servlets/anything.example, and you should see the servlet's output shown below:

How It Works

The first parts of the code simply import the required resources and set up the class, which extends `HttpServlet`:

```java
package com.wrox.servlets;

import java.io.*;
import javax.servlet.*;
import javax.servlet.http.*;

public class ExampleServlet extends HttpServlet
```

373

The `doGet()` method first sets the content type of the response to be HTML, which the client uses to render it. The method then creates a `PrintWriter` object called `out`, acquired from the response object:

```
response.setContentType("text/html");
PrintWriter out = response.getWriter();
```

A series of HTML statements are printed to out and the `close()` method is called, which flushes and closes the output stream, returning the response to the client.

This class showcases a common strategy when a servlet can treat GET and POST requests exactly the same: routing any POST requests directly to the `doGet()` method:

```
public void doPost(HttpServletRequest request,
                   HttpServletResponse response)
        throws ServletException, IOException
{
  doGet(request, response);
}
```

The `web.xml` file that we created starts with these two lines:

```
<?xml version="1.0" encoding="ISO-8859-1"?>
<web-app xmlns="http://java.sun.com/xml/ns/j2ee"
  xmlns:xsi="http://www.w3.org/2001/XMLSchema-instance"
  xsi:schemaLocation="http://java.sun.com/xml/ns/j2ee
  http://java.sun.com/xml/ns/j2ee/web-app_2_4.xsd" version="2.4">
```

The first line simply declares that this is an XML version 1.0 file, encoded with the ISO-8859-1 (that is, Latin-1) character set. The second line provides schema information for validating the file (that is, to ensure that it meets the requirements of JSP `web.xml` files). We look at XML and schemas in more detail in Chapter 14.

The next line starts the `<web-app>` element, which contains the XML tags that configure our web application. It is the mandatory first tag of any `web.xml` file.

The `<servlet>` element assigns our servlet a name and indicates the location of the class that defines it:

```
<servlet>
  <servlet-name>Example</servlet-name>
  <servlet-class>com.wrox.servlets.ExampleServlet</servlet-class>
</servlet>
```

This name can be used elsewhere in `web.xml` to refer to our servlet when providing additional configuration information for it, as when we provide a **mapping** for the servlet. Our mapping tells the servlet container to route any request to any URL ending with `.example` to our servlet:

```
    <servlet-mapping>
      <servlet-name>Example</servlet-name>
      <url-pattern>*.example</url-pattern>
    </servlet-mapping>
  </web-app>
```

The Servlet Lifecycle

The **lifecycle** of servlets is the sequence of events in which a servlet is created, utilized, and finally destroyed. The servlet container manages this for us, creating the servlet object and calling its methods as required. The figure below illustrates the servlet lifecycle in generic terms:

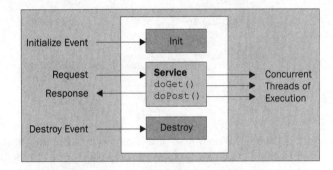

Loading, Instantiation, and Initialization

A server loads and instantiates a servlet dynamically when its services are first requested. The servlet's `init()` method should perform any necessary initialization and is called once for each servlet instance before any requests are handled. You only need to override `init()` in your servlet if a specific function needs to be accomplished at initialization. For example, we could use `init()` to load default data, or to create database connections.

Handling Requests

Once the servlet is properly initialized, the container can use it to handle requests. For each request, the servlet's `service()` method is passed an `HttpServletRequest` representing the request and an `HttpServletResponse` object that the servlet can use to create the response for the client.

The Request Object

The HttpServletRequest object allows the servlet to access all the information sent to the servlet container from the client. We have in fact already been introduced to the HttpServletRequest object earlier in this book – the implicit JSP request object is an example of this same object.

The information HttpServletRequest contains includes the URL and querystring, the request headers, and in some cases additional information called the **request body**. There are several methods for accessing this information. As you are already familiar with how to access this information in a JSP page, we'll provide a comparison of the JSP method with the Java method:

Description	JSP Expression Language	HttpServletRequest Method
Retrieve a request parameter	${param.myParam}	getParameter("myParam")
Retrieve a request header	${header.headerName}	getHeader("headerName")
Retrieve multiple request values	${paramValues.myParam}	getParameterValues ("myParam")

The Response Object

A servlet's end product is the HTTP response object encapsulating all the information to be returned to the client, and the HttpServletResponse interface defines methods that servlets use to construct this response.

An HttpServletResponse object provides two ways of returning data to the user, through the Writer object or the ServletOutputStream object, obtained by the getWriter() and getOutputStream() methods respectively. You should use the first object when the output is text data, and the second when the output is binary data (such as an image or a PDF file). Closing the Writer or ServletOutputStream objects with the close() method on either object once the response is created indicates to the server that the response is complete and ready to return to the client.

There are also a number of other useful methods provided by HttpServletResponse:

❑ sendRedirect()
   Redirects the client to a different URL. Here the URL must be an absolute URL. An example of this method is:

```
httpServletResponse.sendRedirect("http://www.amazon.com");
```

❑　sendError()
Sends an error message (For example: SC_METHOD_NOT_ALLOWED) to the client using the current error code status, an optional descriptive message can be provided as well. An example of this method is:

```
httpServletResponse.sendError(HttpServletResponse.SC_FORBIDDEN);
```

Alternatively, an error message can also be provided:

```
httpServletResponse.sendError(HttpServletResponse.SC_FORBIDDEN,
                        "You don't have access, get lost");
```

The complete list of error codes can be found in the JavaDoc documentation for the HttpServletResponse object.

Try It Out　　The Request and Response Objects

1. In this exercise, we'll make use of some more features of the request and response objects into our earlier servlet. Make a copy of ExampleServlet.java called DisplayServlet.java, and modify it with the highlighted code:

```
package com.wrox.servlets;

import java.io.*;
import java.util.Enumeration;
import javax.servlet.*;
import javax.servlet.http.*;

public class DisplayServlet extends HttpServlet
{

  public void doGet(HttpServletRequest request,
                    HttpServletResponse response)
        throws ServletException, IOException
  {
    response.setContentType("text/html");
    PrintWriter out = response.getWriter();
    out.println("<html><head><title>");
    out.println("Servlet Example");
    out.println("</title></head><body>");

    out.println("Query String being processed: <br>");
    out.println(request.getQueryString());
    out.println("<p>");
    out.println("Request Parameters:<p>");
```

```
      Enumeration enumParam = request.getParameterNames();
      while (enumParam.hasMoreElements())
      {
        String paramName = (String) enumParam.nextElement();
        String paramValues[] = request.getParameterValues(paramName);
        if (paramValues != null)
        {
          for (int i = 0; i < paramValues.length; i++)
          {
            out.print(paramName);
            out.print(" (" + i + "): ");
            out.print(paramValues[i]);
            out.println("<br>");
          }
        }
      }

      out.println("</body></html>");
      out.close();
    }
  }
```

2. Compile the servlet with the following command:

> **javac com/wrox/servlets/DisplayServlet.java
> -classpath %CATALINA_HOME%\common\lib\servlet-api.jar**

3. Now we need to change web.xml to use the new servlet like this:

```
<?xml version="1.0" encoding="ISO-8859-1"?>
<web-app xmlns="http://java.sun.com/xml/ns/j2ee"
         xmlns:xsi="http://www.w3.org/2001/XMLSchema-instance"
         xsi:schemaLocation="http://java.sun.com/xml/ns/j2ee
               http://java.sun.com/xml/ns/j2ee/web-app_2_4.xsd" version="2.4">
  <servlet>
    <servlet-name>Example</servlet-name>
    <servlet-class>com.wrox.servlets.DisplayServlet</servlet-class>
  </servlet>
  <servlet-mapping>
    <servlet-name>Example</servlet-name>
    <url-pattern>*.example</url-pattern>
  </servlet-mapping>
</web-app>
```

4. Restart Tomcat. Then, open your browser, and navigate to a URL something like http://localhost:8080/Servlets/an.example?name=Anne&team=Galatasaray. You should see the request parameters displayed like this:

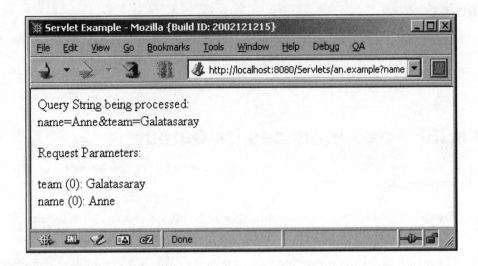

How It Works

This example simply reads the query string parameters and displays them on an HTML page. All the functionality is contained in the class's `doGet()` method. We get the entire query string using the `getQueryString()` method:

```
out.println("Query String being processed: <br>");
out.println(request.getQueryString());
```

The `HttpServletRequest` object contains all the query string parameters, and we get all their names as an enumeration (a collection of objects) called `enumParam` by calling the `getParameterNames()` method, which returns a collection of parameter names:

```
Enumeration enumParam = request.getParameterNames();
```

An `Enumeration` functions very much like an `Iterator`, by the way, so we can iterate through the contents of `enumParam` using a `while` loop, storing each parameter name in string called `paramName`:

```
while (enumParam.hasMoreElements())
{
   String paramName = (String) enumParam.nextElement();
```

We can find the value associated with this name by calling `getParameterValues()`:

```
String paramValues[] = request.getParameterValues(paramName);
```

Unloading

A servlet is typically unloaded from memory once the container is asked to shut down, at which point the container calls the servlet's `destroy()` method. It is only necessary to provide an implementation of this method for servlets that require certain specific actions before shutdown, such as closing open files or database connections.

How a JSP Page Produces its Output

As we stated earlier, a JSP page is converted into a servlet by the servlet container. This transformation occurs in two steps:

1. The JSP page is transformed from its text form into Java source code by the JSP **compiler**. Tomcat's JSP compiler is known as **Jasper**.

2. The Java source code is compiled into a Java class file, just as you have compiled your own Java code into class files.

To better understand this process, let's take a look at the code that Jasper generates when it compiles a JSP.

Try It Out   **A JSP Transformed into a Servlet**

1. For this example, we'll use the JSTL tags, so copy the JSTL `lib` subdirectory and all its contents to the `Servlets` folder as we've done in earlier chapters, and restart Tomcat.

2. Save the code below as `transform.jsp` in your `Servlets` folder:

```
<%@ taglib uri="http://java.sun.com/jstl/core_rt" prefix="c" %>
<html>
  <head>
    <title>
      JSP Compilation Demo
    </title>
  </head>
  <body>
    <h1>
      <c:if test="${param.username != null}">
        Hello ${param.username}.
      </c:if>
      Welcome!
    </h1>
  </body>
</html>
```

3. Navigate to http://localhost:8080/Servlets/transform.jsp, and you should see the following cheerful message:

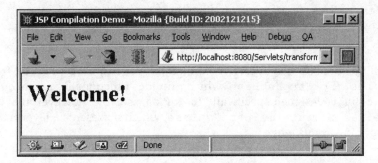

4. If you instead go to transform.jsp?username=Joe+Gillespie, you'll get a more personal message because our JSP recognizes the username request parameter:

How It Works

You shouldn't have too much trouble understanding this JSP code – what's interesting is what's happening behind the scenes. Inside the directory where you installed Tomcat, you'll find a subdirectory called work. Have a look inside that directory, and you should find another one named Standalone. Inside that, one called localhost containing another with the name Servlets. There will be a file there called transform_jsp.java, which is in fact the Java code that Jasper, the JSP compiler, has created from our JSP.

Go ahead and open the file. You'll find that the code is quite daunting, as indeed almost all machine-generated source code has a habit of being. We'll print the whole excerpt here, for the curious, and make some comments on it:

```
package org.apache.jsp;

import javax.servlet.*;
```

```
import javax.servlet.http.*;
import javax.servlet.jsp.*;

public final class transform_jsp extends
org.apache.jasper.runtime.HttpJspBase
    implements org.apache.jasper.runtime.JspSourceDependent {
```

Take a look at the three lines above. All compiled JSP pages must be derived from the class
`javax.servlet.jsp.HttpJspBase`, which provides functionality analogous to
`HttpServlet`, but is designed specifically for JSP pages. Note, however, that this class extends
`org.apache.jasper.runtime.HttpJspBase`, which represents a layer that makes life
easier for Jasper in various ways.

```
private static java.util.Vector _jspx_dependants;

private static org.apache.jasper.runtime.ProtectedFunctionMapper
              _jspx_fnmap;
private org.apache.jasper.runtime.TagHandlerPool _jspx_tagPool_c_if_test;

public transform_jsp() {
   _jspx_tagPool_c_if_test = new org.apache.jasper.runtime.TagHandlerPool(5);
}

public java.util.List getDependants() {
   return _jspx_dependants;
}

public void _jspDestroy() {
   _jspx_tagPool_c_if_test.release();
}
```

Above we see the `_jspDestroy()` method; the JSP equivalent of the `HttpServlet`
`destroy()` method. The method below, `_jspService()`, is the equivalent of `HttpServlet`'s
`service()` method:

```
public void _jspService(HttpServletRequest request, HttpServletResponse
                        response)
       throws java.io.IOException, ServletException {

   JspFactory _jspxFactory = null;
   PageContext pageContext = null;
   HttpSession session = null;
   ServletContext application = null;
   ServletConfig config = null;
   JspWriter out = null;
   Object page = this;
   JspWriter _jspx_out = null;
```

```
try {
  _jspxFactory = JspFactory.getDefaultFactory();
  response.setContentType("text/html");
  pageContext = _jspxFactory.getPageContext(this, request, response,
                                  null, true, 8192, true);
  application = pageContext.getServletContext();
  config = pageContext.getServletConfig();
  session = pageContext.getSession();
  out = pageContext.getOut();
  _jspx_out = out;
```

The Java here means that our JSP page ultimately performs the same tasks as our humble servlet. It takes our HTML and outputs it to the browser via the `HttpServletResponse` object, in much the same manner as our `ExampleServlet`:

```
out.write("\r\n");
out.write("<html>\r\n     ");
out.write("<head>\r\n          ");
out.write("<title>\r\n               JSP Compilation Demo\r\n          ");
out.write("</title>\r\n     ");
out.write("</head>\r\n     ");
out.write("<body>\r\n          ");
out.write("<h1>\r\n               ");
```

Below we see how our JSTL `if` tag was handled. Jasper created a method in this class, `_jspx_meth_c_if_0()`, which performs the custom tag functionality:

```
if (_jspx_meth_c_if_0(pageContext))
  return;
out.write("\r\n               Welcome!\r\n          ");
out.write("</h1>\r\n     ");
out.write("</body>\r\n");
out.write("</html>\r\n");
} catch (Throwable t) {
  if (!(t instanceof javax.servlet.jsp.SkipPageException)){
    out = _jspx_out;
    if (out != null && out.getBufferSize() != 0)
      out.clearBuffer();
    if (pageContext != null) pageContext.handlePageException(t);
  }
} finally {
  if (_jspxFactory != null)
    _jspxFactory.releasePageContext(pageContext);
}
}
```

And below we see that method. Yes, it is hard to follow, but you can see our EL statements being handled as calls to another method, `proprietaryEvaluate()`, and you can also see our "Hello" greeting in there too:

```
    private boolean _jspx_meth_c_if_0(PageContext pageContext)
            throws Throwable {
    JspWriter out = pageContext.getOut();
    /* ----  c:if ---- */
    org.apache.taglibs.standard.tag.rt.core.IfTag _jspx_th_c_if_0 =
(org.apache.taglibs.standard.tag.rt.core.IfTag)
_jspx_tagPool_c_if_test.get(org.apache.taglibs.standard.tag.rt.core.IfTag.clas
s);
    _jspx_th_c_if_0.setPageContext(pageContext);
    _jspx_th_c_if_0.setParent(null);
    _jspx_th_c_if_0.setTest(((java.lang.Boolean)
org.apache.jasper.runtime.PageContextImpl.proprietaryEvaluate("${param.userna
me != null}", java.lang.Boolean.class, (PageContext)pageContext, _jspx_fnmap,
"c", false)).booleanValue());
    int _jspx_eval_c_if_0 = _jspx_th_c_if_0.doStartTag();
    if (_jspx_eval_c_if_0 != javax.servlet.jsp.tagext.Tag.SKIP_BODY) {
      do {
        out.write("\r\n                    Hello ");
        out.write((java.lang.String)
org.apache.jasper.runtime.PageContextImpl.proprietaryEvaluate("${param.userna
me}", java.lang.String.class, (PageContext)pageContext, _jspx_fnmap, null,
true));
        out.write(".\r\n                 ");
        int evalDoAfterBody = _jspx_th_c_if_0.doAfterBody();
        if (evalDoAfterBody !=
javax.servlet.jsp.tagext.BodyTag.EVAL_BODY_AGAIN)
          break;
      } while (true);
    }
    if (_jspx_th_c_if_0.doEndTag() == javax.servlet.jsp.tagext.Tag.SKIP_PAGE)
      return true;
    _jspx_tagPool_c_if_test.reuse(_jspx_th_c_if_0);
    return false;
  }
}
```

You might now be asking yourself the question, "When is this knowledge useful?" Although knowing what goes on behind the scenes when a JSP is compiled is just interesting trivia a lot of the time, occasionally it can be very helpful to know. Examples of these times are:

❑   Really tricky errors
    At times, your JSP pages will fail and you'll have no idea why. In these circumstances, you may receive a line number telling you where in the page's Java source code the error occurred. Looking at that line can sometimes give an indication of where in the JSP code your error lies.

❑   Performance optimization
    If you've determined that a particular JSP is performing in an awfully slow manner, you can examine Java source code to see how your JSP compiler has translated your JSP and look for anything that is particularly nasty.

Web Applications and web.xml

A web application can consist of the following components:

❑ Servlets

❑ JavaServer Pages

❑ JavaBeans and utility classes

❑ Static documents (HTML, images, sounds, etc.)

❑ Configuration information for the above elements

As we have seen, a web application is a structured hierarchy of directories branching out from the root application directory. This physical root directory serves as the web root for serving files that are part of the application. That is, the physical directory in webapps, such as Servlets, is accessed by URLs starting with **Servlets**. This is a mapping, and it tells Tomcat where to look for files requested by browsing users.

The special WEB-INF folder within the web application folder contains:

❑ web.xml
A special configuration file called the **deployment descriptor**. It provides application configuration information for the container, such as the servlet mapping that we set up earlier.

❑ classes
As we have already seen, this folder contains servlets, JavaBeans, and other utility classes, which must be manually compiled into .class files.

❑ lib
Contains Java archive (.jar) files, the archive format for packaging sets of related Java classes, which provide a convenient way of distributing packages such as the Struts framework that we'll be using in later in this book. All the classes – servlets, JavaBeans, or otherwise – in these .jar files will be available to the web application just the same as regular .class files in the classes folder.

The deployment descriptor file can contain various types of configuration, deployment, and custom tag library information: it is the "glue" that holds the web application together. We have encountered a few of its functions in previous chapters. Here is a list of the most important functions it can provide:

❑ **ServletContext initialization parameters**
A set of context initialization parameters can be associated with a web application. Initialization parameters can be used by an application developer to convey setup information, such as the name of a system that holds critical data. This data can be included under the tag <context-param> in the web.xml. It is different to servlet initialization parameters as it defines initialization parameters for the whole application.

❏ **Session Configuration**
The `<session-config>` element defines the session parameters for the web application. For instance, we can define a session timeout for the application. We cover sessions and session timeout in the next chapter.

❏ **Servlet/JSP Definitions**
We can define servlet and JSP related parameters like the name of the servlet and its class, the full path, and initialization parameters.

❏ **Servlet/JSP Mappings**
Under `<servlet-mapping>` tag, mappings specify URLs that invoke particular servlets. We saw this in action in an earlier example.

❏ **Security Configuration**
We can configure security constraints for the web resources concerned with the web application.

These features will be demonstrated in examples throughout this chapter. For a full description of the elements in the `web.xml` file, refer to Appendix C.

Getting Initialization Information

Initialization information such as database connection details can be passed to the servlet through a `ServletConfig` object that is passed to the servlet's `init()` method. The `ServletConfig` object obtains this initialization information from the deployment descriptor file, `web.xml`. In the following example, we will get database login information from the `ServletConfig` object.

As we have already seen, the `ServletConfig` object contains servlet specific initialization parameters, so each servlet has its own. The parameters are stored as name-value pairs, and we use the `getInitParameter()` method to access the value of particular named parameters as a string:

```
String paramValue = ServletConfig.getInitParameter("paramName");
```

We can get the names of all of the initialization parameters using the `getInitParameterNames()` method:

```
Enumeration names = ServletConfig.getInitParameterNames();
```

This method returns an enumeration containing all the parameter names. This method is inherited from the `GenericServlet` class (remember that `HttpServlet` extends `GenericServlet`).

Context Initialization Parameters

The `<context-param>` element in the `web.xml` file associates a set of initialization parameters a web application. These are accessed by calling methods on the `ServletContext` object just as we called methods on `ServletConfig` to get servlet parameters:

```
String contextParam = ServletContext.getInitParameter("contextParamName");
```

Try It Out   Getting Initialization Information

1. Create the servlet below in the same place as the last two, under the name `InitParamServlet.java`. It outputs the database login and port configuration information taken from the `web.xml` file. For demonstration purposes, we even output the password, but it is not normally recommended to display a password in a real application!

```
package com.wrox.servlets;

import javax.servlet.*;
import javax.servlet.http.*;
import java.io.*;
import java.util.*;

public class InitParamServlet extends HttpServlet
{
  public void doGet(HttpServletRequest req, HttpServletResponse res)
            throws IOException, ServletException
  {

    res.setContentType("text/plain");
    PrintWriter out = res.getWriter();

    String url = getInitParameter("URL");

    ServletConfig config = getServletConfig();
    ServletContext context = getServletContext();
    String uid = config.getInitParameter("UID");
    String pwd = config.getInitParameter("PWD");
    String port = context.getInitParameter("some-port");

    out.println("Values retrieved for the init parameters are: ");
    out.println("URL: " + url);
    out.println("UID: " + uid);
    out.println("PWD: " + pwd);
    out.println("some-port: " + port);
  }
}
```

2. Compile the servlet from the same directory as before:

> **> javac com/wrox/servlets/InitParamServlet.java**
> **-classpath %CATALINA_HOME%\common\lib\servlet-api.jar**

3. Open your existing web.xml file and add the highlighted lines below, which provide the initialization information and servlet mapping that our servlet reads:

```xml
<?xml version="1.0" encoding="ISO-8859-1"?>
<web-app xmlns="http://java.sun.com/xml/ns/j2ee"
  xmlns:xsi="http://www.w3.org/2001/XMLSchema-instance"
  xsi:schemaLocation="http://java.sun.com/xml/ns/j2ee
  http://java.sun.com/xml/ns/j2ee/web-app_2_4.xsd" version="2.4">
  <display-name>A Simple Application</display-name>

  <context-param>
    <param-name>some-port</param-name>
    <param-value>5000</param-value>
  </context-param>

  <servlet>
    <servlet-name>Example</servlet-name>
    <servlet-class>com.wrox.servlets.DisplayServlet</servlet-class>
  </servlet>
  <servlet>
    <servlet-name>init</servlet-name>
    <servlet-class>com.wrox.servlets.InitParamServlet</servlet-class>
    <init-param>
      <param-name>URL</param-name>
      <param-value>jdbc:odbc:testdb</param-value>
    </init-param>
    <init-param>
      <param-name>UID</param-name>
      <param-value>scott</param-value>
    </init-param>
    <init-param>
      <param-name>PWD</param-name>
      <param-value>tiger</param-value>
    </init-param>
  </servlet>

  <servlet-mapping>
    <servlet-name>Example</servlet-name>
    <url-pattern>*.example</url-pattern>
  </servlet-mapping>
  <servlet-mapping>
    <servlet-name>init</servlet-name>
    <url-pattern>/init</url-pattern>
  </servlet-mapping>
</web-app>
```

4. Restart Tomcat and navigate to http://localhost:8080/Servlets/init. You should see something like the following:

How It Works

Initialization parameters can be provided under `<init-param>` tags in `web.xml` for particular servlets. Web application wide parameters are declared using the `<context-param>` element. `web.xml` also contains servlet parameter information.

The parameters declared in the `web.xml` file can be accessed from inside a servlet in several ways.

The `InitParamServlet` servlet implements just one method, `doGet()`. This method first sets the content type to plain text, and creates a `PrintWriter` object:

```
res.setContentType("text/plain");
PrintWriter out = res.getWriter();
```

The `init()` method, which this servlet inherits from the `GenericServlet` class, is called when the servlet is created by the web container. This initialization creates a `ServletConfig` object, and if no object is specified, methods are called on this object, as when we store the value of the URL attribute in a string called `url` using `getInitParameter()`:

```
String url = getInitParameter("URL");
```

You can also obtain references to the `ServletConfig` and `ServletContext` objects anywhere in your servlet through the following methods:

```
ServletConfig config = getServletConfig();
ServletContext context = getServletContext();
String uid = config.getInitParameter("UID");
String pwd = config.getInitParameter("PWD");
```

Parameters declared in the `<context-param>` element can only be accessed from the `ServletContext` object:

```
String port = context.getInitParameter("some-port");
```

Collaboration Between Servlets

We've seen in earlier chapters how we can get JSP pages to collaborate. This collaboration is possible thanks to a range of separate mechanisms, such as the `session` and `application` objects, and the `<jsp:forward>` and `<jsp:include>` actions. We can do all these things with servlets too, and that's what we'll look at next.

Session Tracking

Hypertext Transfer Protocol (HTTP) is by design a **stateless** protocol. This means that web servers running our applications can't by default remember details of a page showing in any browser from one request to the next. To overcome this when we require our web applications to maintain data, we must implement a means to store details relevant to each active browser, such as session objects.

Sometimes, it is necessary that a series of requests from a particular client are logically associated with each other through some kind of **session tracking**. Many strategies for this have evolved over time. The Java Servlet API takes a tried-and-tested approach: store objects that pertain to a user on the server in a session object, and then use a cookie stored client-side by the web browser to specify which session object pertains to which browser. The `javax.servlet.http.HttpSession` interface allows us to track a user's session fairly simply. This interface is implemented by the same `session` object that we can so easily make use of in JSP pages.

Session tracking allows servlets to maintain information about a series of requests from the same user for as long as it is required. To make use of this mechanism we need to:

❑ Obtain the `HttpSession` object from the `HttpServletRequest`.

❑ Store and retrieve data from the `session` object.

❑ When you no longer need certain data in the `session` object, remove it. When the entire object is done with, destroy it to conserve server resources by calling `invalidate()`.

The `getSession()` method of the `HttpServletRequest` object returns the session currently associated with the request. If there is no current session object, then one is created. We create name-value pairs to store data in the session. The `HttpSession` interface has methods allowing us to store, retrieve, and remove session attributes:

- ❏ setAttribute()
- ❏ getAttribute()
- ❏ getAttributeNames()
- ❏ removeAttribute()

A **session attribute** is simply an object that has been stored in the session. The invalidate() method invalidates the session, which means all the objects in the session are destroyed.

Try It Out   Session Tracking in a Servlet

1. Let's try a servlet that uses session tracking to keep track of how many times it has been accessed by a particular user, and to display some details of the current session.

Save the following Java code in a file called SessionTracker.java, in the same folder as before:

```java
package com.wrox.servlets;

import java.io.*;
import java.util.Date;
import javax.servlet.*;
import javax.servlet.http.*;

public class SessionTracker extends HttpServlet
{
  public void doGet(HttpServletRequest req, HttpServletResponse res)
            throws ServletException, IOException
  {
    res.setContentType("text/html");
    PrintWriter out = res.getWriter();

    HttpSession session = req.getSession(true);

    Integer count = (Integer) session.getAttribute("count");

    if (count == null)
    {
      count = new Integer(1);
    }
    else
    {
      count = new Integer(count.intValue() + 1);
    }
```

```
        session.setAttribute("count", count);
        out.println("<html><head><title>SessionSnoop</title></head>");
        out.println("<body><h1>Session Details</h1>");
        out.println("You've visited this page " + count + ((count.intValue()
                == 1) ? " time." : " times.") + "<br/>");
        out.println("<h3>Details of this session:</h3>");
        out.println("Session id: " + session.getId() + "<br/>");
        out.println("New session: " + session.isNew() + "<br/>");
        out.println("Timeout: " + session.getMaxInactiveInterval() + "<br/>");
        out.println("Creation time: " + new Date(session.getCreationTime())
                + "<br/>");
        out.println("Last access time: "
                + new Date(session.getLastAccessedTime()) + "<br/>");
        out.println("</body></html>");
    }
}
```

2. Compile the servlet from the `classes` folder, by running the following command:

> **> javac com/wrox/servlets/SessionTracker.java**
> **-classpath %CATALINA_HOME%\common\lib\servlet-api.jar**

3. Add the following entry to the `web.xml` file next to the existing `<servlet>` entries:

```
<servlet>
  <servlet-name>SessionTracker</servlet-name>
  <servlet-class>com.wrox.servlets.SessionTracker</servlet-class>
</servlet>
```

and the following entry next to the existing `<servlet-mapping>` entries:

```
<servlet-mapping>
  <servlet-name>SessionTracker</servlet-name>
  <url-pattern>/Session</url-pattern>
</servlet-mapping>
```

4. Restart Tomcat and browse to http://localhost:8080/Servlets/Session. You should something similar to the output shown below:

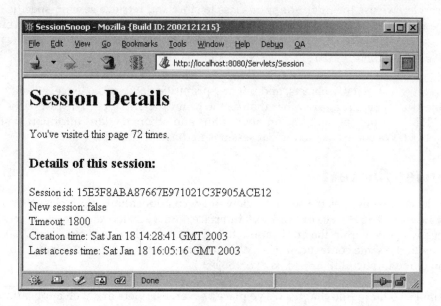

5. Hit your browser's **Reload** button several times. You'll notice that the page shows how many times you've visited it, and also now says **New session: false**.

First, we set the request content type to HTML, create a `PrintWriter` object, and get the current session (a new one is created if needed):

```
res.setContentType("text/html");
PrintWriter out = res.getWriter();
HttpSession session = req.getSession(true);
```

Every time a page is accessed, we get the count from the session by calling `getAttribute()`, increment it and store it back in the session. If the `Session` object returns `null`, meaning that no `count` attribute has yet been set, `count` is initialized to one:

```
Integer count = (Integer) session.getAttribute("count");

if (count == null)
{
   count = new Integer(1);
}
else
{
   count = new Integer(count.intValue() + 1);
}
```

In this servlet, we use the `HttpSession` class to store and retrieve session-specific information (the access count). We store the count in the `session` object by calling `setAttribute()`:

```
session.setAttribute("count", count);
```

A `session` can store only objects, and not any primitive datatypes. Hence, as you can see, we store objects as type `Integer` rather than as the primitive `int` type. The rest of the servlet creates HTML output showing the number of hits and other standard information stored by the session object. We come back to look at sessions in the next chapter.

The Servlet Context

The servlet context defines the servlet's view of a web application. It is a class that implements the `javax.servlet.ServletContext` interface, and a servlet can use it to access all the resources available within the application, to log events, and to store attributes that other servlets with the same context can use. (We encountered the `ServletContext` object earlier in the form of the implicit JSP `application` object.)

For example, so far in this chapter we've placed several servlets in a web application that's based at http://localhost:8080/Servlets; all the resources in our server that are in this application (in other words, that have request paths starting /Servlets) share a single, common servlet context.

A servlet can set an object as an attribute into the context by name, just as it can with the `HttpSession`, providing a convenient place to store resources that need to be shared for general use in an application. Objects can be added, retrieved, or removed from the context using the following methods of `ServletContext`:

❑ `void setAttribute(String name, Object attribute)`
Used to store an attribute in a context

❑ `Object getAttribute(String name)`
Used to get an attribute from the context

❑ `Enumeration getAttributeNames()`
Used to get the names of all the attributes currently stored in the context

❑ `void removeAttribute(String name)`
Call this function to remove an attribute from the context

Try It Out   **Using Servlet Context Information**

1. We'll now enhance our previous example to use the servlet context object to keep count of the total number of accesses to a shared resource.

Add the following lines to `SessionTracker.java` and save it in the same place under the name `SessionTracker2.java`:

```
package com.wrox.servlets;

import java.io.*;
import java.util.Date;
import javax.servlet.*;
import javax.servlet.http.*;

public class SessionTracker2 extends HttpServlet
{
  public void doGet(HttpServletRequest req, HttpServletResponse res)
              throws ServletException, IOException
  {
    res.setContentType("text/html");
    PrintWriter out = res.getWriter();

    HttpSession session = req.getSession(true);

    Integer totalCount = (Integer) getServletContext()
                        .getAttribute("com.wrox.servlets.total");

    if (totalCount == null)
    {
      totalCount = new Integer(1);
    }
    else
    {
      totalCount = new Integer(totalCount.intValue() + 1);
    }

    Integer count = (Integer) session.getAttribute("count");

    if (count == null)
    {
      count = new Integer(1);
    }
    else
    {
      count = new Integer(count.intValue() + 1);
    }

    session.setAttribute("count", count);
    getServletContext().setAttribute("com.wrox.servlets.total", totalCount);

    out.println("<html><head><title>SessionSnoop</title></head>");
    out.println("<body><h1>Session Details</h1>");
    out.println("You've visited this page " + count + ((count.intValue()
                == 1) ? " time." : " times.") + "<br/>");
    out.println("Total number of visits:" + totalCount + "<br/>");
    out.println("<h3>Details of this session:</h3>");
    out.println("Session id: " + session.getId() + "<br/>");
    out.println("New session: " + session.isNew() + "<br/>");
    out.println("Timeout: " + session.getMaxInactiveInterval() + "<br/>");
```

```
    out.println("Creation time: " + new Date(session.getCreationTime())
            + "<br/>");
    out.println("Last access time: "
            + new Date(session.getLastAccessedTime()) + "<br/>");
    out.println("</body></html>");
  }
}
```

2. Now compile `SessionDetails2.java`:

> **javac com/wrox/servlets/SessionTracker2.java**
> **-classpath %CATALINA_HOME%\common\lib\servlet-api.jar**

3. Add the following lines to your `web.xml` file, next to the other `<servlet>` entries:

```
<servlet>
  <servlet-name>SessionTracker2</servlet-name>
  <servlet-class>com.wrox.servlets.SessionTracker2</servlet-class>
</servlet>
```

and add these lines with the other `<servlet-mapping>` entries:

```
<servlet-mapping>
  <servlet-name>SessionTracker2</servlet-name>
  <url-pattern>/Session2</url-pattern>
</servlet-mapping>
```

4. Restart Tomcat. For this demo, open two separate copies of your browser and surf to http://localhost:8080/Servlets/Session2 in each one. If you hit reload a few times in both, you'll get two pages looking something like this:

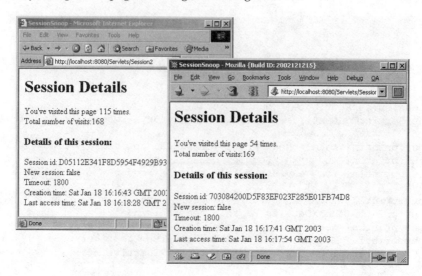

How It Works

We now have two counters. The first one:

You've visited this page 28 times.

tracks the number of times the browser has visited the page in a single session. The second counter:

Total number of visits:39

tracks the number of times all browsers have visited the page.

To accomplish this, we stored information in the `ServletContext` object to track the total number of hits:

```
Integer totalCount = (Integer) getServletContext().
    getAttribute("com.wrox.servlets.total");

if (totalCount == null) {
  totalCount = new Integer(1);
} else {
  totalCount = new Integer(totalCount.intValue() + 1);
}
```

We access this context by calling the `getServletContext()` method, and we can get the attribute from the context by calling `getAttribute()`. We then take this value and increment it by one or initialize it to one if it has not yet been set. We increment this count every time there is an access, irrespective of the session status. We then store information in the context object by calling `setAttribute()`:

```
getServletContext().setAttribute("com.wrox.servlets.total", totalCount);
```

Any servlet can remove an attribute from the context by calling the `removeAttribute()` method; therefore, care must be taken to ensure that other servlets are not using the same name for one of their attributes. This is the reason why it is recommended to use scoped names for context attributes, like `com.wrox.servlets.total` rather than unqualified names such as `total`. Objects placed in the `ServletContext` will stay there until the container shuts down.

Forwarding and Including Requests

It is often convenient when building a web application to forward requests to some other resource for further processing, or to include the output of one servlet or JSP within another. In JSP we do this using the `<jsp:forward>` and `<jsp:include>` actions, and we'll look at this in more detail in the next chapter. A servlet can also forward to or include another resource, using the `javax.servlet.RequestDispatcher` object.

Try It Out — Forwarding and Including Requests in a Servlet

1. Here we will create three servlets, `Include`, `Forward`, and `Goto`, to demonstrate forwarding and including requests. The code for `Forward.java` is shown below:

```
package com.wrox.servlets;

import java.io.*;
import javax.servlet.*;
import javax.servlet.http.*;

public class Forward extends HttpServlet
{

  String forwardingAddress = "Goto";

  public void doGet(HttpServletRequest req, HttpServletResponse res)
              throws ServletException, IOException
  {
    req.setAttribute("option", "forward");
    RequestDispatcher dispatcher = req.getRequestDispatcher(
                                       forwardingAddress);
    dispatcher.forward(req, res);
  }
}
```

The code for `Include.java` follows:

```
package com.wrox.servlets;

import java.io.*;
import javax.servlet.*;
import javax.servlet.http.*;

public class Include extends HttpServlet
{

  String forwardingAddress = "Goto";

  public void doGet(HttpServletRequest req, HttpServletResponse res)
              throws ServletException, IOException
  {
    req.setAttribute("option", "include");
    RequestDispatcher dispatcher = req.getRequestDispatcher(
                                       forwardingAddress);
    dispatcher.include(req, res);
    PrintWriter out = res.getWriter();
    out.println("Response included successfully");
  }
}
```

Both of the above servlets use the `Goto` servlet shown next:

```java
package com.wrox.servlets;

import java.io.*;
import javax.servlet.*;
import javax.servlet.http.*;

public class Goto extends HttpServlet
{

  String forwardingAddress = "Goto";

  public void doGet(HttpServletRequest req, HttpServletResponse res)
              throws ServletException, IOException
  {
    String option = (String) req.getAttribute("option");
    PrintWriter out = res.getWriter();
    if (option != null)
    {
      if (option.equals("forward"))
      {
        out.println("You have been forwarded to this page");
      }
      else if (option.equals("include"))
      {
        out.println("This line will be included in the response");
      }
    }
  }
}
```

2. Now compile these classes, either one by one, or all at once like this:

> **javac com/wrox/servlets/*.java**
> **-classpath %CATALINA_HOME%\common\lib\servlet-api.jar**

3. As before, we need to add some `<servlet>` entries to `web.xml`:

```xml
<servlet>
  <servlet-name>goto</servlet-name>
  <servlet-class>com.wrox.servlets.Goto</servlet-class>
</servlet>
<servlet>
  <servlet-name>forward</servlet-name>
  <servlet-class> com.wrox.servlets.Forward </servlet-class>
</servlet>
<servlet>
  <servlet-name>include</servlet-name>
  <servlet-class>com.wrox.servlets.Include</servlet-class>
</servlet>
```

4. We also need to provide `<servlet-mapping>` entries to map these to particular URLs:

```
<servlet-mapping>
  <servlet-name>goto</servlet-name>
  <url-pattern>/Goto</url-pattern>
</servlet-mapping>
<servlet-mapping>
  <servlet-name>include</servlet-name>
  <url-pattern>/Include</url-pattern>
</servlet-mapping>
<servlet-mapping>
  <servlet-name>forward</servlet-name>
  <url-pattern>/Forward</url-pattern>
</servlet-mapping>
```

5. If you restart Tomcat and navigate to http://localhost:8080/Servlets/Forward, you should see the following screen:

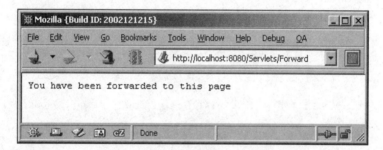

6. If you navigate to http://localhost:8080/Servlets/Include, on the other hand, you should see this:

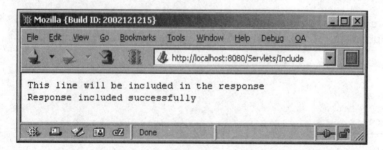

How It Works

As before, the `Forward` servlet implements just a `doGet()` method, which is called when the page is requested using HTTP GET:

```
req.setAttribute("option", "forward");
RequestDispatcher dispatcher = req.getRequestDispatcher(
                                forwardingAddress);
dispatcher.forward(req, res);
```

First, the request attribute `option` is given the value `forward`, and then a `RequestDispatcher` called `dispatcher` is created using the `getRequestDispatcher()` method of the `request` object. Finally, the `forward()` method is called on `dispatcher` which simply forwards the request to another servlet, in this case `Goto`. Here the forwarding path is relative to the application root.

The `Include` servlet also only implements a `doGet()` method, the contents of which are given below:

```
req.setAttribute("option", "include");
RequestDispatcher dispatcher = req.getRequestDispatcher(
                                forwardingAddress);
dispatcher.include(req, res);
PrintWriter out = res.getWriter();
out.println("Response included successfully");
```

This is similar to the previous servlet, but the `option` attribute is set to `include` and the `include()` method is called on `dispatcher`. This includes the response of the `Goto` servlet into the response of this servlet. After the response of the `Goto` servlet a writer object is created using the `getWriter()` method of the `request` object. Then a message **Response included successfully** is printed out.

The `Goto` servlet handles requests in much the same way as the other servlets by implementing a `doGet()` method.

```
String option = (String) req.getAttribute("option");
    PrintWriter out = res.getWriter();
    if (option != null) {
      if (option.equals("forward"))
      {
        out.println("You have been forwarded to this page");
      }
      else if (option.equals("include"))
      {
        out.println("This line will be included in the response");
      }
    }
  }
```

It finds out the origin of the request by querying for request attribute `option` and stores this as a String. A `PrintWriter` called "out" is created; finally, it prints out some text based on the value of `option`.

The `web.xml` file simply maps the servlets to the appropriate URLs.

User Authentication

A web application is expected to provide valuable services to its users. Therefore, you may want to restrict access to a limited set of users, for instance those that have paid a subscription. To do this the server needs to be able to **authenticate** the client – in other words, to make sure that the user is who they say they are. A simple but very effective way is to provide a username and authentication through a password only known to the user.

In some web applications, only certain users are able to access particular resources – for example, it could be that only paying users will be able to use a particular servlet or JSP. With each username/password pair there is associated one or more roles (for instance: user, superuser, etc). It is possible to allow an authenticated user access to only the parts of the web application for which their assigned roles are valid.

Servlets technology provides several methods to implement these procedures in your web application:

- ❑ HTTP Basic
- ❑ HTTP Digest
- ❑ Form-based
- ❑ HTTPS client

We will cover the two most commonly used methods, HTTP Basic and Form-based authentication in detail.

Of the other two methods, HTTP Digest is basically a more secure version of HTTP Basic and HTTPS client is the most secure method available, allowing encrypted communication between client and server. HTTPS client uses digital certificates and the secure sockets layer, which are beyond the scope of this book. Insight can be gained on all these security concepts by visiting http://developer.java.sun.com/developer/technicalArticles/Security/.

HTTP Basic Authentication

The HTTP protocol provides the basic authentication mechanism based on the username/password model. When a user requests access to a protected resource, the server responds by popping up a dialog box for them to enter the user information, which is sent back to the server in plain text. If the submitted username and password match the data in the server's database, then access is granted to that user.

The authentication information can be retrieved by using the HttpServletRequest object's getRemoteUser() method, which returns the remote user's identification and getAuthType() method, which returns the authentication mechanism for a particular request. Typical return values are BASIC or FORM, or null if no authentication was used.

Try It Out   HTTP Basic Authentication

1. This example demonstrates a simple servlet, which you should create in a file called ProtectedServlet.java, that checks authentication details provided by the user:

```
package com.wrox.servlets;

import javax.servlet.*;
import javax.servlet.http.*;
import java.io.*;
import java.util.*;
import java.security.*;

public class ProtectedServlet extends HttpServlet
{
  public void init(ServletConfig cfg) throws ServletException
  {
    super.init(cfg);
  }

  public void doGet(HttpServletRequest req, HttpServletResponse res)
            throws IOException, ServletException
  {
    res.setContentType("text/plain");
    PrintWriter out = res.getWriter();
    String authType = req.getAuthType();
    out.println("You are authorized to view this page");
    out.println("You were authenticated using: " + authType
            + " method of authentication");
    Principal princ = req.getUserPrincipal();
    out.println("The user is: " + princ.getName());
  }
}
```

Compile the servlet from the command prompt as usual.

2. We need a new `web.xml` file to protect our servlet, so replace your existing file with the following:

```xml
<?xml version="1.0" encoding="ISO-8859-1"?>
<web-app xmlns="http://java.sun.com/xml/ns/j2ee"
 xmlns:xsi="http://www.w3.org/2001/XMLSchema-instance"
 xsi:schemaLocation="http://java.sun.com/xml/ns/j2ee
  http://java.sun.com/xml/ns/j2ee/web-app_2_4.xsd" version="2.4">
  <servlet>
    <servlet-name>protected</servlet-name>
    <servlet-class>com.wrox.servlets.ProtectedServlet</servlet-class>
  </servlet>

  <servlet-mapping>
    <servlet-name>protected</servlet-name>
    <url-pattern>/protected</url-pattern>
  </servlet-mapping>

  <security-constraint>
    <web-resource-collection>
      <web-resource-name>Protected Area</web-resource-name>
      <url-pattern>/protected</url-pattern>
    </web-resource-collection>
    <auth-constraint>
      <role-name>private</role-name>
    </auth-constraint>
  </security-constraint>

  <login-config>
    <auth-method>BASIC</auth-method>
    <realm-name>Wrox Area</realm-name>
  </login-config>
</web-app>
```

3. Finally, we need to add an entry to the `tomcat-users.xml` file specifying a user in the `private` role. This file can be found in Tomcat's `conf` directory, and it is where user details for web applications are stored:

```xml
<tomcat-users>
  <user name="tomcat"  password="tomcat" roles="tomcat" />
  <user name="role1"   password="tomcat" roles="role1"  />
  <user name="both"    password="tomcat" roles="tomcat,role1" />
  <user name="fred"    password="tomcat" roles="private" />
</tomcat-users>
```

4. Restart Tomcat and navigate to http://localhost:8080/Servlets/protected, and you'll be asked for a username and password. Enter the values you placed in the `tomcat-users.xml` file. When you are authenticated, the following page will be displayed:

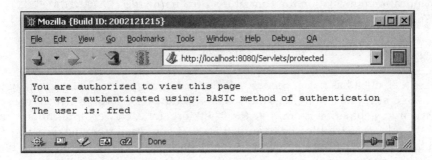

5. If you try one of the other users in the `tomcat-users.xml` file, or make one up, you will not be able to view the page.

How It Works

The setup for all the security mechanism is contained in the `web.xml` file; the resource you are trying to access does not need to know how this works as it is all handled by the web container.

In the `web.xml` file we map the servlet to the path **/protected**. The information of the security setup for your web application is contained within the `<security-constraint>` element. This contains two sub-elements `<web-resource-collection>` and `<auth-constraint>`. `<url-pattern>` sets the path to the protected part of the web application and `<role-name>`, which roles can be authenticated.

```
<security-constraint>
  <web-resource-collection>
    <web-resource-name>Protected Area</web-resource-name>
    <url-pattern>/protected</url-pattern>
  </web-resource-collection>
  <auth-constraint>
    <role-name>begjsp</role-name>
  </auth-constraint>
</security-constraint>
```

The `<login-config>` element defines the configuration of the actual login. We select the BASIC method and the HTTP realm name; this name will be shown in the pop-up login box (on most browsers).

```
<login-config>
  <auth-method>BASIC</auth-method>
  <realm-name>Wrox Area</realm-name>
</login-config>
```

The authentication information for Tomcat is stored in the file `[CATALINA_HOME]/conf/tomcat-users.xml`; we add the following entry to create a new user:

```
<user name="newuser" password="tomcat" roles="begjsp" />
```

Each <user> element has `name`, `password`, and `roles` attributes. The purpose of the `name` and `password` attributes is obvious; the `roles` attribute describes for which roles that this user/password combination is effective for. Therefore, for each web application you only have to define the roles that are allowed to authenticate. If you recall from the `web.xml` file we set the acceptable roles to be role1 and Tomcat, so all of the users listed in the above file would be able to authenticate our application.

When you try to access the **/protected** page the server responds with an "unauthorized" response as part of the response the server returns a **WWW-Authenticate header**, in this case

```
WWW-Authenticate: Basic realm="Wrox Area"
```

The browser then creates a pop-up dialog box asking for a user name and password, which are cached in memory and then returned to the server. If the values are authenticated, the server returns the requested page. As the values entered are cached the user is not prompted for them again when accessing pages within the same realm.

Form Based Authentication

The advantage of form based authentication is that it allows you to write custom login and error pages. The pages you create are responsible for transmitting the username and password to the web container; this is much more flexible than Basic authentication where this is all handled by the browser.

Try It Out   Form Based Authentication

1. For this example, we need to create three JSP pages (in the `Servlets` application folder) and modify the `web.xml` file. First, we create `login.jsp`, which will provide the actual login form:

```
<html>
  <head><title>Login Page</title></head>
  <body>
    <h2>Login page</h2>

    <form method="POST" action="j_security_check" >
      <input type="text" name="j_username">
      <input type="password" name="j_password">
      <input type="submit" value="Login Now">
    </form>
```

```
    </body>
</html>
```

2. We will also provide an error page to deal with users that enter incorrect details, called error.jsp:

```
<html>
  <head><title>Authentication Error</title></head>
  <body>
    You have entered an invalid username/password.<br/>
    Please <a href="login.jsp">try again</a><p/>
    If you continue to experience difficulties please contact the
    administrator at webmaster@sorryfool.com

  </body>
</html>
```

3. The resource that is accessed on authentication is index.jsp:

```
<html>
  <head><title>Protected Page</title></head>
  <body>
    <h2>Authentication mechanism ${pageContext.request.authType}</h2>
  </body>
</html>
```

4. Finally we need to set up the web.xml file. It is not possible for a web application to have more then one authentication mechanism so rather than modifying the previous file, just replace it with this:

```
<?xml version="1.0" encoding="ISO-8859-1"?>
<web-app xmlns="http://java.sun.com/xml/ns/j2ee"
         xmlns:xsi="http://www.w3.org/2001/XMLSchema-instance"
         xsi:schemaLocation="http://java.sun.com/xml/ns/j2ee
                 http://java.sun.com/xml/ns/j2ee/web-app_2_4.xsd" version="2.4">
  <security-constraint>
    <web-resource-collection>
      <web-resource-name>Entire application</web-resource-name>
      <url-pattern>/*</url-pattern>
    </web-resource-collection>
    <auth-constraint>
      <role-name>private</role-name>
    </auth-constraint>
  </security-constraint>

  <login-config>
    <auth-method>FORM</auth-method>
    <form-login-config>
```

```
        <form-login-page>/login.jsp</form-login-page>
        <form-error-page>/error.jsp</form-error-page>
      </form-login-config>
    </login-config>
  </web-app>
```

5. Don't forget to restart Tomcat, and navigate to http://localhost:8080/Servlets/. As we haven't specified a specific web page, the index.jsp file will be opened, which in turn directs you to the login page:

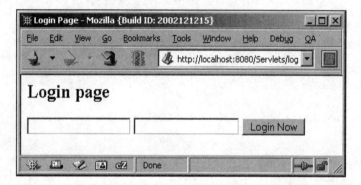

6. Enter the same username and password as before, and click Login Now. You will be redirected to login.jsp, which displays the authentication mechanism used:

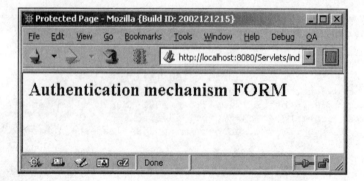

How It Works

If the user tries to access a page in a protected part of the application, a login form is returned instead of the requested resource. The login form contains fields for the user to specify their username and password. These *must* be called j_username and j_password, also the form action must be j_security_check:

```
<form method="POST" action="j_security_check" >
<input type="text" name="j_username">
<input type="password" name="j_password">
<input type="submit" value="Login Now">
</form>
```

The values entered for the username and password are then returned to the server via the POST method. These values are processed in the same way as for BASIC authentication. If the user is accepted the page they wanted to access is returned, otherwise an error page is returned.

Making Servlets Thread-safe

Earlier in this chapter we explained that the servlet container is responsible for receiving requests form browsers and forwarding them to servlets. It turns out that a servlet container can forward multiple requests **concurrently** to the same servlet. "Concurrently", if you didn't know, is a technical synonym of "simultaneously." In the event of multiple concurrent requests forwarded to your servlet, each individual request is made in its own **thread**. A thread is a sequence of execution events that can be performed in isolation from other sequences.

> **Multiple threads might be calling the `service()` method at the same time, and therefore we must write the code in the `service()` method (and, by extension, in `doGet()` or `doPost()`) so that it can safely be called by several threads simultaneously. This is called making the code "thread-safe."**

In other words, because multiple threads might be calling your servlet, you need to make sure that the separate threads won't be interfering with each other. For example, consider the following servlet:

```
import javax.servlet.http.*;
import javax.servlet.ServletException;
import java.io.IOException;

public class UnsafeServlet extends HttpServlet
{
  private int number = 0;

  protected void doGet(HttpServletRequest request,
                    HttpServletResponse response)
              throws ServletException, IOException
  {
    number = Integer.parseInt(request.getParameter("userNumber"));
    number *= 5;
    request.setAttribute("newNumber", new Integer(number));
  }
}
```

The preceding code is *not* thread-safe. The line shown in bold declares number as a **class member**. This means that multiple threads can access and modify number concurrently. In our example, if two threads access doGet() in immediate succession, the first would assign number with whatever its value for request.getParameter("userNumber") happens to be. It then moves on to the next line of code. But wait! The second thread reassigns number using its entirely different value for request.getParameter("userNumber"). Now, when the first thread multiplies number by 5, has it multiplied its value for number by five, or the second thread's value? We just don't know, and that's why this servlet is not thread-safe, and is hence unstable.

The moral of the story is to avoid modifying any class members of your servlet in any method but init() and destroy(). Thus, the thread-safe version of our earlier broken servlet would be:

```
public class SafeServlet extends HttpServlet
{
  protected void doGet(...) throws ServletException, IOException
  {
    int number = 0;
    number = Integer.parseInt(request.getParameter("userNumber"));
    number *= 5;
    request.setAttribute("newNumber", new Integer(number));
  }
}
```

Note the new location of number. Declaring variables inside methods, thus making them **local variables**, is perfectly thread-safe. This is by far the most effective technique for making servlets thread-safe. There are other, more subtle issues that aren't as important. For these, we will leave you in the care of other authors and their books, such as Joshua Bloch's *Effective Java* (Addison-Wesley, ISBN 0-201-31005-8) or Doug Lea's *Concurrent Programming in Java* (Addison-Wesley, ISBN 0-201-31009-0).

SingleThreadModel

We avoid the need to worry about making our code thread-safe if our servlet implements the SingleThreadModel interface, as in this example:

```
public class ThreadSafeServlet extends HttpServlet implements
SingleThreadModel
{
  // Typical servlet code, with no threading concerns in the service method.
  // No extra code for the SingleThreadModel interface.
}
```

Servlets that implement this interface receive the guarantee that the servlet container will not allow two threads to execute its service() method (and thus doGet() et al.) concurrently. To achieve this, the servlet container manages concurrent requests by either queuing requests for a single servlet object or by having a pool of servlet objects and assigning one servlet for each request.

While implementing the `SingleThreadModel` can simplify application development, it may significantly impact your web application's performance. This is because if large numbers of users all try to interact with a single-threaded servlet at once, they would either have to wait for other users to finish, or your poor servlet container would have to create dozens of instances of the servlet.

Summary

When a web browser accesses a web server and makes a HTTP request, the servlet container determines which servlet to invoke based on its configuration settings, and calls it with objects representing the request and response. The servlet processes the request, using the request object to obtain information about the request that the browser sent, and sends data back to the client using the response object.

In this chapter, we have learned:

❑ Features of the servlet technology, how servlets work, and their life cycle.

❑ How JSP pages work behind the scenes: the relevance of servlet technology to JSP developers, and the fact that JSP pages are compiled to servlets.

❑ The role of the `web.xml` file in a web application.

❑ How servlets can collaborate by means of session tracking, the servlet context, and how to forward and include requests when using servlets.

❑ How to ensure only authenticated users can access your web application.

CHAPTER 11

Keeping Track of Users

Most people who shop online and send e-mail using the Internet aren't concerned with how these web sites keep track of all their users so that everyone buys only those things they selected, and only reads their own web-based mail. However, keeping track of users is an essential requirement of e-commerce, and this chapter dips into the technology that makes it possible.

Let's consider an online bookstore as an example. Customers arrive at the main page, where they may search for any particular book. Books appear with the option "add to shopping cart", and when this link is clicked, users are asked to register and login if it is their first visit to the site. Once the book has been added to the shopping cart, the user can continue to browse the site. When they happen upon another item that takes their fancy, they can add it to their shopping cart by clicking the link. When the customer is ready to pay for their chosen times, they click a checkout link, taking them to a page where their chosen items are listed along with their price and shipping charges. The user just has to enter their credit card details to have the books delivered by a particular date.

This sequence of events is probably very familiar to you, because it is just another part of day-to-day business in the 21st century. The real point though is that throughout the shopping experience, the web application can remember every user's choices and preferences, and use them on any pages that they visit. In this chapter, we'll look at techniques and issues for keeping track of users in JSP applications.

It's not just shopping sites that track users – just about all web sites can benefit from providing their users with a personalized experience. A web site can remember users for the duration of each visit, or it can remember users across visits. By the end of this chapter, you will be able to track a user in a web application from login to logout, and you'll know several well-established methods for tracking users that can be applied to JSP.

Session

When a site implements a shopping cart, as in our fictional book site, that cart must exist and remember users' selections as they move from page to page. The cart must exist for the duration of each user's visit to our site; that is, for the duration of a user's **session**. Some sites may remember users beyond a single session.

So the book web application needs a way of tracking sessions. Sessions can be tracked by uniquely identifying the client computer whenever a request is received by the server. In the rest of the chapter, we will discuss session tracking in detail and how to use it to create an improved user experience.

The HTTP Protocol

You may be asking now that if it's so useful for web applications to track sessions, why isn't this feature a fundamental part of the Internet?

The reason is that web browsing is based on a **stateless** model, and the HTTP protocol used provides no way to associate one request with another – each request must be self-contained. This increases the reliability and robustness of web servers, which handle thousands and in some cases millions of requests a day. If it were not the case, and servers had to maintain continuous connections with all current clients at once, it would be a serious hit on server performance and would significantly reduce the maximum number of clients possible..

When a web page is requested, the following sequence of events unfurls:

1. The browser opens an HTTP connection to the web server holding the requested page.

2. It then sends an HTTP request asking for a particular web page.

3. The web server responds to the request by sending either the requested page or an error page in the event of mishap.

4. Once the web server has fulfilled the browser's request for a web page, the connection between the server and browser is closed.

5. Next time the same browser requests another page from the same server, a *new* connection must be opened. HTTP itself provides no way for a web server to determine that any request originates from the same user who accessed a page seconds ago.

Since web servers need to serve many clients at once (some search engines log over a million hits a day), this model helps to keep server performance high, with the drawback that if we wish to track users, we have to add our own 'memory'.

Tracking Sessions

Most web servers can create and maintain **session objects** for each user accessing its pages, and such objects (often just called **sessions**) can hold data relevant to that user's activities. These sessions are available to any page that the user accesses, providing a means for us to persist information the user entered in one page for use in another. We've already looked at session and application state in when we looked at servlets in the previous chapter, but now we'll see how both these can be used in regular JSP pages.

When a web site requires its users to log on to access certain services, a session will often be created at login to hold certain information about each user. This information might have been entered at this visit or an earlier one, and it can be read and written as many times as required by the application. When the user logs out, their session object is either destroyed or stored on the server for use when that user next visits.

Many sites have many thousands of users every day, so this session information could quite easily start to consume large amounts of server memory and bring down performance if we're not careful. Thus, we should create session objects only when required, and destroy them when they're finished with. As we know, HTTP is stateless, so it won't itself tell us when a user has moved off our site to go elsewhere, so typically we would provide a logout link, and sessions can then be identified as finished when the user logs out. Also, we can assume that a session is over if the user is inactive for a certain period (this period is the **session timeout**).

Three main mechanisms have evolved to allow a web server to link any particular session object with the user that it pertains to:

❑   Cookies

❑   URL rewriting

❑   Hidden form fields

Cookies

Cookies are the most widely used session tracking mechanism. A cookie is nothing more than a text file stored on the client machine by the web browser. The cookie stores information as name-value pairs, and it is passed to the server when pages are requested.

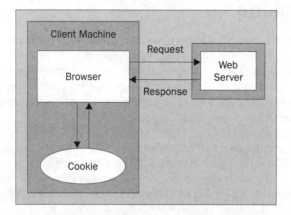

As illustrated in the diagram, the server creates a cookie containing relevant information, and sends it to the client browser. The client stores this cookie, and sends it to the server on every subsequent request.

However, cookies do have some drawbacks. As a minimum, browsers should allow twenty cookies for each web server, a total of 300 cookies, and it may limit cookie size to 4 Kb each. These restrictions are mostly followed and not imposed. Also, sensitive information such as credit card details should not be stored in a cookie, because they could be read by anyone with access to the client computer. In addition, a significant number of users are concerned that cookies compromise their privacy or security, and so disable cookie support in their web browser. Web applications that depend on cookies to track sessions would not work for such users.

Even though JSP makes using cookies relatively straightforward, certain details still need to be handled. These are:

❑   Finding the correct cookie that corresponds to a given session.

❑   Setting an appropriate expiration time for the cookie.

URL Rewriting

Every session is identified internally using a session ID on the server. The URL rewriting method appends the session identifier to the query string at the end of each URL, and the server can then use this to locate the cookie containing information about that user's current session. Such a URL could look something like this:

```
http://www.buystuff.com/buypets.html?jsessionid=12345
```

This solution avoids the issues inherent with cookies, but introduces its own problems, such as:

❑   You have to be sure to append the identifier to every URL in your site.

❑ There is a security risk in making this ID visible, which can sometimes be reduced by encrypting the query string data.

❑ There is a loophole in that users can leave the session and come back using a bookmark, in which case your session information is lost.

This technique is used in case the browser doesn't support cookies or the cookies have been turned off by the user. In general though, hidden form fields are preferable to URL rewriting.

Hidden Form Fields

HTML forms can define a field with a `type` attribute set to `"hidden"`:

```
<input type="hidden" name="jsessionid" value="12345">
```

Such fields will not be visible on the form in the browser (unless the source is viewed), but when the form is submitted the specified name and value will be included in the request message, making them ideal for storing session identifiers.

Hidden fields are supported by all major web browsers and do not require users to permit them. However, their usefulness is limited because they only work for HTML forms, they also require special handling on each form and the HTML source could be intercepted and examined by malicious parties to obtain the session ID.

Using Sessions in JSP Pages

JSP provides a simple way to manage sessions, using the implicit object called `session`. This object internally uses one of the methods described above to track sessions under the hood, but the details are not exposed to the developer. For example, Tomcat uses cookies to identify the client if it can, and if not, it falls back on URL rewriting.

To use the `session` object, we need to follow these basic steps:

❑ Declare that the page participates in a session.

❑ Read from or write to the `session` object.

❑ Either terminate the session by expiring it, or do nothing so it will eventually expire on its own.

We declare that a JSP page uses the `session` object by setting the following attribute on the `page` directive at the start of a JSP page:

```
<%@page language="java" session="true "%>
```

The page can now access the implicit `session` object (which works very much like the `request` object we're familiar with). It will represent the existing session, or if there is no existing session already, a new one will be created.

The default value of the `session` attribute is `true`, meaning pages can access the `session` object unless we explicitly set this attribute to `false`.

Each web application on a server maintains one `session` object for every client currently accessing it. So although JSP pages in one web application can share session data with each other, they can't share it with JSP pages in another web application accessed by that same user.

The Session Object in Detail

To store information in the `session` object, we use the JSTL `<set>` tag:

```
<c:set var="firstVal" scope="session" value="<%new Integer(1)%>"/>
```

This tag creates an `Integer` object and stores it in the session under the name `firstVal`. Note that we must store an `Integer` object rather than the `int` primitive type, because, like the utility classes we saw in Chapter 8, the `session` object can only store objects. The `Integer` object is a **wrapper class**; that is to say, it provides a simple way of "wrapping up" an int value as an object, for just this sort of situation.

Any other JSP page that is in the same session and context can now access our `Integer` object by calling the `session` object's `getAttribute()` method with the name that we gave the object when it was stored:

```
Integer iPrevVal = (Integer) session.getAttribute("firstVal");
```

Notice that we have to cast our object back to its particular class, using `(Integer)`, because objects held in session are stored as the generic `Object` type.

Alternatively, we can use EL, like this:

```
${firstVal}
```

We can get the names of all objects held in session by calling the `getAttributeNames()` method, which returns an `Enumeration` containing the attribute names. Finally, the `removeAttribute()` method removes the named object from the session, which is important as it frees up server memory for other purposes.

Checking for a New Session

We can check whether the session is new by calling the `session` object's `isNew()` method:

```
if (session.isNew()) {
  // Yes it is
}
```

The session is considered new until a client **joins the session**, by returning the session-related information to the server through a subsequent request. Let's look at an example:

- ❏ A client accesses the application by sending an HTTP request to the web server.

- ❏ The server generates a unique ID to identify the client, and passes it on to the client in a cookie sent with the response.

- ❏ When the client makes further requests for that application, it forwards the cookie to the server along with the request.

- ❏ The server then knows that the client is participating in the session.

Obtaining the Session Identifier

Every client's session is identified by a unique ID in the form of a string. We can get this identifier from the `getId()` method:

```
String id = session.getId();
```

Removing the Session

To "kill" a session when it is no longer needed, we call the `session.invalidate()` method.

Session Timeouts

As a stateless protocol, HTTP doesn't tell us whether clients are still active or not, and so we must get rid of old sessions periodically to avoid running out of memory on our server. The best way to determine when a session has become inactive and may be destroyed is by using a timeout period.

Sessions have a default timeout, which for Tomcat is 1. This value means the session expires when the browser is closed. We can change this to another value of our choosing by calling the `setMaxInactiveInterval()` method of the session object with the number of seconds that we want sessions to remain unused before they are destroyed. There is a related method, `getMaxInactiveInterval()`, that returns the current timeout value. We can also set the timeout to –1 if we want the session to *never expire*.

We can define the default session timeout for a Tomcat web application through the `<session-timeout>` element in the application's `web.xml`. For instance, if a web application has the following `web.xml` file in its `WEB-INF` folder, sessions for this application will not expire by default:

```
<?xml version="1.0" encoding="ISO-8859-1"?>

<!DOCTYPE web-app
  PUBLIC "-//Sun Microsystems, Inc.//DTD Web Application 2.3//EN"
  "http://java.sun.com/j2ee/dtds/web-app_2_3.dtd">

<webapp>
  <session-config>
    <session-timeout>-1</session-timeout>
  </session-config>
</webapp>
```

Try It Out   The Session Object

1. This example shows the `session` object at work in a JSP page. The page tracks the number of times any one user accesses it, storing the count in the session. Additionally, it displays the session ID, session creation time, and the time of last access.

Create a folder called `Cookies` in Tomcat's `webapps` folder, and create an empty `WEB-INF` directory inside it. Copy the `lib` directory and its contents from the JSTL folder into `WEB-INF` as we've done previously.

2. Save the file below as `ShowSession.jsp` in the `Cookies` folder:

```
<%@page import = "java.util.*"%>
<%@ taglib prefix="c" uri="http://java.sun.com/jstl/core_rt" %>

<html>
  <head><title>Session Properties</title></head>
  <body bgcolor="white">

    <%-- Increment counter --%>
    <c:set var="sessionCounter" scope="session"
           value="${sessionCounter + 1}" />

    <h1>Session Properties</h1>

    <c:if test="${sessionCounter == 1}">
      This is your first visit to this page!
    </c:if>

    <c:if test="${sessionCounter > 1}">
      This page has been visited <b>${sessionCounter}</b> times within the
      current session.
    </c:if>

    <table border=1 align="center">
      <tr bgcolor="#F9AD00">
```

```
        <th>Info Type</th><th>Value</th></tr>
      <tr><td>ID</td>
        <td> <%=session.getId()%></td></tr>
      <tr><td>Creation Time</td>
        <td><%=session.getCreationTime()%></td></tr>
      <tr>
        <td>Time of Last Access</TD>
        <td><%=session.getLastAccessedTime()%></td></tr>
    </table>
  </body>
</html>
```

3. Start Tomcat, and open http://localhost:8080/Cookies/ShowSession.jsp in your browser, and you should see a screen like that shown below:

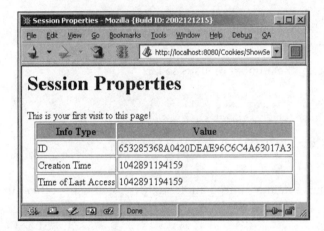

4. Hit your browser's Reload button a few times. Each time the page refreshes, you should see the access count increase:

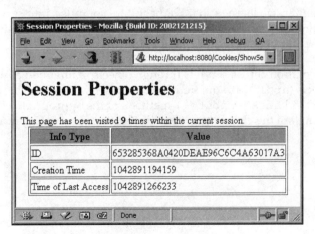

When we first access the page, the `<set>` tag creates a session attribute called `sessionCounter` and initializes it to 0:

```
<c:set var="sessionCounter" scope="session"
       value="${sessionCounter + 1}" />
```

On subsequent page accesses, this tag will simply increment the `sessionCounter` attribute and store the new value in session.

We test if this is the first visit to the page by this user with the following code:

```
<c:if test="${sessionCounter == 1}">
  This is your first visit to this page!
</c:if>
```

Otherwise we display the number of visits so far:

```
<c:if test="${sessionCounter > 1}">
  This page has been visited <b>
  <c:out value="${sessionCounter}" />
  </b> times within the current session.
</c:if>
```

A table displays the remaining information on the session using other attributes of the `session` object.

Collaboration Between JSP Pages

In the previous chapter, we learned that JSP pages are compiled into servlets when they are first accessed. Behind the scenes, servlets collaborate with each other using session and application objects, and by forwarding and including requests.

We can share information across servlets through objects maintained as attributes (a key-value pair) of scope objects (`application`, `session`, and `request`), which can be accessed with the `getAttribute()` and `setAttribute()` methods of the appropriate class representing the scope. The following are the classes that embody the three scopes applicable to servlets:

Scope	Class
Request	`javax.servlet.ServletRequest`
Session	`javax.servlet.http.HttpSession`
Application	`javax.servlet.ServletContext`

We have seen how to access data from the request object in the previous chapter, and now we'll look at the other two.

Session Tracking

Servlets access session objects differently to JSP pages where the session is available as an implicit object. A servlet must access the session object through the request object.

Accessing a Session

Sessions are represented by the `HttpSession` object, which is returned from the `getSession()` method of the `request` object. This method returns the current session associated with this request, or, if the request does not have a session object, it creates one.

Storing Data (Attributes) in a Session Object

We can associate attributes with a session by name. Such attributes are accessible by any web component that belongs to the same application *and* is handling a request that is part of the same session. (Components in the same application are said to reside in the same **web context**.)

We could thus rewrite the previous example to display the access count as a servlet, like so:

```
public class AccessCounterServlet extends HttpServlet {
  public void doGet(HttpServletRequest request,
                    HttpServletResponse response)
            throws ServletException, IOException
  {

    // Get the user's session
    HttpSession session = request.getSession();

    // Get access count from session
    Integer iCount = (Integer)session.getAttribute("count");

    if ( iCount == null )
    {
      iCount = new Integer(1);
      session.setAttribute("count", iCount);
    }
```

```
      // Display count to the user
      StringWriter sw = new StringWriter();
      PrintWriter writer = new PrintWriter(sw);

      writer.println("This page has been viewed " + iCount.increment()
                    + " number of times");
    }
  }
```

Session Management

Session objects consume valuable resources, and overusing them can hamper an application's performance as we've said earlier. It is important to clear out session objects once they are no longer necessary, by **invalidating** them, to use servlet terminology.

As before, there's no guaranteed way of determining if a user has finished browsing our site and gone on their way, and so we have to decide upon a suitable workaround. Generally, this will be one of these two approaches:

❑ **Session Timeouts**
We can specify the session timeout in a web application's deployment descriptor (web.xml). Alternatively, we can set a session's timeout period in code by calling the setMaxInactiveInterval() method on the session object, or we can use the default defined in the application's deployment descriptor. We can call getMaxInactiveInterval() to find out the currently applicable timeout.

❑ **Explicitly Invalidating the Session**
It's often a good idea to provide a logout link when our application uses sessions. In JSP, this link would call the session object's invalidate() method to free up the resources that the user's session was occupying.

For instance, our Log Off link could call the servlet below:

```
public class LogoffServlet extends HttpServlet
{
  public void doPost(HttpServletRequest request,
                     HttpServletResponse response)
            throws ServletException, IOException
  {
    // Get the user session
    HttpSession session = request.getSession();

    // There we go...
    session.invalidate();
    // Session is invalidated
  }
}
```

The Servlet Context

Any information stored at application level is shared between all pages and all sessions. Web components execute in a shared space called the context, which is represented by an object that implements the `ServletContext` interface. We retrieve the `ServletContext` object by calling the `getServletContext()` method. The `ServletContext` object exposes methods for storing and retrieving attributes similarly to the session object. It also has methods for controlling various details of the application, such as setting initialization parameters, controlling resources associated with the web context, and configuring usage logging.

For example, page hit counters often use servlet context to store the total number of times a page has been visited:

```java
public class CounterServlet extends HttpServlet
{
  public void doPost(HttpServletRequest request,
                     HttpServletResponse response)
            throws ServletException, IOException
  {
    StringWriter sw = new StringWriter();
    PrintWriter writer = new PrintWriter(sw);
    ServletContext context = filterConfig.getServletContext();
    Integer hitCounter = (HitCounter)context.getAttribute("hitCounter");

    if (hitCounter == null)
      context.setAttribute("hitCounter", new HitCounter(1));

    writer.println("This page has been viewed " + counter.increment()
              + " number of times");
  }
}
```

In the above example, the `HitCounter` object is created and stored in a context attribute called `hitCounter`. Ideally, the object's `increment()` method should be synchronized to prevent simultaneous access by servlets that are running concurrently, by application of the `synchronized` modifier.

Including Requests

It is sometimes necessary to include another resource (such as another JSP page, image, or HTML file) in the response returned from a web component. We can do this with the `include()` method of the `RequestDispatcher` object:

```java
import java.io.*;
import javax.servlet.*;
import javax.servlet.http.*;

public class IncludeServlet extends HttpServlet
{
```

```
    public void doGet(HttpServletRequest req, HttpServletResponse res)
            throws ServletException, IOException
{
    res.setContentType("text/html");
    PrintWriter out = res.getWriter();

    out.println("<html><head><title>An Include Servlet
                </title></head>");
    out.println("<body>");
```

```
// Show an external resource
    RequestDispatcher dispatcher = req.getRequestDispatcher(
                                "/Folder/servlets/SomeResource");
    dispatcher.include(req, res);

    // Remove the "item" attribute after use
    //do something else
    out.println("</body></html>");
    }
}
```

If the resource is static, such as straight HTML code, this method simply includes it with the response at the point this method is called. If the resource is a web component (a servlet or JSP page), the method sends the request to the indicated component, which processes it and replies with a response for inclusion with the containing servlet's response.

Forwarding Requests

In some situations, we want to divide how requests are processed. For instance, we might have one component that performs preliminary processing on the request and another that generates the response. For example, you might want to partly process a request and then transfer to another component depending on the nature of the request. To do this, you invoke the forward method of a RequestDispatcher. When a request is forwarded, the request URL is set to the path of the forwarded page.

The following code translates a request parameter called isbn into one that the BookDetails.jsp page expects, and then forwards the request on to that page:

```
public class Dispatcher extends HttpServlet
{
    public void doGet(HttpServletRequest request,
                    HttpServletResponse response)
    {
    String bookId = (String)request.getAttribute("isbn");
    request.setAttribute("bookId", bookId);
    RequestDispatcher dispatcher = request.getRequestDispatcher(
                                    "/BookDetails.jsp");
```

```
        if (dispatcher != null) dispatcher.forward(request, response);
    }
}
```

The forward() method passes the responsibility of replying to the user to the forwarded resource. If the current servlet has already accessed a ServletOutputStream or PrintWriter object, you cannot use this method, and it will throw an IllegalStateException.

The same result can be achieved with the following JSP tag:

```
<jsp:forward page="/main.jsp" />
```

Servlets and JSP pages in a web application can collaborate with each other using any of the methods discussed above. Later in the chapter, we'll learn about the MVC framework, which relies on the Servlet-JSP collaboration.

Session Scope

In Chapter 4, we looked at the JSP <useBean> action to instantiate JavaBeans components in a JSP page, and we always set the scope attribute to the value page. In fact, when objects are declared using the <useBean> action, we can set this attribute to any one of the scopes listed below, depending on where we want the bean to be accessible from:

❑   page scope – available to the handling page only.

❑   request scope – available to the handling page and any page to which it passes control. (This will be covered in detail in the next chapter.)

❑   session scope – available to any JSP within the same session.

❑   application scope – available to any component of the same web application. We'll look at this in a few pages.

Using scopes other than page makes the bean accessible to other pages too, and instead of always creating a new bean instance, the action will first look to see if a bean with the specified name already exists in the stated scope. This allows us to share a single JavaBean between multiple pages.

You may think that this sounds rather like storing an object in, say, the session, and you'd be right – in fact, if we specify session scope for a bean, it is stored in the session object just like items that are put there using the setAttribute() method on the session object.

One other caveat: all the objects associated with a session are released once the session is destroyed, and if an attempt is made to use one, an exception will be thrown.

The following `<useBean>` action will look in the `session` object for an existing bean with the ID `ShoppingCart`. If nothing is found, it will attempt to create one. The object will then be available to all pages for the life of the current session:

```
<jsp:useBean id="ShoppingCart" scope="session"
 class="JSPExample.ShoppingCart "/>
```

Try It Out   A Simple Shopping Cart

1. Now let's start building a simple shopping cart to demonstrate use of beans and sessions in JSP pages. We'll provide the user with a list of books to purchase, and options to add books to the shopping cart and to remove them once added.

    Create a new file called `BookStore.jsp` in the `Cookies` folder. It starts off with the usual:

```
<%@ taglib prefix="c" uri="http://java.sun.com/jstl/core_rt" %>
<html>
<head><title>ABC Book Store: For your professional needs</title></head>
<body>
  <center>
```

2. We create a form that posts to itself. The form itself simply contains a dropdown list (the `<select>` element) that offers a choice of books:

```
<form type=post action="BookStore.jsp">
  <h1>ABC Book Store</h1>
  <br>
  Please select a Book and add it to your Shopping Cart
  <p/>

  <!--We now create the dropdown list -->
  <select name='product'>
    <option>Beginning Java 2 by Ivor Horton</option>
    <option>Professional Java Programming by Brett Spell</option>
    <option>Professional Jini by Sing Li</option>
    <option>Professional JSP by Sing Li et al</option>
    <option>Professional XSL by Andrew Watt et al</option>
    <option>XML Applications by Frank Boumphrey et al</option>
    <option>Beginning XML by Nikola Ozu et al</option>
    <option>Instant UML by Pierre-Alain Muller</option>
    <option>Beginning Java Objects by Jacquie Barker</option>
  </select>
  <input type=submit name="submit" value="add">
</form>

<hr/>
```

3. We'll use a JavaBean called `CartManager` to represent our shopping cart:

```
<jsp:useBean id="cart" scope="session"
             class="com.wrox.beans.CartManager"/>
<jsp:setProperty name="cart" property="*" />

<!-- We need to call a method called setRequest in the bean -->
<c:if test="${!empty param.submit}">
  <c:set target="${cart}" property="request" value="${request}" />
</c:if>

<c:if test="${empty cart.products}">
  <h2>Your shopping cart is empty!</h2>
  <h3>$$ Buy now and save 25% on shipping $$</h3>
</c:if>
```

4. If the user has already some items in their cart, we'll display them in an HTML table:

```
<c:if test="${!empty cart.products}">
<h2 align="center">Your Shopping Cart contains the following items</h2>
<p/>
<table width="75%" align="center" border="1">

  <!--iterate through all the shopping cart items and display them -->
  <c:forEach items="${cart.products}" var="product">
  <jsp:useBean id="product" type="java.lang.String"/>
    <tr>
      <td>
        <c:out value="${product}"/>
      </td>
      <td>
        <c:url var="URL" value="BookStore.jsp">
          <c:param name="product" value="${product}" />
          <c:param name="submit" value="remove" />
        </c:url>
        <li>
        <a href="${URL}">remove</a>
      </td>
    </tr>
  </c:forEach>

  </table>
  </c:if>
  </center>
</body>
</html>
```

5. Now let's get onto the JavaBean. Create a `classes\com\wrox\beans` folder in the Cookies WEB-INF directory, and save the Java code below in a new file there called CartManager.java:

```java
package com.wrox.beans;

import java.util.Vector;
import javax.servlet.http.HttpServletRequest;

public class CartManager extends Object
{

  private Vector cart = null;
  String product = null;
  String submit = null;

  public CartManager()
  {
    cart = new Vector();
  }

  public void setProduct(String product)
  {
    this.product = product;
  }

  public void setSubmit(String submit)
  {
    this.submit = submit;
  }

  public Vector getProducts()
  {
    return cart;
  }

  public void addProduct(String product)
  {
    cart.add(product);
  }

  public void removeProduct(String product)
  {
    cart.remove(product);
  }

  public void setRequest(HttpServletRequest req)
  {
    if (submit != null)
    {
      if (submit.equals("add"))
```

```
      {
        addProduct(product);
      }
      else
      {
        removeProduct(product);
      }
      reset();
    }
  }

  public void reset()
  {
    submit = null;
    product = null;
  }
}
```

6. Compile the code by opening a command prompt at the `classes` folder and entering:

> **> javac com\wrox\beans\CartManager.java**
> **‑classpath %CATALINA_HOME%\common\lib\servlet-api.jar**

If you already have `servlet-api.jar` in your `CLASSPATH`, you can miss off that switch here.

7. Restart Tomcat and browse to http://localhost:8080/Cookies/BookStore.jsp. You will see the book dropdown and an **add** button:

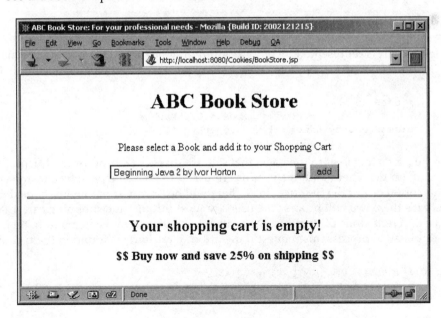

8. Add some items using the **add** button, and then remove them with the **Remove** links:

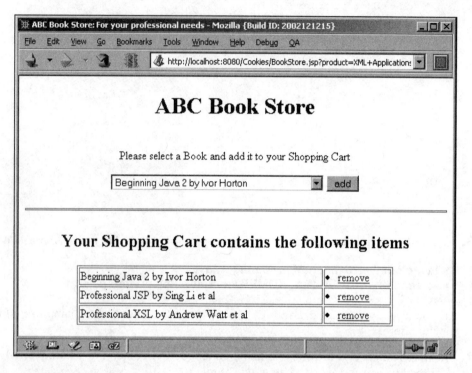

How It Works

The shopping cart is represented by our `CartManager` bean, and we instantiate this bean and store it in `session` scope so that on subsequent requests, we can link users with their carts:

```
<jsp:useBean id="cart" scope="session"
             class="com.wrox.beans.CartManager"/>
<jsp:setProperty name="cart" property="*" />
```

If this is the user's first visit to the page, that's all we display (except for the HTML footer at the very end). If, on the other hand, the user has returned to the same page by clicking either on the **add** button or on one of the **Remove** links, there will be a request parameter named `submit` present. If it's there, we will process the user's request through the shopping cart. Users can make two different kinds of requests: they can either add or remove items from their cart. We ask the cart bean to process this request if the `submit` attribute is found in the request data:

```
<c:if test="${!empty param.submit}">
  <c:set target="${cart}" property="request" value="${request}" />
</c:if>
```

The bean stores the current cart contents as a `Vector` object. We test if this vector contains any elements at all with the following JSTL tag:

```
<c:if test="${empty cart.products}">
  <h2>Your shopping cart is empty!</h2>
  <h3>$$ Buy now and save 25% on shipping $$</h3>
</c:if>
```

If it's empty, we use our marketing skills to lure the user into buying something by showing our current promotion.

If it isn't empty, we display the contents of the cart with a JSTL `<foreach>` tag, looping through displaying each item in a table. The table has two columns, the first displaying the product name and the second a hyperlink that allows the user to remove items from the cart.

The `CartManager` bean is quite straightforward. Every request to add or remove a product from the cart will have two request parameters associated with it: `product`, containing the name of the item, and `submit`, which will be either `add` if we are adding the item or `remove` if we removing it.

The bean's `setRequest()` method is called by this JSTL `<set>` tag, passing in the `HttpServletRequest` object representing the current request:

```
<c:set target="${cart}" property="request" value="${request}" />
```

Depending on the `submit` property of the JavaBean (add or remove), `setRequest()` calls either `addProduct()` or `removeProduct()`.

As mentioned, the list of items in the cart is maintained in a `Vector`. This is instantiated when the bean itself is created, and there is a `getProducts()` method that the page uses to obtain the `Vector`:

```
private Vector cart = null;

public ShoppingCart()
{
  cart = new Vector();
}

public Vector getProducts()
{
  return cart;
}
```

The `ShoppingCart` bean also defines a pair of methods for dealing with the shopping cart, `addProduct()` and `removeProduct()`:

```java
public void addProduct(String product)
{
  cart.add(product);
}

public void removeProduct(String product)
{
  cart.remove(product);
}
```

Requests from the JSP page are processed by the `processRequest()` method. Depending on whether the user wants to add or remove an item (as determined by the value of the `submit` request parameter), it calls either the `addProduct()` or `removeProduct()` method:

```java
public void setRequest(HttpServletRequest req)
{
  if (submit != null)
  {
    if (submit.equals("add"))
    {
      addProduct(product);
    }
    else
    {
      removeProduct(product);
    }
    reset();
  }
}
```

Finally, the `reset()` method tidies up the bean's `product` and `submit` properties ready for the next request:

```java
public void reset()
{
  submit = null;
  product = null;
}
```

The Application Object

Earlier we briefly mentioned that as well as storing application data in session, there are other **scopes** that we can use. We'll round off this chapter with a brief look at the implicit `application` object, which is another useful facility for sharing data between the pages in your site.

The `application` object represents a store for information that pertains to general aspects of the application's behavior. There is only one application object, and it is used by all sessions at the same time, making it useful for sharing data that is widely needed in the application. For example, an e-commerce application might store the product catalog in the `application` object, so that it is readily accessible to all the JSP pages.

Like `session`, the `application` object provides facilities to store and retrieve data in the form of attributes. However, as there is just a single `application` object per application, it never times out nor can it be invalidated, and it doesn't need a unique identifier. However, it will generally be lost when the server is restarted.

Try It Out   The Application Object

1. The `application` object is very similar to the `session` object, with the difference that its values are shared with all clients. Let's create a new page that not only tracks how many times a particular user has accessed it, but also how many times it has been accessed in total by all users.

Create a new file called `HitTracker.jsp` in your `Cookies` folder, and enter the code below:

```
<%@ taglib prefix="c" uri="http://java.sun.com/jstl/core_rt" %>

<html>
  <head><title>Application Object Example</title></head>
  <body bgcolor="white">

  <c:set var="sessionCounter" scope="session"
         value="${sessionCounter + 1}" />

  <c:set var="applicationCounter" scope="application"
         value="${applicationCounter + 1}" />

    <h1 align=center>Welcome. This is visit #${sessionCounter}</h1>
    <h2 align=center>Access Counts</h2>

    <table border=1 align="center">
      <tr bgcolor="#F9AD00">
        <th>Info Type</th><th>Value</th>
      </tr>
      <tr>
        <td>Your Accesses</td>
        <td align="center">${sessionCounter}</td>
      </tr>
      <tr>
        <td>Total Accesses</td>
        <td align="center">${applicationCounter}</td>
      </tr>
    </table>
```

```
    </body>
</html>
```

2. Then open several browser instances and point each at this page. You will see both the number of times each browser has accessed it, and the total number of accesses:

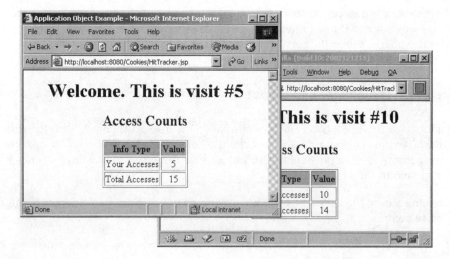

If you find that the server thinks that all of your browser windows belong to the same session, try starting a new copy of the browser for each window, rather than using the File | New menu option, or use two different vendors' browsers, as we have above.

How It Works

The code at the top of `HitTracker.jsp` should look familiar – the first half of it is the same code we used in `ShowSession.jsp`. The remaining code is similar too, except that we are using application rather than session scope. We've called our attribute `applicationCounter` and stored it in the `application` object:

```
<c:set var="sessionCounter" scope="session"
       value="${sessionCounter + 1}" />

<c:set var="applicationCounter" scope="application"
       value="${applicationCounter + 1}" />
```

In the second part of the JSP, we display the values of the `sessionCounter` and `applicationCounter` scripting variables in an HTML table, using EL:

```
<table border=1 align="center">
  <tr bgcolor="#F9AD00">
```

```
      <th>Info Type</th><th>Value</th>
    </tr>
    <tr>
      <td>Your Accesses</td>
      <td align="center">${sessionCounter}</td>
    </tr>
    <tr>
      <td>Total Accesses</td>
      <td align="center">${applicationCounter}</td>
    </tr>
  </table>
```

Summary

We started the chapter off with a look at the reasons why users need to be tracked, and quickly examined the most popular ways for doing this before working through some practical examples of user tracking.

The chapter's key concepts can be summed up as follows:

❑ Session tracking is very important for a range of modern web applications, and we need to choose a session tracking mechanism appropriate to our application.

❑ HTTP is a stateless communication protocol, so we need to use special procedures to track users and sessions.

❑ Session can be tracked using methods like URL rewriting, hidden form fields, and cookies, but these procedures can create a lot of work for application developers.

❑ The HttpSession class provides a simple interface for implementing user tracking.

❑ Objects can be stored with different levels of "scope", so allowing us to determine which JSP pages and users should be able to access them.

You'll have noticed that some of our JSP pages are beginning to get a bit hard to follow, despite our use of JavaBeans and tag libraries. We need to apply some more thought to the best ways of arranging our applications' code to make them easier to write, read, and understand. We'll look at that in the next chapter.

Why Not Try?

1. Rewrite the shopping cart example using servlets. With this workout you will learn the internal workings of the tags used.

2. Rewrite the ShoppingCart.jsp example to use a bean stored in application scope. This bean represents a book catalog, and creates book listings for display on the Shopping Cart page, and would be available for all users.

CHAPTER 12

Securing Web Applications

Developing a web application can quickly diverge from being a fun experience and become a task laden with responsibility and accountability. As developers, then, a crucial factor to consider is how to ensure our applications are secure from malicious or inadvertent misuse.

This moves the focus of this chapter away from general JSP issues and onto the security features of our server software, Tomcat. Nevertheless, we will still make use of all the knowledge gathered so far from previous chapters.

We'll roughly follow this sequence of topics:

❑   Security issues in overview

❑   An investigation of permissions and authentication

❑   Some basic security processes

❑   Some possible security threats

❑   How to secure web applications using Tomcat

❑   A basic HTTP authentication mechanism using JSP and Tomcat

❑   A form based authentication mechanism using JSP and Tomcat

❑   How to build our own simple JSP security tag library

Once this has been done, you should then be able to deploy web applications confident that they meet basic security requirements. Let's get started, shall we?

Security Overview

Web applications provide a way to quickly take, process, and output information in a very elegant and dynamic fashion. Web applications typically conform to the three tier architecture model, working over a disconnected protocol (HTTP) maintaining state and information on the server. Because of this remote and disconnected nature, web applications can be vulnerable to hackers with a little knowledge of the workings of web servers.

Permission and Authentication

Before we get to any practical web security work, we need to cover the building blocks for secure applications. In a very simplistic way, we can divide security into two collaborative layers: authentication and permissions. You can guess what these are, but the distinctions between them can become confused. By definition:

❑ Authentication is the process of verifying whether the user is who they are claiming to be.

❑ Permission is the policy applied to those who are authenticated or not authenticated.

These two are applied in sequence, as we must first **authenticate** before we can determine the **permission** to be applied:

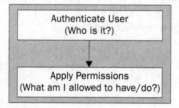

In a way, we all use this "authenticate and permit" security model every day. For example, place yourself in the calm of your own home, reading your favorite web security book, when you hear someone knocking on the front door. Prior to unlocking and opening the door, you may ask, "Who is it?" to determine who is knocking on the door. When they tell you, you apply a certain verification process where you either recognize their voice or come charging out with a baseball bat. This is your own process of authentication! You are basically verifying that the person trying to get in your house is someone you recognize.

Now, suppose a person knocks on the door claiming to be the mailman, and they request to come into your kitchen and make themselves a snack. The authentication itself may succeed, but you might not be too keen on the mailman entering your house and snaffling your Budweiser, so the request will be denied. This is you applying your **permission policy**; anyone attempting to access your resources, such as your precious fridge, must first authenticate themselves, and then they must have been granted prior permission to that resource. For instance, you may have a permission policy for the mailman stating that they:

- ❑ Can drop mail into the mailbox

- ❑ Cannot drop other items into the mailbox, such as fast food wrappings or junk mail

- ❑ Cannot come into the house

- ❑ Cannot try to sell you anything

- ❑ Cannot set up a tent on your front door from which to ply goods to passers-by

- ❑ Can take your dog for a walk (hey, we're not completely mean)

Permissions and authentication can be also very helpful in a process driven model. For example, if your child wanted to have ice cream before dinner, you might say, "You can have ice-cream, but you must finish your dinner first." This type of security requires the authenticated entity – in this case, your beloved offspring – to finish a certain process in order to proceed to another one.

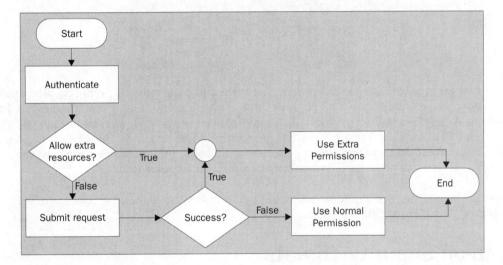

This process can be readily applied to our web security scenario as shown in the flowchart below. The first thing is to authenticate the user. For the mailman to be able knock on your door, they need access to your front door, right? Using the same principle, we must ensure that users can be authenticated on your site by having access to a public login page:

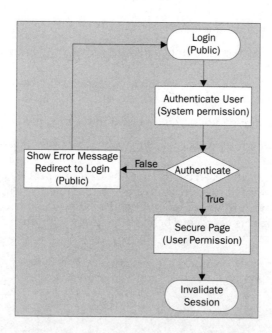

Note that we invalidate the session when it's finished to ensure that it cannot be used again. The above process may seem a bit obvious but it is worth mentioning for many reasons. For example, I can check my account details for my Internet provider at anytime as long as when I am online I am connected using their dialup account. When accessing their public login page, they snoop my IP address to confirm I am connected using their network. This way, they ensure that users accessing account information are at least subscribers.

Later in this chapter, we will look into how Tomcat aids system administrators and developers to protect and authenticate web resources.

Common Security Threats

Without taking into account major design considerations, this section quickly describes some potential security threats when deploying an application. It does not really matter what framework an application is powered by, but here we focus on Tomcat as it's what we've been using throughout the book.

Untrusted User Input

When a user accesses a web application or even a public site, there is an exchange of information between both parties across the HTTP layer, which is also known as the **application layer**. This layer manages and handles communication between client and server. It accepts input from a client, processes it and produces the appropriate response as output. This is the basic pattern, but it is potentially vulnerable to malicious users who 'bake' their own input with the intention of getting output that was not intended by design.

Believe it or not, many companies still fail to take security seriously. For example, consider this real-life scenario that I recently experienced when asked to redesign a JSP-based application in use by an educational institution. The application ran on Linux and used MySQL to present students with an online results checking facility. A student could simply log in to retrieve their entire academic transcript, as well as to update certain personal details.

The existing application that the institution had been using required the student to log in by entering their name and date of birth in an HTML form that was then submitted to the server using HTTP GET. The output returned the student's full transcript as well as a URL containing a querystring such as this one:

getuserequest.jsp?studentid=12345&birthdate=121272&type=transcript

There are two weaknesses to note with this authentication method: firstly, it merely checks to see if the user knows a student number and a matching birth date. Secondly, it uses the GET method instead of POST, so the full query string appears in the address box of the browser. The upshot was that students quickly worked out how to access each other's transcripts by modifying the querystring.

So that's not too harmful, you may think, as indeed did the institution's IT department. However, it does really not matter what actions a malicious user is performing; what really matters is that you have an application that users are misusing by not using the intended interfaces designed for them.

To continue with the story, some students figured out that there was a special 'student' called admin with a 'birth date' of 00000000. It resulted in posting data to the following JSP page:

```
<%@ page import="java.sql.*" %>

<%
   Statement stmt = connection.getStatement();
   String queryStatement = "SELECT * FROM " +
                          request.getParameter("type");
   ResultSet result = Statement.executeQuery(queryStatement);
%>
```

After a while, some students, apparently having nothing better to do, worked out which tables they should be passing as the type parameter to this page in order to retrieve login information for lecturers and administrators. Consequently, many went in and changed their results and some even 'paid' their tuition fees. It was very hard work going back to database backups and comparing records in order to restore those that had been tampered with.

There are many other types of untrusted user input that should be looked at, but for now, I just want you to consider the design of your application, which should ensure users will only be able to use your interfaces and not cut any corners.

URL-Probing Attacks

Probing attacks are very common mostly because they rely on security holes (bugs) on web servers. Tomcat is no exception since it is an open source project, meaning that hackers can simply download its source code and hunt out weak points. Hackers use programs called **sniffers** to sweep the Internet for servers running versions of web servers with known weaknesses.

Some attacks can also be achieved by simply manipulating HTML itself. Such attacks are known as the GET and POST attacks. It is mostly used with the GET method as the user doesn't need to be really aware that an HTML form is being submitted.

Now, consider a malicious user that has key knowledge of the workings of a certain application and its structure (design). This user could then create a web application using a similar design which could post a form to the other application to retrieve sensitive information:

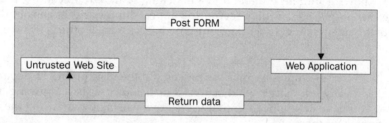

A very quick and easy way to overcome this problem is to check for any unique session attributes within the application. In the case of a JSP application, our code might look similar to this:

```
<%
  if(session.get("CurrentUser") != null)
    //Valid session
  else
    //Kick user out of here!!

%>


<% request.getParameter("GETBANKBALANCE"); %>

<%
  // Perform work, and return sensitive data.
%>
```

As much as this solution can be worked around, it is better to have any fail-safe mechanism rather than none.

Another very irritating URL-probing attack is when you design and implement an application with a login page for authentication and a user finds a way to start from the middle of the process by bypassing some steps. This is often done when malicious users are aware of your JSP code.

Tomcat 5.0 has overcome some of the weaknesses of earlier versions that allowed people to get hold of a JSP page's source code over the Internet. When using the default servlet `org.apache.catalina.servlets.DefaultServlet`, this vulnerability meant that a page you've just deployed, say http://my.site/login.jsp, could be viewed in its original form just by requesting the following URL:

http://my.site/servlet/org.apache.catalina.servlets.DefaultServlet/login.jsp

An older version of Tomcat also had the vulnerability of allowing users to view the original JSP code simply by adding %2570 to the end of the URL. This code was interpreted by Tomcat in two parts, %25 (the URL encoding for %) and 70 (hexadecimal for 'p'). This way a JSP file would be referred to by the server as `myApplication.js%p`:

http://mypage/myapplication.js%2570

This would result in Tomcat's not being able to find the exact filename, and instead returning the JSP page as source code. This is a particularly nasty vulnerability, since JSP source code not only shows paths to databases, what JavaBeans you are using, and the paths to key XML files, but also exposes your intellectual property.

While these tricks are no longer possible with Tomcat 5, the lesson to be drawn is that it's important to keep an eye out for web server updates. As an open source product, bugs are found and reported as and when they occur, and updates are often developed fairly quickly. It's good to know that there are developers around the world working 24 hours a day spotting and fixing bugs, but if you don't regularly check for updates, this process could work against you.

Preventing Misuse of JavaBean Properties

As we already know, JSP supports the JavaBeans specification, which allows for the creation of readily reusable components. The beans encapsulate logic within classes including those members that are hidden by design, providing a level of security by the encapsulation itself.

Looking at the initialization of each object, we know that it merely needs to define the pairs in the query string that depict the desired property that needs to be used.

```
<jsp:useBean id="guessGame" class="com.wrox.secure.GuessClass">
  <jsp:setProperty name="GuessClass" property="*" />
</jsp:useBean>
```

The above `setProperty()` tag uses an asterisk (*) for the `property` attribute to ensure all properties are included (exposed) to the JSP page. This can be very unsafe if the bean is not properly designed with appropriate accessors.

To illustrate this, let's say that this bean represents a guessing game where the user guesses a number between 1 and 100 and the bean processes the guessed number, returning `true` as a Boolean property called `_boolWinner` if the right number was guessed. The user could then use the following code to cheat:

```
http://company/guessnumber.jsp?number=23&_boolWinner=true
```

Entering the code would result in the user becoming world champion at guessing numbers, even if the number guessed was not the right one. This just emphasizes the importance of design when creating your components.

Protecting Applications

In this section, we are going to explore some important settings and functionalities that are available in Tomcat. Even though some of the material presented is not directly JSP specific, it is crucial for any web developer to be aware of these functionalities as they will come and go in your web application requirements.

Tomcat Security

Prior to Tomcat and JSP, Common Gateway Interface (CGI) was very popular (and still is) among UNIX-based servers but the major problem it had was the lack of persistence. Every single POST or GET to the server resulted in an instantiation of a server-side program to process that request, which was destroyed once the request had been serviced. While this makes the CGI model quite independent of the language used for this server-side program, it is also CGI's Achilles' heel.

Firstly, this makes it hard for one request to know anything about any previous request, and consequently it's very hard to keep track of users accessing your web application. This is a major security loophole, as a single client could connect to a web server and execute several pieces of code without being spotted.

Servlets can be an excellent solution for securing web applications, primarily because of their native Java support. This provided user processes inside one recognizable thread entirely managed by a Java Virtual Machine, which was made available by the Java Security Manager.

Security Manager

As many web servers today, Tomcat runs web applications in what we call a **sand-box**. That is, code is tightly controlled, preventing unauthorized behavior such as:

❑ Executing programs

❑ Writing files to disk

❑ Deleting system files

Tomcat uses the Java Security Manager to achieve this. Customizing permission in Tomcat is out of the scope of this book but if you feel like sharpening your knowledge, consult the Tomcat documentation at `%CATALINA_HOME%/webapps/tomcat-docs/security-manager-howto.html`. For information on the Java security manager, go to http://java.sun.com/security.

Without going into details of permissions, we'll not look at a classic example as shown in Tomcat's security documentation. It demonstrates a JSP page that shuts down Tomcat.

Try It Out   Classic Shutdown JSP

1. Save the following line as a file called `shutdown.jsp` in the `%CATALINA_HOME%\webapps\ROOT` folder:

```
<% System.exit(1); %>
```

2. Ensure Tomcat is running and navigate to http://localhost:8080/shutdown.jsp

3. Tomcat should now be shut down completely, and you should receive an error indicating connection to localhost:8080 was refused.

How It Works

This is a very simple page. `System.exit(1)` shuts down the system that runs the code, which in this case is Tomcat.

Customizing Security

In order to customize security, we must have an understanding of **principals** and **roles**. A principal basically identifies an entity that can interact or perform work with a system. It can be a person, company, process – just about anything in fact.

A role groups certain actions together, and we can then specify certain principals as having particular roles, thus giving those principals clearance to perform the actions.

This is similar to an older concept of **users** and **groups**, where users are generally people that may access the system, and groups represent the position that users can hold. For example, a company system may have a user called John Smith, who belongs to the group, Production Manager.

Over the next sections, we will explore how to customize Tomcat's native security using this concept of principals and roles.

The Security Realm Mechanism

The authentication process determines which permissions are granted for entities. Tomcat has three **realms** for storing access information for these entities:

❑ Memory Realm – loads the `tomcat-users.xml` file from Tomcat's `conf` directory into memory, and uses the details given there.

❑ JDBCRealm – stores entity information in a relational database accessed via the JDBC driver.

❑ JNDIRealm – entity information is stored in a Directory service or Lightweight Directory Access Protocol (LDAP) compliant directory server.

We'll just look at Memory Realm here, although there are security risks in storing information in a file on the server's file system, which are reduced by using the more sophisticated JDBCRealm and JNDIRealm. The intricacies of these two realms are beyond the scope of this book however, but if you feel confident, the Tomcat documentation provides more information on these.

Memory Realm

Memory Realm is the least secure method, storing names, roles, *and* passwords in an XML file called `tomcat-users.xml` in Tomcat's `conf` directory. As XML, the file can be readily modified to add more users or roles in any text editor, making this system potentially vulnerable.

The XML file is loaded into memory when an application starts up so you'll have to restart Tomcat if you change it. A typical `tomcat-users.xml` file looks like this:

```
<?xml version='1.0' encoding='utf-8'?>
<tomcat-users>
  <role rolename="tomcat"/>
  <role rolename="role1"/>
  <role rolename="manager"/>
  <role rolename="admin"/>
  <user username="tomcat" password="tomcat" roles="tomcat"/>
  <user username="both" password="tomcat" roles="tomcat,role1"/>
  <user username="role1" password="tomcat" roles="role1"/>
  <user username="admin" password="" roles="admin,manager"/>
</tomcat-users>
```

The single XML root element, `<tomcat-users>`, has child `<role>` elements to define roles and `<user>` elements to describe users (or principals). Note how the `roles` attribute on the `<user>` element can contain multiple `rolename`s by separating them with a comma.

User Authentication

We activate Memory Realm authentication for particular resources using the `<security-constraint>` element in an application's `web.xml` deployment descriptor, in its `WEB-INF` directory. This element is a child of `<web-app>`, and restricts access to one or more resources to the roles defined in `<role-name>` elements. It can appear several times within a `web.xml` file in order to define security constraints for different resources.

```
<security-constraint>
  <web-resource-collection>
    <web-resource-name>
      Name of Resource
    </web-resource-name>
    <description> Optional Description </description>
    <url-pattern>
      /my-protected-page.jsp
    </url-pattern>
    <http-method>
      GET
    </http-method>
    <http-method>
      POST
    </http-method>
  </web-resource-collection>
  <auth-constraint>
    <description> Optional Description </description>
    <role-name>
      manager
    </role-name>
  </auth-constraint>
</security-constraint>
```

The `<web-resource-collection>` element contains three child elements to describe the resource to be protected:

- ❏   `<web-resource-name>` denotes the name of a resource. This is a mandatory element.

- ❏   `<url-pattern>` gives the URL (resource) that will be protected. This can contain from zero to many values.

- ❏   `<http-method>` indicates the methods that will be subject to this security constraint, that is, GET or POST. If omitted, it will apply the constraint to all HTTP methods.

The second element, `<auth-constraint>`, gives the roles that may access the resource. Note that if this element doesn't specify any values, it will apply to all available roles.

The last element is `<login-config>`. This must be present for users to have to authenticate themselves when attempting to access the resource The method of authentication is specified by the child `<auth-method>` element:

```
<login-config>
  <auth-method>
    <!-- BASIC, DIGEST, FORM -->
  </auth-method>
</login-config>
```

Authentication methods include the following:

❑ **Basic** authentication – a method, supported by HTTP 1.1, for requiring a username and password to be supplied for protected resources. If the authentication fails, the server returns HTTP status code 401 (Unauthorized). Basic HTTP authentication transmits usernames and passwords as plain text making it very insecure.

❑ **Digest** authentication – password data is encrypted for transmission using a hashing algorithm. This method is not as secure as others, such as Kerberos or Certificates, but it is a step up from Basic authentication.

❑ **Form** authentication – the login process is performed by a custom web page, allowing us to customize its appearance and the nature of error messages. More importantly, it allows us to apply more secure authentication methods. In order to be secure, form authentication should be used in conjunction with **digital certificates**, but unfortunately these are out of the scope of this book.

There is also `CLIENT-CERT`, but we won't worry about it here. Now let's look at some practical exercises.

Try It Out   Basic HTTP Authentication

1. Create a new folder called `Security` in your `webapps` folder containing an empty `WEB-INF` subfolder.

2. Now, save the following file as `protected.jsp` in the `Security` folder:

```
<%
  out.println("<BR><Center><font size='6' color='Blue'>Authenticated"
          + " User:  </ font> " + request.getUserPrincipal());
  out.println("<BR><font size='6' color='Blue'>Authentication Type:"
          + "</font> " + request.getAuthType() + "</Center>");
%>
```

3. Restart Tomcat, and navigate to:

   http://localhost:8080/Security/protected.jsp

   If everything is OK, you should see the following:

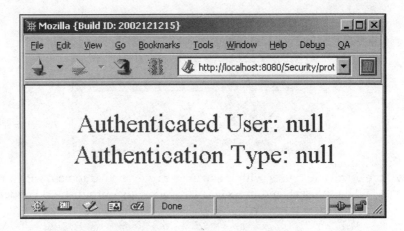

4. We're currently accessing the page without any authentication, so now we'll create a web.xml file in the WEB-INF folder to enforce Basic authentication:

```xml
<?xml version="1.0" encoding="ISO-8859-1"?>
<!DOCTYPE web-app
  PUBLIC "-//Sun Microsystems, Inc.//DTD Web Application 2.2//EN"
  "http://java.sun.com/j2ee/dtds/web-app_2_2.dtd">
<web-app>
  <security-constraint>
    <web-resource-collection>
      <web-resource-name>
        Protected Page
      </web-resource-name>
      <url-pattern>
        /protected.jsp
      </url-pattern>
    </web-resource-collection>
    <auth-constraint>
      <role-name>
        tomcat
      </role-name>
    </auth-constraint>
  </security-constraint>

  <login-config>
  <!--BASIC, DIGEST, FORM-->
    <auth-method>
      BASIC
    </auth-method>
  </login-config>
</web-app>
```

5. When you now navigate to protected.jsp (there's no need to restart Tomcat), you should now see a login dialog like this:

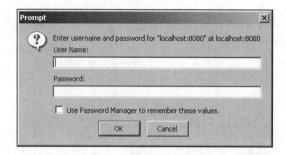

6. Enter the details for a user with the manager role, such as tomcat with a password of tomcat (a default user), and press OK. The following output should appear:

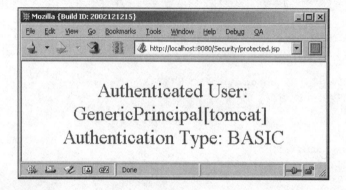

7. If you don't supply correct details or press Cancel at the login prompt, you get the following message:

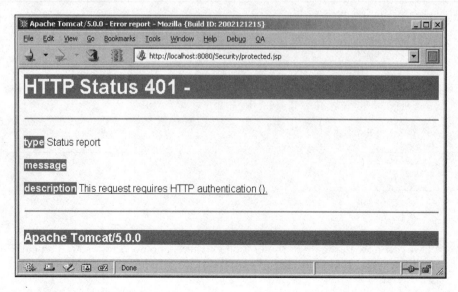

How It Works

When a user requests the `protected.jsp` page, Tomcat calls the `authenticate()` method to ask for a valid username and password. If the details given match an entry in `tomcat-users.xml`, the user is authenticated and granted access to the requested resource.

Form Based Authentication

When using Basic HTTP authentication the login dialog is generated by the web browser. We can specify our own login page in the application's `web.xml` if we wish to use form based authentication.

Try It Out — Form Based Authentication

1. Firstly, open `web.xml` in `WEB-INF`, and change it as highlighted below:

```
        .
        .
        .

<login-config>
  <!--BASIC, DIGEST, FORM -->
      <auth-method>
          FORM
      </auth-method>
      <!-- This element sets up FORM authentication -->
      <form-login-config>
          <form-login-page>
              /login.jsp
          </form-login-page>
          <form-error-page>
              /error.jsp
          </form-error-page>
      </form-login-config>
   </login-config>
 </web-app>
```

2. Then create a new file called `login.jsp` as given below, and save it in your `Security` folder:

```
<html>
  <head>
    <title>Login Page</title>
  </head>
  <body>
    <center>
      <font size='7' color='Blue'>Please Login</font><hr>
```

```
      </center>
      <form action='j_security_check' method=post>
        <table>
          <tr><td><center>Name:</center></td>
          <td><input type='text' name='j_username'/></td></tr>
          <tr><td>Password:</td>
          <td><input type='password' name='j_password' size='8'/></td>
          </tr>
        </table>
        <br>
        <input type='submit' value='login'/></Center>
      </form>
  </body>
</html>
```

3. To see the new login, restart Tomcat and navigate to the `protected.jsp` page again. You should now be directed to the following page:

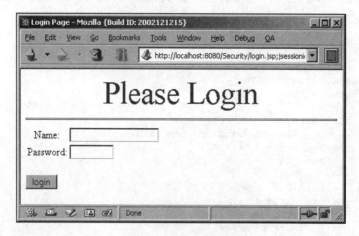

Enter details of a valid user as before, and you should be allowed access to the protected page:

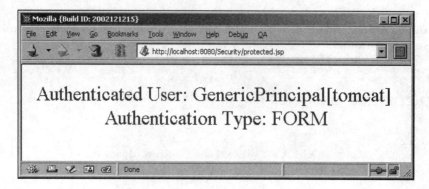

4. Next, we'll create the error page that appears when incorrect details are entered. We named this file `error.jsp` in `web.xml`, so create it now in the `Security` folder and enter the following code:

```html
<html>
  <head>
    <title>Login Error</title>
  </head>
  <body>
    <center>
      <font size='5' color='red'>
        Login Error. Click<a href="login.jsp"> here</a> to try again.
      </font>
    </center>
  </body>
</html>
```

5. Navigate to the protected page again (you may need to restart your browser), and enter an invalid username and password. You should be redirected to the following page:

How It Works

As far as configuring Tomcat is concerned, there are only two modifications to be done from the previous example: modifying the `<auth-method>` element in `web.xml` from BASIC to FORM, and adding the new element, `<form-login-config>`, indicating the URL for the custom login and error page:

```xml
<form-login-config>
    <form-login-page>
        /login.jsp
    </form-login-page>
    <form-error-page>
        /error.jsp
    </form-error-page>
</form-login-config>
```

455

Furthermore when creating the `login.jsp` we must define a form and indicate the method as POST and action to `j_security_check` for the web server authentication.

```
<form action='j_security_check' method=post>
```

The form should contain at least two elements, called `j_username` and `j_password`, for getting the username and password for submission to the web server:

```
<td><input type='text' name='j_username'></td></tr>
    .
    .
    .
<td><input type='password' name='j_password' size='8'></td>
```

We keep the same settings for the `<security-constraint>` element, as they have same function in this method of authentication.

Custom Authentication Tags

So far, the examples given are peculiar to Tomcat but we can create an authentication mechanism from scratch if we want it to be portable rather than web server specific.

Here, we will build an authentication mechanism based on custom tags as introduced in Chapter 9. This hides the complexity in tag handlers rather than inside JSP pages, keeping logic and presentation separate.

Here is the basic idea:

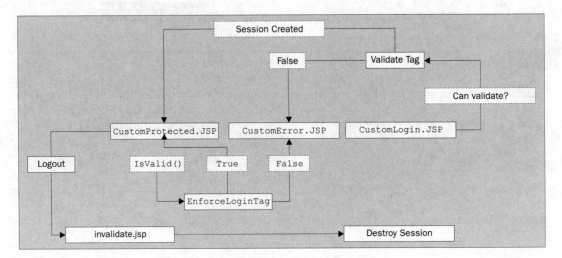

We are going to create tags to implement this authentication mechanism. The principal idea is to authenticate users against a database and create a session once the user is authenticated.

We'll get started with the presentation layer. The `CustomLogin.jsp` page takes the username and password. It is similar to the `login.jsp` form, but instead of sending the username and password to `j_security`, we post it to our own page, `Validate.jsp`.

Custom Authentication Tags

1. Save the following code under the name `CustomLogin.jsp` in the `Security` folder:

```html
<html>
  <head>
    <title>Custom Login Page</title>
  </head>
  <body>
    <center><font size='7' color='Blue'>
      Custom Authentication
    </font><hr>
    <center><font size='7' color='Red'>Please Login</font><hr>
    <form method="POST"
          action="<%= response.encodeURL("Validate.jsp")%>"
          name="loginForm">
      <table>
        <tr><td><Center>Name:</Center></td>
        <td><input type="text" name="username"></td></tr>
        <tr><td>Password:</td>
        <td><input type="password" name="pwd" size='8'></td></tr>
      </table>
      <br>
      <center><input type="submit" value="login"></center>
    </form>
  </body>
</html>
```

2. Our form POSTs the username and password to a custom authentication page called `Validate.jsp`, so we'll write this next. Create it in the `Security` folder with the following code:

```jsp
<%@ taglib prefix="val" uri="WEB-INF/securityTag.tld" %>
<% String username = request.getParameter("username"); %>
<% String pwd = request.getParameter("pwd"); %>

<val:validate username="<%= username %>"
              password="<%= pwd %>"
              securePage="CustomProtected.jsp"/>
```

3. We also need a custom error page. Create a file called `CustomError.jsp` containing the code below in the `Security` folder:

```html
<html>
  <head>
    <title>Login Error</title>
  </head>
  <body>
    <center><font size='5' color='Red'><a href="CustomLogin.jsp">
      Error, click here to retry!! </a>
    </font></center>
  </body>
</html>
```

4. Now create another file called `CustomProtected.jsp`. We'll protect this page using our `forceLogin` custom tag. Save it in the same location as the other JSP pages:

```jsp
<%@ taglib prefix="sec" uri="WEB-INF/securityTag.tld" %>

<sec:forceLogin errorPage='/CustomError.jsp'/>
<%
    out.println("<br><center><font size='5' color='Red'>Authenticated"
           + " User:  </font>" + session.getAttribute("user"));
%>
<center><font size='5' color='Red'><a href="invalidate.jsp">
  Click here to Logout!!!
</a></font></center>
```

5. For users to log out, create a JSP page called `invalidate.jsp` in the same location. It consists of just one line:

```jsp
<% session.invalidate() %>
```

6. Now, let's get started with the Java code for our tags. We'll store all such code in a folder called `classes/com/wrox/secure` inside our application's `WEB-INF` directory. You should create this directory structure now.

7. In the new folder, we'll start with a class that encapsulates a user. Create the following in a file called `User.java` in the `secure` folder:

```java
package com.wrox.secure;

class User
{

  private String name;
  private String password;
```

```
public User(String name, String password)
{

  this.name = name;
  this.password = password;

}

public String getUserName()
{

  return this.name;

}

public String getPassword()
{

  return this.password;

}

}
```

8. Let's now create a class that stands in for the database of users. Save the following code in a file called `UserList.java` inside the `secure` directory:

```
package com.wrox.secure;

import java.util.*;

class UserList
{
  private Vector list = new Vector();

  public UserList()
  {
    list.add(new User("Erick","tomcat"));
    list.add(new User("SevenOfNine","regayov"));
    list.add(new User("Kirk","esirpretne"));
  }

  public boolean isValidUser(User user)
  {

    for(int iCount = 0; iCount < list.size(); iCount++)
    {
      User temp = (User)list.get(iCount);
      if(user.getUserName() == temp.getUserName()
        && user.getPassword() == temp.getPassword())
        return true;
```

```
        else
          return false;
      }
    return true;
  }

}
```

9. The next class makes sure users log in. Save this code in the `secure` directory under the name `ForceLoginTag.java`:

```
package com.wrox.secure;

import javax.servlet.http.HttpServletRequest;
import javax.servlet.http.HttpSession;
import javax.servlet.jsp.JspException;
import javax.servlet.jsp.PageContext;
import javax.servlet.jsp.tagext.TagSupport;

public class ForceLoginTag extends TagSupport
{
  private String errorPage;

  public void setErrorPage(String errorPage)
  {
    this.errorPage = errorPage;
  }

  public int doEndTag() throws JspException
  {
    HttpSession session = pageContext.getSession();

    if(session.getAttribute("user") == null)
    {

      try
      {
        pageContext.forward(errorPage);
        return SKIP_PAGE;
      }
      catch(Exception ex)
      {
        throw new JspException(ex.getMessage());
      }
    }
    return EVAL_PAGE;
  }
  public void release()
  {
    errorPage = null;
  }
}
```

10. Lastly, we'll create a class to act as a tag for authenticating users. It will be called
ValidateTag.java and should be placed in the same folder:

```java
package com.wrox.secure;

import java.io.*;

import javax.servlet.http.HttpServletRequest;
import javax.servlet.http.HttpSession;
import javax.servlet.jsp.JspException;
import javax.servlet.jsp.PageContext;
import javax.servlet.jsp.tagext.TagSupport;

public class ValidateTag extends TagSupport
{
  private String errorPage;
  private String securePage;
  private String password;
  private String username;

  private UserList database = new UserList();

  public void setSecurePage(String page)
  {
    this.securePage = page;
  }

  public void setErrorPage(String page)
  {
    this.errorPage = page;
  }

  public void setPassword(String password)
  {
    this.password = password;
  }

  public void setUsername(String username)
  {
    this.username = username;
  }

  public int doEndTag() throws JspException
  {
    HttpSession thisSession = pageContext.getSession();
    User user = new User(this.username, this.password);

    if(database.isValidUser(user))
    {
      thisSession.setAttribute("user", this.username);
```

```
        try
        {
          pageContext.forward(this.securePage);

          return this.SKIP_BODY;
        }
        catch(Exception ex)
        {
          throw new JspException(ex.getMessage());
        }
      }
      else
      {
        try
        {
          pageContext.forward(this.errorPage);
        }
        catch(Exception ex)
        {
          throw new JspException(ex.getMessage());
        }

      }
      return EVAL_PAGE;
    }

  public void release()
  {
    this.securePage = null;
    this.username = null;
    this.password = null;
    this.errorPage = null;
  }
}
```

11. Rather than specify the classpath using the `-classpath` switch on the `javac` compiler, we'll set up a `classpath` environment variable. Right-click on the **My Computer** icon on your desktop, and choose **Properties**. Click the **Advanced** tab, and then the **Environment Variables** button. Create a new system variable called **classpath**, with the value %CATALINA_HOME%\common\lib\jsp-api.jar;%CATALINA_HOME%\ common\lib\jsp-api.jar. Make sure this value contains no spaces.

12. From the command prompt, change to the `Security/WEB-INF/classes` directory. Compile all our Java classes at once with the following command:

> **> javac com\wrox\secure*.java**

13. Now we need a tag library descriptor file in `WEB-INF` called `securityTag.tld` to describe our tags. It should contain the XML shown below:

```xml
<?xml version="1.0" encoding="ISO-8859-1"?>
<!DOCTYPE taglib PUBLIC
 "-//Sun Microsystems, Inc.//DTD JSP Tag Library 1.2//EN"
 "http://java.sun.com/dtd/web-jsptaglibrary_1_2.dtd">

<taglib>
  <tlib-version>1.2</tlib-version>
  <jsp-version>2.0</jsp-version>
  <short-name>ExampleTags</short-name>
  <description>A set of example tag handlers.</description>
  <tag>
    <name>forceLogin</name>
    <tag-class>com.wrox.secure.ForceLoginTag</tag-class>
    <attribute>
      <name>errorPage</name>
    </attribute>
  </tag>
  <tag>
    <name>validate</name>
    <tag-class>com.wrox.secure.ValidateTag</tag-class>
    <attribute>
      <name>username</name>
      <rtexprvalue>true</rtexprvalue>
    </attribute>
    <attribute>
      <name>password</name>
      <rtexprvalue>true</rtexprvalue>
    </attribute>
    <attribute>
      <name>securePage</name>
    </attribute>
    <attribute>
      <name>errorPage</name>
    </attribute>
  </tag>
</taglib>
```

14. Restart Tomcat. First try to access the `CustomProtected.jsp` page direct. You should be denied access with the following message:

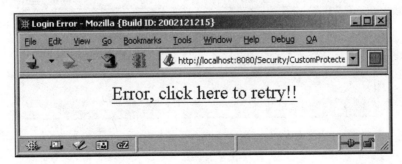

15. Now go to http://localhost:8080/Security/CustomLogin.jsp, or click the link on the above page, and you'll see this:

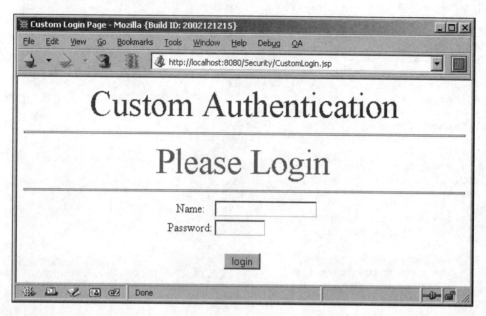

16. Enter any of the following username and password combinations, and click login:

- ❏   Erick, tomcat
- ❏   SevenOfNine, regayov
- ❏   Kirk, esirpretne

You should login successfully and see this page:

How It Works

When the user presses the login button, the username and password entered on the form are passed to `Validate.jsp`:

```
<form method="POST" action="<%= response.encodeURL("Validate.jsp")%>"
 name="loginForm">
```

`Validate.jsp` gets the username and password and stores them as strings:

```
<% String username = request.getParameter("username"); %>
<% String pwd = request.getParameter("pwd"); %>
```

We then use the security tag to check that the username and password match:

```
<%@ taglib prefix="val" uri="WEB-INF/securityTag.tld" %>
<val:validate username="<%= username %>"
              password="<%= pwd %>"
              securePage="CustomProtected.jsp"
              errorPage="CustomError.jsp"/>
```

Note the `securePage` and `errorPage` properties that take the path for the protected resource and the error page URL if authentication fails. We pass the secured page here merely so we can forward the user to that page if authentication succeeds.

Our tag uses the class defined by the `User.java` file. This class is a very straightforward class that is instantiated with a username and password:

```
public User(String name, String password)
{
  this.name = name;
  this.password = password;
}
```

For simplicity, we're using a Java class in place of an actual database. This class, `UserList.java`, creates three users in its constructor:

```
public UserList()
{
  list.add(new User("Erick","tomcat"));
  list.add(new User("SevenOfNine","regayov"));
  list.add(new User("Kirk","esirpretneSSU"));
}
```

It would not be hard to modify this class to access a database or a file in order to get hold of the user details. The `UserList` class also has a public method to perform the actual authentication process. It takes a `User` object and compares it with the `Users` object in memory to see if that username and password match:

```
public boolean isValidUser(User user)
{

  for(int iCount = 0; iCount < list.size(); iCount++)
  {
    User temp = (User)list.get(iCount);
    if(user.getUserName() == temp.getUserName()
       && user.getPassword() == temp.getPassword())
      return true;
    else
      return false;
  }
  return true;
}
```

The `validate` custom tag is defined by `ValidateTag.java`. This class instantiates a `UserList` object:

```
private UserList database = new UserList();
```

It also defines the `doEndTag()` method, which stores the current session in a new `HttpSession` object and a new `User` object is instantiated using the username and password passed by the user:

```
HttpSession thisSession = pageContext.getSession();
User user = new User(this.username, this.password);
```

So if the user is authenticated, we store their username as an attribute of the session object, otherwise they are forwarded to the error page:

```
if(database.isValidUser(user))
{
  thisSession.setAttribute("user", this.username);

  try
  {
    pageContext.forward(this.securePage);

    return this.SKIP_BODY;
  }
  catch(Exception ex)
  {
    throw new JspException(ex.getMessage());
  }
```

```
        }
        else
        {
          try
          {
            pageContext.forward(this.errorPage);
          }
          catch(Exception ex)
          {
            throw new JspException(ex.getMessage());
          }

        }
```

To stop a user directly accessing `CustomProtected.jsp`, we use a tag that specifies the error page to forward to if there is no valid `user` attribute set in session:

```
<sec:forceLogin errorPage='/CustomError.jsp'/>
```

This tag is defined by the `EnforceLoginTag.java` file, which creates a `HttpSession` object from the current session and checks to see if there is an existing `user` session attribute. If so, it loads the rest of `CustomProtected.jsp`, otherwise it forwards to the specified error page:

```
public int doEndTag() throws JspException
{
  HttpSession session = pageContext.getSession();

  if(session.getAttribute("user") == null)
  {

    try
    {
      pageContext.forward(errorPage);
      return SKIP_PAGE;
    }
```

Bear in mind that this is not a bulletproof authentication method. Some of its limitations include its heavy reliance on session objects, not persisting data in a true database and more. Hopefully though I've demonstrated the goals and principles of implementing authentication for JSP applications.

Summary

Securing web applications is a complicated and detailed subject, and in this chapter, we've tried to cover the basics, such as authentication and permissions. We also looked at the processing-based security model and security flow, touching on important considerations when designing secure applications.

We have also touched on some possible security threats, thinking about how to avoid some of them when designing an application.

We looked at Tomcat's Realm mechanisms, covering how to:

❏   secure a web application

❏   apply basic HTTP authentication using JSP

❏   apply form-based authentication using JSP

Finally, we created a custom authentication mechanism, which avoids the dependence on the web server in use that other approaches can suffer from.

Why Not Try?

❏   The obvious enhancement to our last example would be to replace the ListUser.java class with true database connectivity (see Chapter 13). You'd need to create and connect to a MySQL database that has a users table that lists usernames and the corresponding passwords.

❏   Enhance the information held on users in the database to include fields such as Address, Phone number, E-mail address, Department, Position and so on.

❏   As with Realm, try incorporating support for roles into the authentication process. The idea would be to limit access to certain JSP pages to specific groups.

❏   Once roles have been defined for users, create a custom tag that constructs a multi-view JSP page, which presents different output depending on the specific role the current user holds.

❏   Apart from custom authentication, you should also look into your JDBCRealm to link your application with your MySQL, this way authenticating users against larger data stores.

You may also wish to investigate JDBCRealm and JNDIRealm to see how they facilitate keeping user data within a database or directory service such as OpenLDAP (http://www.openldap.org) or Microsoft Active Directory.

CHAPTER 13

JDBC and Advanced Queries

In Chapter 3, we learned about databases, in particular relational databases, and saw how they are preferred to using flat files to store data because of their high degree of internal organization. We installed MySQL, a freely available relational database management system. We created commands to manipulate databases, used the SQL language, and we sent SQL commands directly to the database using the `mysql` command-line tool.

However, remembering that our interest is in accessing databases from Java and JSP, in this chapter we will discuss:

- ❑ The JDBC API and its characteristics
- ❑ The different database access models available to Java programmers
- ❑ JDBC drivers
- ❑ Using JDBC in a Java and JSP program to access a database
- ❑ Adding and populating database tables

In Chapter 3, we learned how to store data, create and alter tables, and to insert and update the actual data itself. We will now see the Application Programming Interface (API) Java provides to facilitate communication with databases. In addition, we will cover in detail how to get the data back *out* of the database.

So, let's get stuck straight in by seeing how we can access a database through JDBC.

Java Database Connectivity

In many programming languages the API used to execute SQL statements is different for each database engine. However, Java programmers do not have these database portability issues as they have a single API, the **Java Database Connectivity (JDBC) API**, which supports various popular database engines.

The JDBC library provides an interface for executing SQL statements and the basic functionality for data access. The classes and interfaces that make up the JDBC API are abstractions of concepts common to database access for any kind of database. The JDBC API makes it easy to send SQL statements to Relational Database Management Systems (RDBMSs) and supports all dialects of SQL. However, the JDBC 2.0 API goes beyond SQL, making it possible to interact with other kinds of data sources, such as files containing tables of data. In other words, with the JDBC library, it isn't necessary to write one program to access a MySQL database, another program to access an Oracle database, and so on. You can write a single Java program that uses the JDBC library, and this program will be able to send SQL or other statements to the appropriate data source. This is in keeping with the *write once, run anywhere* Java ideal.

Drivers

Although we can use the JDBC API to access virtually any data source from a Java application, there is a proviso: we need access to the specific **driver** for the database. A driver is an implementation of the JDBC interface that is suited to a specific database. It is a middleware layer that translates Java method calls into proprietary database API calls, which are then used to manipulate the database. The exact details of how the driver enables this communication between a Java application and the database API depends upon the driver.

A JDBC driver makes it possible to do three things:

❑   Establish a connection with a data source

❑   Run queries and other SQL statements on the data source

❑   Retrieve result sets

A number of drivers are available for MySQL and more information is available at the MySQL homepage at http://www.mysql.com/. The different classifications of JDBC drivers are described in the next section. In this chapter, we will use the MySQL Connector/J driver (http://www.mysql.com/products/connector-j/); this used to be the MM.MySQL driver. MySQL Connector/J is a Type-4 JDBC driver released under the GNU Library License, and we will describe these types in the *JDBC Driver Types* section. It allows Java developers to make connections to MySQL servers from both Java applications and applets. You should download the binary for this driver, and place it somewhere appropriate. We recommend the common\lib directory in the Tomcat root folder. You should then make sure your CLASSPATH environment variable points to the driver. A search facility of available JDBC drivers is available at http://industry.java.sun.com/products/jdbc/drivers.

Data Access Models

The JDBC API supports both two-tier and three-tier models for database access. In the two-tier model, a Java applet or application talks directly to the data source. This requires a JDBC driver that can communicate with the particular data source being accessed. An application's commands are delivered to the database, and the results of those statements are sent back to the user, as illustrated in the following diagram:

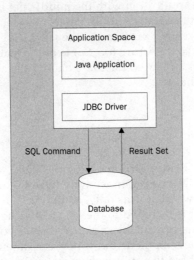

In the three-tier model, commands are sent to a "middle tier" of services, which then sends the commands to the data source. The middle tier of a three tier architecture is the application server which isolates data processing in a central location and maximizes object reuse. It contains problem specific objects called business objects which look after accounts, customers, and transactions that exist independently of how a user might see them. The data source processes them and sends the results back to the middle tier, which then sends them to the user as illustrated below:

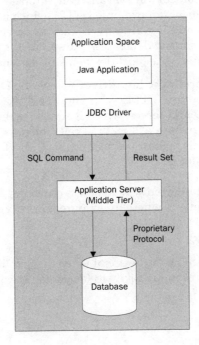

Here a JDBC driver links the application with the middle tier, and the middle tier uses another driver to communicate with the database. With enterprises increasingly using the Java programming language for writing server code, the JDBC API is being used more and more in the middle tier of a three-tier architecture too. Some of the features that make JDBC a server technology are its support for advanced database handling features, such as connection pooling (We'll meet this later in the chapter).

JDBC Driver Types

JDBC drivers are classified into four categories:

- **Type 1: JDBC-ODBC Bridge Driver** – provides JDBC access through drivers that conform to the Open Database Connectivity (ODBC) standard. Originally it was developed for Windows platforms only, and it was later enhanced to work on other platforms. This driver is included in the Java SDK. The bridge is useful when a pure JDBC driver (Type 3) isn't available for the database you want to access. It is also good for prototyping and development, but is not recommended for use in production servers, because the three-tier approach is less optimized for performance.

- **Type 2: Native-API Partly Java Driver** – converts JDBC calls into calls on native methods in the database API for Oracle, Sybase, Informix, IBM DB2, or other DBMS. Like the bridge driver, this style of driver requires that some operating system specific binary code be loaded on each client machine, so it isn't very portable across platforms. However, the two-tier model is faster than the Type 1 driver.

- **Type 3: JDBC-Net Protocol Pure Java Driver** – translates JDBC calls into a DBMS-independent net protocol (for example HTTP), which is then translated to a DBMS protocol by a custom middleware server. This net server middleware is able to connect its pure Java clients to many databases. The specific protocol used depends on the vendor. In general, this is the most flexible JDBC alternative.

- **Type 4: Native-protocol pure Java driver** – converts JDBC calls directly into the network protocol used by a DBMS. This allows a direct call from the client machine running Java to the DBMS server, which is similar to the Type 2 driver but bypassing the need to make a database API method call. The direct approach results in considerable performance improvement. If this class of driver is available to you, then it is the one you should use.

Driver types 3 and 4 are the preferred way to access databases using the JDBC API. Driver types 1 and 2 are interim solutions where direct pure Java drivers are not yet available.

Mapping SQL Data to Java

One tricky subject that you need to be aware of when using JDBCs to access databases is that data types in SQL do not correspond exactly to Java data types.

Indeed there are also significant variations between the SQL types supported by different database products. Even when different databases support SQL types with the same semantics, they may give those types different names. For example, most of the major databases support a SQL data type for large binary values, but Oracle calls this type LONG RAW, Sybase calls it IMAGE, Informix calls it BYTE, and DB2 calls it LONG VARCHAR FOR BIT DATA. Fortunately, you will normally not need to concern yourself with the actual SQL type names used by a target database.

JDBC defines a set of generic SQL type identifiers in the class java.sql.Types. These types have been designed to represent the most commonly used SQL types. While programming with the JDBC API, you will be able to use these JDBC types to reference generic SQL types, without having to concern yourself with the exact SQL type name used by the target database. However, one place where you may need to use SQL type names is in the SQL CREATE TABLE statement. If you want to write portable JDBC programs that can create tables on a variety of different databases, you are faced with two choices:

❑ First, you can restrict yourself to using only very widely accepted SQL type names such as INTEGER, FLOAT, or VARCHAR, which are likely to work for all databases.

❑ Second, you can use the java.sql.DatabaseMetaData.getTypeInfo() method to discover which SQL types are actually supported by a given database, and select a database-specific SQL type name that matches a given JDBC type.

JDBC defines a standard mapping from the JDBC database types to Java types. The Java types do not need to be *exactly* the same as the JDBC types; they just need to be able to represent them with enough type information to correctly store and retrieve parameters, and recover results from SQL statements. For example, a Java String object does not precisely match any of the JDBC CHAR types, but it gives enough type information to represent CHAR, VARCHAR, or LONGVARCHAR types successfully.

The following table illustrates the general correspondence between Java data types and SQL types:

Java Type	SQL Type
String	CHAR, VARCHAR, or LONGVARCHAR
java.math.BigDecimal	NUMERIC
boolean	BIT
byte	TINYINT
short	SMALLINT
int	INTEGER
long	BIGINT

Table continued on following page

Java Type	SQL Type
float	REAL
double	DOUBLE
byte[]	BINARY, VARBINARY, or LONGVARBINARY
java.sql.Date	DATE
java.sql.Time	TIME
java.sql.Timestamp	TIMESTAMP
Clob	CLOB
Blob	BLOB
Array	ARRAY
Struct	STRUCT
Ref	REF
Java class	JAVA_OBJECT

Database Connections

The main classes and interfaces traditionally involved in making a connection to the database are:

- ❑ The java.sql.Driver interface – Responds to connection requests from the DriverManager and provides information about its implementation.

- ❑ The java.sql.DriverManager class – Maintains a list of Driver implementations.

- ❑ The java.sql.Connection interface – Represents a single logical database connection.

The only driver-specific information the JDBC requires from your application is the database URL. Using the database URL, a user ID, and a password, your application requests a Connection from the DriverManager. The DriverManager searches through the known Driver implementations; all being well, one of them recognizes your URL and provides the DriverManager with an instance of a class that implements Connection, which in turn is passed back to the application.

For simple applications, the only method in the DriverManager class that you need to use directly is DriverManager.getConnection(). As its name implies, this method establishes a connection to a database. Drivers are loaded either by setting the jdbc.drivers system property or by using the Class.forName() method call.

This process of passing a driver name and the URL for obtaining a connection seems to be unnecessarily complex when you are trying to write database independent code. Details like registering drivers should be abstracted away from the application, and this is made possible with the **Java Naming and Directory Interface (JNDI)** and the JDBC Optional Package.

Naming and Directory Services

A **naming service** is a means by which names are associated with objects and objects are found based on their names. The primary function is to map people-friendly names to objects, such as addresses, and identifiers. For example, a file system maps a filename to a file handle that a program can use to access the contents of the file. To look up an object in a naming system, you supply the name of the object. The naming system determines the syntax that the name must follow. This syntax is sometimes called the naming system's naming convention.

For example, the Windows and DOS file system naming convention, similar to that used by Unix and Linux, lets us specify files using the path we have to take to reach it, starting at the root directory. Each step in this path is separated with a slash character, so the syntax \usr\hello indicates a file called `hello` that resides in the directory called `usr`, which itself can be found in the root directory.

The association of a name with an object is called a **binding**. For example, a filename is bound to a file. Depending on the naming service, some objects cannot be placed inside the naming service. Instead, they must be stored by reference. A reference is information about how to access an object. Using the reference, you can contact the object and obtain more information about the object. For example a file object is accessed using a file reference, also called a **file handle**.

A **context** is a set of name-to-object bindings. Every context has an associated naming convention. A context provides a lookup operation that returns the object and may provide operations such as those for binding names, unbinding names, and listing bound names. A name in one context object can be bound to another context object, a **subcontext** that has the same naming convention. So, a directory, such as \usr, is a context. A directory contained inside it may be called a subcontext, that is, the directory `bin` is a subcontext of `usr`.

A naming system is a connected set of contexts having the same naming convention and provides a common set of operations. A namespace is the set of names in a naming system. For example, the UNIX file system has a namespace consisting of all of the names of files and directories in that file system.

Many naming services are extended with a directory service. A directory service associates names with objects and also allows such objects to have attributes. An attribute has an attribute identifier and a set of attribute values. A directory is a connected set of directory objects. A directory service is a service that provides operations for creating, adding, removing, and modifying the attributes associated with objects in a directory. Directories often arrange their objects in a hierarchy. When directory objects are arranged in this way, they play the role of naming contexts in addition to that of containers of attributes. The most common directory services are the Network Information Service (NIS), Microsoft Active Directory, and the Lightweight Directory Access Protocol (LDAP).

The Java Naming and Directory Interface (JNDI) is the Java API that allows you to access naming and directory services in a transparent way. The JNDI architecture consists of an API and a service provider interface (SPI). Java applications use the JNDI API to access a variety of naming and directory services. The JNDI SPI enables a variety of naming and directory services to be plugged in transparently, thereby allowing the Java application using the JNDI API to access their services.

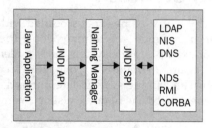

The JNDI PI is divided into five Java packages:

- ❑   `javax.naming`
- ❑   `javax.naming.directory`
- ❑   `javax.naming.event`
- ❑   `javax.naming.ldap`
- ❑   `javax.naming.spi`

The `javax.naming` package contains classes and interfaces for accessing naming services. This package defines a context interface, which is the core interface for looking up, binding/unbinding, renaming objects, and creating and destroying subcontexts. The most commonly used operation is `lookup()`. You supply the `lookup()` method the name of the object you want to look up, and it returns the object bound to that name. In the JNDI, all naming and directory operations are performed relative to a context. There are no absolute roots. Therefore, the JNDI defines an initial context, which provides a starting point for naming and directory operations. Once you have an initial context, you can use it to look up other contexts and objects.

The `javax.naming.directory` package extends the `javax.naming` package to provide functionality for accessing directory services in addition to naming services. This package allows applications to retrieve attributes associated with objects stored in the directory and to search for objects using specified attributes. You use `getAttributes()` to retrieve the attributes associated with a directory object, these can then be modified using the `modifyAttributes()` method allowing you to add, replace and/or modify attributes and their values.

The `javax.naming.event` package contains classes and interfaces for supporting event notification in naming and directory services.

The `javax.naming.ldap` package contains classes and interfaces for using features that are specific to LDAP that are not already covered by the more generic `javax.naming.directory` package. In fact, most JNDI applications that use the LDAP will find the `javax.naming.directory` package sufficient and will not need to use the `javax.naming.ldap` package at all. This package is primarily for those applications that need to use extended operations, controls, or unsolicited notifications.

The `javax.naming.spi` package provides the means by which developers of different naming/directory service providers can develop and hook up their implementations so that the corresponding services are accessible from applications that use JNDI. This package allows different implementations to be plugged in dynamically. These implementations include those for the initial context and for contexts that can be reached from the initial context.

Tomcat provides a JNDI `InitialContext` implementation instance to web applications running under it. Entries in this `InitialContext` are configured in the `server.xml` file in Tomcat's `conf` directory, and may be referenced by the following elements in your web application's `web.xml` file:

- ❑ `<env-entry>` – an environment entry, a single-value parameter that can be used to configure how the application will operate.

- ❑ `<resource-ref>` – resource reference, which is typically to an object factory for resources such as a JDBC DataSource, a JavaMail Session, or custom object factories. A `DataSource` object stores the attributes that tell it how to connect to a database.

- ❑ `<resource-env-ref>` – resource environment reference, a new variation of `resource-ref` that is simpler to configure for resources that do not require authentication information.

The `InitialContext` is configured when a web application is initially deployed, and is then available to web application components. All configured entries and resources will be placed in the `java:comp/env` portion of the JNDI namespace.

The following code snippet shows a typical access to a JDBC DataSource:

```
// Obtain our environment naming context
Context initCtx = new InitialContext();
Context envCtx = (Context) initCtx.lookup("java:comp/env");

// Look up our data source
DataSource ds = (DataSource) envCtx.lookup("jdbc/publish");
```

Each available JNDI Resource is configured by the following elements within the `<Context>` element associated with a particular web application in `server.xml`:

- ❑ `<Environment>` – Names and values for scalar environment entries that will be exposed to the web application through the JNDI InitialContext. This is equivalent to the inclusion of an `<env-entry>` element in the web application deployment descriptor.

❑ `<Resource>` – The name and data type of a resource made available to the application. This is the equivalent of the inclusion of a `<resource-ref>` element in the web application deployment descriptor.

❑ `<ResourceParams>` – The Java class name of the resource factory implementation to be used.

❑ `<ResourceLink>` – A link to a resource defined in the global JNDI context.

Connection Pooling

`DataSources` are also closely associated with **connection pooling**. Connection pooling is a mechanism whereby when an application has finished with a connection, the connection is recycled rather than being destroyed. Because establishing a connection to the database can be time consuming, sharing a pool of connections between all components of an application can dramatically improve performance.

In a standalone application (that is, an application started by the `main()` method), a connection is typically created once and kept open until the application is shut down, because a standalone application serves only one user at a time. However, this isn't very good in real-world server applications, which may have many concurrent connections to the database because they may have many concurrent users.

The interfaces that implement Java's connection pooling mechanism are:

❑ `javax.sql.DataSource` – an alternative to the `DriverManager` facility. A `DataSource` object represents a database, and is a preferred way to get a `Connection`. The class that implements the interface can provide connection-pooling capabilities.

❑ `javax.sql.ConnectionPoolDataSource` – extends `DataSource` and is a factory for `PooledConnection` objects. An object that implements this interface will typically be registered with a naming service that is based on JNDI.

❑ `javax.sql.PooledConnection` – represents a physical connection to a data source. When the application asks the `DataSource` for a `Connection`, it creates a `PooledConnection` object, or gets a new one from its `ConnectionPoolDataSource`.

Using a DataSource

Using a `DataSource` implementation is better than using `DriverManager`, for two important reasons:

❑ It makes code more portable

❑ It makes code easier to maintain

You use `Connection` objects produced by a `DataSource` object in just the same way as ones produced by the `DriverManager`. The `PooledConnection` acts just as the regular `Connection` object from the point of view of the developer. The only difference is that when the application calls the `close()` method, the physical connection to the database is not closed, but returned to the connection pool.

A `DataSource` object represents a real world data source, which can be anything from a relational database to a spreadsheet or a file in tabular format. When a `DataSource` object has been registered with a JNDI naming service, you can retrieve it from the naming service and use it to make a connection to the data source it represents.

The information about the `DataSource` is stored in the form of properties within the object, making the application more portable because it does not need to hard-code the driver and URL name. It also makes maintaining the code easier – for example, if the data source is moved to a different server, all that needs to be done is to update the relevant property; the code using that data source need not be altered.

Tomcat provides similar support to a J2EE Application Server to make available a data source implementation. So database applications developed on Tomcat using this support will run unchanged on any J2EE server. The default data source support in Tomcat is based on the DBCP component from the Jakarta Commons subproject (http://jakarta.apache.org/commons/index.html). However, it is possible to use any other connection pool that implements `javax.sql.DataSource`, by writing your own custom resource factory. We will employ connection pooling via the Jakarta Commons connection pool. So to configure the JNDI data source for our examples, we'll need the following Jakarta Commons Components:

These are all found under the base location of http://jakarta.apache.org/builds/jakarta-commons/release:

- ❑ DBCP (./commons-dbcp/v1.0/)
- ❑ Collections (./commons-collections/v2.1/)
- ❑ Pool (./commons-pool/v1.0.1/)

By default these files are included during the installation of Tomcat, but if these files aren't already in the Tomcat `[CATALINA]\common\lib` folder then download each of these components and copy the relevant JAR file into the `lib` folder.

Try It Out　　　**Using a JNDI DataSource and Configuring Tomcat**

1. Let's create a new database for our examples in this chapter. Start up MySQL and run the following commands:

mysql> create database if not exists books;

mysql> use books;

mysql> grant all privileges

    --> on books.*

    --> to booksuser@localhost

    --> identified by 'bookspass';

2. You now have a database called `books` and a user for it. But your user must be assigned a password or else the driver will fail if you try to connect with an empty password. We assigned the `booksuser` user a password of `bookspass`.

   You will have to register the data source with a JNDI naming service and set its properties. As part of the registration process, you have to associate the `DataSource` object with a **logical name**, which can be almost anything. Usually, it's a name that is easy to remember and describes the data source.

   In the example that follows, the logical name for the data source is `BooksDB`. By convention, logical names for `DataSource` objects are preceded by `jdbc/`, so the full logical name in this example is `jdbc/BooksDB`.

3. Create a directory called `Advanced` in Tomcat's `webapps` folder. Next we create a Java class to actually use our new data source and connection pool.

4. Save the following code as `Connect.java` in the `WEB-INF/classes/com/wrox/library` directory:

```
package com.wrox.library;
import javax.naming.*;
import javax.sql.*;
import java.sql.*;

public class Connect {

  String stat = "Not Connected";

  public void init() {
    try {
      Context ctx = new InitialContext();
      if(ctx == null )
          throw new Exception("Oops - No Context");

      DataSource ds = (DataSource)ctx.lookup("java:comp/env/jdbc/BooksDB");

      if (ds != null) {
        Connection conn = ds.getConnection();
```

```
        if(conn != null) {
          stat = " Got Connection "+conn.toString();
          conn.close();
        }
      }
    } catch(Exception e) {
      e.printStackTrace();
    }
  }

  public String getstat() {
    return stat;
  }
}
```

5. From the command prompt, change to the `%CATALINA_HOME%\webapps\Advanced\`
`WEB-INF\classes` directory and compile the class by running the following command:

> **> javac com\wrox\library\Connect.java**

6. Now create the following file under the name `web.xml` in the `WEB-INF` folder:

```
<?xml version="1.0" encoding="ISO-8859-1"?>
  <!DOCTYPE web-app PUBLIC
  "-//Sun Microsystems, Inc.//DTD Web Application 2.3//EN"
  "http://java.sun.com/dtd/web-app_2_3.dtd">
<web-app>
  <description>mySQL Test App</description>
  <resource-ref>
    <description>DB Connection</description>
    <res-ref-name>jdbc/BooksDB</res-ref-name>
    <res-type>javax.sql.DataSource</res-type>
    <res-auth>Container</res-auth>
  </resource-ref>
</web-app>
```

7. The following code is the JSP page for this application. Save it as `connect.jsp` in the
`Advanced` directory:

```
<html>
  <head>
    <title>Connection Test</title>
  </head>
  <body>

    <%
      com.wrox.library.Connect con = new com.wrox.library.Connect();
      con.init();
    %>
```

```
    <h2>Connection Result</h2>
    <%= con.getstat() %>
  </body>
</html>
```

8. Open the `server.xml` file in Tomcat's `conf` directory, and add a declaration for your resource. The following code should be included between the `</Context>` tag of the examples context and the `</Host>` tag closing the `localhost` definition:

```
<!-- Tomcat Root Context -->
<!--
  <Context path="" docBase="ROOT" debug="0"/>
-->
```

```
<Context path="/Advanced" docBase="Advanced"
   debug="5" reloadable="true" crossContext="true">

<Logger className="org.apache.catalina.logger.FileLogger"
        prefix="localhost_Advanced_log." suffix=".txt"
        timestamp="true"/>

<Resource name="jdbc/BooksDB"
          auth="Container"
          type="javax.sql.DataSource"/>

 <parameter>
   <name>factory</name>
   <value>org.apache.commons.dbcp.BasicDataSourceFactory</value>
 </parameter>
 <parameter>
   <name>maxActive</name>
   <value>100</value>
 </parameter>
 <parameter>
   <name>maxIdle</name>
   <value>30000</value>
 </parameter>
 <parameter>
   <name>maxWait</name>
   <value>100</value>
 </parameter>
 <parameter>
  <name>username</name>
  <value>booksuser</value>
 </parameter>
 <parameter>
  <name>password</name>
  <value>bookspass</value>
 </parameter>
```

```
            <parameter>
               <name>driverClassName</name>
               <value>org.gjt.mm.mysql.Driver</value>
            </parameter>

            <parameter>
               <name>url</name>
               <value>jdbc:mysql://localhost:3306/books</value>
            </parameter>
         </ResourceParams>
      </Context>
    </Host>
  </Engine>
</Service>
```

9. Start Tomcat and direct the browser to http://localhost:8080/Advanced/connect.jsp:

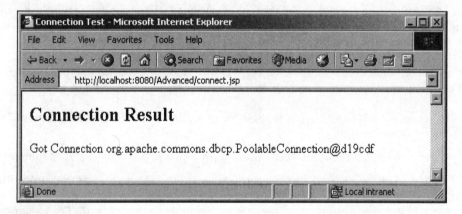

How It Works

The actual code of the JSP page is very simple. First we create an instance of the connect object using a scriptlet and with the help of the getter function, we display the connection status.

Tomcat provides a JNDI InitialContext implementation instance to web applications running under it. Entries in this InitialContext are configured in the server.xml file, and may be referenced in the web application deployment descriptor web.xml) of the web application.

In the Java code, we create an initial context:

```
Context ctx = new InitialContext();
```

And we provide the `lookup()` with the name of the object you want to look up, and it returns the `DataSource` object bound to that name:

```
DataSource ds = (DataSource)ctx.lookup("java:comp/env/jdbc/BooksDB");
```

This `DataSource` object is used to obtain the connection. The status of the connection is stored in a string, which can be obtained using the `get` accessor.

Populating Tables

The next thing we need to do is to populate our tables with data. Let's now dive back into SQL, and refresh how to construct statements that will enable us to fill tables with data.

Creating Statements

Once a connection to a particular database is established, then that connection can be used to send SQL statements. To do this, we need to create a `statement` object that will allow us to create a SQL command and execute it.

There are three kinds of `Statement` object that are used for executing SQL statements on a given connection:

❑ `Statement` objects – these are used for executing a static SQL statement and returning its produced results

❑ `PreparedStatement` objects – these represent a precompiled SQL statement

❑ `CallableStatement` objects – these are used to execute SQL stored procedures

`Statement` objects are objects of a class that implements the `java.sql.Statement` interface, while `PreparedStatement` objects implement the `java.sql.PreparedStatement` interface, and `CallableStatement` objects implement the `java.sql.CallableStatement` interface. You should note that the `PreparedStatement` interface extends the `Statement` interface, and the `CallableStatement` interface extends the `PreparedStatement` interface.

You might want to use a prepared statement when updating a group of objects stored on the same table. A stored procedure is built inside the database before you run your application. You access that stored procedure by name at run time. Stored procedures are generally faster than prepared statements, but this depends on the different databases used. The main point that should be considered when using a stored procedure is that, while JDBC aims at making your Java code portable, the code in your stored procedure will almost never be, because different databases have different syntaxes for their stored procedures.

However, we won't be dealing with `PreparedStatement` and `CallableStatement` objects yet; we'll save those for later in the chapter. In this section, we will focus on how to use `Statement` objects to execute statements.

A `Statement` object is created by the `Connection.createStatement()` method. Here's an example:

```
Statement stmt = con.createStatement();
```

Here we have created a `Statement` object called `stmt`, by calling the `createStatement()` method on the `Connection` object called `con`.

Executing Statements

Once we have created a `Statement` object, we can execute a SQL command by calling a variety of execute methods on the object. The correct method to use is determined by what you expect back when the SQL statement is executed. The SQL statement to be sent to the database is supplied as the argument of the execute method.

The `java.sql.Statement` interface provides three different methods for executing SQL statements:

❑   `executeUpdate()`

❑   `executeQuery()`

❑   `execute()`

The `executeUpdate()` method executes SQL DDL statements such as CREATE TABLE, DROP TABLE, and ALTER TABLE. Its return value is an integer (referred to as the update count) that indicates the number of rows that were affected. For statements such as CREATE TABLE or DROP TABLE, which do not operate on rows, the return value of `executeUpdate()` is always zero.

The `executeQuery()` method is for statements that return a single result set, such as the SELECT statements that we will meet in the next chapter.

The `execute()` method is used to execute statements that return more than one result set, more than one update count, or a combination of the two. We will see more on these last two methods in the later part of this chapter.

Inserting Data into Tables Using JDBC

We can use the `executeQuery()` method on the `Statement` object to create tables. We can also use this same method to insert, delete or modify data.

This example demonstrates the use of a `Statement` object to execute a SQL statement. We will use the `books` database that we created earlier in the chapter. The SQL statement in this example creates the `Book`, `Author`, `Category`, and `Contribution` tables.

Try It Out   Creating and Populating Database Tables

1. Save the following code as `populate.java` to the `Advanced\WEB-INF\classes\com\wrox\library\` folder.

```java
package com.wrox.library;
import javax.naming.*;
import javax.sql.*;
import java.sql.*;

public class populate {
String tstatus = "Error in creating Tables";
String pstatus = "Error in populating Tables";
  public void init() {
    try{
      Context ctx = new InitialContext();
      if(ctx == null )
        throw new Exception("Oops - No Context");

      DataSource ds = (DataSource)ctx.lookup("java:comp/env/jdbc/BooksDB");

      if (ds != null) {
        Connection conn = ds.getConnection();
      Statement stmt = conn.createStatement();
      String upd = "CREATE TABLE Author ("+
                 "Author_ID INTEGER NOT NULL PRIMARY KEY,"+
                 "Author_Name CHAR(50)) type=InnoDB;";
      stmt.executeUpdate(upd);

      upd = "CREATE TABLE Category ("+
            "Category_ID INTEGER NOT NULL PRIMARY KEY,"+
            "Category_Description CHAR(50)) type=InnoDB;";
      stmt.executeUpdate(upd);

      upd = "CREATE TABLE Book ("+
            "Title_ID INTEGER NOT NULL PRIMARY KEY,"+
            "Title CHAR(50),"+
            "Price FLOAT(8,2),"+
            "Category_ID INTEGER) type=InnoDB;";
      stmt.executeUpdate(upd);

      upd = "CREATE TABLE Contribution ("+
            "Contribution_ID INTEGER NOT NULL PRIMARY KEY,"+
            "Title_ID INTEGER,"+
            "Author_ID INTEGER) type=InnoDB;";
      stmt.executeUpdate(upd);
      tstatus = "Tables successfully created";
      upd = "INSERT INTO Category (Category_ID, Category_Description)"+
            "VALUES (1,'Java'), (2,'SQL');";
      stmt.executeUpdate(upd);
```

```
            upd = "INSERT INTO Book (Title_ID, Category_ID, Title, Price)"+
                  " VALUES (1,1,'Professional Java Data',59.99),"+
                        "(2,1,'Professional Java Security',49.99),"+
                        "(3,2,'Beginning SQL Programming',49.99)";
        stmt.executeUpdate(upd);

        upd = "INSERT INTO Author (Author_ID, Author_Name) VALUES "+
            "(1,'Danny Ayers'), (2,'John Bell'), (3,'Carl Calvert Bettis'),"+
            "(4,'Thomas Bishop'), (5,'Mike Bogovich'), (6,'Matthew Ferris'),"+
            "(7,'Rick Grehan'), (8,'Bjarki Holm'), (9,'Tony Loton'),"+
            "(10,'Glen E. Mitchell II'), (11,'Nitin Nanda'),"+
            "(12,'Kelly Lin Poon'), (13,'Sean Rhody'), (14,'Mark Wilcox'),"+
            "(15,'Jess Garms'), (16,'Daniel Somerfield'),"+
            "(17,'John Kauffman'), (18,'Brian Matsik'), "+
            "(19,'Kevin Spencer'), (20,'Tom Walsh');";
        stmt.executeUpdate(upd);
        pstatus = "Tables successfully populated";
        conn.close();

        }
    }catch(Exception e) {
      e.printStackTrace();
    }

  }
  public String gettstatus() {
    return tstatus;
  }
  public String getpstatus() {
     return pstatus;
  }
}
```

2. Open a command prompt, change the directory to `%CATALINA_HOME%\webapps\Advanced\WEB-INF\classes`, and run the following command:

> **> javac com\wrox\library\populate.java**

3. Save the following as `populate.jsp` in the `Advanced` directory. This is the main page for the application:

```
<html>
  <head>
    <title>Populate Database</title>
  </head>
  <body>

  <%
    com.wrox.library.populate pop = new com.wrox.library.populate();
    pop.init();
```

```
%>

<h2>Result</h2>
  <%= pop.gettstatus() %> </br>
  <%= pop.getpstatus() %> </br>

</body>
</html>
```

4. Restart Tomcat and navigate to http://localhost:8080/Advanced/populate.jsp:

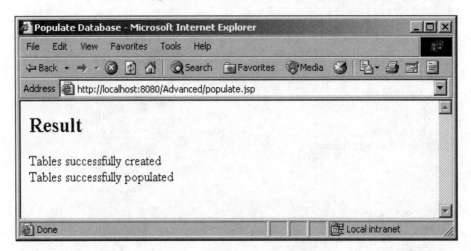

How It Works

We started by obtaining a connection, as in our previous example. We used it to create and execute SQL statements to create tables in our database, using `executeUpdate()`. For instance, we first create a `Statement` object:

```
Statement stmt = con.createStatement();
```

Then we create a `String` that contains our SQL command:

```
String upd = "CREATE TABLE Author (
          Author_ID INTEGER NOT NULL PRIMARY KEY,
          Author_name CHAR(50), Title_ID INTEGER)";
```

Finally we use `executeUpdate()` to execute the command via JDBC:

```
stmt.executeUpdate(upd);
```

Care should be taken here because the JDBC API is not database-specific, and has been written to provide abstraction for database application programming; it does not put any restrictions on the kinds of SQL statements that can be sent. Therefore, it is up to you to ensure the underlying database can process the SQL statements being sent. We then repeated the process for the other tables.

The next thing we did was populate the tables. The process is the same, except we created a `Statement` object, and a `String` containing our SQL `INSERT` command:

```
String upd = "INSERT INTO Book (Title_ID, Category_ID, Title, Price)
              VALUES (1,1,'Professional Java Data',59.99),
                     (2,1,'Professional Java Security',49.99),
                     (3,1,'Beginning SQL Programming',49.99)";
```

Then we do the same kind of thing for the other tables too. You probably noticed that we didn't insert data into the `Contribution` table; we leave that as an exercise for you to do if you wish.

Querying the Database

As we said, we've covered a lot about SQL and databases, but we could also use some means of getting the data back out of the database again! That's where the SQL `SELECT` statement comes in.

Querying with JDBC

OK, so we know the basic SQL for querying the database. Now how do we do this from Java? We've seen the `Statement` interface's `executeUpdate()` method, used to perform SQL statements like `INSERT`, `UPDATE`, and `DELETE`. That method just returned an `int` value to tell us how things went; to perform a `SELECT` statement from our Java code we'll need to use `Statement`'s `executeQuery()` method, which returns us our query results in the form of an object that implements the `ResultSet` interface.

The ResultSet Interface

So, a `ResultSet` contains the results of executing a SQL query (`SELECT` statement) – in other words, it contains the rows that satisfy the conditions of the query. While there are many methods in the `ResultSet` interface, the basic facilities that you'll use most often are:

❑   The `getXXX()` methods, which allow you to access the various columns of the current row. There are different methods available depending on the data type of the column (for example, `getString()` and `getFloat()`); you can specify which column you're interested in by either its name or, as we'll see later, by its position. Column numbering starts with 1 not 0.

❑   The `next()` method, which is used to move to the next row of the `ResultSet` (if there is a next row).

Let's see how we can use what we've learned to query our `Books` database.

Try It Out — Querying the Database using JDBC

1. Enter the following code into your editor and save it as `Querydb.java`:

```java
package com.wrox.library;
import javax.naming.*;
import javax.sql.*;
import java.sql.*;

public class Querydb {

  String title = "No title";
  float price=0.00f;

  public void init() {
    try {
      Context ctx = new InitialContext();
      if(ctx == null )
        throw new Exception("Oops - No Context");

      DataSource ds = (DataSource)ctx.lookup("java:comp/env/jdbc/BooksDB");

      if (ds != null) {
        Connection conn = ds.getConnection();

        if(conn != null) {
          Statement stmt = conn.createStatement();
          ResultSet rst = stmt.executeQuery("select * from book");
          if(rst.next()) {
            title=rst.getString(2);
            price=rst.getFloat("Price");
          }

          conn.close();
        }
      }
    } catch(Exception e) {
      e.printStackTrace();
    }
  }

  public String getTitle() { return title; }
  public float getPrice() { return price; }
}
```

2. Change the directory to `%CATALINA-HOME%\webapps\Advanced\classes` and then compile the file using the following code:

   > **javac com\wrox\library\Querydb.java**

3. The following is the JSP page for our application. Save it as `query.jsp` in the `Advanced` directory:

```
<html>
  <head>
    <title>Query Database</title>
  </head>
  <body>

  <%
    com.wrox.library.Querydb qdb = new com.wrox.library.Querydb();
    qdb.init();
  %>

  <h2>Query Result</h2>
    Title: <%= qdb.getTitle() %><br/>
    Price:$ <%= qdb.getPrice() %>

  </body>
</html>
```

4. Restart Tomcat and direct the browser to the page http://localhost:8080/Advanced/ query.jsp. The output should be something like the following:

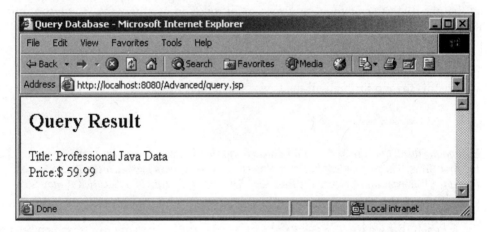

How It Works

Just like before, we start by creating a `Connection` object:

```
Context ctx = new InitialContext();
if(ctx == null )
  throw new Exception("Oops - No Context");
```

```
DataSource ds = (DataSource)ctx.lookup("java:comp/env/jdbc/BooksDB");

if (ds != null) {
  Connection conn = ds.getConnection();
```

After obtaining the connection we created a `Statement` object, which we will use to execute the SQL command:

```
Statement stmt = conn.createStatement();
```

Now for the new bit: we use the `Statement` object's `executeUpdate()` method to perform the query, passing it the SQL code for the query:

```
stmt.executeUpdate(upd);
ResultSet rst = stmt.executeQuery("select * from book");
if(rst.next()) {
  title=rst.getString(2);
  price=rst.getFloat(3);
}
```

The `executeQuery()` returns us a `ResultSet` containing the output from the query. We saw earlier that the `SELECT` statement returns a set of rows, and so the `ResultSet` too contains a set of rows of data. It remembers which is its "current row" in the data, and the `next()` method is used to move it on to the next row.

The `next()` method returns a `boolean` value, indicating whether there are any more results, and we use this to loop through all the rows of data that were returned:

```
while(rst.next()) {
```

You might think that this code would always skip the first row of results as next() is the first thing that gets called; however this isn't the case, because when the ResultSet is created it is positioned before the first row. The first time next() is called it moves onto the first row.

Finally, for each row we use the `getString()` and `getFloat()` methods, which retrieve the values from the `Title` and `Pages` columns and prints them out:

```
title=rst.getString(2);
price=rst.getFloat(3);
```

ResultSet – The Details

Let's look in some more detail at the `ResultSet` interface and its facilities.

A `ResultSet` maintains a **cursor**, which points to its current row, and moves down one row each time the `next()` method is called. When a `ResultSet` object is first created, the cursor is positioned before the first row, so as we saw, the first call to the `next()` method puts the cursor on the first row. `ResultSet` rows can be retrieved in sequence from top to bottom as the cursor moves down one row with each successive call to the method `next()`.

By default this forward movement is the only way you can move a `ResultSet`'s cursor, and it is the *only* cursor movement possible with drivers that implement the JDBC 1.0 API. This kind of result set returns the value `ResultSet.TYPE_FORWARD_ONLY` from its `getType()` method and is referred to as a **forward only result set**.

If a driver implements the cursor movement methods in the JDBC 2.0 core API, however, its result sets can be **scrollable**. A scrollable result set's cursor can move both forwards and backwards, as well as to a particular row, using the `previous()`, `first()`, `last()`, `absolute()`, `relative()`, `afterLast()`, and `beforeFirst()` methods.

The previous example demonstrated moving the cursor forward. It is also possible to iterate through a result set backwards, for example by replacing the `while` loop in the previous code with the following:

```
rst.afterLast();
while (rst.previous()) {
  ...
}
```

The cursor is first moved to the very end of the result set (with the method `afterLast()`), and then the method `previous()` is invoked within a `while()` loop to iterate through the contents of the result set by moving to the previous row with each iteration. The method `previous()` returns `false` when there are no more rows, so the loop ends after all the rows have been visited.

We have already used the `ResultSet.getXXX()` methods for retrieving column values from the current row in the above code fragment. It is always advisable with the forward-only result sets to retrieve the column values from left to right, but with scrollable result sets there are no such restrictions.

Either the column name or the column number can be used to designate the column from which to retrieve data. For example, if the second column of a `ResultSet` object `rst` is named `Title`, and it stores values as strings, either of the following will retrieve the value stored in that column:

```
String s = rs.getString(2);
String s = rs.getString("TITLE");
```

Note that columns are numbered from left to right, starting with column 1. Also, column names used as input to getXXX() methods are not case sensitive.

If the name of a column is known but not its index, the method findColumn() can be used to find the column number. Information about the columns in a ResultSet is available by calling the method ResultSet.getMetaData(), which returns a ResultSetMetaData object which provides you with the following information:

❑ Name of the column

❑ Datatype of the column

❑ Name of the table of the given column

❑ Label of the display header

❑ Whether NULL is a valid value of the column

❑ Display size of the column

❑ Whether the column is searchable

Advanced Queries

Now that we know how to manipulate the results of our queries, let's return to the SQL syntax for a bit and see how we can create more complicated queries, which can do more than just return all the rows from a single table.

Conditional Selection

The first step to enhancing our queries is to be able to retrieve only certain rows from a table. To help us explore the conditional selection of rows, let's add some more data to the Book table, so that it looks like this:

```
mysql> SELECT * FROM Book;
+----------+---------------------------------+-------------+-------+
| Title_ID | Title                           | Category_ID | Price |
+----------+---------------------------------+-------------+-------+
|        1 | Professional Java Data          |           1 | 59.99 |
|        2 | Professional Java Security      |           1 | 49.99 |
|        3 | Beginning SQL Programming       |           2 | 49.99 |
|        4 | Beginning Java Objects          |           1 | 39.99 |
|        5 | Beginning Java 2 - JDK 1.3 Edition |        1 | 49.99 |
|        6 | Java Programmer's Reference     |           1 | 34.99 |
|        7 | Professional ASP.NET            |           3 | 59.99 |
+----------+---------------------------------+-------------+-------+
7 rows in set (0.00 sec)
```

Relational Operators

There are six relational operators in SQL, which behave very much like the Java operators:

Symbol	Meaning
=	Equal to
<>	Not equal to
<	Less than
>	Greater than
<=	Less than or equal to
>=	Greater than or equal to

The WHERE clause is used to specify that only certain rows of the table are to be retrieved, based on criteria described in that WHERE clause. It is most easily understood by looking at a couple of examples.

Firstly, looking at the above data you'll see that Java books all have the value 1 in their Category_ID column. To retrieve only the Java books we could use the "equal to" operator:

```
mysql> SELECT Title, Price FROM Book
    -> WHERE Category_ID = 1;
+-------------------------------------+-------+
| Title                               | Price |
+-------------------------------------+-------+
| Professional Java Data              | 59.99 |
| Professional Java Security          | 49.99 |
| Beginning Java Objects              | 39.99 |
| Beginning Java 2 - JDK 1.3 Edition  | 49.99 |
| Java Programmer's Reference         | 34.99 |
+-------------------------------------+-------+
5 rows in set (0.04 sec)
```

Note that the equal to operator in SQL is a *single* =, not == like in Java. The = operator works just as well on text columns; for example if we wanted to know the price of *Beginning Java Objects* we could use the following SQL:

```
mysql> SELECT Price FROM Book
    -> WHERE Title = 'Beginning Java Objects';
+-------+
| Price |
+-------+
| 39.99 |
+-------+
1 row in set (0.00 sec)
```

We can also use the other relational operators. For example, to see those books that cost $49.99 or more we can use:

```
mysql> SELECT Title, Price FROM Book
    -> WHERE Price >= 49.99;
+--------------------------------+-------+
| Title                          | Price |
+--------------------------------+-------+
| Professional Java Data         | 59.99 |
| Professional Java Security     | 49.99 |
| Beginning SQL Programming       | 49.99 |
| Beginning Java 2 - JDK 1.3 Edition | 49.99 |
| Professional ASP.NET           | 59.99 |
+--------------------------------+-------+
5 rows in set (0.00 sec)
```

Logical Operators

In addition to the relational operators we've just seen, there are various logical operators that allow us to combine conditions:

- ❑ AND
- ❑ OR
- ❑ NOT

The AND operator joins two or more conditions, and displays a row only if that row's data satisfies **all** the conditions. For example, to list the Java books (in other words, having a Category_ID of 1) that cost $49.99 or more we would use:

```
mysql> SELECT Title, Price FROM Book
    -> WHERE Price >= 49.99
    -> AND Category_ID = 1;
+--------------------------------+-------+
| Title                          | Price |
+--------------------------------+-------+
| Professional Java Data         | 59.99 |
| Professional Java Security     | 49.99 |
| Beginning Java 2 - JDK 1.3 Edition | 49.99 |
+--------------------------------+-------+
3 rows in set (0.02 sec)
```

The OR operator joins two or more conditions, but returns a row if **any** of the conditions listed are true. To see books that cost less than $40 or belong to the SQL category (`Category_ID` of 2), we would use the following query:

```
mysql> SELECT Title, Price FROM Book
    -> WHERE Price < 40.00
    -> OR Category_ID = 2;
+-----------------------------+-------+
| Title                       | Price |
+-----------------------------+-------+
| Beginning SQL Programming   | 49.99 |
| Beginning Java Objects      | 39.99 |
| Java Programmer's Reference | 34.99 |
+-----------------------------+-------+
3 rows in set (0.00 sec)
```

Note that this list includes *Beginning SQL Programming* even though it costs $49.99.

The NOT operator displays a row only if that row's data **do not** satisfy the condition. To display all books that are not about SQL (do not have a `Category_ID` of 2) use:

```
mysql> SELECT Title FROM Book
    -> WHERE NOT (Category_ID = 2);
+----------------------------------+
| Title                            |
+----------------------------------+
| Professional Java Data           |
| Professional Java Security       |
| Beginning Java Objects           |
| Beginning Java 2 - JDK 1.3 Edition |
| Java Programmer's Reference      |
| Professional ASP.NET             |
+----------------------------------+
6 rows in set (0.00 sec)
```

Operators can be combined, for example:

```
mysql> SELECT Title, Price FROM Book
    -> WHERE Price > 45 OR Price < 40 AND Category_ID = 1;
+----------------------------------+-------+
| Title                            | Price |
+----------------------------------+-------+
| Professional Java Data           | 59.99 |
| Professional Java Security       | 49.99 |
| Beginning SQL Programming        | 49.99 |
| Beginning Java Objects           | 39.99 |
| Beginning Java 2 - JDK 1.3 Edition | 49.99 |
| Java Programmer's Reference      | 34.99 |
| Professional ASP.NET             | 59.99 |
+----------------------------------+-------+
```

```
7 rows in set (0.00 sec)
```

The SQL engine selects the list of rows that satisfy the condition where the `Category_ID` is 1 and the `Price` is less than $40. Note that this illustrates SQL operators' precedence, where the AND operator takes priority over OR. The WHERE clause will return all books that have a price below $40 and a category ID of 1, and will additionally return all books that have a price over $45 regardless of what category they may be in.

If we wish to perform the OR part before the AND, we need to use parentheses:

```
mysql> SELECT Title, Price FROM Book
    -> WHERE (Price > 45 OR Price < 40) AND Category_ID = 1;
+--------------------------------------+-------+
| Title                                | Price |
+--------------------------------------+-------+
| Professional Java Data               | 59.99 |
| Professional Java Security           | 49.99 |
| Beginning SQL Programming            | 49.99 |
| Beginning Java Objects               | 39.99 |
| Beginning Java 2 - JDK 1.3 Edition   | 49.99 |
| Java Programmer's Reference          | 34.99 |
+--------------------------------------+-------+
5 rows in set (0.00 sec)
```

Using IN and BETWEEN

An easier method of creating compound conditions uses the IN and BETWEEN keywords. To select books that have a `Category_ID` of either 1 or 2 (Java or SQL), we can use the IN operator:

```
mysql> SELECT Title FROM Book
    -> WHERE Category_ID IN (1,2);
+--------------------------------------+
| Title                                |
+--------------------------------------+
| Professional Java Data               |
| Professional Java Security           |
| Beginning SQL Programming            |
| Beginning Java Objects               |
| Beginning Java 2 - JDK 1.3 Edition   |
| Java Programmer's Reference          |
+--------------------------------------+
6 rows in set (0.02 sec)
```

The BETWEEN operator allows us to check for a range of values. To list all books costing between $40 and $50, we'd use:

```
mysql> SELECT Title FROM Book
    -> WHERE Price BETWEEN 40 and 50;
+---------------------------------------+--------+
| Title                                 | Price  |
+---------------------------------------+--------+
| Professional Java Security            | 49.99  |
| Beginning SQL Programming             | 49.99  |
| Beginning Java 2 - JDK 1.3 Edition    | 49.99  |
+---------------------------------------+--------+
3 rows in set (0.00 sec)
```

To list the books that are **not** in this range:

```
mysql> SELECT Title FROM Book
    -> WHERE Price NOT BETWEEN 40 and 50;
+-----------------------------+--------+
| Title                       | Price  |
+-----------------------------+--------+
| Professional Java Data      | 59.99  |
| Beginning Java Objects      | 39.99  |
| Java Programmer's Reference | 34.99  |
| Professional ASP.NET        | 59.99  |
+-----------------------------+--------+
4 rows in set (0.00 sec)
```

Similarly, NOT IN lists all rows excluded from the IN list.

Using LIKE

The LIKE operator allows us to perform inexact textual comparisons. Let's see how we can select all the Wrox *Beginning...* books from our database:

```
mysql> SELECT Title FROM Book
    -> WHERE Title LIKE 'Beginning %';
+-------------------------------------+
| Title                               |
+-------------------------------------+
| Beginning SQL Programming           |
| Beginning Java Objects              |
| Beginning Java 2 - JDK 1.3 Edition  |
+-------------------------------------+
3 rows in set (0.01 sec)
```

The percent sign (%) is used to indicate any possible character or set of characters in a string (number, letter, or punctuation). The % character can occur in any position within the string of characters to be matched, so to find all the books whose titles contain the word Java, we'd use %Java%. There is also a second special character, the question mark (?), which matches any single character in the column being matched. For example, ?SP would match JSP or ASP but not WASP.

We could use NOT LIKE to display rows that do *not* fit the given description.

Joining Tables

A **join** enables you to match a row from one table up with a row in another table. As we saw in Chapter 3, good database design suggests that each table contains data only about a single entity. Relational databases let us use several tables and a join to represent more complex data.

The basic form of join is what is called as the **inner join**. The **outer join** is less commonly used and we will not explore further.

Let's look again at our sample database, this time having added some values into the Category table:

```
mysql> SELECT * FROM Book;
+----------+--------------------------------+-------------+-------+
| Title_ID | Title                          | Category_ID | Price |
+----------+--------------------------------+-------------+-------+
|        1 | Professional Java Data         |           1 | 59.99 |
|        2 | Professional Java Security     |           1 | 49.99 |
|        3 | Beginning SQL Programming      |           2 | 49.99 |
|        4 | Beginning Java Objects         |           1 | 39.99 |
|        5 | Beginning Java 2 - JDK 1.3 Edition |       1 | 49.99 |
|        6 | Java Programmer's Reference    |           1 | 34.99 |
|        7 | Professional ASP.NET           |           3 | 59.99 |
+----------+--------------------------------+-------------+-------+
7 rows in set (0.00 sec)

mysql> SELECT * FROM Category;
+-------------+----------------------+
| Category_ID | Category_Description |
+-------------+----------------------+
|           1 | Java                 |
|           2 | SQL                  |
|           3 | ASP                  |
+-------------+----------------------+
3 rows in set (0.00 sec)
```

You can see here that these two tables are related to each other; the Book table has a column, Category_ID, which relates each book to one of the categories listed in the Category table. The Category table's Category_ID column is its **primary key**; the column of the same name in the Book table is a **foreign key** as it refers to one of the primary key values in a different ("foreign") table.

The primary and foreign keys help us to create the relationship of data across tables, without having to repeat the same data in every table; this is the power of relational databases. For example, you can find the category description of a book without having to list the full description of the category in the Book table. Instead, you can use the Category_ID column to relate the data in the two tables.

For example, the query below lists all books and their category descriptions:

```
mysql> SELECT Book.Title, Category.Category_Description, Book.Price
    -> FROM Book, Category
    -> WHERE Book.Category_ID = Category.Category_ID;
+------------------------------------+-----------------------+-------+
| Title                              | Category_Description  | Price |
+------------------------------------+-----------------------+-------+
| Professional Java Data             | Java                  | 59.99 |
| Professional Java Security         | Java                  | 49.99 |
| Beginning Java Objects             | Java                  | 39.99 |
| Beginning Java 2 - JDK 1.3 Edition | Java                  | 49.99 |
| Java Programmer's Reference        | Java                  | 34.99 |
| Beginning SQL Programming          | SQL                   | 49.99 |
| Professional ASP.NET               | ASP                   | 59.99 |
+------------------------------------+-----------------------+-------+
7 rows in set (0.00 sec)
```

Note that **both** tables involved in the join are listed in the FROM clause. Also, note how the ID columns are related from one table to the next by use of the WHERE Book.Category_ID = Category.Category_ID clause. Only where IDs match across tables will the descriptions from the Category table be listed. Because the joining condition used an equal sign, this join is called an **equi-join**. (Other types of join are possible, but are outside the scope of this book.)

Note the use of the 'dot' notation to prefix the table names to avoid ambiguity with the column names, as in this case they are the same in each table. They do not have to be the same name, however, and if they didn't, it would still be good practice to use the dot notation.

Aliases

As we saw in the previous example, when you use column names that are fully qualified with their table and column name the names can grow to be quite unwieldy. SQL allows you to use an **aliased name** – usually shorter and more descriptive – in place of the longer name. This is done using the AS keyword:

```
SELECT Book.Title AS Title, Category.Category_Description AS Category,
Book.Price AS Price,
Book.Category_ID, Category.Category_ID
FROM Book, Category
WHERE Book.Category_ID = Category.Category_ID;
```

What we have done is provided aliases for column names; likewise, adding table aliases is also permitted.

Miscellaneous SQL Features

SELECT also supports the concept of functions. There are several built-in functions that can operate upon columns of a table, returning their computed value or values. With some functions, the value returned depends on whether you want to receive a numerical or string value. This is referred to as the context of the function. When selecting values to be displayed to you, only text context is used. When selecting data to be inserted into a field or to be used as the argument of another function, the context depends upon what the receiver is expecting. For instance, selecting data to be inserted into a numerical field will place the function into a numerical context, but when returning values from a query the SUM() function returns a string, rather than a number.

Aggregate Functions

There are five important aggregate functions:

❑   SUM()

❑   AVG()

❑   MAX()

❑   MIN()

❑   COUNT()

They are called aggregate functions because they summarize the results of a query, rather than listing all of the rows.

Function	Description
SUM()	Gives the total value of the given column's values that match any condition that was specified
AVG()	Gives the average value of the given column's values that match any condition that was specified
MAX()	Gives the largest figure in the given column that matches any condition that was specified
MIN()	Gives the smallest figure in the given column that matches any condition that was specified
COUNT(*)	Gives the number of rows satisfying any condition that was specified

Let's see how we can use these functions on the tables in our `Books` database:

```
mysql> SELECT SUM(Price), AVG(Price)
    -> FROM Book;
+------------+------------+
| SUM(Price) | AVG(Price) |
+------------+------------+
|     344.93 |  49.275714 |
+------------+------------+
1 row in set (0.04 sec)
```

This query shows the total price of one copy of each title, and the average price of all of the books in the table.

```
mysql> SELECT MIN(Price) FROM Book
    -> WHERE Category_ID = 1;
+------------+
| MIN(Price) |
+------------+
|      34.99 |
+------------+
1 row in set (0.00 sec)
```

This query returns the price of the cheapest Java book.

```
mysql> SELECT COUNT(*)
    -> FROM Book
    -> WHERE Category_ID = 1;
+----------+
| COUNT(*) |
+----------+
|        5 |
+----------+
1 row in set (0.00 sec)
```

This query tells you how many Java books are in the database.

You may be wondering what use these functions can be; if we want to find out how many Java books there are, why not just return a list of all of them and then write some Java code that counts how many times `next()` returns `true`? The answer comes when you consider what would happen if, instead of having 7 rows, our `Book` table had tens of thousands of rows. Then, transferring all that data across the network from the database to our Java program, only for it to be counted and then discarded, would be wasteful in the extreme. These functions allow you to improve performance by moving some of the processor-intensive operations into the database itself.

In addition to the above listed aggregate functions, some DBMSs allow more functions to be used in `SELECT` lists. You should consult your database documentation for detail of these.

GROUP BY

There are a few other SQL keywords that we ought to mention before we leave the subject of queries. One is the GROUP BY keyword, used to associate an aggregate function (especially COUNT(*)) with groups of rows, so that COUNT(*) counts the number of rows in each group rather than in total.

Our Book table has a column named Price, containing the price of each title. The GROUP BY clause allows us to find out the price of the most expensive book in each category. To do this we tell it to group the books together based on their Category_ID, then find the maximum price in each group:

```
mysql> SELECT Category_ID, MAX(Price)
    -> FROM Book
    -> GROUP BY Category_ID;
+-------------+------------+
| Category_ID | MAX(Price) |
+-------------+------------+
|           1 |      59.99 |
|           2 |      49.99 |
|           3 |      59.99 |
+-------------+------------+
3 rows in set (0.05 sec)
```

ORDER BY

The ORDER BY clause allows us to change the order in which results are returned. For example, let's return the books sorted by price:

```
mysql> SELECT Title, Price FROM Book
    -> ORDER BY Price;
+---------------------------------+-------+
| Title                           | Price |
+---------------------------------+-------+
| Java Programmer's Reference     | 34.99 |
| Beginning Java Objects          | 39.99 |
| Professional Java Security      | 49.99 |
| Beginning SQL Programming       | 49.99 |
| Beginning Java 2 - JDK 1.3 Edition | 49.99 |
| Professional Java Data          | 59.99 |
| Professional ASP.NET            | 59.99 |
+---------------------------------+-------+
7 rows in set (0.00 sec)
```

We can also sort them in descending order of price, by adding the DESC keyword:

```
mysql> SELECT Title, Price FROM Book
    -> ORDER BY Price DESC;
+-----------------------------------+-------+
| Title                             | Price |
+-----------------------------------+-------+
| Professional Java Data            | 59.99 |
| Professional ASP.NET              | 59.99 |
| Professional Java Security        | 49.99 |
| Beginning SQL Programming         | 49.99 |
| Beginning Java 2 - JDK 1.3 Edition| 49.99 |
| Beginning Java Objects            | 39.99 |
| Java Programmer's Reference       | 34.99 |
+-----------------------------------+-------+
7 rows in set (0.00 sec)
```

Finally, let's see how we can sort by more than one column. Here we're printing out the title, price, and category description of every book; they are ordered first by the category they're in, then in descending order of price:

```
mysql> SELECT Book.Title, Book.Price,
    -> Category.Category_Description AS Category
    -> FROM Book, Category
    -> WHERE Book.Category_ID = Category.Category_ID
    -> ORDER BY Category, Book.Price DESC;
+-----------------------------------+-------+----------+
| Title                             | Price | Category |
+-----------------------------------+-------+----------+
| Professional ASP.NET              | 59.99 | ASP      |
| Professional Java Data            | 59.99 | Java     |
| Beginning Java 2 - JDK 1.3 Edition| 49.99 | Java     |
| Professional Java Security        | 49.99 | Java     |
| Beginning Java Objects            | 39.99 | Java     |
| Java Programmer's Reference       | 34.99 | Java     |
| Beginning SQL Programming         | 49.99 | SQL      |
+-----------------------------------+-------+----------+
7 rows in set (0.01 sec)
```

It's been a while since we saw some Java, but in fact any of the SELECT statements we've seen could be called from Java, using JDBC. Let's see how that would work for this example.

Try It Out   Using Advanced SQL Queries with JDBC

1. Enter the following code and save it as ComplexQuery.java in the Advanced\WEB-INF\classes\com\wrox\library folder:

```
package com.wrox.library;
import javax.naming.*;
```

```
import javax.sql.*;
import java.sql.*;

public class ComplexQuery {
  Connection conn;
  public ComplexQuery() { }
  public void connect() {
    try{
      Context ctx = new InitialContext();
      if(ctx == null )
          throw new Exception("Oops - No Context");

      DataSource ds =
            (DataSource)ctx.lookup(
                "java:comp/env/jdbc/BooksDB");

      if (ds != null)
        conn = ds.getConnection();
    }catch(Exception e) {
      e.printStackTrace();
    }
  }
  public void disconnect() {
    try {
      if ( conn != null ) {
        conn.close();
      }
    } catch (Exception e) {
      e.printStackTrace();
    }
  }

  public ResultSet viewBooks() {
    ResultSet rs = null;
    try {
      Statement stmt = conn.createStatement();
      rs = stmt.executeQuery
            ("SELECT Book.Title_ID, Book.Title, Book.Price," +
             "Category.Category_Description AS Category " +
             "FROM Book, Category " +
             "WHERE Book.Category_ID = Category.Category_ID " +
             "ORDER BY Category, Book.Price DESC;");

    } catch (Exception e) {
      e.printStackTrace();
    }
    return rs;
  }
}
```

2. From a command prompt, change to the Advanced\WEB-INF\classes directory and run the following command:

> **> javac com\wrox\library\ComplexQuery.java**

3. Then, save the following code as complexquery.jsp in the Advanced folder:

```jsp
<%@ page language="java"
    import="java.sql.*, java.io.*, java.util.*, com.wrox.library.*"
    errorPage="error.jsp" %>

<jsp:useBean id="book" class="com.wrox.library.ComplexQuery" />

<html>
  <head>
    <title> Wrox Press Ltd. </title>
  </head>

  <body>
    <h1> Wrox Press Ltd.</h1>
    <h2> List of Books </h2>

      <table border="1">
        <tr>
          <td><b>ID:</b></td>
          <td><b>Title:</b></td>
          <td><b>Price:</b></td>
          <td><b>Category:</b></td>
        </tr>

        <%
        book.connect();
        ResultSet rs = book.viewBooks();
        while (rs.next()) {
        %>

        <tr>
          <td><%= rs.getString("Title_ID") %></td>
          <td><%= rs.getString("Title") %></td>
          <td><%= rs.getString("Price") %></td>
          <td><%= rs.getString("Category") %></td>
        </tr>

        <%
          }
        %>

      </table><br />

    <% book.disconnect(); %>
  </body>
</html>
```

For more information on the use of `errorpage` see Chapter 8 (*When It All Goes Wrong*).

4. Now, let's create the error handling page which is used in `complexquery.jsp`. Save the following as `error.jsp` in the `Advanced` folder:

```
<%@ page language="java" isErrorPage="true"%>

<html>
  <head>
    <title>Error Page</title>
  </head>

  <body>
    <h2>An error has occurred.</h2>
    <h4>Error:</h4>
    <%= exception.toString() %><br />
  </body>
</html>
```

5. Restart Tomcat and navigate to http://localhost:8080/Advanced/complexquery.jsp, you should see something like this:

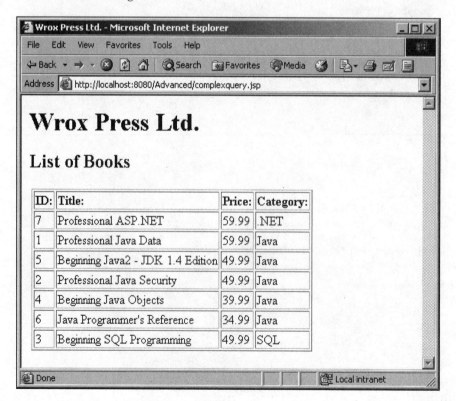

How It Works

The `ComplexQuery` class contains the functionality of this application.
It begins with a standard `package` declaration and imports:

```
package com.wrox.library;
import javax.naming.*;
import javax.sql.*;
import java.sql.*;
```

And a default constructor is declared, so that the class can be used as a JavaBean from within a
JSP page:

```
public ComplexQuery()    { }
```

Now we come to three methods that this class exposes. The first is `connect()`, which creates
the connection to the database. The connection is stored in the `conn` member so that it will be
available to other methods. Next, we have the `disconnect()` method, which closes an open
connection to the database. The `viewBooks()` method returns a `ResultSet` to the caller that
contains the results of a `SELECT` query on the `Book` table. All fields from the table are included
in the `ResultSet`:

```
public ResultSet viewBooks() {
  ResultSet rs = null;
  try {
    Statement stmt = conn.createStatement();
    rs = stmt.executeQuery
        ("SELECT Book.Title_ID, Book.Title, Book.Price," +
         "Category.Category_Description AS Category " +
         "FROM Book, Category " +
         "WHERE Book.Category_ID = Category.Category_ID " +
         "ORDER BY Category, Book.Price DESC;");
  } catch (Exception e) {
    e.printStackTrace();
  }
  return rs;
}
```

The `complexquery.jsp` page calls the `viewBooks()` method on a `ComplexQuery` object and
loops through each record in the `RecordSet` in turn.

Views, Indexes, and Subqueries

It's not feasible to give you full coverage of SQL syntax in the space of one chapter. However, some notable items are **views**, **indexes**, and **subqueries**.

❑   A **view** allows you to assign the results of a query to a new, "virtual" table that you can use in other queries and specify in FROM clauses just like any other table. Views can be used to restrict database access, as well as to simplify a complex query. MySQL does not currently support views, but if it did we could create and use a view Titles like this:

```
CREATE VIEW Titles AS SELECT Title FROM Book;
SELECT title FROM Titles;
```

❑   **Indexes** help the database store data in a way that allows for quicker searches and makes data access quicker. The index is a special data structure in the database that tells the DBMS where a certain row is in the table, given the value of an indexed column; this is much like the way a book index tells you what page a given word appears. Unfortunately, you sacrifice disk space and modification speed for the benefit of quicker searches.

The most efficient use of indexes is to create an index for columns on which you tend to search the most. To create an index for the title in the Book table the code would look like this:

```
CREATE INDEX TITLE_IDX ON Book (Title);
```

❑   **Subqueries** involve the use of operators to allow a WHERE condition to include the output from a second query (the **subquery**). The query below lists the buyers who purchased an expensive item (an item costing at least $50 more than the average price of all the items purchased):

```
SELECT Buyer_ID FROM Buyer
WHERE Price > (SELECT AVG(Price) + 50 FROM Book);
```

Deleting Tables, Indexes, and Databases

The DROP command is used when we want to delete tables, indexes, and even entire databases. To delete an index, we simply type:

```
DROP INDEX TITLE_IDX;
```

It's just as easy to get rid of a table, or a database:

```
DROP TABLE Author;
DROP DATABASE books;
```

SQL in Retrospect

We've seen a lot of SQL in the last section, particularly the SELECT statement. Using SQL you can search for data, enter new data, modify data, or delete data. SQL is simply the most fundamental tool you will need for your interaction with the database.

While we've seen a lot of use of the MySQL command-line interface, all of these SQL commands can equally well be called by a Java program using JDBC, and the Statement and ResultSet interfaces. Let's move back to the Java side, and look at more JDBC features.

More on JDBC

The **JDBC API** provides the basic functionality for data access and a standard way to access the latest object-relational features supported by today's RDBMSs. The new JDBC 3.0 specification builds on an already solid foundation by adding several new features that address a number of areas of missing functionality

JDBC 1.0 introduced with JDK 1.1 had minimal database functionality. JDK 1.2 delivered JDBC 2.0, which contained enhanced features like scrollable result sets, batch updates, BLOB and CLOB support, the ARRAY type, user defined types (UDTs), structured types, and distinct types. This was then followed by the development of the JDBC 2.0 Optional Package; a standard extension that provides the DataSource class (which uses JNDI to connect to any kind of data, such as flat files or spreadsheets), connection pooling, distributed transactions, and RowSets (a higher-level interface on top of ResultSet).

JDBC 3.0 contains the JDBC 2.0 classes and the JDBC Optional Package classes. That means the optional package is being merged into standard JDBC, making the Java platform more flexible and complete. The SQL99 standard has also been finalized, so JDBC 3.0 will attempt to be consistent with that standard. However, JDBC 3.0 will not support the whole SQL99 specification, but the features that are implemented will be consistent with the standard. If a database does not yet support the portions of SQL99 functionality that are supported by JDBC 3.0, the driver can use the metadata APIs to communicate to application developers that the underlying database does not support a subset of the JDBC functionality. This allows database vendors to produce compliant JDBC drivers even though they may not support all of the functionality. The addition of two new data types, as well as support for transactional savepoints, illustrates two of the SQL99-related changes. The JDBC 3.0 specification can be found at http://java.sun.com/products/jdbc/download.html.

JDBC 3.0 defines several standard connection pool properties. Developers are not expected to modify the properties directly with the API, but rather through their application server or data store instrumentation. By reducing the amount of vendor-specific configuration properties and replacing them with standardized properties, it becomes even easier for developers to swap in a different vendor's JDBC driver. The properties are shown in the table below.

Property name	Description
maxStatements	The number of statements that the connection pool should keep open.
initialPoolSize	The number of physical connections that the pool should create when it is initialized.
minPoolSize	The minimum number of physical connections that the pool should contain.
maxPoolSize	The maximum number of physical connections that the pool should contain. Zero specifies that there is no maximum size.
maxIdleTime	The duration, in seconds, that an unused physical connection should remain in the pool before the connection is closed. Zero specifies that there is no limit.
propertyCycle	The interval, in seconds, that the connection pool should wait before enforcing its property policy.

In addition to improved connection pool support, it is now possible to pool prepared statements. A prepared statement allows you to take a commonly used SQL statement and pre-compile it, thereby dramatically improving performance if the statement is executed multiple times. On the other hand, creating a PreparedStatement object introduces a certain amount of overhead, so, ideally, the statement's lifetime will be sufficiently long to compensate for this overhead. Performance-conscious developers sometimes contort their object models to increase the lifetime of a PreparedStatement object. JDBC 3.0 frees the developer from this concern because the data source layer is now responsible for caching prepared statements.

Perhaps the most exciting addition to JDBC 3.0 is the addition of savepoints. The transaction support in JDBC 2.0 gave developers control over concurrent access to their data, thereby ensuring that persisted data is always in a consistent state. Unfortunately, it is sometimes desirable to have finer-grained control over a transaction than simply rolling back every change in the current transaction. With JDBC 3.0 you are given that control with savepoints. The Savepoint interface allows you to partition a transaction into logical breakpoints, providing control over how much of the transaction gets rolled back. You probably won't need to use savepoints frequently. However, a general situation in which savepoints can be useful is when you have a set of changes, but cannot determine what subset of those changes must be kept until all of the results are known.

Now let us look again at some aspects of how an application uses JDBC as the interface through which it passes all its requests to the database.

Accessing the Database

We saw earlier in the chapter that a `Statement` object sends SQL statements to a database once a connection is established. There are in fact three kinds of `Statement` object in JDBC:

❑ `java.sql.Statement` – the most fundamental of the three JDBC interfaces representing SQL statements. It will run all of the basic SQL statements.

❑ `java.sql.PreparedStatement` – this interface extends `Statement` and enables our SQL statements to contain parameters, so we can execute a single statement repeatedly with different values for those parameters.

❑ `java.sql.CallableStatement` – this interface extends `PreparedStatement` to allow us to access **stored procedures** in our database. (These are a special way of embedding bits of program code in the database, for speed). Stored procedures are an advanced database concept and we won't be exploring them any further in this book.

The PreparedStatement Interface

The `PreparedStatement` interface extends `Statement`, and an instance of `PreparedStatement` contains a SQL statement that has already been compiled. The SQL statement contained in a `PreparedStatement` object may have one or more parameters, so that the application can dynamically assign values to it.

The value is not specified when the SQL statement is created. Instead, the statement has a question mark (?) as a placeholder for each parameter. An application must set a value for each parameter in a prepared statement before executing the statement. Execution of `PreparedStatement` objects is faster than that of `Statement` objects, so a `PreparedStatement` is often used when a particular SQL statement needs to be executed many times.

When creating a `Statement` we don't have to supply the actual SQL statement to be run; that's done when calling the `executeUpdate()`, `executeQuery()`, or `execute()` methods. With `PreparedStatement`, on the other hand, the SQL code must be supplied when the object is first created, by passing it to the `Connection.prepareStatement()` method. The statement-execution methods for a `PreparedStatement` don't require any parameters.

The following code fragment creates a `PreparedStatement` object containing a SQL UPDATE statement, with two placeholders for IN parameters:

```
PreparedStatement pstmt = con.prepareStatement
        ("UPDATE Book SET Price = ? WHERE Title = ?");
```

(Note that a `PreparedStatement` object can contain either a query or an update statement.)

Before we execute the `PreparedStatement` we must set an actual value for each of its parameters, represented in the SQL code by the `?` placeholder. This is done using a range of `setXXX()` methods which are analogous to the `getXXX()` methods we used earlier on the `ResultSet` interface.

For example, if the parameter is of type `float` the method to be used is `setFloat()`. This takes two parameters; the first is the **position** of the parameter within the statement. (Remember that there may be more than one parameter; the numbering starts at 1.) The second method parameter is the **value** to which the parameter is to be set. For example, the following code sets the first parameter to 123.45:

```
pstmt.setFloat(1, 123.45);
```

Each `setXXX()` method corresponds to a type in the Java language; it is the programmer's responsibility to make sure that this type maps to a JDBC type that is compatible with the data type expected by the database.

There are a few methods in the `setXXX()` category that need special mention. A programmer can explicitly convert an input parameter to a particular JDBC type by using the method `setObject()`. This method can take a third argument, which specifies the target JDBC type. The driver will convert the instance of `Object` to the specified JDBC type before sending it to the database. The `setNull()` method allows a programmer to send a SQL `NULL` value to the database.

The following code fragment demonstrates the advantage of the parameterized `PreparedStatement` object for populating the `Category` table of our database:

```
int id[] = {4,5,6};
String desc[] = {"XML", ".NET", "Oracle"};
String upd = "INSERT INTO Category VALUES(?,?);";

PreparedStatement ps = con.prepareStatement(upd);

for (int i=0; i < id.length; i++) {
  ps.setInt(1, id[i]);
  ps.setString(2, desc[i]);
  ps.executeUpdate();
```

Advanced ResultSet Use

Just like there are several types of statement in JDBC, there are also various different types of result sets. These may be classified into different types, based on their different capabilities:

❑   TYPE_FORWARD_ONLY – these result sets are non-scrollable, and their cursor can only move forward.

❑ TYPE_SCROLL_INSENSITIVE – the result set is scrollable, so its cursor can move forward or backward and can be moved to a particular row or to a row whose position is relative to its current position. The result set generally does *not* show changes to the underlying database that are made while the result set is open. The order and column values of rows are typically fixed when the result set is created.

❑ TYPE_SCROLL_SENSITIVE – the result set is scrollable; its cursor can move forward or backward, and can be moved to a particular row or to a row whose position is relative to its current position. The result set *is* sensitive to changes made while it is open, so if the underlying column values are modified the new values are visible in the ResultSet, thus providing a dynamic view of the underlying data.

Result sets can also have different **concurrency levels**:

❑ CONCUR_READ_ONLY – Indicates a result set that cannot be updated programmatically. This allows you to read data but not to change it.

❑ CONCUR_UPDATABLE – Indicates a result set that can be updated programmatically, with the changes being transferred to the underlying database.

With the JDBC 2.0 API, it is possible to create statements that will produce result sets that are scrollable and updateable. This is done by using new versions of the createStatement() and prepareStatement() methods that take additional parameters for specifying the type of result set and the concurrency level of the result set being created.

For example, the following code fragment creates a PreparedStatement object that will produce a ResultSet object that is scrollable and updateble:

```
PreparedStatement pstmt = con.prepareStatement
        ("SELECT Title_ID, Title, Price FROM Book WHERE Category_ID = ?",
        ResultSet.TYPE_SCROLL_SENSITIVE,
        ResultSet.CONCUR_UPDATABLE);
pstmt.setFetchSize(25);
pstmt.setInt(1, 6);
ResultSet rs = pstmt.executeQuery();
```

The ResultSet object rs will be scrollable, updateable, and sensitive to changes to its data. We also specified that the driver should fetch 25 rows at a time from the database.

Updatable ResultSets

We saw that a ResultSet object may be updated programmatically if its concurrency type is CONCUR_UPDATABLE. However, to be able to do this, the query should select the primary key, and should reference only a single table. The update*XXX*() methods make it possible to update values in a result set without using SQL commands. (As with the get*XXX*() and set*XXX*() methods we saw earlier, there is an update method for each data type.) This is because the updateable result set only constructs a hidden UPDATE for you, and if it does not know what the unique identifier for the row is, there is no way it can construct a valid update.

517

The update*XXX*() methods take two parameters, the first to indicate which column is to be updated, and the second to give the value to assign to the specified column. The column to be updated can be specified by giving either its name or its index; note that it is the column number in the result set, rather than that in the database table, that is used.

In the following code fragment, the value in the second column of the ResultSet object rs is retrieved using the method getInt(), and the method updateInt() is used to update that column value with an int value of 60:

```
int n = rs.getInt(2);
rs.updateInt(2, 60);
```

These update*XXX*() methods update a value in the current row of the result set, but they do not automatically update the value in the underlying database table. The method updateRow() is used to do this, and so it is very important that the updateRow() method should be called while the cursor is still on the current row (the row to be updated). You can explicitly cancel the updates to a row by calling the method cancelRowUpdates().

The JDBC 2.0 API provides the method deleteRow() to delete the current row from a ResultSet object; before calling deleteRow() you must position the cursor on the row you want to delete. Unlike the update*XXX*() methods, which affect only the data in the result set, this method affects both the result set data *and* the underlying row in the database.

The following two lines of code remove the first row of the ResultSet object rs *and* delete the underlying row from the database (which may or may not be the first row of the database table, depending on the SELECT statement used):

```
rs.first();
rs.deleteRow();
```

New rows may be inserted into a result set table, and into the underlying database table. For this purpose, the API defines the concept of an **insert row**. This is a special row used for building the row to be inserted, and to access it you call moveToInsertRow(), which positions the cursor on the insert row. Then you should call the appropriate update*XXX*() methods to add column values to the insert row.

When all of the columns of the row to be inserted have been set, you should call the insertRow() method. This method adds the inserted row to both the result set and the underlying database, simultaneously. The following code fragment demonstrates these steps for inserting a row:

```
rs.moveToInsertRow();
rs.updateInt(1, 60);
rs.updateString(2, "Book1");
rs.updateFloat(3, 49.99f);
rs.insertRow();
rs.moveToCurrentRow();
```

The call to `moveToCurrentRow()` returns you to the row you were on before you called `moveToInsertRow()`.

Transactions

Transactions are crucial for safe database programming. Often we will have a set of operations that must stand and fall together – the classic example is a transfer of funds between two bank accounts. We have two operations here: withdrawing the funds from one account, and crediting them to the other. If the first fails (perhaps because the account doesn't have sufficient funds) then we shouldn't proceed with the second; on the other hand, if the second fails (perhaps because there is a limit on the amount that account can hold) then the first operation should be undone so that money is not lost.

So, a transaction consists of one or more statements are to be executed as a single unit, and then either **committed** or **rolled back** by calling the connection's `commit()` or `rollback()` methods; the current transaction then ends.

A new `Connection` object is in **auto-commit** mode by default, which means that when a statement is completed the `commit()` method will be called on that statement automatically. In this case, a transaction consists of only one statement. If auto-commit mode has been disabled, a transaction will not terminate until the method `commit` or `rollback` is called explicitly, so it will include all the statements that have been executed since the last call of either `commit()` or `rollback()` is made. In this case, all the statements in the transaction are committed or rolled back as a group.

Transactions not only let us group work on data, but also help us to maintain the integrity of our data. Applications should apply the **ACID** transaction concept to make more robust use of transaction concepts. ACID is an acronym for **Atomicity**, **Consistency**, **Isolation**, and **Durability**:

❑   Atomicity – A transaction allows for the grouping of one or more changes to tables and rows in the database to form an atomic or indivisible operation. That is, either all of the changes occur or none of them do. If for any reason the transaction cannot be completed, it can be restored to the state it was in prior to the start of the transaction via a rollback operation.

❑   Consistency – Data can be said to be consistent as long as it conforms to a set of conditions, such as no two rows in the customer table having the same customer ID, or all orders have an associated customer row. While a transaction executes these invariants may be violated, but no other transaction will be allowed to see these inconsistencies, and all such inconsistencies will have been eliminated by the time the transaction ends.

❑   Isolation – A given transaction should be able to think that it is running all by itself on the database. The effects of other concurrent transactions should be invisible to this transaction, and the effects of this transaction should be invisible to others until the transaction is committed.

❑ Durability – Once a transaction is committed, its effects should be guaranteed to remain even in the event of subsequent system failures. Until the transaction commits, the changes made by that transaction are not durable, but are guaranteed not to persist in the face of a system failures, as crash recovery will rollback their effects.

Most JDBC drivers support transactions; the JDBC 2.0 Standard Extension API also makes it possible for a `Connection` to be part of a distributed transaction.

> **Distributed transactions are transactions that span two or more data sources. This becomes more relevant as businesses move towards an enterprise model, where different types of information of the same business is maintained in different databases and environments.**

Transaction Isolation Levels

There can be conflicts when two transactions are operating on a database at the same time, and we can specify a **transaction isolation level** to indicate how the conflict should be resolved. For example, when one transaction changes a value and a second transaction reads that value before the change has been committed or rolled back, the changed value read by the second transaction will be invalid if the first transaction is subsequently rolled back.

The transaction isolation levels in JDBC allow you to prevent three different types of problems:

❑ A **dirty read** is when a value is read before it has been committed.

❑ A **non-repeatable read** is prevents a situation where reading a row two times within a transaction gives different results since a second transaction has changed the database in the meantime.

❑ A **phantom read** occurs if a SELECT statement is performed twice within a transaction, but another transaction has updated the database in the meantime causing different data to match the WHERE clause.

The `Connection` interface defines five transaction isolation levels, summarized in this table:

Isolation level	Transactions supported?	Dirty reads?	Non-repeat. reads?	Phantom reads?
TRANSACTION_NONE	No	Yes	Yes	Yes
TRANSACTION_READ_ UNCOMMITTED	Yes	Yes	Yes	Yes
TRANSACTION_READ_ COMMITTED	Yes	No	Yes	Yes

Isolation level	Transactions supported?	Dirty reads?	Non-repeat. reads?	Phantom reads?
TRANSACTION_REPEATABLE_ READ	Yes	No	No	Yes
TRANSACTION_SERIALIZABLE	Yes	No	No	No

As you can see, as we move down the table, the number of possible data consistency problems that are prevented is reduced; however, this may well be at the expense of performance as concurrent transactions have to queue for access to database resources.

> The transaction isolation level that can actually be supported depends on the capabilities of the underlying DBMS.

When a new `Connection` object is created its transaction isolation level depends on the driver, but normally it is the default for the underlying data source. You can call the method `setTransactionIsolation()` to change the transaction isolation level, passing it one of the constants mentioned above, and the new level will be in effect for the rest of the connection session.

Transaction Support in MySQL

Old versions of MySQL did not support transactions, but the latest versions do so by supporting additional table types (`BDB`, `InnoDB`, and `GEMINI`) which in turn support transactions. To create a table in the InnoDB format you must specify `TYPE = InnoDB` in the `CREATE TABLE` statement, for example:

```
mysql> CREATE TABLE CUSTOMER (A INT, B CHAR (20)) TYPE = InnoDB;
Query OK, 0 rows affected (0.71 sec)
```

> You also need to be running the "MySQL Max" version of the database, rather than the "normal" version, if you want to use InnoDB tables.

When a connection is created, it is in auto-commit mode; as we saw earlier, this means that each individual SQL statement is treated as a transaction and will be automatically committed right after it is executed. The way to allow two or more statements to be grouped into a transaction is to disable auto-commit mode:

```
con.setAutoCommit(false);
```

Once auto-commit mode is disabled, no SQL statements will be committed until you call the method commit() explicitly. All statements executed after the previous call to the method commit will be included in the current transaction and will be committed together as a unit. The following code snippet, in which con is an active connection, illustrates a transaction:

```
con.setAutoCommit(false);

PreparedStatement updateSales = con.prepareStatement
        ("UPDATE Book SET SALES = ? WHERE Title LIKE ?");
updateSales.setInt(1, 50);
updateSales.setString(2, "Beginning JSP Web Development");
updateSales.executeUpdate();

PreparedStatement updateInvoice = con.prepareStatement(
    "UPDATE Bill SET Amount = ? WHERE Title LIKE ?");
updateTotal.setInt(1, 2500);
updateTotal.setString(2, "Beginning JSP Web Development");
updateTotal.executeUpdate();

con.commit();
con.setAutoCommit(true);
```

In this example, auto-commit mode is disabled for the connection con, which means that the two prepared statements updateSales and updateBill will be committed together when the method commit() is called. Whenever the commit() method is called (either automatically when auto-commit mode is enabled or explicitly when it is disabled), all changes resulting from statements in the transaction are made permanent.

The final line of this example enables auto-commit mode, so that each statement will once again be committed automatically when it is completed. You will then be back to the default state where you do not have to call commit() yourself. It is advisable to disable auto-commit mode only while you want to be in transaction mode. This way, you avoid holding database locks for multiple statements, which increases the likelihood of conflicts with other users.

Calling the method rollback() aborts a transaction and returns any values that were modified to their previous values. If you are trying to execute one or more statements in a transaction and get an SQLException, you should call the method rollback() to abort the transaction.

Batch Updates

The JDBC 2.0 core API provides a batch update facility, which allows a Statement to submit multiple update commands together as a single unit, to improve performance over performing several such commands one at a time. The following code fragment demonstrates how to send a batch update to a database:

```
con.setAutoCommit(false);
Statement stmt = con.createStatement();
```

```
stmt.addBatch(
  "INSERT INTO Order VALUES ('Beginning JSP Web Development', 49.99)");
stmt.addBatch(
  "INSERT INTO Stock VALUES ('Beginning JSP Web Development', 'C100', 60)");
int[] updateCounts = stmt.executeBatch();
```

In this example, a new row is inserted into two different tables, Order and Stock. We start by disabling the Connection's auto-commit mode in order to allow multiple statements to be sent together as one transaction. After creating the Statement object we adds two SQL INSERT commands to the batch with the addBatch() method, then sends the batch of updates to the database with the executeBatch() method.

Because the connection's auto-commit mode is disabled, the application is free to decide whether or not to commit the transaction if an error occurs or if some of the commands in the batch fail to execute. For example, the application may decide not to commit the changes if any of the insertions fail, thereby avoiding the situation where the Stock table is updated without the Order table being updated.

The PreparedStatement interface has its own version of the addBatch() method, which adds a set of parameters to the batch, as shown in the following code fragment:

```
PreparedStatement pstmt = con.prepareStatement(
        "UPDATE Book SET Price = ? WHERE Title = ?");

pstmt.setString(1, "Book 1");
pstmt.setFloat(2, 55.99f);
pstmt.addBatch();

pstmt.setString(1, "Book 2");
pstmt.setFloat(2, 45.99f);
pstmt.addBatch();

int[] updateCounts = pstmt.executeBatch();
```

When we call the PreparedStatement's executeBatch() method it will execute the UPDATE statement twice, once with each set of parameters that we specified.

Database Access and JSP

To round up our discussion of JDBC, we will see how it can be employed in a JSP web application. We will implement a JavaBean to connect and interact with our Books database. First of all, let's place the functionality for connecting and interacting with a database into a JavaBean that we can then use from within a JSP page.

1. Open your editor and save the following as `Books.java` in `begjsp-ch16\WEB-INF\classes\com\wrox\databases` folder:

```java
package com.wrox.library;
import javax.naming.*;
import javax.sql.*;
import java.sql.*;
import java.util.*;

public class Books {
  Connection conn;
  String error;
  public Books() { }
  public void connect() {
    try {
      Context ctx = new InitialContext();
      if(ctx == null )
        throw new Exception("Oops - No Context");

      DataSource ds = (DataSource)ctx.lookup("java:comp/env/jdbc/BooksDB");

      if (ds != null)
        conn = ds.getConnection();
    } catch(Exception e) {
      e.printStackTrace();
    }
  }

  public void disconnect() {
    try {
      if ( conn != null ) {
        conn.close();
      }
    } catch (Exception e) {
      e.printStackTrace();
    }
  }

  public ResultSet viewBooks() {
    ResultSet rs = null;
    try {
      Statement stmt = conn.createStatement();
      rs = stmt.executeQuery
          ("SELECT Book.Title_ID, Book.Title, Book.Price," +
           "Category.Category_Description AS Category " +
           "FROM Book, Category " +
           "WHERE Book.Category_ID = Category.Category_ID " +
           "ORDER BY Category, Book.Price DESC;");
```

```
      } catch (Exception e) {
        e.printStackTrace();
      }
      return rs;
  }

  public void addBooks(int id, String title, float price, int cid)
              throws SQLException, Exception {
    if (conn != null) {
      try {
        PreparedStatement updatebooks;
        updatebooks = conn.prepareStatement(
            "insert into Book values(?, ?, ?, ?);");
        updatebooks.setInt(1, id);
        updatebooks.setString(2, title);
        updatebooks.setFloat(3, price);
        updatebooks.setInt(4, cid);
        updatebooks.executeUpdate();
      } catch (SQLException sqle) {
        error = "SQLException: update failed, possible duplicate entry";
        throw new SQLException(error);
      }
    } else {
      error = "Exception: Connection to database was lost.";
      throw new Exception(error);
    }
  }

  public void removeBooks(String [] pkeys) throws SQLException, Exception {
    if (conn != null) {
      try {
        PreparedStatement delete;
        delete = conn.prepareStatement("DELETE FROM Book WHERE Title_ID=?;");
        for (int i = 0; i < pkeys.length; i++) {
          delete.setInt(1, Integer.parseInt(pkeys[i]));
          delete.executeUpdate();
        }
      } catch (SQLException sqle) {
        error = "SQLException: update failed, possible duplicate entry";
        throw new SQLException(error);
      } catch (Exception e) {
        error = "An exception occured while deleting books.";
        throw new Exception(error);
      }
    } else {
      error = "Exception: Connection to database was lost.";
      throw new Exception(error);
    }
  }

}
```

2. Open a command prompt, change to the `Advanced\WEB-INF\classes` directory and run the following command:

```
> javac com\wrox\library\Books.java
```

3. Then, save the following code as `booklist.jsp` in the `Advanced` folder:

```jsp
<%@ page language="java"
    import="java.sql.*, java.io.*, java.util.*, com.wrox.library.*"
    errorPage="error.jsp" %>

<jsp:useBean id="book" class="com.wrox.library.Books" />

<html>
  <head>
    <title> Wrox Press Ltd. </title>
  </head>

  <body>
    <h1> Wrox Press Ltd.</h1>
    <h2> List of Books </h2>

    <a href="newbook.jsp"><b>Add More Books</b></a>

    <form action="delete.jsp" method="post">
      <table border="1">
        <tr>
          <td><b>ID:</b></td>
          <td><b>Title:</b></td>
          <td><b>Price:</b></td>
        </tr>

        <%
          book.connect();
          ResultSet rs = book.viewBooks();
          while (rs.next()) {
        %>

        <tr>
          <td>
            <input type="checkbox" name="pkey"
                   value="<%= rs.getString("Title_ID") %>" />
          </td>
          <td><%= rs.getString("Title") %></td>
          <td><%= rs.getString("Price") %></td>
        </tr>

        <%
          }
        %>
```

```
    </table><br />

    Check books for deletion.<br/>
    <input type="submit" value="Delete All Checked Books">
  </form>

  <% book.disconnect(); %>
  </body>
</html>
```

4. Now, let's reuse our error handling page from the previous example.

5. Enter the following code in a file called `newbook.jsp`, again in the `Advanced` folder:

```html
<html>
  <head>
    <title>Add a new book.</title>
  </head>

  <body>
    <h1> Add a new book.</h1>
    <form action="add.jsp" method="POST">
      <table>
        <tr>
          <td align="RIGHT">ID:</td>
          <td><input type="text" name="Title_ID" size="5" /></td>
        </tr>

        <tr>
          <td align="RIGHT">Title:</td>
          <td> <input type="text" name="Title" size="30" /></td>
        </tr>

        <tr>
          <td align="RIGHT">Price:</td>
          <td> <input type="text" name="Price" size="10" /></td>
        </tr>

        <tr>
          <td>Category ID:</td>
          <td> <input type="text" name="Category_ID" size="5" /></td>
        </tr>

      </table><br />

      <input type="submit" value="Add to book list" />

    </form>
```

```
    </body>
</html>
```

6. Now, enter the following and save it as `add.jsp` in the `Advanced` folder:

```
<%@ page language="java"
    import="java.sql.*, java.io.*, java.util.*, com.wrox.library.*"
    errorPage="error.jsp" %>

<jsp:useBean id="book" class="com.wrox.library.Books"/>

<html>
  <head>
    <title>Add Books</title>
  </head>

  <body>

    <%
      int id = Integer.parseInt(request.getParameter("Title_ID"));
      String title =  request.getParameter("Title");
      float price =  Float.parseFloat(request.getParameter("Price"));
      int cid = Integer.parseInt(request.getParameter("Category_ID"));
      book.connect();
      book.addBooks(id, title, price, cid);
      book.disconnect();
    %>

    The new book has been added. <br />
    Click <a href="booklist.jsp">Here</a> To Go Back.

  </body>
</html>
```

7. Finally, save the following code as `delete.jsp`, also in the `Advanced` folder:

```
<%@ page language="java"
    import="java.sql.*, java.io.*, java.util.*, com.wrox.library.*"
    errorPage="error.jsp" %>

<jsp:useBean id="book" class="com.wrox.library.Books"/>

<html>
  <head>
    <title>Delete Books</title>
  </head>

  <body>
```

```
<%
    String [] kys = request.getParameterValues("pkey");
    book.connect();
    book.removeBooks(kys);
    book.disconnect();
%>

    The marked books have been deleted. <br />
    Click <a href="booklist.jsp">Here</a> To Go Back.

  </body>
</html>
```

8. Start up Tomcat and navigate to http://localhost:8080/Advanced/booklist.jsp. You should see something like this:

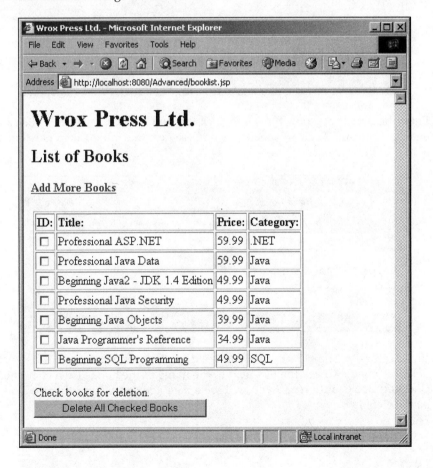

9. If you click on the Add More Books link, you will see the following page:

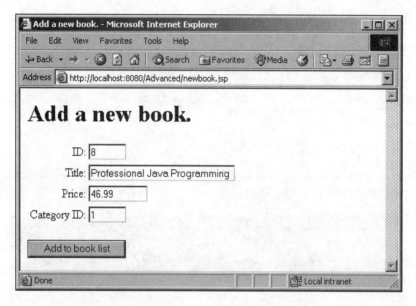

10. Enter the details of a new book and click the Add to book list button. (Be careful not to enter a duplicate ID.) You should see a message confirming that a new book has been added to the database:

11. If you return to `booklist.jsp` you will find that your new book is listed. Now try deleting a book. Check the box next to the name of the book. Then click the Delete All Checked Books button and you will see a message confirming that the book has been deleted:

12. Go back to `booklist.jsp` to see for yourself that the book is no longer listed.

How It Works

The `Book` class contains the functionality of this application; it is responsible for making the connection to the database, retrieving, updating, and deleting records. This works in a similar way to our previous example except now we have two additional methods that this class exposes. The `addBooks()` method is used to add a book to the `Book` table. It takes the ID, title, price and category ID as arguments, creates a statement to insert the new record into the table and executes it.

```
public void addBooks(int id, String title, float price, int cid)
            throws SQLException, Exception {
  if (con != null) {
    try {
      PreparedStatement updatebooks;
      updatebooks = con.prepareStatement(
          "insert into Book values(?, ?, ?, ?);");
      updatebooks.setInt(1, id);
      updatebooks.setString(2, title);
      updatebooks.setFloat(3, price);
      updatebooks.setInt(4, cid);
      updatebooks.execute();
    } catch (SQLException sqle) {
      error = "SQLException: update failed, possible duplicate entry";
      throw new SQLException(error);
    }
  } else {
    error = "Exception: Connection to database was lost.";
    throw new Exception(error);
  }
}
```

The removeBooks() method removes one or more records from the table. It takes an array of String objects as its argument. This is an array of the ID field of the Book table and for each key in turn, a matching record is deleted:

```java
public void removeBooks(String [] pkeys) throws SQLException, Exception {
  if (con != null) {
    try {
      PreparedStatement delete;
      delete = con.prepareStatement("DELETE FROM Book WHERE Title_ID=?;");
      for (int i = 0; i < pkeys.length; i++) {
        delete.setInt(1, Integer.parseInt(pkeys[i]));
        delete.execute();
      }
    } catch (SQLException sqle) {
      error = "SQLException: update failed, possible duplicate entry";
      throw new SQLException(error);
    } catch (Exception e) {
      error = "An exception occured while deleting books.";
      throw new Exception(error);
    }
  } else {
    error = "Exception: Connection to database was lost.";
    throw new Exception(error);
  }
}
```

The JSP pages booklist.jsp, add.jsp, and delete.jsp use the Book class to display a list of all books, create a new book, add a new book, and delete one or more books from the database, by calling the respective method on Book.

booklist.jsp calls the viewBooks() method on a Books object and loops through each record in the RecordSet in turn:

```jsp
<%
  book.connect();
  ResultSet rs = book.viewBooks();
  while (rs.next()) {
%>

<tr>
  <td>
    <input type="checkbox" name="pkey"
```

The value of the Title_ID column is used to set the value of the checkbox:

```jsp
      value="<%= rs.getString("Title_ID") %>" />
  </td>
```

And the values of the `Title` and `Price` columns are included in the HTML.

```
        <td><%= rs.getString("Title") %></td>
        <td><%= rs.getString("Price") %></td>
     </tr>

     <%
       }
     %>
```

If the **Add new book** link is followed from the `booklist.jsp` page, we are sent to a page to fill in the details of a new book. When the form on this page is submitted the details are sent to the `add.jsp` file. The request parameters are passed to the `addBooks()` method, which as we saw earlier will insert a new record into the database.

```
     <%
        int id = Integer.parseInt(request.getParameter("Title_ID"));
        String title =  request.getParameter("Title");
        float price =  Float.parseFloat(request.getParameter("Price"));
        int cid = Integer.parseInt(request.getParameter("Category_ID"));
        book.connect();
        book.addBooks(id, title, price, cid);
        book.disconnect();
     %>
```

If one or more books are selected in `booklist.jsp` and the **Delete All Checked Books** button is clicked we are sent to `delete.jsp`. This page extracts the ID of each book that has been selected for deletion and calls the `delete()` method to remove them from the database:

```
     <%
        String [] kys = request.getParameterValues("pkey");
        book.connect();
        book.removeBooks(kys);
        book.disconnect();
     %>
```

Summary

In this chapter we covered most of the aspects of the JDBC API in depth, and various areas of the SQL language, and provided practical examples of its use in database programming. We learned:

❑   How to use the SQL SELECT statement to query the database.

❑   How to use Statement objects to perform queries from Java code, and how the ResultSet interface makes the query data available to us.

❑ We also covered advanced JDBC topics including connection pooling, `PreparedStatement`, transactions, and batch updates.

Finally we went through how to make a JSP page talk to a database by employing JavaBeans.

Why Not Try?

1. Create a site for storing and retrieving Internet bookmarks instead of having them in a browser. With this you can access them from any web browser.

2. Write an application to dynamically generate a bar chart from a database query to display the area-wise sales information of a Company X.

3. Develop a web service somewhat like a news wire, where some people are authorized to post news items and another group of people can just read it. Everything can be sorted by date and possibly by category.

4. Personalize the above news wire service by providing options for choosing a color scheme and layout, and eliminating articles and sections that are not of interest.

CHAPTER 14

JSP and XML

X (*Extensible*) M (*Markup*) L (*Language*) has become the de facto standard for data interchange on the Internet these days. It has revolutionized the way the web works by defining a standard for electronic exchange of information. It has done the same thing for data that Java did for code: it has made it portable.

What is XML and why is it important to us? We will try and answer these and other questions you may have in this chapter, and have a quick look at how we can use XML in our JSP applications.

Introduction to XML

Before we delve deeper into the guts of XML, let us examine the acronym XML itself. X, for Extensible, means the language can be extended to meet various requirements. ML, for Markup Language, means it is a language for identifying structures within a document.

XML is extensible because it is not a fixed language. It can be extended to create our own languages in order to match our particular needs. In a way, XML is not really a language in itself, rather it is a standard for defining other languages to fit various computing scenarios, typically in the business or academic spheres.

A markup language is used to add meaning to different parts of a document. HTML is another type of markup language. Its tags give particular meaning to parts of a document. For instance, the `<table>` tag **marks up** a section as representing a table.

To clarify things further, let us look at some XML documents. We've already seen the `web.xml` file in previous chapters. Let's look at the one from Chapter 3:

```
<?xml version="1.0" encoding="ISO-8859-1"?>

<!DOCTYPE web-app
    PUBLIC "-//Sun Microsystems, Inc.//DTD Web Application 2.3//EN"
    "http://java.sun.com/dtd/web-app_2_3.dtd">

<web-app>
</web-app>
```

Another XML file type we're acquainted with is the tag library descriptor, such as this one, `exampleTags.tld`, from Chapter 9:

```
<?xml version="1.0" encoding="ISO-8859-1"?>
<taglib xmlns="http://java.sun.com/xml/ns/j2ee"
        xmlns:xsi="http://www.w3.org/2001/XMLSchema-instance"
        version="2.0">
  <tlib-version>1.0</tlib-version>
  <jsp-version>2.0</jsp-version>
  <short-name>ExampleTags</short-name>
  <description>A set of example tag handlers.</description>
  <tag>
     <name>time</name>
     <tag-class>custom.timeTag</tag-class>
  </tag>
</taglib>
```

In many ways, XML is similar to HTML. Both these markup languages use `tags` to enclose items with particular meaning – these tags are enclosed within angle brackets, as in `<table>`, `<web-app>`, `<taglib>`, and so on. Also, there will be a corresponding closing tag that has the same name, but starts with `</`. These closing tags mark the end of the item referred to by the tag, and in XML, the whole section including the start tag and the end tag is known as an **element**. Note that although many HTML elements do not require a closing tag (such as `<p>` and `<br>`), XML elements must always have a start and an end tag. Both HTML and XML allow elements to be contained, or **nested**, within each other as you can see from the examples above (the `<tlib-version>` element is nested within the `<taglib>` element as it appears after the `<taglib>` start tag and before the `</taglib>` end tag). However, XML is much more strict than HTML in this regard, as it does not allow elements to overlap (that is, if an element's start tag appears after another's start tag, the nested element's end tag must appear before the other's end tag).

There are many other ways in which XML is quite different to HTML. XML is not limited to a preexisting set of tags, like HTML is, and while HTML is primarily concerned with describing how a document should be laid out in a browser, XML documents are more concerned with describing the meaning of data contained in a document and they are generally quite independent of how that data may be rendered for display.

Notice that although the later file uses the extension `.tld` and not `.xml`, it is still a valid XML file, because it obeys the rules that XML documents must adhere to. We'll cover these rules in detail shortly.

Both these documents use an XML language, often called an **XML dialect**, to give meaning to the data they contain. The actual mark-up tags (or XML **elements**) each uses are different though. For instance, `web.xml` starts with the `<web-app>` element, while the first element in `exampleTags.tld` is `<taglib>`.

The Structure of XML Data

XML is a vendor-neutral standard, regulated by the **World Wide Web Consortium**, or **W3C** (www.w3c.org). Their specification can be found at http://www.w3c.org/TR/WD-xml, and contains the formal details of XML syntax. We'll cover the essentials here, starting with a look at a very simple XML document:

```
<?xml version="1.0"?>
<!DOCTYPE Book SYSTEM "book.dtd">
<Book>
  <Author-Name>
    <Last>
       Einstein
    </Last>

    <First>
      Albert
    </First>
  </Author-Name>

  <Book-Name>
    General Relativity
  </Book-Name>

  <Edition Year="1930"/>
  <Bestseller/>
</Book>
```

XML documents are composed of data, enclosed within tags that describe that data. There may also be **processing instructions**, which are used to provide specific details required for an application that will read the XML document, and other elements, such as the `xml` declaration or a DTD declaration as seen here.

Note that the `xml` declaration starts with `<?` and ends with `?>`, and doesn't require a closing tag. This notation is also used for processing instructions, but despite the common misconception, the `xml` declaration is not strictly speaking a processing instruction. The `xml` declaration may also specify `encoding` and `standalone` attributes, which specify the character encoding used by the document, and whether or not the document depends on any others:

```
<?xml version="1.0" encoding="ISO-8859-1" standalone="yes"?>
```

The DTD declaration, which starts with < ! and ends with > and also doesn't require a closing tag, specifies what the name of the first element in the file must be (which here is `Book`) and also specifies where to find the **Document Type Definition** (DTD) file that details rules that XML elements in this particular dialect must obey. The `SYSTEM` part indicates that the DTD can be found at either a relative or an absolute URL. If however, the DTD is officially sanctioned by a standards body, we would use `PUBLIC` instead. You can see this in `web.xml` files that have a DTD declaration rather than the XML Schema shown above.

Note that DTDs are falling out of favor now, and the more recent XML Schema standard is often preferred, as it lets us specify more rigorous rules for an XML dialect. However, DTDs are still used in many companies, partly because of legacy issues, and also because DTDs are somewhat easier to create. We will cover this issue further in the section *Well Formed vs. Valid Documents*.

XML Element Syntax

The actual content of an XML document (that is, the data and XML elements it contains) must obey certain syntax rules as we have hinted at already. We've already mentioned the first element in a document, and this element is known as the **root element**, as all other elements must be contained within it. That is to say, all valid XML documents must have one and only one root element. In the XML file shown above, our root element is `<Book>`.

All XML elements can contain other XML elements and/or text data as required – such contained elements are known as **child elements** of the containing element. For instance, the `<Author-Name>` element above has child elements `<Last>` and `<First>`.

If an element has neither child elements nor text data, that is they could be written as:

```
<Bestseller>
</Bestseller>
```

then we can use a shorthand form of:

```
<Bestseller/>
```

Element names can be almost anything you like as long as they start with either a letter or an underscore and do not contain whitespace (such as return characters or spaces). Be aware that XML element names *are* case sensitive. As stated previously, all XML elements must have both a start tag and an end tag, unless they use the short form shown above (`<Bestseller/>`). As we've also said already, XML elements may not overlap. Look at the two examples below of invalid nesting and valid nesting:

Invalid Nesting	**Valid Nesting**

`<Book>`
  `<Author>`
  `</Book>`
`</Author>`
	`<Book>`
	  `<Author>`
	  `</Author>`
	`</Book>`

As the `<Book>` element is the first to be opened, it should be the last to be closed. In the invalid example, its closing element appears before `</Author>` and is therefore wrong.

XML documents that satisfy these rules are known as **well-formed** documents.

Attributes

Attributes of an element are listed in the elements start tag, and give further meaning to that element. Consider the `<Edition>` element from our example:

```
<Edition Year="1930"/>
```

Its `Year` attribute has the value `1930`. Attributes follow the same rule for names as elements and must have their value between quotes. Only one attribute of the same name may be given for an element.

Comments

To improve the readability of our XML documents, we can place comments within them using the same syntax as used in HTML files: we place them between `<!--` and `-->` sequences. Well placed comments can be invaluable when others try to read your XML files (or even when you read them a while after writing them!). As in all programming contexts, prudent use of comments is a very good habit to get into. Note that comments do not form part of the actual content of an XML document, and may be ignored when the document is read, so we should avoid the use of code that depends on them.

Entity References

There are cases when the data in an XML document needs to contain characters that normally have a special purpose, such as the less-than symbol < or the apostrophe '. We can represent these using **entity references**, just as we would in HTML.

An entity reference uses the syntax `&entityname;` XML requires a total of 5 entity references:

Entity Reference	Character	Notes
`&lt;`	<	lt stands for *less than*.
`&gt;`	>	gt stands for *greater than*. Only required in attribute values.
`&amp;`	&	The ampersand sign.
`&quot;`	"	Double quotes.
`&apos;`	'	A single quote – the apostrophe.

So, if we had a book with the title *Learn HTML from < to >*, we could describe it by the following XML element:

```
<Book>
  <BookName>
    Learn HTML from &lt; to >
  </BookName>
</Book>
```

We don't need to use > for the > character because when this character appears in text data, it is clear that it does not mark the end of a tag.

CDATA (Character DATA) Sections

Entity references let us use characters that normally have a reserved meaning, but would not be a great solution if our text data contains many instances of such characters.

The better solution is to place such data inside a section called a **CDATA section**. These sections begin with the sequence <![CDATA[and end with]]>. Text within such sections can contain any characters at all, and their content is preserved as it appears, including any whitespace. Say we had an XML element that contained programming code like so:

```
<Code>
for(int i = 0; i < 10; i++)
{
  if(i < 5) System.err.println("I would rather be fishing.");
  if(i == 5)System.err.println("I would rather be at my PlayStation.");
  if(i > 5) System.err.println("I would rather be at DreamWorld.");
}
</Code>
```

As you can see, this code contains a lot of special characters and it is formatted in a way we may wish to keep. Thus, it would probably be a good idea to put the whole section in a CDATA section as shown below:

```
<Code>
<![CDATA[
for(int i = 0; i < 10; i++)
{
  if(i < 5) System.err.println("I would rather be fishing.");
  if(i == 5)System.err.println("I would rather be at my PlayStation.");
  if(i > 5) System.err.println("I would rather be at DreamWorld.");
}
]]>
</Code>
```

Well Formed vs. Valid Documents

As mentioned before, XML documents follow a set of rules which dictate how an XML document must be structured. XML documents that satisfy these rules are said to be **well formed**. This is not to be confused with the similar concept of validity. A **valid** XML document conforms to the rules specified in the corresponding DTD or Schema for that dialect. The DTD (or XML Schema) details rules that documents in a particular XML dialect must obey. They specify which elements are defined by that dialect, and the attributes that particular elements can have.

Thus, while we can say that our previous example file, book.xml, is well formed because it satisfies the rules of XML, we cannot say just by looking at it whether or not it is valid. To do that, we'd need to see the DTD that it specifies, namely book.dtd. Let's see that DTD file now:

```
<!ELEMENT Book     (Author-Name+, Book-Name, Edition?, Bestseller?) >
<!ELEMENT Author-Name  (Last, First, Middle?) >
<!ELEMENT Last        (#PCDATA) >
<!ELEMENT First       (#PCDATA) >
<!ELEMENT Book-Name (#PCDATA) >
<!ELEMENT Edition EMPTY>
<!ATTLIST Edition
          Year   CDATA  #REQUIRED>
<!ELEMENT Bestseller EMPTY>
```

The first thing to notice is that all items of a DTD start with < ! and end with >. Items define either elements or attributes.

Elements

The < ! ELEMENT> item describes an element that may appear in XML documents that conform to this DTD:

```
<!ELEMENT Book    (Author-Name+, Book-Name, Edition?, Bestseller?) >
```

This line describes an XML element called Book, and states that the <Book> element can have the child elements named in the comma-separated list in parenthesis. The order in which these elements are listed in the brackets corresponds to the order that these elements must appear in XML documents. If the order doesn't matter, we can list the elements using just a space rather than a comma to separate them:

```
<!ELEMENT Book    (Author-Name+ Book-Name Edition? Bestseller?) >
```

The + and ? characters indicate how many times the preceding element may occur, according to the following table:

Symbol	Meaning
,	Strict ordering: elements must be in the specified order
+	1 or more
*	0 or more
?	Optional (0 or 1)

So our DTD states that the `<Author-Name>` element may appear 1 or more times, the `<Edition>` element is optional, and so on. If no symbol is present, that element may only appear once, as is the case with the `<Book-Name>` element.

The `<Last>` element is given the following rule:

```
<!ELEMENT Last        (#PCDATA) >
```

This simply means that this element must contain text data only, as indeed it does in our `book.xml` file:

```
    <Last>
        Einstein
    </Last>
```

The final element to look at is:

```
<!ELEMENT BestSeller EMPTY>
```

`EMPTY` indicates that the `<Bestseller>` element must always be empty and not contain any textual data or other nested tags. In other words, it must be either:

```
<Bestseller/>
```

or:

```
<Bestseller></Bestseller>
```

Attributes

The only remaining item in our DTD we've not discussed is that for the `<Edition>` element. There are in fact two DTD items that relate to this element:

```
<!ELEMENT Edition EMPTY>
<!ATTLIST Edition
        Year    CDATA   #REQUIRED>
```

These two rules state that the `<Edition>` element may not contain any text data or child elements, and that it has an attribute called `Year`. This attribute is required, and it is of the type CDATA (character data). Simply omit the `#REQUIRED` keyword if the attribute is not required.

An XML element may have multiple attributes, and a DTD can restrict each attribute to one of a given set of values, and it can also specify one as a default like this:

```
<!ATTLIST Edition
          Year CDATA #REQUIRED
          Month (Jan | Feb | Mar) 'Jan'>
```

This would add a second attribute to the `<Edition>` element that may have a value of `Jan`, `Feb` or `Mar`, and the default value is `Jan` if the attribute is not specified.

That just about wraps it up for DTDs. We'll now look at XML Schemas, which are rapidly gaining ground over DTDs.

Defining Validity with Schemas

Before we delve into the world of XML schemas, we need to understand the concept of **XML namespaces**.

XML Namespaces

Namespaces are a concept that crops up in other areas of programming as well as XML. In general, namespaces serve two basic purposes:

1. To group related information under one umbrella

2. To avoid name collision between different groups

Namespaces in XML also serve these purposes, by associating elements that belong together with a unique identifier. The unique identifier is a URI, and as these can be quite long and unwieldy, a shorthand form is almost always associated with a namespace. Elements that belong to that namespace are then prefixed by the short form, differentiating them from other elements with the same name but belonging to a different namespace. For instance, our XML file has an element called `<Last>` that contains an author's last name. This same element could quite easily be used in another XML dialect, perhaps one that describes the results of a book awards ceremony. This other dialect's `<Last>` element would probably have a quite different meaning, and by having a unique namespace for each dialect, we can quite easily have an XML document that contains both types of element without ambiguity.

We specify the namespace used through the `xmlns` attribute of the root element of an XML document like this:

```
<Book xmlns="http://www.wrox.com/bookCatalog"
      xmlns:prize="http://www.wrox.com/bookAwards">
```

The unique identifier for these namespaces is given by the value of the xmlns attribute in question, and the short prefix for that namespace is the part preceded by the colon (:).

You can see that the first namespace does not have any prefix – it is called the default namespace, and any elements that do not have a prefix are assumed to belong to it. The second namespace has a prefix of prize. Our XML document can then contain an element such as this without any ambiguity between the two types of <Last> element:

```
<Book-Name>
  <First>
    Joey
  </First>
  <Last>
    Gillespie
  </Last>
  <prize:Awards>
    <prize:Last/>
  </prize:Awards>
</Book-Name>
```

XML Schemas

Schemas do the same thing as DTDs, but they overcome many of the shortcomings that DTDs exhibit when applied to XML. Many of their advantages actually stem from the fact that they are themselves written in an XML dialect.

When elements in an XML document must conform to a certain schema, we specify where a copy of the appropriate schema can be found using the schemaLocation attribute on the document's root element. This attribute is defined by the **schema instance namespace**, which we must therefore declare using an xmlns attribute, typically with the prefix xsi:

```
<Book xmlns:xsi="http://www.w3.org/2001/XMLSchema-instance"
      xsi:schemaLocation="Book.xsd">
```

Note the file extension of .xsd for the schema file (standing for XML Schema Definition).

Below is this Book.xsd file, equivalent to the DTD that we've already seen:

```
<?xml version="1.0"?>
<xs:schema xmlns:xs="http://www.w3.org/2001/XMLSchema">
  <xs:element name="Book">
    <xs:complexType>
      <xs:sequence>
```

```
            <xs:element name="Author-Name">
              <xs:complexType>
                <xs:element name="Last" type="xs:string"/>
                <xs:element name="First" type="xs:string"/>
              </xs:complexType>
            </xs:element>
            <xs:element name="Book-Name" type="xs:string"/>
            <xs:element name="Edition">
              <xs:complexType>
                <xs:attribute name="Year" type="xs:string" use="required"/>
              </xs:complexType>
            </xs:element>
            <xs:element name="Bestseller" />
          </xs:sequence>
        </xs:complexType>
      </xs:element>
    </xs:schema>
```

The first thing to spot is the first line of this schema:

```
<?xml version="1.0"?>
```

This should not be surprising. It is, as we said before, an XML document. After this comes the `<schema>` root element, which defines the xs namespace.

The Root Element

The `<schema>` element is the root element of every XML Schema. Notice that its `xmlns` attribute defines the xs namespace that qualifies the `<schema>` element itself.

Usually, there are a couple more attributes: namely, `targetNamespace` and `elementFormDefault`. `targetNamespace` specifies the URI to uniquely identify this schema, and `elementFormDefault` lets us require our elements to always be qualified with the namespace prefix:

```
<xs:schema xmlns:xs="http://www.w3.org/2001/XMLSchema"
           targetNamespace="http://www.wrox.com/begjsp2"
           elementFormDefault="qualified">
```

Elements

Elements within a schema can be either simple or complex.

A **simple element** does not contain any nested elements and cannot have attributes: it may only contain text between the start and the end tags. An example of a simple element from our example above is:

```
<xs:element name="Last" type="xs:string"/>
```

corresponding to the `Last` tag in our XML.

```
<Last>
  Einstein
</Last>
```

Notice that the `type` attribute qualifies this element as a string type. This means the value of this element is to be interpreted as plain text. Other possible types include `decimal`, `integer`, `Boolean`, `date`, and `time`.

Finally, we can place restrictions on how many times this element may appear by the attributes `minOccurs` and `maxOccurs`. If neither is specified, the element can occur only once. `maxOccurs="unbounded"` allow unlimited occurrences of the element.

Complex Elements

Complex elements can contain child elements and attributes. Below is how we define the `<Author-Name>` and `<Edition>` elements:

```
<xs:element name="Author-Name">
  <xs:complexType>
    <xs:element name="Last" type="xs:string"/>
    <xs:element name="First" type="xs:string"/>
  </xs:complexType>
</xs:element>
```

```
<xs:element name="Edition">
  <xs:complexType>
    <xs:attribute name="Year" type="xs:string" use="required"/>
  </xs:complexType>
</xs:element>
```

We define child elements for `<Author-Name>` and an attribute for `<Edition>` using the schema `<complexType>` element. Just as simple elements, attributes can have a default value or a fixed value specified. Any specified default value is automatically given for an attribute when no other value is supplied. If a fixed value is specified, no other value may be specified for that element.

All attributes are optional by default. To explicitly specify whether the attribute is optional, use the `use` attribute. It can have one of the two values, `optional` or `required`.

Restricting the Content

We have already seen some examples of how to restrict the values contained in our XML documents, when we saw the use of the `type` keyword. With XML Schemas, there are several other ways in which we can restrict content.

Restriction on Element Values

```
<xs:element name="length">
 <xs:simpleType>
  <xs:restriction base="xs:integer">
    <xs:minInclusive value="5"/>
    <xs:maxInclusive value="10"/>
  </xs:restriction>
 </xs:simpleType>
</xs:element>
```

The above example restricts the value of the element `<length>` to the range 5 to 10.

Restriction on a Set of Values

```
<xs:element name="language">
  <xs:simpleType>
   <xs:restriction base="xs:string">
    <xs:enumeration value="C++"/>
    <xs:enumeration value="SmallTalk"/>
    <xs:enumeration value="Java"/>
   </xs:restriction>
  </xs:simpleType>
</xs:element>
```

In the above example, the `<enumeration>` element restricts the value of the `<language>` element to either `C++`, `SmallTalk`, or `Java`.

To limit the content of an XML element to a series of numbers or letters, we use the `<pattern>` element:

```
<xs:element name="choice">
  <xs:simpleType>
    <xs:restriction base="xs:string">
      <xs:pattern value="[abcd]"/>
    </xs:restriction>
  </xs:simpleType>
</xs:element>
```

In the above example, the `<choice>` element can take a value between a and d. We could also do this like so:

```
<xs:pattern value="[a-d]"/>
```

The next example defines an element called `<license-key>` where the only acceptable value is a sequence of five digits, and each digit must be in the range 0 to 9:

```
<xs:element name="license-key">
  <xs:simpleType>
    <xs:restriction base="xs:integer">
      <xs:pattern value="[0-9][0-9][0-9][0-9][0-9]"/>
    </xs:restriction>
  </xs:simpleType>
</xs:element>
```

The following defines an element called <gender>, which can be either Male or Female:

```
<xs:element name="gender">
<xs:simpleType>
  <xs:restriction base="xs:string">
    <xs:pattern value="Male|Female"/>
  </xs:restriction>
</xs:simpleType>
</xs:element>
```

There are several other ways of restricting content. However, to cover them all would probably take another book, so if you would like further information, get hold of a copy of *Professional XML Schemas*, from Wrox Press, ISBN 1-86100-547-4.

This concludes our discussion on XML Schemas. We will next concentrate on how to read and write XML documents. It is time to get our hands dirty by writing some code!

Reading and Writing XML Documents

To be able to read and write XML documents, we need an **XML parser**. An XML parser is a program, typically an API (Application Programming Interface) that can read (and write) XML documents. It **parses** the document (breaks it up into its constituent elements) and makes these available to your own programs. In order to do this, the XML document must generally be well formed, although some parsers can handle XML fragments (these are XML documents that lack a single root element). Validating parsers can tell you if it is valid according to a specified DTD or a schema.

❑   Apache Xerces – http://xml.apache.org/xerces2-j/index.html

❑   IBM's XML4J – http://alphaworks.ibm.com/tech/xml4j

❑   Microsoft's MXSML Parser – http://msdn.microsoft.com/xml/default.asp

We will concentrate on the Apache Xerces parser, as it is part of the open source project at Apache and freely available.

Parsers internally use a set of low-level APIs that allow them to interact with the XML documents in question. There are two approaches to parsing XML documents, known as the **push** and **pull** models. An example of a push parser is SAX, which stands for Simple API for XML, while the DOM, Document Object Model, uses a pull model.

The push model reads an XML document in sequence, firing events whenever a new part of the document is encountered (such as a start or end tag). These events can be linked to our own methods that are then called when that event occurs. This model is quite lightweight and fast, but its main limitation is the sequential access, meaning we cannot go back and forth through elements at random.

DOM on the other hand reads in the entire XML document at once, creating a model of the document in memory (the DOM tree). This allows us to jump about from element to element as we wish, but its main drawback is that loading the whole document can consume a lot of memory and be relatively time consuming, particularly when a document is large.

Try It Out   Download, Install, and Run the Samples for Xerces

1. In this section, we will download, install and run some of the samples provided with the Xerces parser to illustrate how a parser works and to determine the well-formedness of an XML document.

Xerces can be downloaded from http://xml.apache.org/dist/xerces-j/. This location contains both the binary distribution (that we need) and the source code for the parser. Download the latest ZIP or TAR file depending on whether you are running Windows or Linux.

2. Unzip the contents of this file into a folder of your choice, such as C:\java. The Xerces files will be placed in a subdirectory called xerces-2_2_1 (depending on the actual version you downloaded).

3. Add the following paths to your CLASSPATH environment variable (as described in Chapter 1) to point to the Xerces jar files:

;C:\xerces-2_2_1\xercesImpl.jar;C:\xerces-2_2_1\xercesSamples.jar;
C:\xerces-2_2_1\xmlParserAPIs.jar

Make sure that you include the first semi-colon when adding this to your existing CLASSPATH, and do not include any spaces. Note that we've included the xercesSamples.jar also, as we will run these samples. They are not required to run the parser itself.

4. Staying at the command prompt, navigate to the samples directory under the xerces folder and type:

> javac ui\TreeView.java

5. Now run the compiled class like this:

> java ui.TreeView ..\data\personal.xml

This should bring up the following utility that shows the structure of the XML document in the data folder called personal.xml:

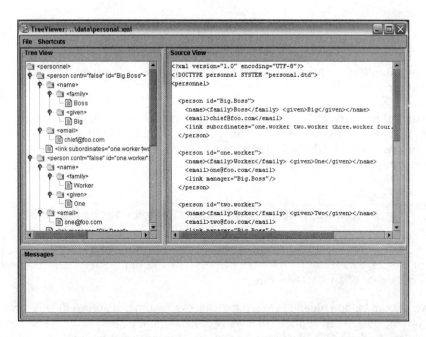

6. Now open this `personal.xml` in a text editor, and remove the end tag for the first `<person>` element (the one with id=`Big.Boss`). Rerun the program by repeating Step 5. This time, the screen will show us an error in big red letters, indicating the XML document is not well-formed:

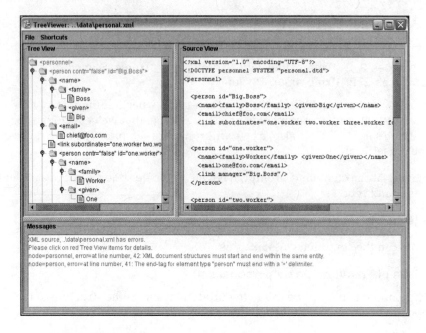

How It Works

This example reads and displays an XML document using a tree structure. The left pane shows the XML elements, and the the right shows the actual document, which is basically the source view. The bottom shows messages, such as the error message that we got when we removed the closing tag.

The source code for this particular file, `TreeView.java`, can be found in the `samples\ui` folder. A quick look at the source code will show that it uses the DOM as the low-level API for parsing the document (Line 127 in the source code).

XML and JSP

Knowledge of XML is becoming increasingly necessary in all areas of programming, and especially so in the web application sphere. We've seen XML in use in configuration files such as `web.xml`. Also, XML is finding a place in data sharing, data storage, messaging, and many other areas of application development. Some of the reasons for XML's widespread acceptance include:

❑ **Content in Plain Text**

Since XML is not a binary format, we can create and edit files with anything from a standard text editor to a visual development environment. That makes it easy to debug your programs, and makes it useful for storing small amounts of data. At the other end of the spectrum, an XML front end to a database makes it possible to efficiently store large amounts of XML data as well. So XML provides scaleability for anything from small configuration files to a company-wide data repository.

❑ **Data Identification**

The markup tags identify the information and break up the data into parts, an e-mail program can process it, a search program can look for messages sent to particular people, and an address book can extract the address information from the rest of the message. In short, because the different parts of the information have been identified, they can be used in different ways by different applications.

❑ **Ease of Processing**

As mentioned earlier, regular and consistent notation makes it easier to build a program to process XML data. And since XML is a vendor-neutral standard, you can choose among several XML parsers, any one of which takes the work out of processing XML data.

With these points in mind, let us look at some areas where XML can be applied in JSP.

Delivering XML Documents with JSP

So far we have learned a lot about JSP as a technology. We know that JSP pages produce HTML content so they can be displayed in a browser as a regular web page. However, some devices cannot interpret HTML, and instead use some reduced form, such as WAP, which makes optimal use of the bandwidth and processing capability available in many mobile phones. Another exciting technology is VoiceXML based voice services. These voice services let users interact with our applications through speech. One thing common with all these technologies is that the content is authored using XML. WML and VoiceXML are XML documents that conform to a particular schema. To be able to display this XML in user-friendly output we need to transform it into either HTML or WML a s the case might be. A process known as unsurprisingly, transformation, can help us then use the same XML to create multiple forms of output. Transformation is done with the help of another standard XML dialect called **XSL** (**Extensible Stylesheet Language**). XSL is similar to CSS (Cascading Style Sheets) which defines styling information for HTML documents, and is also a specification regulated by the W3C. For more information on XSL, check out http://www.w3.org/Style/XSL/.

If our web application creates output as XML, we can apply XSL stylesheets to transform these documents into HTML, WML, or any other XML form that the browser in use may require:

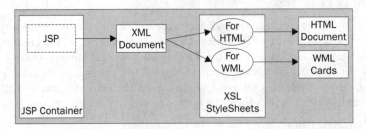

Try It Out   Creating XML with JSP

1. Create the JSP page below and save it as `taglibExample.jsp` in a new subdirectory of webapps called XML:

```
<%@ taglib uri="http://jakarta.apache.org/taglibs/datetime-1.0"
           prefix="dt"%>
<?xml version="1.0"?>
<title>Taglib Example</title>
<content>
  <heading>Sample JSP XML File</heading>
  <text>The date and time is :
    <dt:format pattern="dd-MMM-yyyy hh:mm">
      <dt:currentTime/>
    </dt:format>
  </text>
</content>
```

2. This example uses the Jakarta datetime taglibs, which you'll need to download by going to the jakarta.apache.org/taglibs site, and clicking the DateTime link on the left hand side. From there, look for the download link for the latest binary release. Remember, Windows users want the ZIP file, while Linux bods need the TAR file.

3. Extract the downloaded file to a suitable location, such as `C:\java`. Copy the newly extracted `.tld` file into a subdirectory off the `XML` folder called `WEB-INF`, and copy the `taglibs-datetime.jar` file to a `lib` subdirectory of `WEB-INF`.

4. Now restart Tomcat. When you open our JSP page, it will produce XML as shown below:

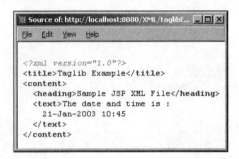

Note that Mozilla/Netscape users will need to choose View Page Source to see the XML elements.

How It Works

As this example shows, creating XML output using JSP is just the same as creating HTML output. Our JSP source contains the XML elements that we wish to appear in the output, mixed in with the same JSP tags we'd use when creating HTML output. These JSP tags create dynamic content in our XML output just as they do when creating HTML output.

By applying a suitable XSL stylesheet (a discussion of XSL is unfortunately beyond the scope of this chapter), XML such as this can be transformed into HTML or other kinds of documents including PDF (portable document format), WML (wireless markup language), and VoiceXML. In other words, we can create the same output for all our users as XML, and simply by supplying suitable stylesheets, provide a readable display for their browser type.

JSP Documents

Providing an XML representation of a JSP page, also called a **JSP Document**, is not a new concept, and has been available since the JSP 1.2 specification. The advantages of a JSP Document include:

❑ JSP documents can be passed directly to the JSP container; this will become more important as more and more content is authored as XML.

❑ The XML view of a JSP page can be used for validating the JSP page against some description of the set of valid pages.

❑ JSP documents can be manipulated by XML-aware tools.

❑ A JSP document can be generated from a textual representation by applying an XML transformation, like XSLT (the Extensible Stylesheet Language Transformations).

❑ A JSP document can be generated automatically, say by serializing some objects.

A JSP Document uses the same file extension (.jsp) as a regular JSP page. The container can distinguish the two because a JSP document has a <jsp:root> root element, and this element cannot appear in a regular JSP page.

As you can see, a JSP Document looks more like XML than JSP:

```
<jsp:root xmlns:jsp="http://java.sun.com/JSP/Page"
xmlns:dt=" http://jakarta.apache.org/taglibs/datetime-1.0"
version="2.0">

<jsp:text><![CDATA[
  <html>
   <body>
     <h1>A JSP Document</h1>
       The date and time is : ]]>
         </jsp:text>
           <dt:format pattern="dd-MMMM-yyyy hh:mm">
             <dt:currentTime/>
           </dt:format>
         <jsp:text><![CDATA[
   </body>
  </html>
 ]]></jsp:text>
</jsp:root>
```

This is equivalent to this standard JSP page:

```
<html>
  <title>Taglib Example</title>
  <body>
    <%@ taglib uri="http://jakarta.apache.org/taglibs/datetime-1.0"
            prefix="dt"%>
    <h1>A JSP Document</h1>
    The date and time is :
    <dt:format pattern="dd-MMMM-yyyy hh:mm">
    <dt:currentTime/>
    </dt:format>
  </body>
</html>
```

XML Tags

XML tags provide easy access to XML content. The JSTL XML tags use XPath, another W3C standard, this time providing a way to specify and select parts of XML documents.

There are three classes of XML tags:

- ❏ **Core** – parse, read, and write XML documents.
- ❏ **Flow Control** – provide looping and decision capability based on XML content.
- ❏ **Transformation** – provide utilities to transform XML content into other classes of documents.

The XML tags use XPath as a local expression language. XPath expressions are specified in `select` attributes. This means that only values specified for `select` attributes are evaluated using the XPath expression language. All other attributes are evaluated using the rules associated with the global expression language or the EL.

In addition to the standard XPath syntax, the JSTL XPath engine supports the following scopes to access web application data within an XPath expression:

- ❏ `$param` – Request parameter
- ❏ `$header` – Header content
- ❏ `$cookie` – Cookie identification
- ❏ `$initParam` – Context parameters
- ❏ `$pageScope` – Any page scope variable
- ❏ `$requestScope` – To access request scope variables
- ❏ `$sessionScope` – Session scope variable access.
- ❏ `$applicationScope` – Application scope variable access.

These scopes are defined in exactly the same way as their counterparts in the JSTL expression language. For example, `$sessionScope:profile` retrieves the session attribute called `profile`.

Let us try out a few simple JSTL XML tags.

Try It Out   Parsing XML with JSP

1. For this example, we'll need the Jakarta XML tag library. From the jakarta.apache.org/taglibs site, click the **XTags** link on the left, and look for the download link on the next page. Get hold of either the latest ZIP or TAR file, depending on your platform.

557

2. Extract the downloaded file to a suitable location, and copy the `.tld` file to the XML application's `WEB-INF` subfolder and the JAR to its `lib` folder.

3. XTags requires the dom4j XML framework for Java to be installed on your machine. Fortunately, the download of XTags that you downloaded earlier contains a `dom4.jar` file in the WAR file called `xtags-examples.war`. You simply need to open the WAR file with an archive utility such as WinZip, and copy `dom4j.jar` to the `WEB-INF/lib` folder.

4. Phew! Almost there. The last thing to do is create the following as the XML application's `web.xml` file, in `WEB-INF`:

```
<web-app>
  <taglib>
    <taglib-uri>
      http://jakarta.apache.org/taglibs/xtags-1.0
    </taglib-uri>
    <taglib-location>/WEB-INF/taglibs-xtags.tld</taglib-location>
  </taglib>
</web-app>
```

5. Save the following as `parseXML.jsp` in the XML folder:

```
<%@ taglib prefix="x"
    uri="http://jakarta.apache.org/taglibs/xtags-1.0" %>

<html>
  <head>
    <title>JSTL XML Support -- Parsing</title>
  </head>
  <body bgcolor="#FFFFFF">
    <h3>Parsing an XML Document using XML tags</h3>

    <x:parse>
      <BOOK>
       <AUTHOR>
         <LAST-NAME>
          EINSTEIN
         </LAST-NAME>
       </AUTHOR>
       <BOOK-NAME>
         GENERAL RELATIVITY
       </BOOK-NAME>
      </BOOK>
    </x:parse>

    <!--printing the LAST-NAME element-->
    LAST NAME :
    <x:valueOf select="/BOOK/AUTHOR/LAST-NAME" />
    <br>
```

```
        <!--printing the BOOK-NAME element -->
        BOOK NAME :
        <x:valueOf select="/BOOK/BOOK-NAME"/>

        <hr />

    </body>
</html>
```

6. Restart Tomcat, navigate to the `parseXML.jsp` page, and you should see this:

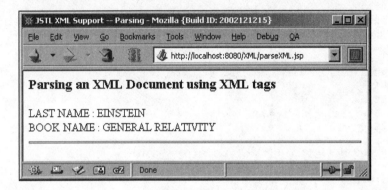

How It Works

The root element in the above XML document is named `<BOOK>`, which contains the two child elements, `<AUTHOR>` and `<BOOK-NAME>`. The element `<AUTHOR>` has another child element called `<LAST-NAME>`. Among these tags, only `<LAST-NAME>` and `<BOOK-NAME>` have content. We retrieve this content using the `<x:valueOf>` tag.

Before the result can be displayed, we need to parse the XML document for which we use the `<x:parse>` tag as shown above. Generally, you would specify a URI rather than embedding XML in the JSP page, by including an appropriate `uri` attribute on the `<x:parse>` tag, like so:

```
<x:parse uri="/book.xml" />
```

Try It Out   XML Flow Control Tags

1. In the last example, we retrieved the required XML elements using XML tags. Now let's look at another example, which iterates through all the elements in an XML document. This example demonstrates the use of XML flow control tags.

Save the following as `iterate.jsp` in the XML folder:

```
<%@ taglib prefix="x"
    uri="http://jakarta.apache.org/taglibs/xtags-1.0" %>

<html>
  <head>
    <title>JSTL XML Support -- Flow Control</title>
  </head>
  <body bgcolor="#FFFFFF">
    <h3>Iterating through an XML document</h3>

    <x:parse>
     <items>
      <item>
       <Fruit Name="Apple">Red Apple</Fruit>
      </item>
      <item>
       <Vegetable Name="Okra">Fresh Okra</Vegetable>
      </item>
      <item>
       <Beer Name="Bud">Fine Beer</Beer>
      </item>
      <item>
       <Beer Name="Kingfisher">Lager Beer</Beer>
      </item>
     </items>
    </x:parse>

    <!--iterate through all the elements -->
    <x:forEach select="/items/item">
      <!--print the current element -->
      ->  <x:valueOf select="." />

      <!--check if the selected element is Beer -->
      <x:if test="./Beer" >
        <!--yes it is beer -->
        * is a Beer
      </x:if>
      <br>
    </x:forEach>

  </body>
</html>
```

2. Now open this new page in your browser:

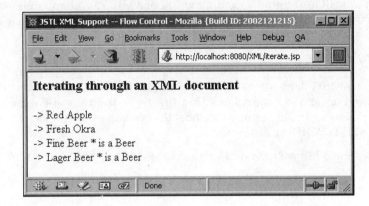

How It Works

Here we parse an embedded XML element called `<items>`. We then iterate over all the child elements of `<items>`, and print * is a Beer next to any `<Beer>` elements. We use a `<x:forEach>` tag to iterate through the document and `<x:if>` to find out if the element name is Beer.

The `<forEach>` tag is used to iterate through all the elements in sequence. We examine all `<item>` elements in the document inside the loop as shown below:

```
<x:if test="./Beer" >
```

Resources

Java API for XML Processing (JAXP) : http://java.sun.com/xml/jaxp

Java API for XML Messaging (JAXM) : http://java.sun.com/xml/jaxm

Jakarta JSTL XML tag library : http://jakarta.apache.org/taglibs/doc/standard-doc/intro.html

Summary

In this chapter we have learned:

❑   XML: its relevance, advantages, and uses.

❑   The difference between validity and well-formedness in the context of XML.

❑   XML parsers: SAX, DOM and XML Tags.

We have taken a small tour into the exciting world of XML. This chapter only serves as a very quick introduction and there is a huge ocean of knowledge out there to be explored.

Why Not Try?

- ❏ The Apache JSTL tags come with some samples in a web application archive called `standard-examples.war`. Place this directly in Tomcat's `webapp` folder and restart Tomcat. Now navigate to http://localhost:8080/standard-examples/xml to access the standard JSTL XML tag examples.

- ❏ Write a simple JSP web application that stores data in XML format using XML tags.

CHAPTER 15

Structuring Applications with Struts

Throughout this book, we have seen how to write JSP pages, use custom tags, and access relational databases. We've discussed how to track users and looked at the architectural options for developing JSP applications, as well as much more.

When putting a certain structure in place for a JSP application, we can use existing **frameworks** that provide a foundation for us to build our applications on. Good frameworks encapsulate best practice in web application architecture, and also implement a lot of common functionality that would otherwise have to be re-implemented for each and every web application. This chapter concentrates on the **Apache Struts Framework**, which has become something of a standard in the field. It takes care of the architecture and a lot of the basic functionality for a web application, letting us concentrate on the remaining features that are unique to that application.

In this chapter, we will cover:

- ❑ **Naïve** (also called **Model 1**) web application architecture
- ❑ **Proper** (or **Model 2**, **Model-View-Controller**) web application architecture
- ❑ How Struts implements Model 2 web application architecture
- ❑ Installing and configuring Struts
- ❑ Struts architecture and its core classes
- ❑ Struts tag libraries, including HTML and templating libraries
- ❑ Dynamic Struts forms that can eliminate Java coding to support HTML forms
- ❑ The Struts Validator for declarative validation without Java code
- ❑ Internationalization of messages, conventions and validation rules

Chapter 16 will support the material discussed in this chapter with an extensive case study based on the Struts framework. These two chapters will take us into the realms of serious, highly structured web programming, so there is quite a lot to take in. Don't worry if you cannot absorb it all in one sitting, and indeed you might want to revisit these chapters as you write your own applications using Struts.

Architecture of Web Applications

One approach to web application development is to gather the requirements and quickly chalk out some JSP pages and JavaBeans. Though this approach would probably work to some degree, the end result is unlikely to be maintainable, and it may well be hard to change a certain feature or to introduce new features without breaking other parts of the application. It is also probably not **reusable**. If we need to introduce new functionality, we would have to repeat a lot of work that we'd already done, but which is locked up in JSP pages and beans in such a way that we cannot make use of it. By structuring our applications correctly, we can go much further towards achieving the goals of maintainability and reusability.

The first part of this chapter will be dedicated to comparing the naïve approach to web applications (the Model 1 architecture) to a more sophisticated Model 2 (Model-View-Controller, or MVC) one. Having gained some understanding of the issues involved, we will look at the way the Struts framework realizes the Model 2 architecture, and we will discover many of the facilities it has to make web application development a much more productive and indeed enjoyable experience.

JSP Model 1 Architecture

If you have been following all the examples in this book so far, you will notice that we have developed the JSP pages to present the view to the user. Along the way, we learned that JavaBeans provide a good mechanism to encapsulate some of your functionality into Java classes. We used these JavaBeans directly in our JSP pages via the `<jsp:useBean>` tags. You would have also noticed that most of our JSP pages not only displayed the data to the user (in other words the JSP pages provide the presentation logic), but they were also responsible for controlling the flow of the application. For instance, they contained the logic to display the next page. This control logic was often coded into the JSP pages as scriptlets or, preferably, using JavaBeans or custom tags. Such architecture is known as a **page-centric** architecture, and this particular page-centric architecture is known as the JSP Model 1 Architecture. This JSP Model 1 Architecture is shown below:

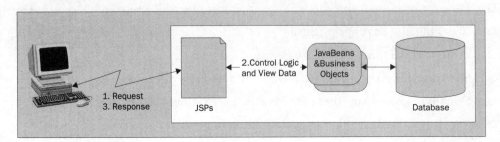

The main features of Model 1 Architecture are:

❑ HTML or JSP files are used to code the presentation. The JSP files can use JavaBeans or other Java objects to retrieve data if required.

❑ JSP files are also responsible for all the business and processing logic, such as receiving incoming requests, routing to the correct JSP, instantiating the correct JSP pages, and so on. This means that the Model 1 Architecture is a page-centric design – all the business and processing logic is either present in the JSP page itself or called directly from the JSP page.

❑ Data access is usually performed using custom tags or through JavaBean calls. Some quick-and-dirty projects use scriptlets in their JSP pages instead.

Therefore, there is a tight coupling between the pages and the logic in Model 1 applications. The flow of the application goes from one JSP page to another using anchor links in JSP pages or the `action` attribute of HTML forms. Let's take a look now at an example that uses the JSP Model 1 Architecture.

We will start with an example of a Model 1 application in which we will build a very simple shopping cart. It might be the core of a simple e-commerce facility offered by a small publisher. During this chapter, we will return to this example a few times to apply the techniques we'll learn, so it is worth creating this example even if you are not interested in the Model 1 architecture per se.

Try it Out   JSP Model 1 Architecture

1. First create a folder in the `webapps` folder called `Shopping-1`, and create the `WEB-INF` and `classes` folders as you have done before. Then copy the entire JSTL `lib` folder into `WEB-INF`, and create the directory structure `com/wrox/shop` under the `classes` folder.

2. The example consists of two web pages and four Java classes. Let's start with the `Book` class, which is a simple JavaBean with two properties, `title` and `price`. Save the code below as `Book.java` in the `shop` folder:

```
package com.wrox.shop;

/** Models a Book offered by the publisher. */
public class Book
{
  private String title;
  private double price;

  public Book(String title, double price)
  {
    super();
```

```
      this.title = title;
      this.price = price;
  }

  public String getTitle()
  {
    return this.title;
  }

  public double getPrice()
  {
    return this.price;
  }
}
```

3. All the books on offer can be found in a `Catalog`. This class extends the standard `ArrayList` class to add a constructor that creates some default content. Save this code as `Catalog.java` in the same directory as before:

```
package com.wrox.shop;

import java.util.ArrayList;

/**
 * The publisher's catalog. Essentially just a List with some
 * Book objects hardwired in the constructor.
 */
public class Catalog extends ArrayList
{
  public Catalog()
  {
    // Start with a call to the superclass's constructor
    super();

    // Create default content
    add(new Book("Professional Java Web Services", 49.99));
    add(new Book("Beginning Java 1.4 Networking", 49.99));
    add(new Book("Beginning Java 2 SDK 1.4 Edition", 49.99));
    add(new Book("Java Server Programming, J2EE 1.4 Edition", 54.99));
  }
}
```

4. As books are added to the shopping cart, we need to keep track of the number of copies of each book that are in the cart. The `ShoppingCartItem` bundles up a `Book` with its associated quantity. Save the following code as `ShoppingCartItem.java` in the same directory:

```
package com.wrox.shop;

/**
 * Models a shopping cart item consisting of a Book and a quantity.
 */
public class ShoppingCartItem
{
  private final Book book;
  private int quantity;

  public ShoppingCartItem(Book book)
  {
    super();
    this.book = book;
    this.quantity = 1;
  }

  public Book getBook()
  {
    return book;
  }

  public int getQuantity()
  {
    return quantity;
  }

  public void setQuantity(int quantity)
  {
    this.quantity = quantity;
  }
```

The following two methods allow us to determine if two ShoppingCartItem are identical. Items are identical if they contain the same book; this will help us to find out if a given book is already present in the shopping cart:

```
public boolean equals(Object obj)
{
  return obj instanceof ShoppingCartItem &&
         equals((ShoppingCartItem)obj);
}

public boolean equals(ShoppingCartItem that)
{
  return this.book == that.book;
}
}
```

5. Finally, a ShoppingCartItem can be put in a ShoppingCart, which is basically just a list of items. Create ShoppingCart.java in the same folder as before:

```
package com.wrox.shop;

import java.util.ArrayList;
import java.util.Iterator;
import java.util.List;

/**
 * Models a shopping cart holding a number of Books.
 */
public class ShoppingCart
{
  private final List items = new ArrayList();
```

We can access items using indexed JavaBean accessor methods, and the getItems() method returns the List itself:

```
public ShoppingCartItem getItem(int index)
{
  return (ShoppingCartItem)items.get(index);
}

public void setItem(int index, ShoppingCartItem item)
{
  items.set(index, item);
}

public List getItems()
{
  return items;
}
```

The getTotal() method calculates the total cost for the items in the shopping cart:

```
public double getTotal()
{
  double total = 0.0;
  for (Iterator i = items.iterator(); i.hasNext(); )
  {
    ShoppingCartItem item = (ShoppingCartItem)i.next();
    total += item.getBook().getPrice() * item.getQuantity();
  }
  return total;
}
```

The addBook() method adds a book to the cart. If it is already in the cart, the quantity for that book is increased by one. Because of the way we defined ShoppingCartItem.equals(), we can use the List.contains() method to find out if we already have the book in the cart:

```
public void addBook(Book book)
{
  ShoppingCartItem newItem = new ShoppingCartItem(book);
  if (items.contains(newItem))
  {
    ShoppingCartItem item = getItem(items.indexOf(newItem));
    item.setQuantity(item.getQuantity() + 1);
  }
  else
  {
    items.add(newItem);
  }
}
```

The `validate()` method goes through the cart and removes any items that have zero or negative quantity:

```
public void validate()
{
  for (Iterator i = items.iterator(); i.hasNext(); )
  {
    ShoppingCartItem item = (ShoppingCartItem)i.next();
    if (item.getQuantity() <= 0) i.remove();
  }
}
```

6. To compile the classes, open the command prompt and change to the `classes` directory inside our application's `WEB-INF` folder, and run the following command:

> **> javac com/wrox/shop/*.java.**

7. The next step is to create the main page, which displays a catalog of all available books. This is quite a straightforward JSP page that retrieves or instantiates the `Catalog` as an application-scoped JavaBean, and then uses the core JSTL tags to loop through all the items it contains. A `<fmt:formatNumber>` tag formats the price with two decimals.

Save the following code as `index.jsp` in the `Shopping-1` folder:

```
<%@page contentType="text/html"%>
<%@taglib prefix="c" uri="http://java.sun.com/jstl/core_rt"%>
<%@taglib prefix="fmt" uri="http://java.sun.com/jstl/fmt_rt"%>

<jsp:useBean id="catalog" class="com.wrox.shop.Catalog" scope="application"/>
<html>
  <head><title>Book Shopping Home</title></head>
  <body>
  <img src="http://www.wrox.com/images/wxmainlogowhitespace.gif"
```

```
      align="left">
   <h2>Book Shopping Home</h2>
   <table style="background:#ffeeee" cellpadding="5" width="80%">
     <tr style="background:#ffdddd">
     <th>Book Title</th><th>Price $</th><th></th>
     </tr>
     <c:forEach items="${catalog}" var="book" varStatus="status">
     <tr>
        <td valign="middle" width="70%">${book.title}</td>
        <td valign="middle" width="15%" align="right">
```

A `<fmt:formatNumber>` tag formats the price with two decimals:

```
      <fmt:formatNumber value="${book.price}" pattern="0.00"/>
      </td>
      <td align="right">
```

The following form is generated for each book listed and allows the user to add the book to the shopping cart:

```
      <form action="showcart.jsp">
         <p><input type="submit" value="Add"></p>
         <input type="hidden" name="index" value="${status.index}">
         <input type="hidden"> <!-- IE layout bug workaround -->
      </form>
      </td>
   </tr>
   </c:forEach>
   <tr>
   <td colspan="3" align="right">
      <form action="showcart.jsp">
         <input type="submit" value="View Cart">
      </form>
   </td>
   </tr>
   </table>
   </body>
</html>
```

8. The other page is only slightly more complicated, consisting of a preamble with business logic code followed by the actual presentation HTML. Save this file as `showcart.jsp` in the `Shopping-1` folder:

```
<%@page contentType="text/html" import="com.wrox.shop.*"%>
<%@taglib prefix="c" uri="http://java.sun.com/jstl/core_rt"%>
<%@taglib prefix="fmt" uri="http://java.sun.com/jstl/fmt_rt"%>
```

9. The page starts with some logic to handle books that are added to the cart, and update cart quantities. A `<when>` element adds a new book:

```
<jsp:useBean id="cart" class="com.wrox.shop.ShoppingCart"
             scope="session"/>
<c:choose>
  <c:when test="${not empty param.index}">
    <c:set var="book" value="${catalog[param.index]}"/>
    <% cart.addBook((Book)pageContext.getAttribute("book")); %>
  </c:when>
```

10. The `<otherwise>` section handles updates of shopping cart item quantities:

```
  <c:otherwise>
    <%
    for (int i = 0; i < cart.getItems().size(); i++)
    {
      String qty = request.getParameter("item[" + i + "].quantity");
      if (qty != null)
      {
        cart.getItem(i).setQuantity(Integer.parseInt(qty));
      }
    }
    cart.validate();
    %>
  </c:otherwise>
</c:choose>
```

11. The presentation part of the JSP uses a JSTL `<forEach>` tag to loop over the items in the cart and display them. A formatting tag is again used to format the prices:

```
<html>
  <head><title>Book Shopping Cart</title></head>
  <body>
  <img src="http://www.wrox.com/images/wxmainlogowhitespace.gif"
       align="left">
  <h2>Book Shopping Cart</h2>
  <table cellpadding="5" style="background:#ffeeee" width="80%">
    <form action="showcart.jsp">
      <tr style="background:#ffdddd">
        <th>Book Title</th><th>Price $</th><th>Qty</th><th>Cost $</th>
      </tr>
      <c:forEach items="${cart.items}" var="item" varStatus="status">
      <tr>
        <td width="60%">${item.book.title}</td>
        <td align="right" width="15%">
          <fmt:formatNumber value="${item.book.price}" pattern="0.00"/>
        </td>
        <td width="10%" align="center">
```

12. Each item in the cart gets its own `<input>` field showing the quantity, allowing the user to amend it and submit their changes:

```
            <input type="text" size="1" maxlength="2"
                   name="item[${status.index}].quantity"
                   value="${item.quantity}">
        </td>
        <td align="right">
          <fmt:formatNumber pattern="0.00"
                            value="${item.book.price * item.quantity}"/>
        </td>
      </tr>
    </c:forEach>
    <tr>
      <td><em>Total</em></td>
      <td colspan="2" align="right">
        <input type="submit" value="Update">
      </td>
      <td align="right">
        <em>
          <fmt:formatNumber pattern="0.00" value="${cart.total}"/>
        </em>
      </td>
    </tr>
  </form>
  <tr>
```

13. A separate HTML form displays options to continue shopping or proceed to the checkout:

```
      <td colspan="3" align="right">
        <form action="index.jsp">
          <input type="submit" value="Continue Shopping">
          <input type="submit" value="Checkout"
                 onClick="alert('Not Implemented')">
        </form>
      </td>
      <td></td>
    </tr>
  </table>
  </body>
</html>
```

14. Start Tomcat and navigate to http://localhost:8080/Shopping-1. You should see the following output:

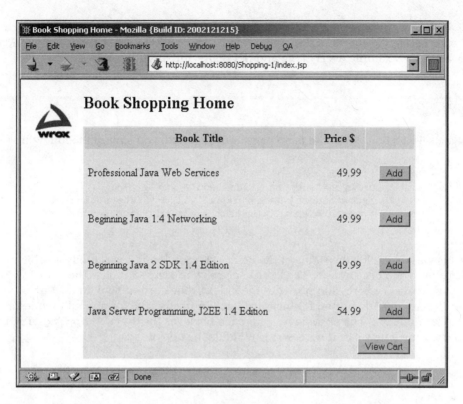

15. From the main index page, you can get to the shopping cart page by either adding a book to the cart or by clicking the View Cart button. You should see something like this (note that if you're not online, you won't see the Wrox logo):

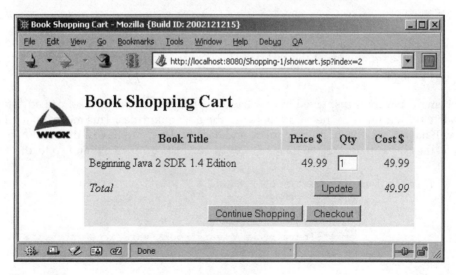

In the cart page, you can adjust the quantities, go back to the shopping page, or proceed to the checkout. We will not implement the checkout facility; it would only make the example overly long and not really add anything.

How It Works

When you select a book from the main page and click **Add**, you submit the following form:

```
<form action="showcart.jsp">
  <p><input type="submit" value="Add"></p>
  <input type="hidden" name="index" value="${status.index}">
  <input type="hidden">  <!-- IE layout bug workaround -->
</form>
```

The status variable holds the status of the `<c:forEach>` loop (it is actually an object of class – deep breath – `javax.servlet.jsp.jstl.core.LoopTagStatus`). The `${status.index}` expression provides the index of the current book in the `Catalog`. So if the user presses the **Add** button for the third book in the list, the form would request showcart.jsp?index=2. The `showcart.jsp` page retrieves the user's `ShoppingCart` from the session (creating a new cart if necessary) and adds the book to it:

```
<jsp:useBean id="cart" class="com.wrox.shop.ShoppingCart" scope="session"/>
<c:choose>
  <c:when test="$
{not empty param.index}">
  <c:set var="book" value="$
{catalog[param.index]}"/>
  <% cart.addBook((Book)pageContext.getAttribute("book")); %>
  </c:when>
```

The `<c:choose>` contains some further logic that deals with cart updates – we'll come to that in a moment. The remainder of the cart page is concerned mostly with displaying the contents of the shopping cart.

Every item's quantity is displayed in an `<input>` element so that the user can edit it; pressing the **Update** button updates the cart items with the new quantities. This means that all quantity fields will have to be part of one big form, and each will have to have a different name. In this example, they are called `item[0].quantity`, `item[1].quantity`, and so forth.

```
<form action="showcart.jsp">
  .
  .
  .
<c:forEach items="${cart.books}" var="book" varStatus="status">
```

```
            .
            .
            .
         <input type="text" size="1" maxlength="2"
              name="item[${status.index}].quantity"
              value="${item.quantity}">

            .
            .
            .
      </c:forEach>
        .
        .
        .
      </form>
```

These field names correspond to the indexed property `item` of the `ShoppingCart` JavaBean, which not only makes them easier to understand but will also help Struts to work later. Pressing the **Update** button will submit a request which looks like showcart.jsp?quantities%5B0%5D=2&...

This request will end up at the `<c:otherwise>` section of the `<c:choose>` tag at the start of `showcart.jsp`:

```
    <c:otherwise>
     <%
     for (int i = 0; i < cart.getItems().size(); i++)
     {
        String qty = request.getParameter("item[" + i + "].quantity");
        if (qty != null)
        {
           cart.getItem(i).setQuantity(Integer.parseInt(qty));
        }
     }
     cart.validate();
     %>
    </c:otherwise>
```

This code loops over all items in the cart, attempts to find a corresponding `item[i].quantity` parameter in the request, and updates the cart for each parameter found. Finally, the `validate()` function removes items if its quantity becomes zero or negative. There is no good way to do all of this using the JSTL tags – if you want to avoid Java scriptlets (and you should!), you'd have to use a custom tag.

Note that the `showcart.jsp` page not only has the control logic to determine whether we are trying to add a new book or update existing quantities, but it also has the presentation logic to display the cart's contents. Since all of the logic is embedded in the JSP pages, this is an example of JSP Model 1 Architecture.

Drawbacks of the JSP Model 1 Architecture

The Model 1 architecture has one thing going for it: simplicity. If your project is small, simple, and self-contained, it is the quickest way to get up and running. But the example above, although by no means large or complicated, already illustrates a number of the disadvantages of Model 1 architecture:

❑   It becomes very hard to change the structure of such web applications because the pages are **tightly coupled**. They have to be aware of each other. What if we decide that, after updating the quantities in the shopping cart, we want to redirect the user back to the catalog? This would require moving the code inside the `<c:otherwise>` tag from the shopping cart page to the catalog page.

Large projects often involve teams of programmers working on different pages and in the Model 1 scenario, each team would have to have a detailed understanding of the pages all of the other teams were working, otherwise modifying pages could break the flow of the application.

❑   Pages that are linked to from many other pages have to handle those other pages' logic, such as the cart update in the example. In this way, they can accumulate a large amount of code that hasn't got an awful lot to do with the page itself. This reduces their **coherence**, making them harder to understand and to maintain.

❑   Presentation and application control logic are mixed up, making it hard for a web designer to change the pages without messing up the Java code. Vice versa, it is very hard for a developer to change control logic that may be hidden between lots of HTML markup. The shopping cart page is a case in point; fortunately logic and presentation are still reasonably well separated, but you will find that as pages and applications get more complex, logic and presentation becomes inextricably intertwined.

❑   The lack of separation between presentation and logic means that providing multiple presentations carries a very high cost. What if it is decided to sell books via WAP or PDA devices as well? These devices are radically different from web browsers and require completely different presentation structure and formatting. Our only choice would be to produce a whole new set of pages and duplicate the application logic. Every subsequent change to the logic would have to be implemented in more than one place. Soon enough, changes will become very hard to manage and the implementations will start to diverge.

Of course, the obvious way to get around these problems is to separate out the presentation code from the application control logic. This leads us onto our next architecture, JSP Model 2.

JSP Model 2 Architecture

JSP Model 2 architecture, also known as **Model-View-Controller** or **MVC** architecture, addresses the problems of the page-centric Model 1 architecture by rigorously separating presentation, control logic, and application state. We had a first look at this architecture in Chapter 10, but let's revisit it now in a little more detail. In the JSP Model 2 architecture, the control flow (or application flow) is embodied in another module called the *controller*, as illustrated in the diagram below:

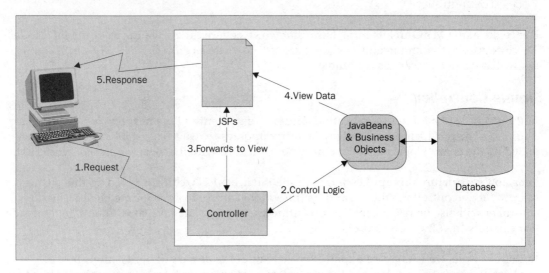

The **Controller** receives all requests for the application, and is responsible for taking the appropriate actions in response to each request. The controller may change some information or initiate some processing by the JavaBeans or other Java objects. Then it will forward the request to the appropriate *view*, usually a JSP page, which contains the presentation logic. The view chosen will often depend on the outcome of the processing.

The **Model** – represented by the JavaBeans, business objects, and database in the above diagram – holds the application state. It is usually understood to cover the whole of the business and data layer in the application. In simple applications like our example shopping cart, it may consist of a number of JavaBeans that model the application state. In more complicated applications there may be a variety of other Java objects that perform operations for us or provide the interface to the database; these objects may even reside on a different server, as in Enterprise JavaBeans. However, such differences do not concern us here.

The sole responsibility of the **View** – or JSP pages – is to take the information provided by the Controller and the Model and present it to the user. It may retrieve data from the model and display it, but it should not change the state of the model or initiate any kind of processing. This is the task of the controller.

By introducing a central controlling mechanism, we cleanly separate presentation logic from control flow. As a centralized component, the controller is a great place for implementing other useful features, like security. We now have three distinct sections within our application:

- ❑ The model
- ❑ The view
- ❑ The controller

Hence the name **MVC** architecture. Now that we've covered the advantages of the JSP Model 2 architecture, let's jump in and see how hard it is to write a controller. You'll be relieved to know that it's not as scary as it sounds!

A Simple Controller

In the example of a Model 1 application, `index.jsp` submitted the new books purchased to `showcart.jsp`, which submitted any quantity updates to itself. The `showcart.jsp` page mixed up the control logic to handle both types of actions with the logic for presenting the data.

Let's now restructure this application to fit the JSP Model 2 Architecture. To do this we need to introduce a controller, which transfers (forwards) control to appropriate pages. This controller will also be responsible for executing the appropriate Java code to update the model (for example the `ShoppingCart`).

In this example, we will create a controller that supports all the different actions our application needs to take. Most of the controller is taken up with code that originally lived in `showcart.jsp`.

Try It Out   **A JSP Model 2 Controller**

1. Create a copy of the `Shopping-1` web application folder named `Shopping-2`, and save the following code in a file named `controller.jsp` in the `Shopping-2` folder:

```
<%@page contentType="text/html" import="com.wrox.shop.*"%>
<%@taglib prefix="c" uri="http://java.sun.com/jstl/core_rt"%>

<jsp:useBean id="catalog" class="com.wrox.shop.Catalog"
             scope="application"/>
<jsp:useBean id="cart" class="com.wrox.shop.ShoppingCart"
             scope="session"/>
<c:choose>

  <c:when test="${param.action=='add'}">
    <c:set var="book" value="${catalog[param.index]}"/>
    <% cart.addBook((Book)pageContext.getAttribute("book")); %>
    <jsp:forward page="/showcart.jsp"/>
```

```
      </c:when>

      <c:when test="${param.action=='cart'}">
        <jsp:forward page="/showcart.jsp"/>
      </c:when>

      <c:when test="${param.action=='update'}">
        <%
        for (int i = 0; i < cart.getItems().size(); i++)
        {
          String qty = request.getParameter("item[" + i + "].quantity");
          if (qty != null)
          {
            cart.getItem(i).setQuantity(Integer.parseInt(qty));
          }
        }
        cart.validate();
        %>
        <jsp:forward page="/showcart.jsp"/>
      </c:when>

      <c:when test="${param.action=='catalog'}">
        <jsp:forward page="/index.jsp"/>
      </c:when>

      <c:otherwise>
        <jsp:forward page="/index.jsp"/>
      </c:otherwise>

    </c:choose>
```

2. Modify the two `<form>` tags in the `index.jsp` page as shown below, also adding one new `<input>` element inside each:

```
      .
      .
      .
    <td align="right">
    <form action="controller.jsp">
      <input type="hidden" name="action" value="add">
      <p><input type="submit" value="Add"></p>
      <input type="hidden" name="index" value="${status.index}">
    </form>
      .
      .

      .
    <td colspan="3" align="right">
      <form action="controller.jsp">
        <input type="hidden" name="action" value="cart">
        <input type="submit" value="View Cart">
```

```
    </form>
      .
      .
      .
```

3. Now delete the `<choose>` tag that occupies first quarter of the showcart.jsp page, as this is now in our controller. Again, modify the two `<form>` tags and add two new `<input>` elements as highlighted:

```
<%@page contentType="text/html"%>
<%@taglib prefix="c" uri="http://java.sun.com/jstl/core_rt"%>
<%@taglib prefix="fmt" uri="http://java.sun.com/jstl/fmt_rt"%>

<jsp:useBean id="cart" class="com.wrox.shop.ShoppingCart"
             scope="session"/>
<html>
  <head><title>Book Shopping Cart</title></head>
    .
    .
    .
    <table cellpadding="5" style="background:#ffeeee" width="80%">
      <form action="controller.jsp">
        <input type="hidden" name="action" value="update"/>
        <tr style="background:#ffdddd">
      .
      .
      .
      <td colspan="3" align="right">
        <form action="controller.jsp">
          <input type="hidden" name="action" value="catalog"/>
          <input type="submit" value="Continue Shopping"/>
      .
      .
      .
```

4. After making these modifications, restart Tomcat, direct your browser to http://localhost:8080/Shopping-2, and try out the new application. The new version should work exactly like the old one:

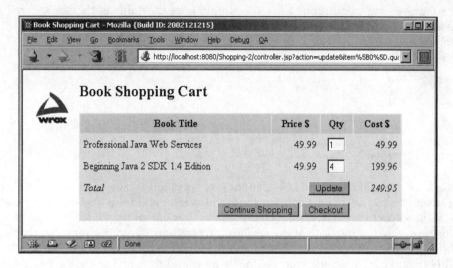

5. Take a closer look at the **Address** bar at the top however, and you will see that all
requests now go via our `controller` JSP page.

How It Works

There's not an awful lot new in the code. The forms in both `index.jsp` and `showcart.jsp`
now all submit to the controller JSP page. In addition, all forms have a new (hidden) field
called `action`, which specifies the kind of action to be taken when submitting the form.

```
<form action="controller.jsp">
  <input type="hidden" name="action" value="add">
```

The catalog (`index.jsp`) and shopping cart (`showcart.jsp`) pages, between them, allow a
number of different actions:

- ❑ The `add` action is used by the catalog page (`index.jsp`) to add items to the shopping cart.

- ❑ The `index.jsp` page also uses the `cart` action. This takes you to the shopping cart
  page without adding a new book to the cart.

- ❑ The shopping cart page (`showcart.jsp`) uses the `update` action to update the
  quantities of the items in the cart.

- ❑ On the cart page, the `shop` action takes you back to the catalog page. This form is
  actually the odd one out, as it has *two* buttons that do different things and should
  ultimately take you to different pages. Had we implemented the **Checkout** facility,
  then the controller would have had to determine which button was pressed and
  handle the request accordingly. We will examine this in some more depth when we
  come to discuss Struts.

The `<c:choose>` tag in `controller.jsp` simply tests the value of the `action` request parameter and compares it to the four possible actions listed above using JSP Expression Language:

```
<c:choose>
  <c:when test="${param.action=='add'}">
    .
    .
    .
  </c:when>
  <c:when test="${param.action=='cart'}">
```

The code inside the `add` and `update` sections has not changed since our Model 1 example. The `cart` and `catalog` actions contain simply forward you to the `showcart.jsp` and `index.jsp`, respectively. Why bother? Remember that one of the disadvantages of the Model 1 architecture was that the flow of the application was hardwired in the pages. By putting the association between an action (`catalog`) and the view (`index.jsp`) in the controller, we gain the ability to make far-reaching changes in site logic and flow just using the controller, without modifying the view JSP pages. The price to pay is increased complexity, and the danger that the controller will keep on growing as new functionality is added to the application.

The `showcart.jsp` page now only has presentation logic built into it. However, by introducing this controller mechanism, you are able to achieve a much cleaner separation of presentation and control logic. There is room for improvement though. Much of the logic in the `controller` JSP page is still contained in a Java scriptlet, and even the bits that use the JSTL are perhaps better written using Java code. As the application grows, our controller will acquire many small chunks of code that have little or nothing to do with each other. The controller will become incoherent and hard to understand. We need a solution to this, as the separation of presentation and business logic is essential to manage complexity and separate responsibilities in medium and large sized projects.

As we will see, the solution is to replace our little controller JSP page with a full-fledged MVC web framework. The Struts framework addresses the issues mentioned in the previous paragraph by spinning off controller functionality into separate Java classes.

Why Use A Web Framework?

If you study almost any real-world application, you will find that its components can be broadly classified into two types:

❑ Business components, such as the logic inside the `<when>` tags of our controller JSP page

❑ Application services, such as the logic which selects the appropriate `<when>` section based on the action passed to the controller

In most scenarios, it is difficult to reuse the business components across different applications, since the functionality provided by these components are **domain-specific**, that is, tailored to the problem you are trying to solve. They could only be reused in applications that dealt with the very same problem domain, and even that can be difficult because different applications often need to model the same domain in a slightly different way.

Application services, on the other hand, are often fairly generic. They provide the foundation that supports the business components and the plumbing that connects them. Application services are not domain-specific and have therefore useful to many different types of application. They can be reused across applications within an organization, and often across organizations. For an MVC web application, such application services might include request routing, data flow between web pages and Java objects, error handling, generating client-side scripts in a generic manner, and tag libraries that supplement the JSTL to support rapid JSP construction.

Software that presents an architecture providing these types of services and that allows you to build your application by slotting in your business components can be termed a **web application framework**. Many big organizations develop in-house frameworks that can be reused by different applications developed within the organization. However, some organizations that can't afford enough time and resources for developing an in-house framework can use third party off-the-shelf frameworks instead. These can be either commercial software or open source. The advantage of this route is that you get a package that is already developed and tested, and therefore ready for use, and moreover often better conceived than most in-house frameworks – saving time, money, resources, and frustration.

This chapter focuses on the most popular open source web application framework, and indeed the de facto standard MVC framework in many places: the **Apache Struts** framework.

The Struts Framework

Apache Struts is an open source web application framework based on the MVC design pattern. It allows us to fully decouple the business logic, control logic, and presentation code of an application, making web applications more reusable and maintainable. Built on the servlet and JSP APIs, it is suited to projects ranging from simple applications to complex enterprise systems. The Struts framework is a part of the Jakarta Project managed by the Apache Software Foundation, and can be downloaded from http://jakarta.apache.org/struts/. The framework provides the following services:

❑   A powerful controller servlet, which delegates the application-specific business logic to *action classes* that you write for a specific application. This controller is configured using an XML file.

❑   A number of JSP tag libraries for JavaBean management, HTML and JavaScript generation, template handling, and flow control in a JSP page. These libraries are integrated with the controller and automate a lot of common web-application functionality that you would otherwise have to code by hand.

- ❑ A **Validator** facility supporting the declaration of validation rules in an XML file. The Validator supports both server-side and client-side (JavaScript) validation.

- ❑ Excellent **internationalization** support. This allows your application to support any number of spoken languages and to use the language and conventions appropriate to any given user. This does not merely include messages, but also dates and number formatting, monetary conventions, and validation logic.

- ❑ A generic error and exception handling mechanism that fully supports internationalization.

- ❑ File upload utilities to allow users to send files to the server using JSP pages.

- ❑ A facility to easily set up JDBC data sources, including a generic implementation which can turn any ordinary JDBC driver into a `DataSource` with built-in connection pool.

- ❑ Various JavaBean manipulation utilities.

Actually, the last two are not part of the Struts framework proper but of the Commons code library (http://jakarta.apache.org/commons). However, they are shipped with Struts so we do not need to worry about the difference. In the remainder of this chapter, we will explain how to use many (although not all) of these features. The next chapter will present a case study that uses them in a full-blown application. But first, we will take a closer look at why we actually need web frameworks such as Struts.

Architecture

Struts is a framework supporting the MVC paradigm (for more information, go to http://java.sun.com/blueprints/guidelines/designing_enterprise_applications_2e/, select The Web Tier, and read section 4.4). It is comprised of a completely general Controller implementation supported by classes and tag libraries that implement the Model and View aspects. The easiest way to understand where its major components fit inside the MVC architecture is to look at the way they work together to process an HTTP request. The collaboration diagram below depicts a high-level overview of Struts' core classes and their interactions:

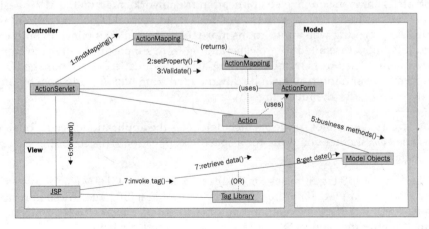

We will now review each of the classes in this diagram in the order in which they are typically invoked. As you would expect in an MVC framework, every request starts at the Struts Controller, the heart of which is the `ActionServlet` class. This servlet is usually mapped to the extension *.do. For example, a request for /payCartItems.do would end up with the `ActionServlet` and tell it that the user wants to pay for the items in our shopping cart.

❑   The first thing the controller servlet does is find out what needs to be done. For every possible action URL, such as /payCartItems.do, it determines what needs to happen next. This information is read from Struts configuration files at runtime into instances of the **ActionMapping** class. So the first thing the controller does is call `ActionMappings.findMapping()` to find what the appropriate `ActionMapping` is for the request URL (/payCartItems.do in our example).

One of the things you often need to do in web applications is store field values from an HTML form in a JavaBean. One of the things an action mapping can do is specify an **ActionForm** associated with the action. An `ActionForm` is a form-specific JavaBean that represents the input data from an HTML form. The controller automatically instantiates this bean if necessary, and populates it with request parameter values.

Let's pretend that /payCartItems.do is invoked by a payment details page asking the user for their credit card number and its expiry date. The HTML form on this page may have a field called `cardNumber`. If we supply Struts with an `ActionForm` that has a `cardNumber` JavaBean property, it will automatically populate that property with the card number entered by the user.

❑   `ActionForms` may be part of the application Model, or they can be used as a convenient way to move data around.

Optionally, the controller servlet can ask the `ActionForm` to validate the data that has been submitted by calling `validate()` on the form. If the `ActionForm` indicates that validation fails, the request is forwarded back to the input HTML page with an error message.

For example, the `ActionForm` could verify that a credit card number has been entered; if it were missing, the request would be forwarded back to the payment details form with a **Please enter your credit card number** message.

❑   The next step is to invoke the **Action** object for the request URL. The `Action` classes provide the application-specific business logic necessary to process the request. We will generally write one `Action` class for every different action in the application.

A good action class is small, focused, and easy to understand; it is merely the "glue" between the controller and the model. Actions are not a good place to implement complicated business logic. An `Action` will generally call one or more business methods in the Model to get the actual work done.

In our /payCartItems.do example, the `Action` would initiate the actual credit card transaction. As such transactions are sensitive and fairly complicated, the action would probably not implement the actual transaction but merely call a business object with the credit card details extracted from the `ActionForm`.

❑ After the Action has been completed successfully, the controller forwards the request to the View component. This view is usually a JSP page. The JSP request is forwarded as configured in the Struts configuration file and – you guessed it – contained at runtime in the `ActionMapping` object. These destinations are represented by **ActionForward** objects.

Struts allows us to set up multiple destinations for a single action, which is useful if an action can have multiple outcomes. For example, the credit card payment could succeed or it could fail if the user's credit limit has been exceeded. You will probably want to forward to different JSP pages depending on the outcome.

❑ The view JSP page can either access the JavaBeans model directly, using `<jsp:getProperty>` or the expression language, or use the **Struts tag libraries** to retrieve data from the model. For example, if you use the tags in the Struts `html` tag library to create HTML forms, they will automatically populate the form fields with the values in your `ActionForm`.

In broad terms, this is how Struts handles a request, although there are some details to flesh out that we will come to in time. First, we will discuss how to install and configure Struts, and then apply our new knowledge to the shopping cart example.

Installing and Configuring Struts

The latest versions source files and binaries for the Struts framework are available from http://jakarta.apache.org/struts. Download the zipped binary distribution of the latest release of Struts 1.1 by following the binaries link on this page. Linux users should download the `.tar.gz` file from the same location. Once downloaded, extract the contents to the `java` folder on your `C:` drive. The unpacked folder will contain the following two subdirectories:

❑ `lib` – includes the following files:

  ❑ The `struts.jar` file containing the actual Struts code

  ❑ The Commons JAR files and other JARs that Struts requires

  ❑ The tag library descriptors (TLDs) for the Struts custom tags

  ❑ The default Validator rules file, `validator-rules.xml`

  ❑ The document-type definitions (DTDs) for the configuration files mentioned above

❑ `web-apps` – contains the web application archive (WAR) files for the example applications and Struts documentation

You usually need only the JAR files and the `validator-rules.xml` file from the `lib` directory. The TLDs and DTDs are packaged inside `struts.jar`, where neither Struts nor the JSP engine have any trouble finding them.

Using Struts in a Web Application

To use the Struts framework in a web application, we need to perform the following steps:

1. When compiling the Java classes, in particular `Action` classes, the `struts.jar` file must appear either in the `CLASSPATH` environment variable or be specified using the `-classpath` switch on the `javac` command line.

2. Applications that use Struts must have a copy of all Struts `.jar` files in their `WEB-INF/lib` folder. The simplest way to do this may be to copy the entire Struts `lib` folder into your application's `WEB-INF` directory.

3. The application's deployment descriptor (`WEB-INF/web.xml`) must declare the Struts `ActionServlet`, and map the required requests to the `ActionServlet` as shown below:

```
<servlet>
  <servlet-name>controller</servlet-name>
  <servlet-class>org.apache.struts.action.ActionServlet</servlet-class>
  <load-on-startup>1</load-on-startup>
</servlet>

<servlet-mapping>
  <servlet-name>controller</servlet-name>
  <url-pattern>*.do</url-pattern>
</servlet-mapping>
```

This excerpt from `web.xml` declares the `ActionServlet` by name, and maps request URIs ending with `.do` to the `ActionServlet`. The (optional) `<load-on-startup>` element must contain a positive integer indicating the priority of this servlet, where lower priorities are loaded before higher ones.

`ActionServlet` takes a host of initialization parameters, but all are optional and in most cases we don't have to worry about them. Refer to the Struts documentation (http://jakarta.apache.org/struts/userGuide/) for further details.

4. You will need to create a Struts configuration file `struts-config.xml` in the `WEB-INF` directory of your web app. This file contains the action mapping information, information on the `ActionForm` beans used in your application, global forwards, exception handling, and other information that you might want to set up such as `DataSources` and Struts plug-ins. We are going to discuss this configuration file next, and we will create one later for our shopping cart application.

5. Finally, to support internationalization, Struts makes heavy use of *resource bundles* that provide the text for each message used in the application. At the very least, you will need to create a default message bundle and tell Struts where to find it. We will discuss resource bundles in a bit more depth later on.

Before starting our exploration of the Struts configuration file and the core Struts classes, we will take a closer look at message resource bundles and how they support internationalization.

Message Resource Bundles and Internationalization

The Struts framework supports **internationalization** (often abbreviated to i18n – 'i' followed by 18 letters and then 'n') and **localization**. When a web browser submits an HTTP request, it provides information about the user's locale within the request that Struts uses to adapt responses.

Among other things, internationalization supports requires us to no longer just embed messages, labels, and other text inside our JSP pages and Java code. Instead, we have to refer to these messages using **message keys**, and for each locale that we support, we must maintain a **message resources** file that provides the text appropriate for that locale for each message key. Chapter 7 discussed internationalization and message resources in connection with the JSTL formatting tags, but let's briefly refresh our memory here.

Message resources are normally read from a Java properties file. For example, the contents of our default message resources file, let's call it `messages.properties`, could be:

```
message.1=The first internationalized message.
message.2=The second internationalized message.
```

We can then refer to these messages as `message.1` and `message.2`, respectively. If we want to support the French language, we could add a `messages_fr.properties` file reading:

```
message.1=Le premier message internationalisée.
message.2=Le deuxième message internationalisée.
```

The `_fr` appended to the filename tells Java that this file is a French message resource. When the user's locale indicates that French is the preferred language (for instance, if they are in France or French-speaking Canada), the messages will be retrieved from this file. We can even distinguish between different regional variants, for instance US or UK English, by taking the user's country code into account as well:

```
message.1=The first internationalised message.
message.2=The second internationalised message.
```

If you saved the messages above as `messages_en_GB.properties` in the same directory as the other files, users favoring British English would see the messages with the word "internationalized" sporting an "s" instead of a "z".

The nice thing is, we only need to provide the messages that are actually *different* to the default resource; if a message cannot be found in `messages_en_GB.properties`, the region-specific file, Java will look in the language-specific `messages_en.properties` (if it exists) and finally in the default `messages.properties` file. This way, we can maintain these files with the minimum amount of work. All the message resource files for the different languages and countries together are called a **message resource bundle**. Having a default resource file in American English means that users whose locale is not specifically supported can at least use the application in its English-language guise.

Java represents the user's locale with the `java.util.Locale` object. In Chapter 7, we saw how the JSTL uses the locale and resource bundles to output messages and format numbers and dates. Struts, too, uses this locale whenever it needs to display a message so it can do so in the correct language, for example in the `<html:error>` tag that displays internationalized error messages. The power of Struts is that application developers need not know about the intricacies of these classes to use internationalized and formatted messages.

The Struts Configuration File

The Struts configuration file is used to configure all components used by the `ActionServlet` to do its work. The root element of the file is `<struts-config>`. It defines the following information, in this order:

❑ **DataSources**
Used to configure connections to external databases in this configuration file. Each data source is defined under a `<data-source>` element, and these elements are in turn grouped together under the element `<data-sources>` in the Struts configuration file.

❑ **ActionForm beans**
Defined within `<form-bean>` element. These elements are grouped together inside the `<form-beans>` element.

❑ **Global Exceptions**
A `<global-exceptions>` tag containing zero or more `<exception>` elements. These define the application exceptions that you want Struts to handle and what action should be taken in response to each of them. You can also define these on a per-action basis (see below).

❑ **Global Forwards**
We can define global forwards for JSP pages that will be used a lot in our application. Each global forward is defined within a `<forward>` element, and these elements are grouped together under `<global-forwards>`.

❑ **ActionMappings**
An `<action-mappings>` element that can contain zero or more `<action>` elements, each mapping a specific action URL to the `Action` class handling it. These action classes are provided by the application developer.

In addition, each `<action>` can have its own private list of exception handlers and forwards.

❑ **Controller configuration**
The `<controller>` element allows a great deal of control over the way the controller operates, including as the debugging level and the automatic capturing of the remote user's `Locale`.

❑ **Message Resources**
There can be zero or more `<message-resources>` elements, each specifying the location of a resource bundle for internationalized messages.

❑ **Struts Plug-Ins**
Defined using the `<plug-in>` element. Each plug-in can receive further configuration information from nested `<set-property>` elements.

The `ActionServlet` loads the XML configuration file on startup. The name and location of the configuration file can be defined as an initialization parameter to the `ActionServlet`. If not specified, it defaults to `/WEB-INF/struts-config.xml` (relative to the web application root). The `ActionServlet` can also be forced to reload this configuration information programmatically.

We will now take a look at how to configure the most important of these elements by building a sample `struts-config.xml` file.

Walking Through a Sample Struts Configuration File

We start off with the top-level `<struts-config>` element:

```
<struts-config>
```

We'll go through the sub-elements in the order in which they must appear under this element.

Configuring JDBC DataSources

Any number of JDBC `javax.sql.DataSource` objects for the application can be defined in the configuration file under the element `<data-sources>`. Every data source is defined within the data-sources element using the `<data-source>` element. The `<data-source>` element defines a number of attributes, the most important of which are listed in the following table.

Element Attribute	Description
key	The name used by `Action` classes for looking up this connection. The default is `org.apache.struts.action.DATA_SOURCE` (defined in the constant `org.apache.struts.Globals.DATA_SOURCE_KEY`)
type	The name of the actual class that implements the `DataSource` interface

Any further configuration information is supplied using nested `<set-property>` tags. These tags can be used to set JavaBeans properties on the `DataSource`; they take `property` and `value` attributes to specify which property to set and what value to set it to.

The default attribute values for `<data-source>` cause it to instantiate a `GenericDataSource` and give it the key. The `GenericDataSource` class wraps an ordinary JDBC `Driver` and turns it into a `DataSource` with a database connection pool. This class has a number of JavaBean properties to configure, the most important of which are listed in the following table.

Element Attribute	Description
Description	A description of this `DataSource`
DriverClass	The fully qualified JDBC `Driver` class used to access the database
url	The JDBC URL used to access the database
User	The username used to log into the database
Password	The password used to log into the database
MaxCount	The maximum number of connections in the connection pool
ReadOnly	If `true`, the `Connections` returned by the `DataSource` are read-only; this has performance advantages with some databases
AutoCommit	If `true`, the `Connections` returned by the `DataSource` automatically commit the transaction after every SQL statement

The excerpt below illustrates how we can use these attributes to define a `DataSource` for a MySQL database:

```
<data-sources>
  <data-source key="mydatabase">
  <set-property property="description" value="My Database"/>
  <set-property property="driverClass" value="com.mysql.jdbc.Driver"/>
  <set-property property="url"
              value="jdbc:mysql://localhost/mydatabase"/>
  <set-property property="user" value="myuser"/>
  <set-property property="password" value="mypassword"/>
  </data-source>
</data-sources>
```

The `DataSource` will be bound in the application context under the name `mydatabase`. It can be used in the JSTL `<sql:query>`, `<sql:update>`, and `<sql:transaction>` tags.

```
<sql:query var="myobject" dataSource="$
  {applicationScope.mydatabase}">
```

It can also be retrieved from within a Struts `Action` using the `getDataSource()` method:

```
DataSource ds = getDataSource(request, "mydatabase");
Connection con = ds.getConnection();
```

Now let's configure a form bean.

Configuring ActionForm Beans

As we have noted, `ActionForm` beans are used by the `ActionServlet` to capture request parameters. These beans have attribute names that correspond to the names of the request parameters. The controller populates the `ActionForm` for the current action from the request, and then passes the instance to the `Action` class to further process the data.

`ActionForm` beans are declared globally within the configuration file using `<form-bean>` elements inside the `<form-beans>` tag. Here are the important attributes of this element; both `name` and `type` attributes are required.

Attribute	Description
name	The name of the form bean in its associated scope (in other words, the name of the request or session attribute that will contain the bean). The Struts `ActionMappings`, below, can refer to the form bean by name.
type	The fully qualified name of the `ActionForm` class.

The excerpt from our sample configuration file below shows how a form bean can be declared:

```
<form-beans>
  <form-bean name="creditCardForm" type="com.wrox.shop.CreditCardForm"/>
</form-beans>
```

Here a form bean of type `com.wrox.shop.CreditCardForm` is declared to use the name `creditCardForm`. After setting up the global exception handling and page forwards, we will look at how an `ActionMapping` can use this bean.

Struts also supports **dynamic action forms**, which need `<form-property>` elements nested inside `<form-bean>` to configure them. We will discuss these in the *Dynamic Action Forms* section near the end of the chapter.

Configuring Global Exceptions

The next section in the Struts configuration file configures, application-wide, how exceptions thrown in your `Action` classes are handled. These are defined using the `<global-exceptions>` element, which contains an `<exception>` element for each exception that we want Struts to catch and handle. Unhandled exceptions are propagated to the servlet container and handled according to the configuration in `web.xml`. The most frequently used attributes of the `<exception>` element are:

Element Attribute	Description
type	The fully qualified class name of the `Exception` to catch.
path	The resource to forward to if this exception occurs. If no path is given, Struts forwards to the input page of the action that threw the exception.
key	The name of the internationalized message to display for this exception.
bundle	The `ResourceBundle` to use to look up the message.
scope	Whether the `ActionError` object used to encapsulate this error should be request-scoped or session-scoped. The default is `request`.

Both `type` and `key` are required. The excerpt below shows how we could handle `SQLExceptions`:

```
<global-exceptions>
  <exception type="java.sql.SQLException" key="errors.database"/>
</global-exceptions>
```

This tells Struts that whenever an `Action` throws an `SQLException`, it should create an `ActionError` object with the message `errors.database` and forward the request back to the `ActionMapping`'s input page. The error message can then be displayed using the Struts HTML tag library, which we will discuss later.

Configuring Global Forwards

Global forwards help us to avoid hardcoding the page flow of our application by associating a page name with the location of the actual JSP page or other resource. They are defined using the `<global-forwards>` element, which contains a `<forward>` element for each global forward. The `<forward>` element is a convenient way to configure logical names for View resources to which an `Action` class can forward. These forwards can be accessed by name using the `findForward()` method on the `ActionMapping`. Hardwiring View page names in our `Action` classes would weaken the separation of responsibilities we are trying to achieve using the MVC architecture; using the logical names provided by `<forward>` tags gets around this problem.

The most frequently used `<forward>` attributes are:

Element Attribute	Description
name	The name of the forward.
path	The resource to forward to.
redirect	If `true`, redirection is used rather than a forward. We covered the difference between these two in Chapter 10.

The `name` and `path` attributes are required. The excerpt below shows a global forward declaration:

```
<global-forwards>
  <forward name="shop" path="/index.jsp"/>
  <forward name="cart" path="/showcart.jsp"/>
</global-forwards>
```

This globally associates the forward name `shop` with the `/index.jsp` page, and the name `cart` with the `/showcart.jsp` page.

Configuring Action Mappings

`ActionMapping` objects are the heart of the Struts configuration file. They map incoming request URIs to `Action` classes, and associate `Action` classes with `ActionForms`. The controller servlet stores these mappings internally. When a request arrives, it examines the request URI, looks up the associated `ActionMapping` and ultimately calls the `Action` class associated with that action mapping. All `Action` classes use an `execute()` method to implement the application-specific code. This method returns an instance of the `ActionForward` class that contains the name of the target resource to which the response has to be forwarded.

`ActionMappings` are defined using the `<action-mappings>` element, which may include zero or more `<action>` elements. The `<action>` element has a number of attributes and sub-elements. The attributes defined for the `<action>` element are listed below. You must specify the `path` attribute, and either a `type` or a `forward`; all other attributes are optional:

Element Attribute	Description
path	The request URI path that will invoke this `ActionMapping`. This path should start with "/" and not include periods; this also means that you should *omit the filename extension* (usually `.do`).
unknown	If the value of this attribute is set to `true`, this action is used as the default action for request URIs that do not correspond to any action mapping path.

Element Attribute	Description
type	The fully qualified name of the Action class this mapping links to. If you specify a type, you cannot specify a forward attribute but you can still supply one or more nested <forward> tags.
forward	The resource path to forward the request to. If you specify a forward attribute, you cannot specify an action type to execute or any nested forwards.
name	This attribute defines the name of the ActionForm bean associated with this action, as used by the Action class. This is the same name used to define the form bean in a <form-bean> element.
attribute	This is the name of the request or session scope attribute under which the ActionForm bean is stored, if different from the name attribute.
scope	The value can be either request or session to indicate the scope of the ActionForm bean. The default is request scope.
validate	If this attribute is omitted, or its value is set to true, the controller will call the validate() method on the ActionForm bean to perform input validation, before the execute() method is called on the Action. If validation fails, the request is forwarded to the input form discussed below.
input	Relative path to the input form, to which the control must be returned if a bean validation error is encountered, or when an exception is thrown that is handled by an <exception> tag without path.
parameter	An additional parameter that will be passed to the action. You can use this to supply extra configuration information to your action.
roles	A comma-separated list of user roles. If this is specified, access to this action is restricted to authenticated users with these roles. This can be used as a convenient alternative to setting up security constraints in web.xml.
prefix	Prefix used to match request parameters to bean properties. This is useful if the attributes to be set are not part of the action form itself, but of a bean contained inside the action form.
suffix	Suffix used to match request parameters to bean properties.

The <action> element can take a number of nested tags; the most important are:

❑ Zero or more <exception> tags can be used to define exception handling rules specific to the action mapping.

❑ Zero or more <forward> tags can provide the action mapping with additional forward destinations. The Action classes can access the forwards by name using the findForward() method defined in the ActionMapping class. This method takes a String representing the name of the forward as an argument, and returns an instance of the ActionForward class to the ActionServlet.

Both of these work in exactly the same way as the global exceptions and forwards discussed above. If there is any overlap or conflict between the global definitions and the ones local to the <action> element, the local definitions take precedence.

The excerpt below shows an example <action> element demonstrating the most important features.

```
<action-mappings>
  <action path="/payCartItems"
      type="com.wrox.shop.PayCartItemsAction"
      name="creditCardForm"
      scope="session"
      input="/creditcard.jsp">
  <exception type="com.wrox.shop.CreditLimitException"
        key="errors.creditlimit.exceeded"/>
  <forward name="success" path="/paid.jsp"/>
  </action>
</action-mappings>
```

This mapping matches to a request for /payCartItems.do, and uses an Action class of the type PayCartItemsAction. A session-scoped form bean with the name creditCardForm is associated with this mapping; the controller will try to match up request parameters with the attributes of creditCardForm and set any values that are appropriate. It will then call the validate() method on creditCardForm. If validation fails, the request is forwarded to the input page, /creditcard.jsp, together with all the original request information.

If validation succeeds, the execute() method of PayCartItemsAction is called. This action will try to forward to a page with (logical) name "success"; this is mapped to the /paid.jsp page. If the execute() call does not complete successfully, but throws a CreditLimitException, the request is forwarded back to the input page with the error message errors.creditlimit.exceeded.

Configuring The Controller

The configuration file can optionally contain a `<controller>` element that can be used to tweak the way the controller operates. The attributes you are most likely to use are:

Element Attribute	Description
debug	Controls the amount of debugging information (indicating such things as the requests being processed by the controller) that should be written to the log file. Higher numbers give more detail. The default is zero.
inputForward	If set to `true`, the `input` attribute of an `<action>` will specify the name of a local or global forward rather than a resource.
locale	If absent, or set to `true`, the Struts controller will store a `Locale` object in the session corresponding to the user's locale.
maxFileSize	The maximum size of a file upload, e.g. `"250M"` (the default), `"100K"`, or perhaps `"7GB"` if you expect people to upload whole DVDs at a time.
tempdir	Temporary directory used to process file uploads.
nocache	Set to `true` if you would like the controller to insert headers that attempt to defeat browser and proxy caching. This is necessary if one and the same URL may produce different results depending on the user's session state or external systems, e.g. news items being updated every few minutes.

For example, you could use the following if browser or proxy caching causes obsolete content to be displayed occasionally:

```
<controller nocache="true"/>
```

Configuring Message Resources

As discussed earlier, the message resource bundles are at the heart of Struts' internationalization support. One or more `<message-resources>` tags can be used to tell Struts where these bundles can be found. Each bundle will be stored as an application-scoped JavaBean. The attributes most often used are:

Element Attribute	Description
key	The key under which the bundle will be stored in the `ServletContext`, and the name by which you can refer to it elsewhere.
parameter	The name of the bundle to load. Message resource bundles are loaded using the Java class loader, so this can include a package name.
null	If set to `true`, an unknown message key will return a `null` message. By default, an error message would be returned to help diagnose the problem.

In many cases, a single bundle is all we need.

```
<message-resources parameter="resources.messages"/>
```

This will cause Struts to load `/WEB-INF/classes/resources/messages.properties` and the other files in the message bundle. The file could also reside inside a `jar` in `/WEB-INF/lib` or somewhere else in the class path. The bundle would be bound as the default message bundle with the special name `org.apache.struts.action.MESSAGE` (this value is defined in the constant `org.apache.struts.Globals.MESSAGE_KEY`).

Configuring Struts Plug-ins

The final items in the Struts configuration file are zero or more `<plug-in>` elements. These are used to hook Struts extensions into the framework. The plug-in class is set using the `className` attribute, and nested `<set-property>` elements can be used to configure the plug-in class by setting its JavaBean properties.

Element Attribute	Description
className	Fully qualified name of the plug-in class.

Commonly used plug-ins include the Struts Validator and Tiles plug-ins, both discussed later in this chapter. The following example illustrates how to set up the Validator plug-in:

```
<plug-in className="org.apache.struts.validator.ValidatorPlugIn">
  <set-property property="pathnames"
      value="/WEB-INF/validator-rules.xml,/WEB-INF/validation.xml"/>
</plug-in>
```

The nested `<set-property>` element will call `setPathnames()` on the plug-in to set the configuration file paths. The properties that can be set will differ from plug-in to plug-in.

Wrapping Up

With all of the configuration done in our `struts-config.xml` file, we need to close the top-level element:

```
</struts-config>
```

Struts configuration is extremely flexible. For advanced use you can tailor the framework and plug in your own classes, setting their JavaBean properties using nested `<set-property>` tags. Graphical configuration and monitoring tools are supported by optional `<icon-name>`, `<display-name>` and `<description>` tags that can be nested inside many of the elements described above. But Struts' power out of the box is more than sufficient for most projects and the features discussed so far will take you a very long way indeed.

Now that we have thoroughly explored the Struts configuration options, before we look a little more deeply at how the core Struts classes fit together, it would be good to first put Struts in action by converting the shopping cart example to use Struts.

In this example, we will take the Model 2 (MVC) shopping cart from the start of this chapter and turn it into a Struts application. The main change is that we will jettison the `controller.jsp` file in favor of the Struts controller and an `Action` class that adds a book to the cart.

Try It Out   A Struts Application

1. Start by copying the `Shopping-2` web application folder and naming the copy `Shopping-3`. You can delete the `controller.jsp` file. Then install the Struts libraries following the instructions in the *Using Struts in a Web Application* section above.

2. Let's start by writing the `web.xml` deployment descriptor to map all *.do requests to the Struts `ActionServlet`. This file belongs in the `WEB-INF` directory:

```xml
<?xml version="1.0" encoding="UTF-8"?>
<web-app xmlns="http://java.sun.com/xml/ns/j2ee"
    xmlns:xsi="http://www.w3.org/2001/XMLSchema-instance"
    xsi:schemaLocation="http://java.sun.com/xml/ns/j2ee
              http://java.sun.com/xml/ns/j2ee/web-app_2_4.xsd"
    version="2.4">

  <servlet>
   <servlet-name>controller</servlet-name>
   <servlet-class>org.apache.struts.action.ActionServlet</servlet-class>
   <load-on-startup>1</load-on-startup>
  </servlet>
```

```
  <servlet-mapping>
    <servlet-name>controller</servlet-name>
    <url-pattern>*.do</url-pattern>
  </servlet-mapping>

</web-app>
```

3. We also need a Struts configuration file. In essence, it defines the same four actions that our old `controller.jsp` implemented. Save the following code in the `WEB-INF` folder as `struts-config.xml`:

```
<?xml version="1.0" encoding="UTF-8"?>
<!DOCTYPE struts-config PUBLIC
       "-//Apache Software Foundation//DTD Struts Configuration 1.1//EN"
       "http://jakarta.apache.org/struts/dtds/struts-config_1_1.dtd">
<struts-config>

  <form-beans>
    <form-bean name="cart" type="com.wrox.shop.ShoppingCart"/>
  </form-beans>

  <action-mappings>

    <action path="/add"
            type="com.wrox.shop.AddBookAction"
            name="cart"
            scope="session">
      <forward name="success" path="/showcart.jsp"/>
    </action>

    <action path="/cart"
        forward="/showcart.jsp"/>

    <action path="/update"
        forward="/showcart.jsp"
            name="cart"
          scope="session"/>

    <action path="/catalog"
        forward="/index.jsp"/>

  </action-mappings>

</struts-config>
```

4. Because we will be updating the `ShoppingCart` using Struts, we've got to turn the cart into a proper Struts `ActionForm`. The changes required to `ShoppingCart.java` are minimal – it has to extend `ActionForm`, and the signature of the `validate()` method needs to be altered to what Struts expects:

```
package com.wrox.shop;

import java.util.ArrayList;
import java.util.Iterator;
import java.util.List;
import javax.servlet.http.HttpServletRequest;
import org.apache.struts.action.ActionErrors;
import org.apache.struts.action.ActionForm;
import org.apache.struts.action.ActionMapping;

/**
 * Models a shopping cart holding a number of Books
 */
public class ShoppingCart extends ActionForm

{

    .
    .
    .


    public ActionErrors validate(ActionMapping mapping,
                                 HttpServletRequest request)
    {
        for (Iterator i = items.iterator(); i.hasNext(); )
        {
            ShoppingCartItem item = (ShoppingCartItem)i.next();
            if (item.getQuantity() <= 0) { i.remove(); }
        }
        return null;
    }
}
```

5. Next thing to implement is the `com.wrox.shop.AddBookAction` class that will add a book to the cart. Save the following as `AddBookAction.java` in the `shop` folder with the other Java classes:

```
package com.wrox.shop;

import javax.servlet.ServletContext;
import javax.servlet.http.HttpServletRequest;
import javax.servlet.http.HttpServletResponse;
import org.apache.struts.action.Action;
import org.apache.struts.action.ActionForm;
import org.apache.struts.action.ActionForward;
import org.apache.struts.action.ActionMapping;

/**
 * Struts Action invoked when the user wants to add a Book to the cart
 */
```

```
public class AddBookAction extends Action
{
  public ActionForward execute(ActionMapping mapping, ActionForm form,
                               HttpServletRequest request,
                               HttpServletResponse response)
  {
    ServletContext ctx = servlet.getServletContext();
    Catalog catalog = (Catalog)ctx.getAttribute("catalog");
    ShoppingCart cart = (ShoppingCart)form;
    int book = Integer.parseInt(request.getParameter("index"));
    cart.addBook((Book)catalog.get(book));
    return mapping.findForward("success");
  }
}
```

6. Finally, the way the controller is invoked changes a little. Instead of, say, the path
   controller.jsp?action=add, we now simply have add.do. We need to make the
   highlighted changes below to our forms' actions in index.jsp:

   ```
        .
        .
        .
     <td align="right">
     <form action="add.do">
       <p><input type="submit" value="Add"></p>
       <input type="hidden" name="index" value="${status.index}"/>
       <input type="hidden">
     </form>
        .
        .
        .
   <td colspan="3" align="right">
     <form action="cart.do">
       <input type="submit" value="View Cart"/>
     </form>
        .
        .
        .
   ```

7. Similarly, make these changes to the showcart.jsp page:

   ```
        .
        .
        .
   <table cellpadding="5" style="background:#ffeeee" width="80%">
     <form action="update.do">
     <tr style="background:#ffdddd">
        .
        .
        .
   ```

```
<td colspan="3" align="right">
  <form action="catalog.do">
  <input type="submit" value="Continue Shopping">
    .
    .
    .
```

Note that we've removed two hidden `<input>` fields from the files in Steps 6 and 7 as well as changing the `<form>` tags.

8. That is it! After making these modifications, recompile the classes by running the following command – all on one line – from the `classes` directory:

> **> javac com/wrox/shop/*.java -classpath**
> **..\lib\struts.jar;%CATALINA_HOME%\common\lib\servlet-api.jar**

If you've changed your CLASSPATH environment variable to include either of these JARs, you can leave them out of the `-classpath` switch.

9. Restart Tomcat, and direct your browser to http://localhost:8080/Shopping-3 and try it out.

<hr>

How It Works

The logic for adding a book to the shopping cart has been moved to a subclass of the Struts `Action` class, `AddBookAction`, which contains the logic to add a book to the shopping cart. It is mapped to /add.do:

```
<action path="/add"
        type="com.wrox.shop.AddBookAction"
        name="cart"
        scope="session">
  <forward name="success" path="/showcart.jsp"/>
</action>
```

Why define the `cart` form (mapped to the `ShoppingCart` class in the `<form-beans>` section) as the action form? After all, the `AddBookAction` takes the book `index` as a parameter, which does not match any of the cart properties. The reason is that the `ShoppingCart` object does not necessarily exist at this point. By letting Struts handle it, we save ourselves the trouble of checking if it exists and, if not, instantiating it and storing the new cart in the session. This is now all taken care of by Struts.

The actual `AddBookAction` class is a bit more verbose than our old JSTL code. It starts by retrieving the `Catalog` from the servlet context, and casting the cart form passed in by Struts to `ShoppingCart` so we can call all the `ShoppingCart`-specific methods:

```
ServletContext ctx = servlet.getServletContext();
Catalog catalog = (Catalog)ctx.getAttribute("catalog");
ShoppingCart cart = (ShoppingCart)form;
```

After retrieving the `index` request parameter indicating the book to add, and turning it into a proper integer, we are ready to call `cart.addBook()`. Finally we forward to the `"success"` view (`/showcart.jsp`):

```
int book = Integer.parseInt(request.getParameter("index"));
cart.addBook((Book)catalog.get(book));
return mapping.findForward("success");
```

That, admittedly, is more code than we had previously because the JSP Expression Language did all the casting and conversion that we now had to do explicitly in Java. The /update.do mapping more than makes up for it, however:

```
<action path="/update"
     forward="/showcart.jsp"
        name="cart"
       scope="session"/>
```

This action mapping defines a simple forward – there is no `Action` class or other Java code at all. The reason is that the field names for book quantities, `item[0].quantity`, `item[1].quantity`, and so forth, correspond exactly to `quantity` of the `item` indexed JavaBean property of our `ShoppingCart`. As we have seen, the first thing the Struts controller does is figure out whether there are any request parameters that match `ActionForm` attributes, and update the form when they do. The next thing it does is call the form's `validate()` method, which in our case just removes the books that have a zero quantity against them from the cart. All we need to do is to let Struts do its job and then forward to the view JSP page.

This matching of HTML form parameters and Struts `ActionForm` classes is a very powerful feature, but it takes some up-front planning to match all the attribute names and types with the HTML forms in your application.

Now that we have seen the Struts controller in action, including an `ActionForm` and an `Action` class, we are ready to explore these and other important Struts classes in more depth.

Core Struts Components

In this section, we are going to discuss the relationships between the main Struts controller components, namely:

- ❑ The `ActionServlet` controller which is at the heart of the Struts framework
- ❑ `ActionMapping` objects describing the mapping of a request URI to an `Action`
- ❑ `Action` classes, which you write to provide the business logic "glue"
- ❑ `ActionMessage` and `ActionError` classes to pass on messages to the View component
- ❑ `ActionForm` beans to capture request parameters

Let's start by examining the main controller component: `ActionServlet`.

The ActionServlet Class

The `org.apache.struts.action.ActionServlet` is the main Struts controller component. We have seen that it's usually mapped to the .do extension in `web.xml`.

The servlet can take a fair number of configuration parameters in its `<servlet>` declaration. The most important of these is the `config` attribute:

Parameter	Description
config	The location and name of the configuration file. The default is /WEB-INF/struts-config.xml.

There are many more, but most of these are either deprecated leftovers from Struts 1.0, or more easily configured using the Struts configuration file.

The `ActionServlet` class exposes a number of public methods; some of these are mandated by the `Servlet` interface, the others are either deprecated or important only when you want to extend the Struts framework itself with custom constructs and configuration objects. These are beyond the scope of this book, but you can find more information about them at http://jakarta.apache.org/struts/ and in the documentation that came with the Struts download.

The ActionMapping Class

As we will see, an instance of the `org.apache.struts.action.ActionMapping` class representing the action mapping for the request is passed to the `execute()` method of the `Action` class. This object encapsulates all the information defined in the `<action>` element of the configuration file. The `ActionMapping` class defines getter and setter methods for these attributes.

The most important methods are those used to manipulate the forward list associated with the mapping.

```
public ActionForward findForward(String name)
```

This method returns the `ActionForward` for the given name; this is an object that encapsulates the destination resource to forward to. For example, you will find the following code snippet often at the end of `Action` classes.

```
return mapping.findForward("success");
```

This finds the local or global forward named "success" and returns it to the `ActionServlet` to act upon. Closely related to this is the `getInputForward()` method:

```
public ActionForward getInputForward()
```

This method returns an `ActionForward` corresponding to the `input` attribute of the `<action>` tag. This can be useful if, after performing some processing in your `Action`, you find that you need to forward the request back to the input form with an error message (although in such cases, throwing an exception and handling it using the `<exception>` tag might be a more transparent alternative).

Finally, the `findForwards()` method finds all *local* forward names associated with this action.

```
public String[] findForwards()
```

This method does not return an exhaustive list of the names recognized by `findForward()`, because it disregards any globally defined forwards.

```
public String getParameter ()
```

Can you remember that when discussing the `<action>` tag in the configuration file, there was a `parameter` attribute that could be used to pass some extra configuration information into actions? This is the method an `Action` can call to obtain the parameter value.

Action Classes

The `org.apache.struts.action.Action` classes we provide are responsible for processing user requests. When the `ActionServlet` needs a specific type of `Action` for the very first time, it instantiates a single object of that class and uses that object to handle *all* requests for that `Action` for the remainder of the application's lifetime.

> This means that all Actions that you write must be thread safe. The safest
> thing to do is only to use method-local variables in your Action classes, and
> never to have any instance variables or static variables in these classes.

The Execute Method

The most important public method in the `Action` class is `execute()`. You must override this
method to implement the business logic you want to execute:

```
public ActionForward execute(ActionMapping mapping, ActionForm form,
                        HttpServletRequest request,
                        HttpServletResponse response)
    throws Exception
```

The first argument is the `ActionMapping` associated with the request. You can use this to
find out about the `<action>` attributes, such as the `parameter`, and to find the forwards
defined for the mapping as discussed in the previous section. The second argument is the
input `ActionForm` defined for the mapping, or `null` if no input form has been defined. You
will usually cast this form to the specific type of form expected:

```
CreditCardForm ccForm = (CreditCardForm)form;
```

The last two arguments are the usual request and response objects. In most cases, it is a good
habit not to actually write anything to the response, as that is the responsibility of the View
resource you are forwarding to. Finally, the `execute()` method should return an
`ActionForward` object encapsulating the destination to forward to. Usually, you will look
this object up in the mapping:

```
return mapping.findForward("success");
```

You can create your own `ActionForward` object if you wish, but this is best avoided. These
forwards really ought to be set up in the Struts configuration file.

The last thing to note is that the `execute()` method can throw any type of `Exception`.
These exceptions can be caught and handled using `<exception>` tags in the Struts
configuration file. If you know that your `execute()` can throw only a few exceptions, for
example `CreditLimitException` and `SQLException`, it is a good idea to make this
explicit in your method declaration:

```
public ActionForward execute(ActionMapping mapping,
            ActionForm form,
            HttpServletRequest request,
            HttpServletResponse response)
        throws CreditLimitException, SQLException
```

```
{
    .
    .
    .
```

This does not make a difference in the behavior or performance of your action class, but it does make the exceptions that can be thrown very explicit and obvious. As such, it is a valuable piece of documentation that someone else can use to find out which <exception> tags to set up.

> *In the Java language, a subclass is always free to throw fewer exceptions than the parent class or interface declares. This is called the "narrowing down" of the* throws *clause. Throwing more or broader exceptions, on the other hand, is never allowed.*

The Action class provides various methods that can be used to pass messages and errors to the view, for internationalization, accessing data sources, and so on. These will be detailed in the next few sections.

Saving Messages and Errors

The saveMessages() method can be used to store informational messages generated by the action code and pass them on to the view for display:

```
protected void saveMessages(HttpServletRequest request,
            ActionMessages messages)
```

We will discuss the ActionMessages object in the next section. Similarly, Action classes can use the saveErrors() method to store error messages when application errors occur:

```
protected void saveErrors(HttpServletRequest request,
            ActionErrors errors)
```

The ActionErrors instance is used to store error messages. Both the ActionMessages and the ActionErrors objects are stored in the request attribute list under special keys. JSP pages can display these error messages using custom tags defined in the HTML tag library. The Struts tags for displaying action and error messages are explained later in the section on the Struts tag libraries.

Accessing Application-Scoped Beans

When you need to retrieve a request or session attribute in your Action, it is obvious how to do this. The execute() method gets the HttpServletRequest giving access to both request-scoped and session-scoped data. It is perhaps less obvious how to access application-scoped (ServletContext) attributes.

```
Catalog cat = (Catalog)servlet.getServletContext()
                .getAttribute("catalog");
```

The protected field `servlet` gives you access to the `ActionServlet` controller that instantiated your `Action`. The line of code above will retrieve the application-scoped `catalog` bean.

Internationalization

There are four methods that deal with message resource bundles and locales.

```
protected MessageResources getResources(HttpServletRequest request)
protected MessageResources getResources(HttpServletRequest request,String
key)
```

The first method retrieves the default `MessageResources` of the application. This object has a number of `getMessage()` methods that you can use to retrieve a given message for a specific locale. For example:

```
MessageResources mr = getResources(request);
String myMessage = mr.getMessage(locale, "my.message.key");
```

The overloaded `getResources()` method that takes an additional key argument can be used to access resources other than the default. The specified key must be identical to the `key` attribute of the `<message-resources>` tag in the Struts configuration file.

```
protected Locale getLocale(HttpServletRequest request)
protected void setLocale(HttpServletRequest request,Locale locale)
```

These methods can be used to get and set the current user's `Locale`. You will normally not have to set this, as Struts will pick up the locale from the HTTP request.

Retrieving Data Sources

A pair of methods provides easy access to the data sources configured using the Struts configuration file:

```
protected DataSource getDataSource(HttpServletRequest request)
protected DataSource getDataSource (HttpServletRequest request,String key)
```

The first method retrieves the application's default `DataSource`, the second one to the data source of the given name (corresponding to the `key` attribute of the configured `<data-source>` tag).

```
DataSource ds = getDataSource(request);
MyObject.businessMethod(ds);
```

Enforcing Application Flow

Finally, the `Action` class provides a few interesting methods to handle the page flow within the application.

```
protected boolean isCancelled(HttpServletRequest request)
```

The Struts HTML tag library, to be discussed below, can generate a special Cancel button for an HTML form. The controller recognizes the Cancel button and treats a cancel request differently from all other requests. Specifically, it bypasses the form validation that would otherwise occur and the `isCancelled()` method returns `true`. A typical usage of this method would be to incorporate the following at the start of the `execute()` method.

```
if (isCancelled(request))
  {
  return mapping.findForward("cancelled");
}
```

The following three methods can be used to enforce a certain flow within your application. Normally, a user is free to open up multiple browser windows for a single session, use the browser history to move between pages in arbitrary ways, and press Refresh to reload certain pages. When that page happens to be a "Thank You" page for an online payment, refreshing that page would resubmit the payment confirmation form and could result in the payment being taken twice. This is of course to be avoided at all costs. It is disturbing to see that some e-commerce sites still do not contain any safeguards against this and have to ask their users not to press Refresh – after reading this section, you will be able to do better!

```
protected boolean saveToken(HttpServletRequest request)
protected boolean isTokenValid(HttpServletRequest request)
protected boolean isTokenValid(HttpServletRequest request, boolean reset)
protected boolean resetToken(HttpServletRequest request, boolean reset)
```

By calling `saveToken()`, you tell Struts to generate a random **transaction token** and save it in the user's session.

```
saveToken(request);
```

You then forward to the JSP page with (say) the payment confirmation form. If you use the Struts HTML tags discussed later to render this form, Struts will incorporate the transaction token as a hidden form field. In the action that process the form submission, you can test the token using `isTokenValid()`:

```
if (!isTokenValid(request, true))
  {
  throw new InvalidTransactionException();
}
```

The second argument (`reset`) tells Struts to remove the token from the session. If, some time later, the user uses the browser history to go back to the payment confirmation page and submits it again, the token embedded in the form will no longer match the transaction token (if any) in the user's session. The code above will detect this and throw an `InvalidTransactionException` to abort the payment.

If we are in the middle of a longer process, we can call `isTokenValid(request, false)` or simply `isTokenValid(request)` to test a token without removing it. Finally, `resetToken()` simply removes the existing token without any checking.

Error and Action Message Classes

Occasionally an action needs to produce one or more status messages or error messages and communicate these to the view JSP page. Although it is not all that difficult to simply store such messages in request attributes, Struts provides `ActionMessage` and `ActionError` mechanisms to accomplish this in a more structured manner. This imposes some uniformity, making our code easier to read and maintain, and enables us to use the Struts HTML tags that assist in displaying these messages. Moreover, it helps internationalization: given the discussion of internationalization earlier in this chapter, it will not surprise you that both of these are designed to contain message keys rather than the actual message texts.

ActionMessage and ActionMessages

An `org.apache.struts.action.ActionMessage` is a Java object that contains a message key and up to four replacement values for the message. The `ActionMessages` (note plural) class, part of the same Java package, acts as a container for an arbitrary number of related `ActionMessage` objects. Before we go on to discuss the API, let's look at a small example first. The following code could be part of an `Action` implementing a credit card payment.

```
String status = paymentGateway.pay(creditCard, amount);
ActionMessages messages = new ActionMessages();
ActionMessage message = new ActionMessage("payment.success.status", status)
messages.add(ActionMessages.GLOBAL_MESSAGE, message);
saveMessages(request, messages);
return mapping.findForward("success");
```

First we perform a payment and retrieve the status message. The second line creates the `ActionMessages` container that, in our case, will contain just a single message. Then we create a new message with key `payment.success.status` and the status string as replacement text, and add it to the `ActionMessages` container. The final line saves the `ActionMessages` object so that Struts tags in the view JSP page can retrieve it. The message resource file for the application would include a line like:

```
payment.success.status=Thanks for Paying (status {0})
```

The `{0}` will be replaced by the payment status code we passed into the `ActionMessage` constructor.

The `ActionMessage` API is extremely simple. It has constructors that take a message key and zero to four replacement values. Finally, there's a constructor that takes an arbitrary array with replacement values:

```
public ActionMessage(String key)
public ActionMessage(String key, Object value0)
public ActionMessage(String key, Object value0, Object value1)
public ActionMessage(String key, Object value0, Object value1,
                     Object value2)
public ActionMessage(String key, Object value0, Object value1,
                     Object value2, Object value3)
public ActionMessage(String key, Object[] values)
```

There are also `getKey()` and `getValues()` methods that retrieve these constructor arguments, but you are likely to simply use the Struts tag libraries instead.

The `ActionMessages` container class is quite simple to use. For our purposes, it has only two interesting methods, `add()` and `clear()`.

```
public void add(String property, ActionMessage message)
```

The `property` argument is useful if the message we are storing relates to a specific JavaBean property of an action form, or a specific area of the HTML page. This makes it easy to display messages close to the visual element they relate to, for example right next to a form field.

To add a message that does not relate to any specific field or area, use the GLOBAL_MESSAGE constant defined in the `ActionMessages` class, as in the example above.

```
public void clear()
```

This clears all existing messages out of the `ActionMessages` object.

ActionError and ActionErrors

In addition to the message classes discussed above, Struts defines `ActionError` and `ActionErrors` classes, also part of the `org.apache.struts.action` package. These actually extend `ActionMessage` and `ActionMessages` without adding any new behavior – the GLOBAL_MESSAGE constant is now called GLOBAL_ERROR and that's about it. They just serve to distinguish application error messages from informational messages.

Typically, you use them in an Action when some type of problem occurs. To continue with our payment example, we could add some code to check for an error status:

```
String status = paymentGateway.pay(creditCard, amount);
if (status.equals(PaymentGateway.PAYMENT_FAILED))
{
  ActionErrors errors = new ActionErrors();
```

```
    ActionError error = new ActionError("payment.failed");
    errors.add(ActionErrors.GLOBAL_ERROR, error);
    saveMessages(request, messages);
    return mapping.getInputForward();
}
ActionMessages messages = new ActionMessages();
ActionMessage message = new ActionMessage("payment.success.status",
                                    status)
messages.add(ActionMessages.GLOBAL_MESSAGE, message);
saveMessages(request, messages);
return mapping.findForward("success");
```

If the `pay()` call returns a `PAYMENT_FAILED` status, we go back to the input page. In fact, this is quite similar to the way Struts validation works under the hood.

While the `ActionErrors` mechanism is a great way to collect multiple errors or warnings, such as invalid field values, it should be emphasized that this is not the best way to handle fatal errors such as a payment failure. Well-conceived Java classes signal a fatal error by throwing an `Exception` of some kind. We can then use a local or global `<exception>` tag in the Struts configuration file to catch this exception and associate it with a message key, and then either forward the request back to the input page or to a special error page. With minimal effort, this does the same job as the Java code listed above.

ActionForm Classes

The `ActionForm` classes we provide must extend the Struts class `org.apache.struts.action.ActionForm` or any of its subclasses. When the controller finds that the `ActionMapping` for a request defines an action form name, it checks if this form already exists in the specified `scope`. If not, it looks up the form type in the `<form-beans>` list and instantiates a new form.

Subsequently, the controller compares the request parameters with the form's JavaBean attributes, and populates any attributes whose names match request parameters. Unless the mapping specifies `validate="false"`, the controller then calls the `validate()` method on the form to give you the opportunity to perform validation. Finally, the controller executes the `Action`.

From this description, you can see that an `ActionForm` serves a dual purpose. Firstly, it is an easy way to capture request parameters; Struts does all the hard work of converting these parameters to the right Java types and calling the setter methods in the form. Secondly, these forms can contain validation code.

We will now have a look at the methods provided by the `ActionForm` class.

Validation

The reset() method is called immediately before the controller starts populating form properties from the request. The default implementation does nothing, and we override this method if we want to perform some initialization of our own at this point.

```
public void reset(ActionMapping mapping, HttpServletRequest request)
```

If validation is enabled for the mapping, the controller will call the validate() method immediately after setting the form properties. The default implementation does nothing and simply returns null to indicate that there aren't any errors. You can override this method to actually do some useful validation.

```
public ActionErrors validate(ActionMapping mapping,
                             HttpServletRequest request)
```

If you do not return an ActionErrors object, or if the ActionErrors object you return does not contain any messages, validation is considered to be successful. If it does contain error messages, the controller will store them as a request attribute and forward to the input form so that the errors can be displayed.

The code snippet below shows how we could implement some simple validation to verify that the credit card number in a CreditCardForm is a 16-digit number. We will leave out the setters and getters and concentrate purely on the validation code:

```
public class CreditCardForm extends ActionForm
{

  private String cardNumber;

    .
    .
    .

  public ActionErrors validate(ActionMapping mapping,
                               HttpServletRequest request)
  {
    ActionErrors errors = new ActionErrors();
```

The Struts controller will have read the value the user entered into the cardNumber HTML input field and it will be stored in the cardNumber field of our CreditCardForm. The first test adds an error message to the list if this number has anything other than 16 digits:

```
    if (cardNumber.length() != 16)
    {
      ActionError error = new ActionError("error.creditcard.16digits");
      errors.add("cardNumber", error);
    }
```

The next test adds an error if `java.lang.Long.parse()` finds that the field is not actually a valid number. These tests are by no means complete; the number can still be negative, for instance:

```
try
{
  Long.parseLong(cardNumber);
}
catch (NumberFormatException e)
{
  ActionError error= new ActionError("error.creditcard.notanumber");
  errors.add("cardNumber", error);
}
```

Finally, the error list is returned. If the list is empty then validation was successful:

```
    return errors;
  }
}
```

A word or two of warning is appropriate here:

❑   An `ActionForm` is not always the best place for validation. Sometimes what constitutes valid input has more to do with the actual Action being undertaken at that moment than with the data item we are working with. In that case, the validation code is best placed inside your `Action` class.

❑   At the end of this chapter, we will explore two Struts technologies, the Validator and dynamic forms, which allow you to create a simple Struts form and define validation rules for it without a single line of Java coding. Even though they have their limitations, they can save you a great deal of work.

Phew! We covered a lot of ground. However, once you've worked your way through this section, perhaps by trying out Struts in your own applications and revisiting a couple of the class descriptions above along the way, you will gain a good grasp of the most important aspects of the Struts controller framework. We will now take a look at the tag libraries that support the framework in our JSP view components.

Introducing the Struts Tag Libraries

A number of tag libraries, which support the development of JSP view components that integrate with the controller, are shipped with Struts. These libraries are:

❑   **Bean Tags** to manipulate JavaBeans

❑   **Logic Tags** to provide conditionals and looping within a JSP page

❑   **HTML Tags** to support the creation of HTML forms and other HTML elements

❑ **Nested Tags** to ease development when your JSP structure mirrors your object structure

❑ **Template Tags** that provide a simple templating mechanism

❑ **Tiles Tags** to extend the template idea to build a framework for assembling JSP pages from component parts

Entire books have been written on the Struts framework, and it is, unfortunately, far too much to cover in this chapter. In particular, we will not be covering Nested Tags or Tiles, but we'll make a solid start.

Looking through the list, it may strike you that there seems to be some overlap with the JSP Standard Tag Library and the JSP 2.0 Expression Language. Doesn't the JSTL support all conditional and loop constructs you might need? Doesn't the EL provide very convenient access to bean properties? This is entirely true. The Struts framework was conceived for older platforms that had neither the expression language nor the standard template library. We will ignore all the tags from the Struts tag library that have been effectively made obsolete and concentrate on what remains.

JavaBean Properties in Struts

Before looking at the tag libraries, we will first have a brief look at the way Struts addresses JavaBean properties. This is important in many of the tags and also determines how the controller matches up request parameters with `ActionForm` properties.

With Struts tags, you usually provide a JavaBean name and the property you want to manipulate, rather than the simple `beanName.propertyName` syntax that the EL uses. The property part supports the following features:

❑ **Simple JavaBean properties**. For example, our `ShoppingCart` class early in this chapter had a simple read-only property `total`, defined by the `getTotal()` method.

❑ **Indexed JavaBean properties**. The `ShoppingCart` class defines an indexed property `item` by defining `getItem(int index)` and `getItem(int index, ShoppingCartItem item)` methods. Note that the JSP Expression Language does not support indexed properties defined in this way.

Support for properties that are `Lists`, such as the `books` property in our `ShoppingCart`, is incomplete at the time of writing. A `List` property will work fine with the Struts tags but the controller will ignore them as request parameters.

❑ **Nested JavaBean properties**. For example, the title of the first book in our cart corresponds to the property `item[0].book.title`. This is quite similar to the EL approach, but the alternative square-bracket syntax (which would be `item[0]['book']['title']`) is not supported by Struts.

❑ **Mapped properties**. These do not use the Java `Map` interface supported by the EL, but require that the bean class implement getter and setter methods that take an additional `String` parameter denoting the key. The syntax, too, is a complete departure from the EL-like syntax and uses parentheses around the key, for example `myProperty(myKey)`.

All of the above can be combined in arbitrary ways. Hopefully, the next version of Struts (or rather, the BeanUtils package used under the hood) will bring full convergence with the JSP Expression Language.

With the preliminaries out of the way, let's take a more detailed look at the tag libraries themselves.

The Bean Tag Library

The Struts framework provides a variety of custom tags for handling JavaBeans within JSP pages. The URI for this **bean tag library** is `http://jakarta.apache.org/struts/tags-bean-1.0`. With the enhanced capabilities for expressions and manipulation offered by the JSP EL and the JSTL Core and Formatting tags, however, most of the bean tags have been effectively superseded.

❑ `<bean:message>` renders an internationalized message string. Similar to the JSTL `<fmt:message>` tag, but the tight integration with the Struts message resource handling and the replacement string feature make using this tag worthwhile.

❑ `<bean:define>`, `<bean:page>`, `<bean:cookie>`, `<bean:header>`, and `<bean:parameter>` all define a variable based on some request or page context attribute. The same thing can be achieved using `<c:set>` and the expression language, so we won't use these tags.

❑ `<bean:size>` defines a variable containing the number of elements in a given `Map` or `Collection`.

❑ `<bean:write>` renders the value of the specified bean property. Superseded by the JSP Expression Language, `<c:out>` and the JSTL formatting tags.

❑ `<bean:include>` includes an external resource, like `<c:import>`.

❑ `<bean:resource>` loads a web application resource and makes it available as a bean.

❑ `<bean:struts>` exposes a named Struts internal configuration object as a bean.

We will go on to review the most relevant of the tags listed above.

Message Tag

We noted earlier that internationalizing your web-app means messages displayed by your web-app are in the preferred language of the user. In effect this means that when the web-app needs to print a message, it refers to a *message resource bundle* and finds the file containing all of the messages written in the correct language. A web-app may use more than one bundle if the number of messages starts to become unwieldy.

The `<bean:message>` tag allows easy access to any of the resource bundles that have been set up in the Struts configuration file. It allows you to write internationalized messages, labels, prompts, and so on in your JSP page. You can either specify the message key directly, or specify a JavaBean name and optionally a property that will yield the key. The most important attributes, which can all take runtime expressions, are listed in the following table:

Attribute	Description
key	The key of the message in the resource file. If you specify the key, you cannot specify name or property attributes.
name	The name of the JavaBean that contains the message key. If you specify name, you cannot specify the key attribute directly.
property	The JavaBean property that will be used as the message key. If you specify the JavaBean name but no property, the bean itself will be converted to a string and used as the message key.
arg0	First replacement string value.
arg1	Second replacement string value.
arg2	Third replacement string value.
arg3	Fourth replacement string value.
arg4	Fifth (and last) replacement string value.
bundle	The name of the application attribute under which the resources object is stored. If not specified, Globals.MESSAGES_KEY is used (its value is org.apache.struts.action.MESSAGE). When specified, this attribute must match the key specified in `<message-resources>` in the Struts configuration file.
scope	Specify page, request or application if you want to find the bean specified using name in a specific scope.

The example below illustrates the use of the `<bean:message>` tag. Suppose there is a message defined in the resources file as follows:

```
info.myKey=The numbers entered are {0}, {1}, {2}, {3}
```

Further suppose that we use the following message tag:

```
<bean:message key="info.myKey" arg0="5" arg1="6" arg2="7" arg3="8"/>
```

The output written to the JSP page by the `message` tag would then be **The numbers entered are 5,6,7,8.**

Size Tag

This tag defines a scripting variable specifying the size of a `Collection` (such as a `List`) or `Map`. This collection can be specified either directly, or using a JavaBean name and optionally a property.

Attribute	Description
id	The name of the variable to be defined. This will be of type `Integer`.
collection	A runtime expression that evaluates to a `Collection` or `Map`.
name	The name of the JavaBean that contains the `Collection` or `Map`. If you specify `name`, you cannot specify the `collection` directly.
property	The JavaBean property that returns the `Collection` or `Map`. If you specify the JavaBean `name` but no `property`, the bean itself will be used.
scope	Specify `page`, `request`, or `application` if you want to find the bean specified by `name` in a specific scope.

This tag can be useful when you need to know a `Collection`'s size, as EL doesn't provide an easy way to get this. For example, if we have a `List` called `books` and we need to define a table cell that spans as many rows as we have `books`, we can use the following code:

```
<bean:size id="numberOfBooks" name="books">
<table>
  <tr>
    <td rowspan="${numberOfBooks}">
```

Resource Tag

This tag will retrieve a web application resource, and introduce a variable of type `InputStream` or `String`. The difference with `<c:import>` is that the resource is loaded directly from the file and not processed as a server request; for example, loading a JSP page using this tag would not execute the JSP page but simply give you the JSP source code.

If there is a problem retrieving the resource a request time exception is thrown. The attributes of this tag, which can all take are runtime expressions, are explained in the following table:

Attribute	Description
id	The name of the variable to be defined.
name	Relative path to the resource.
input	If this attribute is not present the resource is made available as a `String`.

An example of the `<bean:resource>` tag is shown below:

```
<bean:resource id="myResource" name="/WEB-INF/xml/myResource.xml"/>
```

Here the name of the scripting variable is `myResource`, and the name of the resource to retrieve is `myResource.xml`.

The Logic Tag Library

Struts provides a **logic tag library** that provides a set of tags for handling flow control within a JSP page; for instance, iteration or conditional evaluation of the tag body. The URI defined for this tag library is `http://jakarta.apache.org/struts/tags-logic-1.0`. Note that most of the logic tags duplicate JSTL core tag functionality and so will not be discussed in detail:

❑ `<logic:empty>`, `<logic:notEmpty>`, `<logic:equal>`, `<logic:notEqual>`, `<logic:greaterEqual>`, `<logic:greaterThan>`, `<logic:lessEqual>`, and `<logic:lessThan>` all compare some bean property or attribute. These tasks are better performed using the JSTL core conditional tags and the JSP Expression Language.

❑ `<logic:present>` and `<logic:notPresent>` test for the presence or absence of values. Their main utility for us is that they can test whether the user has a specific security role.

❑ `<logic:match>` tests whether a bean or attribute has a specific substring.

❑ `<logic:messagesPresent>` and `<logic:messagesNotPresent>` detect if any `ActionErrors` or `ActionMessages` have been forwarded to the JSP page.

❑ `<logic:iterate>` loops over an array or collection. Effectively superseded by the JSTL core `<c:forEeach>` tag.

❑ `<logic:forward>` forwards or redirects to a logical page names from the Struts configuration file.

❑ `<logic:redirect>` performs redirects.

Let's take a closer look at the most important of these tags now.

Present and NotPresent Tags

The `<logic:present>` and `<logic:notPresent>` tags can test for the presence of a many different things, including cookies, headers, request parameters and the like. However, you can achieve this just as easily using the JSTL and expressions, in particular the `empty` operator. So we will restrict ourselves to the one thing which cannot readily be done otherwise; testing whether the user has the specified security role.

Attribute	Description
role	A comma-separated list of one or more security roles. The presence of any one of the roles is sufficient.

For example, if your company's management approves of business news but not of geeks:

```
<logic:present role="ceo,cfo,manager">
  <a href="http://www.reuters.com">Reuters</a>
</logic:present>

<logic:notPresent role="ceo,cfo,manager">
  <a href="http://www.slashdot.org">Slashdot</a>
</logic:notPresent>
```

MessagesPresent and MessagesNotPresent Tags

In the *Error and Action Message Classes* section, we saw how our validation code and our actions can communicate messages and errors to the views by binding `ActionMessages` and `ErrorMessages` objects to the request. The `<logic:messagesPresent>` and `<logic:messagesNotPresent>` tags provide easy and clean ways of detecting such messages' presence or absence.

Attribute	Description
message	If `true`, test for the presence of action messages bound to the key specified by `Globals.MESSAGE_KEY`. If absent or `false`, test for the presence of error messages bound to the key specified by `Globals.ERROR_KEY`. Note that as in many such attributes, yes can be used for `true`, and no for `false`.
name	Overrides the request attribute key used to find the messages object. Valid only if `message` is either not specified or `false`.
property	The name of the property for which messages should be retrieved. If not specified, all messages are retrieved regardless of the property they belong to.

The following code snippet should illustrate these tags in use:

```
<logic:messagesPresent>
  There are error messages!
  <logic:messagesPresent property="cardNumber">
  There seems to be a problem with the credit card number.
  </logic:messagesPresent>
</logic:messagesPresent>

<logic:messagesNotPresent>
  There are no error messages.
</logic:messagesNotPresent>

<logic:messagesPresent message="yes">
  The action has left us some messages.
</logic:messagesPresent>

<logic:messagesNotPresent message="yes">
  No word from our action, sir.
</logic:messagesNotPresent>
```

Obviously, in a real application, you are much more likely to display the error messages themselves, for example using the <html:errors> tag discussed later. These tags are mainly used in cases where the page layout needs to be modified depending on whether there are any error messages to display or not.

Forward Tag

The Struts logic tag library defines a tag for forwarding or redirecting the request to a global forward from the Struts configuration file. The configuration file determines whether a forward or a redirect is used.

Attribute	Description
name	The name of the global forward to use.

In our configuration file walkthrough, we defined:

```
<global-forwards>
  <forward name="shop" path="/index.jsp"/>
  <forward name="cart" path="/showcart.jsp"/>
</global-forwards>
```

With these definitions, the following code will forward the request to /index.jsp:

```
<logic:forward name="shop"/>
```

Redirect Tag

The `<logic:redirect>` tag is a powerful mechanism for performing a HTTP redirect. The redirect can be achieved in different ways, depending on the attributes specified. It also lets the developers specify query arguments for the redirected URL. The attributes for the tag, all of which can take runtime expressions, are explained below:

Attribute	Description
forward	The logical name of a global forward to use. If you specify a forward, you cannot specify href or page attributes.
href	The fully qualified URL of the resource. If you specify a href, you cannot specify forward or page attributes.
page	The relative path of the resource. If you specify a page, you cannot specify forward or href attributes.
anchor	The # anchor to append to the URL. Do not include the # character itself!
name	If the property attribute is *not* specified: the name of a Map that contains the name-value pairs of the query arguments to be attached to the URL. If the property attribute *is* specified: the name of a bean with a property of type Map that contains the same information.
property	The name of the bean property that is a Map. The bean's name is given by the name attribute above.
scope	The scope in which the bean is searched for.
paramId	Allows adding a single request parameter, as an alternative to the Map method discussed above. Defines the name of the parameter.
paramName	If the paramProperty attribute is *not* specified: the name of a bean of type String that contains the value of the request parameter indicated by paramId. If the paramProperty attribute is specified: a bean that has a property that returns the parameter value.
paramProperty	The name of the String bean property that contains the parameter value.
paramScope	The scope in which the bean defined by paramName is searched for.

Table continued on following page

Attribute	Description
transaction	Set to true if you want the current transaction token to be included. Transaction tokens were discussed in the *Enforcing Application Flow* section above.

The tag should specify exactly one of the forward, href or page attributes to identify the resource to which the response should be redirected. A couple of examples are shown below.

```
<c:set var="manager" value="Ranieri"/>
<logic:redirect href="http://www.myclub.co.uk"
                paramId="manager"
                paramName="manager"/>
```

This will redirect the browser to http://www.myclub.co.uk?manager=Ranieri. Here we have a bean that contains the value from the name-value pair that is used in the URL query argument. Now compare this with the following example:

```
<jsp:useBean id="queryParams" class="java.util.HashMap"/>
<% queryParams.put("manager","Ranieri"); %>
<logic:redirect href="http://www.myclub.co.uk"
                name="queryParams"/>
```

This will redirect the browser to the same URL as before. Here, however, we supply a parameter Map.

The HTML Tag Library

The Struts **HTML tag library** provides a variety of HTML generation tags that are tightly integrated with the Struts controller. Its URI is http://jakarta.apache.org/struts/tags-html-1.0. Other than with the bean and logic libraries, there is virtually no overlap with the JSTL and JSP Expression Language here.

❑ Most of the HTML tags provide HTML form generation support that is tightly integrated with the Struts ActionForm concept. For the most part, these tags closely follow their HTML counterparts: <html:form>, <html:text>, <html:textarea>, <html:password>, <html:checkbox>, <html:multibox>, <html:select>, <html:option>, <html:options>, <html:optionsCollection>, <html:radio>, <html:file>, <html:hidden>, <html:button>, <html:image>, <html:submit>, <html:reset>, and <html:cancel>.

❑ <html:errors> and <html:messages> render the contents of any ErrorMessages or ActionMessages that have been passed on to the view JSP page.

❑   `<html:javascript>` renders the JavaScript validation code generated by the Struts Validator, to be discussed later.

❑   `<html:html>`, `<html:frame>`, `<html:base>`, and `<html:img>` all work like the HTML tags of the same name, but support some extra Struts integration features such the ability to use global forwards instead of resource names.

❑   `<html:link>` renders an anchor or hyperlink that can refer to Struts' logical forwards; `<html:rewrite>` performs many of the same functions but renders just the URI rather than the entire hyperlink.

Quite a few tags, and although we cannot possibly discuss them all we will be taking a look at most of them. Before doing this, though, we will start with a brief discussion of the way the Struts HTML tags support the many HTML element attributes.

Standard HTML Element Attributes

The tags that directly correspond to HTML elements, such as `<html:form>`, support all the attributes that their ordinary HTML counterparts could have. These attributes are simply copied straight into the generated HTML. They will not be listed below as they are in no way Struts-specific and would only clutter things up. The attributes in question include the JavaScript event hooks, such as `onsubmit` and `onclick`, and attributes such as `style`, `tabindex`, `accesskey`, and `alt`. It should be noted that these attributes are always fully lowercase. HTML may not be case-sensitive, but JSP tags are.

There are two cases where the Struts attributes work slightly differently from their HTML counterparts.

❑   The CSS-related attributes `id` and `class` have to be handled differently because these names have a special meaning in JSP tags. The Struts HTML tags use `styleId` and `styleClass` attributes to define them. For example, to incorporate the attribute `class="news"` in the generated HTML element, you'd specify `styleClass="news"` in your Struts HTML tag.

❑   The HTML input field attributes `disabled` and `readonly` do not receive a value, but make a field disabled or read-only respectively merely by their presence. This does not fit the JavaBean tag model, so the Struts input field tags have `disabled` and `readonly` attributes that take a Boolean value. In other words, `disabled="false"` will cause the `disabled` attribute to be completely omitted from the generated HTML element.

The standard attributes, like the additional attributes discussed below, can take runtime expressions in addition to simple string values.

Let's now look at the core of the library, these are the tags that render forms and form controls.

Form Construction Tags

Struts enables you to associate an HTML form with an action mapping, and thereby with the `ActionForm` that has been configured as the mapping's input form. The name of the form fields should correspond to properties of the `ActionForm` bean. This can include nested, indexed and mapped properties in any combination. When the HTML form is rendered, the input fields are populated with the actual values of the bean properties; conversely, when the user submits the HTML form, the bean properties are updated to reflect the values entered into the form.

Form Tag

The `<html:form>` tag is used to render, you guessed it, a HTML `<form>` element. The main reason to use a `<html:form>` tag over a normal `<form>` is that the Struts tag associates its `action` with a Struts action mapping, and the action mapping in turn dictates which `ActionForm` bean to use to render the contents of the input elements. If the bean specified in the action mapping is not found, a new bean is created and stored.

The `<form>` tag will generally contain child tags corresponding to the different HTML input fields; these tags are explained later in this section. The attributes for the `<html:form>` tag are explained in the following table:

Attribute	Description
action	The action associated with the form, without the .do extension. This is specified relative to the web-app root and must match one of the mappings in your Struts configuration file; the mapping should identify the `ActionForm` bean associated with the form.
focus	The field within the form that should have initial focus. Setting this will generate a small chunk of JavaScript that assigns focus to the named field, which will be ignored by clients that do not support JavaScript or have it disabled.

As usual, the tag also takes the `method`, `enctype`, `style`, and JavaScript event hook attributes that a normal HTML `<form>` understands.

By way of an example, consider the first form in the `showcart.jsp` page of the last Try It Out.

```
<form action="update.do">
   ...
</form>
```

The `<html:form>` equivalent is shown below:

```
<html:form action="/update">
   .
```

```
     .
     .
   </html:form>
```

There isn't a lot of difference. Behind the scenes, however, the `<html:form>` tag has inspected the action mapping for its action:

```
<form-bean name="cart" type="com.wrox.shop.ShoppingCart"/>
   .
   .
   .
<action path="/update"
    forward="/showcart.jsp"
      name="cart"
       scope="session"/>
```

The form knows that its associated `ActionForm` bean is the `cart`; if this form bean does not yet exist, it knows that it should instantiate it as an object of type `com.wrox.shop.ShoppingCart`. The form then makes this information available to its nested input elements, as we shall see in a moment.

You can have any number of `<html:form>` tags in an HTML page.

Text, Hidden and TextArea Tags

The `<html:text>`, `<html:hidden>` and `<html:textarea>` tags must be nested inside an `<html:form>` tag. They render HTML `<input type="text">`, `<input type="hidden">` and `<textarea>` elements, respectively. The following table lists the most important attributes these tags support over and above what their HTML counterparts can take:

Attribute	Description
property	The `ActionForm` property this field corresponds to. This will be used as the field name, and the value will default to the form property's value.
name	Indicates a JavaBean that should be used in place of the form's normal `ActionForm`. This is useful if we need to include data from more than one form object in a single HTML form.
value	Specified to use a field value other than the `ActionForm` property value. The value may also be specified in the body of the tag.
altKey	Generates an `alt` attribute by looking up the given message key in the default message resources bundle. Use this for internationalization.
titleKey	Generates a `title` attribute by looking up the given message key in the default message resources bundle. Use this for internationalization.

The action form property associated with these tags must be a simple scalar, that is, a `String`, a primitive Java type, or any of their wrapper types (such as `int` or `java.lang.Integer`).

This gives us all the ingredients we need to finish the `showcart.jsp` form we started modifying in the previous section, replacing the following `<input>` element:

```
<td width="10%" align="center">
  <input type="text" size="1" maxlength="2"
     name="item[$
  {status.index}].quantity"
     value="$
  {item.quantity}">
</td>
```

with its `<html:text>` equivalent:

```
<td width="10%" align="center">
  <html:text size="1" maxlength="2"
       property="item[$
  {status.index}].quantity"/>
</td>
```

The main difference is that we no longer have to specify the `value`; Struts can figure this out from the `property` name and the action form associated with the `<html:form>` tag.

Password Tag

The `<html:password>` tag can be used for rendering a HTML password control. The difference between a password control and the ordinary text input field is that the password control displays its contents as asterisks. With the exception of `redisplay`, it supports exactly the same attributes as the `<html:text>` tag:

Attribute	Description
property	The `ActionForm` property this field corresponds to.
name	Specified to use a JavaBean other than the form's `ActionForm`.
value	Specified to use a field value other than the `ActionForm` property value. The value may also be specified in the body of the tag.
redisplay	If absent or `true`, the current value (if any) of the `ActionForm` property is used as the value for this password field. The browser will show it as a row of asterisks, but the level of security provided is very limited – anyone can view the actual password by selecting the browser's View HTML Source option.

Attribute	Description
altKey	Generates an `alt` attribute by looking up the given message key in the default message resources bundle. Use this for internationalization.
titleKey	Generates a `title` attribute by looking up the given message key in the default message resources bundle. Use this for internationalization.

In addition to these, the normal HTML attributes for the `<input>` element are of course also supported.

Checkbox and Multibox Tags

The `<html:checkbox>` and `<html:multibox>` tags can be used for rendering checkbox controls. They must be nested within an `<html:form>` tag and recognize the same set of attributes as the `<html:text>` tag. The difference between them is the following.

❑ The `<html:checkbox>` tag must be associated with a Boolean action form property. You would typically use this in cases where there were only a few such properties, or when the properties were unrelated.

❑ The `<html:multibox>` tag must be associated with a property returning an array of `String` values. A multibox is considered "on" when its value (specified either using the `value` attribute or in the tag body) occurs somewhere in this array. The multibox tag is useful when there are a fair number of related on/off options. Each multibox is associated with the same property, but has a different value. Each element in the property's array corresponds to a checkbox that is "on".

An example of the use of `<html:checkbox>` is shown below.

```
<tr>
  <td><html:checkbox property="married"/></td>
  <td>Check here if you are married</td>
</tr>
```

Here we have a checkbox called `married` associated with a Boolean action form property. The `ActionForm` would probably define the methods:

```
public boolean getMarried();
public void setMarried(boolean married);
```

If you have ever set up an account with an online retailer or banks, you have probably been presented with a list of options allowing you to control how your contact details can be used. This would be a good use for the `<html:multibox>` tag.

```
<tr>
  <td><html:multibox property="doNotContact" value="ourselves"/></td>
  <td>Check if you do not wish to be contacted by us.</td>
<tr>
<tr>
  <td><html:multibox property="doNotContact" value="partners"/></td>
  <td>Check if you do not wish to be contacted by our partners.</td>
</tr>
<tr>
  <td><html:multibox property="doNotContact" value="others"/></td>
  <td>Check if you do not wish your contact details to be forwarded to
      selected third parties.</td>
</tr>
```

All these options are associated with the array-valued bean property doNotContact:

```
public String[] getDoNotContact();
public void setDoNotContact(String[] doNotContact);
```

An example value for this property could be the two-element array {"partners", "others"}. On the HTML page, this would correspond to the second and third checkboxes being ticked. We could have achieved the same thing by defining three ordinary Boolean properties and using three checkbox tags, but where the number of options is large this clutters up your ActionForm with lots of methods.

Select and Option Tags

The <html:select> tag, nested inside an <html:form>, can be used for rendering a HTML select control. The important attributes of this tag, above and beyond those of the corresponding HTML element, are listed in the following table:

Attribute	Description
property	The ActionForm property this field corresponds to. This will be used as the field name, and the value will default to the form property's value.
name	Specified to use a JavaBean other than the form's ActionForm.
multiple	If true, multiple options can be selected.
value	Specified to use a field value other than the ActionForm property value. It may also be specified in the body of the tag. The value determines which of the options is currently selected.
altKey	Generates an alt attribute by looking up the given message key in the default message resources bundle. Use this for internationalization.

Attribute	Description
titleKey	Generates a `title` attribute by looking up the given message key in the default message resources bundle. Use this for internationalization.

The type of `ActionForm` property associated with this tag depends on the value of the `multiple` attribute.

❏ If `multiple` is `false` or omitted, the action form property must be a scalar, for example a `String`, a primitive Java type or any of their wrapper types (`int` or `java.lang.Integer`). The value of this property corresponds to the selected option.

❏ If `multiple` is `true`, the action form property should be an array of any of the types mentioned above. Each element of the array is a scalar corresponding to a selected option.

Inside an `<html:select>` tag, the list of available options can be provided using any of the three types of option tag included in the library (or indeed a mixture, if you wish).

The simplest is `<html:option>`, which generates a single HTML `<option>` element. Its attributes include:

Attribute	Description
value	The value represented by this option. This attribute is required.
key	The message key to look up in the message resources bundle. If omitted, you must specify the option text (not a key) in the tag body.
bundle	The name of the message bundle to use. Uses the default bundle if omitted.

An example of the select and option tags would be the following dropdown for selecting a credit card type:

```
<html:select property="cardType">
  <html:option value="" key="payments.select.please"/>
  <html:option value="MC">MasterCard</html:option>
  <html:option value="VI">Visa</html:option>
  <html:option value="AE">American Express</html:option>
</html:select>
```

This would set the `cardType` property to `MC`, `VI`, or `AE` depending on the type selected. Note that the first option uses a message key to display an internationalized message displaying something like **Please Select** in the local language, while the others use hardwired credit card brand names.

Often, we do not have a limited set of hardwired options as above, but a long list of possible options or perhaps a list that is populated from the data in a database table. One way to handle this would be to loop over the list of options with the `<c:forEach>` tag, and extract the label and value from each. Struts provides a convenient way to achieve the same thing using the `<html:optionsCollection>` tag. Its attributes are described below:

Attribute	Description
name	The name of the JavaBean that provides us with the options. If omitted, the tag will use the `ActionForm` associated with the current `<html:form>`.
property	The property of the JavaBean indicated by `name` (or the current `ActionForm`, if omitted) that will return the collection of option beans.
value	The option bean property that will return the value. Defaults to `value`.
label	The option bean property that will return the label. Defaults to `label`. If there is no difference between your labels and your values, it is perfectly valid to use a single property name for both `value` and `label`.
filter	If `true` or omitted, characters such as `<` that might mess up the generated HTML are filtered out.

Supposing our `ActionForm` provides a `getSupportedCardTypes()` method returning an array of `CardType` objects:

```
public class CardType
{
    .
    .
    .
  public String getLabel() { return label; }
  public String getValue() { return value; }
}
```

Then we could amend the previous example to read simply:

```
<html:select property="cardType">
  <html:option value="" key="payment.select.please"/>
  <html:options property="supportedCardTypes"/>
</html:select>
```

There is another, older, `<html:options>` tag to generate a list of options. This tag can be used in a large number of ways and can be quite confusing. In most cases, the `<html:optionsCollection>` tag will do the job just fine and is much clearer.

Radio Tag

We can use the `<html:radio>` tag nested within an `<html:form>` tag for rendering one or more HTML radio button controls. The attributes of this tag are explained below:

Attribute	Description
property	The `ActionForm` property this field corresponds to.
name	Specified to use a JavaBean other than the form's `ActionForm`.
value	The value this radio button selection corresponds to. This attribute is required.
idName	Name of a bean that will provide us with the value of the radio tag. If an `idName` is provided, then `value` is not interpreted as the value itself, but as the property of the bean that returns the value. This attribute is most often used when iterating over a collection of possible values.
altKey	Generates an `alt` attribute by looking up the given message key in the default message resources bundle. Use this for internationalization.
titleKey	Generates a `title` attribute by looking up the given message key in the default message resources bundle. Use this for internationalization.

For example, if the `supportedCardTypes` property of `cardForm` returns an array of `CardType` objects, each with `value` and `label` attributes, a radio group for selection between the credit card types could be rendered with the following code snippet:

```
<c:forEach items="${cardForm.supportedCardTypes}" var="type">
  <html:radio property="cardType" idName="type" value="value"/>
  ${type.label}<br>
</c:forEach>
```

This is how the dropdown box from the previous example could be rendered as a radio group. The generated HTML would look something like the following:

```
<html:input type="radio" name="cardType" value="VISA"/>
Visa<br>

<html:input type="radio" name="cardType" value="EUMA"/>
Eurocard/Mastercard<br>

<html:input type="radio" name="cardType" value="AMEX"/>
American Express<br>
```

Button Tags

The Struts HTML tag library supports four different button tags:

❑ `<html:submit>` renders a Submit button that will submit the enclosing form to the server.

❑ `<html:cancel>` renders a Cancel button. This is actually no more than a submit button with a special name. The Struts controller recognizes this name and bypasses its form validation code. The `Action` is invoked as normal and will have to call `isCancelled()` to find out whether the form has been cancelled or not.

❑ `<html:reset>` renders a Reset button that will reset all form fields to their initial values.

❑ `<html:button>` renders an HTML push button control without default behavior, so you need to add JavaScript to the `onclick` attribute to actually make it do something useful.

These tags must be nested inside an `<html:form>` tag and include the following attributes above and beyond those of their normal HTML counterparts:

Attribute	Description
`property`	Name of the request parameter that will be submitted for the button. Do not specify this for a Cancel button!
`name`	Specified to use a JavaBean other than the form's `ActionForm`.
`value`	The value of the button label. This may also be specified in the body of the tag. The value is also submitted as part of the request.
`altKey`	Generates an `alt` attribute by looking up the given message key in the default message resources bundle. Use this for internationalization.
`titleKey`	Generates a `title` attribute by looking up the given message key in the default message resources bundle. Use this for internationalization.

For example, the following code would render a Submit and a Cancel button for a payment form, complete with an internationalized button label rendered using the `<bean:message>` tag:

```
<html:submit><bean:message key="payment.button.submit"/></html:submit>
<html:cancel><bean:message key=" payment.button.cancel"/></html:cancel>
```

Message Retrieval Tags

When discussing the core controller classes, we found that `ActionErrors` and `ActionMessages` were the Struts way to communicate errors and other messages from the validation code and the actions to the View components. Correspondingly, the HTML tag library contains a pair of tags that allow you to easily and quickly turn the contents of these objects into HTML.

Errors Tag

The `<html:errors>` tag retrieves one or more messages from an `ActionErrors` objects and displays them. To help you with the HTML layout of these messages, this tag also allows you to include four special keys in your message resources that will be included at specific points in the list:

- ❏ `errors.header`, if defined, will be printed before the first error message.
- ❏ `errors.footer`, if defined, will be printed after the last error message. If there are no messages, neither header nor footer will be printed.
- ❏ `errors.prefix`, if defined, will be printed before every error message.
- ❏ `errors.suffix`, if defined, will be printed after every error message.

In addition to `ActionErrors` objects, the tag can also be used to display errors from keys stored in simple `String` objects and `String` arrays. The most important attributes supported by the tag are:

Attribute	Description
property	Name of the property for which error messages should be displayed. This filter functionality allows you to print error messages right next to the relevant form field. If this attribute is omitted, all messages are displayed regardless of the property they belong to.
name	The name under which the errors object is stored. You will not usually specify this, as the `ActionErrors` object is normally stored under `Globals.ERROR_KEY` (`org.apache.struts.action.ERROR`), which is the default value of this attribute.
bundle	The name of the application attribute under which the resources object is stored. If not specified, `Globals.MESSAGES_KEY` is used (its value is `org.apache.struts.action.MESSAGE`). When specified, this attribute must match the key specified in `<message-resources>` in the Struts configuration file.

When all messages are being displayed (that is, there's no `property` attribute), the messages are displayed by property, with the properties in the order in which they were first added. Within a property, the associated messages are displayed in the order in which they were added.

For example, assume the default message resource would contain the following messages:

```
errors.creditlimit.exceeded=You exceeded your credit limit.
errors.payment.failed=The payment has failed.
     .
     .
     .
errors.header=There were problems!<ul>
errors.footer=</ul>
errors.prefix=<li><font color="red">
errors.suffix=</font>
```

Assume also that the `ActionErrors` object contained two messages, one `errors.payment.failed` and the other with key `errors.creditlimit.exceeded`.

```
<html:errors/>
```

The single line of JSP code above would generate the following HTML:

```
There were problems!
<ul>
  <li><font color="red">The payment has failed.</font>
  <li><font color="red">You exceeded your credit limit.</font>
</ul>
```

Once you buy into the Struts way of doing things, a lot can be accomplished with very little code indeed.

Messages Tag

Depending on the value of the `message` attribute, the `<html:messages>` tag will display messages from `ActionMessages` or `ActionErrors` objects. It can also be used to display errors from keys stored in simple `String` objects and `String` arrays. A key difference between this tag and `<html:errors>` is that it does not handle the actual printing of the messages; instead, it acts as an iterators tag, making the text for each message in turn available to the tag body through a scripting variable. In effect, this tag is the more flexible big brother of the `<html:errors>` tag. It may have the following attributes:

Attribute	Description
id	The name of the scripting variable holding the message. This variable will hold a `String` with the actual message text.
message	If `true`, retrieves `ActionMessages` bound to the key specified by `Globals.MESSAGE_KEY`. If absent or `false`, it uses the object specified by the `name` attribute or, in absence of a `name`, the `Globals.ERROR_KEY` that is normally associated with `ActionErrors`.
name	Overrides the request attribute key used to find the messages object. Valid only if `message` is either not specified or `false`.
property	Name of the property for which error messages should be displayed. This filter functionality allows you to print error messages right next to the relevant form field. If this attribute is omitted, all messages are displayed regardless of the property they belong to.
header	An optional key for a message to be printed before the first action message.
footer	An optional key for a message to be printed after the last action message.
bundle	The name of the application attribute under which the resources object is stored. If not specified, `Globals.MESSAGES_KEY` is used (its value is `org.apache.struts.action.MESSAGE`). When specified, this attribute must match the key specified in `<message-resources>` in the Struts configuration file.

The following JSP snippet could be used to display a credit card number form field, complete with an internationalized label in front of it, and any credit card related error messages listed behind it.

```
<td><bean:message key="payment.creditcard.label"/></td>
<td><html:text property="creditCard" size="16" maxlength="16"/></td>
<td>
  <html:messages id="message" property="creditCard"
                 header="payment.errors.header"
                 footer="payment.errors.footer">
  <li><font color="red">$
  {message}</font>
  </html:messages>
</td>
```

The <html:messages> tag was used instead of the <html:errors> tag because it allows for the specification of a page-specific header and footer. The property attribute ensures that we are only displaying messages here that are actually related to the credit card number. When you use this filtering capability, it is your responsibility to ensure that every message that can be generated is displayed *somewhere* on the screen.

URL Generation Tags

There is a fair amount of overlap between the Struts URI generation tags and the JSTL <c:url> tag, and in general you should give preference to the latter. However, the Struts tags can do a few things that the JSTL one cannot do: they can refer to global forwards by name, they can include the transaction token, and they can extract request parameters from a Map.

The Link Tag

The <html:link> tag generates an HTML <a href="location"> hyperlink or an anchor. It supports a large number of attributes. With the exception of the linkName attribute used to generate anchors, all of these attributes are identical to those of the <logic:redirect> tag. Please leaf back to the *Redirect Tag* section for a detailed discussion.

You must specify exactly one of the forward, href, page or linkName attributes.

Attribute	Description
forward	The logical name of a global forward to use.
href	The fully qualified URL of the resource.
page	The relative path of the resource.
linkName	The name of the #anchor to generate.
anchor	The #anchor to append to the URL. Do not include the # character itself!
name	The name of a Map that contains the name-value pairs of the query arguments to be attached to the URL, or the name of a bean with a property of type Map that contains the same information.
property	The name of the bean property that is a Map.
scope	The scope in which the bean is searched for.
paramId	Allows adding a single request parameter, as an alternative to the Map method discussed above. Defines the name of the parameter.
paramName	The name of a String to use as the value of the request parameter indicated by paramId, or a bean that has a property that returns the parameter value.

Attribute	Description
paramProperty	The name of the String bean property that contains the parameter value.
paramScope	The scope in which the bean defined by paramName is searched for.
transaction	Set to true if you want the current transaction token to be included.

In addition, all the normal attributes for the HTML <a> element are supported. A quick example:

```
<html:link forward="account" transaction="true">Your Account</html:link>
```

This creates a hyperlink to the account page, while preserving the user's transaction token.

The Rewrite Tag

In some cases, we need to use a URI outside the context of a redirect or a hyperlink, for example when URIs are manipulated by our JavaScript code. For this reason, the library contains a <html:rewrite> tag that supports all the features that <html:link> and <logic:redirect> do, but it will only generate the actual URI and not the actual <a> tag.

```
var accountURI = '<html:rewrite forward="account" transaction="true"/>';
```

This is the last tag from the HTML tag library that we will discuss. There are more tags to explore, but the tags discussed so far should be more than enough to get you started.

The Template Tag Library

Dynamic templates are a powerful way of modularizing web page layout. Assume your web application has got hundreds of web pages using the same layout with a header section, footer section, and the main content section. The simplistic way of implementing a common layout is to use HTML tables and JSP includes as shown below:

```
<html>
  <head><title>Template Madness</title></head>
  <body>
  <table width="100%">
    <tr height="10%">
      <td><jsp:include page="header.html"/></td>
    </tr>
    <tr height="80%">
      <td><jsp:include page="employeeList.jsp"/></td>
    </tr>
    <tr height="10%">
      <td><jsp:include page="employeeFooter.jsp"/></td>
```

```
      </tr>
    </table>
  </body>
</html>
```

The problem with the code above is that the template is hard-coded into the JSP page. If you decide to change the height of the header to 15% and you have hundreds of JSP pages it will become a massive change. This is where dynamic templates come into their own. Dynamic templates encapsulate the layout, and the template page is included in all your JSP pages rather than hard coding the details. So if you decide to change the template, the only place you need to make changes is the template JSP page.

The Struts **template tag library** defines custom tags for implementing dynamic templates. The standard URI for this tag library is `http://jakarta.apache.org/struts/tags-html-1.0`. In this section we will cover those tags in detail.

Insert Tag

The `<template:insert>` tag can be used within JSP to insert a dynamic template. It has only a single attribute.

Attribute	Description
`template`	The name of the template JSP page to use. This attribute is required.

The pages to be inserted into the template are specified using multiple `<template:put>` tags nested inside the body of the `<template:insert>` tag.

Put Tag

One or more `<template:put>` tags are nested inside the `<template:insert>` tag to specify the resources to be inserted in the template. The attributes for the tag are:

Attribute	Description
`name`	The name for the content to be inserted. This attribute is required.
`content`	The content to be inserted. Depending on the value of the `direct` attribute, this is either the path to a resource, such as a JSP page or HTML file, or a simple `String`. Alternatively, the content can be put in the tag body.
`direct`	If `true`, the content of this tag is inserted as-is. If `false` or absent, the content is interpreted as the path to a resource to be retrieved.
`role`	If specified, the content is inserted only if the currently authenticated user has the specified role.

Get Tag

The `<template:get>` tag is used within the template JSP page to retrieve the resources that have been defined by the `<template:put>` tags. Its attributes are:

Attribute	Description
name	The name for the content to be inserted. Required.
role	If specified, the content is inserted only if the currently authenticated user has the specified role.

Using Template Tags

Now we will see how the Struts template tags can be used to create dynamic templates. First we will write a template JSP page that will be used by all our web pages. That JSP page may look as shown below.

```
<%@taglib uri=" http://jakarta.apache.org/struts/tags-html-1.0"
          prefix="/template" %>
<html>
  <head><title>Template Sanity</title></head>
  <body>
  <table width="100%">
    <tr height="10%">
      <td><template:get name="header"/></td>
    </tr>
    <tr height="80%">
      <td><template:get name="content"/></td>
    </tr>
    <tr height="10%">
      <td><template:get name="footer"/></td>
    </tr>
  </table>
  </body>
</html>
```

Let's call this file `template.jsp`. This JSP page uses the `<template:get>` tag to get the contents inserted by our content JSP pages using the `<template:put>` tag, and lays out the contents in an HTML table. The three content names expected are `header`, `content`, and `footer`. A typical application JSP page is now no more than a definition of how its contents should be assembled, as shown below:

```
<%@taglib uri="http://jakarta.apache.org/struts/tags-html-1.0"
          prefix="/template" %>
<template:insert template="template.jsp">
  <template:put name="header" content="header.html"/>
  <template:put name="content" content="employeeList.jsp"/>
  <template:put name="footer" content="employeeFooter.jsp"/>
</template:insert>
```

This page uses the `<template:insert>` tag to define the template to use for the page, and then uses the `<template:put>` tag to push three resources identified by unique `content` names to the template JSP page. If we have hundreds of JSP pages using the same scheme, and we suddenly decide to change the template, the only place we will have to make a change now is the `template.jsp` file.

Templates and Tiles

As you can see, the Template library is simple but very effective. In large projects, or cases where more versatility is required, the **Tiles tag library** is worth a look. It is based on the same concepts as the Template library – indeed, you can replace the Template library with Tiles without change – and it offers the following additional features:

- ❑ An XML file or a Struts action can be used to define pages, as an alternative to assembling pages using a JSP page such as the one shown above.

- ❑ Page definitions can inherit each other to decorate each other's contents or override parameters.

- ❑ Better internationalization support; you can define language- and locale-specific "tile bundles" that work in the same way as message resource bundles.

- ❑ Better support for dynamic lists and dynamic decisions regarding the tiles to load. This is essential in portal-like applications.

We will not discuss Tiles any further; what we've seen so far of the Template library should be an ideal starting point to experiment with Tiles.

More Struts Components

The preceding sections provide all the information you need to do a lot of productive work with the Struts framework. However, there are two more facilities that, although they are not really part of the core framework, can really aid development of Struts applications. Our discussion would be incomplete without them. These facilities are:

- ❑ Dynamic action forms
- ❑ The Struts Validator

Dynamic Action Forms

In the preceding sections we have seen how the Struts controller and HTML tag library provide a two-way channel between HTML forms and `ActionForm` objects. This takes a lot of the routine work out of HTML form manipulation.

In our shopping cart example, the `ShoppingCart` object could immediately and quite naturally be converted to an `ActionForm`. This is not always the case. Sometimes, your Java object needs to extend some other class than `ActionForm`, and as we know Java does not support multiple inheritance, or the class is also used in a different context, for example in a standalone GUI application that isn't browser-based, which should not require Struts.

> *Based on considerations such as this, it could be argued that `ActionForm`, like `Action`, should have been an interface rather than a class.*

At other times, your HTML form captures some information that does not easily map to properties in the object model. Rather than clutter up our source code with additional one-off Java classes that exists just to support a single HTML form, we can use Struts' **dynamic action forms** facility.

This consists of a single class, `org.apache.struts.action.DynaActionForm`, which can model an arbitrary JavaBean and allows us to declare what properties it will have in the Struts configuration file.

Configuring Dynamic ActionForm Beans

`DynaActionForm` beans are declared in the Struts configuration file using the same `<form-bean>` elements that are used to declare ordinary `ActionForm` beans. The difference is that for a dynamic form, we also specify the form's attributes using nested `<form-property>` tags. This tag takes the attributes listed in the following table:

Element Attribute	Description
name	The name of the property to define. This attribute is required.
type	The fully qualified Java class name of the property type. Array types are denoted by appending square brackets `[]` to the type name. This attribute is required.
initial	The initial value for the property. If omitted, primitives will be initialized to zero and objects will default to `null`.

The property types supported include:

❑ Primitives: `byte`, `char`, `short`, `int`, `long`, `float`, `double`, and their wrapper classes: `java.lang.Byte`, `java.lang.Character`, and so on

❑ Big numbers: `java.lang.BigDecimal` and `java.lang.BigInteger`

❑ SQL types: `java.sql.Date`, `java.sql.Time` and `java.sql.TimeStamp`

❑ `java.lang.String` and `java.lang.Class`

The following code shows how a credit card form bean might be declared:

```
<form-beans>
  <form-bean name="creditCardForm"
             type="org.apache.struts.action.DynaActionForm">
    <form-property name="cardNumber" type="java.lang.Long"/>
    <form-property name="cardExpiry" type="java.sql.Date"/>
    <form-property name="cardType" type="java.lang.String" initial=""/>
  </form-bean>
</form-beans>
```

The `creditCardForm` has three attributes, `cardNumber`, `cardExpiry`, and `cardType`. Both the Struts controller and the HTML tags will treat it like any other form, populating its properties with the values submitted by the HTML form and vice versa. Our actions, too, can easily access the properties of the `DynaActionForm`, as we shall see in the next section.

The DynaActionForm Class

Arbitrary JavaBeans cannot be created on the fly, and behind the scenes a `DynaActionForm` does not work in exactly the same way as a normal `ActionForm` bean. In essence, a dynamic action form is little more than a glorified `Map` mapping property names to their corresponding values. We can even retrieve this underlying `Map`:

```
public Map getMap()
```

This `map` attribute is the easiest way to extract data from dynamic forms using the JSP Expression Language, as demonstrated in the following excerpt from a JSP confirmation page:

```
     .
     .
     .
<tr>
  <td><bean:message key="confirmation.card.number"/><td>
  <td>$
  {creditCardForm.map.cardNumber}</td>
</tr>
<tr>
  <td><bean:message key="confirmation.card.expiry"/><td>
  <td><fmt:formatDate value="$
  {creditCardForm.map.cardExpiry}"/></td>
</tr>
<tr>
  <td><bean:message key="confirmation.card.type"/><td>
  <td>$
  {creditCardForm.map.cardType}</td>
</tr>
     .
     .
     .
```

This snippet displays all three attributes of the credit card form for the user to confirm.

Although we can also use the `map` attribute in our `Actions`, there are a number of other methods that can give us easier access to `DynaActionForm` properties from Java code. There are two methods that deal with scalar properties (the supported types listed above):

```
public Object get(String name)
public void set(String name, Object value)
```

Wrapper types are used to represent primitives, for example, a `java.lang.Integer` object will be used to represent an `int` property. Two further methods are provided to handle indexed properties:

```
public Object get(String name, int index)
public void set(String name, int index, Object value)
```

Finally, there are three methods that deal with mapped properties:

```
public Object get(String name, String key)
public void set(String name, String key, Object value)
public boolean contains(String name, String key)
```

Essentially, they are similar to an indexed property except they use a key `String` rather than an integer index, analogous to the difference between a Java `List` and a `Map`. The `contains()` method can be used to determine if a mapped value exists – allowing you to distinguish between a mapped value which does not exist and one which does exist but has the value `null`.

There is also a `DynaValidatorForm` class that enhances the `DynaActionForm` with Validator functionality. We will discuss this class in the next section, after looking at the Validator itself.

The Struts Validator

One of the most important aims of the Struts framework is to take routine web application development tasks off our shoulders as much as possible. Form validation must surely count as one of the most routine and mind-numbing tasks there is; perhaps as a consequence, it often ends up being done patchily or in a clumsy, inflexible, difficult way to maintain.

What we have been doing so far, putting Java validation code in our `ActionForm` or `Action` classes, is certainly neither clean nor flexible. The validation code ends up being mixed in with other concerns – data representation in the case of `ActionForms`, business logic in the case of `Actions` – and Java code is hard to change once a system has been deployed and is in active use. Validation can also be moved to the browser by incorporating validation JavaScript in our web pages, but what if the browser doesn't support JavaScript or has it disabled for security reasons? Really, we need to validate user input on the server side regardless of whether we also use JavaScript validation or not. Needless to say, having both server-side and client-side validation makes the code even harder to write and maintain.

The Struts Validator facility provides a way to replace validation Java and JavaScript code by an XML file, which declares our validation constraints. In many cases, no coding is required, and both server-side and client-side validation can be generated from one and the same set of constraints; there is no longer any risk of the two getting out of sync.

Configuring Validation Rules

The Struts Validator is a controller plug-in. In order for it to work, we need to configure the plug-in in the Struts configuration file (`WEB-INF/struts-config.xml`) by adding the following entry right before the closing `</struts-config>` tag:

```
    <plug-in className="org.apache.struts.validator.ValidatorPlugIn">
      <set-property property="pathnames"
          value="/WEB-INF/validator-rules.xml,/WEB-INF/validation.xml"/>
    </plug-in>
  </struts-config>
```

This plugs in the Validator and tells Struts to read its configuration information from the `validator-rules.xml` and `validation.xml` files in the `WEB-INF` directory.

Supported Validator Rules

The `validator-rules.xml` file defines the *types* of validation constraints we can apply. It defines the Java classes and methods that implement the server-side validation and contains the JavaScript code that handles the client-side part. It is shipped with a fairly extensive set of rules out of the box; while it is possible to add your own rules, we will not go into this. The rules supported out of the box are:

- ❑ The `required` rule is used to indicate that a form field is required and must have a value. If violated, this rule will produce an error with message key `errors.required`.

- ❑ The `minlength` rule is used to enforce a minimum length for the contents of a text field or text area. This rule requires a parameter, `minlength`, specifying a minimum length. Its error message uses the message key `errors.minlength`.

- ❑ The `maxlength` rule is used to enforce a maximum length; it requires a `maxlength` parameter and violations produce a message with the key `errors.maxlength`.

- ❑ The `mask` rule checks whether the contents of a text field or text area match the **regular expression** provided in its `mask` parameter. If violated, this rule will produce an error with message key `errors.invalid`. Regular expressions describe patterns within strings in a very concise machine-readable form.

- ❑ The `byte`, `short`, `integer`, `long`, `float` and `double` rules check that the field is a valid value for the given data type. If the rule is violated, the error message will have key `errors.byte`, `errors.short`, etc.

- ❑ The `date` rule checks that the field is a valid date; if not, an error message with key `errors.date` is produced.

❑ The `range` rule verifies that a number is within the range given by its `min` and `max` parameters; its error key is `errors.range`.

❑ The `creditCard` rule checks whether the text field is a valid credit card number; this includes verification of number's built-in checksum. If the number is invalid, a message is displayed corresponding to the key `errors.creditcard`.

❑ Finally, the `email` rule performs some sanity checks on an e-mail address field. The error message produced has key `errors.email`.

Between them, these rules will cater for most common validation needs. We will now see how we can use these rules to put together validation constraints for our forms and actions.

Specifying Validation Constraints

Validation constraints can be specified in the `validation.xml` file and any further files you configured the Validator plug-in to use. We will walk through an example configuration file such as we might use for a credit card form (not entirely coincidentally, the very same form we defined in the `DynaActionForm` section above).

```
<form-validation>
  <formset>
```

A Validator `<formset>` works much like a file in a message resources bundle, and for the same reason: validation rules may be locale dependent. For instance, a ZIP code or telephone number in the US differs from one in Britain or France, and should be validated differently. The `<formset>` element can take `language` and `country` attributes that identify the locale for the rules contained in the set; the Validator will try to find validation rules specific to the country; failing that, the language; and failing that, it will use the rules defined by the default `<formset>`. There can be any number of form sets inside the file.

```
    <form name="creditCardForm">
```

A `<formset>` can contain zero or more `<form>` elements. A `<form>` defines a set of configuration rules for the fields inside the form. In this case, the `<form>` corresponds to our (Dyna)ActionForm, that is with the `name` attribute of the Struts action mapping. As we will see later, we can also associate a Validator `<form>` with the action itself, that is with the `path` attribute of the mapping.

```
      <field property="cardType" depends="required">
        <arg0 key="payment.cardtype"/>
      </field>
```

The `cardType` property is mapped to a dropdown or radio control, so the only thing that needs to be checked is that a choice has been made in the first place. Making this field depend on the `required` rule is all we need to do here. So what is the nested `<arg0>` tag about, then? Well, as we have seen, when the Validator finds that a required field is missing, it will display an error with key `errors.required`. This message usually reads:

```
errors.required={0} is required.
```

The field name is a replacement value that we must supply. Nested `<argX>` tags, where X is a given value, provide the error message(s) with the replacement values they need. In this case, the replacement value is the message corresponding to the `payment.cardtype` key, which could be something like the following:

```
payment.cardtype=The card type
```

The `<argX>` tags have an optional `resource` attribute that can be used if we want to specify the message directly, rather than via a message key:

```
<arg0 key="The card type" resource="false"/>
```

The next field to consider is the credit card number. Fortunately, the Validator comes with a ready-made validation rule for this.

```
<field property="cardNumber" depends="required,creditCard">
  <arg0 key="payment.cardnumber"/>
</field>
```

Again the error message has a replacement value that we must supply. For example:

```
errors.creditcard={0} is not a valid credit card number.
    .
    .
    .
payment.cardnumber=The number you entered
```

A further thing to note here is that the `depends` attribute provides *two* rules that this field depends on. The field is `required` and must contain a valid `creditCard` number; if either condition is not met, a suitable error message (`errors.required` or `errors.creditcard`) will be displayed:

```
    <field property="cardExpiry" depends="required,date">
      <arg0 key="payment.cardexpiry"/>
    </field>
  </form>
```

There are no new elements to the last validation rule. This concludes the form. There can be any number of forms following this one. Before we go on to the Validator classes, let's examine a more complicated rule where we are checking an item quantity field in a shopping cart against a possible range.

```
<form name="cart">
  <field indexedListProperty="items" property="quantity"
         depends="required,integer,range">
```

This tells the Validator to retrieve the `items` list, and apply its validation rules to the `quantity` property of each item in the list. The rules applied are `required`, `integer` and `range`.

We mentioned earlier that that the `range` rule allows for two parameters, `min` and `max`. These parameters are supplied using nested `<var>` elements, each of which must have a `<var-name>` and a `<var-value>` child element. These supply the parameter name and the parameter value respectively. For example:

```
<var>
  <var-name>min</var-name>
  <var-value>0</var-value>
</var>
<var>
  <var-name>max</var-name>
  <var-value>10</var-value>
</var>
```

These parameters tell the `range` rule that the quantity must be somewhere between 0 and 10. The error message used by the `range` rule is also a bit more complicated than we've seen so far:

```
errors.range={0} is not in the range {1} through {2}.
```

The second and third replacement strings indicate the range. We could of course simply specify this in our replacement string arguments, setting the `resource` attribute to `false` to indicate that we are dealing with literal strings rather than message keys:

```
<arg1 key="0" resource="false"/>
<arg2 key="10" resource="false"/>
```

The problem is that the range would now be defined in two different places, which increases the chance of inconsistencies when the validation rule is being modified at some later date. It would be a lot cleaner if we had a little expression language with which we could retrieve the values of the `min` and `max` parameters defined above. Indeed, the Validator supports simple expressions that almost (but not quite) look like JSP EL expressions:

```
<arg0 key="shoppingcart.quantity"/>
<arg1 name="range" key="${var:min}" resource="false"/>
<arg2 name="range" key="${var:max}" resource="false"/>
```

An expression ${var:*variableName*} will be substituted by the variable's value. Note also that both <arg1> and <arg2> have an extra name="range" attribute. Because the error message produced by the required rule needs only a single replacement value, we need some way to indicate that the last two replacement values are associated with the range rule only.

```
        </field>
    </form>
    </formset>
```

After the <formset>, there can be a number of further form sets for other locales:

```
    <formset language="en" country="GB">
    .
    .
    .
    <formset>
    </form-validation>
```

This concludes our walkthrough of the Validator configuration file. If you'd like to see more, the case study in Chapter 16 uses the Validator for validation purposes throughout. We will now see how we can use the Validator form classes to use these rules in our applications.

Validator Form Classes

So how do we actually use the validation rules defined in our validation.xml file? Don't worry; once the Validator configuration file has been written, things get amazingly simple. Struts has four different classes that you can use instead of ActionForm (or DynaActionForm). All of these classes belong to the package named org.apache.struts.validator, and provide implementations of the validate() method that use the Validator configuration file to perform the validation. Other than choosing the right class, there's nothing for us to do.

> *If there is some validation that cannot be done using the Validator, you can roll your own Validator rule (which we will not discuss here; see the Validator documentation at http://jakarta.apache.org/commons/validator/ for more information) but it is also perfectly fine to override the validate() method in your ValidatorForm subclass and add some code to do the extra validation. Do not forget to call super.validate()!*

The ValidatorForm Class

The ValidatorForm class is a version of ActionForm that performs validation based on the form name, that is the name attribute of the Struts action mapping must correspond to the name attribute of the form tag in the Validator configuration file. The configuration file walkthrough above had two examples of this.

Use this class if the validation is related directly to the ActionForm object in itself, rather than what you happen to be doing with it.

The ValidatorActionForm Class

The `ValidatorActionForm` class performs its validation based on the action taken, i.e. the `path` attribute of the Struts action mapping must correspond to the `name` attribute of the form tag in the Validator configuration file.

```
<form name="/update">
```

This is most useful if one and the same `ActionForm` object has to be validated in completely different ways, depending on the precise action taken with the information.

The DynaValidatorForm and DynaValidatorActionForm Classes

The `DynaValidatorForm` and `DynaValidatorActionForm` classes are versions of `ValidatorForm` and `ValidatorActionForm` that use the dynamic form facility. They work exactly like their non-dynamic counterparts, except that we have to define their properties in the `<form-beans>` section of the Struts configuration file.

To illustrate this, we can convert the credit card form example in the section on dynamic action forms to use the Validator facility as well. The code could appear as follows:

```
<form-beans>
  <form-bean name="creditCardForm"
             type="org.apache.struts.validator.DynaValidatorForm">
  <form-property name="cardNumber" type="java.lang.Long"/>
  <form-property name="cardExpiry" type="java.sql.Date"/>
  <form-property name="cardType" type="java.lang.String" initial=""/>
  </form-bean>
</form-beans>
```

That's all there is to it – we just change the class name. We chose `DynaValidatorForm` because validation of credit card information is intimately tied up with the information itself, rather than what we do with it.

Validator Tags in the HTML Tag Library

What we have been discussing so far is enough to implement server-side validation, but as mentioned in the introduction, the Validator can give us client-side JavaScript validation based on the very same configuration file. The Struts HTML tag library makes this a fairly straightforward procedure.

JavaScript Tag

We can use the `<html:javascript>` tag to generate all the necessary validation code for a given form. This JavaScript code is composed of two parts:

❑ **Dynamic JavaScript** is generated specifically for the form. You want to generate this for every (validating) form on your page. By default, a JavaScript function is generated with the name `validate` followed by the form name, such as `validateCreditCardForm()` for instance. We need to call this function explicitly using JavaScript in our form tag's `onsubmit` attribute.

❑ **Static JavaScript** is effectively a function library independent of the actual form. You should generate only a single copy of this code per page; in fact, you might even want to make your pages a bit smaller by moving this into an external JavaScript file. This code is generally not called directly.

The attributes of the `<html:javascript>` tag are explained in the following table:

Attribute	Description
formName	The Validator form to generate validation code. If you are using the (Dyna)ValidatorActionForm class, this is the path for the action mapping rather than the name of the ActionForm.
method	Used to specify a method name for the dynamic JavaScript validation function. This is useful when the default name ("validate" followed by the formName) would give problems.
staticJavaScript	If absent or true, the tag will generate the static JavaScript code. If false, no static code is generated.
dynamicJavaScript	If absent or true, the tag will generate the dynamic JavaScript code. If false, no dynamic code is generated.
src	If set, generates a corresponding src attribute on the <script> tag.

It is up to us to ensure that the validation code actually gets called, but putting a JavaScript call in the `<html:form>`'s onsubmit event handler. For example, to perform client-side validation on a credit card form, we first need to generate all the necessary JavaScript validation code:

```
<html:javascript formName="creditCardForm"/>
```

Then we call `validateCreditCardForm()` in the onsubmit event handler so that all the information in the form is validated when the user presses the submit button:

```
<html:form action="/payCartItems"
        onsubmit="return validateCreditCardForm(this);">
```

```
          .
          .
          .
      <html:submit>
        <bean:message key="pay.submit.button.label"/>
      </html:submit>
```

When the form is canceled, validating the form serves no purpose and can even be annoying. The generated JavaScript provides a bCancel flag that can be set to bypass the validation code; we can set this flag in the cancel button's onclick event:

```
      <html:cancel onclick="bCancel=true;">
        <bean:message key="pay.cancel.button.label"/>
      </html:cancel>
    </html:form>
```

This does not exhaust all the features supported by the Struts Validator, but it should be enough to get you started.

Summary

In this chapter, we examined how we can optimize the architecture of a JSP application. In particular, we discussed how we could use the Apache Struts framework to efficiently write applications that are maintainable, reusable, and flexible. Throughout the chapter, we have used a small and simple e-commerce application to illustrate points and try out techniques. The most important issues covered were:

- ❏ JSP Model 1 Architecture, where the JSP pages contain both the presentation logic and the application logic, and its impact on the key success factors of maintainability, reusability, and the way developers with different skill sets can work on the same problem.

- ❏ JSP Model 2 or Model-View-Controller Architecture, which uses a controller to overcome the drawbacks of the JSP Model 1 Architecture; how it facilitates the cooperation of developers with different skill sets, and how it promotes maintainability and reusability.

- ❏ The reasons for using third party web application frameworks.

- ❏ The Model 2 (MVC) architecture as implemented by Struts, including the operation of the core ActionServlet, ActionMapping, ActionForm, and Action components.

- ❏ Struts configuration and deployment in an application.

- ❏ The most important tags from the Struts bean, logic, html, and template tag libraries.

❑ Dynamic action forms which can help us to eliminate some of our Java `ActionForm` classes.

❑ Declarative validation using the Validator.

Chapter 16 contains a detailed case study, which develops a real web application using Struts.

Why Not Try?

If you would like to consolidate and build upon the Struts knowledge you've acquired in this chapter, there are a number of things you could try.

Use the Struts HTML tags with the Shopping Cart

In our last Try It Out, we rewrote the shopping cart to make use of the Struts controller and `ActionForms`. To see the full power of Struts, the cart should also make use of the Struts internationalization features and the HTML tag library.

❑ Create a default message resources file for the application and set it up in the configuration file. Then systematically go through the JSP pages and replace all English text with `<bean:message>` tags. Try adding a messages file for a different locale, change your computer's time zone and look at the pages again. Do they pick up the new messages?

❑ Modify the four forms in the JSP pages to use the Struts HTML tag library. In our discussion of the Struts HTML tag library, we have already discussed some of the modifications that need to be made.

❑ If you wish, you can make good use of the template library as well.

Use the Struts Validator with the Shopping Cart

Currently, any two-digit quantity can be entered for the items in the shopping cart. It would make sense to impose a ceiling for this and invite any customer ordering more than 10 copies of a single book to contact customer support to discuss discount and shipping arrangements. The Struts Validator is ideal for the job.

You will have to configure the Validator plug-in, create a configuration file for it, and create a message resources file (if you have not already done so) with the appropriate messages. The shopping cart page will have to display any error messages generated by the validation code (client-side validation does not work with indexed properties at the moment). `ShoppingCart` will have to extend `ValidatorForm`.

Add A Checkout to the Shopping Cart

In numerous examples throughout the chapter, we have discussed how a credit card form could be realized. If you would add the customer's name and address information to this form, you have all the ingredients to extend the shopping cart with a checkout facility (although you will unfortunately have to omit the bit of code that interfaces with a bank or e-commerce company to take the actual credit card payment).

❑ There is a fair bit of validation to do on this form, and the Validator facility can help you there.

❑ You can decide whether to create a Java ValidatorForm or a DynaValidatorForm. It is worthwhile to experiment with both and get a better picture of the pros and cons of each.

❑ The Checkout button on the showcart.jsp page will have to work differently from the Continue Shopping button. The easiest approach would be to turn the Continue Shopping button into an <html:cancel>, and to map the form to an Action that checks isCancelled() and returns different forwards depending on whether Continue Shopping or Checkout was pressed.

❑ If you implemented the validation from the previous suggestion, you will find that pressing the Checkout button will allow you to go to the checkout with "invalid" quantities. Consider giving this action the cart as an input form, too.

CHAPTER 16

A Struts Web Application

In this final chapter, we'll design and develop an intranet web application using the Struts framework. The application will allow publishers to maintain details of books to be published. Staff can view these details and add news items about the progress of each book. The homepage is accessible to anyone and shows the book titles and the most recent news.

The topics we'll be covering in this chapter include:

- ❑ All aspects of the design, development, and deployment phases of the project
- ❑ Almost all aspects of the Struts framework explained in the last chapter
- ❑ Different aspects of security such as authentication and authorization
- ❑ Use of Model 2 architecture for partitioning the components of the application
- ❑ Use of data access objects and business objects to implement the application model
- ❑ Database access
- ❑ Dynamic template management
- ❑ And of course JSP, JSP, and more JSP

We will start by looking at what the application must do, its overall structure, security requirements, and how we represent the data that it needs to maintain. Finally we'll move on to create the Struts objects and JSP pages that form the web interface to the system.

Requirements

Let's get down to business. Once we've decided that it's feasible to go ahead with a project, our first step is to perform a detailed **requirements analysis** to identify the functionality the system should provide. This will give us a clear idea of what we need the application to do *before* we actually start creating it.

There are a number of tools that can help us with requirements analysis, including a **requirements catalog** listing requirements, **use case UML diagrams** which provide a visual overview of the requirements and their relationships, and **screen mock-ups** to help users visualize functionality. We will go through each of these.

Our application is to be run on an intranet with a small portal on the Internet that lists books and recent news items associated with these books. It provides the following functionality:

❑ Allow anyone to view the list of planned books

❑ Allow anyone to view the list of books in progress

❑ Allow anyone to view the latest ten news items

❑ Allow authorized users to log into and out of the application if they wish to modify book details or news items

❑ Allow authorized users to view the details for any book after logging in

❑ Allow editors to enter details for a new book after logging in

This list is in fact part of a requirements catalog. The screenshot below illustrates one possible way to realize these requirements. In this case of course, rather than create a mock-up (or several), the screen below depicts the application that we'll build later in this chapter:

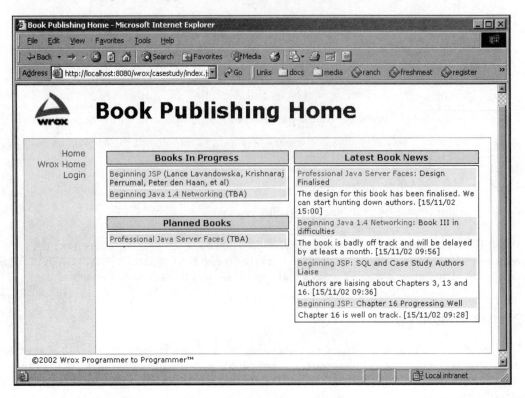

Once books are in print, they are ignored by the system. They remain in the database for archival purposes and perhaps for future expansion.

After logging in and selecting a book to view or edit, a page allows users to:

❑ View the book details

❑ View the last ten news items related to that specific book

❑ Add a new news item and select items previously entered by the user

Editors have some additional functionality not enjoyed by ordinary users:

❑ Add a new book, edit the book details, or delete the book

❑ Select any news item regardless of the author

The screenshot below shows the system after an editor has logged in and selected the "Beginning JSP" book to view or edit:

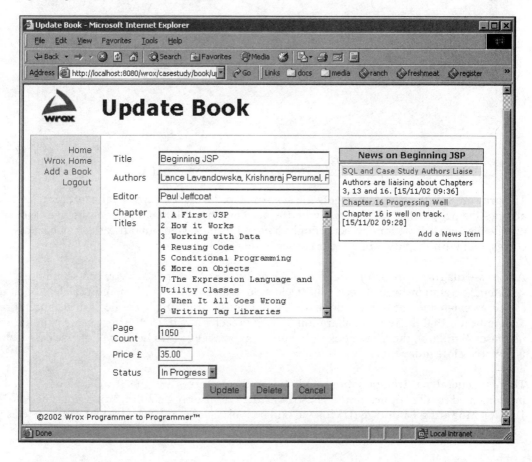

Finally, a news item form will allow allows users to add a new news item for a book, and edit or delete any item previously entered by that user. Editors can edit or delete any news item regardless of who created it.

The layout of this news screen is analogous to that of the book update screen, with the news items at the right hand side omitted.

A **use case diagram** is a great way to get a visual overview of the functionality required, who is interacting with the system in what way, and the relations between the various use cases.

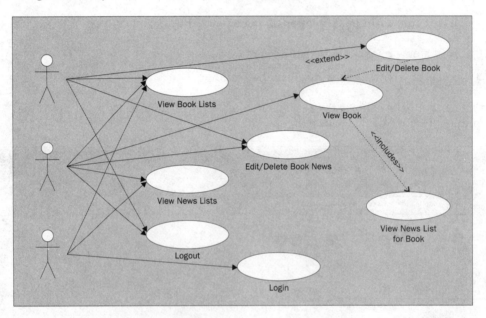

The gray area on the right represents the system, and the stick figures on the left represent the **actors** – the people that will interact with the system. The balloons represent the **use cases**; they are the discrete interactions an actor might have with the system. In our case, they broadly correspond with the bullet point lists earlier in this section.

A use case diagram can also model the relations between use cases, as you can see in the <<extend>> relationship between Edit/Delete Book and View Book. The Edit/Delete Book use case is an extension of the View Book use case: it does everything View Book does, and more. This indicates that the two can share some code; in fact we will use the very same page for both use cases. Similarly, the View Book <<include>>s the View News List for Book use case (which is not accessible independently).

There is generally a strong relationship between the use cases and the Struts actions implemented by the application. The use case diagram is only one of the diagram types of the **Unified Modeling Language** (UML); we will be looking at another important type, the **class diagram**, shortly.

Application Architecture

So now we know what we want the system to do, we can move on to choosing an appropriate architectural model for the web application. As we saw in the last chapter, the **Model-View-Controller (MVC)** paradigm provides high levels of decoupling, maintainability, and separation of presentation from content. We will put the theory into practice in this chapter by using the MVC architecture to develop our application.

❏   The **Model** of our application consists of three parts: the "book" and "book news" **entities**, a layer of **business objects** that manipulates these entities and enforces business rules such as the authorization rules mentioned above, and finally a data access layer which access the database through **data access objects**.

❏   The application **View**s will be implemented using JSP pages. We will make good use of, among other things, JSTL tags and the JSP 2.0 expression language.

❏   For the **Controller** element, rather than reinventing the wheel, we will use the Apache Struts framework. The Struts action classes implement the logic that operates upon the model.

As both the MVC architecture and Struts have been discussed extensively in the previous chapter, we will not go into much detail here.

The servlet container will handle the basic authentication and authorization needs of our application, although we will have to write some Java code to enforce the distinction between editors and ordinary users.

Exception Handling

Before we get into the application in depth, we need to create an exception class that will be the root of all application-level exceptions we will encounter. This will allow us to distinguish between recoverable exceptions that occur due to erroneous user input for example (like a new a book title duplicating an existing title), which will be a subclass of the PublishException defined below, from others that indicate more serious problems such as database SQLExceptions. If you wish to refresh your knowledge of Java exception handling, leaf back to Chapter 8.

Having a well thought out exception hierarchy will greatly help error handling in your applications. In larger applications, you might subclass your application-wide exception to give you separate root exceptions for each major functional area in your application.

PublishException

A PublishException signifies an application-level problem in the system such as a duplicate title or an action the user does not have enough privileges to perform. It will not be thrown directly; rather, we will define subclasses of PublishException to indicate the precise nature of each problem.

```
package com.wrox.publish;

/* The root class of all publishing application exceptions */
public abstract class PublishException extends Exception
{
  public PublishException(String msg)
  {
    super(msg);
  }

  public PublishException(Throwable cause)
  {
    super(cause);
  }
}
```

The Application Entities

Now we will start looking in detail at the objects that form the core of our application. They represent the persistent data stored in the underlying database, where we typically have one table for each entity type. The requirements analysis has identified two major entities that are required for modeling the state of the application:

❑   Book: This entity represents a prospective book.

❑   BookNews: This entity represents a news item associated with a book. It is named BookNews rather than simply News to indicate the relationship with books and because other types of news might be introduced into the system at some future point.

Books have a many-to-one relationship with BookNews items. Each book has zero, one, or many news items associated with it; conversely, each news item is associated with exactly one book.

We now break down each entity into the individual data items that each must contain – these are its **attributes**. This list of required attributes is usually established during the requirements capture and analysis phase.

The Book entity has the following attributes:

❑   id to uniquely identify a book.

❑   title, authors, editor, price, and pageCount attributes to describe a particular book.

   The authors attribute can be a simple text field. We could have modeled this by representing each author as a separate entity in a book_author table, but this would complicate our sample application unnecessarily.

❑ chapters contains the table of contents for the book as a simple list of chapter names, one per line. Like authors, you could make a case that this is actually best modeled in a book_chapter child table.

❑ The status attribute indicates the book's current state, as one of three values, Planned, In Progress, or Complete.

❑ Finally, the news attribute lists the news items associated with the book.

The BookNews entity has the following attributes:

❑ The id uniquely identifies a news item.

❑ The book attribute links the news item to its book.

❑ The title and body attributes contain the item's title and the actual text.

❑ The user attribute records who created the item. This is necessary for the authorization rule that ordinary users can only edit their own news items.

❑ published indicates when this news item was created. This attribute allows us to determine which news items are the most recent.

The **class diagram** below depicts the entity model for our system. A class diagram is a type of UML diagram representing the individual classes within the system. Each box represents a particular class with a list of its attributes; for example, Book has a long property called id and a String property called title. The dash in front of each attribute name indicates that the attribute itself is private (a public attribute would be indicated using a + sign).

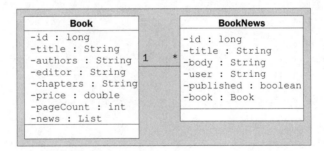

The line connecting the classes describes an association. In this case, a book is associated with any number (indicated by the *) of BookNews items, but each such item is associated with exactly one (indicated by the 1) Book.

Implementing the Entities

We need to implement a database table for each entity to provide a long-term store for the data. We also require some Java classes to access these tables easily within our application.

Database Scripts

Let's start by creating the database itself. Start up the `mysql` command-line utility and create a new database called `publish`:

```
CREATE DATABASE IF NOT EXISTS publish;
```

For security reasons it is always a good idea to limit database accessibility as much as possible, so let's create a user called `publish` with password `wrox` who can only connect locally:

```
USE publish;

GRANT ALL PRIVILEGES
    ON publish.*
    TO publish@localhost
    IDENTIFIED BY 'wrox';
```

Book

We'll store the book information in a table called `book`, using the `id` as the primary key, with the `auto_increment` option specified so this field will be generated for us whenever a new record is created. We define essential columns in the table as `not null`, to prevent their being left blank:

```
CREATE TABLE book (
    id              integer         NOT NULL
                                    AUTO_INCREMENT
                                    PRIMARY KEY,
    title           VARCHAR(255)    NOT NULL,
    authors         VARCHAR(255),
    editor          VARCHAR(255),
    chapters        TEXT,
    page_count      INTEGER,
    price           NUMERIC(5,2),
    status          CHAR(1)         NOT NULL DEFAULT 'P',
    UNIQUE INDEX (title)
) type=InnoDB;
```

The penultimate line defines a unique index on the `title` field. Indexes help us find records with a specific title quickly and efficiently. Because it is a *unique* index, it also prevents users from entering the same book with the same title in the database more than once.

> The `type=InnoDB` part at the end makes MySQL create the table to support JDBC transactions. You must be using MySQL Max for this. If you do not use MySQL Max, MySQL will automatically select an appropriate alternative table type. The `DELETE CASCADE` defined below will not work and you will not be able to delete a book unless you delete all its news items first. You will of course also lack transactions, but they are not required by this application.

Book News

The `book_news` table holds book news items. It has a foreign key field called `book`, which refers to the primary key (`id`) in the `book` table. The database itself will prevent users associating a news item with a book that doesn't exist:

```
CREATE TABLE book_news (
    id              INTEGER         NOT NULL
                                    AUTO_INCREMENT
                                    PRIMARY KEY,
    book            INTEGER         NOT NULL,
    title           VARCHAR(255)    NOT NULL,
    body            TEXT            NOT NULL,
    user            VARCHAR(40)     NOT NULL,
    published       DATETIME,
    INDEX (book),
    FOREIGN KEY (book)
        REFERENCES book(id)
        ON DELETE CASCADE
) type=InnoDB;
```

The `ON DELETE CASCADE` option on the foreign key clause tells MySQL that, when a book is deleted, all its associated news items should be automatically deleted with it. Identifying the foreign key constraints is one of the most important tasks in designing a relational database.

Java Classes

Now we will define the Java classes that will form the **object model** for our entities. Later, we'll move on to the data access and business logic classes. The entity classes can also serve as Struts `ActionForm` beans that can be associated with the forms for entering the book and news item details. To take advantage of the validation features of Struts 1.1, they do not extend `ActionForm` directly but instead extend the subclass called `org.apache.struts.validator.ValidatorForm`.

These object model classes will be placed in a package called `com.wrox.publish.om`.

Book

This class models a book. As you would expect, there is a close resemblance between this class and the `book` table, and it consists of JavaBean accessors for all fields apart from the `Book` class's `news` attribute that details `BookNews` items associated with the book. This attribute has no corresponding field in the database table, and we have to find relevant news items by searching through the `book_news` table for items where the `book_news.book` foreign key matches the `book.id` primary key.

You may remember the `TreeSet` that we saw in Chapter 7. We'll use one here to keep track of news items. This class from the Java Collections framework acts as a container for a set of objects, and it implements the `SortedSet` interface, which has two important properties:

- ❑ Like any `Set`, a `SortedSet` will hold only one copy of a given object. This is just fine, because we really want to show any given news item just once.

- ❑ The objects are held in sorted order; in this case, the latest news item first.

As we shall see in the next section, the sorting order is actually defined by the `BookNews` class itself:

```java
package com.wrox.publish.om;

import java.util.SortedSet;
import java.util.TreeSet;
import org.apache.struts.validator.ValidatorForm;

/*
 * JavaBean encapsulating a single book. This class extends
 * ValidatorForm for easy population and validation with the
 * Struts framework.
 */
public class Book extends ValidatorForm
{
    public static final char PLANNED = 'P';
    public static final char IN_PROGRESS = 'I';
    public static final char COMPLETED = 'C';

    private long id;
    private String title;
    private String authors;
    private String editor;
    private String chapters;
    private int pageCount;
    private double price;
    private final SortedSet news = new TreeSet();
```

A book starts life with a `PLANNED` status:

```java
    private char status = PLANNED;

    public long getId()
    {
        return this.id;
    }

    public void setId(long id)
    {
        this.id = id;
    }

    public String getTitle()
    {
        return this.title;
```

```
}

public void setTitle(String title)
{
  this.title = title;
}

public String getAuthors()
{
  return this.authors;
}

public void setAuthors(String authors)
{
  this.authors = authors;
}

public String getEditor()
{
  return this.editor;
}

public void setEditor(String editor)
{
  this.editor = editor;
}

public int getPageCount()
{
  return this.pageCount;
}

public void setPageCount(int pageCount)
{
  this.pageCount = pageCount;
}

public String getChapters()
{
  return this.chapters;
}

public void setChapters(String chapters)
{
  this.chapters = chapters;
}

public double getPrice()
{
  return this.price;
}
```

```
public void setPrice(double price)
{
   this.price = price;
}

public char getStatus()
{
   return this.status;
}
```

The setter method for the `status` attribute performs some validation to ensure that a book has one of the three status values defined above:

```
public void setStatus(char status)
{
   switch (status)
   {
     case PLANNED:
     case IN_PROGRESS:
     case COMPLETED:
       this.status = status;
       break;

     default:
       throw new IllegalArgumentException("Invalid status " + status);
   }
}

public SortedSet getNews()
{
   return this.news;
}
```

BookNews

This class models the `book_news` table and defines attributes for columns in that table, together with their get and set accessors. In addition, `BookNews` implements the `Comparable` interface to define a **natural sorting order** by publishing date descending. This will be useful because we will generally want to display news in this order, with the most recent news first. As we saw in Chapter 7, the Java Collections framework has various methods to quickly and easily sort collections of `Comparable` objects, including the `TreeSet` used in the `Book` object:

```
package com.wrox.publish.om;

import java.sql.Timestamp;
import org.apache.struts.validator.ValidatorForm;
```

```
/*
 * JavaBean encapsulating a single news item for a book. This class
 * has a natural sorting order which is by publishing date descending.
 * It extends ValidatorForm for easy population and validation within
 * the Struts framework.
 */
public class BookNews extends ValidatorForm implements Comparable
{
  private long id;
  private Book book;
  private String title;
  private String body;
  private String user;
```

The `published` timestamp defaults to the current date and time:

```
  private Timestamp published =
             new Timestamp(System.currentTimeMillis());
```

Now we have the accessors for our class attributes:

```
  public long getId()
  {
    return this.id;
  }

  public void setId(long id)
  {
    this.id = id;
  }

  public Book getBook()
  {
    return this.book;
  }

  public void setBook(Book book)
  {
    this.book = book;
  }

  public String getTitle()
  {
    return this.title;
  }

  public void setTitle(String title)
  {
    this.title = title;
  }
```

```
   public String getUser()
   {
     return this.user;
   }

   public void setUser(String user)
   {
     this.user = user;
   }

   public String getBody()
   {
     return this.body;
   }

   public void setBody(String body)
   {
     this.body = body;
   }

   public Timestamp getPublished()
   {
     return this.published;
   }

   public void setPublished(Timestamp published)
   {
     this.published = published;
   }
```

Remember from Chapter 7 that in order to properly implement `Comparable`, we need a `compareTo(Object)` method and we must override the `equals(Object)` method to be consistent. That is, if `a.compareTo(b) == 0` then `a.equals(b)` must be `true` and vice versa. And if we override `equals()`, we should really override `hashCode()` so that whenever `a.equals(b)`, a and b have identical `hashCode()` values. The JavaDoc documentation for `java.lang.Comparable` and `java.lang.Object` has more information about this.

```
   public int compareTo(Object o)
   {
     return compareTo((BookNews)o);
   }

   public int compareTo(BookNews that)
   {
     int cf;

     if (this.published == null)
     {
       cf = (that.published == null) ? 0 : 1;
     }
     else if (that.published == null)
```

```
        {
          cf = -1;
        }
        else
        {
          cf = -this.published.compareTo(that.published);
        }

        if (cf == 0 && this.id != that.id)
        {
          cf = (this.id > that.id) ? -1 : 0;
        }
        return cf;
      }

    public boolean equals(Object o)
    {
      return o instanceof BookNews && equals((BookNews)o);
    }

    public boolean equals(BookNews that)
    {
      return this.id == that.id;
    }

    public int hashCode()
    {
      return (int)id;
    }
  }
```

Now that we've defined the classes that form the object model for our entities, we'll start looking at how they map to the database.

Data Access Objects

We are now ready to move on to the **data access objects** (**DAO**s) that will access the database. These objects encapsulate the database calls to transform the database records to entity class instances, and vice versa.

There will be a one-to-one correspondence between the entity objects and data access objects, with each Book and BookNews entity object having a corresponding data access object that encapsulates the database calls for that entity.

Each class will have:

❑   A method for creating the entity in the database

❑   A method for removing the entity from the database

❑   A method for updating the information regarding an existing entity

❑   One or more methods for finding entities from the database based on specific criteria. (Each data access object will at least have a method to find a single entity from its primary key.)

When we create an instance of a data access object, we will pass its constructor a JDBC connection for it to use when executing SQL statements on the database.

Supplying a connection rather than allowing the DAO to obtain its own connection from the Struts connection pool makes it possible for the calling code to make multiple DAO calls within a single database transaction.

Exception Handling in Data Access Objects

Before we look at the data access objects themselves, we need to create a specialized set of exception classes to deal with application-level problems that might occur when accessing the database. These exceptions will be subclasses of the PublishException discussed above.

EntityNotFoundException

An EntityNotFoundException will be thrown if, for some reason, we fail to find a book or news item in the database when we try to load or update it:

```
package com.wrox.publish.db;

import com.wrox.publish.PublishException;

/* Exception thrown when an entity could not be found in the database. */
public class EntityNotFoundException extends PublishException
{
  public EntityNotFoundException(String msg)
  {
    super(msg);
  }
}
```

InvalidFieldException

An InvalidFieldException will be thrown if the entity we are trying to create or store violates a database-level constraint, such as the uniqueness constraint on book.title. This exception is a little different from the previous one, because it takes a Throwable rather than a message as its constructor argument. The reason is that a constraint validation actually causes the database to throw a SQLException. Since this represents a user input error rather than a fundamental problem with the database, we will catch the SQLException and, if an invalid field is the cause, re-throw it as an InvalidFieldException. Field constraint problems are identified by a SQLException SQL state code of S1009.

```
package com.wrox.publish.db;

import com.wrox.publish.PublishException;

/*
 * Exception thrown when a database create or update infringes a
 * database field constraint such as a uniqueness constraint.
 */
public class InvalidFieldException extends PublishException
{
    /* SQL State corresponding with an Invalid Argument error */
    static final String SQL_STATE = "S1009";

    public InvalidFieldException(Throwable cause) {
        super(cause);
    }
}
```

We'll now move on to look at how our data access objects will operate, without (at this stage) looking at the actual code. Once we've thought through how each of the methods will work, we'll look at the actual data access object classes for both Book and BookNews.

Create Methods

Each data access object defines one create method, which takes an instance of the corresponding entity class as an argument, and can throw InvalidFieldException. The steps involved in implementing the create method are:

1. Create a PreparedStatement object for the connection, passing it the specific SQL to create this type of entity.

2. Set the input parameters of the PreparedStatement according to the entity object attributes. In our case, the entity object may be a Book or BookNews object.

3. Execute the SQL.

4. Retrieve the primary key (id) generated by the database for the inserted record, and update the entity object with this id. If we neglect to populate the id attribute, a subsequent update using the same object would fail.

5. If a SQLException was thrown in any of the above steps, check whether it was due to an invalid field. If this is the case, throw an InvalidFieldException, otherwise re-throw the SQLException.

6. Finally, close the PreparedStatement.

Update Methods

Next, we'll look at the methods for updating the entities in the database. Each data access object defines one update method, which again takes an as an argument an instance of the corresponding entity class. The steps involved in implementing an update method are:

1. Create a `PreparedStatement` object using the connection, passing it the relevant SQL code to update the entity.

2. Set the input parameters of the `PreparedStatement` using the entity object attributes.

3. Execute the SQL. As we're using the primary key, we should only ever update a single record, so if the update count is not equal to 1, we throw an `EntityNotFoundException`.

4. If an `SQLException` was thrown in any of the above steps, check whether it was due to an invalid field. If this is the case, throw an `InvalidFieldException`, otherwise re-throw the `SQLException`.

5. Finally, close the `PreparedStatement`.

Remove Methods

Next, let's look at the methods for removing entities from the database. Each data access object defines one remove method that takes the primary key (in our case, `id`) of the corresponding entity. The steps involved in implementing the remove method are:

1. Create a `PreparedStatement` from the connection, passing the delete SQL specific to the entity being deleted as an argument.

2. Set the input parameters of the `PreparedStatement` from the entity object passed to the method.

3. Execute the SQL. If the update count is not equal to one, throw an `EntityNotFoundException`.

4. Finally, close the `PreparedStatement`.

Because we have added an ON DELETE CASCADE option to the referential constraint between book and book_news, whenever we delete a book the database will automatically delete all the news items for that book. This saves us quite a bit of coding.

Finder Methods

The data access objects may define one or more finder methods to retrieve an entity or a collection of entities from the database. At a minimum, each object must define a finder that takes a primary key value and returns an entity instance corresponding to that primary key.

Finder methods can be either single or multi object finders:

❑ Single object finder methods return a single instance of the entity. The argument to the method is usually the primary key, as it must uniquely identify a single object. We expect the object with the given primary key to exist, so if the record is not found the method will throw an `EntityNotFoundException`.

❑ Multi object finders return a `Collection` of entity instances. A key difference with single object finder methods is that multi object finders use criteria other than the primary key, and it is therefore perfectly possible not to find any matching records. An exception would be inappropriate because we are not dealing with a problem or exceptional condition, and so if no entities are found matching the specified criteria, an empty collection is returned instead.

Before we can discuss the finder methods in detail, we first have to understand some of the differences between the Java object model and a relational database.

The Object/Relational Impedance Mismatch

In the requirement stage, we determined that news items are associated with a book in a many-to-one fashion. In UML form, with only the relevant attributes shown, the Java implementation we chose was:

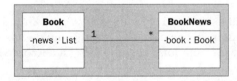

This is a **bi-directional association**, where the `Book` class contains references to all associated `BookNews` items, and these items in turn refer to their parent `Book`. In other words, when we have a `Book` object, we expect all `BookNews` objects to be accessible under its `news` attribute. This means that when we retrieve a book from the database, we do not simply need to retrieve a `Book` object; we need to retrieve what is called an **object graph**, which consists of both the book from the `book` table and all its associated news items from the `book_news` table.

Mapping an object model to a database can quickly become tricky. Inheritance is quite thorny, for one. What if `BookNews` were a subclass of a class `News` representing a generic news item that is not necessarily book-related? We could store both types in a single database table, or have completely separate `news` and `book_news` tables. A third option would be to store all news of any type in the `news` table, and have a `book_news` table that contains the primary key for news (`id`) and those fields that are unique to `BookNews` objects (in this case just `book`). All three approaches have their own advantages and disadvantages.

677

The issues encountered when mapping object models to relational databases are sometimes collectively referred to as the **object/relational impedance mismatch**.

> *In the following sections, we will develop our own Data Access Objects to retrieve object graphs from the database, and store changes to these objects back into it. While this is fine for very small projects, DAOs quickly become cumbersome and error-prone as the object model grows in size and complexity. There are powerful object/relational mapping tools available that will automate much of this task, typically by either implementing the Java Data Objects (JDO) specification or as Entity Bean mappers in Enterprise JavaBean (EJB) containers.*

Single Object Finders

Let's start by examining the logic for single object finders. The number and type of arguments taken by a finder method will depend on the `where` condition in the SQL code used to query the database; the methods for finding an entity by primary key will take the corresponding primary key values as arguments. The steps involved in implementing these finder methods are:

1. Create a `PreparedStatement` for the connection, with a SQL `SELECT` statement matching the entity being selected.

2. Set the input parameters of the `PreparedStatement` using arguments passed to the method.

3. Execute the SQL. If the result set is empty, throw an `EntityNotFoundException`.

4. Create an entity instance, and set its attributes using the values of the result set.

5. Find the other entities referred to by the object by calling their finder methods, and set the relevant attributes. In some cases, we can combine this step and the previous one by selecting all the information in one go using a database join.

6. Return the entity instance.

7. Finally, close the `PreparedStatement`.

Multi Object Finders

The logic for multi-object finders is much like that for single object finders, with the difference that they return a `Collection` of objects and never throw an `EntityNotFoundException`. If no objects are found, they simply return an empty collection.

In this project, we will use just one multi-object finder that the DAO for `Book` uses to retrieve all the associated `BookNews` items for a given `Book`. We would normally need a few more multi-object finders to get the books and news items lists for the homepage, but we're using that as an opportunity to use the SQL tags from the JSTL instead.

BookDAO

BookDAO is the data access object that encapsulates the data access calls for maintaining the state of Book entities. It defines public methods to create, update, and remove Book objects, and to find a Book by id. In addition it provides a package-private loadById(long) method that will load up a Book without its associated BookNews objects for use by the BookNews DAO.

Let's have a look at the source code for the BookDAO class:

```
package com.wrox.publish.db;

import com.wrox.publish.om.Book;
import java.sql.Connection;
import java.sql.PreparedStatement;
import java.sql.ResultSet;
import java.sql.SQLException;
import java.sql.Statement;
import java.util.Collection;

/*
 * Data Access Object responsible for reading, writing, and deleting
 * records in the Books database.
 */
public class BookDAO
{
  private final Connection conn;
```

The constructor takes a single argument of a JDBC connection object to provide the database access:

```
public BookDAO(Connection conn)
{
  super();
  this.conn = conn;
}
```

The create() method takes a Book object as its single parameter. An instance of PreparedStatement is created, for executing the SQL INSERT statement, and the populate() method is called to set the statement parameters. We then try to execute the statement:

```
public void create(Book book)
      throws SQLException, InvalidFieldException
{
  PreparedStatement insert = conn.prepareStatement(
    "INSERT INTO book (title, authors, editor, chapters, " +
    "page_count, price, status) VALUES (?, ?, ?, ?, ?, ?, ?)",
    Statement.RETURN_GENERATED_KEYS);
```

```
        try
        {
          populate(insert, book);
          insert.executeUpdate();
```

The next step is to retrieve the primary key that has been generated by the database. By passing in a RETURN_GENERATED_KEYS parameter into the PreparedStatement above, the database will tell us the value it generated for the primary key. The Statement.getGeneratedKeys() method will provide us with the value in the form of a ResultSet. We can retrieve the results from this ResultSet as we would do for any other:

```
          ResultSet key = insert.getGeneratedKeys();
          if (!key.next())
          {
            throw new RuntimeException(
              "Can't retrieve generated primary key!");
          }
          book.setId(key.getLong(1));
          key.close();
        }
```

We will now catch any SQLException that might have been thrown by the code above. We re-throw it as an InvalidFieldException if the database indicates that we have been trying to create an invalid field, which in this case must mean a duplicate title. A finally clause ensures that the PreparedStatement is properly closed whatever happens:

```
        catch (SQLException e)
        {
          if (InvalidFieldException.SQL_STATE.equals(e.getSQLState()))
          {
            throw new InvalidFieldException(e);
          }
          else
          {
            throw e;
          }
        }
        finally
        {
          insert.close();
        }
    }
```

A finally clause can optionally follow a try...catch block. Its contents will *always* be executed, regardless of whether an exception is thrown inside the try block or not. It is an ideal place for cleanup, such as the connection closing code presented here.

> Always use **try...finally** to guarantee that your statements and connections will be closed whatever happens. Notice that we don't actually close the **Connection** or commit the database transaction at this point – the business object that creates the data access object is responsible for obtaining a **Connection**, managing the database transaction, and closing the **Connection** once it has finished, as we'll see later.

The update() method also takes a Book object. It works much like the create() method, creating a PreparedStatement, populating the query parameters, then executing the query. We do not need to retrieve the primary key in this case, as this is already known; we do however need to test the number of records updated, returned by Statement.executeUpdate(), to verify that the database has actually found the book we want to update. If not, we throw an EntityNotFoundException with a suitable error message key:

```
public void update(Book book)
        throws SQLException, InvalidFieldException,
        EntityNotFoundException
{
  PreparedStatement update = conn.prepareStatement(
    "UPDATE book SET title=?, authors=?, editor=?, chapters=?, " +
    "page_count=?, price=?, status=? WHERE id=?");

  try
  {
    populate(update, book);
    update.setLong(8, book.getId());
    if (update.executeUpdate() != 1)
    {
      throw new EntityNotFoundException(
        "Book " + book.getId() + " not found");
    }
  }
  catch (SQLException e)
  {
    if (InvalidFieldException.SQL_STATE.equals(e.getSQLState()))
    {
      throw new InvalidFieldException(e);
    }
    else
    {
      throw e;
    }
  }
  finally
  {
    update.close();
  }
}
```

The `populate()` method is used by both `create()` and `update()` to populate the book fields in a `PreparedStatement`:

```
private void populate(PreparedStatement stmt, Book book)
       throws SQLException
{
  stmt.setString(1, book.getTitle());
  stmt.setString(2, book.getAuthors());
  stmt.setString(3, book.getEditor());
  stmt.setString(4, book.getChapters());
  stmt.setInt(5, book.getPageCount());
  stmt.setDouble(6, book.getPrice());
  stmt.setString(7, String.valueOf(book.getStatus()));
}
```

The `remove()` method is overloaded to take either a `Book` object or the `id` identifying the book to be removed. An instance of `PreparedStatement` is created that is used for executing the `DELETE` SQL statement, and if the specified record is not found an `EntityNotFoundException` is thrown:

```
public void remove(Book book)
       throws SQLException, EntityNotFoundException
{
  remove(book.getId());
}

public void remove(long id)
       throws SQLException, EntityNotFoundException
{
  PreparedStatement delete = conn.prepareStatement(
                      "DELETE FROM book WHERE id=?");
  try
  {
    delete.setLong(1, id);
    if (delete.executeUpdate() != 1)
      throw new EntityNotFoundException("Book " + id + " not found");
  }
  finally
  {
    delete.close();
  }
}
```

Remember that the database is set up with an `ON DELETE CASCADE` constraint between `book` and `book_news` so that, when a book is deleted, all associated news items are deleted along with it. This saves us from having to do this explicitly in our `remove()` method.

We now end up at the only finder method we will need here, findById(). It gets a single book from its ID. This method will return a Book object that includes all the BookNews objects associated with it. The first step is to load the book itself by calling the package-private loadById method:

```
public Book findById(long id)
        throws SQLException, EntityNotFoundException
{
  Book book = loadById(id);
```

Then we use the BookNews DAO discussed below to populate this book with its associated news items, and sort the news items so that the most recent item comes first in the list:

```
  Collection news = new BookNewsDAO(conn).findByBook(book);
  book.getNews().addAll(news);
  return book;
}
```

The loadById() method does all the hard work of finding the actual Book object. It is a package-private method so that the BookNews DAO can call it as well:

```
Book loadById(long id)
      throws SQLException, EntityNotFoundException
{
  PreparedStatement select = conn.prepareStatement("SELECT"
            + " title, authors, editor, chapters, page_count,"
            + " price, status FROM book WHERE id=?");
  try
  {
    select.setLong(1, id);
    ResultSet results = select.executeQuery();
    if (!results.next())
    {
      throw new EntityNotFoundException(
        "Book " + id + " not found");
    }
    else
    {
      Book book = new Book();
      book.setId(id);
      book.setTitle(results.getString(1));
      book.setAuthors(results.getString(2));
      book.setEditor(results.getString(3));
      book.setChapters(results.getString(4));
      book.setPageCount(results.getInt(5));
      book.setPrice(results.getDouble(6));
      book.setStatus(results.getString(7).charAt(0));
      return book;
    }
  }
}
```

```
      finally
      {
        select.close();
      }
    }
  }
}
```

BookNewsDAO

BookNewsDAO is the data access object for BookNews entities. It defines public methods to
create, update, and remove BookNews objects, and to find a BookNews item by id or a
collection of news items for a given book. The last method is used by BookDAO.

The BookNewsDAO class is very similar to the BookDAO class:

```
package com.wrox.publish.db;

import com.wrox.publish.om.Book;
import com.wrox.publish.om.BookNews;
import java.sql.Connection;
import java.sql.PreparedStatement;
import java.sql.ResultSet;
import java.sql.SQLException;
import java.sql.Statement;
import java.util.ArrayList;
import java.util.Collection;

/*
 * Data Access Object responsible for reading, writing and deleting
 * BookNews in the database.
 */
public class BookNewsDAO
{
  private final Connection conn;

  public BookNewsDAO(Connection conn)
  {
    super();
    this.conn = conn;
  }
```

The create() method takes an instance of the BookNews class, creates a
PreparedStatement that is used to execute the SQL INSERT statement, populates it from the
news object, executes it, and then retrieves the generated primary key (id). The code is largely
analogous to that in BookDAO:

```
/*
 * Creates a new BookNews item in the database.
```

```
 * @param news The BookNews item to create.
 * @throws SQLException If there was a problem accessing the
 *          database.
 */
public void create(BookNews news) throws SQLException
{
  PreparedStatement insert = conn.prepareStatement("INSERT INTO "
            + "book_news (book, title, body, user, published)"
            + "VALUES (?, ?, ?, ?, ?)",
            Statement.RETURN_GENERATED_KEYS);
  try
  {
    populate(insert, news);
    insert.executeUpdate();

    ResultSet key = insert.getGeneratedKeys();
    if (!key.next())
    {
      throw new RuntimeException(
              "Can't retrieve generated primary key!");
    }
    news.setId(key.getLong(1));
    key.close();
  }
  finally
  {
    insert.close();
  }
}
```

Note that the code above does not catch SQLException or throw InvalidFieldException because there are no special constraints on the user-editable fields in book_news.

Next, the update() method. Once again this is completely analogous to the code in BookDAO except for the absence of InvalidFieldException:

```
public void update(BookNews news)
      throws SQLException, EntityNotFoundException
{
  PreparedStatement update = conn.prepareStatement(
                    "UPDATE book_news "
                    + "SET book=?, title=?, body=?, user=?, "
                    + "published=? WHERE id=?");
  try
  {
    populate(update, news);
    update.setLong(6, news.getId());
    if (update.executeUpdate() != 1)
    {
      throw new EntityNotFoundException("BookNews " + news.getId()
```

```
                                                  + " not found");
      }
    }
    finally
    {
      update.close();
    }
  }

  private void populate(PreparedStatement stmt, BookNews news)
          throws SQLException
  {
    stmt.setLong(1, news.getBook().getId());
    stmt.setString(2, news.getTitle());
    stmt.setString(3, news.getBody());
    stmt.setString(4, news.getUser());
    stmt.setTimestamp(5, news.getPublished());
  }
```

The overloaded `remove()` method takes either a `BookNews` object or the `id` identifying the book_news record to be removed. As usual, we use an instance of `PreparedStatement` to execute the SQL statement, here a `DELETE`. If the specified record is not found, an `EntityNotFoundException` is thrown:

```
public void remove(BookNews news)
        throws SQLException, EntityNotFoundException
{
  remove(news.getId());
}

public void remove(long id)
        throws SQLException, EntityNotFoundException
{
  PreparedStatement delete = conn.prepareStatement(
                        "DELETE FROM book_news WHERE id=?");
  try
  {
    delete.setLong(1, id);
    if (delete.executeUpdate() != 1)
    {
      throw new EntityNotFoundException("BookNews " + id +
                                   " not found");
    }
  }
  finally
  {
    delete.close();
  }
}
```

The `findById()` method takes the `id` for which the `book_news` record needs to be found. In the normal way, an instance of `PreparedStatement` is used to execute the `SELECT` SQL statement. If the record is not found, an `EntityNotFoundException` is thrown:

```
public BookNews findById(long id)
        throws SQLException, EntityNotFoundException
{
  BookDAO bookDAO = new BookDAO(conn);
  PreparedStatement select = conn.prepareStatement(
                  "SELECT book, title, body, user, published"
                + " FROM book_news WHERE id=?");
  try
  {
    select.setLong(1, id);
    ResultSet results = select.executeQuery();
    if (!results.next())
    {
      throw new EntityNotFoundException("BookNews " + id +
                                        " not found");
    }
    else
    {
      BookNews news = new BookNews();
      news.setId(id);
```

In the following code, the `BookNews` item is populated with its parent `Book`. So again an object graph rather than a single object is being returned, although we are cheating a bit because the `Book` object does not have its `news` attribute populated! Although it is quite usual in object/relational mapping to truncate the object model in places – loading up the entire model can take a very long time and may even be impossible if the database is large – a professional object-relational mapping is likely to do better. However, for our purposes, the DAO does everything we need.

```
      news.setBook(bookDAO.loadById(results.getLong(1)));
      news.setTitle(results.getString(2));
      news.setBody(results.getString(3));
      news.setUser(results.getString(4));
      news.setPublished(results.getTimestamp(5));
      return news;
    }
  }
  finally
  {
    select.close();
  }
}
```

Finally there is the `findByBook(Book)` method that retrieves all news items for a given book:

```
public Collection findByBook(Book book) throws SQLException
{
  PreparedStatement select = conn.prepareStatement(
              "SELECT id, title, body, user, published"
           + " FROM book_news WHERE book=?");
  try
  {
    select.setLong(1, book.getId());
    ResultSet results = select.executeQuery();
    Collection items = new ArrayList();
    while (results.next())
    {
      BookNews news = new BookNews();
      news.setId(results.getLong(1));
      news.setBook(book);
      news.setTitle(results.getString(2));
      news.setBody(results.getString(3));
      news.setUser(results.getString(4));
      news.setPublished(results.getTimestamp(5));
      items.add(news);
    }
    return items;
  }
  finally
  {
    select.close();
  }
}
}
```

Business Objects

Business objects encapsulate the business rules and processes that the system must follow. They usually have a higher level of abstraction than the data access objects as they deal more with the business processes in a system, processes that a user would probably recognize, than with the individual entities and tables that represent the model internally. The business objects often manage the database transactions as well.

In our application, we need business objects for enforcing the authorization rules for `Book` and `BookNews` entities. Other than that, the application does little more than storing and retrieving simple objects in the database. When the business objects need to perform data access, they'll call the data access objects.

Exception Handling

Just like the data access objects, our business objects need specialized exceptions for handling error conditions. As our business objects do little more than enforcing the authorization rules, there is only a single exception that we may encounter, an `ActionDeniedException`. This will be thrown when an action cannot be performed because the user lacks the necessary privileges.

ActionDeniedException

This exception is thrown by the `create()`, `update()`, and `delete()` methods when the user has insufficient privileges as determined by the user's security role:

```
package com.wrox.publish.bo;

import com.wrox.publish.PublishException;

/* Thrown when a user action is being denied for authorization reasons. */
public class ActionDeniedException extends PublishException
{
  public ActionDeniedException(String msg)
  {
    super(msg);
  }
}
```

BookBO

The `BookBO` class encapsulates our application's business logic. Because the application doesn't have an awful lot in the way of business processes, this object is not much more than a thin layer over the data access classes, exposing methods to create, update, delete, and find `Book` and `BookNews` objects.

Note that we've now moved away from database access issues – our Struts action classes can call `BookBO` methods without caring how the data is stored, and without taking any interest in the authorization rules at all.

We could have dispensed with the business object altogether and accessed the data access objects directly from our Struts `Actions`, but that means that the authorization rules would have to be encoded there as well. As the application grows and the number of actions dealing with the same data increases, we would inevitably start duplicating these rules. Eventually, inconsistencies will almost inevitably creep into the system and the application will start to behave in odd and unpredictable ways that would be very hard to put right.

OK, let's have a look at the source code for the `BookBO` class:

```
package com.wrox.publish.bo;

import com.wrox.publish.db.BookDAO;
import com.wrox.publish.db.BookNewsDAO;
import com.wrox.publish.db.EntityNotFoundException;
import com.wrox.publish.db.InvalidFieldException;
import com.wrox.publish.om.Book;
import com.wrox.publish.om.BookNews;

import java.sql.Connection;
import java.sql.SQLException;
import javax.servlet.http.HttpServletRequest;
import javax.sql.DataSource;

/*
 * Business Object providing access to the functionality of the
 * Book Publishing application; everything related to either
 * Books or BookNews items.
 */
public class BookBO
{
    public static final String EDITOR_ROLE = "editor";
    private final String user;
    private final boolean editor;
    private final DataSource dataSource;
```

While users of the class don't need to worry about database connections, the class will need database connections in order to use our data access objects. To do that, the `BookBO` constructor gets an instance of the `DataSource` and stores it in an instance variable. In addition, it needs to know about the name of the user and whether the user has editor privileges or not in order to perform the authorization checks.

The constructor is package-private. There is a static factory method that should be used to create `BookBO` objects. The factory method knows how to extract the authorization information required by the constructor from an `HttpServletRequest`. If a `BookBO` instance is required in other contexts where a `HttpServletRequest` may not be available, it is easy to add more factory methods as required.

```
BookBO(String user, boolean editor, DataSource dataSource)
{
    super();
    this.user = user;
    this.editor = editor;
    this.dataSource = dataSource;
}
```

The following method wraps the `findById()` method of `BookDAO`. There are no security or other business rules to enforce here, so all this code does is manage the database connectivity and transactions:

```
public Book findBookById(long id)
        throws EntityNotFoundException, SQLException
{
  Connection conn = dataSource.getConnection();
  try
  {
    Book book = new BookDAO(conn).findById(id);
    conn.commit();
    return book;
  }
  catch (EntityNotFoundException e)
  {
    conn.rollback();
    throw e;
  }
  catch (SQLException e)
  {
    conn.rollback();
    throw e;
```

The database connection is closed in a `finally` clause so that we are absolutely sure that it will be released no matter what happens. If we didn't do this, we'd leak connections whenever exceptions are thrown. Sooner or later the application would malfunction because no more connections can be created. On a high-traffic public-facing web site, "sooner" might easily be measured in minutes!

```
  }
  finally
  {
    conn.close();
  }
}
```

In addition to managing the database connectivity, the `create(Book)`, `update(Book)` and `remove(Book)` methods enforce the rule that only editors can create, update or delete books. This rule is encapsulated in a `mustBeEditor()` method that throws an `ActionDeniedException` if the user is not an editor.

```
public void create(Book book)
        throws ActionDeniedException, InvalidFieldException,
            SQLException
{
  mustBeEditor();
  Connection conn = dataSource.getConnection();
  try
  {
    new BookDAO(conn).create(book);
    conn.commit();
  }
```

691

```
    catch (InvalidFieldException e)
    {
      conn.rollback();
      throw e;
    }
```

Whenever we encounter a database error, we back out of all the work we have done so far in this transaction. In this application, we actually don't do more than a single operation at a time. However, in more complicated systems where a number of closely related database operations are performed in a single transaction, it is often very important that either all operations succeed or none at all.

```
    catch (SQLException e)
    {
      conn.rollback();
      throw e;
    }
    finally
    {
      conn.close();
    }
  }

  public void update(Book book)
        throws ActionDeniedException, InvalidFieldException,
              EntityNotFoundException, SQLException
  {
    mustBeEditor();
    Connection conn = dataSource.getConnection();
    try
    {
      new BookDAO(conn).update(book);
      conn.commit();
    }
    catch (InvalidFieldException e)
    {
      conn.rollback();
      throw e;
    }
    catch (EntityNotFoundException e)
    {
      conn.rollback();
      throw e;
    }
    catch (SQLException e)
    {
      conn.rollback();
      throw e;
    }
    finally
```

```
    {
      conn.close();
    }
}

public void remove(Book book)
        throws ActionDeniedException, EntityNotFoundException,
            SQLException
{
  mustBeEditor();
  Connection conn = dataSource.getConnection();
  try
  {
    new BookDAO(conn).remove(book);
    conn.commit();
  }
  catch (EntityNotFoundException e)
  {
    conn.rollback();
    throw e;
  }
  catch (SQLException e)
  {
    conn.rollback();
    throw e;
  }
  finally
  {
    conn.close();
  }
}

private void mustBeEditor() throws ActionDeniedException
{
  if (!editor)
  {
    throw new ActionDeniedException("Only editors can do this.");
  }
}
```

The findBookNewsById() method is again mostly a wrapper around a DAO method, this time BookNewsDAO.findById():

```
public BookNews findBookNewsById(long id)
        throws EntityNotFoundException, SQLException
{
  Connection conn = dataSource.getConnection();
  try
  {
    BookNews news = new BookNewsDAO(conn).findById(id);
```

```
    conn.commit();
    return news;
  }
  catch (EntityNotFoundException e)
  {
    conn.rollback();
    throw e;
  }
  catch (SQLException e)
  {
    conn.rollback();
    throw e;
  }
  finally
  {
    conn.close();
    conn.close();
  }
}
```

The create(BookNews), update(BookNews), and remove(BookNews) methods enforce the rule that only editors or the original author can create, update, or delete a news item:

```
public void create(BookNews news)
        throws ActionDeniedException, SQLException
{
  mustBeEditor();
  Connection conn = dataSource.getConnection();
  try
  {
    new BookNewsDAO(conn).create(news);
    conn.commit();
  }
  catch (SQLException e)
  {
    conn.rollback();
    throw e;
  }
  finally
  {
    conn.close();
  }
}

public void update(BookNews news)
        throws ActionDeniedException, EntityNotFoundException,
               SQLException
{
  mustBeOwnerOrEditor(news.getUser());
  Connection conn = dataSource.getConnection();
```

```
    try
    {
      new BookNewsDAO(conn).update(news);
      conn.commit();
    }
    catch (EntityNotFoundException e)
    {
      conn.rollback();
      throw e;
    }
    catch (SQLException e)
    {
      conn.rollback();
      throw e;
    }
    finally
    {
      conn.close();
    }
  }

  public void remove(BookNews news)
          throws ActionDeniedException, EntityNotFoundException,
                  SQLException
  {
    mustBeOwnerOrEditor(news.getUser());
    Connection conn = dataSource.getConnection();
    try
    {
      new BookNewsDAO(conn).remove(news);
      conn.commit();
    }
    catch (EntityNotFoundException e)
    {
      conn.rollback();
      throw e;
    }
    catch (SQLException e)
    {
      conn.rollback();
      throw e;
    }
    finally
    {
      conn.close();
    }
  }

  private void mustBeOwnerOrEditor(String owner)
          throws ActionDeniedException
  {
    if (!editor && !user.equals(owner))
```

```
        {
            throw new ActionDeniedException(
                "Only owners or editors can do this");
        }
    }
```

Finally the getInstance() factory method takes an HttpServletRequest and extracts the necessary authentication and authorization information from it. On one hand, this makes it unnecessary for the rest of the BookBO object to know where the information comes from. On the other, it shields client code from having to know what information is necessary for BookBO to do its work. New factory methods can be added as the need arises:

```
    public static BookBO getInstance(HttpServletRequest request,
                                     DataSource dataSource)
    {
        return new BookBO(request.getRemoteUser(),
                          request.isUserInRole(EDITOR_ROLE), dataSource);
    }
```

This concludes the design and development of the components for the application tier. In the next few sections, we will finish off by creating the part of the application that actually interacts with the users through a dynamic web interface – the **web tier**. Once that's done, we'll tidy up all the loose ends and see how to deploy the application and get it up and running.

Implementing the Web Tier

After all this dry Java- and SQL-dominated back-end work, let's get stuck into implementing the web tier. There are quite a lot of things we need to do:

- ❑ Identify our Struts action forms
- ❑ Deal with error messages and internationalization
- ❑ Look at how we can use dynamic web page templates to make the page design easier
- ❑ Then, for each use case, we'll need to write the Struts action class and the JSP pages that implement the view

Struts Action Forms

In the *Implementing the Entities* section above, we mentioned that we would be reusing our Book and BookNews entity objects as the Struts action forms as well. Accordingly, both these classes extend org.apache.struts.validator.ValidatorForm, which indirectly extends ActionForm. You won't always want to do this – it's not often true that the forms in your web page correspond exactly to the entities that you want to store in the database as they do in this case.

The excerpt shown below from the Struts configuration file illustrates how the action form beans are declared:

```
.
.
.
<form-beans>
  <form-bean name="bookForm"
             type="com.wrox.publish.om.Book"/>
  <form-bean name="bookNewsForm"
             type="com.wrox.publish.om.BookNews"/>
</form-beans>
.
.
.
```

This defines two action form beans, with the names bookForm and bookNewsForm, corresponding to our Book and BookNews classes respectively. These names will be used later in the action mapping elements that associate the beans with action classes.

Validation

One of the great features of the Struts framework is that it can take the hard work out of basic input validation. Normally, this requires a fair amount of boring but error-prone code. As discussed in Chapter 15, Struts allows us to associate validation rules defined declaratively in an XML file with either actions or forms. All we have to do is write this validation.xml file and add the following snippet to the Struts configuration file to tell the validator where to find it:

```
.
.
.
<plug-in className="org.apache.struts.validator.ValidatorPlugIn">
  <set-property property="pathnames"
    value="/WEB-INF/validator-rules.xml,/WEB-INF/validation.xml"/>
</plug-in>
.
.
.
```

The validator-rules.xml file defines the validator rules that we can use in validation.xml. We will be using the validator rules that come out of the box with Struts and won't have to modify this file.

The validation.xml File

In the publishing application, there are two forms, `bookForm` and `bookNewsForm`, corresponding to the two entities. We will start by defining the validation rules for the `bookForm`:

```
<form-validation>
  <formset>

    <form name="bookForm">
```

Every book should have a title. To make the title required, we make this field depend on the `required` rule. If this check fails, an error message `errors.required` is displayed (such as {0} is required.) with the argument in braces replaced by the `book.title` message (The title). The validation framework is fully integrated with Struts and will use the Struts message file to look up the appropriate internationalized message texts.

```
<field property="title" depends="required">
  <arg0 key="book.title"/>
</field>
```

We will skip the authors and editor fields and not impose any validation rules for them, as when a book is in the planning stage it is quite possible that these fields are not yet known. An estimated page count is not an implausible thing to require, though, and should always be a number somewhere between 10 and 1999. The `pageCount` field therefore uses both the integer `validation` rule, which requires the page count to be a whole number, and the `range` validation rule to test that this number is within a certain range:

```
<field property="pageCount" depends="integer,range">
```

We must define two variables called `min` and `max` so that the `range` rule knows what the required minimum and maximum values are:

```
<var>
  <var-name>min</var-name>
  <var-value>10</var-value>
</var>
<var>
  <var-name>max</var-name>
  <var-value>1999</var-value>
</var>
```

Finally, both rules need to give intelligible error messages if validation fails. Both need the name of the field as their first argument:

```
<arg0 key="book.pagecount"/>
```

The range rule's error message (`errors.range`, for example "{0} is not in the range {1} through {2}.") needs two additional arguments, namely the minimum and maximum values. Rather than duplicate these values, we use an expression to retrieve the values of the `min` and `max` variables. The `resource="false"` attribute tells the validator that the `key` attribute specifies a literal string rather than a message resource key:

```
            <arg1 name="range" key="${var:min}" resource="false"/>
            <arg2 name="range" key="${var:max}" resource="false"/>
        </field>
```

The expression in the `key` attribute looks a little bit like a JSP expression, but don't let that fool you. It is a small, separate expression language integrated in the validation framework. Hopefully a future revision of the framework will remove the difference between the two languages.

Finally, we require the book price to be a floating-point number:

```
        <field property="price" depends="double">
          <arg0 key="book.price"/>
        </field>
      </form>
```

The next form to consider is the news item form. The only user-editable fields are the item's title and the body, and we require both to have some text in them:

```
      <form name="bookNewsForm">
        <field property="title" depends="required">
          <arg0 key="booknews.title"/>
        </field>
        <field property="body" depends="required">
          <arg0 key="booknews.body"/>
        </field>
      </form>

    </formset>
  </form-validation>
```

None of these rules are particularly difficult, but writing both client-side JavaScript and server-side Java validation code would have required between 50 and 100 lines of code spread out over two Java classes and two JSP pages. The Struts validator achieves the same thing with a single 36-line XML file.

Error Handling

A vital element of enterprise application development is the proper handling of exceptions to inform users what went wrong. In this section, we will have a look at how we can implement an efficient error handling mechanism in our application. Ideally, error messages are sent in the user's preferred language. There are two ways to go about this, and we will look at both.

As discussed in the last chapter, we can tell Struts to catch exceptions of a specific type and associate these with a message key, either in a specific action or globally:

```
    .
    .
    .
<global-exceptions>
    <exception type="java.sql.SQLException" key="errors.database"/>
</global-exceptions>
    .
    .
    .
```

This means that whenever an `SQLException` is thrown by an `Action`, Struts will go back to the action's input page and the `<html:errors/>` tag will display the message associated with the `errors.database` key. In English, this message might read: "An unexpected database error has occurred."

This method does not work if, for a given action, we want to display different messages for a single exception. This can easily happen if our exception hierarchy is not very large and different problems might cause the same exception to be thrown. A common technique to deal with this is to use the appropriate Struts message key as the exception message. For example, we could have handled authorization problems by simply throwing a `RuntimeException`:

```
throw new RuntimeException("errors.action.denied");
```

Our error handling code would then catch this exception and use the `errors.action.denied` key to populate an `ActionError` object for use by the `<html:errors/>` tag. There are a number of problems with this approach:

❑ If you are logging exceptions for diagnostic purposes, the log file can become rather hard to read because it will usually contain the exceptions' message keys rather than the actual error messages.

❑ We may want to incorporate extra information in the exception's detail message for debugging purposes. This information would be meaningless or confusing to the user.

❑ In Struts 1.1, this method requires far more Java coding.

Unsurprisingly, the publishing application will use the first method, although the second method is quite prevalent in earlier code written for the Struts 1.0 framework.

Database Access

We can configure database access in two different ways: either via the web container as discussed in Chapter 13, or using Struts as mentioned in the previous chapter. We will illustrate the Struts way here. Below is the relevant snippet from the Struts configuration file:

```
.
.
.
<data-sources>
  <data-source>
    <set-property property="description" value="Publish Database"/>
    <set-property property="driverClass"
                  value="com.mysql.jdbc.Driver"/>
    <set-property property="url"
                  value="jdbc:mysql://localhost/publish"/>
    <set-property property="user" value="publish"/>
    <set-property property="password" value="wrox"/>
    <set-property property="autoCommit" value="false"/>
  </data-source>
</data-sources>
.
.
.
```

We state the JDBC driver to use, the JDBC URL, username, and password. Struts uses this information to create a `DataSource` with integrated connection pool and binds it in the application context under the name `org.apache.struts.action.DATA_SOURCE`. The `Action.getDataSource()` method makes accessing the `DataSource` from a Struts action class particularly easy.

Web Page Templates

In the previous chapter, we saw how using dynamic templates can help us to modularize web page layouts, and in this section we'll come up with a template for our application's web pages. The default template for our pages will have a logo, title, sidebar menu, main content area, and footer laid out in an HTML table as follows:

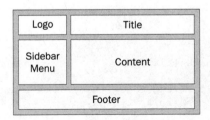

The logo, sidebar menu, and footer are part of the template; the title and content are passed in as template parameters and included using the Struts `<template:get>` tag.

The default.css Stylesheet

Before we start looking at the template pages, we'll first set up a **Cascading Style Sheet** (**CSS**) file. CSS files are one of the most versatile and maintainable ways to provide a consistent look and feel throughout a web site. The default template will link to this stylesheet to define fonts, colors, and borders. Save the following code as `default.css` in a subdirectory called `templates` off our web application folder:

```
body, th, td { font-family : Verdana, Arial, sans-serif ; font-size :
        10pt }
td.header { font-size : 24pt ; font-weight : bold }
td.footer, td.portlet td { font-size : 8pt }
th.portlet, td.portlet { border : solid 1px black }
th.portlet { background : #FFDDDD }
td.title, td.sidebar { background : #FFEEEE }
td.sidebar, td.content { border : solid 1px #CCBBBB ; padding : 1em }
td.sidebar { border-right : none ; text-align : right }
td.footer { padding-left : 1em }
a:link, a:visited, a:active { color: #990000 ; text-decoration : none }
a:hover { text-decoration : underline }
```

The default.jsp Page

The page that implements our template will be `default.jsp`, also in the `templates` folder. We start by importing the Struts template, `html`, `bean`, and `logic` tags:

```
<%@page contentType="text/html"%>
<%@taglib prefix="template"
        uri="http://jakarta.apache.org/struts/tags-template-1.0"%>
<%@taglib prefix="html"
        uri="http://jakarta.apache.org/struts/tags-html-1.0"%>
<%@taglib prefix="bean"
        uri="http://jakarta.apache.org/struts/tags-bean-1.0"%>
<%@taglib prefix="logic"
        uri="http://jakarta.apache.org/struts/tags-logic-1.0"%>
```

The page title and the title displayed in the first table row both use the `<template:get>` tag to retrieve the `title` parameter passed to the template:

```
<html>
  <head>
    <title>
      <template:get name="title"/>
    </title>
    <link href="<html:rewrite page='/templates/default.css'/>"
          type="text/css" rel="stylesheet">
  </head>
  <body>
    <table width="100%" cellspacing="0">
      <tr>
```

```
        <td width="15%">
          <img
              src="http://www.wrox.com/images/wxmainlogowhitespace.gif"
              align="left">
        </td>
        <td class="header" width="85%">
          <template:get name="title"/>
        </td>
      </tr>
```

The first table cell in the next row contains the sidebar menu. The first two items use Struts `<html:link>` tags to link to the application homepage and the Wrox homepage, respectively. Note that the application homepage is not linked to directly, but referred to using its name in the Struts global forwards list. If we later introduce a new homepage with a different name, we would only have to update the Struts configuration file and this link would adjust automatically.

A second advantage of the `<html:link>` tag is that, if the user's browser has cookies disabled, URL rewriting is used to keep track of the user's session. Normally this would require some simple but cumbersome coding.

```
      <tr>
        <td class="sidebar" valign="top">
          <html:link forward="index">
            <bean:message key="sidebar.home.link"/>
          </html:link><br/>
          <html:link href="http://www.wrox.com">
            <bean:message key="sidebar.wrox.link"/>
          </html:link><br/>
```

The remainder of the menu is more interesting, because its contents depend on whether the user is logged in and whether they have editor privileges or not. We use the Struts `<logic:present>` tag to see if the user is an editor. Because editors can add books, we give them that option:

```
        <logic:present role="editor">
          <html:link page="/book/add.do">
            <bean:message key="booklist.add.link"/>
          </html:link><br/>
        </logic:present>
```

If the user is not logged in, a login link is displayed; otherwise a logout link is displayed. To make it easy to find out if a user has logged in or not using the Struts logic tags, we will give every application user the `user` role:

```
        <logic:notPresent role="user">
          <html:link page="/login.do">
            <bean:message key="sidebar.login.link"/>
          </html:link>
        </logic:notPresent>
        <logic:present role="user">
          <html:link page="/logout.do">
            <bean:message key="sidebar.logout.link"/>
          </html:link>
        </logic:present>
      </td>
```

In larger applications with complicated menu structures or a few radically different menus, we might move the menu into a separate include file.

The next cell displays the main content of the page. This is where the life of our actual application will be. All we do is retrieve the content template parameter using the trusty <template:get> tag and include it in the HTML output:

```
        <td class="content"><template:get name="content"/></td>
      </tr>
```

Finally, the footer displaying a static copyright message:

```
        <tr>
          <td colspan="2" class="footer">
            &copy;2003 Wrox Programmer to Programmer&trade;
          </td>
        </tr>
      </table>
    </body>
  </html>
```

The portal.jsp Page

The homepage screenshot shown at the very start of this chapter is a portal-like page. A portal gathers several pieces of information or functionality, often from completely different locations, and displays them all together on a single page. Each bit of information or functionality is displayed in its own **portlet**. A popular example of a typical portal is My Yahoo! (http://my.yahoo.com). Portals usually allow the user to assemble their own homepage containing just information that is relevant to them.

Now this homepage is by no means a full-blown portal, and the Struts template tags are not the best foundation for a portal site (Struts Tiles would be a better choice, and a dedicated portal product better still). But we can define a small sub-template that makes it very easy to add any number of "portlets" to the homepage, and that will be plugged into the content area of the default template above. Create the following file in the templates directory under the name portal.jsp:

```
<%@page contentType="text/html"%>
<%@taglib prefix="c" uri="http://java.sun.com/jstl/core_rt"%>
<%@taglib prefix="template"
         uri="http://jakarta.apache.org/struts/tags-template-1.0"%>

<table width="100%">
  <tr>
    <td width="50%" valign="top">
      <table width="100%">
        <tr><th class="portlet">
          <template:get name="title[1]"/></th></tr>
        <tr><td class="portlet">
          <template:get name="portlet[1]"/></td></tr>
        <tr><td> </td></tr>
        <tr><th class="portlet">
          <template:get name="title[2]"/></th></tr>
        <tr><td class="portlet">
          <template:get name="portlet[2]"/></td></tr>
      </table>
    </td>
    <td width="50%" valign="top">
      <table width="100%">
        <tr><th class="portlet">
          <template:get name="title[3]"/></th></tr>
        <tr><td class="portlet">
          <template:get name="portlet[3]"/></td></tr>
        <tr><td> </td></tr>
        <tr><th class="portlet">
          <template:get name="title[4]"/></th></tr>
        <tr><td class="portlet">
          <template:get name="portlet[4]"/></td></tr>
      </table>
    </td>
  </tr>
</table>
```

This page can display up to four portlets, each with its own title and a content area.

Book Maintenance

Finally we are getting to the meat of the web tier: the book maintenance form. Before we launch into Struts actions and JSP, let us first take another look at the prototype screenshot from the requirements section, stripped of everything provided by the default template:

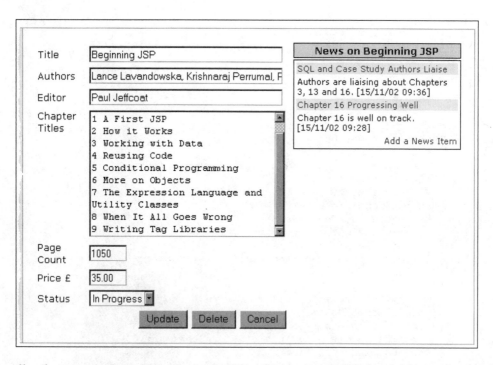

Visually, the page comprises two major building blocks: an HTML form for entering book details, and a list of news items for the book. There are several different actions associated with this page:

❑ When the user goes to the page by clicking **Add a Book**, we need to create a fresh Book object so the form can pick up the right default values for all the fields. In addition, it would be nice to be able to pass a default value for the book status as part of the request, so that a user can easily add a book of a given status.

❑ When the user goes to the book maintenance page by selecting a book from the home page, we need to retrieve the book details from the database for display.

❑ On the form above, we are editing an existing book. Let's call this "edit mode", and we see three buttons: **Update, Delete,** and **Cancel**. For a newly added book ("add mode"), the buttons would read **Add** and **Cancel**.

❑ On the news item list at the right hand side, users with appropriate permissions can edit an existing news item or add a new one. These actions will be discussed in the section on news maintenance below.

If you have read the discussion of Struts in the previous chapter, it will not surprise you that all the actions described above are mapped to Struts Action classes.

The /book Mappings

We will gently ease ourselves into things before discussing the action classes by taking a look at the action mappings in the Struts configuration file.

Requests for /book/add.do are handled by the com.wrox.publish.action.AddBookAction class. The action uses a session-scoped Book object called bookForm; as we shall see, this is actually just used to capture the value of the status parameter. After the action has completed successfully, the request is forwarded to the book.jsp view (discussed below) in add mode. The mode is passed to the page as a request parameter:

```
<action path="/book/add"
        type="com.wrox.publish.action.AddBookAction"
        name="bookForm"
        scope="session"
     validate="false">
  <forward name="success" path="/book.jsp?mode=add"/>
</action>
```

The /book/edit.do action is mapped to the com.wrox.publish.action.EditBookAction class. Like the /book/add.do mapping, it uses the bookForm object to capture request parameters. In this case, the relevant parameter is the primary key (id) of the book to be edited. This action finishes by forwarding to the book.jsp view in edit mode:

```
<action path="/book/edit"
        type="com.wrox.publish.action.EditBookAction"
        name="bookForm"
        scope="session"
     validate="false">
  <forward name="success" path="/book.jsp?mode=edit"/>
</action>
```

Finally we get to handle the Add, Update, Delete, and Cancel buttons. Because they are all located in the same form, they all invoke the same action, /book/aud.do. It is the action class, com.wrox.publish.action.PerformBookAUDAction, that is responsible for verifying which button has been pressed and doing the right thing. The action parameter passed in contains the name of the form buttons from the HTML file:

```
<action path="/book/aud"
        type="com.wrox.publish.action.PerformBookAUDAction"
        name="bookForm"
        scope="session"
        input="/book.jsp"
     validate="true"
    parameter="action">
    .
    .
    .
```

There's more to this mapping. This is where we are actually going to edit the Book and store it in the database, so we need to execute the validation code for this class. To do this, the validate attribute is set to true. Remember that the Struts ValidatorForm class handles the actual validation with the aid of an XML configuration file, so setting this attribute is all we need to do.

Of course, when the ValidatorForm finds fault with the data the user entered for a book, we need to redisplay the book form with an error message. The input attribute tells Struts where the book form lives.

This is a good moment to take a closer look at the scope attribute. As discussed in the previous chapter, the form being used (bookForm in this case) can have either request or session scope. When editing an existing book, we need to keep track of the book's id so we know which record to update or delete from the database.

❑   By giving the bookForm session scope, this form (which is a Book object) simply retains the id value that has been set by the EditBookAction. When the time comes to update the object in the database after Struts has stored the new values into it, the id will still be there.

❑   Had we given it request scope, the bookForm object would have expired after completion of the /book/edit.do request and we would have lost track of the id field. A common workaround is to include it as a hidden field in the form. This would actually be fine for Book, but it is unacceptable for the BookNews form discussed below because it would allow a malicious user to add, update, or delete any news item simply by modifying the id field in the HTML form.

The remainder of the mapping reads as follows:

```
            .
            .
            .
        <exception type="com.wrox.publish.db.InvalidFieldException"
                   key="errors.book.duplicatetitle"/>
        <forward name="added" path="/index.jsp" redirect="true"/>
        <forward name="updated" path="/index.jsp" redirect="true"/>
        <forward name="deleted" path="/index.jsp" redirect="true"/>
        <forward name="cancel" path="/index.jsp" redirect="true"/>
    </action>
```

The <exception> tag catches any InvalidFieldException that may be thrown in our action due to a duplicate title, and redisplays the input form with the errors.book.duplicatetitle error message.

After a successful add, update, delete, or cancel, we simply redirect to the index page. Why redirect instead of simply forward? The difference is how the browser behaves when the user presses their Refresh button. If we simply forward, the browser would try to resubmit the form which, could cause all kinds of odd behavior. After a redirect, a refresh simply reloads index.jsp.

The AddBookAction Class

The first Struts action is executed just before we forward to the Book Maintenance page in order to add a book. It creates a fresh `Book` object and binds it in the session as the new `bookForm` to use. Any old `bookForm` that may still be present in the user's session from previous editing operations is discarded. The request specifies a status for the new book, and a typical request would look like /book/add.do?status=P.

```
package com.wrox.publish.action;

import com.wrox.publish.om.Book;
import javax.servlet.http.HttpServletRequest;
import javax.servlet.http.HttpServletResponse;
import org.apache.struts.action.Action;
import org.apache.struts.action.ActionForm;
import org.apache.struts.action.ActionForward;
import org.apache.struts.action.ActionMapping;

public class AddBookAction extends Action
{
```

The `execute()` method is where the work in an action gets done:

```
public ActionForward execute(ActionMapping mapping,
                             ActionForm form,
                             HttpServletRequest request,
                             HttpServletResponse response)
{
   Book book = new Book();
```

Remember that the action mapping specifies `bookForm` as the input form. Struts will have created this form if necessary and stored the value of the `status` request parameter in it. All we have to do now is retrieve the form and copy the value of the `status` field into our new book:

```
book.setStatus(((Book)form).getStatus());
```

Finally, we can replace the old `bookForm` with our new, pristine book. All old data that might still have been lingering around is gone:

```
request.getSession().setAttribute(mapping.getName(), book);
return mapping.findForward("success");
   }
}
```

The EditBookAction Class

This action is executed when we want to update or delete an existing book. It uses the id request parameter to retrieve the book details from the database and binds it in the session as the new bookForm. An example request mapping to this action would be **/book/edit.do?id=123**.

```
package com.wrox.publish.action;

import com.wrox.publish.bo.BookBO;
import com.wrox.publish.om.Book;
import javax.servlet.http.HttpServletRequest;
import javax.servlet.http.HttpServletResponse;
import org.apache.struts.action.Action;
import org.apache.struts.action.ActionForm;
import org.apache.struts.action.ActionForward;
import org.apache.struts.action.ActionMapping;

public class EditBookAction extends Action
{
   public ActionForward execute(ActionMapping mapping,
                                ActionForm form,
                                HttpServletRequest request,
                                HttpServletResponse response)
        throws Exception
   {
```

Thanks to all the hard work we have done in the first half of this chapter, retrieving an existing book is hardly more complicated than creating a brand new one. The action mapping configured bookForm to be the input form for this action, so that's where we find the value for the id parameter. The findBookById() method in BookBO will then give us the Book, which we finally bind in the session as the new bookForm to use:

```
      BookBO bookBO = BookBO.getInstance(request,
                                         getDataSource(request));
      Book book = bookBO.findBookById(((Book)form).getId());
      request.getSession().setAttribute(mapping.getName(), book);
      return mapping.findForward("success");
   }
}
```

The PerformBookAUDAction Class

Now things are getting slightly more complicated. Because an HTML form can have only one action, the Add, Update, Delete, and Cancel buttons on the book maintenance form all submit to **/book/aud.do**. This action will have to figure out which of the four buttons was pressed and then perform the actual add, update, or delete.

Fortunately, Struts comes to the rescue with an Action subclass called LookupDispatchAction which we can extend to tell it what method to invoke for each button, and Struts will do the rest:

```
package com.wrox.publish.action;

import com.wrox.publish.bo.BookBO;
import com.wrox.publish.om.Book;
import java.util.HashMap;
import java.util.Map;
import javax.servlet.http.HttpServletRequest;
import javax.servlet.http.HttpServletResponse;
import org.apache.struts.action.ActionForm;
import org.apache.struts.action.ActionForward;
import org.apache.struts.action.ActionMapping;
import org.apache.struts.actions.LookupDispatchAction;

public class PerformBookAUDAction extends LookupDispatchAction
{
```

The `Map` method is where we tell Struts how the buttons map to methods in the action class. For example, the first `map.put` call says that when the button with the `book.add.button.label` message (as specified in the `bookform.jsp` file below) is pressed, we want the `add()` method to be called:

```
protected Map getKeyMethodMap()
{
  Map map = new HashMap();
  map.put("book.add.button.label", "add");
  map.put("book.update.button.label", "update");
  map.put("book.delete.button.label", "delete");
  return map;
}
```

The Struts `<html:cancel>` button is unfortunately incompatible with `LookupDispatchAction` because, as explained in Chapter 15, it has a non-standard request parameter name. We override the `execute()` method to handle Cancel before doing anything else. The call to `super.execute()` ensures that all other buttons are handled by the `LookupDispatchAction` superclass.

```
public ActionForward execute(ActionMapping mapping,
                             ActionForm form,
                             HttpServletRequest request,
                             HttpServletResponse response)
      throws Exception
{
  if (isCancelled(request))
  {
    return mapping.findForward("cancel");
  }
  else
  {
    return super.execute(mapping, form, request, response);
```

```
      }
   }
```

The `add()` method is called when the form was submitted using the **Add** button. It gets a `BookBO` business object and calls `create(Book)` on it to create the book.

```
      public ActionForward add(ActionMapping mapping,
                               ActionForm form,
                               HttpServletRequest request,
                               HttpServletResponse response)
            throws Exception
      {
        BookBO bookBO = BookBO.getInstance(request,getDataSource(request));
        bookBO.create((Book)form);
        return mapping.findForward("added");
      }
```

The `update()` and `delete()` methods handle the **Update** and **Delete** buttons respectively. They are completely analogous to the `add()` method:

```
      public ActionForward update(ActionMapping mapping,
                                  ActionForm form,
                                  HttpServletRequest request,
                                  HttpServletResponse response)
            throws Exception
      {
        BookBO bookBO = BookBO.getInstance(request,
                                           getDataSource(request));
        bookBO.update((Book)form);
        return mapping.findForward("updated");
      }

      public ActionForward delete(ActionMapping mapping,
                                  ActionForm form,
                                  HttpServletRequest request,
                                  HttpServletResponse response)
            throws Exception
      {
        BookBO bookBO = BookBO.getInstance(request,
                                           getDataSource(request));
        bookBO.remove((Book)form);
        return mapping.findForward("deleted");
      }
   }
```

This is all there is to it! There isn't an awful lot of code in these `Action` classes, and that's exactly how it should be. Actions are merely the glue between the Controller and the Model in the MVC architecture. If you find yourself writing a lot of code for your Action, it's time to look at putting that code in a Business Object.

The book.jsp Page

The book.jsp page is surprisingly short, thanks to the Struts templating mechanism. All it does is use the <template:insert> tag to insert the default.jsp file, and place the page title and the contents of bookform.jsp in the template using the <template:put> tag:

```
<%@page contentType="text/html"%>
<%@taglib prefix="template"
          uri="http://jakarta.apache.org/struts/tags-template-1.0"%>
<%@taglib prefix="bean"
          uri="http://jakarta.apache.org/struts/tags-bean-1.0"%>

<template:insert template="/templates/default.jsp">
  <template:put name="title">
    <bean:message key="book.${param.mode}.page.title"/>
  </template:put>
  <template:put name="content" content="/content/bookform.jsp"/>
</template:insert>
```

The bookform.jsp Page

And finally we reach our first content page, bookform.jsp. As with the other content pages, it should be placed in a folder called content off of our web application root. This file is pretty dynamic and contains the main content to be displayed on the book maintenance page. Not only do we have the book details to display, but the form appears differently depending on whether we are adding a new book or editing an existing one, and on whether the user is an editor or not.

We start by declaring a whole raft of tag libraries: the JSTL core library, the formatting library to format the book price, the Struts HTML tags for the form, and the Struts bean tags for the <bean:message> tag that displays internationalized messages. Finally, the Struts logic library contains a nice pair of tags to determine if the current user has a given role. We have already used these tags in the sidebar menu:

```
<%@page contentType="text/html"%>
<%@taglib prefix="c" uri="http://java.sun.com/jstl/core_rt"%>
<%@taglib prefix="fmt" uri="http://java.sun.com/jstl/fmt_rt"%>
<%@taglib prefix="html"
          uri="http://jakarta.apache.org/struts/tags-html-1.0"%>
<%@taglib prefix="bean"
          uri="http://jakarta.apache.org/struts/tags-bean-1.0"%>
<%@taglib prefix="logic"
          uri="http://jakarta.apache.org/struts/tags-logic-1.0"%>
```

As we saw in the /book mappings above, the mode request parameter has the value add or edit depending on the action taken by the user. Using the JSP 2.0 expression language, we can access this parameter as param.mode. A variable isEditor is set to true if the current user is an editor, and to false otherwise:

```
<c:set var="isEditor" value="${false}"/>
<logic:present role="editor">
  <c:set var="isEditor" value="${true}"/>
</logic:present>
```

If the user is not an editor, they are not allowed to amend any book details and the book form should be read-only. As you will see below, there is a `readonly` attribute on the form tags to do this:

```
<table width="100%">
  <tr>
    <td width="60%" valign="top">
```

We now open the Struts book form. We give it the action **/book/aud** (without **.do** – this is generated automatically). In the last chapter, we discussed that the Struts validation features can generate client-side JavaScript to validate user input in addition to the normal server-side validation. We have to invoke this validation script explicitly by defining an `onsubmit` JavaScript event handler:

```
<html:form action="/book/aud"
           onsubmit="return validateBookForm(this)">
```

When you are just starting to build your own web applications, it can sometimes be difficult to keep track of which code is executing where. In our JSP page on the server, this JavaScript is not really code. It is just dumb text that is generated together with the HTML. When the browser receives the generated page, it recognizes our JavaScript as executable code and runs it. If JavaScript is not supported or disabled there is no harm done – the Struts Validator implements server-side validation in addition to JavaScript-based client-side validation.

In this particular case, the statement `"return validateBookForm(this)"` is a string that will be copied to the generated HTML. The browser will execute it when the user attempts to submit the form by clicking one of the buttons.

When the form is submitted and an exception is thrown or Struts validation finds a problem, the request is forwarded back to this page (the input page). The error messages generated are stored in a request-scoped `ActionErrors` object, so we use a `<html:errors/>` tag to extract and display the errors that occurred:

```
<table>
  <tr>
    <td colspan="2"><html:errors/></td>
  </tr>
```

The second table row uses the Struts `<html:text/>` tag to display the book's title. This tag will output an HTML `<input type="text">` element:

```
<tr>
  <td width="20%"><bean:message key="book.title.label"/></td>
  <td>
    <html:text property="title" maxlength="255" size="40"
                  readonly="${not isEditor}"/>
  </td>
</tr>
```

You might find it a little hard to decipher what is going on here! An example should help: if the book title were "Beginning JSP 2.0", and the user did not have editor privileges, the HTML generated for this row would end up as the following:

```
<tr>
  <td width="20%">Title</td>
  <td>
    <input name=title maxlength=255 size=40
            readOnly value="Beginning JSP 2.0">
  </td>
</tr>
```

The `<html:text/>` tag above is probably most remarkable for the things we did *not* have to do.

❑   We did not have to provide the `value` of the input field. Struts is intelligent enough to understand that we want to display the current value of the `title` property of the form bean.

❑   There was no need to specify that the title should be retrieved from a form called `bookForm`. Struts already knows this because we started this form with `<html:form action="/book/aud">` and the mapping for this action configures `bookForm` to be its input form.

This level of automation takes a lot of the hard work out of JSP form development. The next couple of fields are all very similar to the `title` field:

```
<tr>
  <td>
    <bean:message key="book.authors.label"/>
  </td>
  <td>
    <html:text property="authors" maxlength="255" size="40"
                  readonly="${not isEditor}"/>
  </td>
</tr>
<tr>
  <td>
```

```
            <bean:message key="book.editor.label"/>
          </td>
          <td>
            <html:text property="editor" maxlength="255" size="40"
                       readonly="${not isEditor}"/>
          </td>
        </tr>
        <tr>
          <td valign="top"><bean:message key="book.chapters.label"/>
          </td>
          <td>
            <html:textarea property="chapters" cols="31" rows="10"
                       readonly="${not isEditor}"/>
          </td>
        </tr>
        <tr>
          <td>
            <bean:message key="book.pagecount.label"/>
          </td>
          <td>
            <html:text property="pageCount" size="5"
                       readonly="${not isEditor}"/>
          </td>
        </tr>
```

The next field to tackle is the book price field. We would like to format the price with two decimal places behind the dot, but the `<html:text/>` tag does not support formatting. Not to worry. We can generate the HTML `<input>` element directly and use the JSTL `<fmt:formatNumber/>` tag to get the format we want:

```
        <tr>
          <td>
            <bean:message key="book.price.label"/>
          </td>
          <td>
            <input type="text" name="price" size="5"
                   <c:if test="${not isEditor}">readonly</c:if>
                   value="<fmt:formatNumber value='${bookForm.price}'
                                            pattern='0.00'/>">
          </td>
        </tr>
```

The book status is an HTML `<select>` element containing three `<option>` tags. Struts takes care of translating the message keys (such as `book.status.planned`) into proper internationalized messages. It also ensures that the right option is selected according to the book's status:

```
        <tr>
          <td>
```

```
        <bean:message key="book.status.label"/>
      </td>
      <td>
        <html:select property="status">
          <html:option key="book.status.planned" value="P"/>
          <html:option key="book.status.inprogress" value="I"/>
          <html:option key="book.status.completed" value="C"/>
        </html:select>
      </td>
    </tr>
    <tr>
      <td></td>
      <td align="right">
```

Finally, we come to the row of buttons at the bottom. Except for the Cancel button, they are only available for editors, which we determine with the isEditor flag:

```
<c:if test="${isEditor}">
```

Then either the Add button or the Update and Delete buttons are displayed depending on the mode:

```
        <c:choose>
          <c:when test="${param.mode=='add'}">
            <html:submit property="action">
              <bean:message key="book.add.button.label"/>
            </html:submit>
          </c:when>
          <c:otherwise>
            <html:submit property="action">
              <bean:message key="book.update.button.label"/>
            </html:submit>
            <html:submit property="action"
                         onclick="bCancel=true;">
              <bean:message key="book.delete.button.label"/>
            </html:submit>
          </c:otherwise>
        </c:choose>
      </c:if>
```

Note that these buttons are all called action. Looking back at the action mapping for /book/aud.do, we find this is the button name we told LookupDispatchAction to look for:

```
<action path="/book/aud" ... parameter="action">
```

Everyone gets a Cancel button. Struts treats the <html:cancel/> tag as a special case. For example, when a cancel button is pressed, Struts skips its validation phase. However, we have to explicitly disable the client-side JavaScript validation code by setting the bCancel flag in the onclick event:

717

```
              <html:cancel onclick="bCancel=true;">
                <bean:message key="book.cancel.button.label"/>
              </html:cancel>
            </td>
          </tr>
        </table>
```

There are two further details related to this form to take care of. First, remember that when the form is submitted and there are any exceptions or validation errors, Struts returns us to this page. This means we need to keep track of whether we were in add or edit mode. The simplest way is to store the mode in a hidden field that will be submitted with the rest of the form:

```
        <input type="hidden" name="mode" value="${param.mode}">
```

Second, we need to tell Struts to generate the JavaScript validation code for the form. This includes the validateBookForm() function called from the form's onsubmit event handler:

```
          <html:javascript formName="bookForm"/>
        </html:form>
      </td>
```

The next thing to worry about is the list of news items at the right hand side of the book maintenance page. Fortunately this is pretty straightforward. A new book cannot have any news items associated with it, so we use a JSTL <c:if> tag to only include the list in edit mode:

```
    <td width="40%" valign="top">
      <c:if test="${param.mode == 'edit'}">
        <table>
          <tr>
```

The list's heading reads News on *title*, where *title* is the title of the book. Of course, the precise heading text depends on the language, and the book title may not come right at the end in all languages. Instead of simply concatenating a <bean:message> with the book title, the title should be a message argument. The message can incorporate the title at the appropriate point within the text:

```
              <th class="portlet">
                <bean:message key="book.news.title"
                              arg0="${bookForm.title}"/>
              </th>
            </tr>
```

For example, the English message file will have an entry:

```
book.news.title=News on {0}
```

The {0} is replaced by the first argument, in this case, the book title.

Next, we need to iterate over the news items for the book. Looking back to the Book class, we find that a Book holds its associated news items in a property called news that returns a SortedSet. All we need to do is use the <c:forEach> JSTL tag to iterate over bookForm.news:

```
<tr>
    <td class="portlet">
      <table>
        <c:forEach var="item" items="${bookForm.news}"
                   end="10">
```

The end="10" attribute tells <c:forEach> to omit any items after the tenth; anything more is old news.

For each news item, we display its title. When the user is an editor, or the author of the news item, we need to link the title to the news item maintenance page so that user will be able to edit the item:

```
<tr>
  <td class="title">
    <c:choose>
      <c:when test="${isEditor ||
          item.user==pageContext.request.remoteUser}">
        <html:link
          page="/book/news/edit.do?id=${item.id}">
          ${item.title}
        </html:link>
      </c:when>
      <c:otherwise>${item.title}</c:otherwise>
    </c:choose>
  </td>
</tr>
```

The formatting library formats the date of publication of the item. We want to display both date and time in short format, according to the conventions of the user's locale as determined from the request by the JSTL library:

```
<tr>
  <td>
    ${item.body}
    [<fmt:formatDate value="${item.published}"
                     type="both"
                     dateStyle="short"
                     timeStyle="short"/>]
  </td>
</tr>
</c:forEach>
```

When there is no news to display, it is a good idea to display a user-friendly message to that effect rather than simply showing an empty list:

```
<c:if test="${empty bookForm.news}">
  <tr>
    <td class="title">
      <bean:message key="book.news.nonews"/>
    </td>
  </tr>
</c:if>
```

Finally, any user is able to add a new news item, so we finish with an **Add a News Item** link:

```
        <tr>
          <td align="right">
            <html:link page="/book/news/add.do">
              <bean:message key="book.news.add.link"/>
            </html:link>
          </td>
        </tr>
      </table>
    </td>
  </tr>
</table>
      </c:if>
    </td>
  </tr>
</table>
```

Phew! That's the entire book maintenance part of the application, and if you have never worked with Struts it may seem a lot to absorb. However, as we create the Book News Maintenance page in the next section, we will cover a lot of the same ground. You'll soon start to see how all the different pieces of the Struts puzzle fit together, and you are halfway there – the pieces themselves are actually quite straightforward.

Book News Maintenance

For this section of the application, we again start with a look at what the page should look like, stripped of everything provided by the template:

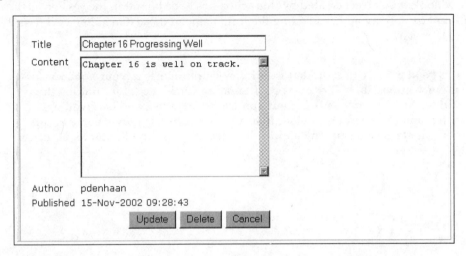

This page consists of just a single HTML form for news item details, similar to the book form but a lot simpler. The actions associated with this page are:

❏ When the user goes to the page by clicking **Add a News Item**, we need to create a fresh `BookNews` object. We need to make sure that it will be attached to the right `Book`.

❏ When the user goes to the news maintenance page by selecting an item from a news list, we need to retrieve the news item's details. We can either try to find it in the news items of the current `bookForm`, or load it directly from the database.

❏ The user should be able to **Add**, **Update**, **Delete**, and **Cancel** the news item using the buttons.

Once again, these actions map directly to Struts `Action` classes, but before we start to examine these we will first have a look at their mappings in the Struts configuration file.

The /book/news Mappings

The /book/news/add.do URL invoked when the user is about to start adding a new news item is mapped to the `com.wrox.publish.action.AddBookNewsAction` class. To properly initialize the new `BookNews` item, the action needs to know what `Book` the news item is for. By configuring `bookForm` to be the input form for this action, we kill two birds with one stone:

❏ When going from the Book Maintenance page to Book News Maintenance, we already have a fully populated `bookForm` in the user's session. No additional parameters are necessary.

721

❏   If, in a future enhancement, we want to be able to edit `BookNews` objects directly from the homepage, we can pass the information we need to populate the `bookForm` object as request parameters. In fact, as we shall see, all we really need is the book's `id`.

The new `BookNews` object created by this action has to be bound in the session as the new `bookNewsForm`. To avoid hard-coding the form name in the action class, we'll pass it in as an action parameter.

> **It is good practice to avoid hard-coding resource names in your `Action` classes as much as possible. The Struts configuration file is the "glue" linking the various MVC components in your application together, and hard-coding object and other resource names in `Actions` effectively moves some of this glue into Java code, making applications less flexible and harder to maintain.**

```
<action path="/book/news/add"
        type="com.wrox.publish.action.AddBookNewsAction"
        name="bookForm"
        scope="session"
    validate="false"
    parameter="bookNewsForm">
  <forward name="success" path="/booknews.jsp?mode=add"/>
</action>
```

The /book/news/edit.do mapping works exactly like the /book/edit.do action for books. It uses `bookNewsForm` to capture the object's id, used by the action to load it up from the database, and finally (if successful) we forward to the actual maintenance page.

```
<action path="/book/news/edit"
        type="com.wrox.publish.action.EditBookNewsAction"
        name="bookNewsForm"
        scope="session"
    validate="false">
  <forward name="success" path="/booknews.jsp?mode=edit"/>
</action>
```

The last of the mappings is /book/news/aud.do implementing add, update, delete, and cancel actions. This is analogous to the /book/aud.do action for books, but with one new feature: after a cancel, we simply forward back to the book page. But after a successful add, update, or delete, the list of news items for the current book has changed in some way, so rather than forwarding directly to `/book.jsp` we chain to another Struts action mapping, /book/edit.do. As you will recall, the edit action will load up the book details from the database, including any changes to news items the user just made.

```
        <action path="/book/news/aud"
                type="com.wrox.publish.action.PerformBookNewsAUDAction"
                name="bookNewsForm"
              scope="session"
              input="/booknews.jsp"
           validate="true"
          parameter="action">
          <forward name="added" path="/book/edit.do" redirect="true"/>
          <forward name="updated" path="/book/edit.do" redirect="true"/>
          <forward name="deleted" path="/book/edit.do" redirect="true"/>
          <forward name="cancel" path="/book.jsp?mode=edit"/>
        </action>
      </action-mappings>
```

This ability to chain multiple actions allows us to break complicated procedures down into small, atomic, self-contained `Action` classes that are much easier to understand and more likely to be reusable than one big `Action` that does all the work.

AddBookNewsAction

This action, invoked when the user wants to start adding a new book news item, brings few surprises. A new `BookNews` object is created, populated with its parent `Book` and the current user, and finally bound in the session as the new `bookNewsForm`:

```
package com.wrox.publish.action;

import com.wrox.publish.om.Book;
import com.wrox.publish.om.BookNews;
import javax.servlet.http.HttpServletRequest;
import javax.servlet.http.HttpServletResponse;
import org.apache.struts.action.Action;
import org.apache.struts.action.ActionForm;
import org.apache.struts.action.ActionForward;
import org.apache.struts.action.ActionMapping;

public class AddBookNewsAction extends Action {
    public ActionForward execute(ActionMapping mapping,
                                 ActionForm form,
                                 HttpServletRequest request,
                                 HttpServletResponse response) {
        BookNews news = new BookNews();
        news.setBook((Book)form);
        news.setUser(request.getRemoteUser());
        String bookNewsFormName = mapping.getParameter();
        request.getSession().setAttribute(bookNewsFormName, news);
```

```
                return mapping.findForward("success");
        }
}
```

EditBookNewsAction

This action is executed to update or delete an existing news item; it uses the id request parameter to retrieve the item from the database and binds it in the session as the new bookNewsForm. A typical request would be /book/news/edit.do?id=813.

```
package com.wrox.publish.action;

import com.wrox.publish.bo.BookBO;
import com.wrox.publish.om.BookNews;
import javax.servlet.http.HttpServletRequest;
import javax.servlet.http.HttpServletResponse;
import org.apache.struts.action.Action;
import org.apache.struts.action.ActionForm;
import org.apache.struts.action.ActionForward;
import org.apache.struts.action.ActionMapping;

public class EditBookNewsAction extends Action {
  public ActionForward execute(ActionMapping mapping,
                               ActionForm form,
                               HttpServletRequest request,
                               HttpServletResponse response)
    throws Exception {
    BookBO bookBO = BookBO.getInstance(request,getDataSource(request));
    BookNews news = bookBO.findBookNewsById(((BookNews)form).getId());
    request.getSession().setAttribute(mapping.getName(), news);
    return mapping.findForward("success");
  }
}
```

In the introduction to this section, it was said that to retrieve the news item to edit, we could either try to find it in the news items of the current bookForm, or load it directly from the database. The current implementation chooses to do the latter, as it will then still work correctly if we have not instantiated the Book object yet. That way, we could link to /book/news/edit.do from the news item list on the homepage if we wanted to.

PerformBookNewsAUDAction

This action is executed when the Add, Update, Delete, or Cancel button is pressed on the news item form. As in the equivalent action for books, we rely on the Struts LookupDispatchAction class to invoke the add(), update(), or delete() method depending on which button has been pressed:

```
package com.wrox.publish.action;

import com.wrox.publish.bo.ActionDeniedException;
import com.wrox.publish.bo.BookBO;
import com.wrox.publish.om.BookNews;
import java.util.HashMap;
import java.util.Map;
import javax.servlet.http.HttpServletRequest;
import javax.servlet.http.HttpServletResponse;
import org.apache.struts.action.ActionForm;
import org.apache.struts.action.ActionForward;
import org.apache.struts.action.ActionMapping;
import org.apache.struts.actions.LookupDispatchAction;

public class PerformBookNewsAUDAction extends LookupDispatchAction
{
  protected Map getKeyMethodMap()
  {
    Map map = new HashMap();
    map.put("booknews.add.button.label", "add");
    map.put("booknews.update.button.label", "update");
    map.put("booknews.delete.button.label", "delete");
    return map;
  }

  public ActionForward execute(ActionMapping mapping,
                               ActionForm form,
                               HttpServletRequest request,
                               HttpServletResponse response)
         throws Exception {
```

The following few lines of code prevent a user from supplying a new id or user for the news item. If we failed to check for this, a malicious user would be able to modify or delete any given news item, something that can normally be done only by editors.

> *This may strike you as rather paranoid. When you are working on secure systems, however, paranoia is a required frame of mind. Somewhere in your system there should be a clearly defined **trust boundary**; anything coming in from outside the boundary should be examined for possible security problems. In this case, the Struts Action objects mark the trust boundary.*

> *Alternatively, we could have moved the boundary deeper into the system, into BookBO for instance, which would be advantageous if there are many different Action objects operating on a single business object.*

The published field is not editable for anyone, so this is also checked for:

```
if (request.getParameterMap().containsKey("id") ||
    request.getParameterMap().containsKey("user") ||
```

```
              request.getParameterMap().containsKey("published"))
    {
      request.getSession().removeAttribute(mapping.getName());
      throw new ActionDeniedException(
                "id, user, and published are immutable");
    }
```

The **Cancel** button is a special case; all others are handled by the `LookupDispatchAction` code:

```
    if (isCancelled(request))
    {
      return mapping.findForward("cancel");
    }
    else
    {
      return super.execute(mapping, form, request, response);
    }
  }
```

The `add()`, `update()`, and `delete()` methods are three lines each. All they need to do is retrieve the `bookNewsForm`, call the relevant method in `BookBO`, and return the page to forward to:

```
public ActionForward add(ActionMapping mapping, ActionForm form,
                         HttpServletRequest request,
                         HttpServletResponse response)
      throws Exception
{
  BookBO bookBO = BookBO.getInstance(request,
                                     getDataSource(request));
  bookBO.create((BookNews)form);
  return mapping.findForward("added");
}

public ActionForward update(ActionMapping mapping,
                            ActionForm form,
                            HttpServletRequest request,
                            HttpServletResponse response)
      throws Exception
{
  BookBO bookBO = BookBO.getInstance(request,
                                     getDataSource(request));
  bookBO.update((BookNews)form);
  return mapping.findForward("updated");
}

public ActionForward delete(ActionMapping mapping,
                            ActionForm form,
                            HttpServletRequest request,
```

```
                              HttpServletResponse response)
        throws Exception
    {
      BookBO bookBO = BookBO.getInstance(request,
                                getDataSource(request));
      bookBO.remove((BookNews)form);
      return mapping.findForward("deleted");
    }
}
```

The /booknews.jsp Page

The templating mechanism makes /booknews.jsp a short and simple affair. The template is default.jsp, and the page content is provided by booknewsform.jsp, in the content folder:

```
<%@page contentType="text/html"%>
<%@taglib prefix="template"
        uri="http://jakarta.apache.org/struts/tags-template-1.0"%>
<%@taglib prefix="bean"
        uri="http://jakarta.apache.org/struts/tags-bean-1.0"%>

<template:insert template="/templates/default.jsp">
  <template:put name="title">
    <bean:message key="booknews.${param.mode}.page.title"/>
  </template:put>
  <template:put name="content" content="/content/booknewsform.jsp"/>
</template:insert>
```

The booknewsform.jsp Page

Compared to the Book Maintenance page, the Book News page is easy going. Create this file in the content folder under the name booknewsform.jsp. It starts as usual:

```
<%@page contentType="text/html"%>
<%@taglib prefix="c" uri="http://java.sun.com/jstl/core_rt"%>
<%@taglib prefix="fmt" uri="http://java.sun.com/jstl/fmt_rt"%>
<%@taglib prefix="html"
        uri="http://jakarta.apache.org/struts/tags-html-1.0"%>
<%@taglib prefix="bean"
        uri="http://jakarta.apache.org/struts/tags-bean-1.0"%>
```

A Struts <html:form> and its nested <html:text/> and <html:textarea/> tags take care of populating the form and JavaScript validation. The Struts configuration file establishes the association between the form action /book/news/aud.do and the bookNewsForm which is our news item object. A <html:errors/> tag displays errors such as validation problems that may have occurred when submitting the form:

```
<html:form action="/book/news/aud"
           onsubmit="return validateBookNewsForm(this)">
  <table>
    <tr>
      <td colspan="2"><html:errors/></td>
    </tr>
    <tr>
      <td width="20%"><bean:message key="booknews.title.label"/></td>
      <td>
        <html:text property="title" maxlength="255" size="40"/>
      </td>
    </tr>
    <tr>
      <td valign="top"><bean:message key="booknews.body.label"/></td>
      <td><html:textarea property="body" cols="31" rows="10"/></td>
    </tr>
```

As is clear from the screenshot at the start of this section, neither the news item's user nor its publication timestamp are editable, so we simply insert their values using the JSP expression language. The publication timestamp is formatted according to the conventions from the user's locale using a JSTL <fmt:format> tag:

```
<tr>
  <td>
    <bean:message key="booknews.user.label"/>
  </td>
  <td>
    ${bookNewsForm.user}
  </td>
</tr>
<tr>
  <td>
     <bean:message key="booknews.published.label"/>
  </td>
  <td>
    <fmt:formatDate value="${bookNewsForm.published}"
                    type="both"/>
  </td>
</tr>
```

A JSTL <c:choose>...<c:when>...<c:otherwise> construct, discussed in Chapter 5, ensures that the Add button is only displayed when the mode is "add", and that Update and Delete buttons are shown only in "edit" mode:

```
<tr>
  <td></td>
  <td align="right">
    <c:choose>
      <c:when test="${param.mode=='add'}">
```

```
            <html:submit property="action">
              <bean:message key="booknews.add.button.label"/>
            </html:submit>
          </c:when>
          <c:otherwise>
            <html:submit property="action">
              <bean:message key="booknews.update.button.label"/>
            </html:submit>
            <html:submit property="action" onclick="bCancel=true;">
              <bean:message key="booknews.delete.button.label"/>
            </html:submit>
          </c:otherwise>
        </c:choose>
        <html:cancel onclick="bCancel=true;">
          <bean:message key="booknews.cancel.button.label"/>
        </html:cancel>
      </td>
    </tr>
  </table>
```

As in the book maintenance page, we need to keep track of the page's mode in a hidden field, in case validation errors mean Struts must redisplay the page. Finally, we tell Struts to generate the client-side validation JavaScript:

```
  <input type="hidden" name="mode" value="${param.mode}">
  <html:javascript formName="bookNewsForm"/>
</html:form>
```

The Home Page

The next page to create is the home page. In the requirements section, we saw a screenshot of the full page; below is the homepage as an editor might see it, shorn of all the decoration provided by the default template:

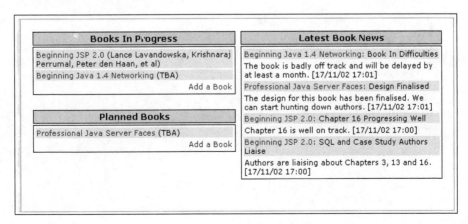

729

This is much like a portal page with three portlets. We will use the `portlet.jsp` template. There are two types of content, so we use two different content pages – one for the book lists and another for the news list – to render this page.

The actions a user can take on the homepage are:

❑   View or edit an existing book (/book/edit.do)

❑   Editors can add a new book (/book/add.do)

Both actions have been discussed in the Book News Maintenance section above. They are available to authenticated users only, but container security will take care of that.

The index Global Forward

Because the home page is forwarded to from a number of different places, we will set up a global forward in the Struts configuration file `/WEB-INF/struts-config.xml`. This forward can be used anywhere both in `mapping.findForward()` calls in `Actions` and in `<html:link forward="index"/>` tags:

```
<global-forwards>
  <forward name="index" path="/index.jsp" redirect="true"/>
</global-forwards>
```

If we ever want to start using a different homepage, we should only have to change it here and all links would adjust automatically.

The index.jsp Page

Like `book.jsp` and `booknews.jsp`, this is no more than a short page that combines the required template with the content pages, and it is also placed in our web application's root folder. There is an added twist though, in that the content area for the main template is produced using our second template, `portal.jsp`:

```
<%@page contentType="text/html"%>
<%@taglib prefix="template"
          uri="http://jakarta.apache.org/struts/tags-template-1.0"%>
<%@taglib prefix="bean"
          uri="http://jakarta.apache.org/struts/tags-bean-1.0"%>

<template:insert template="/templates/default.jsp">
  <template:put name="title">
    <bean:message key="home.page.title"/>
  </template:put>
  <template:put name="content">
```

This is where the content for `/templates/default.jsp` should go. Instead of specifying a `content` attribute or including the content directly in the body of the `<template:put>` tag, we want to use the portal template to render the content. Fortunately, Struts templates can actually be nested. We can simply use a second set of `<template:insert>`...`<template:put>` tags:

```
<template:insert template="/templates/portal.jsp">

  <template:put name="title[1]">
    <bean:message key="home.booksinprogress.title"/>
  </template:put>
  <template:put name="portlet[1]"
                content="/content/booklist.jsp?status=I"/>
```

The `booklist.jsp` page is used twice, with a different status parameter each time, to render the "Books in Progress" and "Planned Books" lists:

```
  <template:put name="title[2]">
    <bean:message key="home.plannedbooks.title"/>
  </template:put>
  <template:put name="portlet[2]"
                content="/content/booklist.jsp?status=P"/>

  <template:put name="title[3]">
    <bean:message key="home.booknews.title"/>
  </template:put>
  <template:put name="portlet[3]"
                content="/content/booknewslist.jsp"/>

  </template:insert>
  </template:put>
</template:insert>
```

The booklist.jsp Page

This page, held in the `content` folder, generates a list of books with a given status, passed in as a request parameter. The natural way to do this would be to implement a `findByStatus()` finder method in `BookDAO`, a corresponding method in `BookBO`, and use them to retrieve the list in an `Action` that is executed before we get to this page. However, portlets for portal pages are often written in a fairly ad hoc way, interfacing with systems that sometimes were not conceived for a web interface at all and provide no easy access to the data. In such cases it is not uncommon to directly read the data from the database using techniques such as the JSTL SQL tags. Note that this is certainly not best practice, and it's better to use data access objects instead, but we will use this method here so we can compare it with the DAO method later:

```
<%@page contentType="text/html"%>
<%@taglib prefix="c" uri="http://java.sun.com/jstl/core_rt"%>
<%@taglib prefix="sql" uri="http://java.sun.com/jstl/sql_rt"%>
```

```
<%@taglib prefix="html"
          uri="http://jakarta.apache.org/struts/tags-html-1.0"%>
<%@taglib prefix="bean"
          uri="http://jakarta.apache.org/struts/tags-bean-1.0"%>
<%@taglib prefix="logic"
          uri="http://jakarta.apache.org/struts/tags-logic-1.0"%>
```

Now we get to the actual SQL query. Struts binds the default `DataSource` set up in its configuration file in the application scope, under the name `org.apache.struts.action.DATA_SOURCE`. Because this name is qualified (it has dots in it), we'll have to use the `applicationScope['x']` expression language syntax instead of simply `applicationScope.x`.

The query itself is quite simple. The question mark denotes a query parameter, in this case the required status. We specify the parameter's value in a `<sql:param>` tag nested inside `<sql:query>`:

```
<sql:query var="books" dataSource=
          "${applicationScope['org.apache.struts.action.DATA_SOURCE']}">
    SELECT *
      FROM book
     WHERE status=?
  <sql:param value="${param.status}"/>
</sql:query>
```

We could easily have substituted the parameter value directly into the query like so:

> *SELECT * FROM book WHERE status='${param.status}'*

but this would have been considerably less efficient.

SQL statements have to be compiled by the database in much the same way that Java source code is compiled into bytecode. To improve efficiency, many databases remember the compiled versions of your most recent SQL in a statement cache. If you use query parameters and run the query a hundred times with a hundred different parameter values, it will still be compiled just once. If, on the other hand, you hard-code the parameter values in each query, all one hundred queries have to be compiled individually. The performance difference can be quite significant. This applies to JDBC (`Prepared`)`Statement`s as well as to the JSTL SQL tags.

The query tag will have bound the result set in the variable `books`. The `<c:forEach>` core tag can be used to iterate over the results, storing each individual book in turn in the `book` variable:

```
<table width="100%">
  <c:forEach var="book" items="${books.rows}" end="10">
```

For each book, we display title and authors. The title is linked to the **/books/edit.do** action so that a user can edit or view a book simply by clicking on it:

```
    <tr>
      <td class="title">
        <html:link page="/book/edit.do?id=${book.id}">
          ${book.title}
        </html:link>
        (${book.authors})
      </td>
    </tr>
  </c:forEach>
```

As in the news list in Book Maintenance, we display a message if the book list is empty.

```
    <c:if test="${empty books.rows}">
      <tr>
        <td class="title"><bean:message key="booklist.nobooks"/></td>
      </tr>
    </c:if>
```

Finally, editors get an "Add a Book" link to **/book/add.do**. This is most easily done using the Struts `<logic:present>` tag to test whether the user has the editor role.

```
    <logic:present role="editor">
      <tr>
        <td align="right">
          <html:link page="/book/add.do?status=${param.status}">
            <bean:message key="booklist.add.link"/>
          </html:link>
        </td>
      </tr>
    </logic:present>
  </table>
```

The booknewslist.jsp Page

The second type of list in the home page is the news item list. This page is completely analogous to the book list page, and is also kept in the `content` folder:

```
<%@page contentType="text/html"%>
<%@taglib prefix="c" uri="http://java.sun.com/jstl/core_rt"%>
<%@taglib prefix="sql" uri="http://java.sun.com/jstl/sql_rt"%>
<%@taglib prefix="fmt" uri="http://java.sun.com/jstl/fmt_rt"%>
<%@taglib prefix="html"
          uri="http://jakarta.apache.org/struts/tags-html-1.0"%>
<%@taglib prefix="bean"
          uri="http://jakarta.apache.org/struts/tags-bean-1.0"%>
```

For each news item, we will display the title of the book it refers to. We do this using a database join that combines both the `book` and `book_news` tables. We also have to give the join condition that tells the database how the tables should be combined, which will be `book_news.book = book.id`. This corresponds exactly with the foreign key constraint in the definition for the `book_news` table:

```
FOREIGN KEY (book)
    REFERENCES book(id)
    ON DELETE CASCADE
```

Whenever you need to use joins in a database query, you will usually join on foreign keys.

```
<sql:query var="news"
          dataSource="${applicationScope
                           ['org.apache.struts.action.DATA_SOURCE']}">
    SELECT book_news.*, book.title AS booktitle
      FROM book_news, book
     WHERE book_news.book = book.id
  ORDER BY published DESC
</sql:query>
```

The actual listing brings no surprises. We use the JSTL `<c:foreach>` tag to loop over the records returned by the query, and the `<c:fmt>` tag to display the news item's publication date. Finally, `<c:if>` tests whether the list was perhaps empty and displays a user-friendly message if it was:

```
<table width="100%">
  <c:forEach var="item" items="${news.rows}">
    <tr>
      <td class="title">
        <html:link page="/book/update.do?id=${item.book}">
          ${item.booktitle}
        </html:link>: ${item.title}
      </td>
    </tr>
    <tr>
      <td>
        ${item.body}
        [<fmt:formatDate value="${item.published}" type="both"
                         dateStyle="short" timeStyle="short"/>]
      </td>
    </tr>
  </c:forEach>
  <c:if test="${empty news.rows}">
    <tr>
      <td class="title"><bean:message key="booknewslist.nonews"/>
          </td>
    </tr>
  </c:if>
</table>
```

Data Access Objects or SQL Tags?

Looking back at the previous two pages, you might think that using the JSTL SQL tags is a lot simpler and more straightforward than the whole apparatus of Data Access Objects, finder methods, Business Objects, actions, and so on, and in this case, it is. There are a number of significant disadvantages associated with this approach, however:

❑ *Poor Error handling I*
You will often discover problems only after starting to generate HTML. Once enough HTML code has been generated, the first part of the response, including the response header, will be committed (sent to the browser). From that moment onwards, it is no longer possible to gracefully handle the error, forward to an error page, or set an error response code. You can increase the size of the response buffer to delay the commit, but this increases memory consumption and it can be difficult to determine how large the buffer should be.

❑ *Poor Error handling II*
We have seen that it is very easy to associate any number of possible exceptions and their error messages with any Struts action. When an exception is thrown from inside a JSP, all you have is the crude global error handling mechanism of the servlet container.

❑ *Hard to implement business logic*
The two pages we've seen have no serious business logic associated with them. When there are complicated requirements as to who can see what, and certainly when you try to handle database updates with JSP tags as well and have to deal with their usually more complicated business logic and transaction handling, your JSP pages will quickly become hopelessly complicated and cluttered.

❑ *Tight coupling*
Embedding SQL in JSP introduces a direct, tight coupling between your view and the database. Whenever you make a database change, you will have to go through all your JSP pages to find out if they need to be modified. With the DAO approach, you usually have just one Java class to modify for every table you change and, unless the DAO's interface changes in an incompatible way, you do not have to worry about the rest of the application.

❑ *Poor reusability*
Data Access Objects and Business Objects are reusable. When, say, you are asked to build a web site feature offering some information on books that are in progress, you can usually use the existing DAO and BO classes. The two JSP pages presented here would be unusable in their present form; you would have to copy and change them, making the entire system even harder to modify and maintain. Any logic that such JSP pages contain makes the situation even worse as it is almost impossible to keep such logic consistent across multiple implementations.

❑ *Mixing of responsibilities*
The ideal application component, be it a Java class, JSP file or something else, has *one* and just *one* clearly defined responsibility. The further you drift away from this ideal, the harder it is to understand the components, and the more obscure the interactions between them are. The SQL tag approach tends to mix a number of different responsibilities in one file: understanding and querying the database schema, implementing the business logic, and presenting an HTML view.

❑ *Mixing of skills*
This actually follows from the previous point. The skills you need to write database queries, the business tier logic, and JSP pages are completely different. In all but the smallest organizations, these tasks are generally carried out by different people. The SQL tag approach makes this specialization very difficult if not impossible.

It should be clear that in all but the smallest projects, you should avoid using the SQL tags whenever possible.

Logging In, Logging Out

In the *Application Architecture* section, it was discussed how the servlet container's security features can take care of users and roles. We will use form-based security to provide a login form that blends in well with the rest of the application. It can look really simple:

Username	
Password	
	login

The default template will add a header, sidebar menu and footer to this form. In addition, the menu provides a logout link that we still need to implement.

The /login and /logout Mappings

Setting up the Struts action mappings for logging in and logging out is straightforward. Logging in is handled by the servlet container, so all we have to do is forward the user to the next page, in this case the homepage:

```
<action path="/login" forward="/index.jsp"/>
```

Logging out needs a bit of Java code, so we set up a mapping to a `LogoutAction` class to do this. After logging out, the user should be forwarded to the homepage. Because there already is a global forward for this page, we do not need to specify it in the action:

```
<action path="/logout"
        type="com.wrox.publish.action.LogoutAction"/>
```

This is a lot simpler than any of the mappings we've seen so far. The login form and the `LogoutAction` are almost as simple.

The login.jsp Page

In the `web.xml` web-app deployment descriptor, we will configure this page (held in the application's root directory) as the login page for the application. The relevant excerpt from the descriptor is:

```
      .
      .
      .
<login-config>
   <auth-method>FORM</auth-method>
   <form-login-config>
      <form-login-page>/login.jsp</form-login-page>
      <form-error-page>/login.jsp</form-error-page>
   </form-login-config>
</login-config>
      .
      .
      .
```

According to the servlet specification, this login page must have a form that posts its contents to the action `j_security_check`, with two fields called `j_username` and `j_password`. These are "magic names" that the servlet container will recognize as a login form:

```
<%@page contentType="text/html"%>
<%@taglib prefix="template"
          uri="http://jakarta.apache.org/struts/tags-template-1.0"%>
<%@taglib prefix="bean"
          uri="http://jakarta.apache.org/struts/tags-bean-1.0"%>

<template:insert template="/templates/default.jsp">
  <template:put name="title">
    <bean:message key="login.page.title"/>
  </template:put>
  <template:put name="content">
```

In the previous template pages, we used the `content` attribute of `<template:put>` to produce the content for the template. Alternatively, we can put the content directly inside the `<template:put>` tag body. Because the login page is so simple, it is tempting to do just that. The price to pay is that it is not easily reused elsewhere:

```
<form action="j_security_check" method="post">
  <table>
    <tr><td colspan="2"> </td></tr>
    <tr>
      <td width="20%">
        <bean:message key="login.username.label"/>
      </td>
      <td>
          <input type="text" name="j_username" size="40"/>
        </td>
    </tr>
    <tr>
      <td>
          <bean:message key="login.password.label"/>
        </td>
      <td>
          <input type="password" name="j_password" size="40"/>
        </td>
    </tr>
    <tr>
      <td></td>
      <td align="right">
        <input type="submit" value="login">
      </td>
    </tr>
  </table>
</form>
</template:put>
</template:insert>
```

LogoutAction

This class is mapped to the /logout.do action. The HttpSession.logout() method logs the
user out of the application and all other applications that use the same authentication
information, so we call this method and forward to the index page:

```
package com.wrox.publish.action;

import javax.servlet.http.HttpServletRequest;
import javax.servlet.http.HttpServletResponse;
import org.apache.struts.action.Action;
import org.apache.struts.action.ActionForm;
import org.apache.struts.action.ActionForward;
import org.apache.struts.action.ActionMapping;

public class LogoutAction extends Action
{
  public ActionForward execute(ActionMapping mapping, ActionForm form,
                               HttpServletRequest request,
                               HttpServletResponse response)
```

```
    {
      request.getSession().logout();
      return mapping.findForward("index");
    }
}
```

After this call, the HTTP sessions associated with the login will have been invalidated, including all information about the user's identity and roles.

The Error Page

All exceptions not handled by Java code or Struts end up with the servlet container itself. To avoid bewildering our users with nasty exception stack traces, we direct such exceptions to an error page using the following entry in /WEB-INF/web.xml:

```
    .
    .
    .
  <error-page>
    <exception-type>java.lang.Exception</exception-type>
    <location>/error.jsp</location>
  </error-page>
    .
    .
    .
```

This will cause any otherwise unhandled exception to end up at error.jsp.

The error.jsp Page

The actual error page does nothing more than display a generic message and the exception's message string. As in the login page, it is so small and simple that it is hardly worth splitting off the content into a separate page.

Note that the <%@page%> directive has the attribute isErrorPage set to true, so that the container knows this is an error page and the exception we're handling should be made available as an object:

```
<%@page contentType="text/html" isErrorPage="true"%>
<%@taglib prefix="template"
          uri="http://jakarta.apache.org/struts/tags-template-1.0"%>
<%@taglib prefix="bean"
          uri="http://jakarta.apache.org/struts/tags-bean-1.0"%>

<template:insert template="/templates/default.jsp">
  <template:put name="title">
    <bean:message key="errors.page.title"/>
```

739

```
      </template:put>
      <template:put name="content">
```

The `Exception` object is accessible from the page context object. Its message is passed as an argument to our "Unexpected Application Error" message:

```
      <bean:message key="errors.unexpected"
                    arg0="${pageContext.exception.message}"/>
      </template:put>
   </template:insert>
```

Application Messages

Key to the Struts internationalization features, and indeed Java internationalization in general, is the notion of a **resource bundle**. This is a properties file associated with a particular **locale**, consisting of the language (such as `en` for English or `fr` for French) and, optionally, the regional variant (such as `en_GB` for British English or `fr_CA` for Canadian French). You can support additional locales by simply adding more files to the bundle.

When mapping a message key to the actual message, for example in the `<bean:message>` tag, Struts attempts to find the message in the region-specific file (like `publish_en_GB.properties`). If that file does not exist, or does not contain the required message, it tries to find the message in the language-specific file (`publish_en.properties`) and ultimately the default bundle (`publish.properties`).

The location of the messages resource bundle is configured in the Struts configuration file:

```
      .
      .
      .
   <message-resources parameter="resources.publish"/>
      .
      .
      .
```

The bundle is loaded using the Java class loader, so it can reside in any location where you can store Java class files, including JAR files. The entry above tells Struts to look for the `publish` bundle in the `resources` package. A good place therefore is `/WEB-INF/classes/resources/`.

The publish.properties Resource Bundle

The `publish.properties` default resource bundle listed below corresponds to the American English locale. As it is just a long list of message keys and their corresponding messages, most of it is rather boring. Lines starting with the hash character # are comments:

```
# Homepage
home.page.title=Book Publishing Home
home.booksinprogress.title=Books In Progress
home.plannedbooks.title=Planned Books
home.booknews.title=Latest Book News

booklist.nobooks=None Found
booklist.add.link=Add a Book
booknewslist.nonews=No News Found

sidebar.home.link=Home
sidebar.wrox.link=Wrox Home
sidebar.login.link=Login
sidebar.logout.link=Logout

# Login
login.page.title=Login
login.username.label=Username
login.password.label=Password

# Book Maintenance
book.add.page.title=Add Book
book.edit.page.title=Edit Book

book.title=The title
book.title.label=Title
book.authors.label=Authors
book.editor.label=Editor
book.chapters.label=Chapter Titles
book.pagecount=The page count
book.pagecount.label=Page Count
book.price=The price
book.price.label=Price $
book.status=The status
book.status.label=Status
book.status.planned=Planned
book.status.inprogress=In Progress
book.status.completed=Completed

book.add.button.label=Add
book.update.button.label=Update
book.delete.button.label=Delete
book.cancel.button.label=Cancel
```

As we have seen before, Struts messages can take arguments, which appear as {0}, {1}, and so on inside the message text:

```
book.news.title=News on {0}
book.news.nonews=No News Found
book.news.add.link=Add a News Item
```

```
# BookNews Maintenance
booknews.add.page.title=Add News Item
booknews.edit.page.title=Edit News Item

booknews.title=The title
booknews.title.label=Title
booknews.user.label=Author
booknews.body=The content
booknews.body.label=Content
booknews.published.label=Published

booknews.add.button.label=Add
booknews.update.button.label=Update
booknews.delete.button.label=Delete
booknews.cancel.button.label=Cancel

# Application Error Messages
errors.page.title=Unexpected Error
errors.header=<font color="red"><ul>
errors.prefix=<li>
errors.footer=</ul></font>
errors.notfound=Entity not found (probably deleted by another user).
errors.denied.editorsonly=This action can be performed by editors only.
```

If a message is getting rather long for a single line, you can put a backslash at the very end of the line and continue the message on the next line. Leading spaces on the next line are ignored. This is completely equivalent to having the entire message on a single line – the line break will *not* show up in the message. This technique also works for any properties file:

```
errors.denied.owneroreditor=This action can be performed \
    by owners or editors only.
errors.database=An unexpected database error has occurred. \
    Please try again later.
errors.unexpected=An unexpected application error has occurred ({0}). \
    Please try again later.
errors.book.duplicatetitle=The book has an existing title \
    or another invalid field.
errors.required={0} is required.
errors.range={0} is not in the range {1} through {2}.
errors.integer={0} must be a whole number.
errors.double={0} must be a valid number.
```

Adding More Locales

To demonstrate how easy it is to add new languages to the application, try adding the following file. Save it as /WEB-INF/classes/resources/publish_en_GB.properties.

```
# Book Maintenance
book.price.label=Price £
```

Reconfigure your computer so that it thinks it is located in the UK, and access the application again. You will find that the price in the Book Maintenance screen now has a pound prefix rather than a dollar prefix. All other messages are still retrieved from the default resource bundle. Obviously, this is not very useful unless we actually maintain a price list in various currencies, but more about this in the *Why Not Try* section!

Configuring and Running the Application

We did it – that's all the Java code and JSP pages for our application written! Our site comprises many components, but they are all pretty straightforward and self-contained. Hopefully you should be able to see that writing the site this way was a lot easier than creating a "bowl of spaghetti" application, with everything tossed together so that it's hard to figure just which bits of code do what.

We do still have a little work left: we need to pull together all the entries we need to place in our Struts configuration file, and we need to do the same for the web.xml deployment descriptor.

The Struts Configuration File

We have already covered all the elements of the struts configuration file, struts-config.xml. The complete listing for this file is shown below:

```xml
<?xml version="1.0" encoding="UTF-8"?>
<!DOCTYPE struts-config PUBLIC
          "-//Apache Software Foundation//DTD Struts Configuration 1.1//EN"
          "http://jakarta.apache.org/struts/dtds/struts-config_1_1.dtd">
<struts-config>

  <data-sources>
    <data-source>
      <set-property property="description" value="Publish Database"/>
      <set-property property="driverClass"
                    value="com.mysql.jdbc.Driver"/>
      <set-property property="url"
                    value="jdbc:mysql://localhost/publish"/>
      <set-property property="user" value="publish"/>
      <set-property property="password" value="wrox"/>
      <set-property property="autoCommit" value="false"/>
    </data-source>
  </data-sources>

  <form-beans>
    <form-bean name="bookForm" type="com.wrox.publish.om.Book"/>
    <form-bean name="bookNewsForm"
               type="com.wrox.publish.om.BookNews"/>
  </form-beans>
```

```xml
<global-exceptions>
  <exception type="java.sql.SQLException" key="errors.database"/>
</global-exceptions>

<global-forwards>
  <forward name="index" path="/index.jsp" redirect="true"/>
</global-forwards>

<action-mappings>
  <action path="/login" forward="/index.jsp"/>

  <action path="/logout"
          type="com.wrox.publish.action.LogoutAction"/>

  <action path="/book/add"
          type="com.wrox.publish.action.AddBookAction"
          name="bookForm"
          scope="session"
      validate="false">
    <forward name="success" path="/book.jsp?mode=add"/>
  </action>

  <action path="/book/edit"
          type="com.wrox.publish.action.EditBookAction"
          name="bookForm"
          scope="session"
      validate="false">
    <forward name="success" path="/book.jsp?mode=edit"/>
  </action>

  <action path="/book/aud"
          type="com.wrox.publish.action.PerformBookAUDAction"
          name="bookForm"
          scope="session"
          input="/book.jsp"
      validate="true"
     parameter="action">
    <exception type="com.wrox.publish.db.InvalidFieldException"
               key="errors.book.duplicatetitle"/>
    <forward name="added" path="/index.jsp" redirect="true"/>
    <forward name="updated" path="/index.jsp" redirect="true"/>
    <forward name="deleted" path="/index.jsp" redirect="true"/>
    <forward name="cancel" path="/index.jsp" redirect="true"/>
  </action>

  <action path="/book/news/add"
          type="com.wrox.publish.action.AddBookNewsAction"
          name="bookForm"
          scope="session"
      validate="false"
     parameter="bookNewsForm">
    <forward name="success" path="/booknews.jsp?mode=add"/>
```

```
    </action>

    <action path="/book/news/edit"
            type="com.wrox.publish.action.EditBookNewsAction"
            name="bookNewsForm"
          scope="session"
        validate="false">
      <forward name="success" path="/booknews.jsp?mode=edit"/>
    </action>

    <action path="/book/news/aud"
            type="com.wrox.publish.action.PerformBookNewsAUDAction"
            name="bookNewsForm"
          scope="session"
          input="/booknews.jsp"
        validate="true"
      parameter="action">
      <forward name="added" path="/book/edit.do" redirect="true"/>
      <forward name="updated" path="/book/edit.do" redirect="true"/>
      <forward name="deleted" path="/book/edit.do" redirect="true"/>
      <forward name="cancel" path="/book.jsp?mode=edit"/>
    </action>
  </action-mappings>

  <message-resources parameter="resources.publish"/>

  <plug-in className="org.apache.struts.validator.ValidatorPlugIn">
    <set-property property="pathnames"
        value="/WEB-INF/validator-rules.xml,/WEB-INF/validation.xml"/>
  </plug-in>

</struts-config>
```

The Application Deployment Descriptor

In this section, we will have a look at the complete listing of the deployment descriptor file, web.xml. As we have already seen, the deployment descriptor will contain the following pieces of information:

- ❑ Struts controller servlet declaration
- ❑ Mapping of all requests for *.do to the controller servlet
- ❑ Welcome file mapping to /index.jsp
- ❑ Security constraints
- ❑ Login configuration

The source listing for the deployment descriptor is as follows:

```xml
<?xml version="1.0" encoding="UTF-8"?>
<web-app xmlns="http://java.sun.com/xml/ns/j2ee"
         xmlns:xsi="http://www.w3.org/2001/XMLSchema-instance"
         xsi:schemaLocation="http://java.sun.com/xml/ns/j2ee
                     http://java.sun.com/xml/ns/j2ee/web-app_2_4.xsd"
         version="2.4">

    <display-name>Wrox Struts Case Study</display-name>
```

The controller servlet is the Struts `ActionServlet`. Normally, a servlet is instantiated only when the first request for this servlet comes in. Because the application's welcome page relies on initialization performed by the controller, such as setting up the message resource bundle, we provide a `<load-on-startup>` tag so that the controller is instantiated straight away:

```xml
<servlet>
  <servlet-name>controller</servlet-name>
  <servlet-class>
    org.apache.struts.action.ActionServlet
  </servlet-class>
  <load-on-startup>1</load-on-startup>
</servlet>

<servlet-mapping>
  <servlet-name>controller</servlet-name>
  <url-pattern>*.do</url-pattern>
</servlet-mapping>

<welcome-file-list>
  <welcome-file>index.jsp</welcome-file>
</welcome-file-list>

<error-page>
  <exception-type>java.lang.Exception</exception-type>
  <location>/error.jsp</location>
</error-page>
```

The resources that should be accessible only by an authenticated user with the `user` role are:

❑   `/book/*` – any modification of books or book news items

❑   `/login.do` – so that the login screen appears when the user clicks Login

We declare the `editor` role as well, but handle the difference between users and editors completely programmatically because it doesn't map cleanly to URLs:

```xml
<security-constraint>
  <web-resource-collection>
    <web-resource-name>View or Edit Books</web-resource-name>
```

```
      <url-pattern>/book/*</url-pattern>
      <url-pattern>/login.do</url-pattern>
    </web-resource-collection>
    <auth-constraint>
      <role-name>user</role-name>
    </auth-constraint>
  </security-constraint>

  <login-config>
    <auth-method>FORM</auth-method>
    <form-login-config>
      <form-login-page>/login.jsp</form-login-page>
      <form-error-page>/login.jsp</form-error-page>
    </form-login-config>
  </login-config>

  <security-role>
    <description>Publish Editor</description>
    <role-name>editor</role-name>
  </security-role>
  <security-role>
    <description>Publish User</description>
    <role-name>user</role-name>
  </security-role>

</web-app>
```

Building the Application

Finally, we need to put all the pieces together. Here's a recap of where our files should be found:

1. Use the `mysql` command-line interface to create all the database tables from the scripts we described at the start of this chapter. If you downloaded the code, the script can be found as `create-tables.sql` in this chapter's code folder.

2. We need to put all the pieces of the web application itself together. Create a folder called `publish`, inside Tomcat's `webapps` folder, to hold all the pieces of our application; its name will be something like `C:\jakarta-tomcat-5.0\webapps\publish`. This will be the root directory of the application.

3. The following files go straight into the root directory:

   `book.jsp`

   `booknews.jsp`

   `error.jsp`

   `index.jsp`

   `login.jsp`

The other JSP pages go into the `contents` and `templates` subdirectories of the root:

contents/

    bookform.jsp

    booklist.jsp

    booknewsform.jsp

    login.jsp

templates/

    default.css

    default.jsp

    portal.jsp

The configuration files go into the `WEB-INF` subdirectory. For `validator-rules.xml` we can use the copy of the file that ships with Struts in its `lib` directory.

WEB-INF/

    struts-config.xml

    validation.xml

    validator-rules.xml

    web.xml

Create a `WEB-INF/lib` directory and copy all `*.jar` files from the `lib` directories of both JSTL and Struts into it. You need only the jars – you do not need any of the `*.tld`, `*.dtd` or `*.xml` files that also live in Struts' `lib` directory. Finally, copy the MySQL JDBC driver file (`mm.mysql-2.0.14-bin.jar` or similar) into the `WEB-INF/lib` directory as well.

WEB-INF/lib/

    *.jar

The Java source files and the resource bundle go into `WEB-INF/classes`.

WEB-INF/classes/com/wrox/publish

    PublishException.java

WEB-INF/classes/com/wrox/publish/action

    AddBookAction.java

    AddBookNewsAction.java

    EditBookAction.java

    EditBookNewsAction.java

LogoutAction.java

PerformBookAUDAction.java

PerformBookNewsAUDAction.java

WEB-INF/classes/com/wrox/publish/bo

ActionDeniedException.java

BookBO.java

WEB-INF/classes/com/wrox/publish/db

BookDAO.java

BookNewsDAO.java

EntityNotFoundException.java

InvalidFieldException.java

WEB-INF/classes/com/wrox/publish/om

Book.java

BookNews.java

WEB-INF/classes/resources

publish.properties

4. Compile all the Java classes. You need both `servlet.jar` (the Sun Servlet API) and the Struts `struts.jar` file in the `CLASSPATH` for this to work. You'll find that in the code download for the book we've provided a Windows batch file `compile.bat` in the `WEB-INF\classes` directory; running this will compile all the code for you.

5. Finally, add an authentication realm to Tomcat. To do this, you need to add two entries to Tomcat's `server.xml` file. You may find this file a bit intimidating; by all means, make a backup before you start. What you need to do is find the bit near the top of the file where it says:

```
        .
        .
        .
    </ResourceParams>

  </GlobalNamingResources>
        .
        .
        .
```

Add the following immediately before the `</GlobalNamingResources>` closing tag:

```
  .
  .
  .
</ResourceParams>
```

```
<Resource name="PublishUsers" auth="Container"
          type="org.apache.catalina.UserDatabase"
   description="User database for the Publish application">
</Resource>
<ResourceParams name="PublishUsers">
   <parameter>
     <name>factory</name>
     <value>
       org.apache.catalina.users.MemoryUserDatabaseFactory
     </value>
   </parameter>
   <parameter>
     <name>pathname</name>
     <value>conf/publish-users.xml</value>
   </parameter>
</ResourceParams>
```

```
</GlobalNamingResources>
  .
  .
  .
```

This tells Tomcat to set up an authentication database called `PublishUsers` that reads its information from a file called `publish-users.xml` in the Tomcat configuration directory. Then find the bit about three-quarters of the way through where it says:

```
        .
        .
        .
      </Context>

    </Host>

   </Engine>

 </Service>
   .
   .
   .
```

Add the following immediately before the `</Host>` closing tag:

```
      .
      .
      .
    </Context>

    <Context path="/publish" docBase="publish" debug="0"
            reloadable="true">
      <Realm debug="0" resourceName="PublishUsers"
          className="org.apache.catalina.realm.UserDatabaseRealm"/>
    </Context>

  </Host>
      .
      .
      .
```

This associates the application with a **security realm** that uses `PublishUsers` for its authentication information. This concept is described in Chapter 13, but in essence, a realm denotes a logical group of users, roles, and access control lists. The application now has a realm of its own, but if you later develop a separate but related application used by the same users in similar roles, it probably makes sense to have that application share the same security realm.

6. Save the following file as `publish-users.xml` in the Tomcat configuration directory (`conf`):

```
<?xml version='1.0'?>
<tomcat-users>
  <role rolename="user"/>
  <role rolename="editor"/>
  <user username="user" password="user"
        fullName="Uwe Ser" roles="user"/>
  <user username="editor" password="editor"
        fullName="Edward Ditor" roles="user,editor"/>
</tomcat-users>
```

This file sets up two users, `user` who is an ordinary user, and `editor` who is, you guessed it, an editor. Their passwords are identical to their usernames. Not exactly an example of good security, but it keeps things simple for our example!

7. All done. To run the application, you need to start your MySQL database, start Tomcat, and point your web browser to http://localhost:8080/publish/. And explore!

Summary

In this final chapter, we have put together everything we've learned in the book to architect and develop a real world web application built on Struts. We covered:

- ❏ Some requirements analysis including screenshots, the requirements catalog, and use case UML diagrams

- ❏ Using the Model 2 Model-View-Controller architecture to properly partition the web application

- ❏ The detailed design of the Model part of MVC using a Java object model, business objects, and data access objects, using some UML class diagrams

- ❏ The impedance mismatch between an object model and a database model, and some aspects of object/relational mapping

- ❏ All important aspects of the Struts framework, including actions, validation, and error handling

- ❏ Dynamic templates using the Struts template tag library to separate generic site layout from page-specific content

- ❏ The use of a Struts `DataSource` and proper handling of connections and transactions

- ❏ Various aspects of security, including form-based authentication and both declarative and programmatic authorization

- ❏ Internationalization using locales, resource bundles, and the Struts internationalization support

- ❏ Deployment of the application on the Tomcat server

- ❏ And of course JSP pages, the JSP Expression Language, and most JSTL taglibs

We've come a long way since the start of the book; we hope you're now confident and eager to get developing your own web applications using JSP, Servlets, and Java. Have fun!

Why Not Try?

If you would like to expand your JSP, Struts, and Java knowledge, there are a number of directions you could take the case study.

Convert the Application to Use a JNDI DataSource

Chapter 13 discussed how the application server can provide a web application with a `DataSource` using JNDI. Compared to a Struts `DataSource` this takes a bit more work. An important advantage is that the person deploying the application will not have to modify `struts-config.xml` file to provide the right database details. Ideally, a web application is a sealed unit, possibly packaged in a WAR archive, which can be deployed without modification.

BookBO would be a good place to put the JNDI lookup code. It would be something along the following lines:

```
Context ctx = new InitialContext();
DataSource ds = (DataSource)ctx.lookup("java:comp/env/jdbc/PublishDB");
```

As you would not expect the DataSource to change while the application was running, you could call this code from the BookBO.getInstance() factory method and store the acquired DataSource in a static variable. You would be able to remove the DataSource argument from the getInstance() method, and the action classes can be divested of any responsibility for database access. Don't forget to modify the <sql:query> tags in booklist.jsp and booknewslist.jsp!

Add a Portlet displaying a News Feed

The publishing application's home page is, in effect, a miniature portal page. Underneath the news item list, there is an empty portlet (number 4) waiting to be used. What about taking a news feed, for example about the book publishing industry?

http://www.moreover.com/cgi-local/page?o=rss&c=Book%20publishing%20news provides an around-the-clock aggregated feed of publishing-related news. If you type this URL in a browser, you will see an XML file in RSS format. This is a very simple format widely used to syndicate headlines around the Internet. You can use the JSTL Core and XML tags to retrieve the feed, parse it, and loop through the headlines:

```
<c:import var="feedXml"
          url="http://www.moreover.com/cgi-
               local/page?o=rss&c=Book%20publishing%20news" />
<x:parse var="feed" xml="${feedXml}"/>
<x:forEach select="$feed/rss/channel/item" var="item">
  <tr><td class="title"><x:out select="$item/title"></td></tr>
  .
  .
  .
</x:forEach>
```

For more information about RSS, see http://my.netscape.com/publish/formats/rss-spec-0.91.html. One of the best places to find out about the feeds available is Syndic8, http://www.syndic8.com. One last word of warning: the approach above retrieves the news feed every time the page is requested. This is fine for experimental purposes but not a good idea in production environments, because of the resultant load on the RSS server among other things. In the real world, you would use a local copy of the feed which is refreshed every half an hour or so.

Add an International Price List

In the *Adding More Locales* section, we looked at a possible requirement to hold multiple prices for a book, corresponding to different countries. This could be modeled as a `BookPrice` object having a book, a price, and a country abbreviation; a `Book` would have a `Collection` or `List` of `BookPrice` objects associated with it. The object would be mapped to a new `book_price` table. It would all work in much the same way that the `BookNews` object does. As the exchange rate between currencies is only one of the factors affecting price differences between countries, it is best to treat each price independently.

The Book Maintenance form could be modified to show, where possible, the price for the current user's country. The country is part of the full `Locale` (`Locale.getCountry()`), and we can get the user's locale either from a request object, from `getLocale()` inside an `Action`, or from the `Locale` object that the Struts controller stores in the session with the name `org.apache.struts.action.LOCALE`. This price would also be editable. If you feel really ambitious, you could add new pages allowing an editor to view and maintain the full price list for a book.

APPENDIX A

JSP Syntax Reference

This appendix describes the syntax for JavaServer Pages 2.0. Our intention is to provide you with a reference that is complete and useful, but more compact than the specification. (The JSP 2.0 Proposed Final Draft specification weighs in at 415 pages!)

> JSP specifications from version 2.0 upwards are available by visiting http://java.sun.com/products/jsp/.

This appendix looks in turn at:

- ❑ Various preliminary details: the notation we're using, how URLs are specified in JSP code, and the various types of commenting you can use.

- ❑ The JSP **directives** – the `page`, `taglib`, and `include` directives.

- ❑ JSP **scripting elements** – declarations, scriptlets, and expressions.

- ❑ JSP's **standard actions** including the `<jsp:useBean>`, `<jsp:setProperty>`, `<jsp:getProperty>`, `<jsp:include>`, and `<jsp:forward>` actions.

- ❑ A brief review of the syntax for using **tag libraries**.

- ❑ The **implicit objects** that are available within a JSP such as `request`, `response`, `session`, and `application`. We will cover these in more detail in Appendix B – *JSP Implicit Objects*.

- ❑ Various predefined request and application **attributes** that you may find useful.

Preliminaries

Before we get stuck into the details, a few miscellaneous observations.

Notation

A word on the notation we've used in this appendix:

- ❑ *Italics* show what you'll have to specify.

- ❑ **Bold** shows the default value of an attribute. Attributes with default values are optional, if you're using the default. Sometimes, where the default value is a little complicated, we use **default** to indicate that the default is described in the following text.

- ❑ When an attribute has a set of possible values, those are shown delimited by |.

```
import="package.class, package.*, ..."
session="true|false"
```

URL Specifications

URLs specified within JSP tags can be of two sorts:

- ❑ **Context-relative** paths start with a "/"; the base URL is provided by the web application to which the JSP belongs. For example, in a web application hosted at http://localhost:8080/begjsp-appendixA/, the URL `/pageurl.jsp` would be equivalent to http://localhost:8080/begjsp-appendixA/pageurl.jsp.

- ❑ **Page-relative** paths are relative to the JSP page in which they occur. Unlike context-relative paths, page-relative paths do not start with "/". For instance, a page application hosted at http://localhost:8080/begjsp-appendixA/morespecs/urlspec.jsp might give a page as `subfolder/urlspec.jsp`, which would be equivalent to http://localhost:8080/begjsp-appendixA/morespecs/subfolder/urlspec.jsp.

Comments

Two sorts of comments are allowed in JSP code – JSP and HTML:

```
<!-- HTML comments remain in the final client page.
     They can contain JSP expressions, which will be ignored by the JSP
     container.
-->

<%-- JSP comments are hidden from the final client page --%>
```

Remember too that within scriptlets (inside <% %>, <%! %>, or <%= %> tags), you can use standard Java comments:

```
<%
   /* This Java comment starts with a slash asterisk, and continues
      until we come to a closing asterisk slash
```

```
    */

    // Comments starting with a double slash continue to the end of the line
%>
```

Directives

Directives are instructions to the JSP container regarding page properties, importing tag libraries, and including content within a JSP; because directives are instructions rather than in-out processes, they can not produce any output via the `out` stream.

The page Directive

The `page` directive specifies attributes for the page – all the attributes are optional, as the essential ones have default values, shown in bold.

```
<%@ page language="java"
        extends="package.class"
        import="package.class, package.*, ..."
        session="true|false"
        buffer="none|default|sizekb"
        autoFlush="true|false"
        isThreadSafe="true|false"
        info="Sample JSP to show tags"
        isErrorPage="true|false"
        errorPage="ErrorPage.jsp"
        contentType="TYPE|
                     TYPE; charset=CHARSET|
                     text/html; charset=ISO-8859-1"
        pageEncoding="default"
%>
```

- ❑ The default buffer size is defined to be *at least* 8kb.

- ❑ The `errorPage` attribute contains the relative URL for the error page to which this page should go if there's an un-handled error on this page.

- ❑ The specified error page file must declare `isErrorPage="true"` to have access to the `Exception` object.

- ❑ The `contentType` attribute sets the MIME type and the character set for the response. The default value is `"text/html"` for standard JSP Pages and `"text/xml"` when implementing JSP Documents in XML format.

- ❑ The `pageEncoding` attribute defines the character encoding for the JSP page. The default is that specified in the `contentType` attribute, or `"ISO-8859-1"` if none was specified there.

This is an example of the code that may be used for an error page:

```
<%@ page language="java"
         isErrorPage="true" %>

<html>
  <body>
    <!-- This displays the fully-qualified name of the exception -->
    <%= exception.toString() %>
    <br>

    <!-- This displays the exception's descriptive message -->
    <%= exception.getMessage() %>
  </body>
</html>
```

The page will print out the error message received.

This directive can also switch on support for scripting and EL in the JSP document, using the following two attributes:

❑   isScriptingEnabled – sets scripting support.

❑   isELEnabled – sets EL (Expression Language) support. Settings in web.xml may influence the behavior of this attribute.

For both of these attributes, a value of true enables support, false disables it, and the default values are both true.

The taglib Directive

A tag library is a collection of tags used to extend a JSP container functional model. The taglib directive defines a tag library namespace for the page, mapping the URI of the tag library descriptor to a prefix that can be used to reference tags from the library on this page.

```
<%@ taglib uri (or tagdir)="/WEB-INF/taglib.tld" prefix="tagPrefix" %>

    .
    .
    .

<tagPrefix:tagName attributeName="attributeValue" >
  JSP content
</tagPrefix:tagName>

<tagPrefix:tagName attributeName="attributeValue" />
```

We assume that the tag library descriptor (TLD) defines a tagName element.

`tagdir` indicates this prefix is to be used to identify tag extensions installed in the `/WEB-INF/tags/` directory or a subdirectory. If a `tld` is present in the specified directory, it is used. Otherwise, an implicit tag library is used. A translation error must occur if the value does not start with `/WEB-INF/tags/`. A translation error must occur if the value does not point to a directory that exists. A translation error must occur if used in conjunction with the `uri` attribute.

The File Tag Directive

Most JSP directives can be used in simple tag handler code files. Note that the `page` directive itself isn't used, and instead we use the `tag` directive, which may only be used in tag files. The directives available are:

- ❑ `taglib` – used just as in JSP pages
- ❑ `include` – used just as in JSP pages
- ❑ `tag` – only available in tag files
- ❑ `attribute` – only available in tag files
- ❑ `variable` – only available in tag files
- ❑ `fragment-input` – only available in tag files

Here's an example `tag` directive:

```
<%@ tag name="msg"
   display-name="Message"
   body-content="scriptless"
   dynamic-attributes="true"
   small-icon="/WEB-INF/small-icon.jpg"
   large-icon="/WEB-INF/large-icon.jpg"
   description="Simple usage of a tag directive"
%>
```

The include Directive

There are two include tags – the `include` directive and the `jsp:include` action.

The `include` directive includes a static file at translation time, adding any JSP in that file to this page for runtime processing:

```
<%@ include file="header.html" %>
```

See also the `jsp:include` action.

Scripting Elements

Scripting elements are used to include snippets of Java code within a JSP: to declare variables and methods, execute arbitrary Java code, and display the result of Java expressions.

Declarations

The following syntax allows you to declare variables and methods for the page. These are placed in the generated servlet *outside* the _jspService() method, in other words variables declared here will be instance variables of the servlet. Declarations do not produce any output:

Here's an example of declaring a variable:

```
<%! String  message; %>
```

The code below declares a variable and initializes it:

```
<%! String message = "variable declarared"; %>
```

We can define a method for use on the global page like so:

```
<%! public String showMessage() { return message; } %>
```

Declaration tags are mainly used in conjunction with scriptlets.

Scriptlets

Scriptlets enclose Java code (on however many lines) that is evaluated *within* the generated servlet's _jspService() method to generate dynamic content:

```
<%
  // Java code
%>
```

Take care when using adjacent scriptlet blocks – this code:

```
<% if(user.isLoggedIn) { %>
    <p>Hi!</p>
<% } %>
<% else { %>
    <p>Please log in first...</p>
<% } %>
```

is not legal since we've broken the else block into two scriptlets.

Expressions

Expressions return a value from the scripting code as a `String` to the page:

```
<p>Hello there,
<%= userName %>
Good to see you.</p>
```

Standard Actions

The standard actions provide various facilities for manipulating JavaBeans components, including and forwarding control to other resources at request-time, and generating HTML to use the Java Plug-in.

<jsp:useBean>

The `<jsp:useBean>` tag checks for an instance of a bean of the given `class` and `scope`. If a bean of the specified class exists it references it with the `id`, otherwise it instantiates it. The bean is available within its `scope` with its `id` attribute.

You can include code between the `<jsp:useBean>` tags, as shown in the second example – this code will only be run if the `<jsp:useBean>` tag successfully instantiated the bean:

```
<jsp:useBean id="aBeanName"
             scope="page|request|session|application",
             typeSpecification
/>
```

or:

```
<jsp:useBean id="anotherBeanName"
             scope="page|request|session|application"
             typeSpecification
>
  <jsp.setProperty name="anotherBeanName"
                   property="*|propertyName" />
</jsp:useBean>
```

There is a lot of flexibility in specifying the type of the bean (indicated by `typeSpecification` above). You can use:

❑ `class="package.class"`

❑ `type="typeName"`

❑ `class="package.class" type="typeName"` (and with terms reversed)

❑ `beanName="beanName" type="typeName"` (and with terms reversed)

763

where:

- ❑ typeName is the class of the scripting variable defined by the id attribute; that is, the class that the Bean instance is cast to (whether the class, a parent class or an interface the class implements).

- ❑ beanName is the name of the Bean, as used in the instantiate() method of the java.beans.Beans class.

<jsp:setProperty>

The <jsp:setProperty> tag we used above sets the property of the bean referenced by name using the value:

```
<jsp.setProperty name="anotherBeanName"
                  propertyExpression
/>
```

The *propertyExpression* can be any of the following:

- ❑ property="*"
- ❑ property="*propertyName*"
- ❑ property="*propertyName*" param="*parameterName*"
- ❑ property="*propertyName*" value="*propertyValue*"

where:

- ❑ The * setting tells the tag to iterate through the request parameters for the page, setting any values for properties in the Bean whose names match parameter names.

- ❑ The param attribute specifies the parameter name to use in setting this property.

- ❑ The value attribute can be any runtime expression as long as it evaluates to a String.

- ❑ Omitting value and param attributes for a property assumes that the Bean property and request parameter name match.

- ❑ The value attribute String can be automatically cast to boolean, byte, char, double, int, float, long, and their class equivalents. Other casts will have to be handled explicitly in the Bean's set*PropertyName*() method.

<jsp:getProperty>

The final bean-handling action is <jsp:getProperty>, which gets the named property and outputs its value for inclusion in the page as a String:

```
<jsp:getProperty name="anotherBeanName" property="propertyName" />
```

<jsp:param>

The `<jsp:param>` action is used within the body of `<jsp:forward>`, `<jsp:include>`, and `<jsp:plugin>` to supply extra name-value parameter pairs. It has the following syntax:

```
<jsp:param name="parameterName" value="parameterValue" />
```

<jsp:forward>

To forward the client request to a static resource, whether it be an HTML file, a JSP page, or a servlet class in the same context as the page, use the following syntax:

```
<jsp:forward page="relativeURL" />
```

or:

```
<jsp:forward page="relativeURL" >
  <jsp:param name="parameterName" value="parameterValue" />
</jsp:forward>
```

where:

- ❏ The `page` attribute for `<jsp:forward>` can be a runtime expression

- ❏ The `value` attribute for `<jsp:param>` can be a runtime expression

<jsp:include>

The `<jsp:include>` action includes a static or dynamically-referenced file at runtime:

```
<jsp:include page="relativeURL" flush="true|false" />
```

or:

```
<jsp:include page="relativeURL"
             flush="true" >
  <jsp:param name="parameterName" value="parameterValue"/>
</jsp:include>
```

where:

- ❏ The `page` attribute can be the result of some run-time expression.

- ❏ The optional `flush` attribute determines whether the output buffer will be flushed before including the specified resource. The default value is `"false"`. (Note that in JSP 1.1 this attribute was mandatory and the only permissible value was `"true"`.)

❑ The jsp:param tag allows parameters to be appended to the original request, and if the parameter name already exists, the new parameter value takes precedence, in a comma-delimited list.

<jsp:plugin>

The <jsp:plugin> action enables the JSP to include a bean or an applet in the client page. It has the following syntax:

```
<jsp:plugin type="bean|applet"
            code="class"
            codebase="classDirectory"
            name="instanceName"
            archive="archiveURI"
            align="bottom|top|middle|left|right"
            height="inPixels"
            width="inPixels"
            hspace="leftRightPixels"
            vspace="topBottomPixels"
            jreversion="1.2|number"
            nspluginurl="pluginURL"
            iepluginurl="pluginURL" >
  <jsp:params>
    <jsp:param name="parameterName" value="parameterValue">
  </jsp:params>
  <jsp:fallback>Problem with plugin</jsp:fallback>
</jsp:plugin>
```

Most of these attributes are direct from the HTML spec (http://www.w3.org/TR/html4/) – the exceptions are type, jreversion, nspluginurl, and iepluginurl.

❑ The name, archive, align, height, width, hspace, vspace, jreversion, nspluginurl, and iepluginurl attributes are optional.

❑ The <jsp:param> tag's value attribute can take a runtime expression.

❑ The jreversion is the Java Runtime Environment specification version that the component requires.

❑ nspluginurl and iepluginurl are the URL where the Java plug-in can be downloaded for Netscape Navigator and Internet Explorer.

Tag Libraries

The syntax for using tag libraries is very similar to that for the standard actions, except of course that the tag names and attributes are defined in the tag library itself rather than by the JSP standard. Each tag library is associated with a **prefix**, by using the taglib directive to map the prefix to a URI identifying the tag library. For example, using the Jakarta Taglibs project's request tag library (http://jakarta.apache.org/taglibs/doc/request-doc/intro.html):

```
<%@ taglib uri="http://jakarta.apache.org/taglibs/request-1.0" prefix="req"
%>
```

Within the JSP, tags from the library can then be used by using the prefix defined in the `taglib` directive and the tag's name, for example:

```
<req:attributes id="loop">
  Name: <jsp:getProperty name="loop" property="name"/>
  Value: <jsp:getProperty name="loop" property="value"/>
</req:attributes>
```

The mapping between a particular URI (as used in the `taglib` directive) and the tag library descriptor can be set up in one of two ways. In JSP 1.2, it is possible to package tag libraries so that the mapping is automatic, based on settings contained in the tag library descriptor file. Alternatively, an entry can be made in the `web.xml` file to map a URI to a tag library descriptor file:

```
<taglib>
  <taglib-uri>http://jakarta.apache.org/taglibs/request-1.0</taglib-uri>
  <taglib-location>/WEB-INF/request.tld</taglib-location>
</taglib>
```

Implicit Objects

JSP defines a number of implicit objects that JSP scripting elements can make use of:

- ❑ request, of type `javax.servlet.http.HttpServletRequest`
- ❑ response, of type `javax.servlet.http.HttpServletResponse`
- ❑ out, of type `javax.servlet.jsp.JspWriter`
- ❑ session, of type `javax.servlet.http.HttpSession`
- ❑ application, of type `javax.servlet.ServletContext`
- ❑ exception, of type `java.lang.Throwable`
- ❑ config, of type `javax.servlet.ServletConfig`
- ❑ page, a reference to the implementing servlet class for the JSP
- ❑ pageContext, of type `javax.servlet.jsp.PageContext`

Appendix B gives details of these objects, and the methods that each makes available. There are many more classes and interfaces defined by the JSP and servlet specifications; to find out more about them, you should consult the online documentation as described in Appendix D.

Predefined Attributes

The servlet and JSP specifications define a number of special request and context (application) attributes.

Security-related Attributes

These attributes are only available when a request has been made over SSL. SSL, the Secure Sockets Layer, allows us to set up secure communications between the server and a client.

javax.servlet.request.cipher_suite

`javax.servlet.request.cipher_suite` is a request attribute of type `String` containing the **cipher suite** used for an SSL request.

javax.servlet.request.key_size

`javax.servlet.request.key_size` is a request attribute of type `Integer` containing the bit size that was used for an SSL request.

Here's an example:

```
public boolean isOver128bit(HttpServletRequest request)
{
   Integer reqSize = (Integer) request.getAttribute(
                          "javax.servlet.request.key_size");
   if(reqSize != null)
   {
     if (reqSize.intValue() < 128)
     {
       return false;
     }
     else
     {
       return true;
     }
   }
}
```

javax.servlet.request.X509Certificate

`javax.servlet.request.X509Certificate` is a request attribute of type `java.security.cert.X509Certificate` containing any certificate associated with an SSL request.

Inclusion-related Attributes

These attributes apply when a servlet or JSP is accessed via a `<jsp:include>` or a `RequestDispatcher.include()` like so:

```
request.getRequestDispatcher("servelt_path/myservlet").forward(req, res);
```

javax.servlet.include.request_uri

`javax.servlet.include.request_uri` is a request attribute of type `String` containing the URI under which this included servlet or JSP is being accessed.

```
String reqURI = (String) request.getAttribute(
                         "javax.servlet.include.request_uri");
```

javax.servlet.include.context_path

`javax.servlet.include.context_path` is a request attribute of type `String` containing the context path of the URI under which this included servlet or JSP is being accessed.

```
String contextPath = (String) req.getAttribute(
                         "javax.servlet.include.context_path");
```

javax.servlet.include.path_info

`javax.servlet.include.path_info` is a request attribute of type `String` containing the path info of the URI under which this included servlet or JSP is being accessed.

```
String pathInfo = (String) req.getAttribute(
                         "javax.servlet.include.path_info");
```

javax.servlet.include.servlet_path

`javax.servlet.include.servlet_path` is a request attribute of type `String` containing the servlet path of the URI under which this included servlet or JSP is being accessed.

```
String pathInfo;

if(req.getAttribute("javax.servlet.include.servlet_path") != null)
{
  pathInfo = (String)req.getAttribute("javax.servlet.include.path_info");
}
```

javax.servlet.include.query_string

`javax.servlet.include.query_string` is a request attribute of type `String` containing the query string of the URI under which this included servlet or JSP is being accessed.

```
String reqQueryString = req.getAttribute(
                         "javax.servlet.include.query_string");
```

Servlet Error Page Attributes

These attributes are only available within an error page declared in `web.xml`.

javax.servlet.error.status_code

`javax.servlet.error.status_code` is a request attribute of type `Integer` containing the status code of the servlet or JSP that caused the error.

```
Integer statusCode = (Integer) req.getAttribute(
                          "javax.servlet.error.status_code");
String error = "HTTP Status Code - " + statusCode.intValue();

return error;
```

javax.servlet.error.exception_type

`javax.servlet.error.exception_type` is a request attribute of type `Class` that contains the type of the exception thrown by the servlet or JSP. It is now redundant with the introduction of the `javax.servlet.error.exception` attribute.

```
Exception e = (Exception) req.getAttribute(
                          "javax.servlet.error.exception_type");
```

javax.servlet.error.message

`javax.servlet.error.message` is a request attribute of type `String` containing the message contained within the exception thrown by the servlet or JSP. It is now redundant with the introduction of the `javax.servlet.error.exception` attribute.

```
String statusCode = (String) req.getAttribute(
                          "javax.servlet.error.status_code");

String message= (String)req.getAttribute("javax.servlet.error.message");

if message == null)
{
  message = "Unknown error";
}
```

javax.servlet.error.exception

javax.servlet.error.exception is a request attribute of type Throwable containing the exception thrown by the servlet or JSP.

```
public void doGet(HttpServletRequest req, HttpServletResponse res)
                            throws ServletException, IOException {

PrintWriter out = res.getWriter();

Throwable = (Throwable) req.getAttribute(
                        "javax.servlet.error.exception");

 .
 .
 .

if (throwable != null)
  throwable.printStackTrace(out);
 .
 .
 .
```

javax.servlet.error.request_uri

javax.servlet.error.request_uri is a request attribute of type String containing the URI of the request that caused the servlet or JSP to throw an exception.

```
String reqErrorUri = (String) req.getAttribute("
                            javax.servlet.error.request_uri");
```

JSP Error Page Attributes

This attribute is available within error pages declared in a JSP page directive.

javax.servlet.jsp.jspException

javax.servlet.jsp.jspException is a request attribute of type Throwable containing the exception thrown by the JSP page.

```
<%
 .
  try
  {
    InputStream in = pageContext.getServletContext()
                    .getResourceAsStream(fileName);

    if(in == null )
```

771

```
    {
        throw new JspException( "Error while opening file: '"+ fileName + "'");
    }
}

catch(Exception ex )
{
    .

    .

    .
}
%>
```

Temporary File Directory Attribute

This attribute allows a web application to make use of a temporary working directory.

javax.servlet.context.tempdir

`javax.servlet.context.tempdir` is a context attribute of type `java.io.File` referencing a temporary working directory that can be used by the web application.

```
File tempDir = (File) getServletContext()
                    .getAttribute("javax.servlet.context.tempdir");
```

APPENDIX B

JSP Implicit Objects

JSP defines a number of implicit objects that scripting elements can make use of. This appendix gives details of these objects, and the methods that each of them exposes. There are many more classes and interfaces defined by the JSP and servlet specifications; to find out more about them, you should consult the online documentation as described in Appendix D.

*This appendix lists **all** the methods available for each object (except those defined in `java.lang.Object`), irrespective of which class or interface defines the methods.*

The implicit objects are:

❑ request
❑ response
❑ out
❑ session
❑ application
❑ exception
❑ config
❑ page
❑ pageContext

The request Object

The `request` object is an instance of a class that implements the `javax.servlet.http.HttpServletRequest` interface. It represents the request made by the client, and makes the following methods available:

```
public Object getAttribute(String name)
```

getAttribute() returns the value of the specified request attribute name. The return value is an `Object` or sub-class if the attribute is available to the invoking `ServletRequest` object, or `null` if the attribute is not available.

```
public java.util.Enumeration getAttributeNames()
```

getAttributeNames() returns an `Enumeration` containing the attribute names available to the invoking `ServletRequest` object.

```
public String getAuthType()
```

getAuthType() returns the name of the authentication scheme used in the request, or `null` if no authentication scheme was used. It returns one of the constants `BASIC_AUTH`, `FORM_AUTH`, `CLIENT_CERT_AUTH`, or `DIGEST_AUTH`, or `null` if the request was not authenticated.

```
public String getCharacterEncoding()x
```

getCharacterEncoding() returns a `String` object containing the character encoding used in the body of the request, or `null` if there is no encoding.

```
public int getContentLength()
```

getContentLength() returns the length of the body of the request in bytes, or -1 if the length is not known.

```
public String getContentType()
```

getContentType() returns a `String` object containing the MIME type ("text/plain", "text/html", "image/gif", etc.) of the body of the request, or `null` if the type is not known.

```
public String getContextPath()
```

getContextPath() returns the part of the request URI that indicates the context path of the request. The context path is the first part of the URI and always begins with the "/" character. For servlets running in the root context, this method returns an empty `String`. For example if there is an incoming request from request: http://localhost/guide/suburbs/index.jsp then getContextPath() would return "/guide"

```
public Cookie[] getCookies()
```

getCookies() returns an array containing any `Cookie` objects sent with the request, or `null` if no cookies were sent.

```
public long getDateHeader(String name)
```

getDateHeader() returns a long value that converts the date specified in the named header to the number of milliseconds since January 1, 1970 GMT. This method is used with a header that contains a date, and returns −1 if the request does not contain the specified header.

```
public String getHeader(String name)
```

getHeader() returns the value of the specified header expressed as a String object, or null if the request does not contain the specified header. Here is an example HTTP request:

```
GET /search?index=servlets+jsp HTTP/1.1
Accept: image/gif, image/jpg, */*
Accept-Encoding: gzip
Connection: Keep-Alive
Cookie: userID=id66589
Host: www.mycompany.com
Referer: http://www.mycompany.com/getproducts.html
User-Agent: Mozilla/4.6 [en] (WinXP; U)
```

For example, if the usage is getRequest("Connection"), it would return "Keep-Alive"

```
public java.util.Enumeration getHeaderNames()
```

getHeaderNames() returns an Enumeration containing all of the header names used by the request.

```
public java.util.Enumeration getHeaders(String name)
```

getHeaders() returns an Enumeration containing all of the values associated with the specified header name. The method returns an empty enumeration if the request does not contain the specified header.

```
public ServletInputStream getInputStream()
        throws java.io.IOException
```

getInputStream() returns a ServletInputStream object that can be used to read the body of the request as binary data.

```
public int getIntHeader(String name)
```

getIntHeader() returns the value of the specified header as an int. It returns −1 if the request does not contain the specified header, and throws a NumberFormatException if the header value cannot be converted to an int. This method was made for convenience when the header type is known to be an integer, this way it can be absorbed by the code without any conversion.

```
public java.util.Locale getLocale()
```

getLocale() returns the preferred locale of the client that made the request.

    public java.util.Enumeration **getLocales**()

getLocales() returns an Enumeration containing, in descending order of preference, the locales that are acceptable to the client machine.

    public String **getMethod**()

getMethod() returns the name of the HTTP method used to make the request. Typical return values are "GET", "POST", or "PUT".

    public String **getParameter**(String *name*)

getParameter() returns a String object containing the value of the specified parameter, or null if the parameter does not exist.

    public java.util.Map **getParameterMap**()

getParameterMap() returns a Map containing the request parameters.

    public java.util.Enumeration **getParameterNames**()

getParameterNames() returns a Enumeration containing the parameters contained within the invoking ServletRequest object.

    public String[] **getParameterValues**(String *name*)

getParameterValues() is used when a parameter may have more than one value associated with it. The method returns a String array containing the values of the specified parameter, or null if the parameter does not exist.

    public String **getPathInfo**()

getPathInfo() returns any additional path information contained in the request URL. This extra information will be after the servlet path and before the query string. It returns null if there is no additional path information. For example, in the incoming request from http://localhost/guide/suburbs/innersuburbs/ then getContextPath() would return "/innersuburbs"

    public String **getPathTranslated**()

`getPathTranslated()` returns the same information as the `getPathInfo()` method, but translated into a real path.

```
public String getProtocol()
```

`getProtocol()` returns the name and version of the protocol used by the request. A typical return `String` would be `"HTTP/1.1"`.

```
public String getQueryString()
```

`getQueryString()` returns the query string that was contained in the request URL without any decoding from the container, or `null` if there was no query string.

```
public java.io.BufferedReader getReader()
        throws java.io.IOException
```

`getReader()` returns a `BufferedReader` object that can be used to read the body of the request as character data.

```
public String getRemoteAddr()
```

`getRemoteAddr()` returns a `String` object containing the IP address of the client machine that made the request.

```
public String getRemoteHost()
```

`getRemoteHost()` returns a `String` object containing the name of the client machine or the IP address if the name cannot be determined.

```
public String getRemoteUser()
```

`getRemoteUser()` returns the login of the user making the request, or `null` if the user has not been authenticated.

```
public RequestDispatcher getRequestDispatcher(String path)
```

`getRequestDispatcher()` returns a `RequestDispatcher` object that acts as a wrapper around the resource located at the specified path. The path must begin with `"/"` and can be a relative path.

```
public String getRequestedSessionId()
```

getRequestedSessionId() returns the session ID that was specified by the client, or null if the request did not specify an ID.

```
public String getRequestURI()
```

getRequestURI() returns a sub-section of the request URL, from the protocol name to the query string.

```
public StringBuffer getRequestURL()
```

getRequestURL() reconstructs the URL used to make the request including the protocol, server name, port number, and path, but excluding the query string.

```
public String getScheme()
```

getScheme() returns the scheme ("http", "https", "ftp", etc.) used to make the request.

```
public String getServerName()
```

getServerName() returns a String object containing the name of the server that received the request.

```
public int getServerPort()
```

getServerPort() returns the port number that received the request.

```
public String getServletPath()
```

getServletPath() returns the part of the request URL that was used to call the servlet, without any additional information or the query string.

```
public HttpSession getSession(boolean create)
public HttpSession getSession()
```

getSession() returns the HttpSession object associated with the request. By default, if the request does not currently have a session calling this method will create one. Setting the boolean parameter create to false overrides this.

```
public boolean isRequestedSessionIdFromCookie()
```

isRequestedSessionIdFromCookie() returns true if the session ID came in from a cookie.

```
public boolean isRequestedSessionIdFromURL()
```

isRequestedSessionIdFromURL() returns true if the session ID came in as part of the request URL.

```
public boolean isRequestedSessionIdValid()
```

isRequestedSessionIdValid() returns true if the session ID requested by the client is still valid.

```
public boolean isSecure()
```

isSecure() returns true if the request was made using a secure channel, for example HTTPS.

```
public boolean isUserInRole(String role)
```

isUserInRole() returns true if the authenticated user has the specified logical role, or false if the user is not authenticated.

```
public void removeAttribute(String name)
```

removeAttribute() makes the specified attribute unavailable to the invoking ServletRequest object. Subsequent calls to the getAttribute() method for this attribute will return null.

```
public void setAttribute(String name,
                         Object o)
```

setAttribute() binds a value to a specified attribute name. Note that attributes will be reset after the request is handled.

```
public void setCharacterEncoding(String env)
       throws java.io.UnsupportedEncodingException
```

setCharacterEncoding() overrides the character encoding used in the body of this request.

```
public static final String BASIC_AUTH
public static final String FORM_AUTH
public static final String CLIENT_CERT_AUTH
public static final String DIGEST_AUTH
```

These String constants are used to identify the different types of authentication that may have been used to protect the servlet. They have the values BASIC, FORM, CLIENT_CERT, and DIGEST respectively.

```
public String getRealPath(String path)
public boolean isRequestedSessionIdFromUrl()
```

These methods are deprecated and should not be used in new code – they exist for compatibility with existing code.

Use `ServletContext.getRealPath(java.lang.String)` instead of `getRealPath (String path)` and use `ServletContext.isRequestedSessionIdFromURL()` instead of `isRequestedSessionIdFromUrl()`.

The response Object

The `response` object is an instance of a class that implements the `javax.servlet.http.HttpServletResponse` interface. It represents the response to be made to the client, and makes the following methods available:

```
public void addCookie(Cookie cookie)
```

`addCookie()` adds the specified cookie to the response (more than one cookie can be added).

```
public void addDateHeader(String name,
                          long date)
```

`addDateHeader()` adds a response header containing the specified header name and the number of milliseconds since January 1, 1970 GMT. This method can be used to assign multiple values to a given header name.

```
public void addHeader(String name,
                      String value)
```

`addHeader()` adds a response header with the specified `name` and `value`. This method can be used to assign multiple values to a given header name.

```
public void addIntHeader(String name,
                         int value)
```

`addIntHeader()` adds a response header with the specified name and `int` value. This method can be used to assign multiple values to a given header name.

```
public boolean containsHeader(String name)
```

`containsHeader()` returns `true` if the response header includes the specified header name. This method can be used before calling one of the `set()` methods to determine if the header value has already been set.

```
public String encodeRedirectURL(String url)
```

encodeRedirectURL() encodes the specified URL or returns it unchanged if encoding is not required. This method is used to process a URL before sending it to the sendRedirect() method.

```
public String encodeURL(String url)
```

encodeURL() encodes the specified URL by including the session ID or returns it unchanged if encoding is not needed. All URLs generated by a servlet should be processed through this method to ensure compatibility with browsers that do not support cookies.

```
public void flushBuffer()
        throws java.io.IOException
```

flushBuffer() causes any content stored in the buffer to be written to the client. Calling this method will also commit the response, meaning that the status code and headers will be written.

```
public int getBufferSize()
```

getBufferSize() returns the buffer size used for the response, or 0 if no buffering is used.

```
public String getCharacterEncoding()
```

getCharacterEncoding() returns a String object containing the character encoding used in the body of the response. The default is "ISO-8859-1", which corresponds to Latin-1.

```
public java.util.Locale getLocale()
```

getLocale() returns the locale that has been assigned to the response. By default, this will be the default locale for the server.

```
public ServletOutputStream getOutputStream()
        throws java.io.IOException
```

getOutputStream() returns an object ServletOutputStream object that can be used to write the response as binary data.

```
public java.io.PrintWriter getWriter()
        throws java.io.IOException
```

getWriter() returns a PrintWriter object that can be used to write the response as character data.

```
public boolean isCommitted()
```

isCommitted() returns true if the response has been committed, meaning that the status code and headers have been written.

```
public void reset()
```

reset() clears the status code and headers, and any data that exists in the buffer. If the response has already been committed, calling this method will cause an exception to be thrown.

```
public void resetBuffer()
```

resetBuffer() clears the content of the response buffer without clearing the headers or status code. It will throw an IllegalStateException if the response has been committed.

```
public void sendError(int sc,
                      String msg)
        throws java.io.IOException
public void sendError(int sc)
        throws java.io.IOException
```

sendError() sends an error response back to the client machine using the specified error status code. A descriptive message can also be provided. This method must be called before the response is committed (in other words, before the status code and headers have been written).

```
public void sendRedirect(String location)
        throws java.io.IOException
```

sendRedirect() redirects the client machine to the specified URL. This method must be called before the response is committed (in other words, before sending it to the client).

```
public void setBufferSize(int size)
```

setBufferSize() requests a buffer size to be used for the response. The actual buffer size will be at least this large.

```
public void setContentLength(int len)
```

setContentLength() sets the length of response body.

```
public void setContentType(String type)
```

setContentType() sets the content type of the response sent to the server. The String argument specifies a MIME type and may also include the type of character encoding, for example "text/plain; charset=ISO-8859-1".

```
public void setDateHeader(String name,
                          long date)
```

setDateHeader() sets the time value of a response header for the specified header name. The time is the number of milliseconds since January 1, 1970 GMT. If the time value for the specified header has been previously set, the value passed to this method will override it.

```
public void setHeader(String name,
                      String value)
```

setHeader() sets a response header with the specified name and value. If the value for the specified header has been previously set, the value passed to this method will override it.

```
public void setIntHeader(String name,
                         int value)
```

setIntHeader() sets a response header with the specified name and int value. If the int value for the specified header has been previously set, the value passed to this method will override it.

```
public void setLocale(java.util.Locale loc)
```

setLocale() specifies the locale that will be used for the response.

```
public void setStatus(int sc)
```

setStatus() sets the status code and should be one of SC_ACCEPTED, SC_OK, SC_CONTINUE, SC_PARTIAL_CONTENT, SC_CREATED, SC_SWITCHING_PROTOCOLS, or SC_NO_CONTENT.

```
public static final int SC_CONTINUE
public static final int SC_SWITCHING_PROTOCOLS
public static final int SC_OK
public static final int SC_CREATED


public static final int SC_FOUND
public static final int SC_ACCEPTED
public static final int SC_NON_AUTHORITATIVE_INFORMATION
public static final int SC_NO_CONTENT
public static final int SC_RESET_CONTENT
public static final int SC_PARTIAL_CONTENT
public static final int SC_MULTIPLE_CHOICES
public static final int SC_MOVED_PERMANENTLY
public static final int SC_MOVED_TEMPORARILY
public static final int SC_SEE_OTHER
public static final int SC_NOT_MODIFIED
```

```
public static final int SC_USE_PROXY
public static final int SC_BAD_REQUEST
public static final int SC_UNAUTHORIZED
public static final int SC_PAYMENT_REQUIRED
public static final int SC_FORBIDDEN
public static final int SC_NOT_FOUND
public static final int SC_METHOD_NOT_ALLOWED
public static final int SC_NOT_ACCEPTABLE
public static final int SC_PROXY_AUTHENTICATION_REQUIRED
public static final int SC_REQUEST_TIMEOUT
public static final int SC_CONFLICT
public static final int SC_GONE
public static final int SC_LENGTH_REQUIRED
public static final int SC_PRECONDITION_FAILED
public static final int SC_REQUEST_ENTITY_TOO_LARGE
public static final int SC_REQUEST_URI_TOO_LONG
public static final int SC_UNSUPPORTED_MEDIA_TYPE
public static final int SC_REQUESTED_RANGE_NOT_SATISFIABLE
public static final int SC_EXPECTATION_FAILED
public static final int SC_INTERNAL_SERVER_ERROR
public static final int SC_NOT_IMPLEMENTED
public static final int SC_BAD_GATEWAY
public static final int SC_SERVICE_UNAVAILABLE
public static final int SC_GATEWAY_TIMEOUT
public static final int SC_HTTP_VERSION_NOT_SUPPORTED
```

These constants represent the status codes defined in the HTTP specification. (Go to http://www.w3.org/TR/html401/ for more information.)

```
public String encodeUrl(String url)
public String encodeRedirectUrl(String url)
public void setStatus(int sc,
                      String sm)
```

These methods are deprecated and should not be used in new code – they exist for compatibility with existing code.

The out Object

The out object is an instance of the `javax.servlet.jsp.JspWriter` class. It is used to create the content returned to the client, and has the following useful methods available:

```
public abstract void clear()
        throws java.io.IOException
```

`clear()` clears the contents of the buffer; it throws an exception if some data has already been written to the output stream.

```
public abstract void clearBuffer()
        throws java.io.IOException
```

clearBuffer() clears the contents of the buffer, but does not throw an exception if some data has already been written to the output stream.

```
public abstract void close()
        throws java.io.IOException
```

close() flushes and then closes the output stream.

```
public abstract void flush()
        throws java.io.IOException
```

flush() flushes the output buffer and sends any bytes contained in the buffer to their intended destination. flush() will flush all the buffers in a chain of Writers and OutputStreams.

```
public int getBufferSize()
```

getBufferSize() returns the size in bytes of the output buffer.

```
public abstract int getRemaining()
```

getRemaining() returns the number of bytes still contained in the buffer. It will return 0 if is unbuffered.

```
public boolean isAutoFlush()
```

isAutoFlush() returns true if the buffer flushes automatically when an overflow condition occurs.

```
public abstract void newLine()
        throws java.io.IOException
```

newLine() writes a new line character to the output stream.

```
public abstract void print(boolean b)
        throws java.io.IOException
public abstract void print(char c)
        throws java.io.IOException
public abstract void print(int i)
        throws java.io.IOException
public abstract void print(long l)
        throws java.io.IOException
```

```
public abstract void print(float f)
        throws java.io.IOException
public abstract void print(double d)
        throws java.io.IOException
public abstract void print(char[] s)
        throws java.io.IOException
public abstract void print(String s)
        throws java.io.IOException
public abstract void print(Object obj)
        throws java.io.IOException
```

print() prints the specified primitive datatype, Object, or String to the client.

```
try
{
  boolean b = false;
  out.print(b);
  JspWriter out = pageContext.getOut();
  out.print(b);
}
catch(IOException ioe)
{
  //Catch error.
}
```

output:

false

```
public abstract void println()
        throws java.io.IOException
public abstract void println(boolean x)
        throws java.io.IOException
public abstract void println(char x)
        throws java.io.IOException
public abstract void println(int x)
        throws java.io.IOException
public abstract void println(long x)
        throws java.io.IOException
public abstract void println(float x)
        throws java.io.IOException
public abstract void println(double x)
        throws java.io.IOException
public abstract void println(char[] x)
        throws java.io.IOException
public abstract void println(String x)
        throws java.io.IOException
public abstract void println(Object x)
        throws java.io.IOException
```

`println()` prints the specified primitive datatype, `Object`, or `String` to the client, followed by a new line character at the end. The no-argument version simply writes a new line character. For example:

```
try
{
  JspWriter out = pageContext.getOut();
  out.println("<HTML><TITLE>Page Title</TITLE></HTML>");
}
catch(IOException ioe)
{
  //Catch error.
}
```

The session Object

The `session` object is an instance of a class that implements the `javax.servlet.http.HttpSession` interface. It can be used to store session state for a user, and makes the following methods available:

> `public Object` **`getAttribute`**`(String name)`

`getAttribute()` returns the `Object` bound to the specified name in this session, or `null` if it doesn't exist.

> `public java.util.Enumeration` **`getAttributeNames`**`()`

`getAttributeNames()` returns an `Enumeration` of `String` objects containing the names of all the objects bound to this session.

> `public long` **`getCreationTime`**`()`

`getCreationTime()` returns the time when the session was created in milliseconds since midnight Jan 1, 2003 GMT.

> `public String` **`getId`**`()`

`getId()` returns a `String` object containing a unique identifier for this session.

> `public long` **`getLastAccessedTime`**`()`

`getLastAccessedTime()` returns the last time a client request associated with the session was sent. The return value is the number of milliseconds since midnight Jan 1, 1970 GMT.

> `public int` **`getMaxInactiveInterval`**`()`

`getMaxInactiveInterval()` returns the number of seconds the server will wait between client requests before the session is invalidated. A negative return value indicates that the session will never time out.

```
public void invalidate()
```

`invalidate()` invalidates the session and unbinds any objects bound to it.

```
public boolean isNew()
```

`isNew()` returns `true` if the server has created a session that has not yet been accessed by a client.

```
public void logout()
```

`logout()` logs out the current client from the web server and invalidates all existing sessions connected with this client.

```
public void removeAttribute(String name)
```

`removeAttribute()` removes the `Object` bound to the specified name from this session.

```
public void setAttribute(String name,
                         Object value)
```

`setAttribute()` binds an `Object` to the specified attribute name in this session. If the attribute name already exists, the `Object` passed to this method will replace the previous `Object`.

```
public void setMaxInactiveInterval(int interval)
```

`setMaxInactiveInterval()` specifies the number of seconds the server will wait between client requests before the session is invalidated. If a negative value is passed to this method, the session will never time out.

```
public HttpSessionContext getSessionContext()
public Object getValue(String name)
public String[] getValueNames()
public void putValue(String name,
                     Object value)
public void removeValue(String name)
```

These methods are deprecated and should not be used in new code – they exist for compatibility with existing code.

The application Object

The `application` object is an instance of a class that implements the `javax.servlet.ServletContext` interface, and allows the page to obtain and to set data information about the web application in which it is running. It makes available the following methods:

    public Object **getAttribute**(String *name*)

`getAttribute()` returns the value of the specified attribute name. The return value is an `Object` or sub-class if the attribute is available to the invoking `ServletContext` object, or `null` if the attribute is not available.

    public java.util.Enumeration **getAttributeNames**()

`getAttributeNames()` returns an `Enumeration` containing the attribute names available to the invoking `ServletContext` object.

    public ServletContext **getContext**(String *uripath*)

`getContext()` returns the `ServletContext` object for the resource at the specified path on the server. The path argument is an absolute URL beginning with "/".

    public String **getInitParameter**(String *name*)

`getInitParameter()` returns a `String` object containing the value of the specified initialization parameter, or `null` if the parameter does not exist.

    public java.util.Enumeration **getInitParameterNames**()

`getInitParameterNames()` returns a `Enumeration` containing the initialization parameters associated with the invoking `ServletContext` object.

    public int **getMajorVersion**()

`getMajorVersion()` returns the major version of the Java servlet API that the server supports. For servers supporting version 2.3 of the servlet specification, this method will return 2.

    public String **getMimeType**(String *file*)

`getMimeType()` returns the MIME type of the specified file or `null` if the MIME type cannot be ascertained. Typical return values will be `"text/plain"`, `"text/html"`, or `"image/jpg"`.

```
public int getMinorVersion()
```

getMinorVersion() returns the minor version of the Java servlet API that the server supports. For servers supporting version 2.3 of the servlet specification, this method will return 3.

```
public RequestDispatcher getNamedDispatcher(String name)
```

getNamedDispatcher() returns a RequestDispatcher object that will be wrapped around the named servlet.

```
public String getRealPath(String path)
```

getRealPath() returns a String object containing the real path, in a form appropriate to the platform on which the servlet is running, corresponding to the given virtual path. An example of a virtual path might be "/blah.html".

```
public RequestDispatcher getRequestDispatcher(String path)
```

getRequestDispatcher() returns a RequestDispatcher object that acts as a wrapper around the resource located at the specified path. The path must begin with "/", and is interpreted relative to the current context root.

```
public java.net.URL getResource(String path)
        throws java.net.MalformedURLException
```

getResource() returns a URL object that is mapped to the specified path, or null if there is no resource mapped to the path. The path must begin with "/" and is interpreted relative to the current context root.

```
public java.io.InputStream getResourceAsStream(String path)
```

getResourceAsStream() returns the resource at the specified path as an InputStream object.

```
public java.util.Set getResourcePaths()
```

getResourcePaths() returns all the paths to resources held in the web application as Strings beginning with a "/".

```
public String getServerInfo()
```

getServerInfo() returns a String object containing information on the server on which the servlet is running. At a minimum, the String will contain the servlet container name and version number.

```
<% out.print(application.getServerInfo()); %>
output:
```

Apache Tomcat/5.0.0

```
public String getServletContextName()
```

getServletContextName() returns the name of the web application, as specified in the
<display-name> element in web.xml.

```
public void log(String msg)
public void log(String message,
                Throwable throwable)
```

log() is used to write a message to the servlet engine's log file. The second version writes both
an explanatory message and a stack trace for the specified Throwable exception to the log file.

```
public void removeAttribute(String name)
```

removeAttribute() makes the specified attribute unavailable to the invoking ServletContext
object. Subsequent calls to the getAttribute() method for this attribute will return null.

```
public void setAttribute(String name,
                         Object object)
```

setAttribute() binds a value to a specified attribute name.

```
public Servlet getServlet(String name)
        throws ServletException
public java.util.Enumeration getServlets()
public java.util.Enumeration getServletNames()
public void log(Exception exception,
                String msg)
```

These methods are deprecated and should not be used in new code – they exist for
compatibility with existing code.

The exception Object

The `exception` object is an instance of the `java.lang.Throwable` class. It is available in error pages only, and represents the exception that occurred that caused control to pass to the error page. Its most useful methods are:

```
public String getLocalizedMessage()
```

`getLocalizedMessage()` returns a localized description of this `Throwable` object. In many cases, this will return the same result as `getMessage()`.

```
public String getMessage()
```

`getMessage()` returns the error message string of this `Throwable` object.

```
public void printStackTrace()
public void printStackTrace(PrintStream ps)
public void printStackTrace(PrintWriter pw)
```

`printStackTrace()` prints information about this `Throwable` object, along with a listing of the method calls that led to the error condition arising. The output can be directed to the standard error stream, or to a specified `PrintStream` or `PrintWriter` object.

```
public String toString()
```

`toString()` returns a short description of this `Throwable` object. If an error message was supplied when the object was created, the result is the `Throwable` class's name, followed by a colon and a space, followed by that message. For example:

```
<%
  try
  {
    throw new Exception("Here's my Exception");
  }
  catch(Exception e)
  {
    out.print(e.toString());
  }
%>
```

outputs:

java.lang.Exception: Here's my Exception

The config Object

The config object is an instance of the javax.servlet.ServletConfig interface. It is used to make initialization parameters available, and has the following methods:

```
public String getInitParameter(String name)
```

getInitParameter() returns the value of the specified initialization parameter, or null if the parameter does not exist.

```
public java.util.Enumeration getInitParameterNames()
```

getInitParameterNames() returns an Enumeration of String objects containing the names of all of the servlet's initialization parameters.

```
public ServletContext getServletContext()
```

getServletContext() returns the ServletContext object associated with the invoking servlet. A ServletContext object contains information about the environment in which the servlet is running.

```
public String getServletName()
```

getServletName() returns the name of the servlet. If the servlet is unnamed, the method will return the servlet's class name.

The page Object

The page object is a reference to the servlet object that implements this JSP page. JSP page authors do not often use this object, as it is very expensive memory-wise.

The pageContext Object

The pageContext object is an instance of the javax.servlet.jsp.PageContext class, and is used by the container-generated servlet code for your JSP page to access the various scopes available within the JSP page. JSP page authors do not often use this object, as they were intended to be generated by the container, but it is important when writing tag libraries.

```
HttpSession thisSession = pageContext.getSession();
```

APPENDIX C

XML Configuration Files

This appendix documents in detail the three most commonly used XML configuration files in JSP applications:

- ❑ **The web application deployment descriptor file (`web.xml`)**
  This is a configuration file used by servlet containers that meet the J2EE specification, such as Apache Tomcat. This file is read by the servlet container on startup. This file is placed in the WEB-INF folder of your web application.

- ❑ **Tag library descriptor (`.tld`) files**
  This is a descriptor file for a tag library, as covered in Chapter 9. This file describes the tag library implementation contained in a JAR file to the servlet container. This file too is generally stored in the WEB-INF folder of your web application.

- ❑ **The Struts configuration file (`struts-config.xml`)**
  This file configures web applications based on the Struts Framework, discussed in Chapters 15 and 16. The Struts framework is an open source MVC implementation using JSP servlet technology.

Common Elements of web.xml

The <description>, <display-name>, and <icon> elements can occur in several places as sub-elements of other elements within web.xml.

<description>

The <description> element is used in a number of places within the web.xml file to provide a description of its parent element.

<display-name>

The `<display-name>` element contains a short name for its parent element, and is displayed by GUI tools.

<icon>

The `<icon>` element references icons that will be used by a GUI tool to represent its parent element. It contains:

- ❏ An optional `<small-icon>` element containing the location within the application of a 16x16 pixel icon

- ❏ An optional `<large-icon>` element containing the location within the application of a 32x32 pixel icon

<web-app> – Root Element

The `<web-app>` element is the root element of the web.xml file. This means that every web.xml file must contain one and only one such element, and all other elements must be contained within it. It contains:

- ❏ An optional `<icon>` element
- ❏ An optional `<display-name>` element
- ❏ An optional `<description>` element
- ❏ An optional `<distributable>` element
- ❏ 0 or more `<context-param>` elements
- ❏ 0 or more `<filter>` elements
- ❏ 0 or more `<filter-mapping>` elements
- ❏ 0 or more `<listener>` elements
- ❏ 0 or more `<servlet>` elements
- ❏ 0 or more `<servlet-mapping>` elements
- ❏ An optional `<session-config>` element
- ❏ 0 or more `<mime-mapping>` elements
- ❏ An optional `<welcome-file-list>` element
- ❏ 0 or more `<error-page>` elements
- ❏ 0 or more `<taglib>` elements
- ❏ 0 or more `<resource-env-ref>` elements

- ❑ 0 or more `<resource-ref>` elements

- ❑ 0 or more `<security-constraint>` elements

- ❑ An optional `<login-config>` element

- ❑ 0 or more `<security-role>` elements

- ❑ 0 or more `<env-entry>` elements

- ❑ 0 or more `<ejb-ref>` elements

Child Elements of `<web-app>`

The permissible child elements that `<web-app>` may have (other than those already described) are:

`<distributable>`

The `<distributable>` element, if present, declares that this web application can be deployed in a distributed servlet container or servlet container executing across multiple JVMs either running on the same host or different hosts.

`<context-param>`

The `<context-param>` element declares a context initialization parameter. It contains:

- ❑ A `<param-name>` element containing the parameter's name

- ❑ A `<param-value>` element containing the parameter's value

- ❑ An optional `<description>` element (see earlier description)

`<filter>`

The `<filter>` element declares a filter. A filter is a Java class that preprocesses the request data received from clients. This preprocessing may include decryption, formatting, or other processes. This element contains:

- ❑ An optional `<icon>` element

- ❑ A `<filter-name>` element containing the filter's name

- ❑ An optional `<display-name>` element

- ❑ An optional `<description>` element

- ❑ A `<filter-class>` element containing the filter's class name

- ❑ 0 or more `<init-param>` elements containing initialization parameters for the filter

Each `<init-param>` element contains:

- ❑ A `<param-name>` element containing the parameter name
- ❑ A `<param-value>` element containing the parameter value
- ❑ An optional `<description>` element

<filter-mapping>

The `<filter-mapping>` element is used to map a filter to a servlet or a set of URLs. It contains:

- ❑ A `<filter-name>` element containing the name of a filter declared by a `<filter>` element
- ❑ Either a `<url-pattern>` element containing a URL pattern to match, or a `<servlet-name>` element containing the name of a servlet declared by a `<servlet>` element

<listener>

The `<listener>` element is used to declare an application listener. It contains:

- ❑ A `<listener-class>` element containing the listener's class name.

<servlet>

The `<servlet>` element declares a servlet. It contains:

- ❑ An optional `<icon>` element
- ❑ A `<servlet-name>` element containing the servlet's name
- ❑ An optional `<display-name>` element
- ❑ An optional `<description>` element
- ❑ Either a `<servlet-class>` element containing the listener's class name, or a `<jsp-file>` element containing the location within the web application of a JSP file
- ❑ `<init-param>` elements
- ❑ An optional `<load-on-startup>` element indicating that the servlet should be loaded when the web application starts up, and containing an optional positive integer value indicating the order in which servlets should be started. If a `<jsp-file>` was specified, then the JSP should be precompiled and loaded.
- ❑ `<security-role-ref>` elements

Each <init-param> element contains:

- ❏ A <param-name> element containing the parameter name
- ❏ A <param-value> element containing the parameter value
- ❏ An optional <description> element

A <security-role-ref> element maps a role name called from within the servlet, and the name of a security role defined for the web application. It contains:

- ❏ An optional <description> element
- ❏ A <role-name> element containing the role name used within the servlet
- ❏ A <role-link> element containing the name of a role defined in a <security-role> element

<servlet-mapping>

The <servlet-mapping> element maps a servlet to a URL pattern. It contains:

- ❏ A <servlet-name> element containing the name of a servlet declared by a <servlet> element
- ❏ A <url-pattern> element containing a URL pattern to match

<session-config>

The <session-config> element configures the session tracking for the web application. It contains:

- ❏ An optional <session-timeout> element containing the default session timeout for this web application, which must be a whole number of minutes. The default behavior of the container without this attribute is never to timeout.

<mime-mapping>

The <mime-mapping> element maps a filename extension to a MIME type. It contains:

- ❏ An <extension> element containing a filename extension
- ❏ A <mime-type> element containing a defined MIME type

<welcome-file-list>

The <welcome-file-list> element defines an ordered list of welcome files. It contains:

- ❏ 1 or more <welcome-file> elements containing a filename to use as a welcome file

<error-page>

The <error-page> element maps an error code or exception type to a resource ("error page") to use if that error condition arises. It contains:

- ❑ Either an <error-code> element containing an HTTP error code, or an <exception-type> element containing the class name of a Java exception type
- ❑ A <location> element containing the location of the error page resource within the web application

<taglib>

The <taglib> element declares a JSP tag library. It contains:

- ❑ A <taglib-uri> element containing a URI to identify the tag library
- ❑ A <taglib-location> element containing the location within the web application of the tag library descriptor file (.tld file)

<resource-env-ref>

The <resource-env-ref> element declares that the web application references an administered object such as JMS resource destination. It contains:

- ❑ An optional <description> element
- ❑ A <resource-env-name> element containing the name of the resource environment
- ❑ A <resource-env-ref-type> element containing the type of the resource environment reference – J2EE web containers are required to support javax.jms.Topic and javax.jms.Queue

<resource-ref>

The <resource-ref> element declares that the web application references an external resource such as a datasource reference. It contains:

- ❑ An optional <description> element
- ❑ A <res-ref-name> element containing the name of the resource factory reference
- ❑ A <res-type> element specifying the type of the data source
- ❑ A <res-auth> element indicating whether the application code signs on to the resource programmatically, or whether the container should sign on based on information supplied by the application deployer. Contents must be either Application or Container.
- ❑ An optional <res-sharing-scope> element specifying whether connections can be shared. Contents must be either Shareable (the default) or Unshareable.

<security-constraint>

The <security-constraint> element applies security constraints to one or more collections of web resources. It contains:

- ❑ An optional <display-name> element

- ❑ One or more <web-resource-collection> elements

- ❑ An optional <auth-constraint> element

- ❑ An optional <user-data-constraint> element

A <web-resource-collection> element identifies a set of resources within the application; it can be qualified by specifying particular HTTP method(s) such as GET or POST. (By default, the security constraint applies to all HTTP methods.) It contains:

- ❑ A <web-resource-name> element containing the name of the web resource collection

- ❑ An optional <description> element

- ❑ 0 or more <url-pattern> elements, each containing a URL pattern to match

- ❑ 0 or more <http-method> elements, each containing the name of an HTTP method

An <auth-constraint> element indicates that certain user roles should be permitted to access these web resources. It contains:

- ❑ An optional <description> element

- ❑ 0 or more <role-name> elements each containing a role referenced in a <security-role-ref> element, or the special name * that indicates all roles in this application

A <user-data-constraint> element indicates how data transmitted between the client and the application should be protected. It contains:

- ❑ An optional <description> element

- ❑ A <transport-guarantee> – can have one of the three values in this table:

Value	Description
NONE	No transport guarantee is required
INTEGRAL	The data must not be changed in transit
CONFIDENTIAL	Others may not view the data en route

<login-config>

The `<login-config>` element configures the authentication mechanism for this application. It contains:

❑ An optional `<auth-method>` element specifying the authentication mechanism. Must contain the text `BASIC`, `DIGEST`, `FORM`, or `CLIENT-CERT`.

❑ An optional `<realm-name>` element specifying the realm name for HTTP basic authorization

❑ An optional `<form-login-config>` element to configure form-based authentication. Contains a `<form-login-page>` element specifying the login page, and a `<form-error-page>` element specifying the error page used if login is unsuccessful.

<security-role>

The `<security-role>` element declares a security role used in the web application's security-constraints. It contains:

❑ An optional `<description>` element

❑ A `<role-name>` element containing the name of the role

<env-entry>

The `<env-entry>` element declares an application's environment entry. It contains:

❑ An optional `<description>` element

❑ An `<env-entry-name>` element containing the environment entry's name

❑ An optional `<env-entry-value>` element containing the environment entry's value

❑ An `<env-entry-type>` element containing the environment entry value's Java type. Legal values are `java.lang.Boolean`, `java.lang.String`, `java.lang.Integer`, `java.lang.Double`, and `java.lang.Float`.

<ejb-ref>

The `<ejb-ref>` element declares a reference to an Enterprise JavaBean. It contains:

❑ An optional `<description>` element

❑ An `<ejb-ref-name>` element containing the JNDI name of the EJB

❑ An `<ejb-ref-type>` element containing the expected type of the EJB, either `Entity` or `Session`

❑ A `<home>` element containing the type (name of the class) of the EJB's home interface

❑ A `<remote>` element containing the type of the EJB's remote interface

❑ An optional `<ejb-link>` element specifying that this EJB reference is linked to the named EJB in the encompassing J2EE application

❑ An optional `<run-as>` element specifying the security role (defined for this application) that should be propagated to the EJB

Common Elements of the Tag Library Descriptor

The `<description>`, `<display-name>`, `<large-icon>`, and `<small-icon>` elements can occur in several places in a TLD file, and they have the same meanings described for web.xml.

<taglib> – Root Element

The `<taglib>` element is the root element of a .tld file. It contains:

❑ A `<tlib-version>` element

❑ An optional `<jsp-version>` element

❑ A `<short-name>` element

❑ An optional `<uri>` element

❑ An optional `<display-name>` element

❑ An optional `<small-icon>` element

❑ An optional `<large-icon>` element

❑ An optional `<description>` element

❑ An optional `<validator>` element

❑ Zero or more `<listener>` elements

❑ One or more `<tag>` elements

Child Elements of <taglib>

The permissible sub-elements of `<taglib>` are as follows.

<tlib-version>

The `<tlib-version>` element contains the version number of the tag library.

<jsp-version>

The `<jsp-version>` element contains the JSP version that the tag library requires (1.2 by default).

<short-name>

The <short-name> element contains a short name for the tag library.

<uri>

The <uri> element contains a URI uniquely identifying the tag library.

<validator>

The <validator> element defines a validator to check that a JSP page uses the tag library correctly. It contains:

❑ A <validator-class> element containing the name of the TagLibraryValidator class

❑ 0 or more <init-param> elements

An <init-param> element defines initialization parameters for the validator, and contains:

❑ A <param-name> element containing the parameter name

❑ A <param-value> element containing the parameter value

❑ An optional <description> element

<listener>

The <listener> element defines an event listener for the web application using the tag library. It contains:

❑ A <listener-class> element containing the name of the listener class

<tag>

The <tag> element defines a tag. It contains:

❑ A <name> element containing the tag's name

❑ A <tag-class> element containing the name of the tag handler class

❑ An optional <tei-class> element containing the name of the TagExtraInfo class for the tag

❑ An optional <body-content> element describing the body content of the tag: either tagdependent, JSP, or empty

❑ An optional <display-name> element

❑ An optional <small-icon> element

❑ An optional <large-icon> element

- ❑ An optional `<description>` element

- ❑ 0 or more `<variable>` elements

- ❑ 0 or more `<attribute>` elements

A `<variable>` element declares that this tag defines a scripting variable. It contains:

- ❑ Either a `<name-given>` element containing the name of the scripting variable, or a `<name-from-attribute>` element containing the name of the tag attribute that will give the scripting variable's name at runtime.

- ❑ An optional `<variable-class>` element containing the class name of the scripting variable. The default is `java.lang.String`.

- ❑ An optional `<declare>` element whose contents indicate whether the scripting variable is to be defined; the default is `true`.

- ❑ An optional `<scope>` element whose contents indicate the scope of the scripting variable. Possible values are `NESTED` (the default), `AT_BEGIN`, or `AT_END`.

An `<attribute>` element defines an attribute of the tag. It contains:

- ❑ A `<name>` element containing the name of the attribute.

- ❑ An optional `<required>` element whose contents indicate whether the attribute is required or optional. Legal values are `true`, `false` (the default), `yes`, and `no`.

- ❑ An optional `<rtexprvalue>` element whose contents indicate whether the attribute value can be a run-time expression scriptlet rather than a static value. Legal values are `true`, `false` (the default), `yes`, and `no`.

- ❑ An optional `<type>` element containing the type of the attribute's value. (For static values, this is always `java.lang.String`.)

Common Elements of the Struts Config File

Note that within the Struts configuration file the ordering of elements is significant. You should additionally note that:

- ❑ All URL paths are context-relative, in other words they must start with a `/` and are relative to the root of the web application.

- ❑ In addition to the attributes listed below, all elements in the Struts configuration file have an implied `id` attribute.

The `<set-property>`, `<description>`, `<display-name>`, `<icon>`, `<large-icon>`, and `<small-icon>` elements can occur in several places within the Struts configuration file, and so we will describe them only once.

<set-property>

The `<set-property>` element is used to configure JavaBeans components by specifying a property name and value. It has no content, but the following attributes:

❑ `property` specifies the name of the bean property to be set

❑ `value` specifies the new property value, in a string representation

<description>

The `<description>` element contains a description of the parent element.

<display-name>

The `<display-name>` element contains a short name for its parent element, for GUI tools to display.

<icon>

The `<icon>` element references icons that will be used by a GUI tool to represent its parent element. It contains:

❑ An optional `<small-icon>` element containing the location, relative to the file, of a 16x16 pixel icon

❑ An optional `<large-icon>` element containing the location, relative to the file, of a 32x32 pixel icon

<struts-config> – Root Element

The `<struts-config>` element is the root element of the Struts configuration file. It contains:

❑ An optional `<data-sources>` element

❑ An optional `<form-beans>` element

❑ An optional `<global-forwards>` element

❑ An optional `<action-mappings>` element

<data-sources> and <data-source>

The `<data-sources>` element describes a set of DataSource objects. The individual DataSource objects are configured through nested `<data-source>` elements.

Each `<data-source>` element describes a DataSource object that will be instantiated, configured, and made available as a servlet context attribute Any object can be specified so long as it implements `javax.sql.DataSource` and can be configured entirely from JavaBean properties. The following attributes are required:

❑ className – the configuration bean for this DataSource object. If specified, the object must be a subclass of the default configuration bean.

❑ key – the servlet context attribute key under which this data source will be stored.

❑ type – a fully qualified Java class name for this DataSource object. The class must implement javax.sql.DataSource, and the object must be configurable entirely from JavaBean properties.

❑ loginTimeout – the maximum number of seconds to wait for a connection to be created or returned.

There are several additional attributes whose use is now deprecated (that is, no longer recommended) as they only applied to the default DataSource class.

<global-exceptions> and <exception>

The <global-exceptions> element describes a set of exceptions that might be thrown by an Action object. The handling of individual exception types is configured through child <exception> elements. An <action> element may override a global exception handler by registering a local exception handler for the same exception type.

The <exception> element registers an ExceptionHandler for an exception type. The following are the important attributes:

❑ className – the configuration bean for this ExceptionHandler object. If specified, className must be a subclass of the default configuration bean org.apache.struts.config.ExceptionConfig.

❑ handler – the fully qualified Java class name for this exception handler. (org.apache.struts.action.ExceptionHandler)

❑ key – the key to use with this handler's message resource bundle that will retrieve the error message template for this exception.

❑ path – the module-relative URI to the resource that will complete the request/response if this exception occurs.

❑ scope – the context (request or session) to access the ActionError object (org.apache.struts.action.ActionError) for this exception.

❑ type – the fully qualified Java class name of the exception type to register with this handler.

<form-beans> and <form-bean>

The <form-beans> element describes the set of form bean descriptors for this application module. An attribute called type is defined for this element, but this attribute is deprecated in Struts 1.0.

This element has <form-bean> child elements that each define a form bean that will be configured to handle form submissions. It may have the following attributes:

❑ className – allows you to override the default class Struts uses to represent a form bean internally.

❑ name – specifies a unique identifier for this form bean, which will be used to reference it in <action> elements. (Required.)

❑ type – specifies the name of the form bean class to be used. Must extend org.apache.struts.action.ActionForm. (Required.)

<global-forwards> and <forward>

The <global-forwards> element contains zero or more <forward> child elements, specifying named forwards that will be available to all Struts actions (unless overridden within an <action> element). It also has a type attribute, but this is again deprecated in Struts 1.0.

The <forward> element maps a logical name to a web resource, and has the following attributes:

❑ className – allows you to override the default class Struts uses to represent a forward internally. You will not commonly use this attribute.

❑ name – specifies a unique identifier for this forward, which will be used to reference it within your application. (Required.)

❑ path – specifies the location of the web resource. (Required.)

❑ redirect allows you to specify whether control should be redirected to this resource (value true), rather than forwarding to it (false). The default is false.

❑ ContextRelative – set to true if, in a modular application, the path attribute starts with a slash / and should be considered relative to the entire web application rather than the module.

<action-mappings> and <action>

The <action-mappings> element contains zero or more <action> elements, which map request URLs to Action classes. It also has a type attribute, which represents a fully qualified Java class to use when instantiating ActionMapping objects.

Each <action> element maps a request path to an Action class. Its attributes are listed below; exactly one of forward, include, or type must be specified:

❑ type – specifies the class name of the action class (which must extend org.apache.struts.action.Action) to be used to process requests for this mapping if the forward or include attribute is not included.

- ❏ `forward` – specifies the path of the servlet or JSP that will process this request, instead of instantiating and calling the `Action` class specified by `type`.

- ❏ `include` – specifies the path of the servlet or JSP that will process this request, instead of instantiating and calling the `Action` class specified by `type`.

The remaining `<action>` attributes are:

- ❏ `path` – defines the path of the submitted request that will be processed by this action, starting with a "/" character. If Struts was used with an extension-based `<servlet-mapping>` element then the filename extension should be omitted here. (Required.)

- ❏ `name` – specifies the name of the form bean (if any) associated with the action.

- ❏ `attribute` – specifies the name of the request-scope or session-scope attribute under which the form bean is accessed, if it is something other than the bean's specified `name`. It is optional if `name` is specified, but otherwise is not allowed.

- ❏ `scope` – specifies the scope (`"request"` or `"session"`) in which the form bean is located, if any. It is optional if `name` is specified, but otherwise is not allowed.

- ❏ `input` – specifies the path of the input form to which control should be returned if a validation error is encountered. It is required if `name` is specified and the input bean returns validation errors, is optional if `name` is specified and the input bean does not return validation errors, and is not allowed if `name` is not specified.

- ❏ `parameter` – specifies configuration information for the action.

- ❏ `prefix` – specifies a prefix used to match request parameter names to form bean properties, if any. It is optional if `name` is specified, but otherwise is not allowed.

- ❏ `suffix` – specifies a suffix used to match request parameter names to form bean properties names, if any. It is optional if `name` is specified, but otherwise is not allowed.

- ❏ `unknown` – specifies whether this action should be configured to handle all requests not handled by another action.

- ❏ `validate` – specifies whether the form bean's `validate()` method should be called prior to calling the action.

- ❏ `className` – allows you to override the default class Struts uses to represent an action mapping internally. You will not commonly use this attribute.

APPENDIX D

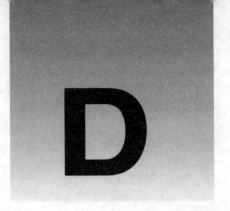

Getting More Information

Java Development Kit Documentation

You should definitely download and install the Java Development Kit documentation; this provides a huge amount of information about the Java platform itself, such as:

- ❑ Instructions on using the Java command line tools (javac, java, and so on).

- ❑ Guides to Java features such as I/O, networking, .jar files, and so on.

- ❑ Most importantly, documentation on the various classes that make up the Java platform; these are commonly known as **Javadocs** because they are generated by a tool known as javadoc.

You can download the documentation from http://java.sun.com/j2se/1.4.1/docs/index.html. If you are using Windows, the file comes in the form of a .zip file, which you should unzip into your JDK directory (for example, into C:\jdk1.4.1), alternatively packages in .rpm and .gzip format are also available for Linux users. Once this is done, you can browse to the index.html to start reading – typically this means pointing your web browser to C:\jdk1.4.1\docs\index.html:

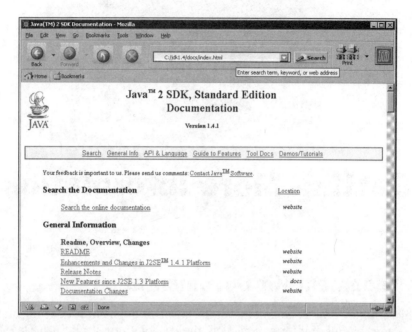

As you'll see if you scroll down this page, there is a lot of information; it's well worth spending some time exploring what's available. However, we'll focus here on one particular part of the documentation, the API guide. If you scroll down to the **API & Language Documentation** section, you'll find a link called Java 2 Platform API Specification. Clicking on this link takes you to a page similar to the following:

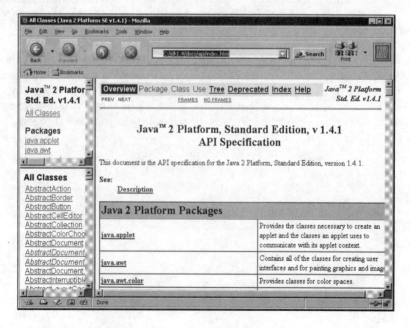

There is rather a lot of information here; there are a lot of classes and interfaces in the Java platform, in fact there are more than 1800 classes and interfaces listed! Fortunately they are all nicely categorized into packages, which makes it easier to find what you're looking for.

You'll see that the screen above is divided into three areas. The main area, on the right, initially contains a descriptive list of packages, while on the top left there is a quick summary of packages and on the bottom left there is a complete list of classes and interfaces.

If you click on a package's name in the list at the top left, the bottom left frame is replaced with a list of the classes and interfaces in that package only. Clicking on a package's name in the main part of the screen replaces that frame with a descriptive overview of that package only.

So, let's say we're interested in the `java.io.File` class. In the top left frame we scroll down to java.io, and click on that link. The bottom left frame now contains a list of the contents of that package only; to get to the overview of that package, we click on the text java.io at the top of the bottom left frame:

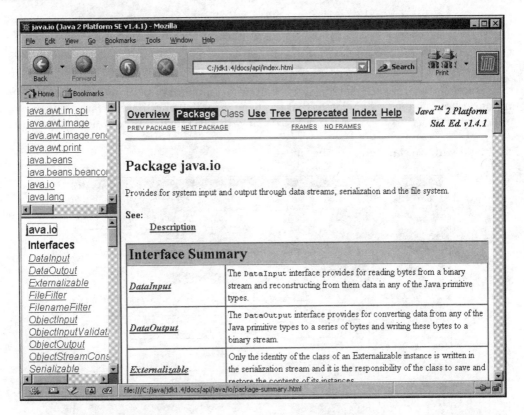

We can now locate information about the `File` class by clicking on the appropriate link in either the bottom left or the main frames, this takes us to the documentation for that class:

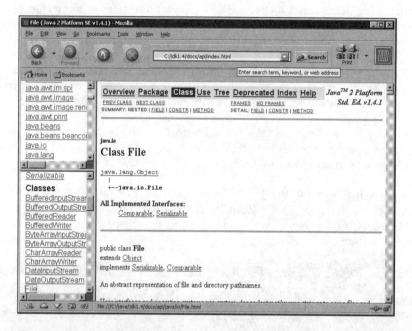

The documentation for each class is divided up into a number of sections. At the top, there is a summary showing the tree of classes that has been extended and the interfaces that have been implemented, to get us to `java.io.File`. Below this is a textual description of the class.

Scrolling down, we start to get to the "meat":

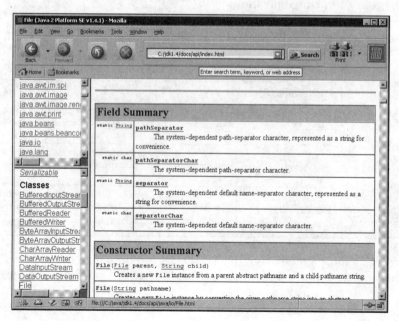

As you can see, we're given summaries of the fields, constructors, and methods declared for this class, with links to fuller descriptions further down the page. There is also a section listing methods inherited from the parent class.

Finally, towards the bottom, come detailed descriptions of each field, constructor, and method:

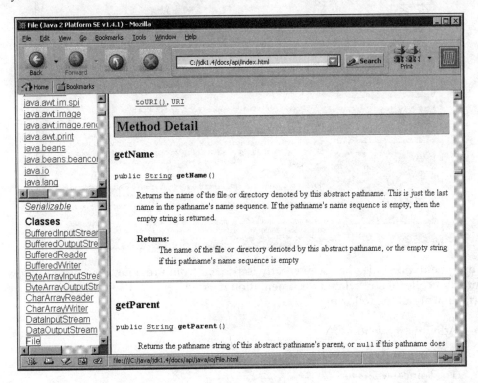

The whole set of API documents is liberally hyperlinked, and it is actually very easy to find your way around.

Tomcat and JSP/Servlet Documentation

You should know about the documentation that comes with Tomcat. When you installed Tomcat 5.0, you may have seen this page:

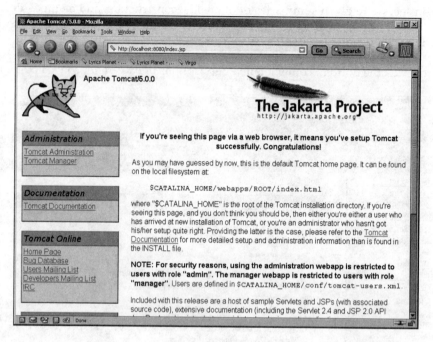

The documentation index has been greatly improved from previous versions, as it now maintains a collection of related documentation making very easy to find basic start up information about the following:

- Administrative tools
    - Tomcat Administration Manager
    - Tomcat Manager
- Startup configuration
    - Web server
    - Proxy support
    - Realm
    - Security Manager
    - SSL
    - JNDI
- APIs
    - JSP 2.0
    - Servlet 2.4
    - Catalina
    - Jasper

The two sections of this which are particularly important are the **Administrators** section, which contains very good startup configuration guides, and the **Application Developers** section, which includes the API docs for Servlet 2.4 and JSP2.0 Packages.

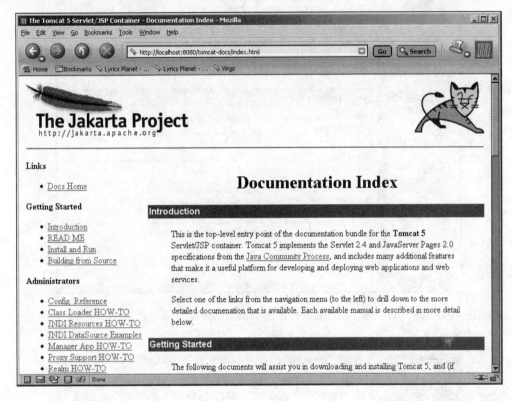

The Servlet API is the Javadocs for `javax.servlet`, `javax.servlet.http`, `javax.servlet.jsp`, and `javax.servlet.jsp.tagext`. You will find these documents (shown in the screenshot below) a handy supplement to the information on JSP implicit objects given in Appendix B:

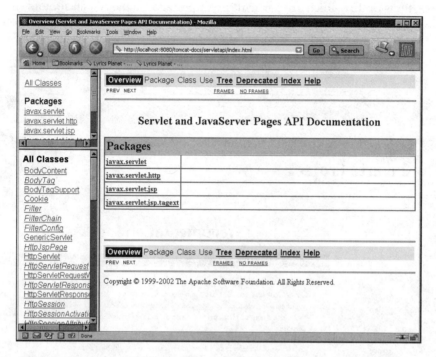

Furthermore the JSP API documentation is the Javadocs for the `javax.servlet.jsp`, `javax.servlet.jsp.el` and `javax.servlet.jsp.tagext`:

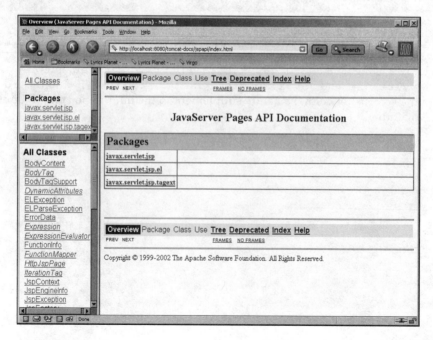

Other Resources

We've put together a list of some other resources you may find helpful as you continue to learn about JavaServer Pages and Java.

Several Wrox Press books will help you to take forward what you have learned in this book. You may be particularly interested in:

- ❑ *Beginning Java Objects*, by Jacquie Barker, ISBN 1-86100-417-6, which teaches object-oriented programming in Java from the ground up, by introducing you to the concepts of object orientation and how to model your system as a set of objects, and then showing you how to translate this into Java sources.

- ❑ *Beginning Java 2 – JDK 1.3 Edition*, by Ivor Horton, ISBN 1-86100-366-8, which teaches you about the fundamentals of the Java programming language and APIs, together with how to use the Swing API to create graphical client-side applications in Java.

- ❑ *Professional JSP, 2nd Edition*, ISBN 1-86100-495-8 takes you beyond what has been covered in this book with extensive coverage of advanced topics such as using XML with Java, more discussion of Servlets, generating non-textual types of web content such as images and PDFs, and further use of the Struts framework.

- ❑ JavaServer Pages and Servlets are only part of the **Java 2 Enterprise Edition (J2EE)**. *Professional Java Server Programming, J2EE Edition*, ISBN 1-86100-465-6, covers the whole J2EE platform – including XML, Enterprise JavaBeans, and the Java Message Service, giving you an excellent overview of the possibilities of Java technology.

Next, here are a few web sites that may be of use:

- ❑ Sun Microsystems' official web site provides information about JSP and Servlets at http://java.sun.com/products/jsp/ and http://java.sun.com/products/servlets/ respectively. This site is particularly useful for official information such as the JSP specification, Servlet specification (hard reading, though), and occasional articles.

- ❑ The Jakarta project, http://jakarta.apache.org/, has many useful subprojects offering useful (and free) server-side Java software. Particularly notable are Tomcat, the JSP/Servlet container we've been using throughout this book (information can be found at http://jakarta.apache.org/tomcat/), the Struts framework (information can be found at http://jakarta.apache.org/struts/), and the Taglibs project (information can be found at http://jakarta.apache.org/taglibs/), which offers a host of ready-made JSP tag libraries ready for you to download and use.

- ❑ JSPInsider, http://www.jspinsider.com/ offers a host of JSP-related information including the helpful articles and useful (free) JavaBeans and tag libraries.

Lastly, there are a number of mailing lists that you may find helpful if you run up against problems in your code:

❑ The Wrox Programmer's Resource Centre, http://p2p.wrox.com/, has a number of Java mailing lists, including lists on JSP, tag libraries, and servlets.

❑ The Jakarta project also has mailing lists for their projects; each has a "user" list for questions about using the product, and a "developer" list where the people who created the projects live. You'll probably be mainly interested in the "user" lists; see http://jakarta.apache.org/site/mail.html for more information.

INDEX

Index

Important entries have page numbers in **bold** type.

executeUpdate method, Statement interface, 487, 490, 494, 515

Expression Language (EL), 39, **239-44**
- arithmetic operators, 244
- collections, **241**
  - map collections, **241-42**
- logical operators, 244
- relational operators, 244
- variables, **240-41**

expressions, scripting elements, 40, **763**

extends keyword, 184, 187

extension elements, web.xml file, 801

F

file handles, naming services, 477

filter attribute, Struts HTML optionsCollection elements, 634

filter elements, web.xml file, 798, **799-800**

filter-class elements, web.xml file, 799

filter-mapping elements, web.xml file, 798, **800**

filter-name elements, web.xml file, 799, 800

final keyword, 190

finally keyword, 250, **264-65**

findByBook method, 688

findById method, 687

findByStatus method, Struts, 731

finder methods, data access objects, 677
- multi object finders, 678
- single object finders, 678

findForward method, ActionMapping class, 595, 608, 730

findForwards method, ActionMapping class, 608

findMapping method, ActionMappings class, 587

first normal form, databases, **72**

FLOAT data type, SQL, 81

flush attribute, include directives, 765

flush method, out implicit object, 787

flushBuffer method, response implicit object, 783

focus attribute, Struts HTML form elements, 628

font-family attribute, CSS, 34

font-size attribute, CSS, 34

footer attribute, Struts HTML messages elements, 639

for statements, 157-59, 165

forEach elements, JSTL, 45, 93, 104, 158-59, 168, 433, 573, 576, 719, 734

foreign keys, databases, **70-71**, **502**

form based authentication, 406-9, 450, 453-56

form elements, HTML, 46-48, 581
- action attribute, **46-47**, 583
- method attribute, **47**
- name attribute, **47**
- target attribute, **48**

form elements, Struts HTML, 628-29, 649
- attributes, 628

format method, SimpleDateFormat class, 235, 312

formatNumber elements, JSTL, 571

formatting, dates, 234-35

formatting, HTML, 31-33

form-bean elements, Struts configuration file, 591, 645, **810**
- className attribute, 810
- name attribute, 594, 810
- type attribute, 594, 810

form-beans element, Struts configuration file, 591, 594, 697, 808, **809**

form-error-page element, web.xml file, 804

form-login-config element, web.xml file, 804

form-login-page element, web.xml file, 804

formName attribute, Struts HTML javascript elements, 654

form-property elements, Struts configuration file, 645

forms, HTML, 46-48
- checkboxes, 48, **54**
- dropdown lists, 48, 57
- hidden fields, **417**
- listboxes, 57, **58-60**
- radio buttons, 48, 56
- textboxes, 48, **50-52**
  - multi-line textboxes, 60, **61**

formset elements, Struts configuration file, 649

forward attribute, Struts configuration action elements, 597, 811

forward attribute, Struts HTML link elements, 640

forward attribute, Struts logic redirect elements, 625

forward elements, Struts configuration file, 591, 595, 624, **810**
- className attribute, 810
- contextRelative attribute, 810
- name attribute, 596, 624, 810
- path attribute, 596, 810
- redirect attribute, 596, 810

forward method, RequestDispatcher interface, 401, 426-27

forward only result sets, **495**

forward elements, JSP, 397, 765
- page attribute, 765

fragment attributes, tags, 294-95

fragment elements, TLD files, 329

fragment-input directives, 761

fragments, JSP, **111**, 298

G

GenericDataSource class, Struts, 593

get method, ArrayList class, 217

get method, Calendar class, 233-34

get method, DynaActionForm bean, 647

get method, HashMap class, 227

GET method, HTTP, 47

get elements, Struts template, 643

getAttribute method, application implicit object, 791

getAttribute method, HttpSession interface, 393

getAttribute method, request implicit object, 775-76

getAttribute method, ServletContext interface, 394, 397

S

Notes

Notes

ASPToday - Your free daily ASP Resource . . .

A discount off your ASPToday subscription with this voucher!!! see below for more details.

Expand your knowledge of ASP.NET with ASPToday.com - Wrox's code source for ASP and .NET applications, with free daily articles!

Every working day, we publish free Wrox content on the web:

- Free daily article
- Free daily tips
- Case studies and reference materials
- Index and full text search
- Downloadable code samples
- 11 Categories
- Written by programmers for programmers

And for just-in-time, practical solutions to real-world problems, subscribe to our Living Book - our 600+ strong archive of code-heavy, useable articles.

Find it all and more at http://www.asptoday.com

This voucher entitles you to a discount off your annual ASPToday subscription; to claim your reduced rate please visit:

http://www.asptoday.com/special-offers/

If you have any questions please contact customersupport@wrox.com

wrox
Programmer to Programmer

p2p.wrox.com
The programmer's resource centre

A unique free service from Wrox Press
With the aim of helping programmers to help each other

Wrox Press aims to provide timely and practical information to today's programmer. P2P is a list server offering a host of targeted mailing lists where you can share knowledge with your fellow programmers and find solutions to your problems. Whatever the level of your programming knowledge, and whatever technology you use, P2P can provide you with the information you need.

ASP
Support for beginners and professionals, including a resource page with hundreds of links, and a popular ASP.NET mailing list.

DATABASES
For database programmers, offering support on SQL Server, mySQL, and Oracle.

MOBILE
Software development for the mobile market is growing rapidly. We provide lists for the several current standards, including WAP, Windows CE, and Symbian.

JAVA
A complete set of Java lists, covering beginners, professionals, and server-side programmers (including JSP, servlets, and EJBs)

.NET
Microsoft's new OS platform, covering topics such as ASP.NET, C#, and general .NET discussion.

VISUAL BASIC
Covers all aspects of VB programming, from programming Office macros to creating components for the .NET platform.

WEB DESIGN
As web page requirements become more complex, programmer's are taking a more important role in creating web sites. For these programmers, we offer lists covering technologies such as Flash, Coldfusion, and JavaScript.

XML
Covering all aspects of XML, including XSLT and schemas.

OPEN SOURCE
Many Open Source topics covered including PHP, Apache, Perl, Linux, Python, and more.

FOREIGN LANGUAGE
Several lists dedicated to Spanish and German speaking programmers; categories include: NET, Java, XML, PHP and XML.

How to subscribe:
Simply visit the P2P site, at http://p2p.wrox.com/

Register your book on Wrox.com!

When you download this book's code from wrox.com, you will have the option to register.

What are the benefits of registering?

- You will receive updates about your book
- You will be informed of new editions, and will be able to benefit from special offers
- You became a member of the "Wrox Developer Community", giving you exclusive access to free documents from Wrox Press
- You can select from various newsletters you may want to receive

Registration is easy and only needs to be done once for each book.

Just go to www.wrox.com

Got more Wrox books than you can carry around?

Wroxbase is the new online service from Wrox Press. Dedicated to providing online access to books published by Wrox Press, helping you and your team find solutions and guidance for all your programming needs.

The key features of this service will be:

- Different libraries based on technologies that you use everyday (ASP 3.0, XML, SQL 2000, etc.). The initial set of libraries will be focused on Microsoft-related technologies.
- You can subscribe to as few or as many libraries as you require, and access all books within those libraries as and when you need to.
- You can add notes (either just for yourself or for anyone to view) and your own bookmarks that will all be stored within your account online, and so will be accessible from any computer.
- You can download the code of any book in your library directly from Wroxbase.

Visit the site at: www.wroxbase.com

Programmer to Programmer™

Registration Code: | 8317Q955C6SS0A01 |

Wrox writes books for you. Any suggestions, or ideas about how you want
information given in your ideal book will be studied by our team.
Your comments are always valued at Wrox.

Free phone in USA 800-USE-WROX
Fax (312) 893 8001

UK Tel.: (0121) 687 4100   Fax: (0121) 687 4101

Beginning JSP 2.0 – Registration Card

Name _____

Address _____

_____

_____

City _____ State/Region _____

Country _____ Postcode/Zip _____

E-Mail _____

Occupation _____

How did you hear about this book?

☐ Book review (name) _____

☐ Advertisement (name) _____

☐ Recommendation _____

☐ Catalog _____

☐ Other _____

Where did you buy this book?

☐ Bookstore (name) _____ City _____

☐ Computer store (name) _____

☐ Mail order _____

☐ Other _____

What influenced you in the purchase of this book?

☐ Cover Design   ☐ Contents   ☐ Other (please specify):

_____

How did you rate the overall content of this book?

☐ Excellent   ☐ Good   ☐ Average   ☐ Poor

What did you find most useful about this book? _____

_____

_____

What did you find least useful about this book? _____

_____

Please add any additional comments. _____

_____

_____

What other subjects will you buy a computer book on soon?

_____

What is the best computer book you have used this year?

_____

Note: This information will only be used to keep you updated
about new Wrox Press titles and will not be used for
any other purpose or passed to any other third party.

Programmer to Programmer™

Note: If you post the bounce back card below in the UK, please send it to:

Wrox Press Limited, Arden House, 1102 Warwick Road,
Acocks Green, Birmingham B27 6BH. UK.

Computer Book Publishers